HOUSE OF LORDS
HOUSE OF COMMONS

SES

JOINT COMMITTEE ON FINANCIAL SERVICES AND MARKETS

First Report

DRAFT FINANCIAL SERVICES AND MARKETS BILL

Volume II

Minutes of Evidence and Appendices

Ordered by The House of Lords *to be printed*
27 April 1999

Ordered by The House of Commons *to be printed*
27 April 1999

LONDON: THE STATIONERY OFFICE

HL Paper 50-II
HC 328-II

ORDERS OF REFERENCE

HOUSE OF LORDS

Tuesday 2 March 1999

Financial Services and Markets—It was moved by the Chairman of Committees that the Commons message of yesterday be now considered and that a Select Committee of eight Lords be appointed to join with the Committee appointed by the Commons, as the Joint Committee on Financial Services and Markets, to report on the consultative document on the draft financial services and markets bill presented by Her Majesty's Command on 21st December 1998 and any further draft of the bill which may be laid upon the Table of both Houses by a Minister of the Crown;

That, as proposed by the Committee of Selection, the following Lords be named of the Committee:

L. Burns	L. Montague of Oxford
L. Eatwell	L. Poole
L. Fraser of Carmyllie	L. Taverne
L. Haskel	V. Trenchard

That the Committee have power to agree with the Commons in the appointment of a Chairman;
That the Committee have leave to report from time to time;
That the Committee have power to appoint specialist advisers;
That the Committee have power to adjourn from place to place within the United Kingdom;
That the minutes of evidence taken before the Committee from time to time shall, if the Committee think fit, be printed and delivered out;
That the Committee shall report by 30th April 1999;
and that the Committee do meet with the Committee appointed by the Commons this day at half past four o'clock in Committee Room 3A;
the motion was agreed to and a message was ordered to be sent to the Commons to acquaint them therewith.

HOUSE OF COMMONS

Friday 26 February 1999

Financial Services and Markets,—*Ordered,* That a Select Committee of eight Members be appointed to join with a committee to be appointed by the Lords, to be the Joint Committee on Financial Services and Markets, to report on the consultative document on the draft Financial Services and Markets Bill presented by Her Majesty's Command on 21st December 1998 and any further draft of the Bill which may be laid upon the Table of both Houses by a Minister of the Crown;

Ordered, That three be the quorum of the Committee;
Ordered, That the Committee shall have power—
   (i)   to send for persons, papers and records;
  (ii)   to sit notwithstanding any adjournment of the House;
 (iii)   to report from time to time;
 (iv)   to appoint specialist advisers;
  (v)   to adjourn from place to place within the United Kingdom;
 (vi)   to communicate to any Select Committee appointed by either House its evidence and
       any documents of common interest;
Ordered, That the Committee shall report by 30th April 1999;

Ordered, That Mr Nigel Beard, Mrs Liz Blackman, Dr Vincent Cable, Mr David Heathcoat-Amory, Mr David Kidney, Mr Tim Loughton, Mr James Plaskitt and Mr Barry Sheerman be members of the Committee.—*(Mr Jim Dowd.)*

LIST OF WITNESSES

LIST OF APPENDICES TO THE MINUTES OF EVIDENCE

[1]See also Appendix 62
[2]See also Appendix 61
[3]See also Appendix 63
[4]See also Appendix 66

[5]See also Appendices 64 and 65

LIST OF MEMORANDA
REPORTED TO THE HOUSE BUT NOT PRINTED

The following Memoranda have been reported to the House, but they have not been printed and copies have been placed in the House of Commons Library, where they may be inspected by Members. Other copies are in the Record Office, House of Lords, and are available to the public for inspection. Requests for inspection should be addressed to the Record Office, House of Lords, London SW1A 0PW (tel. (0171) 219 3074). Hours of inspection are from 9.30 am to 5.00 pm on Mondays to Fridays.

Association of Friendly Societies
Association of Solicitor Investment Managers
Association of Unit Trusts and Investment Funds
Barclays PLC
Campaign for Community Banking Services
Chancery Bar Association and Combar Spring Lecture, March 1999, given by Mr Howard
    Davies
Mr Charles Flint QC: Due Process and the FSA
Ms Reziya Harrison
Institutes of Chartered Accountants in England and Wales, Scotland and Ireland
National Consumer Council
Real Time Club
Society of Pension Consultants
Theatrical Management Association and Society of London Theatre

HOUSE OF LORDS
HOUSE OF COMMONS

SESSION 1998–99

JOINT COMMITTEE ON FINANCIAL SERVICES AND MARKETS

MINUTES OF EVIDENCE

Tuesday 16 March 1999

Financial Services Authority

Mr Howard Davies, Mr Michael Foot and Mr Phillip Thorpe

Printed pursuant to the Order of the House of Lords of 2 March 1999
Ordered by The House of Commons *to be printed*
16 March 1999

LONDON: THE STATIONERY OFFICE
£5.30

HL Paper 50-i
HC 328-i

MINUTES OF EVIDENCE

TAKEN BEFORE THE JOINT COMMITTEE ON FINANCIAL SERVICES AND MARKETS

TUESDAY 16 MARCH 1999

Present:

Lord Burns (in the Chair)	Mr Nigel Beard
Lord Eatwell	Mrs Liz Blackman
Lord Haskel	Dr Vincent Cable
Lord Montague of Oxford	Mr David Heathcoat-Amory
Lord Poole	Mr David Kidney
Lord Taverne	Mr Tim Loughton
Viscount Trenchard	Mr James Plaskitt
	Mr Barry Sheerman

Examination of witnesses

MR HOWARD DAVIES, Chairman, MR MICHAEL FOOT, Managing Director and Head of Financial Supervision, and MR PHILLIP THORPE, Managing Director and Head of Authorisation, Enforcement and Consumer Relations, Financial Services Authority, called in and examined.

Chairman Lord Burns

1. Good afternoon. It appears that we have under-estimated the demand for this event! Welcome to the first public session of this Joint Committee which, as you know, is part of what you described last week as the unusual and scenic route from the Treasury to Buckingham Palace which this Bill is taking. The Committee has decided to look at a range of issues which we set out last week in the press release. The main text is the Treasury's response to the consultation on the draft Bill which is described as a "Progress Report". What we would like to do is investigate how far this meets the concerns of those people who commented on the draft Bill and to the extent that there are outstanding issues we hope to be able to clarify them or try to see if there is common ground in taking them forward. One of the main objectives of this pre-legislative scrutiny stage is to see if we can short-circuit some of the more contentious issues. As you also know, we do not have very much time. We have been asked to report by 30 April which is a very tight remit and contrasts with the process that seems to have overrun most of its timescales so far. After taking evidence from yourself and the Economic Secretary to the Treasury we are proposing to invite a group of witnesses to each session and to take the issues one by one as set out in the press release. We are in new territory and we are going to have to find our way as we go along. We are very grateful to you for coming here today with your team and also for the prompt delivery of the paper you put to us, copies of which are available for people who want them. I would like to begin, Howard, by asking you if you could introduce your team and ask if there are any introductory comments that you would like to make.

(Mr Davies) Thank you very much, Chairman. I apologise for the crowd. I know that Queens Park Rangers are not used to large crowds! The team I have brought with me is Mr Michael Foot on my right, who is the Managing Director responsible for financial supervision across the whole of our area of responsibilities. Mr Foot was Executive Director for Banking Supervision in the Bank of England and came

out of the Bank to the FSA with me. On my left is Mr Phillip Thorpe who is Managing Director responsible for authorisation, enforcement and consumer affairs and in the previous regime was Chief Executive of IMRO. We are the only three executive members of the FSA Board which in addition has ten non-executives and one *ex-officio* member. Thank you for giving me the opportunity to make one or two preliminary remarks. I would make six very brief points. First, in spite of my characterisation of this as the scenic route to Buckingham Palace, I should say that we do very much welcome the Joint Committee process. It is clear to us that it is important to build consensus around the new legislative framework for financial regulation. We want to end up with legislation which is generally accepted by both practitioners and consumers as fair and reasonable. To an important extent we do regulate by consent and that consent will be facilitated by a process which allows people to have their say. As far as the timing is concerned we and the self-regulators are working on the basis that the legislation will be through early next year. If there were to be no new Act beyond the spring of next year we could run into difficulties but between now and then the priority must be to produce legislation which is workable and fair and we are working to contribute to that process as far as we can. Second, we have of course, put together in management terms a single regulatory structure already, albeit within the constraints of the different pieces of legislation within which we operate. The main reason for that was that all concerned, particularly the boards of the previous self-regulators, agreed that it was necessary to preserve the integrity of the regulatory system. We also of course have the Bank of England Act to contend with and a body which consisted of the old SIB and the Bank of England Banking Supervisors would not have made much sense. Third, our experience of operating as a single regulator over the last nine months has so far been very positive. The market reaction has been enthusiastic and we have already begun to find many synergies, not just in the obvious areas of cost but also in crisis management where we can take a broader

[Chairman *Cont*]

view than before and in handling issues like pensions mis-selling where you need to integrate the views of conduct of business regulators and the prudential regulators of insurance companies. Also it has helped in handling new product introductions like ISAs or stakeholder pensions which will be sold by many different types of institutions. Furthermore, even over the last two years since the Chancellor's announcement market consolidation has reinforced the trend towards regulatory consolidation. Groups like Citigroup or last week Prudential buying M&G cut across the old sectoral boundaries and made it necessary to take a view of them in the round. So we become keener on a single regulator as time goes by. Perhaps we are conditioned to do so but it is nonetheless true. Fourth, I think we are in the vanguard of international regulatory developments but not out on a limb. We have supplied the Committee with a review of the regulatory structures elsewhere and how they are changing. Two general trends are observable. First, banking supervision is increasingly being moved out of central banks. In only three of the G10 countries does the central bank now have sole responsibility for banking supervision. There is also a general trend towards consolidation, sometimes banking and insurance, often banking and securities. Not everybody is going for a single body. There are single bodies mainly in Scandinavia and the Far East so far but the trend towards consolidation is gathering pace. Fifth, my Board welcome the overall shape of the Bill, in other words the statutory objectives with provisos and the flexibility within them to keep regulations up to date. We think the balance of objectives and provisos is about right and manageable in practice. We recognise that a balance must be struck between flexibility and parliamentary accountability but if we want a durable system there will have to be a good deal of flexibility. One answer has been for us to try to illuminate the ways in which we would use this as we go along through consultation papers, etcetera, and we continue to do that. Also we think the powers overall are broadly appropriate. In fact, for the firms we regulate they are no more than a consolidation of the powers the different regulators have now. Lastly, my Board are nonetheless very conscious of the risks of an excessive concentration of power and responsibility in one body and of their own role in holding the staff to account. Perhaps that makes us excessively cautious about proposals for the extension of the scope of regulation, although I have to say I regard caution as a virtue in that context. It has also encouraged us to introduce accountability measures such as a Consumer Panel and Practitioner Forum which Ministers have now adopted as part of the legislative framework. It has also pushed us towards a very open style of consultation but we think that will pay off in terms of improvements in the long run in the quality of decisions. With that preamble we are very happy to take the Committee's points and questions.

Chairman: Thank you very much. We are going to begin with the general issue of accountability and Mr Beard is going to put the first question.

Mr Beard

2. Mr Davies, the FSA are required to be accountable to the Treasury and through it to Parliament and to consumers and to the financial market industry itself who are your supporters. Do you see any conflict between these various strands of accountability?

(*Mr Davies*) I think we would see the prime accountability route as being through Ministers to Parliament but that we have to take account of the views of the consumers and of financial institutions themselves. It is clear to us that the responsibility we have is to Parliament for the way in which we interpret the statutory objectives and the provisos on them but nonetheless we have to recognise that it will have an impact either on consumers if we do not exercise those powers in an appropriate way or on institutions if we exercise those powers in an unbalanced way. I think it would be wrong to think of there being conflict therefore between these different strands. I can see that there could be tension from time to time but I do not think there is conflict because the prime accountability route is absolutely clear and what we have tried to do in designing the architecture of the system is to establish a Practitioner Forum which will keep us honest, if you like, in terms of those objectives and provisos that relate particularly to the regulated community and a Consumer Panel which will keep an eye on how far we are delivering the objectives that relate to consumers. Clearly the Board will have to reconcile those points of view and I would not be surprised if from time to time they did differ. I do not think that is so much conflict as a way of ensuring we hear all points of view as we deliver against this single prime line of accountability.

Mrs Blackman

3. On this point of accountability, one of the major mechanisms of accountability is the annual report which will be driven by the objectives and principles of the FSA. Obviously the devil is in the detail of that report. Will there be any consultation as to the shape of the report and what will be in it and the way that those objectives are measured?

(*Mr Davies*) We are already discussing with the Consumer Panel and the Practitioner Forum as we call it, although I imagine it will be called the Practitioner Panel now it has been made statutory, about how we should measure what we do and the Practitioner Panel in particular are likely to launch quickly some surveys of industry opinion which will provide a sort of benchmark about regulatory sensitivity and regulatory intensity against which they can measure us in the future. We also would expect the Practitioner Panel and the Consumer Panel to have their own sections, if you like, of the annual report and so in that sense we would be consulting them. We had not thought of consulting on the overall shape of our report which is for our Board to determine although of course there are also certain requirements imposed by the Treasury on what we put in that report. We certainly could do so, but we have primarily consulted on prospective things rather than on retrospective things.

[Mrs Blackman Cont]

(Mr Thorpe) There is perhaps a point that influences that. We have said in our terms of reference for the Consumer Panel—and I think this is mirrored with the Practitioner Forum or Panel—that they should anticipate publishing their own reports without interference from the FSA, so there is a check and balance there in terms of their review of us and their unfettered right to say what they feel about our performance on those objectives.

4. But they will have an opportunity to comment in the report that goes to the Chancellor as well?
(Mr Davies) Yes.

Mr Plaskitt

5. It is a follow-on question from that really. You have already indicated that the Government has said that the Consumer Panel will be put on a statutory basis and the model you used is that of the PIA Consumer Panel. Do you think that is the correct model? Secondly, I would like you to say a little bit about how you envisage you are going to act and relate to the Consumer Panel. Can you give us some reassurance that you are not producing an annual report, they are producing annual reports, but that the two are never speaking to each other. I want to know how you are going to react to them.
(Mr Davies) First of all, it is true to say that we did build to some extent on the PIA Consumer Panel and we did ask the current chair to chair our Consumer Panel through to the point at which the legislation comes into place and we are pleased she accepted, but in other respects we have changed it quite substantially. The breadth of its remit is significantly wider than before and we have also introduced Nolan procedures to appoint the members of the panel so we advertised publicly and had independent assessment of candidates, etcetera. We have moved it along quite a bit already. What we have set up is a regular relationship between the Panel and our Board whereby the chair of the Panel will attend our Board periodically and so it is not just a question of reports going off separately, there will be practical, face-to-face encounters between the Consumer Panel and our Board. In fact, one of them will take place on Thursday of this week. So we undoubtedly recognise that we need to respond to the Consumer Panel in a clear way. We would expect to produce reasoned response to points they made to us.
Chairman: We will have to adjourn at this stage for five minutes or so to allow some of our members to vote.
The Committee suspended from 16.10 to 16.17 for a division in the House of Lords.
Chairman: Thank you all very much for returning so promptly. We were dealing with the question of the Consumer Panel. Lord Haskel has a question.

Lord Haskel

6. I do feel that this is a matter which is absolutely central to the work that we are doing and the lines of authority and as you explained them the manner in which you are accountable seemed to me to be satisfactory if everything is going well but you are going to be accountable to both a buyer and a seller and when the buyers and the sellers fall out then there is trouble. Do you think that the accountability as you described it to us will be able to withstand the stresses and strains of that situation?
(Mr Davies) I think that the previous regulatory system, albeit with its flaws mainly related to the different tiers of responsibility, has nonetheless shown itself to be capable of dealing with that kind of problem. I am reluctant to pray in aid pensions mis-selling as a shining example of anything since it is an unhappy episode, but regulators have in the end been able to get the agreement of the industry to a major programme of compensation as long as their views were soundly based and I think in that we have steered a course between the interests of consumers and the interests of the industry. I think the other point I would also add is that most of the time most businesses are clearly trying to stay comfortably within the regulatory framework and regard most of the regulatory requirements as simply good business. Compliance with the law, good record keeping, good advice to their customers is part of what good business ought to be. I think there is a danger sometimes in seeing this as more confrontational an activity than it typically is. Most of our work is involved in a constant process of debate and negotiation with the industry and with consumer groups to try to set the parameters appropriately and most of it is not in fact highly confrontational.

Lord Poole

7. I would like to ask, if I may, a question about your own personal position as Chairman. I assume you have some form of terms of reference. Could you tell us a little of how your own performance is going to be judged and who that will be judged by and whether there are formal criteria laid down?
(Mr Davies) The contract that I have is a five year term which began on 1 August 1997 as Chairman of the SIB. My office is, as they say, at the disposal of the Chancellor. The arrangements for assessment of my own performance are at the moment twofold. One is that there is a system of upward appraisal in the Financial Services Authority for all our staff. With the benefit of an external consultant my performance, as perceived by the people who work for me, was assessed at the end of last year and the results reported to the Board. In addition to that there is a remuneration committee of the Board composed of non-executives which is charged with assessing my performance from time to time. They assess also the performance of my two managing directors but in that case with my assistance. We have introduced also, in the case of the managing directors, an arrangement whereby the chair of both the Consumer Panel and the Practitioner Panel will give their views to us on the performance of the Authority as a whole and of the parts of the Authority which they control. But I think that is probably best suited to their performance whereas I think my performance is assessed by my non executive Board members.

8. Are there criteria we should know about?

[Lord Poole *Cont***]**

(*Mr Davies*) There are absolute criteria in the sense that we set out for the Board a budget and performance against the budget. We set out objectives in terms of deliverables, at the moment that is heavily based on getting the new regulatory regime up and running. The Board also in addition to the regular financial performance, they monitor staffing, performance, turnover of staff which is quite a good indicator of whether we are managing effectively.

Mr Sheerman

9.   Mr Davies, I am fascinated by the often quoted failure of the previous Act and I wondered whether when you were making your introductory remarks pertaining to this particular first question where you see the real improvement between the old FSA system and the new? I would like just to draw your attention to a City Editor yesterday who said that "the degree of bullying, intimidation and seedy vindictiveness in the old system was the greatest hidden regulatory scandal". Now, first of all, do you think that is a fair criticism of the old system and do you think the new system will meet that criticism?

(*Mr Davies*)   No, I do not think that is in any way a fair characterisation of the old system. I have not heard that point of view advanced by trade associations or by city institutions. I simply do not recognise it as a characterisation of the old system. I think that where we are seeking to make improvements in the old system are twofold. One is undoubtedly that there is some genuine new change in powers in relation to market abuse, which I am sure we will come on to in due course, but more importantly it is in trying to ensure that the regulatory system is able to take a view of the financial services market place which reflects the structure of that market place. The old regulatory system was built on a set of sectoral divisions which are no longer relevant to the way in which business is actually done in that nowadays you can buy life insurance from a traditional life insurance company, from a financial advisor, from a bank, from a unit trust or a company that owns unit trusts or indeed from a supermarket. These old divisions on which the previous regulatory system was built no longer apply. Also the old system had in the investment business area an unsatisfactory two tier split which was put in place for some understandable motives but which generated dysfunctional conflicts but also complicated overlaps and underlaps within the system, whose significance and importance became gradually apparent during the course of the ten years in which the old system operated. Lastly we think also, and this comes back to the remarks I made at the beginning, that if you are interested in the integrity of markets and in looking at risks to market stability overall, then it makes sense also to be able to look at banks, securities houses, insurance companies, fund management overall and to look at the interactions between them in order to get an assessment of the health of the overall financial system. In that, in the old system there was a lot of coming together of regulators, undoubtedly attempts were made to do that but it is much easier within one organisation than it was before.

Chairman: Could we move on to the question now of fine income and its definition and what happens to it. That is one issue raised under the heading of accountability in the progress report.

Mr Loughton

10.   Mr Davies, the press has made good sport about the costs of the new FSA structure and some criticism has come of course by the potential capacity of the FSA to levy fairly hefty fines. Now how are you going to assuage public perception that one may be subsidising the other?

(*Mr Davies*)   If I could say just on the overall costs of the system, this year we are going to come in around £10 million below our budget, and our budget for next year is 1.9 per cent up on this year in budgetary terms and we put out a consultation paper on our costs and on our fees. We have had a very small number of responses and all of them have accepted our fees and our budget for next year. So the controversy about our costs in the market place I think can be much overstated, certainly we have found that institutions have been quite understanding of our cost base and appreciated our need to recruit good people and indeed constantly say to us that what worries them is not so much our out of pocket costs but the costs imposed on them if we have poor quality people who do not understand their business well enough. As far as the fine income point is concerned, we have tried to present our budgets and our management accounts in a way which demonstrates that we see fine income not as going to the FSA but as going through the FSA back to the regulated community. The way we present our budget is by publishing what we call a control total which is mainstream regulatory cost and that is for next year £158.5 million, and that includes all of the in-house costs of supervision and the in-house costs of enforcement but it excludes the case-specific costs of enforcement when you hire in law firms, etc.. Then we show the outturn against that control total and that is what we and our Board are managing against. The enforcement costs are somewhat unpredictable depending on the number of cases that arise during the year and the fine income is also wholly unpredictable depending on the number of fines which are levied during the year. So we present that separately: the external enforcement costs and the fine income. Where there is a surplus of fine income over out of pocket enforcement costs there is then a discount applied at the level of the fees but it does not run through our P&L, if you like, it is accounted for quite separately to demonstrate that it goes back in the form of lower fees and is not used retrospectively to justify a higher level of budgeted expenditure than would otherwise be the case. We hope that with this presentation we can make people see where the fine income goes in and where it goes out and that it is not used by us as a back door way of justifying an increase in our budget or an increase in our salaries.

11.   It sounds like a very good way of a firm shopping the competition in order to reduce their own fees if they go down, which I am sure is good competition. Are you sure it is watertight in terms of

[**Mr Loughton** Cont]

appeals going to the independent tribunal from firms trying to take just that tack but in fact the fines are for other reasons?

(Mr Davies) Well, we think that operating in this way it would be because there would be no benefit accruing to the FSA from these fines except in so far as we are recouping our enforcement costs but they would be related to the case in question. We do not anticipate that being a problem. I am not aware that it has been a problem in relation to the old system which had the same arrangements for fines.

Lord Montague of Oxford

12. I think it is very important, and I am sure you will agree, that the Consumer Panel has a feeling of total independence. Have you given any thought to how you determine the budget for the Consumer Panel and whether those who work for the Consumer Panel can be the employees of the Consumer Panel from that budget rather than your employees?

(Mr Davies) Yes, we have given some thought to the budget for the Consumer Panel and we have set, from memory, a budget of £420,000 for the Consumer Panel next year, about half of which will be on consumer research which will be carried out outside the FSA and about half of it is on the staffing support and the costs of the Panel itself and its publications etc.. We do have staff who spend most of their time working for the Consumer Panel but I am slightly reluctant and I can understand the case for a complete separation but also the point of having a Consumer Panel which is inside the FSA is of course that it therefore has a legitimacy within the organisation and its views are conveyed through the organisation and not just in the form of points that are lobbed in from the outside. Therefore we have taken the view that it makes sense for the Consumer Panel to have exposure to quite a number of our staff and for a number of our staff to go and present to them, our regulatory staff, Michael Foot's staff go and present to the Consumer Panel on the way they are doing regulation of sales of personal pensions or whatever. We would not want to see I think the Consumer Panel off completely separated from the FSA, at which point I think it will lose some of its feel.

13. Will they be independent?

(Mr Thorpe) That is one of those issues we have looked at long and hard and discussed with members of the Consumer Panel. The rather lame answer I suppose is the proof of the pudding being in the eating. We have approached the matter on the basis that the Consumer Panel should put forward a budget proposal and a programme of work, that should be something that the FSA Board—which at present is underwriting this—should see and be content with. The work then taken forward is a matter for the Panel. As I was mentioning before, the Panel should be free to publish its own reports without hindrance from us. We see the independence coming more in its freedom of action within that published and acknowledged budget. Going further away, as my Chairman suggests, decreases our capacity to influence our own staff with the Consumer Panel's thinking. In some senses it would create

another public consumer body which we are already aware of and already take note of. For us this is an important informing aspect of our own structure.

Lord Montague of Oxford : I find that worrying.

Chairman: We will have a chance to speak to others about this in due course.

Mr Plaskitt

14. Just a supplementary following on from Lord Montague, you said £420,000 was the budget allocated to the Consumer Panel.

(Mr Davies) Yes.

15. Your enforcement budget is about £150 million?

(Mr Davies) No, the total budget is £158 million, that includes everything. The Consumer Panel is £420,000 but that is not of course all of our consumer related work. Our own work on consumer relations, consumer education, town meetings around the country and all of that, that is separately accounted, that is just specifically what the Consumer Panel itself is.

16. That is your consumer work but the Consumer Panel at some stage may want to stand up to you and tell you off about something.

(Mr Davies) Yes.

17. How do you arrive at that figure? It is about a quarter of a per cent of the total budget you are talking about. How do you arrive at that figure and are you sure it is enough for the Consumer Panel to do a proper job?

(Mr Davies) I suspect that in the long run it would not be but I ought to say that at the moment we are operating of course primarily under the old powers and therefore while we have broadened the remit of the Consumer Panel in terms of the issues which it can cover, and we have changed the membership of the Panel, essentially we are operating on the back of the old powers we have through the PIA. We have taken therefore what the PIA spent on the Consumer Panel and increased it a little bit but I think until we have our full statutory responsibilities, and in particular our new statutory objective of promoting consumer understanding of the financial market place, we do not think that we can justify to ourselves, therefore to our fee payers, spending a large amount on the Consumer Panel where they might reasonably say "You do not have statutory authority in some areas for doing that". We believe that we do have in relation to the old PIA areas.

18. Will you commit to an early review of the budget?

(Mr Davies) Absolutely.

Chairman: I think we need to move on. Lord Haskel, you have a question about complaints.

Lord Haskel

19. You are required to consult on your arrangements for independent investigation of complaints against you, against the FSA. Can you tell

[Lord Haskel *Cont]*

us how your consultation is going and when you expect it to be concluded?

(Mr Davies) When we brought the different regulators together into the FSA we overhauled the arrangements for complaints against regulatory staff both in the SROs and in the FSA. I should have to say that in some cases in coming in there were no arrangements at all in the past and we have painted those on, the Bank of England did not have such an arrangement for a complaints commissioner against the Bank of England in the past. The Board have approved an independent complaints commissioner, Mr Jock Worsley, who has terms of reference which have been revised to take account of our new responsibilities and that is operating. I believe there is only one current complaint which he is looking at but that is an operating system. We do recognise however that for the full new regime we will have to amend that because what we have done is patch the old system on to the new. We will be consulting, during the course of this year, we expect to complete that process by the end of this year, that is on our critical path this year.

20. You are obliged to consult and I am rather interested to know who you consult who is likely to complain against you? Do you find likely complainants with whom you can consult?

(Mr Davies) Inspite of what I said about the comment by the *Evening Standard* we can nonetheless find some people who want to complain about us if we try hard enough. I think that the trade associations but also the consumer groups do have a point of view on how complaints have been handled in the past so I do not think we will find it difficult to generate some responses there.

Mr Sheerman

21. Mr Davies, I do not want to go back to the City Editor but in terms of complaints in a sense do you see a responsibility in terms of the consultation process? How widely do you consult? What worries me, our job with a pre-legislative inquiry it seems to me is not to make the mistakes that were made over the last Bill. People keep coming back to us and saying "We do not want that process of the 1986 Act" and I am sure the Government does not want to make the same mistake. The consultative process has been much better, there is a longer period of time. Very often what we do not get is a voice from any view which says "The reason this is better is because we have improved it to suit a more dynamic situation". You have mentioned a more dynamic situation, the diversity of the markets but your initial reply to my colleague from the House of Lords seems to say we are really patching up what was there before and we do not see there is much room for improvement.

(Mr Davies) No, sorry, that was purely on the question of the Complaints Commissioner, where in the past you could complain to the SIB about an SRO, etcetera. We had to have an independent Complaints Commissioner in order to cope with the fact that we had managerially merged different regulators. That was all I meant by patching up that particular system. For the future we will need in the complaints area and

many other areas an overhaul of the system in a fundamental way. We will overhaul our rule books. We aim to reduce them in complexity and size. We will overhaul our disciplinary procedures. We are in the middle of consultation on that. That was just a very narrow point about the Complaints Commissioner.

Chairman

22. We will be coming to rule books. That is probably as much as you can give us today on the question of accountability. The Government did cover quite a number of these issues when it responded to the consultation. One of our topics will be this subject generally, where we will invite in people who are on all sides of this debate. We will see the extent to which they are content with what you have said today; and also with the way the Government have responded to the consultations. The next subject we would like to deal with is the whole question of the statutory objectives and principles in the Bill. These are obviously an innovation from the point of view of regulation of United Kingdom financial services. It would be helpful, by way of introduction to this section, for you to set out for us what difference you actually see this making. Do they really matter, these objectives and principles? How are they going to influence your work?

(Mr Davies) We think they do matter a lot. We think they are helpful. Indeed, we have already found that they are a very effective discipline on our internal processes. You are right that in the past the objectives of regulators have not been clearly set out in the legislation. The Banking Acts and the Financial Services Act are really silent on the point. That has been the cause of some difficulty, both in terms of allocation of resources, but also in the event of failures there has been a lot of debate about just what it was the banking supervisors should have been doing; how much they should have been trying to protect the institution itself, etcetera. So we think that having a framework of objectives, particularly also with a set of provisos about the things we need to take into account in pursuing the objectives, is a helpful one. I think it is particularly helpful for the board—here I think I speak for both the executive and non-executive, particularly for the non-executive members of the board—who have, ready-made in the legislation, a kind of checklist of things that they need to think about whenever we and our staff put up proposals to the board for a new regulation, for a case they might take, whatever. Then the board can say: Have you taken account of the impact of this on competition? Have you done your cost benefit analysis? Is this going to harm innovation? Is this going to drive business offshore? Is it going to worsen the competitive position of the United Kingdom financial services industry and are you doing it, even if it is worth doing, in the most economic and efficient way that you can? This, therefore, provides an important point of purchase for our board on what we do. At the same time, of course, it provides an important purchase for the outside world. The outside world can require us to explain just how we have felt that this new rule, (or rule book or whatever it might be), is contributing to our statutory

[Chairman Cont]

objectives and does not fall foul of the various things that we must take into consideration. So we have found already that it is becoming a kind of disciplined framework within which we assess what we do. We have told our staff all the time that they have to come back to us with ideas as to what initiatives they wish to pursue to work towards our statutory objectives.

Lord Taverne

23. In working out how this is actually going to make a difference in practice, may I take the example of (perhaps to my mind the most basic objective of all) consumer protection. Now, in which sort of way do you think you are going to be able to provide better safeguards to ensure that people do not get sold the wrong product?

(Mr Davies) I think it would be fair to say that the statutory objectives in themselves do not guarantee that we do that. But I think a combination of the statutory objectives, plus the learning we have had over the last decade of operating the old system, do mean that we hope we are getting better at doing that. We hope we are getting better at understanding where the opportunities for consumer detriment arise and how best to counter them. But that can only be done up to a certain point. We cannot guarantee that the consumers do not buy products which are unsuitable to them, but we can ensure that the process gets as close to the suitability criterion as it can.

(Mr Foot) An example of the current situation which might help: the case of Y2K now. We have some 8,000 firms. We clearly have to prioritise. When we looked across the individual regulators we established that their concept of what was high impact in terms of retail consumers was very different between the regulators who had formed the predecessors to the FSA. Now we have a coherent and consistent framework across the piece in the context of the draft objectives for the protection of retail customers and market confidence, which enables to us to prioritise consistently across the piece in the framework that Howard was describing.

24. The legislation still seems to have a slightly worrying bit of it, which seems to enshrine the principle of caveat emptor. Now you are dealing with things which are very complicated and difficult to understand, and you have had a product campaign which has got under way. Do you think that it is a mistake to apply the old doctrine of caveat emptor in the case of these complicated products?

(Mr Davies) This is a matter where reasonable people might disagree, but I think I reflect the balance of the opinion on our board if I say that we favour an element of caveat emptor in the legislation; partly, you might say, for slightly selfish regulatory reasons; which is that without that it might be possible for people to argue that regulators should go to any extent possible to remove the possibility of misbuying. I think there is only so much that a regulator can do to eliminate misbuying. We can probably do rather more to eliminate mis-selling, we hope, but there will be judgments that individuals need to make about their own personal circumstances and where we think it

would be very dangerous for markets, as a whole, if you had legislation which allowed unpicking of contracts because they did not happen to have turned out the way people would have liked them to turn out. Furthermore, there is no way you can remove the need for individuals to take responsibility for making decisions themselves. What I would say, however, is that in the way the draft Bill is currently formulated, there is a danger—and this is something which consumers associations and others have pointed out— that it might be read that we do this, this and this in terms of rules and education, etcetera, but bearing in mind the fact that consumers take responsibility for their own decisions. I think there is a danger that this could be read in the sense of negating everything that went before. We have come to believe that we would prefer in the legislation something which referred to the need for consumers to pay due care and attention. I am not quite sure I am drafting at this point but to take due care in making their decisions, which we think is an appropriate caveat, if you like, on our regulatory effort. We would like to see the concept reworked a little.

Chairman

25. In your speech to the Chancery Bar Association on 3 March, you said you thought the drafting could be improved a little bit. It was in that direction you had in mind?

(Mr Davies) Yes.

Lord Poole

26. Could we look at the word "consumer" for a moment. There is a whole range, as you have commented already, of people who can be called consumers. There are the very, very important retail consumers. Then there are the wholesale consumers. An important sub-objective for you is the international character of financial services and the desirability of maintaining the United Kingdom's international competitiveness. How do you see that you are going to be able to have an appropriately light touch for dealing with the wholesale market between consulting adults, and the retail market where I would be the first to say that the greatest possible attention to detail is required?

(Mr Davies) The legislation points us in this direction in a number of different ways. One is the one you referred to about the international character of financial markets. Also, we are required to ensure that our regulation is appropriate to different financial markets. As to the way in which we will implement that, obviously we have not yet completely revised our rule books but, for example, in our principles, where we set out the new FSA principles, we disapply certain principles in the wholesale area; so the principles about how you must understand the nature of your customers' needs, etcetera, are disapplied in wholesale market transactions. We have also set out for consultation a three-way classification of consumers because we think that the wholesale/retail split, which people colloquially talk about, is perhaps not the best way of thinking about the different types of consumers

[**Lord Poole** *Cont*]

which you have in the markets. We have suggested a three-way split which has market professionals at the top where, broadly speaking, we are content for them to exploit each other in private, though we obviously deal with complaints if there is market abuse or whatever. We do not think Goldman Sachs needs to spend a lot of its time worrying about whether Merrill Lynch knows what it is doing. Secondly, what we called expert end-users, who might be the treasurer of a corporation, who might be broadly expected to understand the nature of the derivatives markets, but nonetheless should not be grotesquely over-sold or have his portfolio churned by people blinding him with science. Thirdly, the retail consumer, where we believe the full range of protection should apply. The market reaction to that idea—though we have not yet had all the consultation responses back—but the market reaction to that seems to be reasonably positive.

Mr Heathcoat-Amory

27. Following that, I understand your point that there is not a completely clear distinction between the retail and the wholesale markets. Nevertheless, there is a workable destination there. My question is: what work has been done on assessing the regulatory burden, the compliance costs on the wholesale market, which is almost by definition international and therefore highly vulnerable to the danger of being undercut by other jurisdictions? We will know a good deal about your own costs but I would like to know from you whether you have done any work, and whether you should do any work, on trying to assess these compliance costs. And, in particular, trying to compare them in our market, as proposed, with other countries where the regulatory burden may be lighter; and whether there was a risk of regulatory arbitrage, or simply migration of sectors of the market away from what may be an overburdened and over-regulated sector here.

(*Mr Davies*) Part of the answer to that is that, yes, in future it is not just that we might not only feel that we want to do that, but we would be required to do that because it is part of the cost benefit analysis requirement. Clearly, the in-house costs, which are easy to assess, are dwarfed by the out-of-house costs of compliance. We will be required in future to do that kind of work before we propose any change in the regulatory environment. As for what has happened so far, the old SIB, the old regulators, did some cost benefit analysis on particular points. There are two external sources which are useful. One was work done by the City Research Project, by the London Business School on their behalf, which compared the costs of regulation in different centres; and, broadly speaking, in most areas identified the United Kingdom as a low cost area in terms of regulation. Also, the Australian Government commissioned some research as part of their research into regulation before they made their regulatory change, the Wallis Commission, which shows that the cost per unit, if you like, of transactions in London is lower than in any other international centre. So such evidence as one can find is reasonably reassuring, but we also believe that the requirement on us is not only to consider competitiveness in the

international dimension, it requires us also to watch out for any signs that activity is moving offshore, particularly where it is moving offshore to a less regulated environment but selling back into the United Kingdom consumers, where we would have scored an obvious own goal if that happened. So we are keen for trade associations to bring that evidence to our attention but I have to say we have not had any examples of that put to us recently.

(*Mr Foot*) That is true. It is a regular topic on the agenda for LIBA and for all the other major wholesale associations. The only other point to make is that looking obviously at the costs of regulation, and looking at the change in patterns of business with Japanese and other firms retrenching within Europe, London has won net far more than you might have thought, or certainly internal costs were not seen as unduly high.

Lord Eatwell

28. May I come back to the statutory objectives. Could you tell us a little bit about the objective of maintaining confidence in the financial sector. Is that about probity and honesty? What is it about?

(*Mr Davies*) I think there are a number of component parts to it and certainly the question of fair markets is a very important one. So we would see the market abuse regime as contributing to that objective, as much as to anything else, because we think it is people's confidence that market prices are fair prices and that is a crucial part of that objective. We would also, however, see much of our prudential work as contributing to that. We think it important that consumers—and, indeed, financial institutions—should believe that we run a tight ship as far as prudential requirements are concerned; therefore, that banks and insurance companies operating in our markets are prudentially sound within international best practice standards. So we would see at least those two dimensions as contributing to our work.

29. I see that objective as rather confusing because it is a bundle of things. I thought one of the main tasks of the regulator was to manage systemic risk, yet it is extraordinarily odd that our regulator is not told to do this. Now you are telling me that it is bundled into market confidence but it is put in with all these other aspects of market abuse. It is quite different from market abuse. Do you not think there should be a clear objective of managing systemic risk?

(*Mr Davies*) We would feel that a combination of our statutory objectives, and the Memorandum of Understanding we have with the Bank of England and the Treasury, are a respectable way of handling this problem. Indeed, the IMF, who recently reviewed these arrangements, confirmed that they regarded them as operating satisfactorily. It was rather a good model. Our contribution to systemic risk is trying to ensure that institutions are prudentially sound. Also, if they are in trouble and come to us, to see if market solutions to their problems can be found. We contribute to a process of overseeing systemic risk, which is shared with the Bank of England and the Treasury through the Standing Committee framework, on which Michael Foot sits regularly.

[Lord Eatwell *Cont*]

(Mr Foot) It is certainly our experience in the first year or so that the MOU has shown that what was drafted in the summer of 1997 stands up. We have only had "small" external crises from Asia, Russia, Long-Term Capital Management, and we will no doubt see, (although we would not want to see), in due course, something closer to home.

30. This is odd because this is not an objective. It is not a defined objective of the financial regulator in the United Kingdom to manage systemic risk. It is not one of your statutory objectives. Do you not think that is a little odd?

(Mr Davies) I have to say that set against the continuing responsibilities of the Bank of England and the MOU, I do not find it odd. I think that these responsibilities sit quite comfortably alongside each other. As a practical matter we have not found this, in any way, handicapping our work.

(Mr Foot) If we take the example of Y2K, high impact firms are those with large numbers of retail consumers and sometimes (and sometimes not) because of their position in the market place, this would cause major problems if there were a market failure. That is one example.

Viscount Trenchard

31. I would like, if I may, to return to the question of costs of regulation. It may well be that the UK has been a country with a relatively low cost regulatory regime, but I am worried that this may not be the case for very much longer. If you look at the public awareness objective, it seems to me it is cast in very broad terms. I can understand that promotion of the awareness of risks is a very sensible and a proper objective, but I would like to ask whether you think that the provision of education and advice on the benefits of investment itself are quite so appropriate, particularly when we have already looked at the difficulty of having a single regime that applies both to the wholesale and to the retail markets? If, for the benefit of the retail investor, you have to provide education and advice on investment generally, do you think that foreign practitioners involved only in the wholesale market will be happy to pay the costs?

(Mr Davies) That would not be where I would start in looking for the income to carry out that objective. I think it will be important for us to consider the way in which that should be funded and to ensure that it is funded by those people who might either be potentially responsible for consumer detriment on the one hand or who might benefit from our consumer education work on the other. We have not determined at this point to spend a lot of money on this activity yet in advance of our statutory responsibilities. We have put out a consultation paper which says how we might go about meeting this objective and that has generated 100 or so responses, most of which are rather enthusiastic about the notion of a regulator operating in that area. They have been enthusiastic partly from a consumer point of view and from a point of view related to the overall cost of the regulatory regime because there is an attraction in the long run in being able to improve the buying process from the consumer end as well as from the regulated firm end

which may, over time, allow one to take a slightly different view about the requirements for suitability and the best advice that you put on people if you have got better educated consumers. I would encourage you not to think of the consumer awareness objective as one which is to be seen purely as a regulatory burden. The industries we have talked to who are most interested in this market can see quite a lot of attraction in the FSA lending its name to advice and, indeed, a number of independent financial advisers have taken up publications and are using them in their offices because they show that they give the consumer greater confidence in the regulatory regime, greater confidence in the products available and, all other things being equal, consumers are more confident of what they are being sold and more likely to buy it. That is a side product of our work, but I should say that quite a number of people in the industry have found this an attractive area of work for the regulator for precisely that reason.

Mr Sheerman

32. Mr Davies, do you not think there is going to be a revolution of rising expectations? Here we have nine regulatory bodies rolled into one, the FSA, and that is going to have a high public profile. Then, if you build into that public awareness and the mission to protect consumers, are we not actually going to see an inability by the FSA to meet those expectations? I was looking at the *Financial Times* last week where they make the point that a third of people taking up mortgages at the present moment are sold inappropriate endowment policies linked to their mortgages, and so in terms of public awareness there is a very important role there. I did not realise until fairly recently that if you had a complaint about bank overcharging you could complain to the FSA, as it is now, if you were a personal customer of the bank but you could not if you were a one-person business. Are we going to get this legislation right if we have these bold statements, one FSA with this broad sweep of powers? It is going to attract a lot of attention. Do you think you are actually going to cope with that kind of revolution in terms of perceived demand?

(Mr Davies) Could I just try to disentangle the regulatory side from the complaints side because there will be a separate body, although parallel, if you like. It will be the Financial Services Ombudsman, which has a different board and a different chairman, who will be responsible for handling all of the consumer complaints. We think that will be an attraction to consumers because there will be a single point of entry for complaints. People will not have to worry, as they currently do, which particular door they go into to complain. As far as the issue of expectation is concerned, I think I would find it difficult to say that that is not potentially a problem. I think that it could well be. I think it is important that people do not have unrealistic ambitions about what regulators can achieve. I think that is part of the justification why we believe that an element of *caveat emptor* is appropriate in the legislation and that consumers should not be given the idea that somehow we are sitting alongside every financial adviser or bank clerk ensuring that she

[Mr Sheerman *Cont*]

does the right thing in relation to every consumer. What we can do is wrap a regime of suitability and good advice around the present system and police that within reason. I hope that people do not have unrealistic ambitions of regulators. In fact, my impression from our so far limited meetings with the public is that—we have held three large open meetings to talk directly to investors about what they think and want from the regulatory regime—people, interestingly, have quite realistic objectives. They are interested to know what the complaints framework is, they are interested to know that we monitor the soundness of firms, they are interested to know that there are a set of expectations that they should have about what they get from companies and on the whole we have not heard individuals say, "Why are you not doing more and preventing every single bad financial decision?" I think people are reasonably realistic about it, but I can see there is a danger.

33. I do not mean to deride them, but it seems to me that here you have rather waffly objectives that you are not quite sure you could meet, whereas with something that you could be much more focussed on in terms of systemic risk the Government has not put that in at all.
(Mr Davies) I am not sure that I would regard systemic risk as a very easily measurable objective either, frankly. I think that confidence in the markets is something that it is equally hard to measure when you have got it, although you tend to know when it is not there.

Chairman

34. Could I wrap up this section on objectives and principles, although obviously we are going to have to come back to it. There is one issue that has come up before which we have not touched on today. I just invite you to confirm your position that you are very reluctant about the idea of raising one of the principles, about the competitive position of the UK, into an objective which is what some people have argued should happen. Part of that, as I understand it, is the concern about raising unrealistic expectations about what it is that you can actually deliver.
(Mr Davies) I think so. Competitiveness as an objective would be a rather different in character from the others and could take us into either areas of explicit City promotion where I think there are other people involved, i.e. the City Corporation, British Invisibles and the Bank of England to some extent are involved in that area, but also, perhaps more importantly, could drag us into commercial issues about just what is competitiveness and could we not bias our regulations in order to promote the interests of this particular market which people could come along and plausibly argue to us was the way of the future, which it might or might not be. I think it would risk dragging the regulator into essentially commercial issues. Lastly, I think that there would be considerable concern overseas in relation to a regulator who had an explicit competitiveness objective. I think we would find some difficulty with some of our overseas counterparts who would say, "What are you really trying to achieve? Are

you really trying to work with us collectively"—to pick up Lord Eatwell's point—relating to systemic risk, to guarantee safe markets internationally, or is your real objective to promote the particular interests of the City of London because you are aiming for competitiveness?" I think that could create international confusion.

Mr Sheerman

35. Could I put a very quick supplementary on that. The other principle that stands out here is innovation. How are you going to handle innovation? Why is that in principle? What role does the regulator have in stimulating innovation?
(Mr Davies) I think not. I think if you read the construction of the clauses it is that we must have regard in performing our duties—and our duties are about rule-making, etc.—to the need not to damage the prospects for innovation. So we are not promoting innovation, we are just doing that. So the way we read that is, for example, to lead us to be very cautious about certain forms of product regulation. We could not completely ban a new product because we thought it might be dangerous for a lot of consumers, because that might hinder innovation. So it would be in relation to our rule-making powers that we would consider the impact on innovation, not promoting innovation in its own right.
Chairman: I would like to move on now to the third section we wanted to look at, which is the issue of discipline, enforcement and the tribunal. This has created a good deal of comment and, of course, the Government has responded to it. Lord Eatwell?

Lord Eatwell

36. I would like to start on the issue of rules and rule-making. One of the most striking propositions in the Board of Banking Supervision's report on the Barings affair was that the Bank of England did not understand the industry it was regulating. How are you going to ensure that your staff understand the industry for which they are making rules and which they are regulating?
(Mr Davies) I think there are two main ways in which we hope to ensure that. The first is that we do aim quite deliberately to recruit people from the market. We aim to have a balanced recruitment policy whereby we do take in some people and grow our own but the greater part of our recruitment, as I say, as a whole is from people who have some market experience and we will certainly continue with that. But secondly, we will involve practitioners to a high degree in our processes, both in the rule-making processes and in the enforcement processes. At the moment we have what we call our handbook of rules and guidance and we have a Handbook Advisory Group, which met this morning, senior market practitioners who are helping us and steering our process of revising our rule books. So there are two ways: one, recruiting in and out of the market and by involving practitioners we hope to ensure that we do understand the market we regulate.

[Lord Eatwell *Cont]*

37. But your relationship with practitioners is a bit arm's-length, is it not, in the sense that a practitioner who is an adviser is very much representing his or her firm, his or her industry, maybe from a trade association or whatever it might be, whereas a practitioner who has responsibility, which will not be the case in the FSA, actually then has the interests of the organisation at heart for which he or she is responsible?

(Mr Davies) I do not think that is entirely the way I would see it because we do, after all, have some very senior practitioners on our main Board. Keith Whitson, who is the Chief Executive of HSBC, Christopher Rodrigues, Chief Executive of Bradford and Bingley, etc. So we do have, and have carried over from the old system, the notion of having senior practitioners on the board and they are clearly fully responsible. We have suggested in our enforcement paper that we would have practitioners on our top Enforcement Committee and we have said that we are prepared to envisage them having a voting right, if that is what people think would be appropriate. We also do deliberately recruit as part of our staffing now a group whom we call colloquially the "Grey Panthers". They initially started off not liking it but I notice they have now got themselves a tie with a grey panther on it. They are more senior people who are very recently retired, who actually work directly with our banking supervision teams, because we did acknowledge, in response to the Board of Banking Supervision Barings inquiry, that banking supervision—in particular the Bank of England typically staffed by recruiting from university and growing their own—was lacking in people with real live market experience. So in those areas we do have this grey panther brigade who are employees and who are responsible and who are on review committees, etc.

Lord Poole

38. I share Lord Eatwell's concern. I am interested in what you say about people at a senior level, in a sense sharing his concern, but I am much more concerned about what really happens when your people turn up to regulate real businesses. I do not mean this rudely in any way but I think there is a very long way to go indeed before you meet the objectives you have been talking about of having people who know what they are doing when they arrive in many companies. Over the years I have observed a major transition into box-ticking and just making sure that everything has been neatly done according to rules that have been laid down, and what was really needed was somebody who understood the business sufficiently to know what the right question was to be asked. I appreciate that is a problem for you. I would not have worried about it so much if you had said it was a problem. I think I am more concerned because you did not.

(Mr Davies) I would not deny that it can be a problem in some areas and I would not deny that in a perfect world we would have a longer average tenure in our organisation with longer market experience. Unfortunately, the fairness at work legislation does not include any provision for us to be able to ban our employees from taking offers of higher salaries from the market and I am afraid that is something to which we are very vulnerable and it is very difficult for us to pay top dollar. But as a general rule what we have moved towards—and I think this is the case really across all regulators but I know most about it in relation to banking so perhaps I can quote that as an example—is an approach which attempts to assess the overall risks of an institution from the top down and, therefore, to create a framework within which we can focus on the things that really matter rather than on the dignified parts of regulation (if I might characterise them in that way) and certainly post Barings we have introduced a new process called the RATE process, Risk Assessment Tools and Evaluation process, which very much starts at the top and says, "What are the areas of this bank which cause us concern because they are high-risk, because they are new, because the bank is not clear that it really understands how to manage them properly?" and that is where we should focus our attention, pinning senior management responsibility on those areas and making sure they know what our regulatory expectations are. So that is our overall philosophical approach but, of course, when you get down to the small firm you also have to ensure that the requirements have been kept and that there is decent record-keeping, and at the retail end you really do have to ensure that because we have demonstrated that in pensions mis-selling and in other areas poor record-keeping can be very damaging for consumers. So I do not apologise for the odd box receiving the odd tick.

Mr Plaskitt

39. It is down at the small firm end that I wanted to ask a question, which follows directly on from Lord Poole's. For example, looking at enforcement in the case of the independent financial adviser, the very small business, giving independent advice, how are you going to be a presence there? How is your enforcement going to apply in that very micro end of the market? Attached to that, the draft Bill gives you the power, as I understand it, to delegate enforcement, if you wish to, to—the phrase is—"body or persons who in your opinion are competent to perform them." Are you minded to do some delegation of enforcement, and if so, to whom, and might it be in the area of this enforcement at the very local, very small-scale level?

(Mr Davies) I think it is important to distinguish between supervision and enforcement here because at the low level, and, indeed, any other level, what we have is people who, under Michael, go around and try to make sure things are proceeding as they should and they have got proper record-keeping and proper procedures, etc. Sadly, from time to time his teams find that there is something not right and then they hand over to Phillip's team. So I might ask Phillip to speak specifically on the enforcement point.

(Mr Thorpe) I suspect that you were talking about the supervision aspect, the day-to-day monitoring of the activities that are undertaken in the firms?

40. Or by independent financial advisers.

(Mr Thorpe) Yes. I do not want to play tennis, but that is an issue which is primarily supervisory. That

[Mr Plaskitt *Cont]*

goes back to an earlier comment about box ticking where you are dealing with a mass market of, as in the case of the old PIA community, some 4,000 either one or two-men firms or individuals and getting out to see them is a very difficult task with any kind of regularity.

41. So will you delegate?

(Mr Foot) We would consider delegating in particular areas in terms of, let us say, the recognised professional bodies, but only where we are convinced that it is more cost-effective to do so and only where we are convinced that the standards that we would get meet those that we require.

42. Can you give an example of where you might delegate?

(Mr Foot) One possibility would be with the recognised professional bodies, the ones who become authorised for investment advice such as accountancy firms. We would consider the possibility of delegating supervision to the relevant professional body if they met the criteria I have just set out. We have not begun to discuss with the bodies concerned whether they would (a) be interested and (b) could meet those needs.

43. Would you envisage delegating to Trading Standards Officers, for example, at the very local level?

(Mr Foot) I have heard of these proposals that Trading Standards Officers have made. We have not considered that in detail. At the moment we have not got a viable package to put out to tender to consider how we would assess different capabilities of performance. One would not want to rule it out, but I think I would go no further than that at this stage.

(Mr Thorpe) Enforcement as such cannot be delegated under the legislation as envisaged. Breach of a rule or a principle has to be something that the FSA gets involved in. Supervision, yes, but enforcement, no.

Mr Loughton

44. The term practitioner has been used a lot to support the FSA keeping in touch with the real world and how business is done. Is it not the case—and certainly we saw this from the conference last week—that many people that you have taken on board as practitioners are in fact compliance officers? Were they necessary, though they may be, those people with experience in the City may see compliance officers as a somewhat stifling enterprise. What is the balance going to be between real practitioners, i.e. those people who do the business at the sharp end and make money for their customers, and those people whose whole life revolves around the rule book?

(Mr Davies) I think it is typically true that our committees include people who are in your terminology "real practitioners", though I immediately will get lots of letters from compliance officers which I will pass on to you. I think that the real practitioners are quite keen and extraordinarily willing to give up time in policy areas, have been in the SROs in the past and we do find it perfectly possible in our policy work now. It is undoubtedly true that quite a lot of the

people whom we recruit as monitoring officers are the sort of people whose jobs might otherwise be in compliance functions. At the junior and middle levels I agree that it is the case that we would—not always—typically get people who are that sort of person. I think it is difficult for us and I am not sure entirely appropriate for us to want to attract derivatives traders, etcetera. We do get some who come in from front-line business areas, but typically we are getting people who see their careers in that way.

(Mr Thorpe) I would add that the compliance side of the business, certainly in the more clear thinking firms, is viewed as a business function rather than merely a robot function and, in fact, the people that are involved in that have the unusual advantage of having oversight of a whole range of activities in a firm and for us that is a very valuable skill.

Dr Cable

45. The Treasury recently confirmed to me in a written answer that there was not a single case in the last five years where they had felt that the abuse of regulation was sufficiently serious to have referred the matter to the police. Do you think that in your own enforcement procedures you will not be looking to make more use of the criminal law and, if so, what is the process by which the relationship with the police would be developed?

(Mr Thorpe) We are having to confront this much more in terms of the draft legislation because we will have our own criminal provisions to enforce. That has caused us to look at how we would make referrals through to other agencies, particularly the police and we have put forward a set of propositions about how we will determine to deal with something as a criminal or a civil matter and we are proposing to use the guidelines that are commonly used by the Crown Prosecutors in doing that, that has been part of our consultation and we have also embarked on the process of establishing memoranda of understanding with the various agencies, whether it is the Crown Prosecution Service, the Serious Fraud Office or the police to allow us to know when to talk to each other and to determine who goes first and in what circumstances. We do anticipate that when the legislation is in place we will be looking to use the criminal powers from time to time. Experience has shown us that the civil powers that have been available in the past have tended to be powers of choice because they allow more rapid resolution of matters and particularly when we are focussing on consumer issues and wishing to see compensation delivered, they do give us the flexibility to deliver those matters quickly, but we will have in place mechanisms for passing matters to the criminal authorities.

Mr Kidney

46. Mr Davies, the present prosecutors of criminal offences in financial crime are the DTI, the Crown Prosecution Service and the Serious Fraud Office and presumably they all apply the Crown Prosecution Service code of when to decide to prosecute and your Chancery Bar speech shows that as a result there are

[Mr Kidney Cont]

very few prosecutions. I think from 1993-98 there were five successful prosecutions and eight acquittals. In the same period, not in your speech, the RIEs have referred over 100 suspected cases. It is a pretty dismal record of criminal prosecutions. Do you not welcome the civil proceedings simply because you can ditch criminal prosecutions and go along with an easier burden of proof and impose the fines yourself and very nice fines they are with an unlimited top level?

(Mr Davies) A seductive question, Mr Kidney, but that is not quite the way that we would see it. We would not see the civil route as a cheap alternative to the criminal route. We think that if there is criminal intent then the criminal route should be chosen and that is what you should attempt to do, but we do believe that there can be a category of market manipulation-type offences which are more in the character of civil offences and, therefore, where a civil regime is the appropriate one as long as it is backed by a code of market conduct which clarifies the regulator's expectations in terms of what is and is not market manipulation.

Chairman

47. Perhaps I could move the questioning on to this whole question of your various functions as prosecutor, judge, jury, etcetera. There have been a lot of complaints that there are dangers in the process as it has been set up in the Bill. One of your responses has been to propose an Enforcement Committee. I wonder if you could take us through how you have responded; what you think of the worries that there are undoubtedly on this front; how it is that you have responded to them; and the extent to which you think that this now meets people's concerns.

(Mr Davies) Initially, of course, what people saw was the draft Bill last July without seeing the way in which we proposed to operate our general enforcement processes and in the absence of any clarity from us about how we would operate our processes I think people did react and say that this was potentially oppressive and burdensome, etcetera. We then put out a consultation paper on our enforcement processes which made it clear that we did envisage an Enforcement Committee with public interest representatives, of whom some would be practitioners. Since then I think the debate, whilst it has not stopped, has moved on to more detailed questions about the precise composition of that committee and also its relationship with our enforcement staff. Then also the Treasury have made a change to the draft Bill. The new clauses have not yet appeared but they have announced a change whereby it is clear that the tribunal, which was previously characterised as an appeal tribunal with a window open to it largely on points of law, will now be more in the character of a first instance tribunal able to hear evidence and hear the facts of a case. If you take that change and look at our procedures alongside that change, then my own judgment is that the level of anxiety has reduced again. Nonetheless, there remain some issues about how we structure that and I might hand over to Phillip, who is going to pick up the story.

(Mr Thorpe) We have been continuing discussions with commentators who have expressed this "judge, jury, prosecutor" fear and one of the late realisations on all our parts was that the conversion of the tribunal to a tribunal of first instance had a material effect in terms of dealing with that separation. As that is a first instance tribunal it can hear, as the name suggests, matters afresh and it does meet concerns about the ECHR proposals and their impact. What we have been trying to do—and I think we are close to concluding—is produce an administrative procedure beneath that that allows cases to be settled wherever possible, and it does so again with an eye to the ECHR requirements. We think we are close to having a procedure which will meet the objections of the commentators that we have heard voice concerns so far and in part that seems to be likely best met by providing a form of mediation between the party who is accused of having breached a rule and the FSA in the course of that settlement process. So we think we are quite close to having an agreed approach with the industry and their advisers. That will maintain the ability to refer the matter to that independent first instance tribunal set up by the Lord Chancellor but nevertheless meet our concern that we try to provide an administrative process which, hopefully, has the advantage of promptness, cost-efficiency and relative flexibility.

Mr Kidney

48. I am still not quite clear. Let me go through it. If there is a possibility of a criminal prosecution, your staff investigate and you can actually be the prosecutor, as it happens, but at least there is going to be a criminal court, judge and jury at the end of the case. If there is a supervisory breach I understand that you investigate and then there is going to be an Enforcement Committee and they will make decisions about whether to issue the notices or not. Is that right?

(Mr Thorpe) The intention at the moment, as evidenced by the Bill, is that if we believe there has been a breach of a rule or principle that is sufficient to require regulatory discipline, we will issue a notice to the firm of that intention. The option then is for the parties to sit down and discuss it and determine whether there is agreement about it. If agreement is not reached, then as the Bill is currently drafted the FSA will issue a notice indicating what its view of the matter is. If neither party were content with that as a mechanism for resolving it, it can go on to the tribunal where a full judicial avenue is available.

49. For those people who do not choose the tribunal, as far as a supervisory breach is concerned, it is inside the FSA. You have your investigating staff and then the enforcement staff who are separate from the investigating staff?

(Mr Thorpe) What we are talking with the industry and their advisers about is creating an internal mechanism that within that general framework allows right of representation, the right to make submissions, allows the use of the Enforcement Committee. It is independent of the staff who are prosecuting, yes.

50. I see that has been consulted upon rather than actually being a Bill decision yet?

[**Mr Kidney** *Cont*]

(*Mr Thorpe*) Indeed. We have consulted once. We have a lot of very keen interest in those proposals and we are doing as good consultants ought to do, going back and thinking about it some more and discussing it.

51. Just to complete the picture, that is the prosecutions and the breaches of regulations. Now the new civil power that sits in the middle between those two. The Enforcement Committee would be the one that decides levels of fines as well?

(*Mr Thorpe*) Forgive me if I am getting the wrong end of the stick here but from our perspective the regulatory action and the criminal action—I am using the terms inexactly here but that is the civil. The regulatory is the civil. Is that what you mean?

52. Yes, but imposing a fine for market abuse is a new civil power that has been developed for the first time in our jurisdiction. I am just asking, on top of the regulatory stuff is the new fine for market abuse to be via the Enforcement Committee?

(*Mr Thorpe*) It could be progressed in the same chain of discussion and decision, indeed.

53. Could I say it does worry me a bit about the confusion. Civil is just a bit more on the regulatory side and I really think it is much more fundamental than that. Could I push you on one point. It is a seductive question, Howard. If you want an injunction you will go to a judge in the court, if you want an order for disgorgement you will go to the court and the judge will make the order and in both cases the judge can also award a fine to the FSA, so why do you not just say, why does not the legislation just say, you go to the court to start proceedings for fines? What is wrong with that?

(*Mr Thorpe*) What I believe the Government's intention is, and our own experience bears out as being good experience, is that the civil structure or the administrative structure or the regulatory structure, whichever term you fasten on, has worked very well for dealing with a myriad of essentially administrative offences. I think you may have said yourself the track record in taking forward criminal prosecutions is not one which seems particularly exciting. What it does show, I believe, rather than failure necessarily on the part of the prosecutors to do a good job is the difficulty in achieving criminal prosecutions in a wide variety of cases. What we have found, and I think the industry supports this, is that a lot of the matters which we deal with as civil are not matters that are amenable to criminal resolution and I do not think we are suggesting anything which is unusual in terms of the history of this and I do think the proposition which the legislation puts forward is one which will lead to the most expeditious disposal of cases.

Viscount Trenchard

54. I do not want to leave this theme alone just yet. I would like to come back to it because by your own admission, Mr Davies, the Authority does have very considerable powers and we have talked about the need to separate the functions of prosecution and decision-making, but I still think for a body which has

the considerable powers that you have acknowledged the proposals contained in your Enforcement Committee do not go as far as, say, the SEC in the United States, where I think those who are performing the judicial role or the decision-making role are completely separate and separately accountable from those who are carrying out the prosecution role. In your speech last week I think you referred to the third way, about which we hear a lot these days. I am a little bit sceptical about what it actually means and either you separate the functions of prosecutor and judge or you do not and it seems to me that we have not quite got there yet. On the subject of the European Convention on Human Rights, which I believe requires such a separation, it also requires the need for offences of which individuals are accused to be made clear. I think also in the Bill there is, as yet, a lack of an adequate degree of clarity in the definition of offences. It seems that the Authority is going to discipline people for breaches of general principles, such as behaviour—"behaviour" is used extensively in the Bill—and I wonder whether we have drawn offences and breaches tightly enough to be compatible with the requirements of ECHR?

(*Mr Davies*) You raise a great complexity of issues there. I just make two or three points on it. One is that the question of whether we have achieved an adequate separation, people can take different points of view but we have set up an Enforcement Committee which would have, as we envisage it, a chair appointed specifically for that purpose and appointed quite separately from the rest of the staff, and the other members of the committee would be people drawn from outside the FSA as public interest representatives, either consumer representatives perhaps or practitioners. We think this creates a very separate structure, albeit within the overall administrative framework of the FSA. The second point really is that, as I understand this, perhaps imperfectly, the ECHR question, which I think ultimately will be a matter on which ministers will have to make a statement, is determined by the totality of the processes available, both taking into account the tribunal and the administrative procedures within the FSA, and in order to meet the ECHR requirements you look at the two alongside each other. We have, therefore, taken the view that if you do that, if you look at this first instance tribunal alongside our administrative procedures, their separation but also the ability of the tribunal to hear things afresh, our view is that those requirements are met in the totality of the system.

55. I think, though, there is a valid point especially for foreign firms here, which is that they may well think that if they choose to go to the tribunal they are going to incur the displeasure of their regulator and that represents a considerable incentive for them to say, "Well, let us keep it within the FSA because if I go to the tribunal then the regulator is going to be very much stricter on me and regulate me more severely than he would have done otherwise."

(*Mr Davies*) I could not make a window in men's minds and work out what their motivation might be in terms of staying within the system or going out of the system. It is true to say that one of our principles is

[Viscount Trenchard *Cont]*

that we will take account of the openness with which firms deal with their regulators in terms of all our disciplinary processes. We think that that creates a positive incentive and typically most firms who encounter problems will come to us at a very early stage and say, "We have encountered this problem. We recognise a regulatory breach has occurred. These are the measures that we think are appropriate in response to it. How does that look to you?" Most of the time this is a collaborative process. In the figures that I quoted in my lecture last week, on average out of 100 cases something like four go to tribunals. It would be difficult for me to disprove a contention, that some people settle because they did not want a tribunal. Why did they not want a tribunal? I doubt if it was particularly because they wished to keep their regulators sweet. Sometimes they are not sure how strong their case is or they would like to get things settled and move on without dragging things out. I would not under-estimate this. Many firms say to us that what they are keen to ensure is that there are administrative processes to handle regulatory breaches in an expeditious way and what they do not want is a very long drawn out process whereby on the word processor of every City journalist it says, "Bloggins and Bloggins, a firm under a regulatory cloud for their activities in so and so" which stays for the whole three-year process of going to tribunals. They would like to be able to achieve rapid resolution in many of these cases and move on with their business.

Lord Poole

56. Lloyd's is not just a wholesale market, it has a very important retail component. It would seem to me to be a situation which is very unsatisfactory because of the existence of the Lloyd's Act and other Government decisions not to fold Lloyd's into the FSA. What are you going to be able to do from an enforcement point of view to ensure that the sort of standards you have been enforcing in other industries will be applied within the Lloyd's market for the protection of policy holders, customers in general and, to the extent that they are still remaining, the investors?

(Mr Davies) You are right that we will have to operate within the existing Lloyd's Acts, but the Government have given us some new powers in the draft Bill to take responsibility for oversight of the regulation of the Lloyd's market and we have set out some preliminary proposals in a consultation paper which explain that there are roughly two options, i.e. either we could do a lot of the Lloyd's regulatory work in-house or we could have a relatively small team in-house and delegate the functions of direct day-to-day regulation of the market to the Lloyd's regulatory division and we are genuinely open minded on which course we should go down. But for those powers that we have we would bring Lloyd's into the enforcement framework of the rest of the FSA and therefore the same enforcement procedures as we have been describing would apply to breaches of those elements of the Lloyd's market which we will be able to oversee.

57. Did you worry about people falling through holes?

(Mr Davies) I worry about little else.

Mr Heathcoat-Amory

58. You have stressed the advantages of a speedy resolution by administrative procedures and I understand that, but am I right in saying that you have the power to levy unlimited fines and to deprive people of their livelihoods on a balance of probabilities and not beyond reasonable doubt which would be required in criminal proceedings? It seems to me that you have the advantage of being essentially a rule maker and investigator and a prosecuting authority and yet you can levy these really draconian penalties on a balance of probability. What is more, it does not have to be proved that the culprits intended any wrongdoing, you can be judging by their actions, so they could be bowled out for incompetence rather than any malicious intent. This worries me. Although you have made efforts to separate out your investigative and your decision-making powers, it is all in one huge organisation and although the Government has moved on the question of the tribunal, it still does not seem to me to measure up to the standards of impartial judicial decision-making and that standard of proof that is commensurate with the penalties that may be levied.

(Mr Thorpe) Could I perhaps take, firstly, the point on the standards of proof. It is often put to us as being highly attractive that we should work to a balance of probabilities standard and in the normal course of events that would be attractive from the point of view of the prosecutor. What we have found in practice is that in dealing with matters of the type that you describe, matters where a business may be closed down, where an individual might be banned from the industry or where substantial fines might be imposed or, indeed, where severe reputational damage might be incurred, it has been put to us—and tribunals have determined that it is correct—that the standard of proof is on a sliding scale and it slides very close to the criminal level of proof in cases of the type you describe. We find that we are going nine-tenths of the distance in terms of the standard of proof for cases that carry that heavy penalty.

59. But that is up to you, that is your discretion.

(Mr Thorpe) Like all bodies, we are bound by the precedents that go before us and we have to take the arguments of those we try and take through the disciplinary process. We are also very concerned, as any administrative body exercising administrative powers is, that if that should be reviewed then our actions would be found to be reasonable and we do take our reasonableness quite seriously. I think the totality of that is that we have a very high burden of proof to discharge when it comes to the serious offences. On the more general point about the accumulation of powers, it is a point that has a bit of history to it, but the powers that we are looking at receiving under this legislation, save for the area of market abuse where there are some genuinely new powers that have not existed in the past and we are not looking at a new panoply of particularly onerous

[**Mr Heathcoat-Amory** *Cont*]

powers, they have been onerous before, they were there before and we are of the view that put together with the process that we have been working at with the industry and their advisers it will deliver the fairness that must be required of us and will meet the ECHR requirements as well.

Chairman: We will come to market abuse in a moment.

Lord Eatwell

60. I have one extra question on rules. Mr Davies, in your introduction you said that if there was no new Act beyond the spring of next year then you would run into difficulties and yet in your speech to the Chancery Bar Association you said that it is not realistic to think all the codes of practice and rule books have been finally overhauled. So why will it cause difficulties when you will not be ready to do the job anyhow?

(Mr Davies) The difficulties to which I refer are (1) practical and (2) potentially legal. When the self-regulatory boards agreed that it was reasonable to delegate their staff to the FSA and have the FSA carry out their functions on their behalf, reporting back to the boards, they did so on the basis of advice that it was reasonable for them to do this on the basis that they were organisations with a limited life and the Government had clearly declared that they would be removed in a finite period, and the boards took the view that, based on that legal advice and their expectation that legislation would be brought forward in a timely way, this was a reasonable exercise of their functions. I think legally it would have been open to the SROs in the past to have had their enforcement work or their supervision work done by somebody else on their behalf. There is no reason why they should employ staff. However, the sort of time horizon at which people were looking was some time in the spring or summer of 2000 as the end point for this process. I think the risk is that if the legislation is not through by then people may argue that the decision made by the SRO boards might have been a different decision if they had known that they were going to stay in existence for a longer period. The second point is a more practical one, which is, of course, that our system at the moment depends very heavily on the goodwill of the members of the SRO boards to continue working, even though they know, of course, that there is no future in the organisations that they run, and I am very conscious that we prevail on a lot of people still to spend a lot of time managing the old system, which must become an activity with diminishing returns. It is true to say that not every jot and tittle of the rule books will be revised in time for the spring of next year but the key point is that those rules which we took over, which we could adopt where we were not going to change them, the old SRO rules can be adopted as FSA rules. That would be our system to manage with a new set of practitioner panels and groups and boards, etc. within that, and that would still allow us some time to achieve the final change of the rule books to the new form, but the legislative responsibility would have come to us. So I think there is a distinction to be drawn between the legislative responsibility and the amendment of the system, where

I should say that the pressure on us from the market typically is in favour of lengthening that process because of the year 2000 problem and not wanting to have to change a lot of detailed systems over the next 12 months. So the market on the whole would like the legislation to come through reasonably soon so that there was certainty about the overall environment and we could restock our committees and organise ourselves for the long term and then proceed in a more measured way to revise the rule books, which in any case have to be subject to consultation and cost-benefit analysis before we can change them materially.

Chairman

61. Thank you very much. I would like to move on to the question of scope but might I ask one last question on this. Is there any case for making the Enforcement Committee part of the Bill? We have seen the move to the suggestion that the Consumer Panel and the Practitioner Panel should now become statutory components. What about the Enforcement Committee?

(Mr Thorpe) We are looking now again, as I mentioned before, with the industry at how much separation needs to be achieved to satisfy both perceptions and legal requirements and we will be taking that matter up with the Treasury. Certainly one of the issues we will look at is whether greater detail needs to go into the Bill on that point. At this stage it does not show itself as an immediate case.

Chairman: On the question of scope, we have two broad areas that it might be sensible to do today. One is the issue of territorial scope and the other is the vexed question of mortgages, which I would like to move on to. Mr Heathcoat-Amory is going to raise the question of territorial scope.

Mr Heathcoat-Amory

62. Scotland. I am a little surprised, and perhaps I can put this as a question. Is it the case that regulating Scottish solicitors, in so far as they give financial advice, will now come under the FSA? If so, this is a curious devolution in reverse and I wonder if you consulted with Scottish interests on this and in particular whether you foresee a possible difficulty with the Scottish Parliament, who will be guiding all the legislation governing Scottish solicitors, and whether you could either find yourself reporting to two different bodies or arbitrating in a rather unhealthy English/Scots type of war on this issue?

(Mr Davies) I hope not. As I understand it, the Government's intention is that financial regulation remains a power for this Parliament. In the case of solicitors in Scotland, in the case of solicitors in general, if they are regulated to do investment business in the future they will need to be regulated by us. There is perhaps a separate issue that you might not have time to come on to, about how you define investment business, and our general proposition would be to define it in such a way that we only captured in our regulatory regime those people who were genuinely doing investment business as a business and not as business incidental to their legal

[Mr Heathcoat-Amory *Cont*]
or accounting professional work. But it is true to say that by making that change solicitors who do carry out investment business as a business will be regulated by their professional body for their legal work and by the FSA for their investment work and that will be the case throughout the United Kingdom. So they will have a dual regulation both north and south of the border.

63. So it will come from Scotland down to the FSA in London?
(Mr Davies) No.

64. At the minute it can be done by the Scottish Law Society?
(Mr Davies) Yes, sorry. That aspect, if they are running investment business as a business under the terms that the Bill eventually defined, then it will come to the FSA, yes. We have an Edinburgh office but it will come to us.

Dr Cable

65. You made a very powerful plea at the beginning for unitary regulation but the banks have persuaded the Government that one aspect of their business, and specifically one aspect of their loan business, should be taken out and regulated separately under a self-regulating structure. Could you, first of all, tell us where you stand on this issue? Is it such an anomaly and do you feel strongly about it?
(Mr Davies) I think it is not quite right to say that it has been taken out because it was not ever in, in that there has not been in the old regime conduct of business regulation of the mortgage-selling process. The conduct of business regulation that there is applies to long-term investment products—personal pensions, life insurance, unit trusts, etc.—and mortgages, which are a liability not an asset, have not been captured by a conduct of business regulation. In awareness of the fact that there was considerable consumer anxiety about mortgage-selling practices, the industry itself decided to set up a self-regulatory regime, which I think it is fair to say has only in the last six to nine months got going in its full form, and that is attempting to improve the standards of mortgage-selling, and the position that the Government have taken is that it will be for ministers to reach a view on whether that code is delivering an improved standard of consumer protection, or if not, whether a more cost-effective means of achieving that would be to put it into the FSA. Ministers have clearly said that they wish to make that decision and that our role will be to provide analysis for them of the costs of putting the regulation into the FSA if that is what they decided. It is clear that in general terms the Bill gives a very rigorous framework to the FSA in terms of deciding on any extension of its scope. It requires us to go through cost-benefit analysis, both our own costs, industry's costs, and also to explain why it is that the examples of consumer detriment that we might find would be corrected by this new regulatory framework. We have not done that analysis in relation to the mortgage market as it is currently operated because it is new, with a new CML code, so we will need to go through a process of looking at how far the CML code has dealt with the kind of problems that there were in the

market and whether going beyond that into our regulation would achieve a better outcome at a reasonable cost. It follows from that that I think it would be not just unwise but actually wrong for us to give a view on what the outcome of that process should be now because I think I could then reasonably be accused of having made up my mind beforehand and then produced a cost-benefit analysis to justify the decision I had made. So I am afraid I am not prepared to be tempted by yet another seductive question to decide at this point whether it would be right to extend the FSA regime to mortgages.

Chairman

66. Could I ask a possibly more practical question? If it were to be, and the conclusion was that it were to become part of your business, how would it change the nature of the FSA? What would you have to do? What would it do to your size? Have you any ideas about what it would do to the mortgage industry generally if it were to be brought within your remit?
(Mr Davies) I think it is fair to say that, of course, quite a lot of the institutions which deliver mortgages are already regulated by us one way or another, either prudentially and usually also for Conduct of Business and for some of them adding Conduct of Business regulation of mortgages would not make a huge amount of difference either to us or them because we are visiting them anyway and we could look at their mortgage business as well as, for example, their personal pensions business. However, the mortgage market remains quite a diverse market and our estimate is that there are probably 6,000 or so unregulated mortgage providers or intermediaries who would be brought within the net if we were to regulate mortgages. What we cannot be sure of is how many of them would wish to get themselves authorised by the FSA. Some might decide that they did not have the procedures, that they did not have the personnel who were trained to cope with regulatory requirements, so some of them might vanish away. If we did have another 6,000 or so then we would be talking about quite a considerable increase in our activity. As I have mentioned before, we have 4,000 PIA firms and this would be potentially another 6,000 and therefore we would not be talking tens of people but 100 to 200 people if you were going to do a proper job on assessing the effectiveness of that selling process.

Mr Sheerman

67. We can see the need for the concentration on whether mortgages should be in or should be out. Mr Davies, looking at the Bill as a whole, is there any other activity that you would have thought—and this legislation has been in progress since July—on mature reflection you would like to see included in the scope of the legislation that has not been put in up to this present moment but which at the moment seems to be a hole in the legislation?
(Mr Davies) The Government have announced one extension of prepaid funeral plans which seemed to us to meet the criteria that we have in place in terms of extensions. I am happy to give you a straightforward

[Mr Sheerman Cont]

answer to that, but essentially what we look for is a methodology which says that if we see some new product area or area where people want to come to us and suggest we should regulate it we ask ourselves a whole series of questions, such as how far does it look as if this justifies regulation? Is it something where the costs of being locked into the product are so high that the decision is very important to start with? Is it something which is characterised by many repeat purchases, like *Bureaux de Change* where you may say that if people pay high commission one day presumably they will go across the street for the next transaction? We ask ourselves a series of questions. If you asked yourself those questions then I think prepaid funeral plans score quite highly. I would say that long-term care insurance probably also scores quite highly. The Royal Commission on Long Term Care recommended that it should be regulated. It is a relatively immature market at the moment, but I suspect that if you ran a complete cost-benefit analysis on that you would find that scoring quite highly. The one other area that I draw attention to is Credit Unions, where the Government put out a consultation paper which suggested two ways of approaching Credit Union regulation, i.e. either just as is, with rather simple regulation which is essentially by registration really rather than supervision, or a more FSA-type framework and we have responded to that consultation by saying that we think there is a case for bringing them into the FSA because we are quite bullish about the prospects for Credit Unions overall in the UK, but we think they are more likely to flourish if they have a proper regulatory regime put around them, although we have some caveats about how that will be paid for, but those are the cases where we can see cases for extension at the present time.

Mrs Blackman

68. The FSA will regulate the financial advice that recognised financial bodies give. The House of Commons Treasury Select Committee recommended that the definition of that advice be drawn quite narrowly. Has there been any progress on that? Is it difficult to do?

(Mr Davies) I think it probably is not totally straightforward to do, but our point of view on this is quite clear. We would like the legislation to be drawn up in such a way that there was no need for authorisation if a professional firm was retailing advice from an authorised provider of that advice already so that if you were just a conduit for an authorised person then you should be outside. Secondly, where investment business is supplementary to the practice of a profession, and there are for instance some bits of incidental business attached to probate or family law business which arise which could be counted as investment business, we would like them to be excluded because we believe at the moment there is a lot of precautionary authorisation and I think the Treasury are thinking about that at the moment.

Chairman: The next question is on the Ombudsman and compensation schemes.

Mr Beard

69. The Government has said that they will give the FSA discretion as to whether disputes relating to activities which could be regulated by the FSA under the Bill should be brought within the compulsory jurisdiction. What are the advantages of doing that and will you be required to carry out consultation if you use that discretion?

(Mr Thorpe) We are looking at a position with the various Ombudsmen schemes which is only slightly less complicated than that which the FSA has had to deal with in terms of numbers of schemes and their approach to their task. The key point here is that some of the eight schemes that are going at present operate with a compulsory jurisdiction, some operate a voluntary jurisdiction and some expand beyond the scope that the Financial Services Authority will have in terms of investment business. What we are keen to do is ensure that in bringing together a single Ombudsman we do not cut out a complaints handling mechanism that is already up and running and serving consumers well, hence the need to provide legislation which allows the Ombudsman to go beyond our scope in dealing with those complaints. There are two requirements that we understand will apply to any expansion beyond that compulsory FSA scope: firstly, the need to consult and, secondly, a cost-benefit analysis yet again must come into play, but consultation most certainly will have to take place. It will be the industry, after all, that has to bear the cost of its voluntary inclusion.

70. The Government has declined to change the requirement that a respondent firm but not a complainant should be bound by the Ombudsman's decision. Is that inherently unfair?

(Mr Thorpe) I suppose it depends whether you are the firm or the complainant in this case. If it is unfair, it is the same unfairness that exists in most of the schemes at the moment. I do not think I would make an apology for it. I think it repeats a positive discrimination in favour of those who are likely to be less able to take their cause through other channels through the courts. I believe it is intended that those who are in that position should have the advantage of having all of their rights available to them, the Ombudsman scheme and then, should they choose, the courts.

Lord Montague of Oxford

71. I would like us to turn our minds to the public. What do they do if they have got a complaint? Are they going to ring you? Are you going to shove them off to somebody else and is somebody else in turn going to shove them off to somebody else? How is it all going to work? We have heard of the one-stop shop. It does not sound like that to me in terms of consumer complaints. Will you try and see if you could move to that?

(Mr Thorpe) I think you have described correctly the system that we are looking at the moment because it is very difficult for most consumers to be able to identify to whom they should take their complaint in the first instance. In many instances there will be

[Lord Montague of Oxford Cont]

several jurisdictions which might overlap. We are with this legislation intending to see a single complaints resolution mechanism, a single ombudsman scheme, as an important precursor to the action of that scheme. We are not seeking to see a change on the primary responsibility that the firm will have for resolving the complaint and our advice to all people who have complaints will be, "You should go to the person who gives rise to that complaint first and seek its resolution." What we are then trying to put in place is a one-stop shop for those who do not obtain satisfaction from the firm or individual that they are dealing with, and yes, it will be a one-stop shop. It will not be us but it will be our ombudsman scheme.

72. Very often with a complaint a consumer wants advice. I wonder if there is a role for you with your education objective to see if some of this advice can be given in a slightly more professional way by Citizen's Advice Bureaux? People are comfortable with going to Citizen's Advice Bureaux, partly because they know it does not cost them any money. They are hesitant about going to a lawyer because straightaway they are incurring costs.

(Mr Thorpe) I would add on that last point it is not intended that the ombudsman scheme, indeed none of the existing schemes, require you to be legally represented to take advantage of them. In fact, from my own knowledge of the way these schemes operate, they are very keen to try and assist complainants to put their complaints in a useable and progressable form. The use of Citizen's Advice Bureaux is a matter we have looked at and certainly one of the initiatives we have taken is already to start publishing booklets that will be helpful to the consumers and we will look for any channel to distribute those and the Bureaux are very valuable channels for that form of distribution.

73. And the training of the personnel within the Bureaux?

(Mr Thorpe) We have not gone that far but we will certainly be happy to talk to the Bureaux to discuss that.

Lord Haskel

74. As I see it, there will be an ombudsman scheme and a separate compensation scheme. Will one follow automatically from the other or will the consumer have to go to the compensation scheme having had a decision from the ombudsman?

(Mr Thorpe) Sadly, sometimes the sequence does not have to be that way because firms make the mistake of going immediately into liquidation, in which case the first port of call for the consumer will be the compensation scheme. We are looking at the pass-over. What we find at the moment is that the majority of complaints are resolved whilst the firm is still in existence, the vast majority. It is very rarely that a case goes to the ombudsman and then suddenly the firm is out of business and falls into another category. Where that does happen there have been problems in the past and we are looking at how we can use the information twice so that we

do not put the compensation process through the business of re-establishing the facts.

(Mr Davies) But it is worth underlining that for the most part the compensation awarded by the ombudsman is awarded against an existing, continuing firm and there is no way that goes to the compensation scheme to be handled. The compensation scheme only comes in if you have a complaint against a firm which has then gone into liquidation. So that is a tiny proportion of the cases involved. There are some enforcement cases, of course, in the past there have been, but it is not the normal route. You do not need to go to the compensation scheme to get an ombudsman award enforced.

Mr Sheerman

75. Could I ask a quick supplementary on that, Chairman. Every time that someone makes a complaint to the ombudsman about an account with a building society, what is the cost of that to the building society regardless of who wins or loses?

(Mr Davies) I think we will have to come back to you on that.

76. I have heard from the building society organisations that it is substantial and they have a number of people who have threatened to make a complaint in order to get a quick pay-off. Are you aware of that?

(Mr Davies) It is a wicked world. I could not rule out that possibility. I should say that at the moment the building societies scheme is a scheme which we have no great insight into. We have not been responsible for managing that scheme. It will gradually be folded into the ombudsman scheme. In general principle the ombudsmen are fairly discriminating in taking up only the cases that they feel are reasonable and it is only in a case they actually agree to take up that the bank or building society would incur significant costs.

77. So just an initial reference to the ombudsman does not cost anything? He has actually to take it up to incur a cost for the building society?

(Mr Davies) It might cost the building society something because the ombudsman might say, "Here is a complaint" and he might initially refer it to the building society and he might get a letter back which actually removes it completely, where the ombudsman says, "I do not wish to pursue this any further." So it is unlikely that an ombudsman would reject a complaint completely out of hand without getting any kind of answer but quite a number would fall at the fence of just getting one letter back which explains the position; perhaps somebody has misunderstood something.

Chairman

78. Thank you very much. That leaves us with one question. Unfortunately, it is the rather burning issue of market abuse. But maybe we can short-circuit this as far as possible and maybe we are going to have to come back another day. We

[Chairman *Cont]*

are going to have some of our evidence sessions on this. Some of us were at a conference last week which you ran where we got a better feel for this issue. But it might be helpful to the Committee if you could explain reasonably briefly what you see to be the state of this particular game at the moment. Where you are in the process of batting backwards and forwards the views and the concerns about this question?

(Mr Davies) I think the first point to make is that we do believe that it would be right to have a code. It would be possible to have some offences in the Bill and then for case-law effectively to develop as the regulators took cases and in some other jurisdictions that is what has happened. We believe that it would be better from the point of view of certainty in the marketplace for there to be a code which set out as clearly as possible what the regulators saw as the offences and what they saw as market abuse and what they did not. But we recognised that this was going to be a difficult exercise and, therefore, we set about it rather early in the process. We will not need this code until a year from now at the earliest, we would guess, but we did put out a first version of it last summer and we gave people an extensive period of time for consultation and we have then digested those consultation responses and, as you say, last week held a conference at which we published a feedback statement on the main points that had been made to us about the code. I guess the main points would be around intent. I do not have to tell you we mentioned that. We continue to believe that markets can be damaged even where there is no intent to so do. Indeed, the rest of the law provides for offences of recklessness or negligence. Nonetheless, we believe we do need to clarify the extent to which we take intent into account or take the absence of intent into account, and it is quite clear that we do not propose to prosecute people for accidental offences. We have said that many times in relation to our enforcement procedures. But undoubtedly the market is looking for more clarity from us in that area. The second area is the general question of definitions of what we mean and how the code relates to particular types of market transaction. There is undoubtedly a need for greater clarity there and we are working through a variety of market circumstances with practitioners to try to tease out what we mean. The third area is the interrelationship between the market abuse code and the enforcement processes. I think we have probably handled that this afternoon. I guess the fourth big area is the issue of waivers or no action letters, as they are sometimes called in the US jurisdiction, and the market is asking us in what circumstances we would be prepared to say, "This transaction we will not regard as in conflict with the code," etc. We are currently working on a policy statement which I hope to take to our board next month about the circumstances in which we will be prepared to issue clarificatory guidance and waivers, etc. So where we are going is, we press on to try to revise the code in a way that will meet people's concerns; the enforcement process we are dealing with separately; the waiver process we are dealing with separately, and we hope that in the next few months we can resolve these issues to a reasonable degree. I cannot be sure we will ever end up with a code which everybody thinks is a splendid thing but we are not discouraged from our belief that it is possible to achieve it.

Lord Poole

79. May I ask on the question of waivers, leaving aside the consumer market, where I can see that that perhaps might be very difficult, in the professional marketplace when I was running a bank it was incredibly helpful to be able to go along to the Bank of England, talk to one's regulator and say, "I am thinking about doing something along these lines. How would you feel about it? What sort of issues would it raise with you?" The same has applied in other marketplaces that I have operated in and it does lead to things being very speedily resolved and that is often very important in terms of a competitive edge for London. I do not want you obviously to commit yourself to something you have still got under discussion but do you feel at all well disposed towards practitioners of the sort that I am and have been who would like to be able to have conversations rather than 45-page documents?

(Mr Davies) Broadly speaking, yes, I would agree with that. The Bank of England has done that in the past and we do it now and I would expect us to carry on doing that and, indeed, there are some benefits from that because while some people who come in are entirely reasonable folk who are seeking the truth, there are some others where you get some interesting information which you do not like the sound of because people come in and talk to you and so we certainly do not want to get into a position where people are afraid to come and discuss things with us. I do not think that that is an issue. The specific request put by some in response to the market abuse document, however, relates to particular transactions and to some kind of legal quasi indemnity. That is not characterised in the kind of relationship that you are talking about in the past and that raises much more difficult issues. You have to be very very clear about the terms of the transaction you are approving because you do not want to approve something and then discover that when it is actually effected the transaction is rather different in crucial ways from the one that was put to you. Of course, you also have to address the question of whether it is right for everybody in the market to pay for that or whether the firms asking for this specific exemption should be asked to pay for it. That in itself raises rather complex issues. No, we are not trying to rule out the kind of informal discussions we have about what our guidance means, what our rules mean, how transactions fit in with them. What we are addressing is a specific point.

Chairman

80. It was quite clear to me at the conference, and this goes back to the conversation we were having earlier, that there is some concern that people may walk into a problem that they had not foreseen. And that you were then going to come after them with some pretty tough penalties. This raises the whole question about whether or not the guidance is clear, whether or not they are going to be caught, in a sense, off-side in this way and if the penalty is going to turn out to be extremely substantial. This is obviously something that you have very much in mind and it is going to be an issue of how far there will be a meeting of minds on this. But I was struck by what I regarded as quite a high degree of nervousness in the market about these powers.

(*Mr Thorpe*) I think we agree with the nervousness. We would hate to see the development of this code evidenced by a series of enforcement cases. That would be evidence of failure in terms of prescribing a code to cope with the alternative bits of the market. I would just reinforce the point that our Chairman was making, that we are in the process of reviewing the comments and it will be a matter of issuing another draft of this code at some point when we feel we have reached a consensus with the Chairman.

81. I think that probably is as much as we can usefully do this afternoon, Mr Davies. Thank you very much. I know it has been a very long session. We would like to keep open the possibility, after we have had our deliberations both with the Minister and with others in the world outside, that we might come back to you at a later stage. On the other hand, looking at the timetable, time may very well not allow that. But we have had a very useful session and we are very grateful for the way in which you have answered our questions. Thank you very much.

(*Mr Davies*) Thank you. Of course, we would be happy to return.

Printed in the UK by The Stationery Office Limited
3/99   418843   78344

Published by The Stationery Office Limited
and available from:

The Publications Centre
(Mail, telephone and fax orders only)
PO Box 276, London SW8 5DT
General enquiries *Lo-call* 0345 58 54 63
Order through the Parliamentary Hotline *Lo-call* 0345 02 34 74
Fax orders 0171 873 8200

The Stationery Office Bookshops
123 Kingsway, London WC2B 6PQ
0171 430 1671 Fax 0171 831 1326
68-69 Bull Street, Birmingham B4 6AD
0121 236 9696 Fax 0121 236 9699
33 Wine Street, Bristol BS1 2BQ
0117 926 4306 Fax 01179 294515
9-21 Princess Street, Manchester M60 8AS
0161 834 7201 Fax 0161 833 0634
16 Arthur Street, Belfast BT1 4GD
0123 223 8451 Fax 0123 223 5401
The Stationery Office Oriel Bookshop
The Friary, Cardiff CF1 4AA
0122 239 5548 Fax 01222 384347
71 Lothian Road, Edinburgh EH3 9AZ
0131 228 4181 Fax 0131 622 7017

The Parliamentary Bookshop
12 Bridge Street, Parliament Square,
London SW1A 2JX
Telephone orders 0171 219 3890
General enquiries 0171 219 3890
Fax orders 0171 219 3866

Accredited Agents
(see Yellow Pages)

and through good booksellers

ISBN 0-10-432399-X

HOUSE OF LORDS
HOUSE OF COMMONS

SESSION 1998–99

JOINT COMMITTEE ON FINANCIAL SERVICES AND MARKETS

MINUTES OF EVIDENCE

Thursday 18 March 1999

HM Treasury

Ms Patricia Hewitt, MP and Mr David Roe

Printed pursuant to the Order of the House of Lords of 2 March 1999
Ordered by The House of Commons *to be printed*
18 March 1999

LONDON: THE STATIONERY OFFICE
£4.65

HL Paper 50-ii
HC 328-ii

THURSDAY 18 MARCH 1999

Present:

Lord Burns (in the Chair)   Mr Nigel Beard
Lord Eatwell   Mrs Liz Blackman
Lord Haskel   Mr David Heathcoat-Amory
Lord Montague of Oxford   Mr Tim Loughton
Lord Poole   Mr James Plaskitt
Viscount Trenchard   Mr Barry Sheerman

Examination of witnesses

Ms PATRICIA HEWITT, a Member of the House, Economic Secretary to HM Treasury, and MR DAVID ROE, Head of the Bill Team, HM Treasury, called in and examined.

Chairman

82. Good afternoon, Economic Secretary, welcome to the second public session of the Joint Committee. As you can see this is becoming quite a popular activity. As you know, we have decided to look at the range of issues that we set out in our press release. We are taking the Progress Report, which the Treasury published a week or two ago, as our main text and asking ourselves how far this meets the concerns of those who commented on the Bill and what are the outstanding issues. After the session with you we are then going to have a number of sessions with consumers and practitioners, taking the issues one by one, to see if we can find out how people are responding to the updated position of where we are. We are very grateful to you for coming today. The first thing is to ask whether you have an opening statement.

(Ms Hewitt) If I could, please. Perhaps I could begin, Chairman, by introducing my colleague, David Roe, who is the Head of the Bill team within the Treasury and who will be working very closely with you. I should also like, if I may, Chairman, to thank not only yourself but every Member of the Committee for taking on this task. I think pre-legislative scrutiny by a Joint Committee of this kind is almost without precedent. I am very aware, as my colleagues are, that you do have a very substantial task in front of you and also a pretty challenging timescale. We are extremely grateful to you for taking it on. Obviously I want to make sure that I, but also my officials, work very closely with you. What is important about this process is that we have an opportunity for the executive branch and the legislative branch to work together in getting the best possible system of regulation for our financial services industry. That industry, of course, is a very important part of the British economy: seven per cent of GDP, employing over one million people. I think it is important to have that context in mind when we look at the principles underpinning the Bill and the details of it. The financial markets support enterprise, provide funds for investment, but using for that purpose the savings which millions of people entrust to the industry. All of us as savers, as consumers, as business people, have a shared interest in a regulatory structure that is clear, robust, accountable and fair. It needs to provide proper consumer protection particularly to the small man and woman, the retail consumer who may be quite unsophisticated in financial affairs, but at the

same time it needs to work with the grain of the market and take full account of the needs of competition, of innovation and international competitiveness. The standpoint from which we have approached the drafting of this Bill is light touch regulation where possible, protection where necessary. I am happy to say that we have had an excellent, very constructive response to the public consultation on the draft Bill that we published last summer. As you said, Chairman, we have now produced a Progress Report on the main areas on which people commented and our reactions. We have also had a very helpful report from the Treasury Select Committee in the House of Commons which we have taken very careful note of and I am sure that this Committee will also have the opportunity to study it. It is particularly good to see some Members of the Treasury Select Committee on this Joint Committee so that some of the ideas developed in this report can be taken forward further here. I think it might be helpful if I just say a little bit about the six topics which I understand this Committee has decided to focus on. First of all, on the issue of accountability because getting the accountability of the FSA right is crucial. We believe that one of the advantages of having a single regulator, which has been very widely welcomed in the consultation, is that it offers the possibility of much clearer lines of accountability. We want to capitalise on that. I think that the arrangements we proposed last summer in the draft Bill were a very big advance on the present arrangements but a number of respondents had concerns about them and because of that we have reflected further and we have announced several more improvements to the accountability regime. That includes the periodic independent reports into the Authority's efficiency and value for money, the statutory creation of Consumer and Practitioner Panels and annual public meetings. All of these proposals were in response to the constructive comments that we have had. The second issue, which of course is critical to proper accountability, is the question of clear objectives. What we have done in the Bill is to give the FSA statutory objectives on market confidence, consumer awareness, consumer protection and financial crime. I think the responses to the consultation suggested that, with the possible need for clarification in some areas, we have got the balance and the coverage of those objectives and the supporting principles about right but

[**Chairman** *Cont*]

obviously that is a conclusion we hope this Committee will test. The third issue, again closely linked to accountability, is fairness and openness in how the FSA uses its powers. A number of points were put to us about the process by which the Authority might use the extensive discipline and enforcement powers that we propose to give them and how the FSA's role relates to that of the independent tribunal that will be set up by the Lord Chancellor. Again, we have responded to the consultation with some significant improvements, including a duty on the FSA to act in accordance with its published procedures and a right for firms and individuals to see the evidence on which the case for regulatory action rests. The fourth issue has to do with the scope of regulated activities, another area, not surprisingly, of great interest. We are very interested in your views and obviously those of the Treasury Select Committee on the case for and against regulating mortgage advice and also on the question of when financial services regulation is appropriate for members of the recognised professions. Those are both issues where we have to balance the objective of appropriate consumer protection with the desire to avoid unnecessary or even overlapping regulation. Fifthly, our plans for a single Ombudsman and single compensation scheme have generally been very well received. There have been some useful detailed suggestions for improvements and again we have signalled our intention to act on them. Finally, there is the issue of market abuse. We are still looking very carefully at whether we need to make any changes in the Bill's regime for the imposing of administrative fines on people who abuse our financial markets. I really want to underline this Government's determination to take firm action against people who harm the efficiency of the financial markets or undermine confidence in the financial services industry in this way because damage to the financial markets undermines the economy as a whole. Again, we will give very careful thought to your views before we reach a final conclusion on the detail of the measures and whether any further drafting changes are needed to the Bill before it is introduced in the House. I look forward very much to your questions and to working with you and members of the Committee during your enquiry.

83. Thank you very much, Minister. We would like to begin with the general subject of accountability. The Government has stressed its commitment to accountability and, as you say, following the consultation process you have proposed a number of ways of strengthening that. However, I think it is still fair to say that there are quite a lot of people who remain concerned that here we are putting together a single large organisation which has a lot of powers across a wide range of areas and quite a lot of discretion in terms of rules and codes of conduct, etc. We would like to explore the extent to which you think that balance of accountability is now right; or whether there are any other ways that one can go if there is still unease about it. We have not yet had much feedback in terms of the revised proposals that you have made.

(Ms Hewitt) Indeed.

84. But I think it would be helpful if we could begin by just looking at the issue generally and asking whether you think you have now got this right or whether there are any other ways in which you can reassure people that we have here an organisation which is going to be properly accountable.

(Ms Hewitt) I think we have gone a very long way towards getting it right. There are some new suggestions being made but there may well be further changes that we should consider. What I would stress is that we are really putting in place here two lines of accountability. There is the accountability to ministers and to Parliament which is absolutely crucial given the public purposes of the FSA. We are achieving that because the Treasury has the powers to appoint but also to remove the board. The Treasury will have the power to commission statutory enquiries in the public interest. There will be an annual report to ministers on the FSA's performance measured against its statutory objectives and any other matters that the Treasury specifies. Those reports, of course, will be laid by the minister to Parliament and will thus be available for parliamentary scrutiny. We obviously hope, and I think the Treasury Select Committee in particular has indicated that it would wish to play a full role in holding the FSA accountable to Parliament. We have also suggested, in light of the consultation responses, that we as the Treasury should have the power to commission specific enquiries into the efficiency and economy with which the FSA carries out its responsibilities. I think that is a full line of public accountability. There is also the second line of accountability to the industry itself. What we have sought to achieve is accountability both to practitioners and to consumers through the annual open meeting that the Authority will have a statutory obligation to hold, through the annual report, through the fact that the board will have a majority of non-executives. They will have a particular responsibility, and powers, to monitor the FSA's compliance in terms of its fulfilment of its objectives but will also be responsible for ensuring that the FSA is efficient in its operation. Some of those non-executives, of course, are and will be practitioners. There will also be a Practitioner Panel, that has already been constituted, and there is a very clear obligation upon the Authority to consult with practitioners and others in introducing new rules and also on its fee arrangements. Again with consumers, in addition to the open meeting and the annual report, they too, or consumer representatives and organisations, will have to be consulted on rules. I think it would be impossible to constitute an effective board for the FSA without having amongst the non-executive directors some people with a specific interest in and experience of consumer matters. Of course there will also be the Consumer Panel currently modelled on the PIA's Consumer Panel but to be expanded in line with the new Bill. So I think that is a pretty substantial set of arrangements for accountability. We had announced, I think in response to the consultation, more specification of the process, for instance the requirement to give feedback when the FSA is consulting on new rules but we are very happy to look at further suggestions on that. What we do not

[Chairman *Cont]*

want to do is put so much procedural detail into the legislation in the name of accountability that we then tie the FSA down to procedures that in some years' time may not be appropriate but where it will be impossible to change them without coming back for primary legislation.

Chairman: Thank you very much. Lord Montague?

Lord Montague of Oxford

85. May I start with the consumer arrangements and say how pleasing it is to learn that the Consumer Panel is going to be on a statutory basis, but I am just wondering how that will work and whether you feel it has got sufficient independence. It is customary, as you are no doubt aware, for such organisations to have their own budgets and an appropriate amount of freedom. When we asked Mr Davies about the budget he told us what budget exists at the present time and it seemed to be plucked out of the air. I do not mean that unkindly but it might be worth reflecting on how we can have a budget that has some sort of formal basis and it is not a whim, as it were, of the FSA. Secondly, when it comes to the feeling of security of people on the Consumer Panel that they can be independent without fear they are going to lose jobs, I think they might be happier if they felt they were employed by the Consumer Panel rather than employed by the FSA. That is certainly something that goes through one's mind and your views on that would be very helpful. Staying with the aspect of consumers there was a statement put out in relation to the public at large which said that the new architecture provided investors with a one-stop shop for information and redress. It seems to me it is more of a two-stop shop. I am thinking of the Ombudsman scheme and wonder whether there will be any relationship and whether you would consider some benefit to a relationship between the Consumer Panel and the Ombudsman scheme. Finally, the final thought coming from me is there are the public, and if they are uncertain in some particular situation, what do they do? Who do they go to? Who can they expect a response from? How will the rules work?

(Ms Hewitt) Let me take those in turn. Starting with the Consumer Panel, I have a very strong belief that the Consumer Panel, and you could just look at the people that are already on that Panel, have exactly the qualities of independence of mind and commitment to the interests of consumers that will enable them to play a very effective role in relation to the FSA. By putting that Panel on to a statutory basis we have really underlined our commitment to consumer protection and helped to ensure that the FSA board and the FSA staff take the views of the Consumer Panel very seriously indeed. On the issue of the budget I think with a new organisation, albeit one that is building upon the old foundations, it may be quite difficult to decide in the first instance what the appropriate level of budget is. I am sure that is a matter on which the Consumer Panel itself will be putting forward views, but if there are suggestions for a clearer basis for that budget to be set I am sure Howard Davies in particular would want to look at them very sympathetically. In

terms of the FSA staff, I have met and been very impressed by several of the staff in the consumer affairs section of the FSA. Were you suggesting they should all be employed by the Panel rather than the Authority?

86. Those who are working, as it were, for the Panel are employed by this statutory body, the Panel.

(Ms Hewitt) That is something that I would need to look at. I would not want the Panel to have to set itself up as an employer with some additional, almost bureaucratic administrative requirements there. I suspect it is much easier if their secretariat and their office is provided by the FSA but if there are concerns there from members of the Panel I would be very happy to look at them. The next issue was to do with the Ombudsmen and also the related question of whether consumers will know where to go. I think this is very important and one of the difficulties, it seems to me, with the old system of financial regulation that we inherited was that there were nine different regulators and a large number of different Ombudsman people and compensation schemes and all the rest of it and the ordinary consumer found it extremely bewildering. I believe that with a single Ombudsman and with the publicity and concentration of resources that we are establishing with a single regulator consumers will find it much easier to know where to go and of course the advertising campaign that the Financial Services Authority has itself been sponsoring this year to launch phase two of the personal pensions review has helped to publicise it as a very active body that is out there looking after consumer interests.

87. Where will they go? Do they go to the FSA or do they go to the Ombudsman? Will the Ombudsman people be advertising? Where do they go to? Do they go to the FSA to respond to all the fears and worries and questions they have? I am not talking about selling products or anything like that.

(Ms Hewitt) The FSA is going to put in place and is already creating a single helpline for consumers behind which they will develop a call centre with trained staff. People who phone into that will be able to get information about financial services and about products. They will be able to get hold of leaflets and information and so on. Some of it of course is in pursuit of the FSA's objective of raising financial awareness. If what the person writes or phones to the FSA about is a particular complaint about a particular financial services organisation then the FSA will be able to advise them on the appropriate complaints process. If they have gone through that complaints process and they are not happy then they will go to the Ombudsman. If they happen to ring the FSA helpline at the point where they need to go to the Ombudsman then the FSA will direct them to the Ombudsman but, as I understand it, although the company that will operate the Ombudsman is only now being established, the Ombudsman him or herself will wish to publicise their existence so that a consumer who has gone through a complaint without satisfaction against a provider will know where to go.

Lord Montague of Oxford: Perhaps we can sort this out even tighter than you have so helpfully explained.

Lord Poole

88. Could I preface my question by just asserting, so that there should be no misunderstanding, that I hugely support and would have chosen it back in the 1980s the establishment of a central regulator, but I am very concerned that the steps taken to make the FSA in general and its chairman and chief executive in particular accountable will prove inadequate. I say that because listening to you and hearing you talk about accountability through you to Parliament, I find it rather less impressive and persuasive than I suspect that you do. I feel that something more is required than that. There are two ways of doing more it seems to me. One is what sort of reporting takes place, annually or bi-annually, what sort of follow-up there is for the things they do and, secondly, what constraints can be placed upon their discretion to implement. I do not think in either of those cases that enough is there. Why do I mind? I operate in this market and I and 1,000 people who work for me and their livelihoods will quite properly be subject to this organisation. We will be looking at enforcement and discipline later but I personally would be interested to know whether you would be prepared to listen to suggestions that would make something much more clear about Howard Davies being answerable for how he runs it in a more public way and for the decisions that they make in terms of the rules?

(Ms Hewitt) Thank you because I am, of course, extremely aware of your expertise in this area and I am appreciative of the fact that you, like many others, welcome the creation of a single regulator. Of course, I will look at further suggestions to strengthen lines of accountability. What I would say is it is obviously not for the Government to dictate to Parliament how it fulfils its part of the accountability process, but it does seem to me that if publication by the Minister to Parliament of the annual report were to be followed by a Treasury Select Committee or Joint Committee or whatever, by a Parliamentary Committee hearing that took place annually on the basis of the annual report where the chairman and chief executive were held to account by Parliament, and were quizzed on what was in the report and what further action was going to be taken on points of concern and so on, then that would be immensely important. I know as a Minister appearing before scrutiny committees it is a very powerful form of scrutiny for those of us who hold executive positions. As I say, I am not sure that is something we could properly specify in the Bill but I think it is a very important part of the process. In terms of action on recommendations, for instance recommendations that might come out of the Treasury commissioned inquiry into how they are operating financially and whether they are actually operating efficiently, we would obviously expect the FSA and its board and its chairman to be implementing the recommendations of such an inquiry and of course the fact the Treasury appoints the board and can disappoint the board is a rather powerful sanction in terms of ensuring that recommendations and concerns are properly followed up and acted on.

89. I think that would be another issue of some concern to quite a lot of us here as well as outsiders

because there is something terribly cosy about a Treasury that appoints the people in the Financial Services Authority and the board. I suspect we may be coming back to you on that when we have had a chance to take other evidence. I believe that the transparency of how this is made to be the world's leading regulatory environment will be critical to the survival in London of the financial services business that has been built up over the last century or so.

(Ms Hewitt) I completely agree with that. What is increasingly clear is that in the modern world regulation is a vital source of competitive advantage providing you get it right; it is a source of competitive disadvantage if you do not. On the appointments, I would just underline all appointments to the board will be in line with the Nolan procedures. They will be completely consistent with the principle of ministerial accountability for appointments that were set out in the first report of the Nolan Committee and all those procedures will be properly followed.

Lord Eatwell

90. Can I follow on from something you said in your answer to Lord Poole. It is genuinely regarded these days as very bad governance practice to have the chairman and the chief executive being the same person. I am rather puzzled that in the design of this organisation you have committed that sin against good governance.

(Ms Hewitt) The Financial Services Authority is not, I think, entirely equivalent to a private company producing goods and services, although its output is obviously rules and regulatory judgments. In the interests of accountability it seems to me that there is a good case for having one person who fulfils the functions of both chairman of the board and chief executive of the Authority and he is the person with whom the buck stops. If you or others consider that there is merit in separating those functions then of course we will have a look at that but I am not aware that it is an issue on which there was any great comment in the consultation.

Chairman

91. Your proposal is to have the position of vice chairman as the senior non-executive who has particular responsibilities with regard to scrutiny?

(Ms Hewitt) That is perfectly true. The board itself we have decided, and it is certainly proposed for the Bill, should have a majority of non-executives so it is not a question of the board being dominated by the executives with the chief executive also being the chairman. The majority of the board are non-executives.

Lord Poole

92. I think it is fair to say that you may not have received it as a component of representation but there is a growing concern that he can set the agendas of meetings, for example, and we all know this is the single most powerful thing that anyone can do. A lot of the issues and the worries about accountability could

[**Lord Poole** *Cont*]

perhaps be greatly modified by taking Lord Eatwell's point.

(*Ms Hewitt*) I would be very grateful if the Committee were to pursue this point further. I think the test has to be whether separating the two functions enhances accountability or whether it weakens it.

Chairman

93. Could I take the example which came up the other day. Suppose we were going through a process of consultation and suppose that the FSA, having listened to the consultation, decided to take little notice of the consultation and decided to head on as it originally thought. What is the response to this? The Treasury has deliberately not taken the power to instruct. After the event, several months after the event, there may be a Treasury Committee hearing in which they criticise or raise questions of the chairman. One can imagine circumstances where people could begin to feel quite frustrated that they have the power to say things and they have the power to comment but in the end the Authority just do as they wish.

(*Ms Hewitt*) What we have tried to do is build into the Bill, strengthened by the proposals summarised in the Progress Report, a number of duties upon the FSA so that for any rules that they make or wish to amend they have to publish drafts, they have to consult, they have to publish the results of the consultation, they have to undertake and publish cost benefit analysis and make the methodology as well as the conclusions of the cost benefit analysis open to public scrutiny. We are really seeking to put in place here a very, very transparent process. We are also putting in place a board that in the ways I have described is accountable to Government, and through Government to Parliament, that will have statutory duties, statutory objectives, to fulfil. If the Authority starts riding roughshod over the overwhelming views of the industry or substantial concerns raised within Parliament I think they will find their position completely untenable. It is always possible in a sense to come up with a nightmare scenario here but I have to say if the FSA ran amok then rather drastic action would be taken and the powers to take drastic action are there in the Bill.

Mr Plaskitt

94. Can I turn to the Treasury's power to commission these independent reports and first of all put a little group of practical questions together. You described these as "periodic" and I wonder if you could expand on that, whether they will follow a simple timetable or whether they could be triggered by some particular issue or concern and you think that is a sufficient reason to go in and commission an independent report on that subject and who would do them? The second question following that arises from a small discussion we had on the Progress Report, paragraph 3.10. A number of respondents have raised the statutory immunity issue and suggested that should be removed. In your response to that you cite the fact that you can have these independent reports as adequate cover for not doing that. I wonder if you

really think that is so given, as I understand it, it is only the Treasury that can initiate that independent report?

(*Ms Hewitt*) On the independent report specifically, that is really to reinforce the duty that we are giving to the non-executive directors to have a particular focus upon the efficiency of the FSA's own operation. Rather than commit ourselves to an annual or a three yearly independent audit process, as it were, we think it is more useful for the Treasury to have the power to commission an independent report as and when it is needed. That could be triggered by concerns expressed by the non-executive directors, it could be triggered by concerns expressed within the industry or concerns that officials within the Treasury or perhaps even the Bank of England were having, a whole variety of things. I think it would be a pity to pin ourselves down at this stage to an annual review that might not be needed when something less frequent or more frequent may turn out to be of more use. On the issue of immunity, this is a matter that I know has aroused considerable concern and has been the focus of some press attention. I wonder if I could just say a bit about this, Chairman. Perhaps I should start by saying that I suspect many, if not all, members of the Committee will have seen the piece by Anthony Hilton in a recent issue of the *Evening Standard* which is inaccurate in almost every respect. I am glad to say that the General Counsel to the Board of the FSA has now sent off a correction letter which I hope will shortly appear. The first point is that immunity from actions for negligence, provided that there is good faith on the part of the FSA, has existed since 1986. It is part of the regime that was put in place by the 1986 Act which was supported and endorsed by Parliament at the time and specifically endorsed by Lord Denning himself, amongst others. Immunity also exists for the SEC and the Commodities and Futures Trading Commission in the USA. There is no immunity for FSA staff or the FSA as an entity from criminal prosecution. If an FSA staff member commits a criminal offence they will be prosecuted in the usual way. There is no immunity for negligence that involves bad faith. If an FSA staff member were maliciously to pursue some firm within the marketplace and make their lives a misery that would clearly be a bad faith action and a negligence action could result. There will be no immunity for actions brought under the Human Rights Act where it is alleged that the FSA or its staff has acted in breach of the European Human Rights Convention. The scenario Mr Hilton describes where some hapless firm is driven into bankruptcy by the actions of some ill-tempered or ill-advised or ill-educated FSA staff member is frankly inconceivable because the FSA enforcement process requires not only that the FSA officer discloses evidence and causes of action to the firm or individual under investigation but also that the matter be referred to the enforcement committee of the FSA itself, a committee appointed by the board and acting in its name. The Bill provides that where the firm is unhappy with the proposed course of action it can have the matter dealt with in the first instance by the tribunal, an independent, judicial body established by the Lord

[Mr Plaskitt Cont]

Chancellor. I have spelt that out at some length because it is a matter of such importance that I do not wish this misunderstanding to take root.

Mr Loughton

95. You have stolen my thunder there. The phrase that Anthony Hilton uses—and I do not take his side— is "the most maladjusted inadequate who slips through the selection procedure can exercise all the powers granted to the body and behave with impunity". The provisos that you describe do not include incompetence and there is a scenario that says the biggest booming industry in the City at the moment is in compliance officers. There is a scenario that says that duff compliance officers will be queuing up to get jobs at the FSA because it is the one place where they will not be prosecuted. So there is a possibility of incompetent new staff. We know the problems that the FSA have had with the haemorrhaging of staff and the problem of getting decent compliance staff for City firms anyway because of the enormous amount of extra work they have to do, they are in short supply and certainly the awards available through the FSA are not nearly as attractive to staff as they are in commercial firms. So there is the scenario, by your own definition Minister, that incompetence of compliance officer recruitees could cause serious problems with firms and be immune from prosecution.

(Ms Hewitt) That is a very interesting point. The FSA itself, and Howard Davies in particular, as I am sure you have discussed with him, is making enormous efforts to ensure that they can recruit and train and retain first-rate staff because clearly the quality of our regulatory system depends upon the quality of individual regulators and compliance officers. I would be very surprised indeed if the FSA, located in the City with a board with very considerable expertise, never mind the expertise of its senior staff, were to appoint somebody who was notorious for being a duff compliance officer within a regular authorised firm. There will be the usual high standard of personnel recruitment and human resource practices within the FSA. But assume that somebody slips through the net who is not very good and the training does not make him better, even then the firm that is the object of that individual's attention can still ensure that the matter goes not only to the enforcement committee but also to the tribunal. If they believe, let's say, before the matter even goes to the enforcement committee that they are being messed around, handled incompetently or given conflicting instructions, whatever, then of course they can go directly to the chairman and chief executive. They can draw the matter directly to the attention of ministers. They can draw the matter directly to the attention of their own Member of Parliament or Members of either House who are known to have an interest in this subject. I think it is most improbable that incompetence on the part of an FSA officer would go unnoted for long either by senior staff or outsiders.

96. That does beggar the question that firms would not wish to draw attention to themselves and incur the wrath of the FSA who may pursue them slightly more aggressively than if they had rolled over and had their tummies tickled. I am afraid I do not share your enthusiasm about a great flood of potential compliance officers queuing up to be recruited by the FSA because there is an enormous shortage along with millennium bug type experts as well. What I want to draw out from you is to ask for your definition of "practitioner". You have used the term a lot and Howard Davies used the term a lot. It is related to a question I will ask in a minute. What is your definition of practitioner?

(Ms Hewitt) I am not sure I have a neat little definition for you. I assumed that we were talking about authorised individuals and firms practising within the financial markets but people also not necessarily authorised but who are practising and operating within the financial markets.

97. The point I am trying to challenge you on is that by practitioners Howard Davies includes an awful lot of compliance officers, and people who are categorised as practitioners are in fact not people at the sharp end who have done the business of selling financial products and making money but people who have been specifically recruited to institute rule books that just happen to be in the City in this case. It may not be through incompetence that firms have their business impinged upon but through a rather slavish dedication to a rule book where on practical implications and impacts on business they are entirely inadequate or entirely wrong and that is where some of the problems may occur. My fear is that compliance officers and practitioners are two entirely different things.

(Ms Hewitt) I think that is an important point but what the Financial Services Authority needs to do and is seeking to do is to ensure that within its staff, and this is also true of the board, we have what you might term "real" practitioners, people who have actually worked within the financial markets through the financial services industry in a variety of roles, not simply as compliance officers (although I would be less scornful of the role of compliance officers than you are implying) but have advised real clients and handled the money and done the business in a serious way. I think despite its recruitment difficulties the FSA has got some very good staff with precisely that kind of experience. If you look at the board of the Authority and also at the Practitioners Panel, again you will see people with real hands-on experience.

Lord Eatwell

98. I just wanted to follow up really and it is a point I put to Mr Davies as well, Minister, which is this: one of the most striking characteristics of the Board of Banking Supervision's report into the Baring's affair was that Bank of England staff, high quality and talented though they are, did not understand the business they were regulating. The attempt to acquire good staff has got it seems to me two good models. One is the SEC model where very bright young lawyers know that having worked for the SEC on their *curriculum vitae* they have a good chance of an illustrious career later in life. There is also the model of using practitioners as decision makers where

[Lord Eatwell *Cont*]

you get very talented people working for you for free because they come in and make decisions, which works with the SRO structure, I think with reasonable success. We seem to have opted in this Bill for the model that has failed and that is the life-long bureaucrat model which is the Bank of England model and it is the model of people making a career of being regulators who actually run too far behind the industry. I think that is the staff fear which is reverberating around this Committee.

(*Ms Hewitt*)   I must say I am surprised to hear you say that about what we are doing with this Bill and with our Authority. I do not think that there is anything in the Bill at all to say that the FSA has to follow perhaps the traditional public service model of a lifetime career. Not at all. The Financial Services Authority, and some have commented on this, is a private company. It is a private company, it is situated in Canary Wharf, it is not part of the public sector in that sense or part of a public service organisation and, in any case, I would say public service organisations are changing pretty rapidly and the lifetime career model, as I think perhaps the Chairman is aware, is not as common as it used to be. The Financial Services Authority, if the board and the chief executive wish, will be pursuing something much closer to the model you described of the SEC where it will become a normal part of a successful career in financial services to spend some time within the regulatory authority. That may be at the start of a career, it may be later, I do not think we need to be prescriptive about that. But, of course, the Enforcement Committee itself, which has an important role in this whole process, might well include, as indeed the tribunal might, very senior practitioners or recently retired practitioners who bring that expertise and that ability to make peer judgments without at that point expecting very large sums of money in return for doing it.

Mr Beard

99.   It is unusual for enforcement authorities to receive the income from fines. Could you say what has caused you to adopt this in this particular case? Could you also say where there are precedents for it elsewhere?

(*Ms Hewitt*)   The thinking behind this, and I have to say we did not design it on the basis of precedent, we looked at what we thought would be right for financial services regulation, the principle is that the people who breach the rules should help to pay the regulatory costs of those who abide by the rules. Therefore, the effect of allowing the Authority to keep the funds is that the fees that it will charge to authorised firms will be less than they would be if the fines were not available to offset and defray the costs of the Authority. It has certainly been suggested that by allowing the Authority to keep the fines we will be giving them a perverse incentive to impose fines unnecessarily and to an excessive extent. I think our feeling was that the transparency and the consultation that the Bill requires around the FSA's budget, the annual report, the consultation around levels of fees, the whole line of accountability to the industry, would ensure that in fact that perverse incentive, although it

might exist in theory, would not exist in fact in reality. If there are alternative suggestions that the Committee would like to put forward then of course I will very happily look at them. One suggestion that was made in consultation was that the fines income should go into the new compensation fund so that one could see very clearly that the fines paid by transgressors were helping in the generality of cases to compensate the victims. In terms of precedents there are some, for example local authorities are now entitled to keep parking fines, but as I say it was not really precedent that we were concerned about but the fitness for this purpose.

Mr Heathcoat-Amory

100.   Can I bring you back to this issue of statutory immunity. It is not absolute that they will not be protected where they are acting with malicious intent, for instance, although I do note that that defence will not exist for the public who come under their scrutiny, for instance market abuse, in that they could be found in breach of the rules even if they did not intend to commit market abuse. The central fact here surely is that the FSA is a private company and it has huge powers of investigation. For instance, in some cases it can enter premises without a warrant. It can also levy unlimited fines, deprive people of their livelihoods. This is quite different from the police, for instance, who do not have statutory immunity. After the Lawrence investigation recently it has actually been proposed that the police should come under some additional legislation. I am not quite clear why you are setting up a new body with these quite awesome powers which are not subject to the laws which the rest of us are.

(*Ms Hewitt*)   I think we need to be very clear that we are not doing anything new in this Bill. The Financial Services Act 1986 gave precisely the same immunity to the predecessor body, to the SIB, and it did so for the very good reason that if the financial services regulator and the officers of the regulator have to spend all their time worrying about the possibility of what may be an ill-founded or malicious negligence action against them then we will tie the regulatory process up in red tape and lawyers and that will be extremely expensive for the industry as well as for the regulators and it will seriously undermine the capacity of the regulators to deal with inefficiency, incompetence or worse within this very important industry. Let me give you one very topical example. You will have seen in the *Financial Times* this morning that the FSA has threatened 12 major firms with having their authorisation withdrawn if they do not sort out their Millennium Bug problem because they are not up to speed on that issue. The FSA would find it virtually impossible to wave that kind of potential sanction against firms if the firms had the option of saying "you are threatening to shut me down, I am going off to sue you for negligence". That is why Parliament, as well as Government, in 1986 decided on the immunity from negligence actions where the FSA was acting in good faith, and I do stress that. That is why the Supreme Court in America, when an action for negligence was brought against the British

[Mr Heathcoat-Amory Cont]

regulator but brought in the American courts in an attempt to get round the immunity that exists in this country, having regard to the fact that Parliament had given this immunity, having regard to the fact that immunity existed in the USA, said that the action could not succeed and indeed could not proceed. Finally, if I may, Chairman, can I just draw your attention to the fact that in 1986 the Minister for Corporate Affairs said on the relevant provisions of the then Financial Services Act, on the Bill, that "a regulator will face a number of difficult choices in deciding when to act. One of the most difficult issues is deciding whether to withdraw a business's authorisation and supervisors should not have the threat of a negligence action hanging over their head when taking difficult decisions. If they do then the quality and effectiveness of regulation and the interests of investors will suffer."[1]

The Committee suspended from 4.02 p.m. to 4.11 p.m. for a division in the House of Commons.

Chairman: I would like to move on to the next section of objectives and principles although I hope we can get through this reasonably quickly because there are issues about discipline and enforcement that are very much on people's minds. You said in your opening remarks that you think there is some clarification needed in the question of objectives as you mentioned in the progress report. You thought you had it broadly right and we just wanted to put two or three questions to you on that. Mrs Blackman?

Mrs Blackman

101. Minister, there has obviously been a lot of discussion about the definition of consumer and the principle of *caveat emptor* which I think the industry expects more of a consumer organisation. You acknowledge that there are some difficulties in your progress report but you did not state where you are in terms of any revisions you would see as being helpful.

(Ms Hewitt) What we are trying to do with the *caveat emptor* clause is to say that consumers, although they have to be protected, also have a role to play in protecting themselves in particular by having a responsibility for decisions about their financial arrangements. We also, of course, want to encourage and enable the FSA to differentiate between different categories of customers and counterparty. That is, we believe, the effect of the clause as currently drafted but clearly it has not been understood in that way and therefore we are looking at it again to see whether we and the Parliamentary draftsman can come up with a better form of words that will make those intentions clear. The *caveat emptor* clause is not there to let the industry off the hook, but equally we do not want a situation to arise where consumers believe that wherever they put their money and whatever decisions they make they will always be protected. They will need to have that responsibility for the decisions they make.

Chairman

102. Will we have the redraft of this before we finish our deliberations?

(Ms Hewitt) I will certainly do my best to make sure that you do. We are to some extent in the hands of the Parliamentary draftsman but we are trying to get the redrafting done as quickly as possible.

Chairman: It is probably sensible to leave that for now. Lord Eatwell had a question about systemic risk.

Lord Eatwell

103. I must confess I am puzzled by the statutory objectives as set out by the FSA particularly objective number 1: "maintaining confidence in the financial system,", which it seems to me covers issues of probity, of honesty and of the absence of market abuse. What it does not cover is the regulator's main job which is managing systemic risk. Since the management of systemic risk is one of the fundamental tasks of the FSA set out also in its Memorandum of Understanding with the Treasury and Bank of England, I really do not understand why it is not one of its objectives. Let me explain why I am particularly worried about this. It is because the management of risk is a crucial element in directing the energies of the FSA to maintain its understanding of market innovation and the implications of market innovation for the economy as a whole. The absence of managing systemic risk as one of the statutory objectives undermines the position of the FSA.

(Ms Hewitt) This is an extremely interesting point and I have had the benefit of reading your paper on proper objectives not only of the national regulators but also what we need to do in terms of the global financial architecture. Of course, at the global level what we are putting in place, in part as a result of the initiative of our own Chancellor, is a financial stability forum that brings together the IMF, the World Bank, the Basle Committee and so on to fulfil that function of managing and trying to avert systemic risk within the world financial markets. At a national level we have what seems to me to be a parallel arrangement contained in the Memorandum of Understanding between the Treasury, the Bank of England and the Financial Services Authority. The position that we have now in this country, and I believe it is the right position, is that these three institutions between them have a joint and shared responsibility for the common objective of financial stability and dealing with systemic risk. The Memorandum of Understanding—and obviously I would be delighted to supply the Committee with a copy if that would be helpful—does state quite specifically that the Bank will be responsible for the overall stability of the financial system and I think this is because the issue of systemic risk and financial stability taken as a whole goes wider than the powers and reach of the FSA, wide and important though those are, and the Bank has this crucial role because it is responsible for the stability of the monetary system and it is responsible for crucial parts of the financial infrastructure including the payments system. The Treasury has a different role. It brings to the joint panel on the issue of financial

---

[1] 11 June 1986, *Official Report*, Cols.406-407.

[Lord Eatwell Cont]

stability the information and expertise acquired, for instance, through our membership of the IMF and the World Bank. The Treasury of course also has a crucial role in terms of, through the Chancellor, deciding whether or not public funds should be committed to deal with potential banking collapse, for instance, which would indeed threaten systemic risk. And then the FSA certainly has a role, a crucial role, to share market information with the other two organisations and its own responsibility as the financial services regulator to contribute to the management of systemic risk and the achievement of financial stability, but I would say that that is a shared and common objective rather than one that needs to be given to the FSA alone.

104. Yes, but I am slightly puzzled about that because, as you quite rightly say, in its regulatory role the FSA has considerable responsibility for management of systemic risk. For example, the statement just today about the Euro 2000 is not just to protect consumers, but it is to make sure that the banking system does not collapse. Similarly, capital adequacy requirement, the value of risk modelling, the whole drive of ensuring that companies take risk effectively into account, which is a regulatory activity, is central really to a whole body of what the FSA does, yet when we look through the objectives we find that promoting public understanding is elevated above actually making sure that the financial system does not collapse.

(Ms Hewitt) The regulatory objectives are not put in any order of importance, but I think what you have said reinforces the point that a very large part of the FSA's activities are in fact directed towards managing systemic risk and that is in a sense embedded within their function and you have described indeed what it is that the FSA brings to the party, to the joint forum of the Treasury, the Bank of England and the FSA. I do not see that anything would be gained by adding this as a separate statutory objective, but of course if the Committee feels that that is going to add something that is not already there, then of course we will have a look at it.

Chairman: I think that is probably as far as we can take it today. One of the other issues about the objectives which has been very much raised has been about competition.

Lord Trenchard

105. Minister, in your introductory remarks, you recognised the importance of the City representing 7 per cent of GDP and more than a million jobs and I was heartened to hear your recognition of the need for light-touch regulation where possible. You said that you had got the balance between the objectives about right. I am, therefore, rather surprised that you have not responded positively to the many suggestions that have been made to include the improvement or the maintenance and improvement of competition and the maintenance or enhancement of international competitiveness as objectives in their own right. Indeed, these two are included only in the principles and you have said that the order is not important, but

it did not escape my notice that they are fifth and sixth in the list of six principles. Looking at the objectives, maintaining market confidence is obviously a proper objective of the regulator, although it is one which it shares obviously with others, like the Bank of England and the Treasury, and obviously the protection of consumers and the reduction of financial crime are essential objectives of the regulator. Public awareness, which includes the promotion of awareness of the benefits of investment and provision of advice, is, I think, a fairly broad and open-ended objective for a regulator, so I am surprised that in comparison with that, and obviously it is highly desirable that everybody should be educated all about the investment opportunities in the derivatives markets, but I think that the costs involved in providing such an education would in fact be prohibitive. Now, your progress report suggests that keeping competition and the maintenance of international competitiveness in the principles would be sufficient. I rather doubt it, but if you think, as you say, that maintaining a regulatory regime under which the City can thrive is of paramount importance, why take the risk? Why not include it there as a proper objective in its own right? The City has been extremely successful for many reasons. One of the greatest of the City's successes was the attraction and the retention of the eurobond market. The reasons the eurobond market came here, as I am sure you are aware, Minister, are that the tax and regulatory regimes here compared with those in the United States were much more favourable. Looking at the regulatory regime, the lightness of touch of the regulatory regime in the City was absolutely key in this and I think that if we have too heavy a regulatory system, it may well damage the City. If it is a proper objective of the regulator to promote awareness and education, surely it must be an equally important and proper objective to maintain international competitiveness?

(Ms Hewitt) What shall I say? No and then yes, I think, meaning yes, I agree with most, if not all, of your general points about the importance of competition and the contribution that good regulation can make to that and to competitiveness, but no, I am not convinced that including competition and competitiveness as objectives in clause 2 is the right way to go about it. The reason for that, and we have thought about this very carefully again in the light of the consultation, is that the FSA's primary role is the protection of consumers and markets. We have a competition authority in this country and it is the Office of Fair Trading and they are the experts charged with enforcing competition policy and indeed we are strengthening it through the Competition Act 1998, so we think it is right that they should continue to carry out the function of a competition authority in the financial services industry as in every other part of the economy. What we do believe, and that is reflected in clause 3 on the principles, is that in carrying out all its work in pursuit of its objectives, the FSA must indeed have regard at all times both to competition between authorised firms, between players in the marketplace, and the overall competitiveness of Britain's financial services industry within the global economy, but I

[Lord Trenchard *Cont*]

think it would be a pity to create confusion about where competition issues actually sat and create a potential overlap between the OFT and the FSA. I am also concerned that if we just keep adding to the number of objectives that we are giving the Authority, we will weaken the accountability of the Authority because inevitably objectives have to be balanced against each other and if there are too many of them, then I think we risk weakening each of them.

Chairman

106. I am conscious that we seem to be suggesting adding to them rather than subtracting from them.

(Ms Hewitt) Perhaps I should, if I may, just say one word or a few words about your comment on public awareness. We are not envisaging educating people about the derivatives market, but the problem is much more basic than that and as Treasury officials informed me shortly after I arrived in the Treasury, 50 per cent of the British public do not know what 50 per cent means, and the annual percentage rates, the APR——

Mr Heathcoat-Amory

107. That is a typical Treasury piece of information!

(Ms Hewitt) It is one of those great facts that goes down very well when you get people thinking about it, but let me show you what this means. We have a very helpful system in this country that lenders are required to publish APRs so that people can see what the real rate of interest is that they are being charged and not have it concealed within some misleading headline rate. There are many people in this country who believe when they look at APRs that if it is a big number, it must be good and if it is an even bigger number, it must be better still, so we have a real problem and it is very well established, I think, in economic theory and practice that well-informed consumers challenging providers are a very important source of competitiveness for the companies who serve those consumers.

Lord Trenchard

108. I think that is absolutely right, Minister, but is it proper that clients of wholesale firms involved in the eurobond market, many of them are foreign and they do not have retail consumers as their customers, so is it right that they should have to bear the costs of this education of retail consumers?

(Ms Hewitt) I think it is reasonable to spread the costs of the FSA's operation across the whole of the industry, but the FSA is currently consulting, I think, on its fees structure, so that may be a point which we may wish to consider further.

Chairman: I would like to leave this topic now and move on to the question of discipline, enforcement and the Tribunal where there are a number of issues which are of interest to the Committee.

Mr Heathcoat-Amory

109. Minister, the European Convention on Human Rights hovers like a bee above this Bill and you have clearly made considerable efforts to comply with its judicial requirements and you have made or indicated some changes for the appeal structure, in particular, the procedures to be adopted by the independent Tribunal, but that still leaves the internal arrangements of the Financial Services Authority and I am a little concerned that it remains the case that the FSA will obviously have these investigative powers, and it will be not exactly making up its own rules, but it will have a very big influence on the rules it is enforcing and of course it can levy fines. I wonder whether if in all respects these do comply with the European Convention. I notice there has been a very important court case in France where the Supreme Court has ruled that the European Convention will apply to regulatory tribunals. Now, of course we are an entirely different legal jurisdiction here, but, nevertheless, I think that was a rather important court case. Do you yourself consider that the internal regulatory procedures of the FSA must be covered by the European Convention and do they yet comply? If they do not yet, can you give us an assurance that well before the end of our own proceedings you will be able to perhaps submit a rather more detailed reply even if you are not able to do so today?

(Ms Hewitt) Can I start by saying, Chairman, in response to that that of course we will ensure that the Bill that is introduced into Parliament is certified as being compliant with the Human Rights Convention. It is this Government that introduced the Human Rights Act and we will certainly ensure that this Bill, like other Bills, is Convention-compliant. Now, having said that, this is a matter on which there is quite legitimate room for disagreement between lawyers. As Lord Lester himself says in his very interesting opinion on this subject, the case law from the European Court of Human Rights in this area is complex and not always consistent. In relation to the French decision, I should say we have got that judgment in French, and legal French is particularly opaque, but obviously we will look at it in considerable detail. I think the important thing to note about the French judgment is that it was made on the basis that the COB's procedures were flawed because the staff member who presented the case, the prosecutor, as it were, also took part in the Tribunal's discussion and vote. Now, that would certainly not be possible under our arrangements. I might just note of course that the French courts do not provide rulings for the United Kingdom law on this point. There are several other things I think I need to address in relation to the Convention.

The Committee suspended from 4.32 pm to 4.41 pm for a division in the House of Lords.

Chairman

110. Please continue.

(Ms Hewitt) I think the next point I wanted to make has to do with the internal procedures of the FSA and of course the FSA will have to publish its

[Chairman *Cont]*

procedures and abide by them, but what we have ensured, and I think we spell it out in the progress report, is that the FSA at that stage, the internal stage, will have to explain to the person being investigated exactly what the basis of the case is. Evidence will have to be made available, the nature of the accusation will have to be spelt out, and the firm or the person concerned will have to be given a chance to come along and put their side of the case. Indeed Lord Lester himself notes that it appears that, for instance, the presumption of innocence within the Convention will not be infringed by action of the FSA before an appeal is heard. Now, the second point is what Lord Lester refers to as an appeal, but which is actually a first instance hearing in front of the Tribunal because what we are putting in place is this internal process, although including the Enforcement Committee, that will allow the FSA to make a reasonably rapid, reasonably informal decision. If the firm is content with that, and in many cases, and I have heard firms say this to me themselves, they say, "Yes, we got it wrong. We did not supervise the staff properly. We had not put in place the proper processes. We put our hands up and we pay the fine", and in that situation, where there is agreement by the firm about the action that is proposed to be taken, then it will simply be dealt with through that internal process and with the Enforcement Committee. However, where the firm, the authorised person is not happy with the action that the FSA is proposing to take or the basis of that action, then of course the matter will go the Tribunal for a first instance hearing and again in many respects or indeed in all of the crucial respects, Lord Lester indicates that that procedure, providing it is a first instance Tribunal, which it will be, is compliant with the Convention, and that is very important and the Tribunal, as I indicated earlier, is an independent, judicial body set up by the Lord Chancellor's Department, operating under the supervision of the Council on Tribunals and so on, so that is very important. Now, there are other Convention issues that really relate to the market abuse regime which we are still considering and of course we will let you have a further and more detailed view on this when we have had a chance to reflect further upon the legal position and obviously we will try and do that in good time given your own timetable.

111.   Would it be fair to characterise this whole area as really following the same procedures that are already in place with the existing regulators, but, if anything, they have been strengthened by the introduction of the Tribunal?

(Ms Hewitt)   We are indeed taking over some of the existing procedures, but of course they are not consistent as between the existing regulators, but we are improving them, I think, significantly and of course the Bill itself will set out some of the basic elements of that internal procedure, including, as I say, the opportunity to make representations and to see the evidence and so on. The FSA itself is consulting on those internal procedures. I think the period for comments on that has only just closed and we have not yet had the FSA's own conclusions and reflections upon that.

112.   Do you have an open mind on the question of the status of the Enforcement Committee? I noticed that you moved to make two of the panels statutory bodies and you now have the proposal for the Enforcement Committee. Should this also be in the Bill along with the whole question of its membership and whether they have voting rights, et cetera?

(Ms Hewitt)   The Enforcement Committee will be appointed by the Board and it will act on behalf of the Board. It will effectively be exercising the powers of the Board. Since, therefore, its entire legal being stems from the Bill, from the Act and from the existence of powers of the Board of the FSA, I do not think it would be necessary, and indeed it might not be appropriate, to give it a separate statutory existence.

Lord Poole

113.   Could I ask you a question which relates quite specifically to a particular sort of case which I think there will be many of as a matter of fact. It relates to the protection of the individual because all too frequently firms want to get on and get everything done. They go to the FSA and they say, "Excuse me, we have discovered that such and such a thing has taken place. Our internal disciplinary procedures have been put into practice. Tell us what the fine is, and unless there is anything else you care about, we will get back to business", and the machine likes that sort of thing because it is a smooth, easy way of dealing with it, but at the heart of it there tends to be an individual who almost certainly is going to find himself unable to work again and there are quite a number of examples where this has happened where, paradoxically, the firms and the FSA are conspiring to whistle something through, but the individual rather gets left out. You might think that from me that is an odd remark, but actually we must really worry about that. It is not obviously a human rights thing, but it is very important that something should be in place to look after individuals in these difficult cases.

(Ms Hewitt)   That is a very interesting point and one that the FSA might well wish to reflect upon as well in terms of its internal procedures. I think what one has to balance here is the fact that yes, an individual is the subject of the agreement between the firm and the regulator and the firm says, "Yes, we have got a chap in there. We should not have recruited him", or "We did not train him", or "We did not supervise him properly", whatever it is, "It's a fair cop and we will pay the fine", and almost certainly will get rid of the person concerned, and it is important that we have a regulatory system that can make those fairly fast, effective decisions. Of course, if the individual is cited, and that is what we are talking about here, where an individual is named in the disciplinary action against the firm, then he or she has the right to make representations of their own.

114.   They are often not.

(Ms Hewitt)   If they are not cited then on the face of it they would not be entitled to make a representation but if they are dismissed by the firm—and I imagine from what you are saying that that would be the normal consequence—then of course

[Lord Poole Cont]

they do have the protection of the normal employment law, strengthened—strengthened, if I may say so—by the Government's new Fairness at Work Bill which we are about to introduce.

115. I hope you are right, maybe we can ask David Roe and his team to consider that a little bit more.
(Ms Hewitt)   Fine.
(Mr Roe)   Yes.

Mrs Blackman

116. You referred a few moments ago to a consultation exercise that has just taken place on enforcement, that has just closed, and responses are now being studied. Will those responses be available to us and be fed into the next revised draft Bill which is out fairly soon? It is a specific question about enforcement but it has a wider issue. I am just concerned that this Committee has access to conclusions to the various forms of consultations that have been going on as quickly as possible.
(Ms Hewitt)   I completely understand that. It is very difficult to keep up with all the documents that both we and the FSA are consulting on. In this case the conclusions of the consultation will not necessarily feed into the revised draft Bill because what we think it is sensible to do here is put some basic elements into the Bill, the right to make representations, the right to see evidence, but we do not want to put all the detailed internal procedures into the Bill because, of course, then we would have to have primary legislation to amend them in future. What the FSA is consulting on is its own internal procedures which they will be under a statutory duty to publish, to consult upon and to follow. They will be bound by their own procedures. Of course they will be publishing the summary of responses, the conclusions of the consultation exercise and their own proposals in respect of them.
Chairman: This is another area where we will be very interested to see what practitioners and consumers have to say. You have made a number of proposals on this whole area in response to the consultation and I am not sure we can take this much further until we have heard the other side of how people are responding to an issue where there has been a great deal of concern. Can I move on now to the question of market abuse where there are some similar issues which arise but nevertheless, as you say, it is a distinct issue of its own. Mr Sheerman?

Mr Sheerman

117. Minister, could I just start by saying that in the Progress Report, given the amount of interest that we have heard in terms of this section on market abuse in the Bill, it is a very short commentary. you mention in the overall aims that though a number would have preferred to see changes in the existing criminal regime rather than just the introduction of a new civil regime, when we came to the conference where we heard you speak last week and the evidence we took on Tuesday, it does increasingly bear upon us that this is a subject on which we are both very concerned. I wonder if you could clarify in a sense whether there

are any further thoughts that the Treasury has on meeting this concern? There is this feeling that there is going to be the possibility of double jeopardy, there is going to be a feeling if you are not caught in one way you are caught in the other. I wonder in terms of a specific question, all of us want to cut out market abuse but we have got to be realistic in the sense that if companies fear heavy penalties they may feel that where they did not intend to abuse the market, unintended consequence, they fall foul of the FSA. Now we have had several explanations. There was a feeling in the Committee, taking the House of Lords totally, of "not content" fully with the remarks of the Chairman of the FSA on Tuesday on this. We would like a little bit more assurance on that matter. He made the point in passing that there are other parts of the law where you do not have to prove intent—dangerous and reckless driving and so on—which still causes injury and you can prosecute it of course under the law. I wonder if you could see your way clear of assuring the Committee that there is some further way to go of assuring those people in the markets that they are not in this situation?
(Ms Hewitt)   Certainly I understand the strength of feeling on this issue and, of course, respect it. I think it is helpful just to start by clarifying, as it were, the two issues here. There is an issue about behaviour and there is an issue about people. In relation to behaviour, there is a category of behaviour called market abuse, abuse of the financial markets, which is a serious matter because it undermines confidence in the financial system as a whole and thus undermines all the objectives that we set out at the beginning. A sub set of market abuse constitutes criminal offences, criminal offences of market manipulation and insider trading in particular, although theft and fraud might come into it as well but clearly market abuse covers a range of behaviours that is wider than simply those criminal offences. Then if you look at the people to whom the laws might apply you have a broad set of market participants, a sub set of those are authorised persons. At the moment the criminal law regime, the narrower set of behaviour, the laws relating to that narrower set of behaviour apply to all market participants whether or not they are authorised. The wider set of rules concerned with the wider behaviour, the rest of market abuse that is not criminal, only applies to the sub set of participants, those who are authorised. So I think we have a gap in the regulatory system that it is simply not possible at the moment to take action in respect of non criminal market abuse by non authorised participants in the market, even though that behaviour may be extremely detrimental to the good working of the markets and confidence in the financial system. When you look at the FSA's consultation on this and learn this fascinating new language of squeezes and bear hugs and all the rest of it, you can see how frustrating it must be for market participants who know perfectly well what is going on but where nothing can be done about it. On the specific question of intent, when we are looking at this broader category of non criminal market abuse then I think it must be right to look at the effects of the behaviour, not the intention behind it. What we are

[Mr Sheerman *Cont]*

concerned about here is the efficient operation of the market, not the moral culpability of the individual player of the market place. Confidence in the market is affected and can be damaged by people's actions even when they do not intend to do something fraudulent. Therefore, what the market abuse regime as drafted does and is designed to do is to alert market participants to the fact that they have to act with due care and attention when they are interacting with the financial market. If we found that somebody was very deliberately pursuing this course of market abuse action then that might have something to say about the appropriate level of fine but I do not think it is integral to the nature of the wrong that one is trying to address.

118. Minister, you would agree that this is probably the most sensitive part of the Bill and getting it right, even if it means building a little more assurance into the Bill, is I think, even from the evidence we have taken so far, absolutely crucial?

(Ms Hewitt) Yes, I think it is very important that we get it right but we have to get it right from the point of view of confidence in the system as well as from the point of view of fairness to the individual market participants because as we all know there are people out there, some of whom acting with criminal intent, and where there is evidence of criminal offences they will be prosecuted in the usual way, but there are also people who where there is not criminal intent, and maybe it is very difficult to prove motivation at any particular point in a highly complex set of virtualised transactions, but through carelessness or whatever are involved in actions that are very, very damaging and we do not want to leave our regulators powerless against abusive behaviour.

Mr Beard

119. Market abuse is very substantially covered in the competition legislation which was passed last year. Where do you see the division being drawn between what will be the responsibility of the FSA under this legislation and the responsibility of the Office of Fair Trading under the competition legislation?

(Ms Hewitt) I think there are two different things here really. There is a market abuse where there are some perhaps unauthorised firms getting together in a cartel-like operation, for instance, where there is anti-competitive behaviour, and that would clearly fall under the Competition Act 1998 and to be dealt with by the competition authorities. The kind of market abuse that the FSA needs to deal with is the various forms of manipulation, whether it is on the demand side or the supply side, which does not necessarily involve anti-competitive behaviour in the sense of monopolistic behaviour that the competition authorities would be dealing with, but does involve perhaps a temporary artificial manipulation of price or a squeezing of the supply in order to put people into unfair positions, and that, I think, is properly dealt with by the FSA under the market abuse regime. If there was behaviour which potentially could fall within both regimes then that would be something which the regulators would sort out between them as to which would be the lead institution dealing with the problem.

Chairman

120. I presume again that this is an area where you are very anxious that this should be ECHR compliant?

(Ms Hewitt) Absolutely, and on that particular issue I think at the heart of that is the question of whether this is a civil or a criminal regime and clearly that in turn has implications for conventions compliance. We still need to reflect upon that and to consider the legal position and, as I indicated earlier, we will obviously provide you with a further memorandum. I can come back on that point if you would like me to.

Viscount Trenchard

121. Minister, in the area of market abuse the Bill makes no special provision for guidance and the issuance of guidance, so the general provisions of clause 87 apply, but the problem is that guidance can be issued without consultation, which I think is a worry. I understand that under the present regime there have been occasions when self-regulatory organisations have issued guidance and subsequently withdrawn it when they found out that they had misinterpreted some of the facts. So would you consider extending the requirement to seek consultation on the issuance of guidance?

(Ms Hewitt) My understanding is that under the Bill there will, of course, be a code of market conduct and on that the authority has to consult market users before it finalises that code. The code itself will set out in detail the types of behaviour which will or will not be acceptable. The FSA, indeed, has already begun to consult on that code. When it is in force the code will carry evidential weight, so that if somebody has complied with the code, that will clearly be material to their defence or argument against any accusation that is made against them. Guidance is a different matter, as I understand it. It is really where the regulators are guiding an individual firm, an authorised person in most cases, about a particular course of action and in that situation, if the FSA gives somebody guidance and they act upon it in good faith, the FSA would really not be able to take action, but I do not think it would be appropriate for the FSA—in fact, I am not quite sure how the FSA could publish draft guidance in such a case and consult on it before giving that guidance to the individual market participant who had requested it. They are two different things.

Mr Sheerman

122. On a supplementary to that, that is the whole dichotomy here from what was said on Tuesday. On the one hand, we have the Chairman of the FSA saying there is going to be a code, the code is not established yet so it is unknown, and then there is going to be a build-up of case-law and this makes it look more like a judicial system. He assures us, on the other hand, that there is going to be thorough guidance. If that advice is taken then the operator in the market that takes that guidance and accepts that advice should not fear any ill consequences. So in a sense you and he

[**Mr Sheerman** *Cont*]

are developing a system which says, on the one hand, it is judicial and the heavy hand of the law will come down, and on the other, here is a nice "touchy-feely" side to this organisation. Is it both or is it one or the other?

(*Ms Hewitt*)   I think it is both. What I think we are trying to do here, by using the code, is to spell out in considerable detail, although it is never going to be exhaustive because the market participants think of things that nobody could have thought of before, but pretty great detail, what constitutes market abuse and what people need to do to avoid market abuse. The FSA, quite rightly, and we do not want to wait for case-law to build up slowly. We want that code to be available very early on so that people know where they stand, but the guidance will, as I understand it, go beyond the code because what it will do is respond to the needs of a particular participant who wants to see, as it were, tailormade advice on a particular course of action. David, do you want to add to that?

(*Mr Roe*)   No, that is right.

(*Ms Hewitt*)   That is my understanding of it.

Chairman: I think we will move on to the question of scope, where there are a number of issues which you mentioned in your opening remarks about what is covered and how the Government has responded. Mr Heathcoat-Amory is going to deal with this.

Mr Heathcoat-Amory

123.   On the question of scope, Howard Davies earlier in the week confirmed that, as regards investment advice given by solicitors in Scotland, that would be taken away from that professional body and would come to be regulated by the FSA. If that is so, are you happy that in the view of the Government's professed devolution policy to give more decision-making and responsibility to Scotland, this apparently goes in the opposite direction? And a second question, if I may: again my understanding is that some of the legislation touching the Scottish investment advice is embedded in specifically Scottish Acts which will fall to the Scottish Parliament to be amended or repealed. As that Parliament is shortly to be elected, they may take a different view about this to the Parliament of which we are Members. That seems to me to have dangers. Have you consulted or thought about how you might anticipate this problem rather than fall into any sort of trap?

(*Ms Hewitt*)   We have certainly considered the devolution issue, as we always do. The financial services industry is a United Kingdom-wide industry and, indeed, a global industry and we believe that consumers who are using the services of the United Kingdom financial services industry should have the same level of protection, the same standards of regulation, wherever they buy the relevant financial products and services. So the regime that we are setting in this Bill will be a United Kingdom-wide regime. This is a reserved power. As far as the recognised professional firms go, there is an issue, which is not simply Scottish, about professionals— solicitors, accountants and so on—who, in the course

of their business, may well give some incidental investment advice and the problem in a sense that has arisen is that quite large numbers of professionals who are regulated by their recognised professional bodies also have sought, as it were, precautionary authorisation in order to ensure that they do not inadvertently fall foul of the financial regulation regime when they are giving advice. As I say, we want to make sure that where people are buying financial products they are benefiting from the same regulatory standards. On the other hand, we do not want every firm of solicitors in the country having to seek authorisation from the FSA, and so the FSA and, indeed, ourselves have been discussing with, amongst others, the Law Societies, both of England and Wales and of Scotland, the issue about where we draw the line in terms of the boundaries between the professional bodies and the FSA. Indeed, we have just issued last month a consultation document on the scope of the Bill that addresses this particular issue. So in terms of the Scottish solicitors specifically and the Solicitors (Scotland) Act of 1980, we are looking at what amendments might be needed to that or to other legislation to ensure that there is the single regulator for financial services that we want and that that is recognised within a reserved power under the Devolution Act.

Chairman

124.   Before we move on to the question of mortgages, could I ask, about the timetable—I just cannot recall it—for dealing with this question of recognised professional bodies? You have issued a document. What you seem to be trying to do is to follow the Treasury Committee's recommendation that this should be drawn as finely as possible to limit the area of what is regarded as financial advice in order to try and avoid having 16,000 people turn up?

(*Ms Hewitt*)   Indeed. As far as the timescale is concerned, the closing date for responses to the Treasury's consultation document on this is also 30 April and the reason for that and the reason why it is not earlier is partly to allow due time for consultation but also because the scope of the Bill, the scope of the Act eventually, falls to be dealt with under secondary legislation and, therefore, issues about scope, including this and also including mortgage advice, is something that we do not have to make a final judgment on at the point where we introduce the Bill. It is something we have to make a final judgment on when we come to publish and introduce the secondary legislation that will determine the scope of the Act and, therefore, we can make this decision later in the year, but we would want that decision obviously to be informed by the views of this Committee.

Mr Beard

125.   I think the Minister has just answered my question because I was going to ask why the question of bringing mortgages in was going to be left until the Bill was introduced but you have essentially answered that?

[Mr Beard *Cont]*

(*Ms Hewitt*) There is one more reason on mortgages, which is, of course, the Council of Mortgage Lenders code. What my predecessor said when that was introduced, and I have said since, is that we want to see how that code works in practice. We are monitoring it very closely, as is the Council of Mortgage Lenders itself, and later this year, before we make a decision on the scope order, we will see whether that code has had the effect that the Council hoped of dealing with the problems that have arisen in some cases. Endowments, of course, sold in connection with a mortgage are already covered by financial regulation.

Chairman

126. I can understand that and if this comes to be decided later I can see the case why you want to postpone it. But are we not going to end up with a lot of debate about these issues of mortgages, etc. whilst the Bill is going through? Would it not be better to get this issue sorted out before we go through that rather than having it tagged on later and end up with a large amount of debate and discussion about it? We know there are a lot of strong feelings about this.
(*Ms Hewitt*) Indeed.

127. It seems to me that it is going to complicate the process by having it on a different timescale. I wondered why you were not bringing it forward for decision now as to whether it should be in or not. Then the information would be before people when we come to put the Bill through both Houses?
(*Ms Hewitt*) I think it is fair to say that this piece of legislation is a very large undertaking—the size of the Bill itself but then the size of the secondary legislation that will follow—that it is actually not possible to get everything determined, or everything proposed, out for consultation, determined and drafted all at the same time. We have had to sequence it, but also in the specific case of mortgages, we did give an undertaking last year that we would give the mortgage code time to bed down and time to be given a fair trial and, therefore, I would not want to try, and it would be quite wrong, to rush into a decision on that in time for the introduction of the Bill. At this stage we do not have a firm timetable obviously for the Bill and I think the debates on this issue when the Bill is introduced will be very helpful in informing the decision that we make and then announce as early as we possibly can.

128. The FSA are due to do a cost-benefit analysis of this and this is going to come somewhat later.
(*Ms Hewitt*) We will take another look at the timing and see whether we can make it tidier.

Mr Beard

129. I wonder, Minister, if you are able to say what are the criteria you will be using in deciding whether to bring mortgages into the Bill or not?
(*Ms Hewitt*) What we are looking at in relation to mortgages, I think the starting-point here is that part of the issue, the endowment side, is already regulated. When it comes to the rest, although the complaints are

often very highly publicised, and very disturbing given the importance of a mortgage to most of us, the number of complaints is actually very small in relation to the total number of mortgages. In 1995, which is the last year I have figures for, it was about 0.5 per cent., 50,000 compared with 10.5 million mortgages. In some cases those complaints relate to unfair terms and, of course, more mortgages were brought within the scope of the existing Consumer Credit Act when the upper limit for that Act was raised to £25,000 and all mortgages are already subject to the Unfair Terms in Consumer Contracts Regulations, whatever the amount of the mortgage involved. This is why the Office of Fair Trading is looking at the issue of redemption penalties—this is on the fixed rate mortgages—which have aroused very considerable concern with people finding themselves faced with a huge bill for early redemption that they apparently had no idea they were likely to face. So that is already being looked at. So what we will want to see is whether the code has improved the situation and I think we could judge by that by whether or not it has reduced the number of complaints, and whether those complaints that are still arising are being dealt with more efficiently, more effectively and more to the satisfaction of the consumer. The other thing we have to look at—and you mentioned the FSA's cost-benefit analysis—is that we have to balance the protection of the consumers who have taken out a mortgage and have a complaint about it with what might be the very substantial additional costs to the FSA if we bring the whole of the mortgage market within their scope.

Mr Sheerman

130. Just on that point, I do not know if I was amused or concerned about your anecdote that the Treasury told you only 50 per cent. of people in this country know about what 50 per cent. means. I cannot believe that is true in Huddersfield. I do not know about any other constituency. The fact of the matter is that many people have always found financial regulatory systems very complicated. That is why, presumably, part of the intent of this Bill is to have one rather than nine. We are going to have this expectation amongst people that the FSA is the place to go if you have a financial worry, concern or complaint, and in a sense, as a mortgage is such a big part, I understand the restrictions in terms of the complexity and timetable and all the rest, but to have it built in as a possibility of growing without new primary legislation would, it seems to me, be wise in the longer term because people are going to come back and say they want one identifiable, knowable way of complaining about the situation?
(*Ms Hewitt*) Surely. I think I would make two points. One is that if we decide, after we have looked at all this, not to bring mortgages within the scope of the Act initially, the FSA, I have no doubt at all, will ensure that people who do come to them with a complaint about mortgages are told how that complaint should be dealt with, but because the scope of the Bill is being dealt with through secondary legislation we will have in any case the flexibility to bring mortgages within the scope of the Act subsequently, if we decide

[**Mr Sheerman** *Cont*]

that is the right thing to do, even if we do not do so at the outset.

Mr Heathcoat-Amory

131. I am a bit alarmed by this. The Bill, which has not been republished yet, will, from what you say, make very heavy use of secondary legislation and one can see that a lot of detail has to be amendable without primary legislation. On the other hand, we all know that in practice secondary legislation does not really get closely scrutinised by either House. Certainly I can speak for my own. Therefore, it is very important that when we proceed to the Bill itself we at least know, and preferably have seen, the scope of the secondary legislation, otherwise how can we make a judgment about what ought to be in the Bill itself, because Parliament will at least want to lay down the skeleton of the Bill and limit the powers and set up the balancing checks in order to be sure that Parliament's intentions are not exceeded. It is going to be very difficult for us to do that if the secondary legislation has not even been published and the scope of the Bill has not yet been announced by ministers. Could I ask you to come back to us at a later date and give us some details about the scope of the secondary legislation, including dates on when it will be exposed for consultation and can we be sure that that will be before Parliament actually enacts the primary legislation?

(Ms Hewitt) We have already begun the consultation on the scope of the Bill and the consultation document that we published last month sets out our view of what the scope of the Bill should be and raises specific issues for consultation and also explains, as I have just done, the approach we propose to take on making a decision on mortgages and why we are doing that. That is already out for consultation. The closing date for that consultation is 30th April. We will then respond publicly to that consultation. The secondary legislation will itself be published for debate, but one of the changes that we have signalled and reported on in the progress report and which will be contained in the new Bill when it is introduced is that the secondary legislation determining or extending scope should be subject to the positive and not the negative resolution procedure so that we somewhat strengthen the Parliamentary accountability at that point.

132. I can quite understand the point about timing. Will we see all the secondary legislation in draft before the primary legislation is given a First Reading?

(Ms Hewitt) No, we will not be able to do that because the current timetable is that your Committee will report by 30th April. We will then need to make appropriate changes to the Bill in the light of your report and other consultation and, indeed, our own progress report. We will then introduce the Bill as quickly as possible. As you know, it is our intention to get the Financial Services Authority on to a full statutory basis as quickly as possible because that is what this industry needs. But the scope Order obviously follows the enactment itself, it does not need to be finalised before First Reading of the Bill. In terms of the consultation process that we need to go

through and the drafting of the secondary legislation, it would not be possible to finalise it. The consultation document itself includes the draft statutory instrument, so that is already part of what we are consulting on.

Chairman: Thank you very much, Minister. We will need to consider this and consider the question of the timetable. But I think there is some concern about this whole question of knowing where we are going and at what timetable.

Lord Eatwell

133. I wonder if I could ask you a question about timing. Since timing started here I had to find some place to put it in. It is about something, as they say, completely different, but it is to do with timing. In a number of comments and speeches that Mr Davies has made recently he has intimated that the rule book for the FSA will not be ready, so to speak, when the legislation comes into effect and when the FSA acquires full statutory responsibility. In evidence to this Committee on Tuesday he took this much further when he said, "Once the legislation is in place we will then organise ourselves for the long term and then proceed in a more measured way to revise the rule books". So it is now clear that the day the FSA actually acquires legal authority it will not be ready to do the job in the sense that the rule book will not be ready. He said what he will do is he will simply be operating the old rule books under the new statutory framework. Are you content with this timing? I must say, I think it is worrying.

(Ms Hewitt) I have discussed this point only fairly briefly so far with Howard Davies. My understanding is that there will certainly be a rule book but it will not be an entirely new rule book and in part it will replicate existing rule books and this is really because of the scale of the task that is required to re-write, to synthesise, to improve, to consult upon, to do a cost-benefit analysis and all the rest of it that we are requiring them to do. There will be a rule book and there will be rules, but the formal process of creating a new and entirely synthesised and integrated rule book will not be complete. Could David perhaps add to that?

(Mr Roe) I understand the FSA have published information about the priorities that they are giving to replacing rules in particular areas where there is a stronger need to do it sooner rather than later. What we will have on the day when the Act comes into force will be partly new, partly old, but they are publicly consulting on the balance of areas and which areas they should deal with first.

134. The rule book is a living thing. It is always trying to catch up with the market and it is following ten yards behind it. The problem is that if you have an old rule book which you are just sitting on for what is now, Mr Davies says, "the long term" whilst in a measured way the rule book is revised then you are likely to ossify a structure. There is no point in modifying the old books or is there? In fact, there is because you will try and keep things going. You have a peculiar dual structure where you are running under an old set of rule books whilst trying to develop a new

[Lord Eatwell *Cont*]

one and yet you have got to keep the old ones up-to-date.

(Ms Hewitt) I am not sure that there is quite the contradiction in that that perhaps you are implying. It seems to me very sensible for the FSA to prioritise this either by reference to where the existing rule books are out-of-date or where innovation is fastest or where there are particular concerns, whether it is to do with the protection of individual consumers or having an appropriate regulatory regime for complex sophisticated wholesale markets. So getting some priorities here is sensible, particularly in view of the fact that they do not have the resources to do everything all at once. They can create new rules for those priority areas and continue to do so after the Act comes into force. They can also update, presumably, the lower priority rule books or sets of rules and that in turn will feed into the process of developing the completely up-to-date rules in those lower priority areas that, of course, they will also wish to do and need to do, but they cannot do it all at once and that does not seem to me a particular problem. Of course it would be nice if they had all the resources in the world and could do everything all at once. We would like to have more Parliamentary draftsmen to draft everything quicker and all at once. But this is the real world and we have got to operate within resource constraints.

Chairman: We have got one more question to put to you in this area, but I am very grateful for your time and I am aware of your time constraint and your need to get away. We have one or two questions on the Ombudsman which I think we will have to leave for now. We will find another way of inserting our questions after we have talked to the outside world about this. One last question from Lord Poole who wants to raise the question of Lloyd's. I hope that he will deal with this quickly and let you get to your engagement.

Lord Poole

135. I will ask my question swiftly. Very many of the professional operators of Lloyd's market consider it a very substantial shame that you have not

been able to include a repeal of the now wholly unsatisfactory Lloyd's Acts as part of this process and inclusion of the regulation of the Lloyd's market by the FSA. I understand that in fact you are trying to find ways around this, that your officials, and possibly for all I know you, are in discussion with the FSA on steps which might be taken. This is very, very important because the regulatory authorities in Lloyd's are finding it not possible to control cases of market abuse by unauthorised people, and that is becoming quite a problem with some major international operators in the insurance market. Can you tell me whether you will indeed see whether you can find ways round this and, if so, how this might be done?

(Ms Hewitt) We are certainly in discussion with Lloyd's and indeed have agreed with them a process whereby the supervision and regulation of Lloyd's does include a statutory base and in particular within the Bill provides for external oversight of that regulation. That is something they very much welcome. Clearly, the provisions of the Bill, and this includes market abuse provisions in relation to unauthorised persons, could not come into effect until the Bill itself comes into effect. In terms of amendment to the Lloyd's Acts themselves, the difficulty here is that as I understand it this is private legislation and I think it would not be possible to amend it in this Bill, it is actually outside the scope of the Bill. In many cases, many of the problems you raise are private matters for the Society of Lloyd's, who may well wish to bring forward private legislation on this matter rather than something for the Government. But officials are very closely in touch with Lloyd's on this. I have on various occasions met with the chairman and other senior members of Lloyd's and I should say they have not specifically raised that concern with me.

Chairman

136. Minister, thank you very much for what has been a long session of evidence. We have covered a lot of very interesting material and we are very grateful.

(Ms Hewitt) Thank you very much indeed, and thank you for your interesting questions.

Published by The Stationery Office Limited
and available from:

The Publications Centre
(Mail, telephone and fax orders only)
PO Box 276, London SW8 5DT
General enquiries *Lo-call* 0345 58 54 63
Order through the Parliamentary Hotline *Lo-call* 0345 02 34 74
Fax orders 0171 873 8200

The Stationery Office Bookshops
123 Kingsway, London WC2B 6PQ
0171 242 6393 Fax 0171 242 6394
68-69 Bull Street, Birmingham B4 6AD
0121 236 9696 Fax 0121 236 9699
33 Wine Street, Bristol BS1 2BQ
0117 926 4306 Fax 01179 294515
9-21 Princess Street, Manchester M60 8AS
0161 834 7201 Fax 0161 833 0634
16 Arthur Street, Belfast BT1 4GD
0123 223 8451 Fax 0123 223 5401
The Stationery Office Oriel Bookshop
The Friary, Cardiff CF1 4AA
0122 239 5548 Fax 01222 384347
71 Lothian Road, Edinburgh EH3 9AZ
0131 228 4181 Fax 0131 622 7017

The Parliamentary Bookshop
12 Bridge Street, Parliament Square,
London SW1A 2JX
Telephone orders 0171 219 3890
General enquiries 0171 219 3890
Fax orders 0171 219 3866

Accredited Agents
(see Yellow Pages)

and through good booksellers

ISBN 0-10-432499-6

9 780104 324998

HOUSE OF LORDS
HOUSE OF COMMONS

SESSION 1998–99

JOINT COMMITTEE ON FINANCIAL SERVICES AND MARKETS

MINUTES OF EVIDENCE

Tuesday 23 March 1999

*Ms Jill Johnstone, Ms Harriet Hall, Mr Bernard Jones, Mr Garry Heath
and Mr Robin Hutton*

*Mr Peter Foster, Mr Mark Boléat, Mr Alastair Ross Goobey, Mr James Stretton
and Mr Jonathan Agnew*

Mr David Roe and Mr Andrew Whittaker in attendance

*Printed pursuant to the Order of the House of Lords of 2 March 1999
Ordered by* The House of Commons *to be printed
23 March 1999*

LONDON: THE STATIONERY OFFICE
£4.65

HL Paper 50-iii
HC 328-iii

TUESDAY 23 MARCH 1999

Present:

Lord Burns (in the Chair)
Lord Eatwell
Lord Fraser of Carmyllie
Lord Haskel
Lord Poole
Lord Taverne
Viscount Trenchard

Mr Nigel Beard
Mrs Liz Blackman
Mr David Heathcoat-Amory
Mr David Kidney
Mr Tim Loughton
Mr James Plaskitt

Examination of Witnesses

Ms JILL JOHNSTONE, Head of Policy, and Ms HARRIET HALL, Legal Adviser, National Consumer Council; MR BERNARD JONES, Chairman, and MR GARRY HEATH, Director-General, Independent Financial Advisers Association; and MR ROBIN HUTTON, Director of Regulation, Singer & Friedlander, called in and examined.

MR DAVID ROE, Head of Financial Services and Markets Bill Team, HM Treasury, and MR ANDREW WHITTAKER, Deputy General Counsel, Financial Services Authority, in attendance.

Chairman

137. Good afternoon and welcome to this the first of these sessions following the evidence that we have had from Howard Davies and from the Economic Secretary to the Treasury. As you know, we set out a number of topics in our press release that we were hoping to cover. As far as possible we would like to arrange the sessions so that we are majoring on a particular topic in each one. Today we want to major on the issue of statutory objectives, although in the full understanding that if later in the proceedings there are one or two points that people wish to make about any of the wider issues, we would be happy to do that. But if we are going to have any order in this process and are going to be able to hear as many people as possible, we have to try to stick broadly with the major topic we want to deal with today. I would like to ask you each to introduce yourselves and to tell the Committee what your main views and concerns are about the Bill. So this is an opportunity to make your general remarks. In particular I would like to hear from you to what extent the Treasury's Progress Report and the responses we have had from the Treasury over the period since the Bill was first published, have met your concerns and what are the main issues that remain outstanding. What we are trying to do in this process is to go through a further iteration. We have had the Treasury's Bill, we have had public consultation, we have now had the Treasury's response to the public consultation. What we are trying to do is to see what is the next round and to have your response as to how far the Treasury has gone. Shall we begin with Jill?

(Ms Johnstone) I will go first and then hand over to Harriet. My name is Jill Johnstone, I am Head of Policy at the National Consumer Council. The National Consumer Council has a remit to represent all consumers of all goods and services, whether they are publicly or privately provided, and we have a particular remit for disadvantaged consumers and we have a long-standing interest in financial services.

Indeed, we worked on the last Bill and I was the policy officer who did that work.

(Ms Hall) I am Harriet Hall and I am the Legal Officer of the National Consumer Council but I also do a lot of policy work in financial services that is not strictly legal work. I think our major concern that we would like to address today is the question of appropriate consumer protection. The Bill says,"the FSA shall have an objective of consumer protection" as if somehow we all know what consumer protection is, but there are different ways of defining it, and I do not think there is a generally understood body of understanding on this, and if there is not some further assistance given in the Act, then one lays oneself open in five years, ten years, 15 years, when outside flavours change, to people saying either it should be much more or it should be much less than what people imagine is appropriate. So we feel that there should be some assistance in defining consumer protection. At the moment the only thing that helps in defining it is the caveat emptor, about which we have serious concerns. This point is in our response to the Treasury, that in ordinary goods and services you have a very basic element of consumer protection, which is that goods shall be satisfactory for the purpose and fit for the purpose for which you want it, but you have huge advantages with buying things like kettles because you buy them, you take them home and you know if they are going to work on the whole, and even if you decided not to pursue your remedies on the kettle that was faulty, you would know not to buy that kind of kettle next time. That is the fundamental difference with financial services. You do not have any of these benefits and yet somehow we do not give this fundamental assurance that people are buying things of a satisfactory quality. There are other things that may arise in questions but that is the main thing we would say.

138. Some of the worries in your evidence have been addressed by the Progress Report?

[Chairman Cont]

(*Ms Hall*) A lot of the other worries we have had, indeed, about the Consumer Panel, about the ombudsman, and we understand the Government's position on scope, those are being addressed but this is an area really that has not, I think, been explored. It is left, in a sense, to the FSA and the principles for businesses. They are producing the principles and we think there should be something on the face of the Bill.

(*Mr Hutton*) Mr Chairman, I would not like to intervene on this particular issue because, first of all, I have no experience of dealing with the retail public, and perhaps I could come back later.

139. Could you respond to my general question about what are your views and concerns about the Bill, not necessarily on the narrow question but with a wider statement? I would like to get each person's views on the table before we go through and take them item by item.

(*Mr Hutton*) My name is Robin Hutton, I am a non-executive director of Singer & Friedlander, which is a relatively small merchant banking group but it deals only peripherally with the retail public. Most of its business is of a wholesale nature. We find the Progress Report encouraging in many respects. However, we have about four main concerns about the regulatory system as it is developing, which I would like to develop a little bit later on. One of those concerns is that we think it is very difficult and, indeed, the Bill does not really answer this point, to cover the whole range of financial services in a single regulatory system. We therefore very much prefer the idea of banks being regulated separately from securities businesses and we believe that many of the criteria and other tests which are applied to the regulation of banks are not appropriate for other kinds of financial services industries. We think that the process of building a regulatory system which is unitary is actually going to produce an enormous bureaucracy in the course of time because people will keep inventing new products, new services, new ways of approaching financial problems and every time they do so there will have to be a new division or a new group of people in the regulatory body which will have to study that and look at it. The second point I wanted to raise with you, my Lord Chairman, is that we think it is going to be very difficult to maintain cost-effectiveness if that happens and at the moment we find the cost of the system really very seriously damaging to us and we are not an untypical firm. We know that Howard Davies has said that he thinks that London is a relatively low-cost location from which to operate in financial services but that is not our experience. There are only about 10 per cent. of the working days of the year when we do not have a visitor from one of the regulatory bodies or even several visitors or some other provocation from the regulators interfering in our business. We welcome a relationship with the regulators, we are not against regulators as such, but this costs us something like £2 million a year in just running a system to cope with all these visits and requests and so on and our profits are £25 million in the United Kingdom. So it is a very heavy cost burden which is only going to go up if the supervisory serpent goes on growing. We therefore think that it

would be perhaps advantageous if the legislation were to be more specific and there were to be less discretion left to the regulatory body than is actually proposed. The third point that I wanted to refer to is the question of the technique of regulation. Regulation at the moment takes place by trying to prevent anything going wrong. The result is that everybody, whether they are good, bad or indifferent, gets the same volume of interference from the regulator and has to pay a very high amount of the costs of the regulator, just in case something is going wrong or to make sure that it is not going wrong. That is a very expensive way of going about it. We therefore think that it would be a much better idea if we could have a more intimate relationship with regulators which is not provided for in the Bill. Indeed, I do not quite see how you could provide for that in the Bill, but it certainly could be provided for in practice. Finally, the last point, which is a rather serious one, my Lord Chairman, is that we are worried about the personal liability of executives, which is not treated specifically in the Bill but which is rather left to the discretion of the regulatory bodies, and we have had some experience of this in the City in the recent past. We feel that it is quite wrong that executives should be separately liable for disciplinary action from their firm. If the firm has made a mistake, then the firm must stand ready to take the rap, and that to go on and attack individuals with a process which can be very damaging to them financially and in their own lives is something which should be provided for specifically in the legislation and the offences should be spelt out in the legislation and it should not be a discretionary matter for the regulators. That briefly, my Lord Chairman, is all I would like to put on to the table for the present as points that concern us.

(*Mr Jones*) I am Bernard Jones, I am Chairman of the IFA Association. We as an Association represent 2,600 registered firms, directly regulated firms, and that comprises some 7,000 individual IFAs in the community. Personally, I have been in the financial services industry 35 years, over 30 of those as a practitioner, and for the last three years I have been Chairman of the Association, so I have had a long connection with financial services. Broadly speaking, the IFA Association welcomes the new Bill and the creation of the FSA. We feel that, as far as professional independent advisers are concerned, they will have nothing to fear from it. Our main concern is the lack of clarity in many of the provisions and it was the lack of clarity which caused an awful lot of problems with the last regulatory regime. We are looking for clarity of definition in all aspects of the Bill because we think that the operators, the IFAs out there, cannot operate successfully unless they are clear on what is expected of them. Beyond that, I would like to take up one or two of Mr Hutton's points because they also concern us, and that is the way in which the provisions are implemented by the monitoring teams. We feel very strongly that an approach of prevention being better than cure is the approach here and we would like to see the development of a partnership between the regulators and the regulated. We would like open dialogue and, hopefully, agreement eventually between the parties concerned and we prefer to see discipline

[Chairman Cont]

as a last resort rather than a first resort, certainly where the breaches discovered are of a minor nature and are just rule breaches. There is a lot to be said for private reprimand and putting things in order rather than going out for public announcements in the first place. Obviously where the misdemeanours are wilful they have to be treated in a different manner. We also have a strong desire to see the return of common law principles to this regulation because that was almost totally absent from what we have been facing with the previous regulators. We would also like to see some form of prescribed fining basis rather than the basis at the moment, which is, how much can the individual organisation afford and what was the last highest amount that we fined anybody. There has been an element of headline-chasing in the fining policies of the previous regulators which I think bears no relationship whatsoever to natural justice. On the costs side of things, again we do need a cost-benefit analysis and I was pleased to see that that was addressed in the Progress Report, because the regulator owes a duty of care to the consumer just as much as the provider or the intermediary does because the costs of regulation ultimately affect the returns on the costs of the financial products that the consumer is buying, so there is a duty of care there from all sides. Finally, I would like to see some acknowledgement and encouragement of proper professional qualifications. I would like to see some element of moderation in the level of regulation for people who can demonstrate that they are properly professionally qualified, and the very fact that that group of people were getting a lighter regulation would surely encourage others through to obtaining qualifications, which ultimately would move the financial services on to a proper professional plane.

140. Mr Heath, do you want to say anything?

(Mr Heath) I just announce my existence, my Lord Chairman, and I look forward to questions.

Chairman: Thank you very much. Shall we take the first subject which we have got down and which has, in a sense, been alluded to already? This is the question of consumer protection. Can we see if we can take that a bit further? Lord Haskel?

Lord Haskel

141. As you said, one of the statutory objectives of the FSA is to protect consumers and I wonder whether we are all agreed as to what a consumer is. Is the consumer just the man in the street because often the man in the street can be an expert in financial services? Is the small businessman, who may know little about financial services, a consumer or is he a professional person, and how far do we have to go to educate or advise the consumer so that they can become more expert? I just wondered whether we were all agreed as to who the consumer is or whether, in fact, the Bill ought to go some way towards defining that?

(Ms Hall) I think our view is that there is a difference between retail and wholesale consumers and if we had been starting off that is where we would have made a distinction, and although there may be very expert men and women in the street who are

nevertheless retail consumers, you have to make the division somewhere and the people who are buying it really not as an expert purchase but as a means to an end, to greater security in old age or whatever, those people need a different level of protection from the people who do it as a business and who pay lots of people large sums of money to look after those interests. I think our concern is that what is encompassed by the term consumer in the Bill is too broad.

(Mr Heath) We would agree with the NCC on that. I think there is a fear in the City that the sort of excesses we have seen in the retail regulation will invade the City and that is something we certainly would not wish to see. Equally, the previous divide was that of the retail consumer and certain people who were members of the public who were deemed to be expert investors. The NCC definition is that of are you doing this for your business or are you doing this without your business? That is not a bad definition. Frankly, wherever you draw the line, my Lord Chairman, it is not a clear line. It is not a bad definition at all, but it does rather leave out protection for your local cabby who takes a mortgage out to buy a cab. Yes, he really is one of the more protected people in need of protection, but he would fall outside of that definition. It is not easy. I suspect we would agree across the table that there must be a clear definition between the foxes and rabbits, i.e. the foxes can look after themselves and the rabbits will need considerable protection in what is a complex market.

Lord Poole: Can we ask David what he thinks?

Chairman

142. David Roe is here from the Treasury. The Progress Report implied that you wanted to look at this issue again and the drafting of it. Do you think that you are going to be able to meet people's concerns about this question of the distinction?

(Mr Roe) I think we will try, although the answers that witnesses have given explain some of the difficulties in doing so. I think it is fair to say that the approach in the Bill at the moment envisages more of a spectrum rather than foxes and rabbits and recognises that there are certainly different degrees of experience and expertise which different consumers of financial services will have. It is really rather difficult to divide them into boxes. It is better to think of them in terms of a spectrum and I think even within the range of retail customers there will be people who are more and less vulnerable depending on their circumstances and we would want the FSA to be able to recognise those kinds of distinctions as well. So the drafting of clause 5 is an issue which Ministers are thinking about, but it is not very easy to come up with black and white difference in legislation.

Lord Poole

143. Have you considered the possibility that professional traders and expert end-users might explicitly be able to contract out in terms of asserting for themselves that they do not require the retail consumer protection and so if I was dealing with you

[Lord Poole *Cont*]

and we both had said we were professional traders then I would know we operated within a different set of rules?

(Mr Roe) It is certainly a thought. In the consultation document that we have just produced on financial promotion we address some of the possibilities of this kind of approach where we are considering the idea that it might be desirable to allow people from whom capital might be raised for start-up ventures and so on to exclude themselves from the regulatory system. Whether you could apply that more generally I think is a good question which certainly does bear thinking about. Some of the practicalities get rather difficult when you deal with a situation where a particular firm may be dealing with a mixture of expert and non-expert investors and you then start having to ask yourself whether those kinds of arrangements apply to a very broad range of transactions which might be quite difficult.

Viscount Trenchard

144.   If it is difficult to put the consumers into specific boxes and you say we are dealing with a spectrum, how does the Treasury think it would be possible to divide up the costs attributable to the different types of regulation? It seems unfair to me that firms who deal only with wholesale customers should have to bear part of the costs of regulating firms that deal with retail consumers who need much more protection.

(Mr Roe) There certainly is a distinction that one can imagine between the kinds of business which incur high costs and those which incur low costs and there is a great amount of discretion for the FSA within the Bill to develop charging structures which reflect those differences.

Chairman

145.   At the moment this distinction is in Clause 5(2)(b), is it not. It refers to the different degrees of experience and expertise which different consumers have in relation to different kinds of regulated activity. Why is that not enough for the purposes of drawing the distinction between different types of user?

(Ms Hall) I think our difficulty is with this idea of consumer protection. I know I have admitted that there are some more and some less expert, but we do not usually divide up consumer protection according to how expert you are. We do not usually give more to some and less to others. That principle is not there. I think I would feel happier if there were a consumer protection principle. The other difficulty is that the general principle that consumers should take responsibility for their decisions applies across the board whether expert or not, retail or wholesale.

146.   If we were able to take care of the issue in terms of the *caveat emptor* clause you would be less worried about what goes before it, would you?

(Ms Hall) Yes, but in a sense in order to take care of *caveat emptor* I think you have to divide them up. You have to divide those who I am happy to leave to *caveat emptor* and those who I think should not be left to it.

Lord Taverne

147.   Howard Davies mentioned that one might substitute for *caveat emptor* a duty of due care to be taken by a consumer which would certainly moderate the principle of *caveat emptor*. Is that something which the Treasury has considered as a way of distinguishing between wholesale and retail markets?

(Mr Roe) It is certainly a possibility that we are considering. I am not sure that it necessarily means the same thing as taking responsibility and I think this is something that we would need to consider further. In other words, it seems to me that the idea of taking care is rather less of a responsibility than taking responsibility. I imagine that Ministers will want to think very carefully about whether they want to make what would be a change in that area.

Chairman

148.   The National Consumer Council offered a different form of this at one stage, did you not?

(Ms Hall) We want to see the *caveat emptor* gone in relation to retail consumers, but we did add that if it is going to stay there then we think that needs to have some kind of provision such as "as far as they are able" because I have to say that all the evidence is that it is very difficult for people to be responsible for their own decisions in this area. As the only consumer principle in this Bill, the suggestion that that is the desirable provision is not the way we think things should go and it does not apply in other consumer protection legislation.

Mr Beard

149.   The principle of *caveat emptor* is not disputed as a principle for the wholesale end. The real problem is where you divide the wholesale from the retail and what you put in place of it at the retail end because, as Mr Howard Davies was saying, it is appropriate that people should take some responsibility for what they are doing. Even if they are not so fully informed, they can take the full responsibility as someone at the wholesale end. What would be your view as to what would satisfy this requirement at the consumer end?

(Ms Hall) As far as we are concerned, the wholesale end can take care of itself from our perspective. I do think it should go at the retail end. In all other areas of consumer protection there are implied terms that in a contract for the sale of goods and services you get what you think you are buying. I am not really clear why financial services should be any different. Clearly the Bill has strong powers for the FSA to involve itself in advice, information, consumer education and those are all desirable and we think it is an extremely good idea that the consumers should gain more expertise in this, but I do not think it should be a principle that consumers should look to be responsible for their own decisions. Of course, you have got to start off with "I think it is about time I thought about a pension", but it is a long way from there to saying, "It is me and only me who is responsible for which one I buy". If there were more

[**Mr Beard** *Cont*]

consumer protection principles in the Bill I would feel less unhappy about *caveat emptor* along with some kind of qualification in relation to the skills and experience of consumers.

150. How would you deal with the inherent risk there is involved in any of these products in respect of the kettle which you quote?

(*Ms Hall*) That would have to be provided for and in that respect would be different from kettles, but I do not necessarily think that it is insuperable to exclude the investment risk.

151. Have you got a form of words which would satisfy what you are saying?

(*Ms Hall*) No, because usually when we draft things people pick them to pieces. If you would like us to take it away and imagine drafting one, we would be happy to have a try.

(*Mr Heath*) However you define the consumer, can we have it defined at the time we advise them and not have it defined in retrospect or because the world has changed or whatever? We rather like the idea of a professional investor against a member of the public-type of investor, because of this rather cloudy area it seems to be one of the cleaner lines, but if we are advising someone who is deemed to be someone who needs special attention, that is one thing, but if we are advising a consenting adult who knows what they are doing then that is another thing and we really need to know that from day one rather than find that at a later date that is imposed upon us. If I can move on to *caveat emptor*. We do not like the phrase *caveat emptor*. We much prefer consumer responsibility. *Caveat emptor* also has the unpleasant effect of anyone to do with consumerism getting the crosses and garlic out. We much prefer the idea that the consumer basically needs to take an active role in their financial future, but they cannot just take little to no attention of what is going on, particularly as we are (a) trying to educate them, and (b) trying to find a regime where we can get information to them in a clear and meaningful way and then for them to have the perfect defence of "I did not understand". Clearly, there is a distance here somewhere that we need to agree a position on. Our fear, and it is very much the same as the NCC's, is that all this regulation is very undefined. Who are you trying to protect and against what? The Act fails to answer that question. We have five of these propositions: who are you trying to protect; against what; is it cost effective; is it fair; and can you explain to the public? At least we are going to explain it to the public, which is a big step forward under this legislation than the previous version. We need to ensure that the consumer has a responsibility, but I think this is a little too strict and it would be strange for us to say that.

Chairman

152. This is more general.

(*Mr Heath*) Yes, exactly. I think we have got to try and find a wording which does not allow members of the public purely to do anything they like in the sure knowledge that it can be put right somewhere down the line whilst at the same time ensuring that members of the public are not exposed to being misled, lied to and what have you and taking responsibility for it. So there is a position somewhere which we call consumer responsibility, but we cannot define it for you.

Lord Poole

153. If somebody puts money on deposit on the assumption that they have not gone for some improbably high rate of interest and the bank is properly regulated then they have certainty that they will have a return of their funds deposited. The uncertainty is merely the rate of interest that will be set by the marketplace whilst that deposit runs. If you wish to make an alternative form of investment, for example in some equity product, you give up that certainty in the hope of future reward. It seems to me that this is why this is such a very difficult conversation because no truthful adviser can say what the outcome of a non-deposit investment is going to be other than in bond markets, for example, which is not quite the point I am trying to make. The word investment is frequently misused when people mean a deposit, but if one can accept for this purpose that the word investment means the giving up of certainty in the hope of future reward, does it make it more difficult to pin bad advice on an adviser and make it even more difficult for the consumer to understand what he is doing? What are your views about this very complicated area?

(*Ms Johnstone*) These products are very complicated products which is why you have had so many difficulties in the past and why we are all sitting here today. I do not know, I think there are no straightforward answers, but it does seem very peculiar to us that we are setting up a system that provides less protection to consumers for very difficult products than we provide for them for easy products like buying a kettle. Whilst we quite agree, we cannot give people a guarantee of what return they are going to get, we still need to give them protection to make sure that they know what they are getting and that it is a product that is suitable for their needs.

Lord Taverne

154. That leads on to the very difficult question about possibly imposing on the regulator some sort of duty to regulate the product rather than just the people or the process. There are obvious disadvantages to regulating a product because you can thereby go for standardisation and lessen competition and provide poorer value for the policy holder, but, nevertheless, is this an area which you have thought about how one might secure some sort of obligation for the regulator to see that suitable products are sold without stifling competition or producing standardisation?

(*Ms Johnstone*) It is certainly an area we have looked at and it is an area that we have found is fraught with difficulties.

(*Ms Hall*) I think we think there are some types of products that we think would be unsuitable and something that should be done and to some extent those will be covered by powers which I think the FSA

[Lord Taverne Cont]

will have to control unfair terms in consumer contract regulations. One might want to look at those sort of powers where there are obnoxious clauses that allow people to do whatever they like in relation to the consumer without the consumer getting any benefit from them. There are difficulties with the unfair terms regulations which I will not go into now, but it is to do with the fundamental subject matter of the contract. So there are things on which we think outright the regulator might want to say. "This is not fair. This should not be in this product." But we also take the point that it may be standardisation, that it may lack competition and that it may stifle innovation. I think that if we were going to approach this, that we would look at it through the regulator having the power to expose, as it were, benchmarks. What a common product across this range looks like, so that you can say, "Oh, yes, this one is inflation proofed and this one is not." The regulator would look at what the central features are and then you would be alerted to the ones which did not have the things that off your own bat might not come into your head to think about.

Viscount Trenchard

155. Ms Johnstone, the London Investment Banking Association in some advice it submitted to the Treasury, suggested that "regulation should be no greater than is necessary to protect reasonable people from being made fools of. It should not seek to achieve the impossible task of protecting fools from their own folly." Would you agree with that?

(Ms Johnstone) I do not know how one would view a definition like that in the Bill. Obviously consumers are very vulnerable and an awful lot of consumers are very vulnerable when they are buying these products, because they are very difficult to understand and they have greater difficulty understanding them. I can see the point you are making, that if they have been properly advised and they still choose to buy something which is highly risky, then that is something they should be taking on themselves. However, at the moment, the way the caveat emptor is in the Bill is that they are taking everything on themselves.

Lord Poole

156. Do you think there might be a case for there being a limited range of very simple approved products, the nature of which would be specialised? Let us say, a ten-year insurance policy. There would be an approved ten-year policy, which would have to come from a company which qualified exactly the same, as you get in Germany. You would say to consumers, If you buy one of these we will make certain ... (whoever "we" is, the FSA or whatever body we wish to evolve). This is very limited range—it may be fairly bog standard, there may be a shortage of bells and whistles, some of which are more for the advantage of the adviser than for the customers but that is another point—but when somebody decided to go for a product, which was not a bog standard approved one, however defined or established, in so doing they would be accepting a significantly greater

degree of personal care and attention to what they were doing, with obviously the normal period for rescinding the contract, a fortnight after, for example. Do you think that would be at all helpful?

(Ms Johnstone) I think the idea of benchmarking is helpful but I am not sure that it helps with the basic problem we started with here, which was different types of consumers—wholesale, retail—where one draws the line.

157. At the very bottom end of the consumers.

(Ms Johnstone) I think having benchmarked products is helpful but it does not deal with the problem we were addressing.

Lord Eatwell

158. May I follow on from that and ask the FSA if that is what they regard as one of their public awareness duties, benchmarking basic products. Is that the requirement in the Bill: to provide appropriate information and advice?

(Mr Whittaker) We strongly support differentiation in the way the regime operates. We operate differentiation in much of what we do at the moment and have already set out proposals to continue to do so. We think that differentiation ought to be something that can be designed to adapt over time and across different sectors. You may want a different differentiation in one market from the one you want in another. We agree with the idea that caveat emptor is a very important issue that needs to be clarified in the Bill. We think it is right that the industry should have assurance that we will not regulate to the nth degree, we will not regulate where there is no need, but we do think there are concerns which need to be clarified as soon as possible. We look forward to seeing the new draft, which Treasury has offered, in the new version of the Bill. On the specific point that has just been raised, as far as the consumer awareness objective is concerned, yes, I think although we are at a very early stage in considering how we will operate the consumer awareness objective, we could see the consumer awareness role being used to alert people to standard features which they might expect to see in particular kinds of products or products designed to achieve particular objectives. What we have been more reluctant about is going from that identification of general issues to any form of product approval in which we were, in some sense, endorsing products that met those particular objectives, which I think we are very reluctant to undertake.

Chairman

159. Thank you very much. Given the time I am going to have to move on.

(Mr Jones) May I just make a point. We have been agonising over the definition of consumer. The problem with the answer is the confines of the procedures themselves. Every adviser has to go through the client fact finding process. Part of that process is identifying whether you are talking to a totally inexperienced investor or a very experienced investor or in between. So the advice that you give that

[**Chairman** Cont]

individual has to be commensurate with the expertise that individual has in financial matters. If you stray very far from that, if you put a non-experienced investor into high risk investments, you would soon be pulled up by the FSA monitoring team visiting you. That is probably as close as you can get to control of this because if you write these definitions into the legislation, there is no guarantee that this is going to stop people selling the wrong contracts to the wrong people. They still have to be found by the FSA monitoring teams.

Chairman: I think this has been very helpful. This does help in terms of clarifying it. We are in a position of waiting for the redraft from the Treasury on these issues. Could I now move on to the question of the market confidence objective.

Lord Eatwell: This may take you a little beyond what this group would like to comment on, but perhaps I may ask you very briefly. In the list of statutory objectives for the Bill is market confidence, public awareness, protection of consumers, and reduction of financial crime. We have been rather puzzled on this Committee that one of the objectives is not reducing systemic risk, reducing risk in the system as a whole, which is what most of us thought regulators actually did. We have discovered that is not one of the objectives and we wondered how you would react: for example, the consumer is enormously important, it seems to me, because the consumer protection will protect the consumer who is signing up to a particular contract. Diminishing systemic risk makes sure that the cash is there at the time when you want to hand it over.

The Committee suspended from 16.33 pm to 16.40 pm for a division in the House of Lords.

Chairman

160. Lord Eatwell's question about systemic risk.

(Ms Johnstone) I have to say it is not an issue that we have thought about a great deal but having looked at the definition of market confidence I think I would rather agree with the Committee. It does seem rather strange that it is not there because the market confidence definition seems quite narrow. We would have sympathy with that point of view.

(Mr Heath) We get rather blasé in the United Kingdom about the stability of our various product providers. We have done very well with the DTI's covering of insurance companies and the Bank of England in the way of regulated banks. With the exception of the BCCI I could not think of too many occasions where there has been systemic collapse in the way we have seen in America. We have been extremely fortunate. I would think whatever this Bill says must continue that tradition. It not only comes in terms of straight preventative regulation being careful in that way, but there are things which could be done within the wholesale sector and the way the retail sector is regulated, which could destabilise providers. This is another area but we would agree. We also need to have a pretty clear definition of the regulation of the Bank of England and FSA. We would not want to see

a situation where somebody fell down the middle somewhere. One of our great legacies, I have to say, in the United Kingdom, is that our tradition of regulation has been so good. It was quite interesting, the comment made that if you are a investor of a building society your money is safe. Not in America it ain't. It is because we have had that wonderful position that has gone on so long.

Chairman: I would like to use the remaining time of this session to deal with the two issues—maybe we will roll them together—of competitiveness and competition and the whole question of the regulatory burden.

Mr Loughton

161. International competitiveness and competitiveness between firms in this country. The Treasury Select Committee looking at this subject did recommend that there should be a fifth objective to improve competition. What are your thoughts on the way the whole FSA structure and the rule book is going to impinge on the competitiveness of the City of London financial services institutions in this country? Are we driving out people? We have 550 foreign banks operating here already. Are they likely to diminish or expand as a result of what we are discussing?

(Ms Johnstone) I do not think we have views or are in a position to have a view on the impact on the industry although we have got views on competition.

(Mr Heath) I am looking at Robin actually but the point I would make is that people do not send money to London because Howard Davies is a good regulator. They send it because the City of London has a very good reputation, and because of the place and time zones and other reasons that is why markets and business is done here. So the cost of regulation can only drive out business. That is something we have to be careful of. In the retail side we have a similar problem, but we now have effectually two systems running, which was picked up by one of your earlier speakers. We have the full blown regulation, advice based research, and now we have CAT standards and attempting to move to benchmarks; where in one area we are trying to protect the consumer from everything and in the other area we are allowing the consumer to misbuy with confidence. These, if you like, are two separate strands. However you benchmark products it does not mean that your client is buying the right product for themselves in the first place. They may end up with a most suitably and cheap wonderful pension but actually need protection insurance more than they need a pension. There will be no-one under the benchmarking system to advise them of that.

Lord Poole

162. You have just said something I really quite strongly disagree with, so I would just like to hear you justify it. I think almost the whole of my life has been spent as one form or another of international operator in the City. I would say that one of the fundamental reasons, for many years, why business came to London, is that London was clean and well regulated.

[**Lord Poole** *Cont*]

Now in some cases, of course, it came because it was not regulated at all, as in the case of the Euro markets. I do not think the quality of advice, as you suggest, is anything like as appalling to external holders of funds, so we are rather at odds.

(*Mr Heath*)   I do not think we are at odds. The point I was making was that the City of London was built on reputation. As you say, a clean market. It was not based on regulation. Since we have had to have regulation, we have it. So my point really is, I do not think we are at odds in any way. If you look round at the magnificence of it, that was not built by regulation, it was built by a market which happened to be self-regulated. Now we cannot trust the market to be self-regulating, so we are told, so we have to bring in regulation. I do not think there are any odds in what we are saying. Purely we are all looking for a clean market.

(*Mr Hutton*)   Could I add, I do not really see any problem with the wording of the clause 2.3. It summarises quite well what this regulatory legislation should try and achieve. As far as ensuring proper competition and conditions of competition are concerned, there are other pieces of legislation to deal with that and other machinery. I personally—and it is a purely personal opinion—find the drafting of those four sub-clauses to be very helpful indeed, in that they say it should not get in the way of competition. It should generally help the competitive environment which, it seems to me, is the best way of doing it.

Chairman

163. In the principles rather than a separate objective?

(*Mr Hutton*)   Yes.

Mr Loughton

164. Would anyone like to make a case, it says here "proportionate to the benefit". If we are all agreed that there is a cost involved in providing an appropriate product or financial service to a client, would anybody realistically suggest that there should be minimum commission, minimum cost to a product, as we used to have in the old days of the Stock Exchange, below which it would just not be physically possible to provide a product with best advice and best compliance regulation costs that went with it? Maybe we should be allowed to charge below that. Nobody is actually suggesting that.

(*Mr Hutton*)   I see no justification for that.

165. Right, so how can we guarantee "with minimal cost" and at the same time comply with all these regulations that a financial company is providing the consumer with the most appropriate products?

(*Mr Hutton*)   Could I just say that I think the word "guarantee" is the key to the whole thing. You cannot guarantee it. Competition in the market place will eventually weed out the ones who do not do the job. It seems to me that in a capitalistic system that is pretty fundamental.

Viscount Trenchard

166. The public awareness objective is fairly open-ended. It talks about the promotion of public awareness of the benefits associated with investment and the provision of appropriate information and advice. It seems to me fairly open-ended and could become more and more extensive. Do you think that, compared with the four regulatory objectives, there is enough about the maintenance of competition and international competitiveness in the Bill, whether or not the maintenance of competition were to be made an objective in its own right? It does seem to me that the Bill may not yet recognise fully how much consumers have benefited from competition in the United Kingdom market. The range of products that have been available to them and the opportunities that have been available have been much greater than would have been the case had we had a much tougher regulatory regime. I know it is a balance. I would like to know whether you think the Bill says enough about the maintenance of competition.

(*Ms Johnstone*)   We would find it helpful if it did have improving competition as an objective. Whilst we have a competitive market, it has not always worked in the consumer's interest. If the regulator is looking to improving the market, as well as not distorting the market, that would be very helpful. The provision of comparative information is one of the things we have been talking about.

(*Mr Heath*)   I think Viscount Trenchard makes a very good point and it picks up the point made earlier about Germany, which has had product regulation since the Second World War and has had—although it is beginning to improve now—a totally stagnating product development there. There was very poor product development there. There was very poor value for money for the clients and consumers and a lot of money flows out of Germany, not only for fiscal reasons but because there is better value elsewhere, not least on the London market, I have to say. For things like death in service benefits for German companies, the Germans discovered some years ago that it was much cheaper in London than in their own area. So we do have to keep an eye on this. Whilst we have to have a regulator looking at particularly poor value products, because the previous regime allowed a poor value product, as long as it was sold correctly it was fine. There was some pretty ropey stuff being thrown about in some cases, I have to say, which really the consumer was very lucky to get a decent return on. But if it was sold correctly that was okay. Equally, we do not want the regulators marching through every product, attempting to second guess the product design, which is what happened in Germany and did their industry unaccountable harm.

Mr Heathcoat-Amory

167. At the heart of this subject seems to be a balance to be struck between the desirability of reducing risk, particularly for the ordinary public, as against the cost of doing so. I am interested in where these costs fall. Would I be right that the costs are ultimately borne by that same public or are they

[Mr Heathcoat-Amory *Cont]*
absorbed by the industry and reduced profit margins and shareholders? To the extent that they are borne by the public, is this a matter which concerns or should concern the Consumers' Council? Do you see yourself as the guardian of a savings culture, which will obviously be undermined if everybody had to pay excessive costs for savings products?

(Ms Johnstone) We assume the costs of regulation are borne by the consumers in the end. That would be our starting point. Obviously I am no expert in the industry cost structure, so I would not be able to say if it was otherwise. Clearly it is a concern to the consumer organisations and to the NCC, if the burden of regulation is disproportionate to the benefit to consumers. But it is very hard to make that kind of judgment because obviously the costs of inadequate regulation are borne by consumers. Those costs can be very heavy indeed when you get to retirement age and your pension is not able to keep you. What do you do?

168. The taxpayer has to provide a social security system to pick up the pieces.

(Ms Johnstone) Yes, that is another issue. You pay for it as a taxpayer instead. But as the intention of Government policy is to move people more and more into making provision for themselves, to relieve the burden on taxpayers, if the regulatory system does not work that policy will not work. It will come back to the taxpayer. It is very hard to make a judgment about what is excess costs; apart from the accidents, the casualties, which is not a particularly good way of measuring the system.

(Mr Heath) From our point of view, we have a problem because we have no access to shareholders' money, so our costs find their way back. It does give an imbalance in the market, particularly if regulators are allowed to have free will as to what they can do. There is a tension here that the Government, in the form of Treasury, is not paying for this system, yet could find itself under very significant pressure to do things. One can think of a Dangerous Dogs Act situation without needing to go to legislation. Effectively, from now on, the Treasury will own this regulation in some form or way. But it does not have to pay for it. The regulator does not have to pay for what is going on. As we have seen previously, product providers can and do accept these costs, whilst sometimes maybe putting up a fight on behalf of the shareholders and policy holders. There is this tension in the whole system. This is why when we go back to our perspective—and the NCC is coming from the same place in a different way—we are coming back to defined regulation; to knowing where we are and to making sure that what we are doing now is actually acceptable. If I can just pick up the kettle analogy for a second because it is a good one, although I do not think it takes us very far. The kettle works on water, which remains the same, and on electricity, where the voltage remains pretty much the same. To give you an example we work in different products. Mortgages in 1992 were 16 per cent and are now down to 6.5 per cent. Returns on pensions fell from 23 to 11 per cent between 1990 and 1999 and between 1991 and 1999

annuity rates of 12.6 per cent were down to 6 per cent. What I am saying is in inventing this kettle we have to invent it in such a way as to ensure that the voltage goes from 100 volts up to 240. In reality we are not buying a thing. When a consumer buys a pension he is not buying a kettle. He is buying a promise from the pension company that they are going to do the best they possibly can for his retirement in the light of 101 different things that can change, not least fiscal policy, Government policy, changes in welfare benefits and a million and one other things. Although the kettle analogy is an interesting one I am not sure it takes us very far because it is very difficult to say at the time you purchase a product that it will be fit for purpose right the way through changes not only in business rates but a thousand and one other things the Government chooses to do.

Lord Taverne

169. In these circumstances is there any role for a league table of costs and charges?

(Mr Jones) There is a culture at the moment that hangs on to this idea of charges being the mythical answer to all investment problems. In the part of the world I originate from there is a saying that you do not get owt for nowt. You basically get what you pay for. I would much prefer rather than have league tables of charges, interesting though they are, to look at performance because at the end of the day it is performance that matters and I could cite you cases from my operational days where pension plans maturing now are coming out at something like three times the original projection. Whilst ever you have got this artificial projection where you are projecting at a given rate which is laid down by the regulator, charges obviously are the major concern, but in the real world out there you will get some funds that massively out-perform others and that is really the role of the adviser to actually sort out the sheep from the goats. Again, you have to do this based on the information you have gleaned about the clients and the amount of risk that the clients can cope with, but I think to link everything to charges is a very dangerous approach to investment. The other danger is that if you have league tables of charges there will be a tendency, and I am sure that there are those out there thinking about it already, to set up their insurance divisions out in Dublin or somewhere like that where they can avoid all this regulation but still operate on the mainland under EC regulations. So it is a difficult one. I can understand why people want to look at the costs and charges of things but, as I say, that is very much only one side of the equation. The other side is just as important. On the question of competition we would like to see polarisation written into this Bill because the retention of polarisation is an effective means of ensuring competition in the market place. If there is a healthy IFA community out there that is the surest way of ensuring that the providers remain competitive than any other way. If we abolish polarisation we will run into the problem of multi-ties and you will see a consolidation of the market where the biggest

[Lord Taverne *Cont*]

providers, effectively, ultimately operate a cartel. The only healthy way as far as the investor is concerned and to ensure competition for the future is that polarisation should actually be written into this new Bill.

Mr Beard

170. What does polarisation mean in this context?

(Mr Jones) The adviser has to declare when speaking to a client for the first time whether he is totally independent and therefore can offer contracts right across the market place or whether he is tied and can only sell the products of one particular provider.

Lord Taverne

171. That is not in the Bill at the moment?

(Mr Jones) No.

Chairman

172. Does the NCC have a view about this?

(Ms Hall) We have always supported polarisation. If we have any concern about it, it is that it does not necessarily help those who were not able to go to independent financial advisers. Nevertheless it is not a principle that we would want to lose precisely for the competition argument.

173. Mr Roe, where are we on polarisation?

(Mr Roe) Polarisation is, of course, a very important part of the existing regulatory structure although it is not set out in primary legislation. I think it is quite right that these sorts of things should be examined from time to time and, indeed, I understand it will be examined, but it demonstrates quite an interesting point which is I do not think it would be consistent with our general approach to write these kinds of specific rules into the legislation because there are views on the investor protection aspects of polarisation and also on the competition aspects which need to be looked at in a way which means that they are not necessarily rules set in stone for all time. So I do not think we would want to write polarisation into the Bill, which is not to say we do not recognise the importance of the issue.

Chairman: I will bring this session to a close because, as you know, we are under tremendous time pressure in terms of reporting for this Committee. We are having to try and fit in an awful lot of witnesses in a very short time. We are very grateful to you for coming and helping us through this. Could I say if there are any points that you would have wanted to make but you have not had a chance to make this afternoon, we are very happy to receive them in writing. We are very grateful for your contributions.

Examination of Witnesses

Mr PETER FOSTER, Finance Director, CGU, and Mr MARK BOLÉAT, Director General, Association of British Insurers; Mr ALASTAIR ROSS GOOBEY, Chief Executive, Hermes Pensions Management Ltd, Member of the Council of Lloyd's; Mr JAMES STRETTON, Chief Executive of UK Operations, Standard Life Assurance Co and Director of the Bank of England; and Mr JONATHAN AGNEW, Executive Chairman of LIMIT plc, called in and examined.

Mr DAVID ROE, Head of Financial Services and Markets Bill Team, HM Treasury, and Mr ANDREW WHITTAKER, Deputy General Counsel, Financial Services Authority, in attendance.

Chairman

174. Good afternoon and thank you all very much for joining us. I think a number of you have been sitting in and have heard some of the discussions we had in the first session. We would like to begin with a similar set of issues. I understand, Mr Stretton, that you have to go at 5.45. If we are still going, if you would just leave when you think you have to leave.
(Mr Stretton) Thank you, I am very grateful for that.

175. I would like to start on the same basis we started the previous session. This is to ask you to introduce yourselves and tell us briefly what your main views and concerns are about the Bill; how far the Government in their responses so far have met your concerns; and what you think the outstanding issues are. We have labelled this section "objectives". We are trying to divide up sessions into broad topics but we will understand, particularly in your opening remarks, if there are wider issues you would like to cover at this point as long as you are reasonably brief. I will start with Mr Stretton.
(Mr Stretton) I am Jim Stretton. I am here as the UK Chief Executive of Standard Life, a company which is a major supplier of products to the retail financial services market so what I would like to talk about briefly is solely in relation to retail customers and taking up the point of what the retail customer needs to do in order to secure his or her own interests. I would like the customer to be as secure as the customer possibly can but I am concerned that we should not promise something that we cannot deliver. The problems arise normally not in relation to the product itself. In the kettle analogy it is very unusual that the kettle actually does not work. People may buy expensive kettles or they may find that they have bought a product that is basically unsuitable for them. It is at that level that the model gets a lot more complicated in financial services than in normal product areas. The decision about what you want to do, how you want to protect yourself or your family is chiefly a subjective one and ultimately nobody else can take that decision for you. Inevitably there is a residual responsibility on customers to decide just what is important. There is a duty on the industry to make sure that the products are properly described, fairly and fully. There is a duty on an adviser to act competently in enabling the customers to get to their priorities as rapidly and accurately as possible but ultimately the decision that says, "I want to insure this. I do not want to insure that. I am going to take a particular risk of either the performance of the contract, if you are talking about an equity against gilts type of investment, or the issues and risks of my own lifestyle", is entirely for individuals themselves. That is the situation today. It is actually going to get worse in the sense that with Individual Savings Accounts and with Stakeholder Pensions there is going to be much less of an advisory process costed into the product. The whole drift of policy is to make it more feasible for customers to act on their own and therefore to operate more cheaply. In that environment it is absolutely imperative that the customers do realise there is a responsibility lying on them otherwise we will finish up eventually with disappointed customers and that will damage them, the industry and the regulators.
(Mr Ross Goobey) My Lord Chairman, I am Alastair Ross Goobey, Chief Executive of Hermes Pensions Plans and a nominated member of the Council of Lloyd's. I am also a member of the executive committee of IFMA, the Institutional Fund Managers Association, which manages over two trillion pounds of assets. Hermes is 100 per cent owned by the BT Pension Scheme, Britain's largest with over £25 billion in assets, and it manages the bulk of the assets of the Post Office pension schemes with over £15 billion in assets. I have been a nominated non-executive member of the Council of Lloyd's since December 1997. I have 30 years' experience working in financial markets businesses. While welcoming the general thrust of the Financial Services and Markets Bill with its integration and regulation, I believe this is an opportunity to make certain that the regulatory regime in the United Kingdom comes as close to the best fit as possible to the appropriate protection for customers, called consumers in the Bill, without over-burdening suppliers as legislative tailoring will make it; not too tight and not too loose. I am concerned that there will inevitably be a tendency to err on the side of reducing the risk to the regulator at the expense of the regulated. The regulatory objectives do not include the principle that the FSA must have due regard to the competitive position of the London financial market and I believe that the DTI Ministers have said that is a matter for them. That is not a statutory objective. The FSA and its Chairman will probably be judged harshly if there is even modest wrongdoing that escapes their gaze. The idea that there can be 100 per cent success in any regulatory regime must be dismissed. Your Lordships and Honourable Members have been passing laws for hundreds of years but I regret there are still some who disobey them without being found out until too late. The Treasury Progress Report acknowledges that there has been

[Chairman *Cont*]

some confusion about the expression "consumer". My strong preference is that the regime should be prepared to treat more consumers as professionals, defined as willing to act under the principle of *caveat emptor*, whilst maintaining a suitably strict regime for those supplying services to the less sophisticated, those more usually referred to as consumers. Let me give you one really concrete example. In February 1993 pension funds came under the occupational pension scheme regime of IMRO. This was a response to the Maxwell scandal, one in which IMRO had proved completely unwilling to intervene when warned, as I know personally. The burden on those providing investment services to such clients exploded. My two client sets of trustees, the largest and fourth largest schemes, were faced with the prospect of receiving many feet high of transaction reports periodically which you may be sure they would never read. Fortunately, they negotiated a waiver with IMRO. However, and this is the point, since the 1995 Pensions Act pension fund trustees are themselves regulated by the pensions regulator OPRA. They are obliged to take professional advice and breaches of self-investment and other restrictions must be reported to the regulator by the scheme secretary or auditors or actuaries, and yet the OPS regime continues. So we have double regulation. We are agents for sophisticated investors. We may even be treated as wholesale counter parties as we are under the current S. 43 of the Financial Services Act for dealing in currencies and money markets, yet the Bill makes a distinction between our status for some of these instruments and that of our clients, even though they are considered to be sophisticated. I am slightly worried about Howard Davies' view that we should subdivide into three areas, which is the professional wholesale investors, the professional investors and the man in the street. I accept entirely that we should have a greater duty of care for retail investors, not that we are addressing them, than our counter parties would to us but regulated entity to regulated entity transactions seem to demand a single *caveat emptor* regime rather than the possibility of three parties becoming subject to three different levels for disclosure and reporting. My last point, if I may Chairman, as a parenthesis, is a point about the regulation of Lloyd's of London which will not come up very often I suspect, although my recent colleague Jonathan Agnew is here. Here I speak in a personal capacity rather than representing the views of the Council. Council members of Lloyd's are to be authorised persons under the putative Act and subject to the disciplinary powers of the FSA. These have a civil burden of proof and the authorised person is assumed to be guilty unless innocence can be proved. The Council of Lloyd's is like a board of a plc. Non-executive directors of insurance companies would not be subject to such potential discipline, having the duty of care that all plc directors must demonstrate and being subject to criminal action only for negligence and similar failings. The working members of the Council of Lloyd's must, by definition, be more familiar with the workings of that market than the nominated members who, as I say, are equivalent to non-executive directors and they should rightly be subject to the normal rules of the FSA for market

professionals. However, under the current proposals I personally would be in double jeopardy. If the Council was deemed to have fallen down on its responsibilities on a matter it might be unreasonable to expect a non-executive to have full information on, I would not only be subject to fines, I might also have my authorisation removed, preventing me from carrying out my day job as an investment manager. Anyone who works as an executive in another part of the financial services industry would be a fool to put themselves in that position. I can say categorically today if the legislation makes no distinction between the position of a nominated member of the Council and working or executive members of it, I shall resign from it. I cannot see why anyone working in another regulated part of financial services would take the risk of being a Council member. That would seem to be a pity for the strategic guidance of Lloyd's in the future. The last thing I would say is I am very, very happy to take questions but I would ask that they remain at a high level. If you want me to delve into the individual clauses of the Bill I think you would find me failing.

176.   You may not be alone! Mr Agnew?

(Mr Agnew) Thank you, my Lord Chairman. My name is Jonathan Agnew, Executive Chairman of LIMIT plc which is the largest underwriting business at Lloyd's. I was a member of the Council of Lloyd's from 1995 until January of this year. I remain a member of the Lloyd's market board. I really wanted to bring up just one single issue in relation to Lloyd's and the Financial Services Bill which since it is a suggested omission from the Bill I think must fall under other issues. I should also say that I am not speaking for the Council of Lloyd's though I understand that the Corporation of Lloyd's has made representations on this point to the Treasury. As members of this Committee will know, Lloyd's has been going through a period of very rapid change. To give just three examples. In the last five years the capital base has changed to such an extent that corporate capital has gone from nil to 73 per cent of the Lloyd's capital base. Secondly, Lloyd's is now in fierce competition with Bermuda and other overseas financial centres for business that was traditionally a London market insurance business. Thirdly, if the Bill or something like it is enacted ultimate regulation of Lloyd's is due to pass to the authority of the FSA, a move which I may say is welcome to most at Lloyd's and indeed was recommended by Lloyd's itself, a very different attitude, parenthetically, to that which Lloyd's took at the time of the passing of the Financial Services Bill in 1986. However, the regulation of Lloyd's is still governed by a series of Lloyd's Acts, the most recent of which is the Lloyd's Act 1982. Some of you on this Committee may think it inappropriate that a collection of commercial businesses in a period of rapid change should be governed by an Act which was passed at a time 17 years ago which long predated the present situation of Lloyd's and the present state of the insurance market. Worse still, as the Committee will be aware, the Lloyd's Act is a private Act and to repeal it and pass a detailed new Act would require a private Bill or more probably a hybrid Bill. Not surprisingly it has been

[Chairman *Cont]*

difficult and is likely to be difficult if not impossible under a Government of either party to find Parliamentary time for the peculiar and lengthy procedures necessary to pass a hybrid Bill. The Committee may ask does this matter? I think it does. Just to give one example. The Lloyd's Act prohibits Lloyd's underwriters from accepting business other than from Lloyd's brokers. Lloyd's brokers under the Act have to be regulated by Lloyd's. This is a very important commercial point at the moment as to whether brokers other than Lloyd's brokers should be allowed to bring business to Lloyd's. Also there is an anomaly in that the present Government has said that it does not consider that commercial insurance brokers should be regulated by statute and on the other hand there is the statute on the books saying that a particular type of commercial insurance broker, Lloyd's brokers, have to be regulated by Lloyd's. How can this be solved? Lloyd's has taken legal advice that it would be possible to insert a simple clause into the Bill to allow the Treasury on the written application of Lloyd's and with the approval of the FSA, to amend by secondary legislation any provision of the Lloyd's Acts which concerns the regulation of Lloyd's. This would be a very simple way of allowing the Treasury with the approval of the FSA to change the Lloyd's Acts to meet changes in the commercial situation and in the regulatory situation which need apply to it. I understand, and I would not wish to enter into discussions on this, that such a clause could be drafted in such a way as to avoid hybridity and that it could come within the present scope of the Bill. I would ask the Committee to consider if that would not be a useful addition to the Bill. Thank you very much.

(Mr Foster) My name is Peter Foster. I am Finance Director of CGU which is an international insurance group formed through the merger of the Commercial Union and General Accident. I welcome the creation of a single regulator for the financial services industry and believe it is important that there is a sensible, legal framework that will enable it to function effectively and adapt to changing circumstances and, very importantly, allow companies to operate on an even playing field with its international competitors. As a director of a company with worldwide premium income of some £18 billion, of which 60 per cent is written outside the United Kingdom—some £11 billion, it is very important to us and I believe to the rest of the insurance industry (which makes a substantial contribution to the UK economy) that we are not exposed to undue regulatory burdens, undue compliance or excessive capital requirements relative to international competition. I therefore think it is very important, and the main point I want to make is that going forward adequate weight is given by the FSA in its deliberations in terms of the insurance industry not being disadvantaged on regulatory matters compared with its international competitors. I think generally that insurance regulation has worked reasonably well in the past and one would wish to see that continue.

177. Mark?

(Mr Boléat) I am Mark Boléat, the Director General of the Association of British Insurers. We have submitted joint evidence to this Committee with the British Bankers Association, an example of joined up trade associations perhaps following the move of the regulators! I want to highlight three points very quickly.

178. Your evidence to the Treasury back in the autumn?

(Mr Boléat) No, we have submitted to this Committee on Friday our formal evidence of the two bodies together. We fully support the objective of a single regulator and obviously we want to do everything we can to bring the new arrangements into effect as efficiently and as quickly as possible. To us the key issues are ones that have been highlighted to the Committee already. In a way they stem from one point. So far the regulation of insurance and banking has been conducted in a fairly informal but effective way and has not been rule-based. We have no doubt that the FSA marks a move towards a more rule-based approach which has advantages and disadvantages and we wish to minimise those disadvantages. A few key issues. Accountability, we note what has been done so far, the announcement recently, but we think there is a need to go further. We do think the Treasury should be empowered not only to receive proposals of the FSA, but also to comment on them. My colleague Peter Foster has already mentioned the need for the FSA to take account of international competitiveness of institutions in Britain and we think that sensibly should be an objective. I am sure you will have heard about enforcement as well. We believe the provisions still go too far.

Chairman: We are having two sessions on enforcement at the end of this week.

The Committee suspended from 17.21 to 17.31 for a division in the House of Commons

Chairman: Thank you very much. We thought that because Mr Stretton has to leave we should start with the whole question of consumer protection and the approach to *caveat emptor*.

Lord Eatwell

179. I want to ask Mr Stretton a question since the point that he made referred to the responsibility of the consumer. He will have heard the discussion previously between the National Consumer Council and the independent advisers and so on. I want to ask him to reflect on that and whether he feels that either through the consumer protection objective or through the advice, the quasi-educational objective, satisfactory consumer protection can be attained?

(Mr Stretton) I think the education aim is very important. I do not think that we can achieve a satisfactory position for consumers without having educated consumers. That is a very important aim to pursue. Based on the discussion I heard I feel that too much attention was being paid to the product and not enough to the actual mechanics of the decision making process, which is the complicated piece. I share the view that product regulation inhibits the development of markets and I do not think that it can play as large

[Lord Eatwell *Cont***]**

a part in making sure that customers do not make the wrong decisions as sometimes is made out. If you take the Stakeholder Pension as an example of a decision that people will have to make, they will have to make the decision as to whether they want to have it and if so to whom will they go, will they seek advice or can they do this by themselves, how much will they contribute, should they contract out of the state scheme and if they have an existing pension should they stay on that or should they use a stakeholder pension? These are things that the customer cannot avoid having some responsibility for and some knowledge of how to address themselves and education will be very, very important.

Lord Poole: I personally find these sorts of issues, such as the ones you have mentioned, utterly incomprehensible and that is after a lifetime spent working at them. That may be a slight exaggeration but these are fiendishly complicated. How do you suggest that can practically be done and, more importantly, how can the regulator ensure that you are doing it?

180. I am a professional economist and I find it completely incomprehensible. It just seems to me that whilst it is highly desirable that one should have an educated consumer, it is simply not credible.

(Mr Stretton) I understand the question and I agree with it. The question really is what do you do about it? Do you pretend that you can protect people in this situation when you cannot or do you just acknowledge that there is a problem and try to make sure that customers are genuinely on their guard and will ask the basic questions like "what does this do for me?, what are the risks involved in what I enter into?", and at least hope that we can get customers able to do that? I really fear an environment in which customers regard any action that they take here as being one which has been sanitised and safe and is bound to work out to their advantage, even though they will find it difficult to make those decisions themselves.

Mr Kidney

181. Just on the back of that, somebody spoke in the last session about being against league tables of costs and charges. Clearly that is too narrow but is it not part of this consumer advice or consumer information to empower consumers to make informed choices by having comparative tables of all sorts of things: persistency rates, performance over years, charges, hidden charges or open charges? Are those not all a part of trying to promote competition through allowing the customers to have the information they need to make their decisions?

(Mr Stretton) I am perfectly happy with league tables, we just need to make sure that in a world where some of the important things are not measurable we do not get people spending all of their time looking at things that you can measure. This is a very strange product, it is not manufactured until some time over the next 50 years, so getting a league table which is really helpful is difficult. We should measure what we can and that should be available to customers.

(Mr Boléat) My Lord Chairman, can I add on that all those league tables are available and are published.

Indeed, a month ago we had the PIA's latest effort which ran to 60 pages of tables giving all of the costs and charges, performance tables are published every month in any number of journals, persistency figures are published by the Personal Investment Authority, and the overall impact of this on consumers is not a lot.

182. Not measurable.

(Mr Boléat) I very much agree with the point that Lord Eatwell mentioned. I am a professional economist, like him, and I stopped buying the *Economic Journal* after 30 years when I realised that I had not understood any of it. It is not just in financial services where there is this problem. We know from any amount of research that consumers do not read literature until they need to. That is not to say we should not do everything we can to make that literature as readable and as user friendly as possible for those who wish to read it, but the majority of people do not read literature until they have a problem. If we actually build a regulatory system on the basis that people read and understand everything it will fail. Having said that, there is more that can be done to make products easier to understand and easier to compare but we need to look at financial services in the context of all other goods and services where the same problems exist.

Mrs Blackman

183. I just want to check out with those members of the panel who have not spoken recently whether they are struggling with this statutory objective of public awareness. Is it too woolly? Have you worked out what you think it means for your area in terms of meeting that statutory objective or does a lot more work need to be done on the objective of public awareness?

(Mr Ross Goobey) I was keeping deliberately quiet because fortunately we do not have to sell directly to the retail customer, thank goodness.

Lord Poole

184. Come on, you are not allowed to get away with it that easily! You know far too much to sit in complete silence, you must have a view.

(Mr Ross Goobey) What worries me as an institutional investor is actually the question of the cost of informing these consumers which does not give us any benefit at all. If we are going to get charged that, there was a question that was raised about the cost of cross-subsidising between the institutional professional investors and the private client investors. I think it is very difficult to inform sufficiently the individual. The individual does not take a great deal of interest in these products and does not understand when they are explained to them. In my limited experience, and I was on the board of Cheltenham and Gloucester for a long time, even in mortgages, which are the most widely taken out products, people do not understand what they have got and there were many complaints to the ombudsman about fixed rate mortgages when people thought they had been robbed by the building society and please could they now have the variable rate because rates had fallen. There was a great danger

[Lord Poole *Cont*]

when we reported to the Building Societies Ombudsman that he was actually taking some notice of it. I am not confident that consumers, even well informed, well educated, exposed to education, will make well informed decisions.

185. That is such an indictment, is it not, of ordinary retail consumers faced with ever increasing complex products on the market and you are saying that you are not even convinced after they have been taken through the process that the majority of them will understand what it is that they are being sold and the ramifications of the product. There is an awful lot of work still to be done on how we can simplify the information and the process that consumers go through. Would anybody else like to comment on that?

(Mr Boléat) The consumers are also balancing the price of the product against the time it takes to discover all of these bits of information. If you apply that analogy to it, why does anybody buy Coca-Cola in a pub when they can go to a garage and buy it at a tenth of the price? If you look at any good and service there is that balance to be made all of the time. That is part of it. How many people can operate a video recorder without the help of a ten year old? The literature is all there, indeed it is there in 18 languages to make it easy for everybody, but do people use it? The chances are they probably cannot programme a video. It is not saying that they are unable to, it is that they do not think that is a sensible use of their time and they are buying sometimes on the basis of the reputation of the product provider or salesman. We know they take far more notice of what a salesman says than what is written down. If a salesman said the opposite of what is written down the chances are that the salesman would be believed, that is human nature. It is not a criticism of consumers.

Lord Eatwell

186. Can I come back to one of the points that was made earlier. I cannot remember whether it was this group or the previous one, it is melding together. Somebody said in regulation in the past if you sold a rotten product but actually went through the procedure correctly you were okay and the regulator thought that you had behaved correctly. That does not sound very pleasant, it does not sound the sort of thing that one would like to encourage. Are we getting into a position, from Mr Stretton's position, that if the company selling the product describes what it does clearly, sets out all the conditions and sells it then as far as the regulator is concerned that is okay even though it might be a quite inappropriate product for the person buying it?

(Mr Stretton) There are duties on the seller to make sure that, if asked, the product is at least relevant to the customer. The customer cannot escape the duty to decide whether it is the most relevant thing that he or she is faced with. There will be people who do buy, and the regulator will regard the sale as perfectly proper, things which they subsequently regard as not having been their priority. There will be expensive products which are sold perfectly properly through that system.

Lord Burns: Maybe at this point it would be sensible to ask whether or not David Roe has anything to say on this issue and the general question we heard earlier that maybe there should be more in terms of the principles, not only about how it should operate with respect to the industry but how it should operate also with respect to consumers. What has come out of this discussion is that the sentences in the Bill are, if anything, rather terse and rather short and they have led to a certain amount of ambiguity. Is there a case for spelling out a little bit more some of these principles; about different kinds of consumers and what are some of the responsibilities are towards consumers and what responsibilities the consumers have themselves?

Lord Haskel

187. Can I just add to that, we have had this discussion about consumers and nobody has mentioned the Consumer Panel. There is to be a statutory Consumer Panel, I wonder if Mr Roe could give us some idea as to whether the Consumer Panel could play some role in this? What we may be doing is saying we will leave a lot of these decisions to the Consumer Panel.

(Mr Roe) I think one thing I would say is that there is a general matter of judgment about how much detail one wants to put in legislation of this nature. The Government has been very keen to take a framework approach and set out very clearly what it is expected that the FSA will achieve and leave the task of actually writing the rules and codifying the behaviour to the regulator. I did want to say something about clause 5 generally before answering the specific question, Chairman. What clause 5 effectively does is to say that the protection of the consumers objective is about securing an appropriate degree of protection. In the second sub-clause it sets out three separate considerations which have to be taken into account in determining what that appropriate degree of protection is. The first one talks about different degrees of risk involved in different kinds of investments and other transactions. The second one talks about different degrees of experience and expertise which different consumers may have in relation to different kinds of regulated activity. I think there is an awful lot in the idea of different experience and expertise, some of which we have touched on, either talking about wholesale/retail or talking about vulnerable or less vulnerable consumers. The ideas are all consistent with subsection 5(2)b. The third of the general things that needs to be taken into account is the general principle that consumers should take responsibility for their decisions, on which we have had some interesting discussion. My point, I think, is that in looking at this we need to look at the clause as a whole. It is very important to talk about particular elements of it but it does help and it will help the Committee if you look at these as three considerations which in some ways are complementary. On the point about whether there should be more in the Bill which sets out the responsibilities of the industry, clearly in the current regulatory regime there is a large amount of material which does set out the responsibilities of the industry

[Lord Haskel *Cont*]

both in terms of broad principles and specific obligations. A lot of that effectively codifies some of the general propositions about agency law and so on. That is broadly the approach that we have been taking forward. Clearly there is an argument for bringing into the Bill some of these ideas about what the particular responsibilities of firms ought to be and I am sure this is something that Ministers would be quite happy to reflect on if the Committee comes to the view that they should. The other question that I was asked to talk about was the role of the Consumer Panel which, as has quite rightly been said, will be a requirement in the Bill, one of the changes that Ministers announced a month or two ago. We do think that the Consumer Panel could have an important role to play in helping to inform the kinds of decisions which the FSA are making about how best to give effect to these objectives.

Viscount Trenchard

188. Yes, Mr Roe, can I just ask you about this protection of consumers objective again? I think you explained that we should look at the clause as a whole and that the FSA would clearly have to write those rules specifically in the interests of the consumers. I assume that those rules will not be available in draft before the Bill is introduced to Parliament? I would also like to ask whether the FSA will be obliged to consult with the practitioner bodies on the appropriateness of the proposed rules before they are introduced as secondary legislation?

(Mr Roe) Yes, the Bill does require quite extensive consultation with the industry and other interested parties on the rules. If I may perhaps refer the question about precisely what the FSA is doing in terms of developing its rules back to my FSA colleague.

(Mr Whittaker) We have a detailed programme that we have published and can make available to the Committee if it is not already available—I thought we had attached it with our submission to the Committee—setting out the way in which we intend to consult on the proposed rule book over the coming year or so. It is the case that because of the process of consultation that we are going through we will not have final rules, or indeed even draft rules, at the time that the Bill is introduced to Parliament. We are doing a very extensive consultation process to ensure that people's views are taken into account.

Lord Taverne

189. I want to put a very general question. We have been running around this subject of how we can define consumer protection more effectively and we have identified a lot of problems but we have not identified any solutions. I hope that perhaps in some way the Civil Service will be able to draft something which is a little more specific but I am not sure if they can. I wonder whether in the end, and this is what I would like to ask you about, is not the most effective guarantee the closest possible consultation at every stage with the Consumer Panel and indeed the practitioners?

(Mr Boléat) Yes, but not just the Panels. I think we would like to see widespread consultation, anybody who has got a view should be able to comment. Recently the Government has been trying to produce a more effective method of consultation with the Cabinet Office having published some guidance which almost every department ignores, except the Treasury, which is quite disturbing. There are many industry bodies— you are going to see some of them—and I think it is important that those looking at the responses are able to weight them according to who they represent. The Panels have a major role but consultation needs to go wider. We hope that the FSA will publish the results of the consultation exercises and where there is a strong view against what the FSA proposes we hope that the FSA, if it decides to do something there is a view against, will justify that to the market.

Chairman: Maybe we can move on to the other issues and wrap up the questions on market confidence, competitiveness, competition and the regulatory burden.

Mr Heathcoat-Amory

190. On the question of international competitiveness, speaking to some City firms one would suppose that the moment this Bill receives Royal Assent the City is going to empty and they are all going to leave and set up in Zurich or New York. Is this a realistic threat? What I want here is some assessment of the sensitivity of location to the regulatory environments and in particular the regulatory costs. On the face of it, even if one grosses up the FSA fees quite considerably, that is really not going to be a tremendously significant item for the larger firms. Possibly the compliance costs are rather larger. Some say that with the narrow margins in international business this is a very real factor and because the City of London is fighting a pitiless struggle for international competitiveness we really have got a duty in this Committee and in this Bill not to disadvantage a colossally important British industry. I would be very interested if one or two of you could give your assessments of the sensitivity.

(Mr Foster) I think the regulatory cost is obviously an important feature. Clearly we want to see a strong regulatory framework but there is always this balance with the amount that it is going to cost. You can never make it foolproof. The balance needs to be maintained in a sensible way. Equally important, there are a number of other factors which give rise to where businesses wish to locate themselves. A regulatory environment is one of those, it is not the only one but it is quite an important one. I think that flows through from the fact that depending what is in the legislation and how that legislation is enacted, particularly in relation to capital as well and the amount of capital requirements that are needed in a regulatory environment, that is at least as important an aspect.

(Mr Ross Goobey) Direct costs in our own organisation—I looked it up before I came here—of compliance and internal audit, which is very closely associated, are six per cent of our net operating costs. That does not include the cost of the time that the other people in the organisation spend meeting the needs of

[Mr Heathcoat-Amory *Cont*]

our compliance and internal audit, so you can possibly double that. That is a huge cost. Perhaps we are just inefficient. Coming from a relatively low start before the imposition of the OPS regime in 1993, I think it is not that they are going to go off to Zurich but some elements of the financial services have already gone to Dublin. Dublin has a regime which is fiscally very attractive, where the language is the same—give or take—and the basic law is much the same as ours and the probity of the regime is thought to be similar. I think the cost base over there is probably lower. I have no direct experience, I just observe that a lot of things like the open end investment companies have almost all gone to Dublin and that is a potential danger.

Chairman

191.   How much is regulation and how much is other factors?

(*Mr Ross Goobey*)   It is impossible to distinguish. I just observe that quite a lot of this sort of thing has gone to Dublin. I can give you an example of where one of the big Italian banks has set up its investment management business in Dublin to service the UK and the rest of Europe rather than in London. Going back to something Mr Heathcoat-Amory was asking, who bears the cost of all this regulation, in our case it is the people we are supposed to be protecting because we are owned by the pension fund that we are managing. That seems rather perverse and that may come back to the point I was making in my opening remarks that we are having to protect them from themselves whereas they are actually protected under the Pensions Act already.

Mr Loughton: Do you think that if it is cheaper to do business in Dublin, and interestingly I think I am right in saying that Ireland is the only place that has higher stamp duty on equity transactions than we do, have you seen any evidence of the cheaper costs being passed on to customers or are they just doing it there because there is far less red tape involved and they can be far more innovative?

Lord Taverne

192.   And less tax.

(*Mr Ross Goobey*)   There are lots of reasons for them being there. Part of it is the taxation of the corporates in the international financial centre which is a tax free zone and the very low rate of corporation tax, of course, which is the lowest now in the EU, if they do have to pay tax. They do not have to transact stock transactions in Dublin, they can transact it anywhere they like. That is one of the things—a completely different subject—about what is going to happen with Frankfurt and London, where is the actual transaction going to take place? If we have got half a per cent stamp duty and the Germans have got none we can be pretty sure that they are going to go to Frankfurt to transact their stocks. There are lots of reasons for going to Dublin, some of which are related to compliance costs.

Mr Loughton

193.   As a general point, do you think that an awful lot of what we are discussing in the FSA is actually retrospective because the way financial services are going to be marketed and the way financial products are going to be produced in the future, using the Internet or whatever, is very different from what happens now? In many respects the whole FSA Bill is being tailored to what has already gone and is quickly being surpassed and that is a very good example of what is happening in Frankfurt and in Ireland.

(*Mr Ross Goobey*)   Yes.

Mr Kidney

194.   Is that not why the Bill is terse and speaks in principles and relies on rules that even the FSA themselves could make, that it is not stuck in a particular time zone and it can actually respond to the way the markets develop in the future?

(*Mr Ross Goobey*)   That is obviously very helpful, not too prescriptive. I agree with everything that the Treasury and the FSA think about this, that they do not want it too prescriptive. We can see what level of cost the FSA has by merging all their SROs together and there is not much sign of it being lower.

Chairman

195.   Would you stick to the view that you would like to see a separate competitiveness objective? You do not think it is sufficient that it should be in the principles? You would like there to be something which is rather stronger than that?

(*Mr Foster*)   That is certainly my comment that I made earlier on, there should be something stronger.

Lord Haskel

196.   Do you think that there is a danger instead of firms moving to Frankfurt or to Dublin that regulated firms will deal with other regulated firms outside regulation, that large firms know each other and will do business with each other outside regulation and save the regulation costs?

(*Mr Goobey*)   Some of the most extensive transactions are not regulated anyway. I think it is going to be much more a matter of cherry picking about where you do bits of business and you will go to the regime that is most suitable for the transaction you want to do and the cheapest and most effective. The base of where you are is not going to determine where the actual business takes place.

Lord Poole

197.   You have said that cost is a factor. Do you think that another factor may be the actual quality of the individuals concerned who engage in the detailed regulation at the interface, the people who come out of the central regulator and come and inspect your business? If they do not really understand your business it is frightfully difficult to get them to work with you. That may be a very important factor and one

MINUTES OF EVIDENCE TAKEN BEFORE
THE JOINT COMMITTEE ON FINANCIAL SERVICES AND MARKETS

56

23 March 1999]   Mr Peter Foster, Mr Mark Boléat, Mr Alastair Ross Goobey, Mr James Stretton and Mr Jonathan Agnew   *[Continued*

[Lord Poole *Cont]*

that certainly the FSA, if not the face of the Bill, needs to concentrate on.

(Mr Ross Goobey) We find that we have a perfectly relaxed relationship with our regulator and IMRO is not notorious for being very soft on these things. Obviously they are not up to date practitioners in many of the areas that they are regulating and that is inevitably true. I do not think that is the real problem, I think it is the tasks that they are set by legislation or by the FSA, they have to go through the process of doing it. Again, like Lord Eatwell, I have forgotten which panel it was but I think it was the previous panel where somebody was saying he only had ten per cent of working days when he did not have one of the regulators in his operation. That is quite a burden on resources.

Chairman

198. Before we close, and I think we should close now, can I ask David Roe and Andrew Whittaker whether there is anything you want to say in response to the issues raised about Lloyd's earlier? Or whether you would rather reflect on them and come back to us at a later stage?

(Mr Whittaker) Perhaps I could try to deal with the issue that has been raised about the way in which regulation of individuals might impact on non-executive directors. The Bill does provide powers to enable the FSA to operate a system for regulation of individuals within an authorised firm. We plan to issue a consultative paper in June setting out how we

expect to exercise those powers. I do not want to do too much by way of anticipating that consultative paper. We do expect that it will treat non-executive directors at Lloyd's no differently from non-executive directors at any other institution that we regulate. So I think that to the extent that there was a suggestion that we might view Lloyd's differently from an insurance company, I do not think that is currently what is planned. We recognise that non-executive directors have a different role from executive directors. The objective of what we are doing will be to try to ensure that responsibility under that regime reflects the role of the people concerned. We are not offering that non-executive directors will be entirely outside the new regulation but the way in which it will apply to them will be commensurate with their responsibilities as non-executive directors and no greater.

Lord Poole

199. And Jonathan's point?

(Mr Roe) I think Mr Agnew gave me a bit of a let off by saying that he did not really want to have a debate about the issue today. We are certainly aware of the point that has been made and are giving it careful consideration.

Chairman: Thank you very much for coming this afternoon. This has been very helpful. As I said to the other group, we are up against sharp time constraints and we want to get as much evidence as possible. We want to get people's reactions to what they see as the outstanding issues that are left and in that context this has been extremely useful. Thank you very much.

Printed in the UK by The Stationery Office Limited
4/99   421287   78344

ISBN 0-10-432899-1

9 780104 328996

HOUSE OF LORDS
HOUSE OF COMMONS

SESSION 1998–99

JOINT COMMITTEE ON FINANCIAL SERVICES AND MARKETS

MINUTES OF EVIDENCE

Thursday 25 March 1999

Mr Kit Farrow, Mr David Mayhew, Mr Chris Bates, Mr Philip Telford, Mr Alan Whiting

and Mr Guy Morton

Mr David Roe and Mr Andrew Whittaker in attendance

Printed pursuant to the Order of the House of Lords of 2 March 1999
Ordered by The House of Commons *to be printed*
25 March 1999

LONDON: THE STATIONERY OFFICE
£4.65

HL Paper 50-iv
HC 328-iv

THURSDAY 25 MARCH 1999

Present:

Lord Burns (in the Chair)

Lord Haskel	Mr Nigel Beard
Lord Poole	Mr David Heathcoat-Amory
Lord Taverne	Mr David Kidney
Viscount Trenchard	Mr Tim Loughton

Examination of Witnesses

MR KIT FARROW, Director General, London Investment Banking Association, MR DAVID MAYHEW, MR CHRIS BATES, Partners, Clifford Chance, MR PHILIP TELFORD, Senior Policy Researcher, Consumers' Association, MR ALAN WHITING, Executive Director: Regulation & Compliance, London Metal Exchange, and MR GUY MORTON, Partner, Freshfields, a member of the City of London Law Society, called in and examined.

MR DAVID ROE, Head of Financial Services and Markets Bill Team, HM Treasury, and MR ANDREW WHITTAKER, Deputy General Counsel, Financial Services Authority, in attendance.

Chairman

200. Good afternoon and welcome to this session of the Joint Committee. As you will know, we are now in the process of trying to major on some particular topics and having along groups of witnesses who will help us to do that. Today the main themes are the question of discipline, enforcement and the tribunal, but we are happy to have additional comments that may be particularly on your mind as this is the opportunity you have to make them. We have a little bit of flexibility, but we would like to concentrate on the subject that we have indicated as far as possible. I think the best way to begin is if you could introduce yourselves and make short introductory remarks about what you think are the main issues and the main things that concern you. Very much in our mind is the fact that we have had the draft Bill. We have had the consultation period and we have had lots of information from that. We have now had the Treasury's Progress Report and I think the Committee is particularly interested to know to what extent you believe that the proposals that were in the Progress Report take us forward and how much is left outstanding to take forward to the next stage. We do not want to go over the ground where the Treasury have responded. What we want to do is to move on to the areas where you feel that we are still facing a shortfall in terms of what you would like. Mr Morton, would you like to start?

(Mr Morton) Thank you, my Lord Chairman. I am Guy Morton. I am a Partner in Freshfields and Chairman of the City of London Law Society's Regulatory Working Party which has the task of commenting on this Bill and matters connected with it. I think I would like to focus on three points by way of introduction. First, on enforcement and the Enforcement Committee structure. I think that there is a fairly general consensus among City lawyers that although very much welcome progress has been made, some further movement is needed to strengthen the independence of the enforcement mechanism within

the FSA. Exactly how that works I think is probably a lesser issue. Whether you have a fully fledged tribunal of first instance within the FSA or leave it to the Enforcement Committee to take the first decision as an FSA decision with appeal to the Appeals Tribunal is a lesser issue. The crucial point, I would submit, is that people who are the subject of enforcement should have access to an independent body and have the opportunity to put their case and, if necessary, to negotiate a settlement having seen the case against them and the evidence on which it is based. I think that costs are always an important issue. As you will know, of course, there have been widespread concerns under the current structure that people have been effectively deterred from pursuing defences because they simply felt they could not afford it and ran the risk of being bankrupted if they tried to do so. That is an issue and it is an issue under the European Convention of Human Rights as well. If I can move on then to market abuse. I think the main point about market abuse is the need for greater certainty in the definition, which does seem to us not to give an adequately clear impression of what behaviour is regarded as objectionable. The second issue I would highlight about market abuse is the fact that the current structure does involve a novel delegation of rule making, law making power, if you will, to a non-public body because it seems to us that although the code is in label only evidential, its practical effect is to make rules and that is particularly so because of the uncertainties in the definition of market abuse. Finally, if I could just mention the European Convention on Human Rights. As the Committee knows, there has been a lot of debate about the categorisation of both the market abuse and the disciplinary regimes. I think we would feel that they ought to be categorised as criminal for the purposes of the Convention, which has some consequences, particularly on the admissibility of evidence obtained compulsorily. The Government up to now has taken the view that they are to be categorised as civil, which would have a different

[Chairman *Cont*]

effect, of course. There are also issues about whether the FSA principles and the market abuse definition meet the test of legal certainty required under Article 7 of the Convention. The point I would like to make there is that whoever is right on these perhaps arcane matters it is essential, I would submit, that the position be clarified before the Bill is passed, because nothing could be more damaging than to proceed and to find that there remained uncertainty or, even worse, that the first time the powers were used they were struck down on Convention grounds.

201. Thank you very much. Mr Farrow?

(Mr Farrow) I am Kit Farrow. I am the Director General of the London Investment Banking Association. I am, as it happens, also the Vice Chairman of the London Metal Exchange, but I am not speaking for them this afternoon. The London Investment Banking Association (LIBA) is the principal trade association for the investment banking industry in London. Its particular concern is the impact of the Bill on the competitiveness of London as an international financial centre. My remarks this afternoon will be directed to inter-professional business and business with experienced investors including high net worth individuals. I will not be addressing my remarks to retail business customers. LIBA shares and supports the principles for the enforcement regime that were set out in the FSA's Consultation Paper 17. They were: the maintenance of an open and co-operative relationship between firms and regulators; transparent, proportionate and consistent exercise of power; and fair treatment for those in the enforcement process, but we are concerned that a number of the specific provisions in the draft Bill and CP17 are contrary to those principles working out in practice. We welcome a number of the changes that have been announced by the Government in recent weeks which have met some of our concerns, but we believe that the proposals still need substantial further change. Maintenance of an open and co-operative relationship is an essential element in the UK's approach to supervision. We believe that the FSA should take as the primary objective of formal disciplinary action the stopping of malpractice and the provision of appropriate remedies to clients who have suffered disadvantage. It should reserve deterrent sentences and retribution for cases of fraud, gross negligence and other rank abuse. We believe that the right approach is for the regulator to operate a system which encourages, reinforces and rewards good compliance within firms. This will not be achieved securely if retribution and deterrents are the primary objectives of the enforcement regime. Good internal control by firms is far more effective in practice than external inspection can ever be; and it should be encouraged and reinforced by the approaches to cases where firms have themselves identified regulatory breaches in their own firm. Where firms have detected a failure, and have promptly set about rectification and redress and have promptly notified their regulator, the only purpose of a fine or public censure will be retribution and deterrence. We think the imposition of a penalty is generally inappropriate in such a case and will prejudice an open and co-operative relationship.

We are concerned that CP17 says, "it is equitable that those who breach regulatory obligations should generally pay a penalty", which seems to be slanted towards an inevitability of imposing penalties every time you find something wrong, i.e. in the way that a parking meter attendant does. The second objective is the transparent, proportionate and consistent exercise of powers. We think it is necessary to make clear any rules which can give rise to disciplinary proceedings. High level principles interpreted with hindsight do not seem to us to be a basis for enforcement and we believe that the FSA should recognise that it should not take disciplinary action for breaches of principles alone. This point is particularly important for investment banks because of the need to avoid over-prescriptive rule books which will deter innovation. The market abuse offence and its evidential code—which will apply to everybody, not merely to authorised persons—are also both vague and subjective. The overlap and the conflict between the criminal law, the market abuse code, the principles, regulatory rules and exchange rules means that we are very far at the moment from the admirable objective of making the rules more user-friendly with which the Bill was launched. We think that the FSA should follow the Better Regulation Guide which was circulated to all Government Departments last year— with a foreword by the Prime Minister—and we think that it should be obliged to act in conformity with the Code for Crown Prosecutors. Specifically, it should be required to take into account the extent to which a firm has sought to compensate persons that have been harmed by its actions. Lastly, the commitment to provide fair treatment. We think that it should meet the standards of the European Convention. We believe on the basis of advice from Leading Counsel that the ECHR does apply and we have provided that opinion to the Committee. However, we think that the Government should be keen to apply the standards of the ECHR because it wants Britain to have a fair and just system, not simply because it has been obliged to apply the principles by international law. While some of the changes already announced by the Government will bring the enforcement regime closer to the standards required, important discrepancies remain in respect of fair process and clarity of rules. In this introduction I have touched on only a few points in which we feel that the substance does not match the broad principles. I would be happy to send the Committee a list of very specific points to substantiate what I have said.

202. Thank you very much. I think that would be helpful because this Committee has to concentrate on what has to be done with the Bill in order to make it as sensible as possible. So we are interested in specifics as well as general information. Mr Mayhew?

(Mr Mayhew) My Partner, Chris Bates, and I are here on behalf of Clifford Chance. As you know, my Lord Chairman, the firm has provided a response to the Bill and to CP17. Chris takes the role of advising clients as to how their businesses can comply with regulation and so he sees the varied ways in which business is conducted both here and abroad because of the international client base. I tend to be on the

25 *March 1999]*   Mr Kit Farrow, Mr David Mayhew, Mr Chris Bates,   *[Continued*
                 Mr Philip Telford, Mr Alan Whiting and Mr Guy Morton

[Chairman *Cont]*

litigation side and see the problems when compliance has not happened or when they have ignored Chris's advice. So we come at it from different angles, but together we have spent the last number of years looking at the system and working with the system, as it were, on the ground under the 1986 Act. We are not here as an academic exercise as lawyers, but more as practitioners who have talked to our clients about the way in which this Bill might impact on their business. Can I just draw back and say that we are talking here—and I hesitate to teach the Committee anything of this nature—about administrative power of a significant amount being handed to a private law body albeit with statutory objectives. It is well-established amongst English law that administrative power is only tolerable if the safeguards of procedural fairness and in the context of the legal regime which is criminal in nature of legal certainty apply and this is why Guy Morton and Kit Farrow have referred to Article 6 and Article 7 of the European Convention on Human Rights, but you do not even need to refer to the Convention because it is part of English law already as it is part of the administrative law that has been built up over a number of years by the Divisional Court in the judicial review proceedings which governments have had to contend with over the years, so it is a matter of our own law anyway. The framework currently envisaged by the Bill does not measure up, in our submission, because we consider that the courts should take the view that the regime is criminal in nature. Even though it is called civil, it is, in fact, substantively criminal and the reasons for that have been worked out in Lord Lester's opinion, which you have seen and to which Kit Farrow has referred, and that has had a consequence, we say, on the Bill as currently drawn. For example, the decision-making powers of the tribunal and, we would hope, also the FSA need to be subject to compliance with the right of a fair trial. It is clear that the tribunal as currently proposed does comply with the provisions of Article 6 of the Convention except in relation to the concept of equality of arms which is one of the concepts underpinning Article 6, i.e. if it applies in a criminal regime. We say to make the system work, to avoid people having to get to the tribunal stage, the FSA's internal adjudication powers should also be subject to an overriding principle of fairness because people will not buy into the results unless they feel they have been fairly arrived at. That involves concepts such as the separation of the investigation and prosecution functions on the one hand and the adjudication function on the other. It involves making sure that decisions are reached with proper consideration of the views of the people affected by them and with no appearance of bias. If that is achieved then the result will be more acceptable and, indeed, better quality. You have kindly circulated the models which we have drawn up to help illustrate the points we are making. I will not take you to them now, but if at an appropriate moment you would like me to explain that, I would be quite happy to do so. There is an element of confusion which has come in because since the Bill was published and since the consultation paper was published we have had pronouncements both from the

Treasury and more recently from the Economic Secretary to this Committee itself which tends to suggest that thinking is moving in a different direction from what is currently in the Bill and I am happy to illustrate that to you to show you where you would want to see that the change coming through the next draft of the Bill. Guy Morton has already touched on the issue of self-incrimination and the admissibility of statements. Essentially what that is saying is that the compulsorily obtained statements, which the FSA will have powers to obtain under threat of imprisonment, should not be used in enforcement proceedings, i.e. they should not be placed before the tribunal. The fruits of those interviews, of course, can be used. If someone under interview gives disclosure of information which can then build the case for the prosecution, that is fine, not a problem. It is actually the self-incriminating statement that cannot be used, that is all and that accords with the principles of both criminal law and the Convention. The third area is the question of certainty and the problem of vagueness of the market abuse provisions which I will not go over again. The key point there, of course, is that you can cure that through the evidential code provided that it is sufficiently descriptive of the conduct you are trying to prohibit, but the corollary of that is that if something is not described in the code you are back into the area of uncertainty and we say that the FSA is wrong to consider that it can take enforcement action against people who have done something which is not covered by the code at all because then you are simply saying to people, "If we do not like it we can effectively take proceedings against you". As Guy said, the code is actually revealed as being in effect a form of legislation and we are troubled by that in terms of the scope, i.e. its regulating conduct of anyone anywhere in the world whose behaviour may indirectly affect the UK markets and this is something Chris can explain in much better detail than I. He has this nice example of the Singapore trader in oil who happens to trade Brent oil. That will affect the Brent oil contract which is traded on the IPE in London. Something that is happening across the other side of the world can have an effect on the market here and would currently be caught by the proposals. It also engages in the FSA having unfettered power to introduce a number of wholly new concepts into UK law in which we believe the case for doing so has not been made out. I think our approach is that traditionally an incremental increase of law is the preferred approach rather than introducing some grand design. We do not believe a case has been made out for not extending the scope of the criminal law if you believe that there is conduct which should be criminalised. Similarly we could have a parallel administrative fine system sitting alongside the criminal law system. What we find difficult is the idea of introducing a new layer of proscribed conduct which introduces uncertainties about what conduct is and is not permissible depending on the description and how certain it is. In any event, and this should be something of particular concern to this Committee, we believe these effectively rule-making powers should be subject at least to Parliamentary scrutiny. Finally, can I just touch on one topic which again has concerned

[Chairman *Cont]*

us and I know it has concerned the Committee and that is the question of intent and the market abuse system. We do not believe that strict liability is an appropriate mechanism in this case. When you have broadly defined concepts you do need to have a mental element, otherwise you have conduct being described which is not culpable and you need to have a mental element to make it sufficiently certain and fair and there the mental element may vary depending on the specificity of the conduct, so broadly speaking a knowledge of consequences of actions or recklessness is sufficient for these purposes. It is very important to us in this respect that we are not seen as being anti the Bill or, indeed, anti the FSA. That is not our remit. We do believe in a strong system of enforcement being good for London. What we do want to avoid is uncertainty and problems that will entail following a system which is not adequately thought out and designed.

(Mr Bates) I think David has taken my points and I would be happy to deal with questions.

(Mr Whiting) My Lord Chairman, I am Alan Whiting, Executive Director: Regulation and Compliance at the London Metal Exchange. I will confine my opening remarks to those aspects of the draft Bill which impinge particularly on the operation and regulatory functions of the LME and the other recognised investment exchanges and clearing houses, namely the recognition regime for investment exchanges and clearing houses, statutory immunity and the market abuse regime. The LME welcomes the retention in the Bill of the special recognition regime for investment exchanges and clearing houses which currently operates under the Financial Services Act 1986. The LME endorses the Government's view that this part of the current regulatory regime has worked well and that where exchanges can demonstrate that they can meet the required standards, "the regulatory system should allow them a wide degree of freedom to set and police their own market rules". We believe it is appropriate for the Financial Services Authority to have a power of direction over the exchanges if they are failing to meet the broadly defined recognition criteria. We are not even calling for this power of direction to be subject to appeal—we are very reasonable people at the exchanges—as long as it is clear that the power relates explicitly to principles in the recognition criterion rather than the detailed means by which they are satisfied. In particular, it should not be a function of the FSA to oversee the commercial direction and decisions of exchanges. In view of the FSA's new power of direction this should be made explicit, rather than implicit, in the legislation. One of the most important of the recognition criteria requires exchanges to run proper markets and to deter market abuse and financial crime. The LME takes its regulatory responsibilities, which it carries out under statute, extremely seriously. It is the exchanges, not the FSA, who are the front-line regulators and who deter and detect abuse on their markets. The exchanges have pressed over the years for statutory immunity from civil suit for their regulatory functions. The draft Bill restricts immunity to actions taken by members of the exchange. This is unsatisfactory for all the reasons we have set out in the detailed submission which we

have given to the Joint Committee as it will impede the effectiveness of regulation of the exchanges and the deterrence of market abuse. The exchanges believe that the balance of public interest versus private rights points firmly to the granting of statutory immunity for the regulatory actions, taken in good faith, of the exchanges and clearing houses. In its Progress Report on the Bill, Her Majesty's Treasury, when rejecting a proposal to remove or reduce statutory immunity for the FSA commented: "The Government considers that if this were done the regulated staff would be unable to go about their business without being unduly hampered by concerns about legal action". We entirely agree and would point out that this applies equally to the regulatory functions of the exchanges and clearing houses. The LME welcomes the extension of the market abuse regime to cover both non-authorised persons and off-exchange activity which has a manipulative effect on official exchange markets. One has only to refer to the Sumitomo affair to appreciate the need for these two extensions. Sumitomo was not a member of the LME or an authorised person, and nearly all of its business was not transacted on exchange but was transacted in a manner which manipulated the exchange's market. The scope of the market abuse regime does, however, need one clarification. While it is right to include behaviour off market which influences the official market and from which the perpetrator will benefit, it cannot be right to include the actions of warehouses, mining companies and metal fabricators, etcetera, who do not participate in investments, whether qualifying or not, even though their actions may influence the official markets. If we were to do that you would be requiring people who have never even heard of the LME to have tremendous knowledge not only of the LME but of the market abuse regime and the law. This cannot be sensible. There is confusion at the moment about whether this class of person is caught within the scope and we need clarification that they are not. Finally, the market abuse regime must provide greater clarity on what will constitute market abuse. It is essential that the code of market conduct is sufficiently well defined to avoid market members and users unwittingly contravening the new regime. That would not only be unjustifiably damaging for the firms concerned and for financial services business in the UK, but it would also bring the market abuse regime itself into disrepute. It is particularly important that it is made explicit, at least in the code, that any conduct which conforms to the rules and guidance of the exchange will not constitute abuse under the code and the legislation. For anyone who is concerned that this may be giving the Exchanges too much power I would point out that this is one of the recognition criteria and we cannot have rules and regulations in relation to investment business which are not approved by the Financial Services Authority. I would be pleased to expand on any of these points and any further points. Thank you.

203. Thank you. Mr Telford?

(Mr Telford) My name is Philip Telford and I am a Senior Policy Researcher working on personal finance issues for the Consumers' Association. If I could say a couple of brief points about the Bill generally and

[Chairman *Cont]*

then go on to talk a little bit about enforcement which is today's topic. Generally as an organisation we are certainly enthusiastic about the Bill and we see a variety of advantages in having a single financial services regulator. We are also very conscious, of course, that the Bill is a widely drawn framework document and much will depend on the rules formulated by the FSA. We have certainly been very encouraged by the attitudes and actions of the FSA to date in a wide variety of areas. If I can turn to the Bill itself, as you can imagine one of our major concerns is about consumer representation and we did have worries about the lack of a statutory basis for the FSA Consumer Panel. We are pleased that has now been addressed as we have seen from the Progress Report. As you may have heard from other organisations we would certainly prefer the scope of the Bill to be widened to include the sale of mortgages. Again we are conscious there are reserve powers in the Bill to bring that in later if that is seen as appropriate. We certainly welcome the statutory duty on the FSA to promote public understanding. There are a couple of areas in which we will be suggesting amendments to clarify the wide definition of consumers in the Bill and also to qualify the principle of *caveat emptor*. On the subject of enforcement we see it as very important not to lose sight of the purpose of the rules and powers of the FSA. We would see it as vital for the functioning of markets and for consumer confidence that the regulator does have wide-ranging disciplinary and enforcement powers and is not afraid to use them, or hindered in doing so. We certainly hope and expect that the FSA will be proactive in identifying problems in the market before they become widespread and that they will target their investigations so that the weight of enforcement falls where it is most appropriate. We are also very strong supporters of individual accountability. We think firms that adopt good practices have nothing to fear from this regime. We think it is essential that there are strong and flexible powers for the FSA and we certainly agree that it is time now to sort those powers out and to clarify them rather than leave it as it is for year after year, once the FSA are fully up and running and have their full powers. We will be happy to contribute any way we can to try and sort out this point.

204. Mr Mayhew, how long will it take to explain your diagram?
(Mr Mayhew) I would hope no more than five minutes.

205. I will give you five minutes!
(Mr Mayhew) I want to illustrate how the various enforcement mechanisms work.[1] Taking the current model, the SRO model, the first chart is to illustrate that you have under the SRO model clear separation between adjudication and prosecution so the investigation team investigates the matter and hands it over to the prosecution which acts as a check on the work done so far. It then goes to the enforcement committee made up of practitioners advised by the executive. At that point in time they authorise the issuing of the disciplinary proceeding. If there is no

---

[1] See Evidence, pp. 73–74.

settlement reached the matter refers over to the SFA Tribunal. The important point here is that there is no power in the regulator to impose the result, it has to go to the tribunal for decision.

Mr Kidney

206. Can I ask about model 1. That is only one SRO out of many. The PIA, for example, do they not impose their own fines?
(Mr Mayhew) Again they do have an adjudicate function which involves some impartial decision-making process or at least an appeal to that process. What I am trying to do is look at what the current SROs have been dealing with and IMRO as well and look to see where the Bill is going. If I could take you to model 2——

207. One more question about model 1. In the whole system when there are disputes what is the standard of proof? Is it the criminal standard of beyond a reasonable doubt to solve the dispute or the civil one that one is more likely than the other to be correct?
(Mr Mayhew) The standard of proof adopted is the civil standard of a balance of probability. They talk about a sliding scale. The more serious the charge the more certain the evidence has to be. Certainly the disciplinary panels I advise in the markets work on the principle that if it is tantamount to theft or tantamount to a crime one effectively applies the criminal standard. That is in accordance with English law. I think the standard of proof issue is, by and large, a red herring because ultimately if it is a serious charge the tribunal will apply the more weighty standard.

208. It is not a red herring when people say to us we should now say that for fines and possibly withdrawal of authorisation it should be the criminal standard of proof when for many years we have all tolerated the civil standard for people who can suffer fines and have their authorisation removed.
(Mr Mayhew) In terms of the application of the civil test of the balance of probabilities the tribunals have regularly said that the more important the charge the more weighty the evidence has to be. It has effectively been akin to the criminal standard.
Chairman: I must ask the Committee to look at all the charts and then ask questions.

209. I have stopped now anyway!
(Mr Mayhew) The next model is what we call the proposed model under the Bill and here the important point is that under the Bill the FSA is proposed to be given power to actually impose the decision. You start with the warning notice setting out the proposed action giving reasons and inviting representations, and then move to a decision by the authority actually imposing the result, giving the effective date, reasons and right of appeal. Then of course there is the right of appeal to the tribunal which is independent of the FSA and the power to review the merits and impose its own decision. Under the modifications proposed in the Progress Report you see the FSA has the duty to establish and publish procedures, the right to see the evidence relied on by the FSA, both welcome improvements and, secondly, in relation to the tribunal

[Mr Kidney *Cont*]

the Government has indicated that they are going to drop the name "appeal" and call it a tribunal at first instance. There will be no restriction on evidence going to the tribunal and there will be appeal to the Court of Appeal. If you turn the page we then have the proposed model with some flesh coming through with the consultation paper CP17. Effectively what this describes is how you get from the warning notice to the decision notice and you see the role in particular of the enforcement committee where it is both a quality check on the prosecution at the stage prior to the issuing of the warning notice but also proposing to play a part in the adjudication process of reaching a decision. This has been the area of most concern to practitioners, that you cannot have an enforcement committee exercising an adjudication function if the prosecution has special access to it. It undermines the concept of impartiality. Howard Davies in his recent speech to the Chancery Bar talked about having two panels drawn from the enforcement committee, one which would handle the first part and one to handle the second part, recognising the need for impartiality.

Lord Poole: Can I just butt in and ask why do you need to have impartiality? Surely, the whole point about this system is that it is almost admitted there is something special about financial services and that those who engage in financial services live in a rough and ready world and have to learn to live by it. I am not talking about the delivery of retail product to consumers, I am talking about the investment bank, metal market, whatever it is, where you have extremely highly paid, hugely intelligent people working very hard to make as much money as they possibly can and looking for every conceivable way of doing so within whatever happens to be the acceptable form of behaviour that applies at the time, in a legal sense or otherwise. It does not seem to me that what you are suggesting is necessary at all. Can I ask you to explain that.

Chairman

210. Can I ask you to hold your explanation until you finish the diagram otherwise your five minutes will become a good deal more.

(Mr Mayhew) If we turn the page to the CP17 model enhanced, I will not dwell on this, this reflects the submissions we made to the FSA essentially to try and make sure there was a separation of the prosecution and adjudication function and in particular introducing a number of checks to ensure that the adjudication system was rigorous. If I can then move on to what I call the preferred model.

211. Five is your preferred model?

(Mr Mayhew) Yes for this reason: that it has the beauty of simplicity I think but also I believe it accords with something the Economic Secretary said to the Joint Committee at page 32 of the evidence. What she said was that they were looking to a system whereby if the parties, that is the FSA and the person affected, could not agree a result then the matter would be referred to the tribunal, which is what we consider to be the most appropriate way of dealing with this. It mirrors to some extent the SRO approach we saw at

the beginning with the FSA but the important point here is that the enforcement committee plays a role in the process both in reviewing the staff recommendation and deciding on the notice of intention to act and indeed in any settlement discussions that might take place to try and achieve the result, but if a decision is not agreed it is then referred to the tribunal for determination in accordance with the rules that will be issued in relation to that tribunal. This alternative model does exist already under the 1986 Act. The Financial Services Tribunal, although it does not have a huge jurisdiction, does operate in this manner. Section 59 offences where directors are being threatened with the prospect of not being allowed to be employed in the industry have this model of the then SIB issuing a notice of intention to act and if it was not agreed it would be referred to the tribunal. One point I want to say is I am not clear if this is what Ms Hewitt was actually referring to in her evidence because it certainly seemed to be a shift away from the Bill model and that is something the Committee may have to clarify at some stage to see if this is the model rather than the one currently proposed in the Bill.

212. If I could hold you and your answer to Lord Poole and ask Mr Whittaker, do you recognise these diagrams as being a description of the various stages you have been through? Mr Mayhew meanwhile can think of his answer to Lord Poole's question.

(Mr Whittaker) I think the substance of most of the description given by David is a description I recognise. I have not studied every part of these diagrams as they relate to the legislation and the rule books since like the Committee I have only seen them as we came here today. In particular in relation to the alternative model I am not in a stronger position than the witness (David Mayhew) in offering a view as to whether or not this is what the Economic Secretary had in mind.

213. David Roe?

(Mr Roe) I fear that the witness is reading rather too much into what the Economic Secretary said. Although she is very interested in hearing these kinds of suggestions, I think she was speaking at a rather higher level of generality than these diagrams operate at. I would not draw the conclusion that you have drawn.

214. If you would now answer Lord Poole and then I will come to Mr Beard.

(Mr Mayhew) The implication of the question, my Lord, is that somehow people who work in the City do not need to have a fair process because they make lots of money, the risks are very high but because they are successful there it is. I challenge that as being an inappropriate premise anyway.

215. It worked very well for quite a long time as a matter of fact.

(Mr Mayhew) With respect, no.

216. It is just because you are a lawyer is it not? It would seem to me you are creating an opportunity to——

(Mr Mayhew) With respect, my Lord, no. The SFA, for example, which has one of the busiest

[Chairman Cont]

tribunal systems, has worked very well indeed and a lot of the cases are settled before they get to the tribunal stage but there is a very clear demarcation between adjudication and the prosecution function and the reason why you need that is because people will not feel that they are being fairly treated or the quality of decisions made is right if they do not have a system whereby they are appealing essentially to a decision maker who has an open mind in listening to both sides. It is inevitable when you are in the prosecution team, and I have acted as a prosecutor for exchanges as well, that you take on the prosecution mind set. You are not there in a position to make decisions as well. If you can get an agreed result, all well and good but the point is that unless people feel that they have the ability to appeal to a fair-minded decision-maker then they will not buy into the result. They may be forced into the result, which is one of the criticisms of the current system, that the chips are all on one side of the table, or they will appeal and take the thing to the tribunal and the whole thing will then get bogged down into the tribunal. What we are looking to achieve is a system whereby most cases are dealt with by agreement and even in that process you would want to have a sense that you are not just talking about prosecution.

Mr Beard

217.   But there is a third party at this feast and that is the public in general who need to be satisfied that justice is being done from their point of view, too. I do not see how this sort of plea bargaining hugger-mugger you end up with in this last diagram is going to enhance that process in the least. I can see why it should be recommended by someone representing your own interests in that the upshot of this is likely to be the amelioration of any penalty that is likely to be delivered, but that is really not the object of the exercise. I would also suggest that if this is going to be the case on every occasion that you end up with this bargaining process the whole process will grind to a halt. There will be very little done, very little will come out of it and the amount of work and the amount of man hours tied up in this process will be enormous.

(Mr Mayhew)   If I can respond to that. We are not suggesting a system of plea bargaining which in some way devalues the process of enforcement. What we are suggesting are ways and means whereby both the regulator and the regulated or indeed the unauthorised, because it includes the market abuse system, can achieve a result without going to the full panoply of a tribunal hearing which is very expensive, very time-consuming and very disruptive.

218.   Can justice be seen to be done in that case?

(Mr Mayhew)   That is the current system we have where we have the SROs reaching agreements with their members and imposing results. You get a Board Notice but you do not see anything more than that. If you want justice to be seen to be done you have to go to tribunal whether on the public interest side or in the interests of the people accused of wrongdoing.

219.   On every occasion?

(Mr Mayhew)   If that is what you want to see but that would grind the whole system down. The regulators would be very opposed to that result. They need to have a system that delivers fast and efficient results. What I am saying is that has to be counter-balanced by a system that which enable people to have fairness incorporated into that result.

Viscount Trenchard

220.   I would like to turn to the question of whether there is sufficient certainty in the Bill as to what constitutes breach of rules and market abuse and whether we should not consider trying to put more into the Bill in this regard. Mr Morton and others have talked about the need for greater certainty and Mr Farrow referred to the paramount importance of maintaining the competitiveness of the City of London and expressed a worry that a lack of certainty might detract from that. In looking at the question of certainty and defining rules and market abuse, to the extent that the ECHR rules apply, the offence of which an individual is accused must be clear. It seems to me looking at the Bill that it could be argued that what we have is a broadly satisfactory balance because clause 56 defines market abuse in broad terms admittedly but the Treasury's Progress Report has explained that its purpose is to set the outer perimeter of abusive behaviour and to make sure that there are no loopholes in coverage. The Economic Secretary explained that there is currently no sanction against abusive but non-criminal acts by non-authorised persons. But clause 56 is of course balanced by clause 57 which requires the Authority to issue a code and the Authority has argued that regulated persons will under this code have more certainty than exists at present. That might also be said to be true if you look at the point that there are nine regulatory regimes and if you are a foreign firm coming into London you have to cope with nine different regimes and it is very complicated and very unclear. I would like a little bit more on why you think there is not enough certainty. In addition, the FSA has set up a Practitioner Group to revise the draft code which means practitioners have the opportunity to be involved in this. Are you satisfied with this framework? If not, what extra do you think should be done?

(Mr Farrow)   Could I take two specific examples where we think it is lacking in clarity. If I start with the FSA principles, one of the points I made in my initial remarks was that the FSA have made very clear that they wish to be able to take disciplinary action for breaches of principle regardless of anything else. I read principle 5: "A firm must observe proper standards of market conduct." Does that tell you, my Lord, as a practising investment banker what you may and what you may not do? I am looking at the consultation paper and the FSA principles for business. Can I just repeat the principle because it is very short: "A firm must observe proper standards of market conduct." I would submit that that does not give you in your work in the financial market great clarity about what is the boundary between what is and what is not proper.

221.   No, so I would expect the Practitioner Group to seek clarification on that.

[Viscount Trenchard *Cont*]

(*Mr Farrow*) It may be that a changed set of documents will achieve the clarity we want. That is exactly what my objective is. All I can say is that the text we have been given to look at so far is not one that achieves the clarity which we need. If I could turn to a second example. If you look at the definition in CP10 of abusive squeezes, and I am not going to read this out because it is rather lengthy, if you go through paragraphs 4.3, 4.4 and 4.5 if you feel that leaves you with knowledge of what transactions you can carry out in the forward market and what you cannot——I have spent ten years looking at that subject from the London Metal Exchange boardroom and I do not find clarity in it on the basis I would be comfortable to tell anybody they had breached a clear provision of law.

Lord Poole

222. How then would you answer those who would say that in a fast-moving market-place to be very specific is extremely difficult and from a regulator's point of view counter-productive? As a matter of fact you will recall, because you have been around for as long as me if not longer, the old rule that says people know where the white line on the road is and if you step to one side or the other you certainly know. The more specific you become the more like America we will become with people merely seeking loopholes because that is how the system particularly in the States works. It would seem to me that it may be to your advantage for the rules to be more specific but it is more to the advantage of the national well-being that it should be about principle, which may become defined over time. I know what proper behaviour is and so do you as a matter of fact. You look doubtful: I find that more worrying than your answer! I would like to ask Andrew Whittaker in due course.

(*Mr Farrow*) I have no wish to force an ever increasing elaboration of rule books, but I think if you are going to exercise the power of prohibiting somebody from earning his living in the City for the rest of his life you need to do so against a clearer standard. It is not what the market thinks is proper behaviour. It was whatever was in the mind of the draftsman or the FSA's enforcement division when they wrote the words "proper behaviour". It is because the sanctions are so potentially severe that such a vague definition is really very problematic.

223. Mr Morton, do you want to comment on this?

(*Mr Morton*) Yes and I would like to come back to the other point Lord Trenchard made in terms of market abuse. He referred to the FSA Practitioner Panel which is a very welcome body, of which I am a member, and that is engaged in examining and trying to improve the code of conduct, the market code, which is very welcome. However, that is only part of the story because the market code obviously only covers the areas which it covers and the Government is making it quite clear that it wishes the possibility to be open to sanction people purely for breaching the definition of market abuse. If you look at the definition of market abuse, clause 56.1(c) in particular, that is not, I submit, a prime example of something that gives

people a very clear indication of what conduct is permissible. I will read it out: "Behaviour which is likely (or if the circumstances were publicly known, or the behaviour became commonplace, or both) would be likely, to damage the confidence of informed participants that the market, so far as it relates to investments of that kind, is a true and fair market". It is asking you to make a hypothetical judgement about the attitude of some other described group of people to a set of behaviour. I do not think that that would give the great majority of people any clear idea what they can and cannot do.

(*Mr Farrow*) Could I make one supplementary comment to Lord Poole. The London Metal Exchange has a very considerable body of rules about what is acceptable behaviour on the market which achieves as much clarity as we have been able to achieve. At the moment the way the Bill is constructed we are faced with the possibility that you might conduct a transaction on the LME in complete conformity with the detailed rules but you would nevertheless be at hazard to somebody saying, "I don't think that is proper." One of the clarifications to avoid these layers of general rules, precise rules and so on, is a specific provision that if you have done it in conformity with all the detailed rules that is a safe harbour guarantee against being accused of having breached a very general statement.

(*Mr Whiting*) Can I give the Committee a practical example which I think might be helpful to Lord Poole who said that surely you know you are abusing the market and that this must be absolutely clear. The normal definition of "market squeezes" which is used the world over, a wonderful definition, is that you cannot use a dominant position to extract a higher price from the market than you would have been able to extract if you did not have that dominant position, ie, you cannot use a dominant position to move the market. It is a beautiful definition but in practice it is not particularly helpful because in my position as the regulator that leaves me with the task of saying what is this price? It leaves the participants, who quite often have dominant positions for perfectly good reasons, saying how much can they charge, although the regulator might come along and take a different view from them; and the first they would know about it was when they were charged with market manipulation which is a very serious charge. What the LME has done is to lay down detailed rules about what we think is acceptable behaviour and what is not. The answer to all this uncertainty in the Bill is not to try to have a more specific definition in the Bill. That is a hopeless task. You cannot define these things in legislation and the definition in the current Bill is more helpful than the definition in the Financial Services Act 1986. My own view is it is not particularly helpful to try and define these things in much greater detail. You have got to get whatever detail you use correct in the code of market abuse. I agree with Kit the way to do this (and the exchanges have done this in terms of the markets) is if the FSA has disputes about what we have done, which they do not because they have signed them off, then they should tell us. If they do not have a dispute there should be an explicit provision that if people act in accordance with the rules and regulations

[**Lord Poole** *Cont*]

of the exchanges then it is deemed to be in accordance with the regulations and code of conduct. I think that would be very helpful for all participants because it would ensure investor protection and would keep down the body of rules enormously.

(*Mr Bates*) I would like to comment on one point in relation to this which is that it has to be remembered that this provision, clause 56, is primarily aimed against the unauthorised person, primarily aimed against people not working in the City and indeed it is, so it seems, primarily aimed against people who are not even operating in the United Kingdom. We are in a situation where we are being asked and Parliament is being asked to prescribe a standard which is a very, very broad generality which applies to anyone anywhere in the world and on which anyone anywhere in the world can be called upon at a later stage and told "sorry, your conduct was unacceptable by British standards". I think there is a suggestion by some people that this only applies to people who have taken advantage of UK markets but in fact it does not matter whether they took advantage of UK markets or not, that is what the Bill says. This is a very, very broad provision aimed at asserting a very universal jurisdiction on the basis of no clear standard at all which I think has raised very serious questions about the proper scope of British legislation. I would suggest that one can focus not only on the effect of this on the authorised community, markets and members of the exchanges but also on the rest of the world and think "is this a standard which we wish as a country to promulgate and impose?"

Chairman

224. I would like to move on to the next issue about pre-clearance, guidance and waiver. Could I ask Mr Whittaker if he would like to wrap up this part of the session in response?

(*Mr Whittaker*) I would like to respond first to Kit Farrow's point and then to Alan Whiting's. Kit expressed concern about one of the proposed principles for businesses that we have issued for consultation on the grounds that it was too short and simple. It is not often that we are criticised for the shortness and simplicity of our requirements. This particular one is based on existing principles that have been in place since the early 1990s. Those principles, which were issued by the SIB, were issued at the request of the industry very largely because of concern on their part that the existing rule books were too long and complicated and made it difficult for people to understand what they had to do and made it difficult to look at the underlying moral content of whether what was being done was right or wrong. The possibility remains available, if desired, for guidance to be given on the application of the principles either on a general basis in published written form or on an ad hoc basis if people want to ring up and find out what the regulators consider the proper interpretation of a principle is. As has been pointed out, we are involving the markets in discussing the way in which we should give guidance on particularly sensitive issues. We have also proposed that there should be a practitioner involved in the Enforcement Committee's

decision on whether to take enforcement action. That will also provide a safeguard against what is described as being arbitrary conduct by the regulator in taking enforcement action. Finally, it is not going to be ultimately what the regulator considers is improper conduct but what the tribunal considers is improper conduct and they are entirely independent from us. That is the way I would respond to Kit's comments. In relation to Alan's proposal that conduct which complies with the rules of an exchange should not be regarded as market abuse, we have some sympathy but also some concerns about this proposal. We think that a Bill provision to this effect would reduce rather than improve certainty. Firstly because market abuse often does not sit neatly within a single exchange and it can involve on and off exchange transactions and it can involve exchange and non-exchange members. If you have more than one exchange's rules applying you will risk the situation where the same transaction is construed differently under the market abuse provisions. You would also want each exchange's rules to be construed in the same way that exchange construed them. So you would have more uncertainty, more different sources of authority and guidance, on what the provisions meant.

Lord Taverene

225. Has this happened? Is this a frequent occurrence?

(*Mr Whittaker*) We do not have market abuse provisions at the moment and certainly conduct that affects more than one exchange is something that happens quite regularly and, indeed, because most of the enforcement mechanisms and investigation mechanisms are within the existing exchanges one particular form of abuse is that you manipulate one market and take the profit on another in the hope that you will avoid detection in that way. Just two more points in relation to Alan's comment, the bits that we regard more sympathetically. We do think that it is desirable that the Code should give weight to the rules of the exchange in the way in which it describes particular abuses. That is the first point. The second is that we have said that where an abuse arises only within a particular exchange we would expect it to be that exchange that would take enforcement action. We ourselves would not get involved.

Chairman

226. Thank you very much. You have thirty seconds to add to the original reply, although you do not have to.

(*Mr Whiting*) Perhaps I can just say one thing. Most of the exchanges are stand alone in the UK, nobody else trades energy apart from the IPE, nobody else trades metals apart from the LME, at least at the moment; who knows where competition is coming from. Market abuse applies to a market. I cannot see anything wrong in having different—I would not call it standards—regimes for different markets. You may want a difference. It may be quite justifiable to have a different regime for a different market. Markets are totally different. The LME is a market which includes

[**Chairman** *Cont*]

delivery; therefore it is a totally different sort of market from a purely financial derivatives market. You therefore have to have different regimes. My concern about putting all of the detail even in a code is that you are going to have a heck of a long code.

(*Mr Farrow*) I would only like to say that the elaboration of the general principles by the SIB was I think a form of guidance and was not expected at the time to be the basis of enforcement action. This is the point I have been trying to make, that while they are excellent principles the very generality of the statements makes them unsuitable as the basis for disciplinary action.

Lord Poole

227. I think that conveniently brings us on to the proposals for guidance to market practitioners. How do you feel about that? Are they adequate and, if not, what else could you do?

(*Mr Bates*) We think the provisions in the Bill on guidance are not adequately framed at the moment. I think one has to distinguish between guidance with respect to the statutory framework and guidance with respect to the FSA's own rules. If we start with the first: if you look at the scope of some of the offences in the Act they are quite broadly defined, the authorisation offence for example, and indeed there is concern about the impact of the new rules on solicitors, whether they will need to be authorised. That is just one of the questions that arises with respect to the scope of the Act. It is suggested in the Treasury's Progress Report, for example, on that point that the role of FSA guidance will be helpful to the market in avoiding the need for unnecessary authorisation but the FSA guidance is given no status in the Act whatsoever on that point. The FSA is not the only prosecutor of the offences, other prosecutors can take action as well. The effect of breaching those requirements is to render contracts unenforceable and to give rise to damages claims against firms. Again, the FSA guidance is given no status with respect to those points. It seems to us right and actually beneficial for the regulator if its guidance were given some interpretative or evidential value. We hear much about evidential value of FSA Codes of Conduct against firms but we hear very little about benefits in favour of firms. Why should the court not be directed to take account of whether somebody has complied with FSA guidance in relation to compliance with the statutory offences and for that to be given some sort of evidential value, for example to show that you have taken reasonable care to avoid the commission of an offence? An example of this in a practical way is in relation to the Internet, a very topical question in relation to the scope of the UK regulatory regime, where the FSA has made some statements about its enforcement policy but it is unable, because it has no powers effectively to interpret the law and there are no powers for the courts to take account of that, to give any real assistance to businesses that are seeking to comply with the law. It may say something but it has no effect and it seems to us that is wrong. We do not need to go so far as to say that what the FSA says binds the court, just that it has some value in the court. That is what we would suggest

in relation to the effect of guidance on the statutory effect of offences. Just very briefly in relation to its own rules, it seems to us right if the FSA has said that certain conduct does not contravene its rules that people can rely on that. That is the position with respect to many of the SROs at the moment in respect of written formal guidance and it seems to us only fair that if the regulator has said: "Here are my rules, this is what you have to do to comply with them" you can rely on that. Again, it might be given some sort of evidential value or whatever: at least it should have some status and you should not be in the position that you can obtain published guidance: it can be standing guidance or whatever: but at any stage the regulator can step back from it and resile from its position. Of course it can change its guidance and develop it in the future but we believe that this will provide an alternative flexible way of developing the regulatory system, both with respect to the FSA's own rules and codes of conduct and with respect to the statutory framework.

Chairman

228. Does anybody else want to comment on this?

(*Mr Morton*) I see it principally as a matter of clarity as to what is the status of guidance. If it is in fact something for which you can be prosecuted then let us be absolutely clear that that is its status. If this is informal friendly advice that you can take or not as you judge in the circumstances, fine, but let us be clear about that. There are places where there are suggestions that doing something which is not actually contrary to the guidance but is getting rather close to being contrary to the guidance might itself cause you trouble. It is necessary to know what you can do and what you cannot.

229. I think it sounds like Mr Whittaker again.

(*Mr Whittaker*) We have no particular problem with the idea that our guidance should be given some special status. We regard it as very much a matter for the Treasury to balance the arguments for and against that from the point of view of the Bill.

230. Mr Roe, at this stage?

(*Mr Roe*) Only really that we did address this particular point in the Progress Report and said in particular that we did not think that giving particular evidential weight to FSA guidance would add very much. I think this is an example of an issue where if the Committee comes up with some new, and I think preferably specific, ideas about precisely what is meant by evidential weight, I am sure that Treasury Ministers will be happy to consider its suggestions. The Treasury is really coming at this I think from the point of view that we are not entirely convinced that anything particular is necessary.

Lord Haskel

231. If the FSA has said something formal, surely a court or a tribunal would take note of what they say irrespective of the status? So I do not quite understand why it is you are so concerned about the status of what the FSA says.

[Lord Haskel *Cont*]

(Mr Bates) The issue is, and there have been some practical examples of this, yes, indeed the courts would look at what the FSA says but because it has no formal status, it is no more of an opinion than my opinion as to what the law is. Therefore the court may say: "Well, obviously we wish to construe the law in a sensible way and we will listen to what the FSA says" but at the end of the day it makes no more difference to the outcome than my opinion or your opinion as to what the law is. Our suggestion is giving it some form of evidential status as to compliance, I might add not so the FSA can purport to extend the law by saying: "Well, we think the law means X" and therefore take the law wider but in the sense of interpreting it to say you are not contravening the law by doing X: the starting point is that compliance with the standard tends to establish that you have complied with the law and then you are starting from a slightly different position with the court. The court is not saying this is not just a matter of their opinion or our opinion, as to which the court can put those on one side and make its own mind up, but it has to effectively look at that and treat it as the starting point from which the court can be moved by rebutting force of argument or evidential evidence as to the conduct.

Lord Taverne

232. Can you give any statutory precedent for that kind of guidance being given special evidential status?

(Mr Bates) The only one which I can think of is in relation to a statutory instrument—others may well be able to think of others—in relation to the money laundering regulations which implement European obligations. Industry guidance is given evidential weight as to whether people have taken the appropriate steps to comply with the identification requirements.

Chairman

233. Could I ask if any of you could respond to Mr Roe's request for some concrete suggestions about how we might deal with this? It is obviously something the Committee would like to look at.

(Mr Bates) We are happy to do so.

Chairman: Can we move on to the next subject.

Mr Heathcoat-Amory

234. I am interested in providing some legal counterweight to what could be excessive administrative powers. It gets me back to this question of statutory immunity. We have heard a call today to extend statutory immunity to exchanges in their regulatory function and I think equality is a powerful point. Am I right that the proposed statutory immunity from the FSA includes reckless or negative behaviour in the course of business? This seems to be excessive if granted to the FSA or to an exchange. As part of that, I do not quite see why in its criminal prosecuting role any body should be given statutory immunity when it is not granted to the police or to the Serious Fraud Office. Am I right about that?

(Mr Whiting) Can I try and answer some of those questions. You are right that the current statutory immunity which is granted to the FSA and other bodies as well, the Bank of England for example has it, does not exempt reckless behaviour. However, it does not apply to action taken in bad faith. It is always open to somebody to go to court to challenge that an issue was taken in bad faith. Where the border line between recklessness and bad faith is drawn I think is very difficult. It would have to be judged on a case by case basis. I am not a lawyer I should say. I am aware that the police and the FSO and even the Director of Public Prosecutions do not have statutory immunity as such. However they do have—my lawyer colleagues will tell me if I am wrong—a body of law which has been built up over the years which amounts to something extremely similar. It is very difficult, if not impossible, to sue the police for operational issues. You have to establish that the police have a duty of care over you and the same with other bodies. It is incredibly difficult to do. One of the problems with financial services is this body of law has not been developed. There is no body of common law which establishes these issues. As far as the LME and recognised investment exchanges are concerned, I think I have tried to point out we have this public duty and we have a very important public duty which in essence is to protect the public or to run proper markets and to protect the public. This is a public function. Clearly if you give people statutory immunity then to some extent you are taking away private rights. Now you are not taking them away totally because all bodies, certainly the LME, are subject to judicial review. At the moment we are in a rather unusual position that we can be sued in the civil courts and taken to judicial review as well. You could say it is the best of both worlds or the worst of both worlds. I think it is a very important point.

(Mr Farrow) I would not entirely agree with Alan Whiting that there is no clear difference between bad faith and recklessness, I think to prove that a public authority has acted in bad faith is an extremely difficult thing for anybody to set up whereas acting without proper thought is perhaps more readily established. As a matter of principle it is hard to believe that a public authority should be allowed to be reckless with impunity as a general statement. What does one do about it? In principle there are two ways in which one can address it. One is one could limit the immunity to say that it does not apply in the event of reckless behaviour. Alternatively in the Bill at the moment there is a provision for investigation of complaints which is quite an attractive way of addressing the same issue but at the moment the provisions are, I think, very much within the control of the FSA and if one were to rely wholly on the investigation of complaints mechanism I think one would want to see it made substantially more robust and independent.

Chairman

235. We were reminded by the Economic Secretary that Lord Denning had spoken on this subject back in 1986 when the original Financial Services Act was going through; about the importance of the regulators not having to look over their

[Chairman *Cont]*

shoulders all the time, just as judges, in terms of how they carry out their duties. I am interested in what you say about the alternative route of looking at this in terms of strengthening the complaints procedure.

(Mr Bates) I just want to make one point which I think is not addressed in the Bill and which I think is important. If we are going to have a complaints procedure it has to involve the idea of the payment of compensation. It is not enough to have a complaints procedure which only censures or requests the reinstatement of the licence. If a very broad immunity is to be given then it seems to be right that in appropriate cases the complaints body ought to have the power, as the Ombudsman does, to propose the payment of compensation. That raises the important question of who pays that compensation because the FSA is funded entirely by the industry and if it is the FSA that has to pay then essentially the industry is being required to fund the costs of maladministration by a body which it did not appoint and whose members it does not control. There is an issue here as to compensation which I think is important, in answer to Alan's comments, but we also have to think about who pays, because who pays the bill at the end of the day is a rather important question.

Lord Haskel

236. I have a short question on that point, if I may. You were raising the point about who pays and what went through my mind was what then should the powers of the FSA be over firms that are not regulated because they do have certain responsibilities over firms that are not regulated? They do not pay towards the upkeep of the FSA. Should the FSA have any powers over them?

(Mr Bates) I think the principal power is in relation to the market abuse power which comes back to the point we were discussing earlier. I think there is an issue not so much as to the payment of the FSA's regulatory costs but more as to the extent of its regulatory— effectively delegated—powers to regulate the unregulated. I think the concern which I was alluding to earlier was the question of a very broad power being given to effectively prescribe conduct with very few limits placed on those powers and with no parliamentary scrutiny, for example, of the way in which those powers are exercised.

(Mr Whiting) Can I just come back to the point about statutory immunity. We just explained very briefly why we think it is important but I suspect that members of the Committee may think we need it for a different purpose from what we actually do need it for. It is not that we are concerned that if we take disciplinary action against the members of the exchange that we fear we will be sued, I think that is extremely unlikely, but a large part of my job is to maintain the markets as fair and proper markets. In order to do this you have to monitor markets very closely and you have to intervene quite often at extremely short notice. When you intervene in the markets, and you do it as best you can, you are bound, unfortunately, from time to time to hurt innocent people as well as the guilty. You hurt the innocent people far less than the guilty people but nevertheless sometimes innocent people are hurt. This is an inevitable consequence. If we have to fear that we are going to be sued every time that we intervene in a market or, worse, that lawsuits will go in that prevent us intervening very quickly in the market this really does make the job impossible. I think people's rights are protected because everything we do has to be Wednesbury reasonable. We are subject to judicial review; we are facing a judicial review at the moment.

237. We discussed the question of tribunals when we were talking about the various models, but one way or another we are going to have to have some sort of independent tribunal. I wonder whether you think that the proposals for the tribunal as they now stand are satisfactory? Do they make sense? What about costs? What about Legal Aid? Can you tell me what your thoughts are about the status of the tribunal?

(Mr Mayhew) Certainly as far as the tribunal is currently proposed we do not have any difficulty or problems with the way it is formulated. We do not know enough about the rules yet because the Lord Chancellor's Department has not made those proposed rules. There are two things I would say. One is that I think it is very important that the tribunal has sitting on it practitioners alongside the qualified chairman because in my experience they bring enormous value to the quality of decision making of tribunals. Secondly, it is very important that the tribunal does have the ability to award costs against either party. Currently in the SFA model in particular the basis on which costs can be awarded against the SFA is only if the prosecution is unreasonable, which I think is a high standard which is unnecessary. Finally, in relation to the way the tribunal operates, I do believe that the equality of arms principle means that we may need to have provision for Legal Aid for people who are impecunious who are caught up in a tribunal hearing because they will require expert evidence and it can be very expensive. Some people have felt very aggrieved by the current system where they are faced with huge legal costs, not only their own but also the regulator's costs, which leads them to abandon the game altogether with a burning sense of injustice. We have seen that in the Morgan Grenfell case where individuals felt that they were very poorly treated.

238. Will equality of arms imply Legal Aid?

(Mr Mayhew) It does effectively in those circumstances. In relatively complex cases and unusual circumstances, yes.

Viscount Trenchard

239. I would like to ask the panel whether they think that the establishment of a tribunal as now proposed is an adequate response to those who think there is a lack of independent review within the disciplinary process? That is my first question. My second question is what about practitioners, in particular foreign practitioners, who are trying to preserve a good relationship with a regulator and who are frightened that they might incur the regulator's displeasure if they go off to the tribunal? I represented a British firm in Japan and I was very concerned at all times to have a good relationship with my regulator

[Viscount Trenchard *Cont***]**

and I would have thought very long and hard before appealing against what he said. Aside from the costs, is the desire to maintain a good relationship with the FSA also going to be a reason working against a practitioner feeling free to appeal to the tribunal?

(Mr Farrow) Yes, as a matter of practice people are quite reluctant to start litigating against the man who is going to be regulating them next year or the year after. That is one of the inevitabilities of things. However, to go back to your first question, my Lord, yes, the establishment of a fully independent tribunal is what we want to be available as a safety net. We do not in any way want to make the enforcement process more litigious or more involvement of lawyers generally than there needs to be but the safeguard to ensure that fairness prevails is an opportunity for a fully independent hearing if you have not been able to resolve matters in any easier way.

Mr Loughton

240. Can we go on to the thorny subject of the European Convention and obviously stemming from the role of FSA as judge, prosecutor, jury, executioner and the beneficiary of the executed to take it to extreme there as well bearing in mind that there are probably two main areas where the Bill may get a conflict within the European Convention in relation to the FSA and competition on the one hand and the claims by investors against practitioners in financial services as well. Could we have potted versions of what the Economic Secretary referred to last week as "room for disagreement amongst lawyers", to put it mildly? Bearing in mind that nobody here is notching up bills of about £350 an hour for their views, could we have potted versions of where we think there are discrepancies that may lead to problems with the European Convention which need to be sorted out before this Bill becomes law as stated earlier on?

(Mr Morton) There are two main areas of potential discrepancy. The first is, as David Mayhew referred to earlier, the classification of market abuse and disciplinary measures as to whether they constitute criminal or civil proceedings for the purposes of the Convention. That is significant because criminal proceedings under the Convention have an additional set of extra protections which include in particular the privilege against self-incrimination and therefore classification as criminal carries with it the consequence that the current provisions which entitle the FSA to use in evidence material which has been compulsorily obtained would fall away as being contrary to the Convention. That is the first issue. The second issue relates to Article 7 of the Convention, which deals with the principle of certainty. There is a fear that some of the provisions, in particular the prohibition on market abuse which we talked about earlier, are insufficiently precise to meet the standard required by that and, therefore, there is doubt about their enforceability should they be challenged under the Convention. Those are the two main areas where there are points at issue.

241. Your views as to how they can be resolved?

(Mr Morton) In the first case I do not see that there is much scope for resolving them other than by

admitting that it is not possible to use evidence compulsorily obtained by putting it in evidence before the proceedings in question. As David Mayhew referred to earlier that probably is not such a dramatic change as you might suppose because it is still possible for the prosecutors to have the evidence in deciding how to present the case. In relation to the question of legal certainty then I think the remedy is clear, that if the provisions are too uncertain then they have to be reworded so they are more certain.

Chairman

242. Mr Morton, is your conclusion as far as the general question of enforcement is concerned, other than market abuse, that your view is that this is now all right and that your uncertainty relates to market abuse, or do you have some questions also about the more general area of enforcement?

(Mr Morton) There is one particular issue outstanding on the general area which is this question of whether evidence which is compulsorily obtained can be used.

243. Right.

(Mr Morton) My view would be that it cannot be used because jurisdiction is properly classified as criminal under the Convention.

(Mr Mayhew) Effectively Clause 104 subclause 5 should be extended to include all enforcement proceedings. The reason for that is that the enforcement proceedings are directed to achieve punishment and deterrence with quite severe fines. In a sense this comes back to an earlier point made in relation to the question "Well, we all know what is misconduct, we all know what is good or bad conduct". That was fine when regulators were about regulating a profession and not allowing people to practise for the protection of the community who were not fit and proper. If that is what the regulatory system is about you do not have to worry about the criminal nature of the process because it can be dealt with in the civil system but having introduced, as has happened over the last few years, substantial fines and substantial punishment that is what has brought the criminal element into play.

(Mr Farrow) If I understood Mr Morton correctly, the problem of an uncertainty would apply to enforcement proceedings for breach of principles?

(Mr Morton) Correct.

244. Do you want to say anything at this stage, Mr Whittaker? You do not have to.

(Mr Whittaker) Why not carry on.

Mr Beard

245. There is no test of intent in the legislation as so far proposed for market abuse. The Government have said this is because unintentional behaviour would still undermine the proper work of the market and confidence in it. Mr Howard Davies when he was here said that he agreed with that but, on the other hand, they have no intention of prosecuting people for accidental offences. The Minister, Ms Hewitt, told us that the degree of intent might affect the penalty but

[Mr Beard *Cont]*

not the character of the offence. Do you find the Government's arguments are persuasive on this question of including or not including intent?

(Mr Bates) Shall I start because no-one else wishes to take this point. I do not think we are convinced that one can ignore the issue of intent altogether. The point which we would make is that if you have very broadly defined offences then in order to decide whether it is culpable or not culpable you have to introduce an element of intent or some sort of mental element. If you have narrowly, specifically focussed offences where the conduct is clearly prescribed then it is much easier to abandon the test of any form of mental element or intention. The parking ticket example where it does not matter that you drove the car and left it on a double yellow line—it is your car, you are liable, you can be fined—that is a very clearly defined act. At the other extreme you can have very broadly defined offences but you find that, generally speaking, to make them workable and to make them fair to people you have to introduce the mental element to make them effective. I think the danger here, particularly with the statutory test—and remembering that the statutory test can be relied on supposedly on its own without any guidance from a code of conduct—the statutory test is both a broad test—we are very unclear what the conduct is precisely proscribed—and no mental element is attached to it either, so you end up with the worst of all worlds on both counts. Even when one moves to the codes, the codes of conduct, I think you find that the FSA have found drafting it that they have had to introduce some sorts of mental elements into the definitions—and they say so themselves—but what they have done in some cases is reduce those mental elements to a very limited extent: for example, and this shows the width of the quasi legislative power being given to the FSA, to criminalise negligent mistakes, which as far as I know is an entirely novel concept, that a fine can be levied on someone for a mistaken false statement, careless or whatever but false. Firstly, that demonstrates the width of the power being given, going back to the delegated powers point, but also demonstrates that even in the context of the Code the FSA has found that it has had to have some mental element. We think that ought to be directed.

Chairman

246. How do you tell? Unless somebody says "Fair cop", how do you show intent other than by looking for other corroborative evidence about what it is that they have been doing? I ask this in a very naive way. If you rely on intent can you ever catch anyone?

(Mr Bates) Can I just make the point that it is not the case in the States. The States is different and yet the American legislation 10b-5, on which most enforcement action is based, is firmly based around the idea of intent or recklessness, that is the test of scienter. The idea is that somehow we have English regulators who need to do away with the intent test because in other jurisdictions they do not have it either, but I do not think that is really truly the case. It is possible to prove intent by inference.

247. Yes, but that is back to evidence.

(Mr Bates) It is back to evidence, that is the point. Let us call a spade a spade: being fined £1 million is a conviction whether you label it civil or not and you should be convicted on the basis of evidence not on the basis of a vague assertion.

(Mr Whiting) Could I just make a personal comment. The LME does not have a formal policy on this; it does not actually need one because it does not really affect it. If we are frank, regulators hate the concept of intent because it is virtually impossible to prove. I cannot recall a single case where anyone has been able to prove intent. On the other hand, firms, quite rightly, not just because they do not want to be found guilty when they have committed offences, do not like the absence of intent because it does lay them open to the possibility of being disciplined for things which they did not intend to do. I think there is a way through this. If we can introduce certainty in what market abuse is then I think the issue of intent falls away.

(Mr Farrow) My Lord Chairman, I think you were present at the FSA Conference a couple of weeks ago. I thought the SEC judge, who addressed the conference and who said he had managed to be satisfied as to intent several hundred times in cases in front of him on the basis of inferring it from behaviour, was not dismissing it. Intent is quite substantial in US law he was saying, he was recognising that the test of intent in the law had to be satisfied but you could reasonably see intent without actually having the man on tape saying "I meant to do it". It seems to me we risk making this a yes/no insoluble problem whereas in a more pragmatic way the US system seems to have found a way of coping with it.

(Mr Mayhew) I think it is important, to follow on from what Kit Farrow said, that we understand clearly that the concept of intent in law is different from how you might use it in everyday parlance. It is not a question of motive or desire that the court will look for in this sort of area but should you have a knowledge of the natural consequences of your actions. This is where the flaw in the Government's position comes in because if the aim of this provision is to deter abusive behaviour, by definition you cannot be deterred if you did not have a knowledge of what you were about to cause. I may not desire it, I may not have had that as my purpose, but if I know what is going to happen then that is sufficient for knowledge.

248. Or you suspect that it might happen?

(Mr Mayhew) Then it is a question of degree. That is a matter of evidence again. If I know the consequences of my actions the court will hold me as having intended those actions, even though that was not my desired outcome.

(Mr Whittaker) On this occasion I would like to agree with one point that Kit Farrow made which is to agree that this is not something where there is necessarily a yes/no answer as between intent and non-intent. I would agree that the correct classification of the issue is what, if at all, should be the mental element for different aspects of market abuse. I would emphasise that the market abuse definition covers a wide variety of different forms of behaviour and it is quite conceivable that you might want to have a

[Chairman *Cont*]

different mental element as between different forms of behaviour covered in the Code of Conduct. We are certainly looking at the Code of Conduct again to see whether there is more scope to introduce a mental element into different parts of it without making it completely impossible to be able to take any enforcement action over market abuse as a result. All that said, I think that Howard made clear when he gave evidence to you that we are not seeking to take action where someone has taken all reasonable steps to avoid committing market abuse. I think there are cases where someone may well not have intended to abuse the market but where they should be expected to take reasonable steps to secure that their conduct does not do so.

249. This is the margin between recklessness and intent?

(Mr Whittaker) It may well be that if there is any sort of general solution it is in that area.

Mr Kidney

250. Could I ask the lawyers about fines. Mr Morton, would you like to start. It is proposed that the FSA can fine authorised persons for regulatory breaches and that the FSA can fine authorised persons and unauthorised persons for market abuse. Do you see those as two limbs of one administrative regime or is the first one an administrative one and the second one a civil regime?

(Mr Morton) I certainly see them as separate regimes. The market abuse regime is there for a significantly different purpose which to my mind is more closely akin to what in layman's terms we would call a criminal regime. I think one can spend an awful lot of time debating academically whether it is administrative or civil or criminal but I would see them as two quite distinct functions. Having said that, I do not see why the power of fining in principle is not appropriate for each of them.

251. Is it a worry that under the proposed scheme fines could be unlimited?

(Mr Morton) I think that is a worry but a greater worry is the need to ensure a reasonable degree of clarity about the probable scale of fines. There are provisions in the Bill, as you know, requiring the FSA to publish, and it has published some material already, the scale of the fines. I would be very concerned to try and ensure that there is as much clarity as possible about the likely level of the fines for what particular kinds of behaviour so that the tariff, using the word loosely, is apparent to people and therefore the deterrent effect which Chris Bates referred to before is maximized.

252. Presumably in due course the tribunal and the civil courts will have a track record of fines themselves?

(Mr Morton) Presumably so because they will have possibly appeals against the level of fines and, therefore, a track record will emerge.

253. Lastly, is it a worry that the FSA is going to keep all the fine income?

(Mr Morton) I think that is a worry. There seem to be differing levels of concern expressed about this but I do think that it gives rise to clear conflicts of interest and it increases the risk that the eye will stray from the ball a little bit in fixing the fine on the basis of the case rather than on the basis of extraneous factors like budget and the performance indicators.

Chairman

254. I assume that those who worry about this do not actually wish the income to come to the Government! It would be extremely unusual for a group to volunteer that it should be handed to the Government. Is it not therefore an issue of trying to find a way of ensuring that in terms of recycling the money it influences the behaviour of the prosecuting body as little as possible?

(Mr Morton) I think that is a fair point.

(Mr Farrow) It is not altogether separate from the question of how should prosecution costs be funded. At the moment the proposal is that in any case where somebody has been found guilty in the enforcement process, all the prosecution costs should be charged against him. One can easily envisage in a case which turns out to be a difficult case to investigate and much argument and expense for witnesses that at the end of the day you are found guilty for something for which the appropriate tariff fine is £10,000 but you are fined £10,000 with £200,000 costs. That seems to be quite an inappropriate way of setting about things. I have no simple solution to offer this afternoon but I think this question that you raised about where do the proceeds go needs to be looked at alongside where do the prosecution costs come from.

255. I think we have probably kept you all long enough. I have one last question and short answers would be preferred. Besides the rules and processes many of the things that in practice are going to matter here are going to be the people who apply them. We wonder what advice you would like to give Howard Davies as he builds his teams and committees as to how we are going to get the people to do the job?

(Mr Telford) Once point particularly is that we focus a lot on the punishments of people who do wrong. One of the greatest things in the minds of those people must be the chance of being caught, the deterrent effect is partly whether you are going to be caught as much as what the fine will be. We are quite clear that there must be effective monitoring and a proactive regime. I think Howard Davies has already sent out a message in a variety of ways saying: "I am on your case, I am looking for potential problems before they become very expensive, very long term problems." I think the message would be "Look at the monitoring as much as much as look at the penalties and the powers in the enforcement regime".

256. Preventing things, getting into this process which we are discussing this afternoon.

(Mr Farrow) Not quite answering your question, I am afraid, but to the extent that the FSA is going to be taking prosecution decisions and perhaps settlements on the basis of very market judgments like what is proper market behaviour, I am conscious of the considerable

[Chairman *Cont*]

efforts that the FSA has made to recruit people with market experience and that it is far from easy. But, nevertheless, it remains absolutely essential that they are found because without some experience of what is market behaviour you cannot be an arbiter of market behaviour.

257.   Mr Whiting?

(Mr Whiting)   I think that the hope must be, and I think it is a realistic hope, that when the FSA becomes established and develops its reputation it will attract extremely good people. I should say there are already extremely good people. The LME on the regulation side has had no difficulty at all finding over the last year extremely capable people. Some times we have taken them from the FSA I am afraid to say although they are probably more valuable within the LME than they are there. This is the experience in the United States where it is perceived to be an extremely good thing indeed to have done two, three, four years in the CFTC or the SEC and then they go back into private practice and sometimes come back into the regulatory body. This can have mutual benefits for all sides.

Viscount Trenchard: Could I ask the panel whether they think that the FSA should have some separation of the powers of chairman and chief executive? We hear a lot nowadays about corporate governance, companies increasingly requiring the functions to be separate. The FSA has very extensive powers and it can be said to be in part legislator, prosecutor, judge, jury and enforcer all within one body, although admittedly it is said that there will be separation of functions within the body. Are the panel satisfied that the powers of chairman and chief executive should be combined in one person?

Chairman

258.   If you do not wish to answer, fine, I understand if it is incriminating!

(Mr Bates)   My own view, if I might express one, is that the corporate model is inappropriate because this is not really a public company. It may be clothed in corporate form but it is not a company in the traditional sense of the word. Therefore the governance models adopted for corporate companies, I do not think necessarily can be thrown straight on to what is essentially a regulatory body or regulatory agency where it is not that uncommon to combine the roles. I would not express a view one way or the other about the appropriate governance model on that particular point but I do not think you can necessarily say that it is a company, therefore we ought to separate the two roles.

Viscount Trenchard

259.   You do not think it should be a company?

(Mr Bates)   On that point I think that the question of whether it is a company or not is not of particular importance. I understand that there are reasons why it is,

not least because the SIB was in that form and therefore continuity was possible. What is important is the role that it has, the powers it has, and the accountability controls that the Bill provides for which the Government has gone a long way in its recent statements to strengthen and enhance in line with and in response to comments made by the industry.

(Mr Farrow)   In our very early submissions when the concept of the FSA was first announced we addressed this by saying that the majority of the board should be non executives and should be independent of the FSA. The Government has agreed with that proposal. I think bearing in mind what Chris has said that is a reasonable way of dealing with the need for both control and supervision.

Chairman

260.   There is of course the position of the senior non-executive in particular. I think it is probably fair that we should not ask Mr Whittaker about that. Mr Telford I am aware that on much of what we have been doing today the detail has not been your concern, but do you have any final comments you want to make?

(Mr Telford)   I think just to emphasise some of my earlier remarks. Of course we support any fairness and transparency in the system, we think that should be pushed as far as it can be. We are aware that in a fast moving market the regulator does need to be flexible. One thing certainly, in a way we are disappointed to hear, as we have been told for many years by people in wholesale and retail markets that they really wish the regulator would just establish clear principles and let them get on with running their business as they know how to run it, are comments that in fact detailed rules are what are required at every turn to give certainty, putting aside the legal argument about certainty in that context. We have been receptive to those views and said, yes, principles are very important and firms should be left to run their businesses as they see fit. We still support that principle and we would rather the regulator was not caught up at every turn at having to go into the detail of every single eventuality. Just one final point I would make is about companies paying for regulators, they have consumers and consumers generally also pay for regulation. Our understanding of where funds go is to reduce the cost of regulation which is to consumers and also to firms. So long as that is transparent and we do not see the regulator issuing large fines to make the budget better then we will be happy with that. Yes, clarity and transparency but also a strong regulator with teeth will give consumers confidence in the market place right across the board. Although you are right to say wholesale markets may seem one step removed from consumers, what happens in those markets, the fact they are not corrupt and they are working efficiently does impact on consumers on the range of investments and institutions they wish to trust. We do have those concerns.

Chairman: Thank you all very much. It has been a very interesting session.

Paper Submitted by Clifford Chance

1. The Current SRO Model*

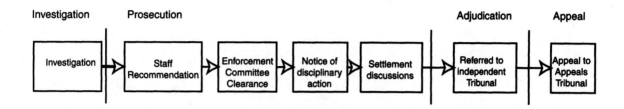

* Taken from SFA Rules

2. Proposed Model - The Bare Bones (Bill)

1. As proposed in the Bill

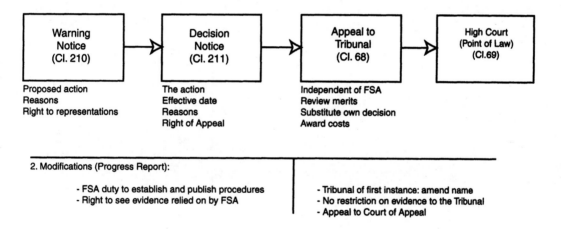

2. Modifications (Progress Report):

- FSA duty to establish and publish procedures
- Right to see evidence relied on by FSA

- Tribunal of first instance: amend name
- No restriction on evidence to the Tribunal
- Appeal to Court of Appeal

3. Proposed Model - The Details (CP17)

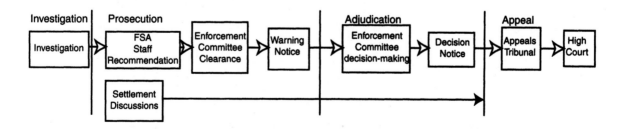

4. The CP17 Model Enhanced

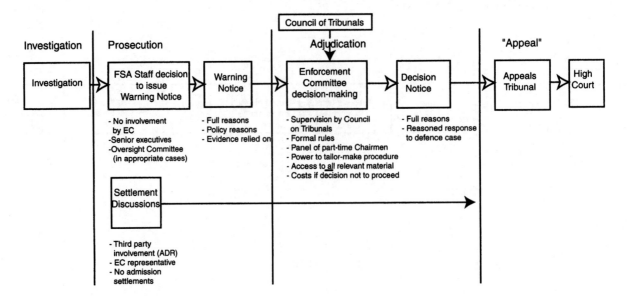

5. An Alternative Model*

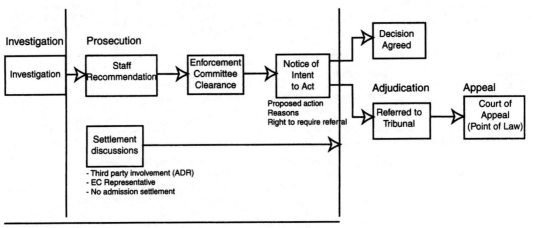

* Precedent: the Financial Services Tribunal established under the 1986 Act
Note: this model reflects the comment by the Economic Secretary to the Treasury to
the Joint Committee that the FSA internal process will not entail an imposed result

Printed in the UK by The Stationery Office Limited
4/99   421665   78344

ISBN 0-10-432999-8

9 780104 329993

HOUSE OF LORDS
HOUSE OF COMMONS

SESSION 1998–99

JOINT COMMITTEE ON FINANCIAL SERVICES AND MARKETS

MINUTES OF EVIDENCE

Tuesday 30 March 1999

Mr Andrew Buxton, Mr Peter Vipond, Mr Marc Sylvain, Lord Archer of Sandwell, QC,

Ms Lucy Hutchinson, Mr Dominic Clarke, Mr Antony Blunden and Mr Geoffrey Turner

Mr David Roe and Mr Andew Whittaker in attendance

Printed pursuant to the Order of the House of Lords of 2 March 1999
Ordered by The House of Commons *to be printed*
30 March 1999

LONDON: THE STATIONERY OFFICE
£5.30

HL Paper 50-v
HC 328-v

TUESDAY 30 MARCH 1999

Present:

Lord Burns (in the Chair)
Lord Eatwell
Lord Fraser of Carmyllie
Lord Montague of Oxford
Lord Poole

Mr Nigel Beard
Mrs Liz Blackman
Dr Vincent Cable
Mr David Kidney
Mr Tim Loughton
Mr James Plaskitt
Mr Barry Sheerman

Examination of Witnesses

MR ANDREW BUXTON, President, and MR PETER VIPOND, Director, British Bankers Association; MR MARC SYLVAIN, Managing Director, Fidelity Investment Management Limited, Association of Unit Trusts and Investment Funds; LORD ARCHER OF SANDWELL, QC, Chairman, Council on Tribunals: MS LUCY HUTCHINSON, Partner, and MR DOMINIC CLARKE, Partner, Herbert Smith, Solicitors; MR ANTONY BLUNDEN, Company Secretary/Head of Compliance, Credit Suisse Financial Products; and MR GEOFFREY TURNER, Chief Executive, Securities Institute, called in and examined.

MR DAVID ROE, Head of Financial Services and Markets Bill Team, HM Treasury, and MR ANDREW WHITTAKER, Deputy General Counsel, Financial Services Authority, in attendance.

Chairman

261. Good afternoon. Welcome to this session of the Joint Committee. As you will have seen from some of the evidence that we have had, we have been dividing our time by certain themes. Today, as we did last Thursday, we have a general theme of discipline and enforcement and the tribunal. We have started with the Bill, as it was published, and we have looked at a lot of the consultation documents that have come in as a result of the Bill. We have now had a Treasury Progress Report. Basically we are trying to find out to what extent the Treasury Progress Report has answered people's concerns, and what are the outstanding issues which still arise. We are also very aware that people may have points that they may wish to make on other issues, apart from our major topic today, and we are happy to take those today as well. What I would like to do is to take each of you in turn. If you would like to introduce yourselves and make any opening statement, which may include any other points you want to get on the record, which do not relate to the topic we are discussing this afternoon. Could I start at this end. Mr Blunden.

(Mr Blunden) My Lord Chairman, I am Tony Blunden. I am Company Secretary and Head of Compliance at Credit Suisse Financial Products. CSFP is a member of LIBA. The single point I would like to make in my introductory remarks is the problem of uncertainty attaching to the proposed market abuse regime issue. The proposed legislation and regulation seeks, as previous legislation and regulation has sought, to protect markets by preventing a large number of possible trading sins, which come under the collective and perhaps ambiguous heading of market abuse. However, identifying such behaviour precisely is not without difficulty. Identify too little and you will have been ineffective. Identify too much and you will have been effective in preventing legitimate trading.

Of course, we agree that the London market should be fair and dependable and viewed internationally as such. Most people would agree that behaviour, which deliberately sets out to mislead and manipulate prices and therefore threatens the financial markets, that this behaviour needs to be prevented. However, it is important to protect the cornerstones of our current market and to give them undisputed safe harbours. In all respects the activities such as hedging activities, investment activities, and the provision of liquidity should be acceptable market activities, irrespective of the market place. Without these safe harbours the existence and evolution of markets could be undermined. It is also vital that we recognise that the markets, by definition, are imperfect. There will always be factors and events that affect the market, which were not anticipated by the participants. For continual evolution and proper price determination these factors and events need to be permitted, so that players such as speculators, market makers, arbitrage players—and, indeed, firms undertaking stabilisation—should all be permitted to be legitimate participants within the market. We acknowledge that the distinction between legitimate behaviour and abusive behaviour, in the context of an evolving market, is likely to be a matter of degree. After all, market abuse can only really be generally understood as behaviour that runs contrary to market practice and commonly understood market practice. Even then, as markets are constantly evolving, so too is accepted market practice. As such, whether the behaviour amounts to market abuse must and can obviously be subjectively determined. It is nevertheless possible to develop criteria, the tests for such behaviour. At the recent FSA conference on tackling market abuse, Tom Sjoblom of the SEC noted that criteria can be very effective in tackling this problem area. As the purpose of the code was to expand the Act and to provide clarity, it is of the utmost importance that the code

30 *March* 1999]

Mr Andrew Buxton, Mr Peter Vipond, Mr Marc Sylvain,
Lord Archer of Sandwell, QC, Ms Lucy Hutchinson,
Mr Dominic Clarke, Mr Antony Blunden and Mr Geoffrey Turner

[*Continued*

[Chairman *Cont*]

itself provides examples of conduct which will be acceptable. If laws are to be drafted generally, and I understand and accept why the Government wants to draft the laws more generally, but the interpretive matter and underlying laws need to provide certainty in order realistically to achieve clear guidance. I noticed in an earlier Committee session that the Chairman of the FSA stated that the code of market conduct should clarify the regulator's expectation in terms of what is and what is not a market manipulation. Unfortunately, we do not yet have a code which indicates what is not market manipulation. It is worth noting that we are only seeking that which the Government believes is the right way to draft regulation. In the Better Regulation Guide, issued by the Better Regulation Unit of the Cabinet Office, the question is asked in paragraph 3.9, "Making sure that regulation works": Is it clear and unambiguous? That is all we are asking for. It is our view that the way forward is now to be found through an open and honest discussion of the constituent components of market abuse. This needs to be supported by clear guidance and the issuance of things such as no action letters, waivers, and the redrafting of the code, to include safe harbours. This will go some way to addressing the lack of certainty. We also hope that this will enable both the market and an understanding of market abuse to evolve. This will assist in maintaining confidence in the United Kingdom financial markets.

(Ms Hutchinson) Perhaps if I can do the introductions, I am Lucy Hutchinson, a litigation partner from Herbert Smith, Solicitors. With me is Dominic Clarke, one of my partners in our corporate department. Our evidence addresses issues relating to discipline and enforcement procedures and, to some extent, market abuse. There have been some notable changes in the approach of the FSA but we still have some concerns that these do not go far enough, particularly in relation to the fairness of the procedures, bearing in mind the European Convention and the fact that the FSA is to remain prosecutor, judge and jury. We are also concerned about the overlap of the criminal and civil procedures, penalties and the regime of fines, plus we have concerns over the lack of certainty as to what constitutes market abuse, which is something that has just been mentioned. For market abuse we think there should be a clearer statutory definition of market abuse; and combined with that the code should be made a safe harbour in the absence of intent to manipulate the market. The need for intent is particularly important where the code may conflict with the statutory definition. For example, trading on the strength of relevant but not disclosable information is apparently permitted by the code but may breach clause 56. We consider that compliance with the code should be a defence in the absence of an intent to abuse the market. We are also concerned that the current proposals may breach Article 7 of the European Convention because of vagueness. We think that the avenues of no action letters and also the status of guidance should be reconsidered. We are particularly concerned about the unregulated because they are subject to the market abuse regime, but they do not have the advantage of compliance officers, in-house

legal advice, training and guidance. We are still of the view that the market abuse regime is criminal in terms of the European Convention. As far as disciplinary procedures are concerned, these might be categorised as criminal but the position is not clear. There are certainly arguments that it only falls within the civil categories. Turning to the procedural framework, what is envisaged at the moment is a two-tier system with an enforcement committee, which can make decisions and impose penalties; and then a tribunal with a final tier of an appeal to the Court of Appeal on a point of law. The difficulty we see here is the inherent conflict of the FSA acting as both prosecutor, and where no agreement is reached, also making a determination of guilt and imposing a punishment. To make this a fair system, we believe it would be necessary to provide for full disclosure of evidence and an independent impartial decision making process, but this would create a cumbersome procedure, which we think the Government and the industry would want to avoid. So, instead, what we think should be considered is a procedure allowing for a quick resolution, if the parties wish this; and, if not, a fair and proper hearing before the tribunal. This could be done by giving a different role to the enforcement committee. It could remain part of the FSA and its duty would be to consider the FSA's case and that of the defendant but without a full hearing. It would not impose sanctions but it would be able to rule that there was no case to answer so it would act as a filter. If it did not make a rule and there was no agreement, then you would go to the tribunal. If instead the enforcement committee is to make first instance decisions, then we think it should be a separate independent body accountable to the Treasury. Whichever scheme you adopt, there should be a right to legal representation before the tribunal. Also, where you are looking at the market abuse regime, because that is criminal for European Convention purposes, the defendant there should have access to legal advice; if necessary, through Legal Aid or some other fund. That would include the cost of investigatory and expert witness assistance because these are particularly important in financial services cases. On a general point, we think there should be the possibility of settlement without the defendant having to make an admission of liability. Turning to the overlap of criminal and civil points, ideally we think the FSA should not have a power to prosecute. We do have concerns that the threat of criminal prosecution could be used to achieve a civil settlement. Under the current proposals, the FSA suggests that generally it will not seek to impose a civil fine for market abuse against someone who has already been prosecuted. We think that should be a commitment. We also think that as the FSA is not the only prosecuting authority, where it decides to prosecute and then it pursues the civil route, there should be some way of ensuring that none of the other prosecuting authorities step in and prosecute. Turning to the question of fines, we remain of the view that the fines should not be paid to the FSA. We think that can only lead to a conflict, or apparent conflict of interests, with fines being seen as an alternative source of funds. Instead, we suggest they should go to the Treasury. We also think that where

[Chairman *Cont*]

costs are awarded against the defendant, that should be dealt with separately from the fine and any costs order must be proportionate and bear in mind the breach upheld and the amount of the investigation related to that breach. We also think that if the enforcement committee is to have decision making powers, it should be able to award costs against both parties; that is, against the FSA as well as the defendant. Finally, on statutory immunity, we think the proposal here may be in breach of the European Convention, but in general we do not think there is a need for statutory immunity anyway.

262. Thank you very much. Lord Archer.

(Lord Archer of Sandwell) My Lord Chairman, I was not proposing to make any specific points at this early stage. However, it may assist the Committee, (and I am subject to your guidance), and it may perhaps help the record if I trespass, just for two minutes on the Committee's time, to explain how I come to be sitting at this end of the table. I am the Chairman of the Council on Tribunals. The Council was established, by statute, by the Tribunals and Inquiries Act of 1958. Its purpose is to advise Government on matters relating to tribunals and ministerial inquiries, either when we are asked for advice or if visits or perambulations disclose something which should be drawn to attention, by unsolicited and sometimes unwelcome advice. The tribunals, which we supervise, are listed in Schedule I to the Tribunals and Inquiries Act of 1992, which is the latest edition of the consolidating legislation. This may be added to from time to time either by primary legislation, as suggested in this case, or by ministerial order. At the last count there were 78 different systems of tribunals which we supervised. There is hardly a human activity which does not come into contact with a tribunal at some stage. We think that our contribution to the process may be a familiarity with the whole tribunal family, and one of the things we try to do is to spread best practice from one tribunal to another. Therefore, our concern is not specifically with financial services. We do not claim any specific expertise on that. However, we do hope that we have some expertise on tribunals and that, I think, is going to be our contribution to the process. We are independent, although we are appointed by the Lord Chancellor and the Lord Advocate. We are totally independent of Government, and we are not subject to their directions, so we have no axe to grind. Our concern is with the three principles—which were set out in the Report of the Franks Committee in 1957—of openness, fairness and impartiality; and to which we have added a fourth, user-friendliness. I will not feel constrained from attempting to answer a question by the fact that the Council may not specifically have considered it but I will try, as far as possible, to distinguish between matters on which the Council has pronounced and matters which carry no greater authority than the fact that I am the respondent. In view of what has already been said may I add this, part of our problem here, in relation to the powers of the FSA, is that we are shooting at a moving target. If you look at the draft Bill, it has very substantial disciplinary and regulatory powers. Clearly, it is acting

in a quasi-judicial capacity. But there has been all sorts of subsequent re-thinking. I understand that Ms Hewitt said, in effect, that it is going to be an adviser and counsellor, and that no-one will actually have any order made which might prejudice them unless they agree to it. (I think she said, unless they virtually settle.) That is what is meant apparently by saying that the tribunal will now be a tribunal of first instance. There are three possibilities. You could have an authority—and I could name quite a few of them, if you wish—which begins by trying to counsel people, sending a warning letter, offering to help, offering to have coffee with them, and regards their disciplinary powers as the end of the line. That gives you certain problems because these two processes sometimes get mixed up. The second possibility is that it is simply a disciplinary authority subject, as it should then be, to an appeal to someone else. The third possibility is that it has no disciplinary powers at all. They are purely there as an advisory authority. It looks as if that is the way the Treasury's mind may be working at the moment, in which case some of the things we have said in one context may not be applicable if the picture has changed.

263. I will ask Mr Roe to comment on that when we have finished. We followed this up last Thursday and it was suggested then that maybe we over-interpreted what the Economic Secretary said. If we did I am sure Mr Roe will tell us in a moment.

(Mr Buxton) I am President of the British Bankers Association, which represents about 320 members from 60 countries, so although it is a British organisation it represents banks and financial institutions in the City of London generally, from whatever country they come from. Firstly, we have in our evidence so far said that we support the creation of the FSA and look to it to be a world class institution. We want robust and effective supervision which works with the market. That is important. It is also important that it should maintain the confidence of the consumers, so somehow it has to tread that path through the middle. We are concerned about a more formal system and how far the formal system goes: more reliance on detailed rules, which is backed by enforcement as the means of implementation. While formalisation and enforcement clearly have a role to play, they can easily undermine the open relationship that currently exists between regulated and regulator, which should continue to do so for the benefit of both parties. With regard to the Bill, we continue to be concerned about discipline, enforcement and market abuse. Our concerns are that the processes should be fair and reasonable, so that after investigation, enforcement should be considered without the presumption that an offence has been committed. We think there is a danger of amendment making matters more legalistic. That may be a fear of the future but the legislation empowers the FSA to make rules. We think there is a danger that since these rules will be empowered by the legislation but not set out, that gradually we could get an even more legalistic process. The internal processes of the FSA, if they are properly established and run, should enable the overwhelming majority of enforcement matters to be resolved

[**Chairman** *Cont*]

speedily and fairly for all parties. Good legislation and legal practice should enable regulatory processes to work, not be a substitute for them. We are also concerned about the competitiveness of the financial services industry. I think we look at this because of our position at the centre of a banking community in London, which is made up of a very large number of foreign institutions, which give rise to the success of London as a financial institution. We are concerned to maintain that international competitiveness by including a statutory objective that would mandate the FSA to take international comparators into account. There is no doubt that regulation in different centres is compared, particularly by the foreign community, and we do need to be aware of that. We feel that accountability to Ministers, and through them to Parliament, is also fundamental. In a powerful statutory system an additional safeguard lies in obliging the FSA formally to consult and report back on how consultation has affected their decisions. Such process contributes to an open public debate on regulatory issues: something which can be reviewed by Parliament. Thank you, Chairman.

(*Mr Vipond*) My name is Peter Vipond. I am a Director of the British Bankers Association. At this stage I do not think I need to add anything to what my colleague has said.

(*Mr Turner*) My name is Geoffrey Turner. I am the Chief Executive of the Securities Institute. My background is that I have been involved with security regulation since 1973: first with the London Stock Exchange and then the FSA; then at APCIMS, the stockbroker trade organisation; and now with the Securities Institute. I would like to start by thanking the Committee for giving the Institute an opportunity to give evidence on this very important Bill. The Securities Institute is the institute for professionals in the securities industry. Our aim is to set standards of professional excellence for individual practitioners, and to provide the means for attaining them. We are the major examining body for the securities and derivatives industry, and provide a wide range of industry exams and courses, which attract considerable support. Unlike the trade associations and the companies which have given evidence here, our particular focus is on individuals and it is that which I would like to concentrate on. For me the key issue in the regulation of retail financial services is simple, it is, does the adviser know his or her stuff and can the saver or investor rely on that person's skill and judgment? For my Institute the issues of training, competence, integrity of individuals and investor education and recognition by the regulatory system of the responsibility of individuals, are of major importance. So we are awaiting with the greatest interest the publication by FSA of its *Suitability of Individuals* paper which is promised for the second quarter of 1999. We do welcome the additional arrangements for the accountability of FSA which have been outlined in the progress report. We believe that effective accountability is in the best interests of both consumers and practitioners, but we have further recommended that the FSA should be subject to value for money audit by the National Audit Office. We know there may be some scepticism in the Committee

that financial services are too complicated to be able to be taught to consumers but we believe they can and that a start must be made now in the education system. I mentioned a minute ago the capable and competent adviser as key to effective investor protection, the other essential of course is the well-informed customer, and we welcome the Committee's thoughts on our proposal to require the FSA to report annually to the Secretary of State for Education and Employment on the progress it is making to promote public understanding of the financial system and awareness of the benefits and risks of different kinds of investment. The Progress Report records industry fears that the FSA could stray into the areas of financial advice and education in discharging its public awareness goals. The report says that the Government believes the FSA does have a legitimate role in financial education but must work in partnership with institutions having relevant expertise and resources, and I would very much like to say here that we have such expertise and we would very much like to play our part in a partnership with the FSA. I cannot speak for other institutes like the Chartered Insurers, the Bankers, the Scottish bodies, but I feel sure that they too would wish to participate and they have a long tradition of activity in the educational and training field. The FSA have said they recognise the importance of the responsibility of management of a regulated firm to run their business in compliance with the regulations. We believe that the legislation should now recognise the special position of compliance officers and we think it is important they should have some legal standing in the new framework. We have circulated to the Committee an excerpt from a recent Jersey law which recognises the role and importance of the compliance officer, and we would ask the Committee to consider a similar recognition of their vital job in the regulatory system. Thank you.

264. Thank you very much. Mr Sylvain?

(*Mr Sylvain*) Thank you, my Lord Chairman. Good afternoon. Let me introduce myself and AUTIF before I turn to the points I would like to make. I am Marc Sylvain and I am managing director of Fidelity Investments, I am a practitioner here. Fidelity is the third largest investment fund company in the UK. I am also representing AUTIF today, which is the Association of Unit Trusts and Investment Funds. AUTIF member firms represent 99 per cent of the unit trust assets under management, mostly the savings of consumers. Before I comment on the points in this Bill, particularly as to AUTIF, I must point out that this Committee itself is not looking at a complete Bill. The specific provisions relating to collective investment schemes, that is the funds we sell to consumers, have not yet been drafted and our concern is that there will be little time left to comment on the provisions which will affect consumer orientated funds. With that proviso, I would like to make two points. The first is that we believe that there is beginning to be some confusion between the enforcement committee idea and the tribunal. We strongly recommend that an independent enforcement committee process be established with six points. That it be enshrined in the Bill; that it have an independent

[Chairman *Cont*]

chairman and otherwise be composed of public interest members and practitioners; that it have the responsibility for overseeing the process of enforcement ensuring it is timely and fair to all sides; that it actually be required to hear evidence from both sides on a case; that it be the body which sets fines; and that it be able to award costs against the FSA where the finding is in favour of the accused. I believe an enforcement committee such as I have just proposed would have no problem dealing with those who breach regulatory obligations wilfully or recklessly. Firms which engage in that sort of behaviour should be hung out to dry and, moreover, consumers will demand that. If I turn to the second point, it is about the accountability of the FSA. Today's agenda will include some discussion of market abuse and the role of intent. I would like to suggest there could also be regulatory abuse without there being any intent; it is not necessary for the FSA to intend to commit regulatory abuse for it to happen just the same. I have no doubt that the FSA will be staffed by well-meaning people, that no one at the FSA intends to carry out actions that a city editor might characterise as bullying or intimidation, but if it appears so to the regulated it can lead to a break-down in the system. I believe this is at the root of the loud concerns you are hearing from the industry about the accountability of the FSA given its wide powers of discipline. AUTIF is keen to know how in practice the Bill will put checks in place to ensure that vigorous regulation does not descend into regulatory abuse, particularly when there will be and can be legitimate differences of opinion about how best the FSA should carry out its duties. Let me end by saying that the industry and the FSA share a strong commonality of interest. Our industry depends on consumer trust and a well-regulated environment is essential to inspire consumer confidence. Thank you, my Lord Chairman.

265. Thank you very much. We are fortunate this afternoon in having both David Roe, who is head of the Bill team in the Treasury, and Andrew Whittaker, who is deputy general counsel of the FSA. We are very careful that these sessions do not become occasions in which we take evidence from them. The idea is that we should be taking evidence from the witnesses of the day but nevertheless we do like to give them the opportunity to respond to some of the things which have been said to see if we can make progress. I would now ask them if there is anything in any of the opening remarks which would cause them to intervene at this point?

(Mr Roe) Thank you, Chairman. I would just respond to your earlier invitation to confirm that what the Economic Secretary said in an earlier hearing is consistent with what is set out in the Bill. If anybody read into that a signal of change in policy, that is not the right interpretation. That is not to say, of course, that Ministers are not taking a very close interest in these proceedings.

266. Andrew?

(Mr Whittaker) Thank you, Chairman. I would like to respond to a fairly small number of points which have been made but it may nevertheless take me a few moments to do so. Can I start first by dealing with the issue which has been raised as to the certainty of some of the provisions which we will be asked to enforce, in particular in relation to the general principles that we have ourselves enunciated in the past and plan to continue to operate by and also in relation to the general provisions in relation to market abuse. In relation to the principles in particular we think that clarity and predictability of operation are important both to ensure fairness and to assist people to understand the standards we set. We do not think this means there needs to be over-prescriptiveness. The Better Regulation Unit, which has been mentioned already this afternoon, has urged that there should be a focus on the outcomes to be achieved rather than necessarily on the methods by which they should be achieved, and that is certainly something that we apply in the formulation of the general principles we operate under. We would also point out that confidence and predictability which we see as being the aims to be achieved in this context can be achieved not only by hard prescription but also by gentler forms of law, by guidance with authoritative effect and by codes of practice. We also think that case law on Article 7 of the ECHR, which has been mentioned earlier, shows that they are prepared to uphold broadly-worded provisions as well as more specific ones, so we think there is a lot to be said for the proposal made by Andrew Buxton that we should not move towards a more rule-driven system but should continue to operate on the basis of some general principles as well as specific rules where those give people the confidence to be able to understand what is and what is not expected of them. Just picking up on the point which was made earlier about what is and what is not expected in the context of market abuse, it was suggested that the code of conduct in issue should be given an express status under the legislation to enable that to become a safe harbour from the market abuse provisions, and certainly that is an idea we would not have any difficulty with if that were something which were to find favour more generally. There are a number of other points which I could raise but I imagine most of them the Committee will be coming back to before long. Just to pick up, in case it is not dealt with later, the point about competitiveness, we do think the existing requirements of the Bill which require us to take into account the international position of the UK will require us to look at international comparators in order to be able to do so in an intelligent way, so it may be there is no need to change the Bill in that respect.

267. Thank you. Could I ask David Roe about this question of the timing of the rules on collective investment schemes. Is there anything you can say about that?

(Mr Roe) There is nothing specific I can say at this stage, Chairman. We are very aware of AUTIF's concerns and we are doing all we can to meet them.

Chairman: I think the order in which we take these issues is very difficult and there is no right order in which to do this. So we will stick broadly to the agenda we have outlined and we will begin with the whole question of certainty. Lord Poole is going to raise questions on this.

Lord Poole

268. Each of you to some extent or another has raised the question of certainty and it may be you want to make some more points about the sort of additional certainty which you would feel comfortable with, but our concern, I have to say, is not with how the rules may subsequently be made so much as with what needs to be put into the Bill to ensure the greater certainty you would seek. To the extent that anybody has specific suggestions which have been thought through, that would be very helpful for us.
(Mr Blunden) My Lord Chairman, I can respond to that. I think there is a natural clash here between the Government's wish to have flexibility and just establish boundaries in the legislation and the industry's wish to have certainty. For our part, we are quite comfortable with the code itself supplying certainty, it does not have to be in the Bill, but there needs to be certainty provided somewhere so that as a compliance practitioner I can look at transactions and to a reasonable degree advise my senior management those transactions will be acceptable or will not be acceptable under law.

269. How do you deal with the point which has been made that says in a rapidly evolving world—and I think any of us who had been operating 20 years ago would be astonished by these markets working now—something could be prescriptively laid down in advance which is going to cause almost more problems than the more open mechanisms which are intended?
(Mr Blunden) I do not think everything can be laid down in advance. Indeed, I would not expect the code to be written in stone and to survive for many years. I would expect it myself to be an evolving document and it would involve, I suspect, very much as the FSA rules have done in the past, a number of no actions and waivers which would be given, but hopefully in the new regime they would be given publicly rather than as they have been under the old regime privately where therefore only the regulator and that particular entity know the waiver exists. I do recognise that the FSA have also from time to time published those waivers that they have thought would affect a wider number of people and the publishing of the waivers has helped itself to move the rules and regulations. I think there is also a balance to be drawn between waivers which are specific to a single transaction and really will only ever apply to a single transaction and those in which there is a quite a wide public interest.

Mr Sheerman

270. So you are looking for building up a sort of case law of publications?
(Mr Blunden) I am sure there will over time be a build up of case law, but hopefully we will not actually need to employ lawyers as an industry. In a sense, working with the regulator, we can build up a two-way flow of what is and what is not acceptable.

Chairman

271. What does this lead you to suggest should be changed as far as the Bill is concerned, which after all is our main concern as a Committee?

(Mr Blunden) Ideally, it would be good to see the Bill going further along the lines of requiring the FSA to give advice and guidance and that is something that undoubtedly will be discussed in the Committee further, but to give some form of certainty to the industry.

Mr Beard

272. Beyond producing codes?
(Mr Blunden) Yes. Things such as the equivalent of no action letters. I recognise in market abuse the regulator cannot possibly give a no action letter for something which might be seen as fraudulent, but at the same time a regulator can give guidance on very specific transactions.

Lord Fraser of Carmyllie

273. One of the issues about guidance is not that it might from time to time be changed but as to, when it is changed, what status it enjoys.
(Mr Blunden) Yes, absolutely. I recognise that is a problem and there are no easy solutions.

274. Do you regard what is proposed at present as the status for guidance as sufficient?
(Mr Blunden) I think it is helpful that it will be evidential in nature. I would like to see it go further in that abidance with the guidance actually is a safe harbour itself.
Lord Poole: Perhaps we can ask others for their views?

Lord Eatwell

275. Before we do that, what was striking in the discussion about certainty was the totally opposite position taken by Mr Buxton from that taken by Ms Hutchinson. Mr Buxton seemed to say that Ms Hutchinson's approach would ruin his business. I may be putting that slightly strongly but it is to bring out the difference between you.
(Ms Hutchinson) We certainly do not intend to ruin your business!
(Mr Buxton) Actually, Sir, I thought there was quite a lot of similarity between what Ms Hutchinson was saying and what I was saying. I think it is a question of where you find the narrow path between everything being in the Bill and nothing being in the Bill. There is a path between the two. Ms Hutchinson may go a little further towards the legislation than I do.
(Mr Clarke) My Lord Chairman, perhaps I can answer? We are going towards the safe harbour route. It is not in our opinion possible to cover in a code all the circumstances which could arise. We feel that the code is also going to lag the market to a degree. The code should provide a safe harbour to those people who carry out transactions in accordance with its terms, but I would accept the caveat "in the absence of actual intent to abuse the market". There are no doubt ways in which activities in compliance with the code could be conducted in a way to abuse the market, and I do not think I would have a great problem with that additional requirement. The example we gave was

[Lord Eatwell Cont]

a situation where apparently the code said one thing and the Bill said another. That may be because they were produced at different times. The background scenario we were describing was this difference between relevant information and discloseable information. To take an example of an industry which would be of more use to those represented here, the electricity industry, at the present moment the forward market in electricity futures is not regulated but it is intended to be regulated in the next 18 months or so and therefore perhaps would become within the ambit of the code. If an electricity supplier takes a plant off the market by closing it down, for repairs or whatever, the relevant market might require him to state he has done that, in which case that will be discloseable information. The code says that you cannot trade on the basis of having discloseable information which you have not disclosed if it is also relevant information, ie information which other market users would like to know about. The code says that providing it is not discloseable information, you can actually trade and that might mean the electricity company which wants to close down its plant can go into the market and find the electricity it needs to supply its customers. That is what the current application of the code says. The Bill suggests that all relevant information will have to be disclosed essentially so this is where you have this sort of conflict, and conflicts are bound to arise because there are different economic views as to whether or not people should be required to disclose that sort of information before they trade. Some people may say, "It is perfectly fair and proper that a person who knows they are going to need the supply of a particular commodity should be allowed to go into the market and buy that commodity before he announces to his competitors and the people who are going to sell it to him that he actually needs it." Others would say, "For a totally fair market the sellers actually need to know he needs it." This is the sort of situation which the code is going to have to sort out. If the code takes the view that a particular activity is acceptable, then people should be able to rely on that code unless they intend to abuse the market.

276. We discover that Andrew Buxton does really agree with that.

(*Mr Buxton*) Can I just make two points? Firstly, Ms Hutchinson mentioned Clause 56 in her first presentation and that is a very key clause which we think it is too broad and too opaque at the moment. The point which has just been made about the differences between the code and the Bill actually is a very important one. At the moment we do not think that firms of investors can be certain of what the law means in that particular clause and the FSA's code of market conduct cannot remedy this because at present compliance with the code does not bring certainty where no offence has been committed. I think that is the point which has just been made. We absolutely agree with that and we think that Clause 56 needs more attention. The other point I would just like to support is the point made earlier about guidance, and really that comes back perhaps to my moving away from the detailed legislation. I do think that it is important for the industry to be able to get guidance from the FSA

rather than the FSA always relying on the law. That is the sort of relationship the industry wants.

(*Mr Sylvain*) My Lord Chairman, we are talking about the guidance and the rules, and often the guidance is how to comply with the rules, whereas we also want waivers of the rules themselves. For instance, if we have a rule which says you have to get something in writing from the consumer, people will start to ask, is a fax okay, is an e-mail okay, is a recorded conversation okay? So there is no intention in this case to continue to abide by the specific rule of "in writing" and more guidance is needed as to whether or not the FSA will waive that rule. Then once people have received that, they need to be able to rely on it. We talk about guidance but I think we have to talk about innovation at the same time, because it is innovation that requires guidance and if the UK is going to be successful you will have people asking the FSA in the face of new innovation, new technology, can they waive a given rule given that it is obsolete now. I am sure you have heard in this Committee before that the rule books do need to be re-written from time to time because they do become obsolete. So I see the request for guidance and waivers for rules as an early warning signal that a rule is becoming obsolete and in that case, as firms move towards the new practice, they cannot then find they are disciplined for that. So we want rule waivers in the Bill and we want to be able to rely on them, absent, as Dominic said, of market intent to abuse.

Lord Fraser of Carmyllie

277. Mr Clarke seems to me to have introduced a qualification which is not at present in the Bill but it might be an extremely desirable one to introduce, and I agree with that. As I understand it, you and Ms Hutchinson and other lawyers who have given evidence here, have been arguing that compliance with the guidance on an issue by the FSA should not just simply have a mitigatory effect on a breach of what is Clause 56 at the moment but should lead to the consequence there is no breach whatsoever?

(*Mr Clarke*) With the one caveat, and other people will decide whether that caveat is a fair one or not but I personally do not see any difficulty with it, that if somebody actually intended to abuse the market and used a loophole in the code, to put it simply, I would not have much sympathy with them.

278. That is what I am trying to get at. So if you comply with the guidance that the FSA has put up, and it will be from time to time modified according to market conditions—and as others have indicated that may lag behind what is happening in the market place—if you meet the guidance at any time that will be a complete answer to any allegation of breach of what is Clause 56 at the moment. What you seem to be suggesting is that notwithstanding your compliance with the guidance if the FSA could look into your conduct and discover behind that in this unique circumstance intent on your part, that would be enough to sustain a breach of Clause 56?

(*Mr Clarke*) Yes, I think the current law in Section 47 of the current Act is very similar.

Lord Poole

279. A code we have all lived by and died by for many, many years which has developed extremely effectively is the takeover panel. I wonder whether you would assert what you have just said applies to the takeover code, because my understanding is that even if you have been to the takeover code and got their approval, or got their approval through an appeals procedure, if it turns out afterwards that the steps you were taking were in some way, for example, against the Companies Act, the fact you went to the takeover panel is neither here nor there? I notice you nod. You are quite sure you are not asking for something from the FSA which is not realistic because there are so many other sorts of laws you can fall over that it could not conceivably be the case you could be excused, as it were, by speaking to them first?

(Mr Clarke) The takeover code is not statutory. I will not pretend to be an expert on it but if I remember there is a spirit of the code and a letter of the code, and notwithstanding what the letter of the code says if you are deemed to be in breach of the spirit of the code, a decision that you have not complied with the spirit of the code may be made by the panel. As far as breaches of the Companies Act are concerned, because it is not statutory the takeover panel has no application under the Companies Act and you have to comply with the Companies Act at the same time. The takeover code is actually dealing with a slightly different area. It is concerned with how do you make a bid which is fair to minority shareholders for example and how the procedures are carried out. The Companies Act says very, very little about procedures in relation to takeovers.

Lord Fraser of Carmyllie

280. Can I try and approach it the other way round? The mischief I would be seeking to avoid is where someone who has complied to the letter with the guidance in place from time to time and has no intent to bring about any abuse of the market, nevertheless is regarded by the FSA as having breached Clause 56 without intent and could find himself in breach of that. That would seem to me to be unfair and the modification you have suggested seems to me to be a helpful way, if I may say so, of avoiding that mischief.

(Mr Clarke) I agree it is unfair. Somebody said at one of the earlier evidence sessions that it was necessary to have offences of strict liability to ensure certain sorts of conduct were not carried out and offences of strict liability do exist under the law but they are usually concerned with "You shall not do a particular course of action." In this case the code can say, "You shall not do a particular course of action and if you then carry out that action in breach of the code you are going to be in trouble, you do not have the code to protect you." The situation I am describing is when you are trying to prevent people manipulating the code or manipulating the market, or whatever, and in those circumstances I believe that intent is a necessary element.

Chairman

281. I think this would be a useful time to return to Mr Whittaker. We have this familiar group of issues to do with guidance, principles and intent or lack of it. I think it would be helpful if we could have your response, particularly to what Lord Fraser has been saying, about the interaction between these.

(Lord Archer of Sandwell) My Lord Chairman, if you are concluding this part of the matter, I wonder if I might make one comment?

282. Of course.

(Lord Archer of Sandwell) The House of Lords Select Committee on Delegated Legislation is also considering this subject. I think you will have the advantage of reading our report before we have the advantage of reading yours, but it might just be worth seeing what each other says before we conclude.

283. Thank you very much.

(Mr Whittaker) As I indicated when we last met, we for our part have no difficulty with the idea that guidance which we issue should have a special status in providing comfort to people who act in accordance with it. This would not legitimise conduct which is criminal under other parts of the law, but could be relevant for the purpose of the market abuse provision which we are discussing. We very much want to have a co-operative relationship with the firms we relate to in which firms feel free to come to us for guidance. We regard this as good for compliance, good for the industry. We are not necessarily very enthusiastic about the idea there should be a duty on us to give guidance in a big range of situations. That seems to us to raise the issue of who determines the resource allocation within FSA. Is it the board of the FSA determining where they think the risks most lie, or is it those in the industry who come to us and ask us to give guidance? We know that some overseas regulators find much of their resource is taken up in giving guidance rather than in the areas they would themselves wish to target. One further point before we leave the issue of guidance. We are conscious there is conflict, or potential conflict, between giving guidance to firms on individual transactions and the responsibilities of the senior management of those firms for the management of their businesses. We would not want to encourage a situation in which there was in any particular area of operation the growing up of a dependency culture in which firms felt unable to take action themselves without seeking guidance from the regulator. With that caveat, we are generally supportive of the idea.

284. Do any of the witnesses want to respond to that? How far do you think that takes us?

(Mr Sylvain) My Lord Chairman, on the issue of intent which the FSA seem to want to keep out, as some of the discussion shows here I do not think you can keep it out. In my experience, market abuse and something that is intentional is just an exaggerated form of normal market behaviour. For instance, every day a large City brokers in the United Kingdom will issue research reports on stock and it might be a stock that they own. If they issue a very glowing report about a stock and the price goes up, was there an intent to

[Chairman *Cont]*

abuse the market or is that just everyday business in the financial services world? Similarly, if you take a short position on a stock and the stock goes down, is the fact that the stock went down evidence that you meant to abuse the market? My point is that I do not think you can distinguish very easily behaviours which have the same impact between the one who intended to have a manipulative impact from the one who simply was engaging in normal markets where in markets it is the behaviour of buying and selling which forces prices up and down. So actions all the time in the market will create outcomes which, with 20/20 hindsight, one might say were intended to drive the price up or down but which are actually just normal. That is what happens if you sell a load of stock that you have. The price will go down but it is not your intent. Your intent is to capture as much price as you can for that while you are selling. So the intent is very important in that and I do not see how you can do any better.

(Mr Vipond) My Lord Chairman, I think that is exactly right. The problem is with market abuse and it is in clauses 56 and 57, which you have discussed already, rather than many other clauses, but the intent issue is so critical. Beyond that I think there is an important issue about guidance, that is, the guidance from the FSA, and that is that if guidance is to be sought, then in general the FSA have an obligation to have an open relationship with firms that will allow them to give that guidance on an informal basis, where possible, and formally, where necessary. The danger I think we face at the moment is that people will be reticent about having that open relationship with their regulator precisely because of the growth in emphasis on enforcement on a more legalistic basis.

(Mr Blunden) Just a very quick point on the resource allocation required for guidance. The FSA could take a leaf out of the industry's book. Where we do not have sufficient resources to do something we out-source it and perhaps the FSA could make whoever is requiring the guidance pay for it and make it available to all on the Internet.

Lord Poole

285. May I say that I do feel there is a very considerable difference of opinion between Mr Buxton and Mr Vipond and Miss Hutchinson, which I suggest is there in graphic terms. Mr Vipond has just said no, the legalistic approach would, he felt, be damaging to a good relationship between the regulator and the industry and Miss Hutchinson's plea for certainty seems to be exactly that. Similarly—and I wrote it down—Mr Buxton said he was against formal rules, which seems also to be contrary to the notion of the continuous desire for categorical certainty. I quite understand the position taken by Mr Buxton and Mr Vipond because it sounds very much like the process by which the SIB rules were interpreted and the rule book developed and so on and so forth. So I wonder if I have interpreted it correctly and if Miss Hutchinson could say if she felt that the regime of the SIB principles and developed rule book equally fell into the dangers to which she has tried to alert us today?

(Ms Hutchinson) I think the concern we have is that, given the strict penalties, the severe penalties, there may be for market abuse, people have to be clear, or as clear as they can be, what is and what is not market abuse, but we do live in a moving world and, as Dominic said, you cannot legislate for everything, the market is always going to be ahead of you, but you do need some safe harbours. If there is a code you ought to be all right if you comply with that code, subject to an intent to abuse it. If you ask for guidance and you are given guidance, you ought to be all right if you comply with it and that is the certainty working, that in certain situations you know you are going to be on the right side of the line. We are not trying to make it more legalistic. What we are trying to do—and I am sorry if this is not coming over—is to make it workable and user-friendly for the people in the market so that they know where the line is, and if they do not, they know where they can go to find out.

(Mr Buxton) I hope I did not say I was against all rules. What I said was that the legislation empowers the FSA to make more rules and what I wanted is for more rules actually to be in the legislation on some points. I mentioned particularly clauses 56 and 57. I think they are very important, but let me give you a practical example. Andrew Whittaker has talked about senior executives and their liability. I do not know whether the Committee is aware that all non-executive directors—I am talking about non-executive directors—of financial companies are also completely liable and actually sign a liability document when they become a director of a financial company. I believe that those people need to know what their liability is and I think it needs to be spelt out because otherwise it may be very difficult to get non-executive directors to be non-executive directors of financial companies. So I am not against the rule book but I think I take really exactly the same view as Miss Hutchinson has just taken. We need as much certainty as we can get within the context of a relationship with the FSA that we have talked about on guidance.

Mrs Blackman

286. Just a small point on this issue. Howard Davies has said on record that he favours an informal pre-clearance on many occasions and Andrew Whittaker mentioned that as one of the courses of action they may well take, and I suspect that course of action may well be taken far more frequently than an official request for guidance. What kind of conversations and what kind of culture need to be developed at the FSA to get that relationship built up?

(Mr Vipond) If I were starting I would pay tribute to the old supervisory culture that the Bank of England had, and some of the old SROs, where I think a great deal of what one would hope exists in the future already existed. It is not beside the point that London's success as a financial centre is partly due to the quality of the regulation and I think you will find that international firms particularly have appreciated the way in which they can talk openly and honestly to regulators about complex deals and get guidance. It is something they cannot do in other parts of the world very often. The culture is one which is very much a

[Mrs Blackman Cont]

sharing, not a symbiotic culture but one that shares values, shares aspirations. One of the biggest tasks Howard Davies has in merging nine different regulatory cultures is to sustain that basic ability to work with businesses in the market place. I think that is something we would all strongly endorse. In a sense the debate about market abuse, which, is, I repeat two clauses in the Bill, is a discrete area of special civil offence and we should not allow that to cloud the overall view of the business of enforcement of the FSA.

Chairman

287. Andrew Whittaker, I think we should wrap up this part of the discussion but do you want to have a last word?

(Mr Whittaker) There are two things I would particularly point to in terms of promoting the right relationship between regulator and regulated. I think, first of all, it needs to start at the top and I think it has started at the top. I think there is a clear message going out to staff that a good relationship with the regulated community is important to us in terms of the regulator we want to be. Secondly, from a personal point of view I would say that I think a degree of empowerment is important, that people need to know that in fostering a good relationship and in taking responsibility in giving views to people in the industry the organisation will back them, and I think we also have that as well. So I think those two things are what I would regard as important. I think they are both in place.

Lord Montague of Oxford

288. Mr Buxton, I want to take up one point you made about non-executive directors and the difficulty you might have in securing them. Would they not be protected by insurance, and, therefore, not be so worried?

(Mr Buxton) There is a degree of insurance that can protect them but they are not completely protected. I believe that the protection they have is knowing that they can only be prosecuted by the FSA for actions for which they are responsible, i.e. policies that they have laid down that have resulted in a breach.

(Mr Roe) There is just one point I might make for balance in some of this discussion. I think it is worth bearing in mind when we are talking about intent what the underlying objective of the policy that we set out in the market abuse provisions is. Essentially the new regime is concerned with the effects of behaviour and very central to the Government's policy here is the idea that we must have efficient, well-run markets which can allocate resources effectively and so on. So we are primarily, I think, concerned with market efficiency and it seems to me and to Ministers to be the case that confidence in markets is affected by actions regardless of intentions, and what is important, I think, is for people to act with due care and attention when they are operating in financial markets. I say this not because the Government necessarily disagrees with all of the points that have been made but I think it is worth keeping in mind that particular background.

Chairman

289. I hate to attempt to sum this up because it will immediately cause a whole series of disagreements. But what I am taking from this is that if there is no intent that can be shown and if people do stick to the guidance and if they do take due care and diligence, then they will be reasonably safe. Is that an over-strong statement?

(Mr Whittaker) I am not sure, Chairman.

Lord Fraser of Carmyllie: If you have regard to the FSA's formal guidance and if you also go along and ask them, "What I am about to do, is that okay?", is that not a proper discharge of due care?

Chairman: And there is no intent to do something else?

Lord Fraser of Carmyllie

290. I go to the FSA and I say, "I am going to do this. I do not know whether you would regard this as abuse. I have looked at your guidance. I cannot see that there is any breach. Can you tell me on any formal basis?" I understand that Howard Davies said there is not going to be a formal procedure but if the qualification that is now being suggested is one of paying due care and attention, if I have gone through both those steps it would seem to me that is a very clear indication that I have discharged that duty that is incumbent upon me, is it not?

(Mr Whittaker) As the Bill now stands, if you were to come to us for guidance on a particular transaction and we were to say that we thought that transaction was consistent with the market abuse provisions, then provided you had been open with us in what you said and the situation was as you described it, I think we would be extremely unlikely to take any action in relation to those provisions. There is not currently in the Bill as it stands at the moment anything that says that anyone who has acted with due care and attention can, in the absence of having gone to the regulator, nevertheless regard themselves as protected from action.

Chairman: I think we may have moved a little way forward on this but we will have to look at the record and we ourselves will have to consider this. I would now like to move on to general issues about FSA powers of discipline and enforcement against authorised persons and their staff.

Mr Sheerman

291. I think it moves seriously on to whether the FSA's powers are coherent and are they sufficient. I want to come back to Lord Eatwell's theme which has really run through this, and what Mrs Blackman mentioned, that, on the one hand, we can hear two voices, one saying, "Let us have a good informal relationship with the FSA backed up by known powers and rules." On the other, there is a voice coming quite strongly—and I am not pointing particularly to Andrew Buxton but one or two of you are saying, "Don't specify too closely. We have a good relationship. It is a very dynamic market, and if that dynamic means the rules get out-of-date, then we need

[**Mr Sheerman** *Cont*]

an informal process by which we can clear that." What would worry some of us in terms of this being too flexible is that there are other players in this and we have to remember there are consumers and very often we hear the views of the big players and the wholesales but the consumers also have to know there is a dynamic and that the rules are changing, are becoming more flexible, that there is a smooth and easy relationship between the wholesale market which may outpace consumer knowledge. So in a sense do we think that the FSA's powers here are coherent and are they sufficient? Can I pick on Antony because Antony is the prime suspect. He has a strong view and most of us have had the benefit of his presentation to the conference two or three weeks ago.

(Mr Blunden) I was rather hoping to leave it to the lawyers.

292. You made it a theme in your presentation that you were concerned about not having a rule book, rules that were understood, guarantees of safe harbours and so on.

(Mr Blunden) Yes, certainly. That concerns me greatly. Again, I apologise, my Lord Chairman, I find myself drifting back to certainty but it seems that most things come back to that. The FSA's powers are huge, they are enormous, and I find it troubling that with a great degree of uncertainty as to what market abuse is the FSA has such an unmitigated amount of powers. I think particularly with regard to individuals, when the FSA is pursuing individuals, there is again such a discrepancy of resources that I welcome Lucy Hutchinson's thought of an independent enforcement committee and the ability for that independent committee to give Legal Aid to individuals. Firms can go one on one against the FSA without too much of a problem but when you are being prosecuted by the FSA you are looking at bills of hundreds of thousands of pounds and very few individuals, even in the financial services sector, can afford that sort of money.

293. The FSA did point out that out of 1,850 staff there are only 110 engaged in enforcement against authorised persons. In a sense are you not getting your fears for this enormous power of the FSA, as you describe it, out of balance? The voice I hear from the other side of the room is "go on, we understand that people want a seamless transition to build on a culture that already exists", okay nine regulatory authorities coming under one, but the aim is to have a seamless transition where one does not disturb a culture that is working very well anyway. Are you not getting these fears out of proportion?

(Mr Blunden) If that bit of the existing culture that is working well, and I acknowledge that part of it does work well, if that was transferred to the FSA and enlarged then it would certainly allay some of our fears, although not all of them. I am aware that a number of times I have had a number of meetings with the FSA in various bodies and Howard Davies and a number of his staff have all said "do not worry, it will be fine". I would love to believe that, and I am sure they genuinely mean it and they want it to be fine, the problem is we cannot have a system that is going to exist for hopefully a considerable number of years relying on the initial chairman, the initial managing

director of enforcement, who I am sure are dedicated to ensuring that it will be fine but five years down the road we do not know who this vast amount of power will be handed to and that does concern me.

(Lord Archer of Sandwell) My Lord Chairman, I think everyone is in favour of an informal relationship where people can talk and get advice. As I said earlier, there are a number of authorities which operate in this way. If I might suggest what I think is probably a good example, the Occupational Pensions Regulatory Authority tries to work in this way. But at the end of the line if there has to be enforcement action then they are in the business of quasi-judicial decisions. I think they rather regard it almost as a failure on their part if it gets that far but if it gets that far that cannot be a reason for slipshod procedures and I think there would be some impact probably of Article 6 on this if we did have slipshod procedures. If I might just suggest one or two things that occurred to the Council on Tribunals on this. First of all, Chinese walls are quite important in this context. Whether they should be Chinese walls or whether they should be written into the Bill, I do not think I would want to be dogmatic. But, for example, if anything was said by someone who was going to be the potential recipient of disciplinary procedure to the staff at an earlier stage they should be able to do that without feeling that it might be disclosed to the enforcement committee at a later stage. There ought to be some sort of barrier between what is said to the staff and what the enforcement committee is told otherwise you will not get people being frank and you will not get them asking for advice. The second thing is that there ought to be an opportunity, we believe, to present your case orally at least to the enforcement committee. It should not be a question of passing judgment on you without you having had an opportunity orally to argue your case. I would support strongly what Ms Hutchinson said about the independence of the enforcement committee. I would want to argue two things about that. The first is that they should not be in any sense employees of the FSA. We would recommend that the chairman should be someone like a High Court judge, or a retired High Court judge if the Lord Chancellor objected to seconding a judge, but someone of that status who would operate as chairman and who would not be in any sense under the control of the committee. In relation to the other members, the representatives of public interest, I think we would want to argue—it is not spelt out in the Bill, it may be intended—that they should have votes together with the chairman so that they might actually outvote the chairman if that arose. If there is a disagreement it should be made known to those concerned. When there is a question, as I think is suggested in the paper, of the chairman issuing a warning we believe that the other members should not be associated with that. If they are then they should be different members who actually hear the complaint. There are a number of these matters. Perhaps it would be quicker if we put in a document about it. There are a number of matters of this kind which we would regard as essential if the FSA is going to make binding decisions on people.

Chairman

294. There are two models that are emerging here as I understand it. One is where the enforcement committee is a body which takes a decision and it comes to a judgment and then the tribunal can go through the whole process if anyone is not happy with it. There is another model which was mentioned which is that the enforcement committee, in a sense, is merely a filtering agent which says whether or not a case should proceed. Meanwhile people try to agree on the outcome and it is only if they fail to agree that the enforcement committee should give some indication of how it feels but basically it then goes to the tribunal.

(Lord Archer of Sandwell) Yes.

295. These are two models which I interpret are being discussed here. Your comments, I take it, are related to the first model which is where the enforcement committee has the power to actually come to a decision. Therefore you want to build in a series of measures to ensure degrees of independence between the different parts of the process and also to ensure that the individuals involved are independent.

(Lord Archer of Sandwell) Yes, thank you, my Lord Chairman, that is so. If that were the pattern then it would be in rather a Pickwickian sense of the word that the tribunal would be a tribunal of first instance. It would be a tribunal of appeal. I think probably what was meant by saying that it was a tribunal of first instance was that it could rehear the case and the Lord Chancellor would not make regulations excluding it from hearing particular evidence. If that was all that was meant then there is no difficulty.

296. Do you have a view between those two models as to which direction you would prefer to see this moving; one is that the enforcement committee is the body that comes to a decision and then you have the tribunal; or is it that the enforcement committee sends the case forward to the next stage which is the tribunal? Maybe that is an unfair question.

(Lord Archer of Sandwell) I cannot be certain it is the view of the Council but my own view is the second one, I think, which was why I was pleased to see what the Economic Secretary had said.

297. It has been dashed from our lips!

(Lord Archer of Sandwell) Like all of us who have been Ministers someone later construes what we said as to what we ought to have said!

Lord Poole

298. Can I just pick that up. So you think there would be some merit in a system that took through the enforcement committee the parties to whatever it is that has taken place in the hope that there would be some sort of agreement, settlement, fines, whatever might be the outcome, and only if that failed then taking it to the tribunal, as it were, for the case to be more formally heard?

(Lord Archer of Sandwell) Yes, that would be the model that I had in my mind. I do not know which building they will operate in but if the two things could happen on different floors that would be an advantage.

Chairman: Can I ask what others think about these two models?

Mr Beard

299. If you take the second model where the FSA becomes a sort of Crown Prosecution Service and the tribunal is the one where the decision is made, is that not going to be a very cumbersome procedure? One can imagine a large number of things that are really quite minor in nature ending up going to the tribunal which really ought to have been settled by the FSA if you took the original interpretation of it as being a regulator, which takes these decisions within itself and then uses the tribunal as an appeal court. It does seem to me that before very long the whole thing will become gridlocked with cases pending, waiting, and all the plea bargaining that is going on to try and avoid it going to the tribunal and little will come out and the result could very well be that which is not very well represented around this discussion, that the public at large lose confidence in it.

(Lord Archer of Sandwell) I do see that argument and I think it is quite an important one. I would envisage, and I rather thought a number of people in the Committee and a number of witnesses were envisaging, that the plea bargaining would be part of the discussion, it would not entail a decision by the enforcement committee. I can see in a particular case where not very much is at stake and you cannot get agreement that it would be better if you could have a quick sharp decision. Possibly you could have a two tier system.

Chairman

300. Can I ask the other witnesses how they feel about these two models?

(Mr Sylvain) I think from the Association of Unit Trusts and Investment Funds we would prefer the model where most problems are resolved at enforcement committee level, very little would go to the tribunals. Most of the issues that are faced by practitioners of the FSA are minor issues, we are not talking about BCCI and Barings every day, we are mostly talking about was a reconciliation done on time. An enforcement committee that is independent, structured the way Lord Archer described it, with an independent chairman, with members who are public interest members and practitioners who could hear in a sensible, relaxed environment in some sense, not as formal as a tribunal, the points being made by the FSA, the points being made by the accused, in this case the firm, and come to a decision on whether it recommended going forward. I would imagine it would develop guidance over time for the FSA on what should be brought forward and what should not. Over time the staff of the FSA will learn what will never get by the enforcement committee, it is too minor, and others obviously will have to be addressed by that committee because they are very serious. In that sense, as somebody mentioned before, case law will develop and it will all be done within this enforcement committee.

[Chairman Cont]

301. This is model one.

(*Mr Sylvain*) The tribunal is really very far down the road, very expensive to go through and probably does not meet the efficiency, quick resolution, that both consumers need to see and that the firms themselves want.

(*Mr Turner*) My Lord Chairman, could I just comment. I favour, and I am sure the Institute favours, model one in that it looks pretty like the system that was used and is used at the FSA where most of our members are. I saw that system for four or five years working fairly and efficiently and it is certainly one that I think the Committee should pay much attention to.

(*Mr Vipond*) I would not be surprised if we too did not favour model one because frankly I do not think model two is workable. Something like 95 per cent of the cases currently concerned in bodies such as the SFA and IMRO are settled without reference to a tribunal. The sheer volume of these cases requires a quicker, more efficient, more informal means of dealing with them. Also I think it is important to remember that we are not talking about criminal cases, we are not talking about civil cases, we are talking about breaches of rules established by the FSA and these are not crimes that are heinous, they are large exposure breaches and that sort of thing. I think it is very important that they can be dealt with. The problem comes with the enforcement committee which in many ways is not spelt out in the Bill very much at all because the enforcement committee has really got to be an adjudicator, it has got to be something that can solve problems, but it has also got to be something that in the last instance can become a formal prosecutor and take things to the next stage. I think it is going to be very difficult to specify precisely how an enforcement committee can work and in many ways it is very difficult to put it down into primary legislation.

302. But you would like to see it in the Bill?

(*Mr Vipond*) Indeed. We would like to see it clear in the Bill that it has this role, as it were, of preventing things going to the tribunal when they can reasonably be settled before.

Lord Poole

303. So you do not think you need the independent chairman that Lord Archer was suggesting?

(*Mr Vipond*) I think if you set it up in the way Lord Archer started to set it up, it looks by the time you have finished awfully like a tribunal. It looks like a formal tribunal with full legal powers and capability and very impressive, but if you have that then you do not need what he went on to describe as the appeal tribunal because you have got a tribunal. What you need to make sure is that the processes internal to the FSA are fair and reasonable and give people a chance to make their case but they can always appeal to a tribunal.

304. I am not worried at any rate about most companies in the business of financial services holding their own against the FSA. It is very expensive, hugely time-consuming and can be very scary but that is fine.

The people I worry about are the individuals in a firm who find that actually the management and the FSA have done a deal which says, "Sorry, guv, you caught us out. We did not know the procedure properly. Can we have a fine." He has very little say in that. How are you going to protect the rights of these employees, to whom I do not think necessarily always enough attention is paid?

(*Mr Vipond*) I think I agree with that and there are two issues, one to do with the enforcement committee and one to do with costs. On the enforcement committee, it is important that individuals have the capacity to appear before it, state their case and state it to the enforcement committee without the FSA, as it were, prejudging it. There must come a point at which the enforcement committee looks again and looks cleanly at the position the individual is in, and that I think has not been spelt out adequately yet. The second point is cost and I think it is very important the distinction you make between firms who have got the money and individuals who, as Antony Blunden said earlier, by and large have not, and it is important, therefore, on grounds of natural justice and fairness that a process is found whereby individuals can be supported to the extent that that is reasonably necessary for them to defend themselves.

Mr Beard

305. Going back to what Ms Hutchinson said earlier in her introductory remarks, that one of the objections to the arrangements was that it was going to be judge, jury and prosecutor all within its own walls: is that not true of any regulator we have? Why is this one different in that respect? Is it not also true of the voluntary organisation that it is taking over from, so why is it especially different in this respect?

(*Ms Hutchinson*) If others do have it that does not make it ideal.

306. No, but the consequence of following your argument is that you get into these convoluted procedures that may be much more theoretically just but will be much more cumbersome, and surely what one is looking for is some compromise between the two?

(*Ms Hutchinson*) That was really why we suggested the second alternative, because our concern is that if the FSA is the prosecutor, judge and jury, we do not think that is the right approach because if anyone wants to take it further they start off on the back foot. They have already been, as it were, found guilty. If you are going to have them doing that, then you should not have that. You should have the adjudication made by a separate person and it comes back to Lord Archer's point about having the enforcement committee as an independent body, and if it is going to make an adjudication it is going to have to look at the evidence. You are going to have to have a proper full oral hearing. You may have individuals who cannot afford to be represented. They may have a right to be represented but that is not much good if they cannot afford it, and the FSA, of course, will no doubt have their in-house legal advisers or whatever, so you do not actually have a level playing-field there,

[Mr Beard *Cont*]

and if the appeal is to a tribunal where it is by way of a re-hearing, you seem to be committing yourselves to two full hearings, and given that the approach, we think, is to have a market that acts quickly and efficiently, there is co-operation, there is a good culture, what we were suggesting was that the enforcement committee would act as a filter, could possibly put forward some type of mediation service. You would be able to have settlements without admitting liability. You would have these other ways of resolving matters, and if you could follow those routes then I would not expect the breaches which have been described as administrative to find their way up to the tribunal.

Chairman

307. Do you hope that the 95 per cent. or whatever it is, of cases that are presently resolved would nevertheless be resolved within the first stage of your proposals?

(Ms Hutchinson) That is right, but I think it is important, if you are going to achieve that, that, if you are a defendant, you have to be able to settle on the basis that you are not admitting liability.

Mr Beard

308. But is not a lot of the anxiety that is being expressed arising from the fact that you as practitioners, whether legal or financial, have become used to a voluntary organisation where you knew one another and it was very much more informal and now you are seeing the thing move to a proposed statutory base with powers which I think to an extent there is a tendency to exaggerate for the FSA, and this is just the anxiety of seeing a new, more distant, more formal procedure replacing a voluntary one?

(Mr Sylvain) My Lord Chairman, I think that is an excellent point that relates to the one made earlier. It all depends who is running the organisation and if we had a Ralph Nader type running the FSA or a Rudolph Giuliani, how would we know that we are not at zero tolerance and that is having moved too far? So I think the powers are very strong and unless they are balanced by a body that can actually act as a brake on what might be overbearing regulation, then I fail to see how the individual is going to be protected in that situation.

Lord Fraser of Carmyllie: If you come to the position that Part VI of this Bill cannot properly have as its heading "Civil Fines for Market Abuse" and what is in procedure there is essentially criminal in nature, if we are to meet our obligations under the European Convention on Human Rights, are we not bound to have a tribunal which allows all the evidence to be heard before it and is not qualified, as the appeal tribunal is, in the restriction that is imposed on it as to the type of evidence that can be heard before it?

Chairman: That has been changed, I think. The Treasury responded to that in the Progress Report.

Lord Fraser of Carmyllie: But we are still going to have an independent tribunal.

Lord Eatwell

309. I am still puzzled about the extent of the powers or activities of the enforcement committee which is envisaged. Some reference has been made to the current structure of enforcement of the SFA, and I declare an interest as a member of the SFA's enforcement committee, and in that operation the vast majority of problems are dealt with by the committee hearing reports from its staff and determining a penalty which is then negotiated with the person who is the defendant. Those negotiations usually reach a settlement and a very small number do not reach a settlement and go on to a tribunal. Some of the penalties imposed are very severe. Sometimes, for example, people are expelled from the industry and they put their hands up and say, "It's a fair cop." The notion of all those sorts of things going on to a tribunal would completely gum up the system.

(Mr Clarke) My Lord Chairman, I think there may have been some misunderstanding. The question keeps getting mixed up between model one and model two. The model we were proposing is exactly the same as the industry is requesting, which is that the committee can, by agreement, reach a settlement for disciplinary action to be taken against somebody. Our difficulty is that that would be a very informal procedure and would be internal to the FSA. If the committee is unable to reach agreement with the defendant, which is probably more likely in the case of an individual who has more to lose than a commercial offender, then the Bill proposes that the committee then makes a formal decision of guilt and imposes a fine.

Chairman

310. Then it goes to the tribunal?

(Mr Clarke) Then it goes on to the tribunal. So the defendant goes to the tribunal with a decision against him having already been made. At that stage he has not been able to present all his evidence; he has not heard all the evidence against him. It seems to us that if you are going to make a formal determination of guilt then you have to go through really a tribunal system, which is that you have to have all the evidence at the first stage. That is not practical. Our suggestion, therefore, is that you can have the informal procedure but if you cannot reach agreement you then proceed to the tribunal without a formal hearing of guilt so that the defendant does not start what I might call the fair process having a formal decision against him already having been made.

Chairman: The key difference between these two models, after all of the negotiations and discussions have gone on, is whether or not the enforcement committee then gives a judgment before it goes on to the next stage; or whether it simply says "we cannot reach agreement, let us move it on to the next stage".

Mr Beard

311. Why should the evidence not be there in the first stage?

(Ms Hutchinson) It could take quite a long time. This is why we were suggesting that you do not have

[Mr Beard *Cont]*

all the evidence at the first stage, at the initial enforcement committee stage, when you try and reach a settlement. The enforcement committee will be able to say to the FSA "you have not presented a case that needs answering" and could filter it out, so the FSA would have to put a certain amount of evidence on the table. You would not go through the full hearing calling witnesses and seeing all the evidence.

(Lord Archer of Sandwell) My Lord Chairman, I was horrified by what I thought was the implication of the question by Lord Eatwell. What he seems to be suggesting is that you have a committee which receives a report from somewhere and then decides that there has been an infringement, it then decides what is the penalty and then it says to the person concerned "are you happy with this" and if he says "no", they say "all right, we will now start to consider it but we will not consider it properly, we will consider half the evidence and somebody else can do the rest". My Lord Chairman, nobody has ever devised a tribunal which operates like that since the Spanish Inquisition.

Lord Poole: This is the most beautifully expressed view of Lord Eatwell's activities!

Chairman: I am sure that other members of Lord Eatwell's committee would be very quick to explain that it does not quite work like that!

Lord Poole

312. So far I am glad to say that I have not found myself in front of Lord Eatwell but the more I listen the more worried I become! I think there is a concern that on the other hand a lot of evidence has been given to us, and we are here talking about the wholesale rather than the retail, that what is wanted is something that is reasonably quick and reasonably dirty but that also will catch and find a way of looking after the hard cases and in particular the individual. It does seem to me this sort of rough justice tends not to be quite as rough as it sounds. I would suggest that you might be prepared to accept it given what you were saying earlier about the need for an independent chairman, for example. Do you feel that would help in preserving what Lord Eatwell is saying works rather well but adding in some protection for the individuals concerned?

(Lord Archer of Sandwell) I think we are discussing the second model rather than the first model now. I was rather minded to say that I would favour the second model. What I do not think we can do is to muddle the two. If it is the second model then it goes on to the tribunal without a finding against the respondent and I do not see anything wrong in that. If it is the first model and there is going to be a finding against the respondent then we do need to have the safeguards that we have been discussing.

Chairman

313. I think this is probably the moment to give David and Andrew a say, if they so wish. Again, you do not have to respond.

(Mr Roe) I am not sure whether I am allowed to ask a question.

314. By all means.

(Mr Roe) I am interested in what Lord Archer said about what the nature of the difference is between these two models in the sense that they are at the point where a decision is taken and the case will go forward to the tribunal and in one case it is a finding and in the other case it is something else. I would be grateful if he could explain precisely what the something else is on the second model. I would like to understand that a bit better.

(Lord Archer of Sandwell) If I may say, something turns here on how the Treasury sees it. The something else could be either of two things. It could be a decision to prosecute, and that can very properly be taken by a committee without hearing anybody: "we think there is enough *prima facie* evidence for the case to go forward". Or it could be a decision to say "we are not prepared to settle for the offer which the respondent has made", and that again happens every day and that is perfectly sensible. What it must not be is a finding against him I would have thought.

(Ms Hutchinson) I think what we were suggesting was that there would not be any findings at all by the committee apart from no case to answer or in giving its blessing to a settlement. If no settlement were reached, the SFA would have to decide if it wanted to prosecute it would then have to, as it were, bring proceedings in the tribunal but it would know that it would have to make its case out.

Lord Eatwell

315. I do not understand that at all. Surely what happens is that the committee has the person they feel has done something or other and they say "Look, we think you have breached principle one of the FSA principles and that means you are out and that is what we believe" and the person says either "I accept that" or "I do not accept that". Without the committee actually making a finding how do you start making a settlement? How do you start having a discussion?

(Lord Archer of Sandwell) In a *prima facie* case you can very properly say "we think there is a case to answer here, do you want to answer it or do you want to settle?"

Lord Poole

316. Which is really what you are doing. I think we are jumping around the language a bit.

(Mr Whittaker) I am conscious that this discussion has revealed that we are all finding it difficult to accommodate the implications of there being a first instance tribunal. Certainly we have found that has been something that we have needed to factor in at a fairly late stage in our decision making processes about what sort of procedure we would like to adopt. It seems on the one hand that we want, given there is to be a first instance tribunal, to avoid duplicating the role of that first instance tribunal by judicialising the decision that we might be asked to take or the process that we might be asked to go through. Therefore, we and the Committee are all left with trying to square a very awkward circle which is trying to work out, given that people who want the fullest possible hearing of

[Lord Poole Cont]

the issues concerned will have the opportunity to go to the tribunal, whether there is anything that is capable of dealing with the vast majority of cases that may not need anything quite so elaborate on a less ambitious basis which provides people with confidence that their decisions have been dealt with fairly but nevertheless with more speed than they might get with the tribunal.

Lord Fraser of Carmyllie: Do you propose to distinguish between circumstances where there is agreement on the facts but not on the penalty? Suppose I put my hands up and accept my abuse of the market is obvious but to be disqualified for life is too much for me.

Lord Poole: Do not forget the case which is the firm saying that about somebody who has not been asked to speak.

Lord Fraser of Carmyllie

317. I am only concerned about this draconian penalty. Do I go straight to the tribunal?

(Mr Whittaker) I am not sure that this is the right forum to try and answer a question like that which has lots of sub-questions built into it.

Lord Fraser of Carmyllie: I would ask you to consider it.

Chairman

318. Before wrapping up this part, can I raise the question of costs which came up in the earlier discussion? This is something which I have been thinking about and I am not at all clear about the extent to which it is sensible that either party should be able to claim costs back from the other. It has always struck me that this becomes a mechanism for causing people to hire yet more and more expensive help and to press the process on and on. Is there any case for saying no costs could be claimed against the other party? Each party simply has to accept its own costs. This then builds in a certain amount of self-regulation about how far and at what expense they press their case on? I keep hearing lots of stories about people who are worried or frightened of taking their case on because they are meanwhile acquiring great liability in terms of the costs of the FSA who they think have very deep pockets.

(Ms Hutchinson) I think there are a number of tribunals where there is not a power to award costs but the current proposals envisage that in a fine there will be two elements. There will be the penalty, the punitive element, and also the costs elements, and we do not think that is right. We think if there is a power to award costs it should be even-handed, so that the FSA might be, as it were, on the wrong end of the costs order as well as the defendant.

(Lord Archer of Sandwell) The Council on Tribunals certainly have the same anxieties as you have, my Lord Chairman. They think that it may deter people from pursuing their remedies. There are a number of different patterns. Most tribunals do not award costs. Some do and I think, if I remember, the present Financial Services Tribunal award costs where someone has been acting "vexatiously, unreasonably or frivolously" and that seems to me a possibility.

319. Perfectly reasonable.

(Mr Sylvain) My Lord Chairman, we are not always talking about firms, as Lord Poole mentioned. We are often talking about individuals and the deep pockets of the FSA as against the individual I do not think represent any situation where fairness and natural justice have taken place if you cannot get your costs back. If you are defending yourself, as Lord Fraser said, for your livelihood and your life, I do not see how that can go forward. So the enforcement committee or the tribunal should be able to award costs against the FSA, but at the same time you could go the other way, of course.

320. So you would prefer the even-handed approach whereby the costs should be separated out and either party can claim against the other depending on the outcome of the case?

(Mr Sylvain) Yes.

Mr Loughton

321. But if that were the case, on the deep pockets of the FSA, those deep pockets will not be as deep if you do not let them have the fine income, as was suggested earlier. So how are you going to gel with that? The implication is that the costs will fall with the fees of the members subscribing to the FSA. Presumably it will not be terribly welcome?

(Miss Hutchinson) We feel it is inherently wrong for the fines to be a source of funding for the FSA because that is bound to lead to people deciding how much they need to fine by comparing it to the budget, as it were.

322. But are they not required to publish their basis for that? To play devil's advocate, Howard Davies would say that, although nearly 70 per cent. is variable income, they are going to set a norm of a budget for a year and that will be the benchmark against which they are fining too much or not. So to take his view, he is looking at it quite closely as to what is a fair amount to fine, and I fully admit that on the face of it I do not like in principle the fines going because it is an incentive to fine if the fee income has gone down because market conditions suggest it has gone down whereas people have gone out of business.

(Miss Hutchinson) It means if you are being an effective FSA in providing all the right guidance and people are not doing anything wrong, you will not have any money.

Chairman

323. Could I press this particular case because as I said last week I was slightly astonished at this suggestion that the industry should volunteer to give money to the Treasury. I have not come across this in many years in the Treasury. It seems to me it should not be beyond the bounds of possibility to design something which avoids the apparent incentive to levy fines in order to cover costs, either by returning the money in its gross form back to the industry in the form of a discount on their fees or by allowing some modest offset of the enforcement cost against it. I find it difficult to believe there is not a way of designing it

30 March 1999]

Mr Andrew Buxton, Mr Peter Vipond, Mr Marc Sylvain,
Lord Archer of Sandwell, QC, Ms Lucy Hutchinson,
Mr Dominic Clarke, Mr Antony Blunden and Mr Geoffrey Turner

[Continued

[Chairman Cont]

such that you can return the money to the people who paid it in the first place as a discount, and which quite clearly avoids the apparent incentive to impose a fine rather than another form of discipline where there is a choice. The extreme conclusion of having the money come to the Treasury surprises me.

(Mr Sylvain) My Lord Chairman, I think we have heard that, as you say, in the proposals that have been put forward by Howard Davies it will be separately accounted for and be discounted. That actually sounds like something you can control and you can do, so that sounds sensible from the point of view of a practitioner.

Mr Loughton

324. But does that not encourage a culture of one firm ratting on another to keep the fees down?
(Mr Sylvain) I hope not.
(Mr Buxton) My Lord Chairman, we would vote in favour of the fines going back to the FSA.

Chairman

325. To the industry?
(Mr Buxton) Then being accountable in the way that has been suggested.
Lord Montague of Oxford: My Lord Chairman, they do not necessarily have to go back to the industry. Perhaps these fines could be considered for consumer education.
Lord Eatwell: All the activities of the FSA have to be funded out of its fees anyhow, so you are having some form of reduction of fees.

Lord Poole

326. I thought it was very interesting that the view over there was as it was.
(Mr Clarke) My Lord Chairman, it would be ideal if you were right and there was a system for making sure that fines were not used as an incentive to the FSA, but I think you would have to add on another independent layer to make sure that it was not impliedly motivating the FSA. Once upon a time, I understand, back in the Middle Ages judges got a percentage of fines they levied but eventually that was thought not a good idea.

Chairman

327. I understand that. I am very familiar with the arguments. I wrestled with them a lot in the Treasury, particularly the question of whether the police authority or whatever should have any access to the fines that were levied, which is why I am taking an interest in this. But I would have thought it would be possible to design something whereby the money went to the industry in a form which did not touch the FSA's pockets in any way. If it did not affect the amount they actually spent, then it would not affect the decision that they took, other than if they suddenly set themselves an objective to maximise the discount going back to the industry.

(Ms Hutchinson) The point may be dealt with to some extent because the body that makes the adjudication, which imposes the fine, I suppose, is the independent tribunal and not a part of the FSA.
(Mr Clarke) It does in a way get back to it, that because of the conflict of interest I think it is actually something the industry does not want. It does want a quicker and better procedure at the first stage and that should be seen to be fair. The other thing one would hope is that the junior members of the staff of the FSA would always act perfectly reasonably, but if a prosecutor has to spend a great deal of money developing a case which could be recovered if there was a decision, it can be, I suspect, in cases of perhaps the less strong-minded prosecutor a strong incentive not to admit halfway through, "I have made a mistake. This person has not acted unreasonably and if you pursue it you can actually recover your costs."
Mr Beard: But there is a requirement for guidelines on fines to be set out and consulted on beforehand. You cannot just decide in the middle of a case what your new principles of fining are. You would have to stick to the guidelines which have been published.

Lord Poole

328. Furthermore, this is a system which has been running for rather a long time in various institutions around the City. Would you like to produce a couple of cases where you are utterly certain that the amount of the fines and the way the thing was handled and generally conducted clearly indicated that the fact that the SRO would keep the fine really influenced the outcome of how that was conducted?
(Mr Clarke) I cannot, but I still believe in this principle and, therefore, the procedures——

329. All of us who have been on the other side of this thing, curiously enough, and some practitioners over there, may say it is possible to envisage this vision but it seems to me it is fair to ask whether you are not envisaging something to do with angels on the tops of pins?
(Mr Clarke) I hope not.

Chairman

330. If I could take the Chairman's privilege, I would like to move on to the question of statutory immunity, which I think was raised by one or two people. Can I put the other side of this, as I see it. I hear a lot about the desire not to have over-regulation. We do not want people to be very bureaucratic and heavy-handed about this. If there were not statutory immunity would that not turn the FSA into a very different sort of body that had to be really immensely concerned about everything that it did? Every time a firm went under and somebody lost any money—and occasionally that is going to happen—we would find they were being sued by the investors. In order to avoid that, you have to pursue a policy of saying no firm can ever go under and

[Chairman Cont]

the whole process becomes enormously cautious. Would not that on its own be a very strong motivating force towards a very heavily regulated business and, therefore, is not the statutory immunity in the Bill a safeguard against excessive regulation?

(Mr Turner) Could I say that why we have statutory immunity in the current system, the self-regulatory system that is fading away, is because way back in 1985 nobody would agree to play, if I can call it that. Practitioners would not take part without the assurance of immunity from discharging their role on SRO boards and committees. What I simply do not know is in moving this system to a statutory system whether that force still applies. Certainly the community believed implicitly a decade ago that without it regulation would not work.

(Mr Buxton) We believe that the FSA should have immunity. I think it is necessary. The other side of that is that we do not believe that the complaints procedures set up in Schedule 1.7 are sufficient. We think they should be more independent and we think they should be more transparent as a result of the complaints.

331. So you see these two things going together. You see statutory immunity requiring that you have a strong and independent complaints system.

(Mr Buxton) Yes, absolutely.

(Mr Sylvain) This is all of a piece, is it not? If there is strong accountability for the FSA, if there is a complaints procedure, if there is a tribunal then, as you say, there are probably enough safeguards that the freedom that immunity might give an over-zealous regulator can actually be checked. I think that is what has to be in place.

(Ms Hutchinson) I think our concern started really because granting statutory immunity may be in breach of the European Convention in a case that the European Court heard last year. Obviously that would be a problem.

332. That would be a problem.

(Ms Hutchinson) We cannot have that, can we? If there is no statutory immunity then is the FSA really going to be on the receiving end of a large number of claims? For a claim to succeed a plaintiff or claimant, as we will have to call them in a few weeks' time, will have to show that the FSA owed it a duty of care in a particular way. If you look at the case law of people who have tried to sue the police and other authorities they probably would not get very far. It may be that if the Convention is a problem and there can be no immunity then it will not be too much of a problem for the FSA anyway. There may be examples of cases where the FSA should be liable, for example if it acts in breach of confidence or there is some act by a member of staff when they have intervened in someone's business or exercising their powers of inspection and have caused some damage there, there should be a claim then.

333. But what about the suggestion that this should be seen alongside a strong complaints procedure too?

(Ms Hutchinson) I think that is a very good idea, yes.

Mr Loughton

334. How would that work in practice? How would that be accountable? Would it come out as a subsidiary to the annual report in terms of complaints investigated and successfully taken up or whatever? It seems slightly against the trend to me where at the moment there is pressure on the police to be far more accountable and for disciplinary action against them to be much more easily taken by members of the public aggrieved by measures they have taken. Putting it the other way, the point I always make is that it will become a haven for duff compliance officers who cannot do their job because they would get prosecuted anywhere else in the City but they can do the job in the FSA with immunity from prosecution, just to take it to its extreme. I am not particularly concerned about the malicious possibilities of somebody acting with immunity for the FSA, and I think Howard Davies reassured us that there are a number of procedures in hand to do that, it is more those of incompetence and various actions taken by the FSA leading to the whole industry being prejudiced in the eyes of its competition.

(Ms Hutchinson) Dealing with the malicious point, that would not be covered by statutory immunity on the current drafting. On the other one, I have not given a huge amount of thought to the complaints procedure but having heard what Andrew Buxton has said I can quite understand that you are going to need a strong complaints procedure if you are not going to have the ability to bring civil proceedings.

(Mr Vipond) The key feature we would see is that it is a continuing and independent body that does produce its annual report. At the moment, as drafted in Schedule 1 of Part 7, it is very much an underdeveloped and un-thought through complaints procedure. It is something that will happen on a case by case basis. Given the power that the FSA has, given the need for accountability, that is simply not adequate, you need something much more robust, particularly if it has statutory immunity. The FSA can come into your offices, it can trash them, it can go around and do a full investigation and they can walk away and come back two days later and say "sorry, we got it wrong, we came to the wrong offices". There has got to be some redress.

Chairman

335. Thank you very much. I think that more or less gets us to the end of our agenda. I would like to offer David Roe and Andrew Whittaker the chance to make any remarks. If they say something particularly controversial we may come back. Do you have anything to say by way of concluding remarks?

(Mr Whittaker) Just on the point of statutory immunity. We have made a number of points about this in the past and the way that it affects us in practice. One point we have not made up until now is to report to the Committee on the extent of statutory immunity available elsewhere in the world.

[Chairman *Cont*]

We understand that the Basle Core Principles on how they relate and operate include a statement that there should be "a suitable legal framework for banking supervision... including... legal protection for supervisors". They expressly refer to "protection ... from personal and institutional liability for supervisory actions taken in good faith in the course of performing supervisory duties..." In accordance with that principle legal protection for the banking supervisors is available in Australia, Canada, Germany, India, Ireland, Malaysia, New Zealand, Philippines, Singapore, South Africa, Sweden, Switzerland, the UK and the US. Thank you.

Lord Poole

336. Do you have anything to say about the complaints procedure because that was a very interesting point?

(Mr Whittaker) It is an entirely fair point. Certainly if the volume of complaints were such as to justify it we would need to have an ongoing continuing complaints arrangement.

337. Does that satisfy you over there?

(Mr Vipond) I think there will be that volume of complaints so there ought to be consequences.

Chairman

338. I think that is something we can return to. David Roe?

(Mr Roe) I was going to make the same point on statutory immunity but I did not have quite such an impressive list as the one that Andrew has provided to you. I do think that it is very important not to under-estimate the importance of statutory immunity and the fact that it is rooted in other jurisdictions and in previous arrangements we have here. On the complaints arrangements, yes, I think this is a very interesting area which I am sure we would welcome the Committee's thoughts on.

Chairman: Thank you very much. David, one of the interesting things is trying to judge your language, particularly the words you use as to whether these are possibilities which may be open or whether they are possibilities which may be closed. Thank you all very much for coming, I have certainly found it very interesting and illuminating. You have given us a lot of evidence which we will do our best with. We have a very tight timetable, as you know, so we are going to have to get down quite soon to the whole question of taking a view about these things. Thank you all very much.

Printed in the UK by The Stationery Office Limited
4/99   422145   78344

Published by The Stationery Office Limited
and available from:

The Publications Centre
(Mail, telephone and fax orders only)
PO Box 276, London SW8 5DT
General enquiries *Lo-call* 0345 58 54 63
Order through the Parliamentary Hotline *Lo-call* 0345 02 34 74
Fax orders 0171 873 8200

The Stationery Office Bookshops
123 Kingsway, London WC2B 6PQ
0171 242 6393 Fax 0171 242 6394
68-69 Bull Street, Birmingham B4 6AD
0121 236 9696 Fax 0121 236 9699
33 Wine Street, Bristol BS1 2BQ
0117 926 4306 Fax 01179 294515
9-21 Princess Street, Manchester M60 8AS
0161 834 7201 Fax 0161 833 0634
16 Arthur Street, Belfast BT1 4GD
0123 223 8451 Fax 0123 223 5401
The Stationery Office Oriel Bookshop
18-19 High Street, Cardiff CF1 2BZ
01222 395548 Fax 01222 384347
71 Lothian Road, Edinburgh EH3 9AZ
0131 228 4181 Fax 0131 622 7017

The Parliamentary Bookshop
12 Bridge Street, Parliament Square,
London SW1A 2JX
Telephone orders 0171 219 3890
General enquiries 0171 219 3890
Fax orders 0171 219 3866

Accredited Agents
(see Yellow Pages)

and through good booksellers

ISBN 0-10-433099-6

9 780104 330999

HOUSE OF LORDS
HOUSE OF COMMONS

SESSION 1998–99

JOINT COMMITTEE ON FINANCIAL SERVICES AND MARKETS

MINUTES OF EVIDENCE

Tuesday 13 April 1999

Ms Barbara Saunders, Dr Oonagh McDonald, CBE, Mr Philip Telford and Ms Francesca Arcidiaco

Mr David Challen, Mr Tim Herrington, Mr Kit Farrow,

Mr Derek Wanless, Mr Mark Boléat and Ms Angela Knight

Mr David Roe and Mr Andrew Whittaker in attendance

Printed pursuant to the Order of the House of Lords of 2 March 1999
Ordered by The House of Commons *to be printed*
13 April 1999

LONDON: THE STATIONERY OFFICE
£5.30

HL Paper 50-vi
HC 328-vi

TUESDAY 13 APRIL 1999

Present:

Lord Burns (in the Chair)
Lord Fraser of Carmyllie
Lord Haskel
Lord Montague of Oxford
Lord Poole
Viscount Trenchard

Mr Nigel Beard
Mrs Liz Blackman
Mr David Heathcoat-Amory
Mr David Kidney
Mr Tim Loughton
Mr James Plaskitt
Mr Barry Sheerman

Examination of witnesses

Ms Barbara Saunders, Chairman of the FSA Consumer Panel, Dr Oonagh McDonald, cbe, and Mr Philip Telford, and Ms Francesca Arcidiaco, Consumers' Association, called in and examined.

Mr David Roe, Head of Financial Services and Markets Bill Team, HM Treasury, and Mr Andrew Whittaker, Deputy General Counsel, Financial Services Authority, in attendance.

Chairman

339.   Good afternoon. Thank you all very much for coming to this session. I am sorry we are a little late. As you know we have been having a number of sessions with groups of people. Basically we have been taking the Treasury's Progress Report as the document that we have been investigating and asking how far it goes to meet people's concerns in relation to the original consultation document that we had from the Treasury. We have been trying to major on particular issues in each of these sessions but we have also recognised that people will sometimes wish to touch on other things as this is their only opportunity to come and speak to the Committee. Although the main theme today is accountability, and many of our questions will be on this subject of accountability, we are happy also for people to make points on other issues if they wish. I would like to begin by asking you each to introduce yourselves and to give us a brief statement of your views on this general subject. Maybe I will start with this side and Ms Saunders.

(Ms Saunders) Thank you very much, Chairman. My name is Barbara Saunders and I am Chair of the Financial Services Authority's Consumer Panel. The Consumer Panel was set up to be an independent voice for consumers within the FSA last November and as a Panel it has met on four occasions to date. My Panel welcomes the Government's announcement that the Bill will contain a statutory requirement for the FSA to establish such a Panel in future but it is far from clear whether the Government will also impose other requirements in addition to its stated objective that the Panel should assess performance in meeting consumer protection and consumer awareness objectives. We believe that the relevant clause in the Bill should actually secure the independence of the Panel, credibility which we believe will come from the members' appointment on merit following open competition, powers for the Panel to establish its own priorities, provide advice and make recommendations, conduct research which is fundamental and publish its views. In order to do that it will have to be provided with adequate human and financial resources to do the job. We believe that those things are important in

addition to the requirement to contribute to the FSA's effectiveness assessments. On wider issues, Chairman, since this is my only opportunity, there are three things that I think are crucial. The first is that the rhetoric surrounding the one stop shop for financial services' regulation needs to be matched by a reality as perceived by consumers and investors in the retail market. That means that the definition of financial services should be wide enough to include mortgages and long term care within the scope of the FSA. It will, I believe, require a review of the interface with OPRA, the pensions' regulator, particularly in the context of stakeholder pensions. We would like to see the deletion of the *caveat emptor* clause from the Bill because we think it is unnecessary and it is already covered by the previous two provisions that the FSA should establish an appropriate degree of consumer protection having regard to the differing degrees of risk and the different expertise and experience of consumers. We think in the context of that the *caveat emptor* provision is unnecessary. Also we support the case which has already been made by the National Consumer Council and others that there should be a suitability and fitness for purpose requirement in the Bill, picking up on the existing PIA rules in that area.

340.   Thank you very much. Dr McDonald?

(Dr McDonald) My name is Oonagh McDonald. I was formerly a board member of SIB and then the FSA for five years in total but I am here to give an entirely independent point of view today. The focus of my submission, which has already been received, to the Joint Committee is on the issue of enforcement and accountability, especially in the context of the European Convention on Human Rights. The main point I want to make is that sufficient safeguards in my opinion have been built into the Bill and in terms of subsequent Treasury announcements to ensure that the FSA continues to operate in a fair, open and accountable manner. In order to see that it is important to recognise some features which I think have been overlooked in the public debate, the continuity between the current system and the FSA under the new legislative regime. Some of the comment I have seen on the issue of accountability would lead one to

[**Chairman** *Cont*]

suppose that an entirely new and uncontrollable regulatory monster is about to come into being, I do not think this is the case. Much has been learnt over the past decade or more about the process of regulation and indeed of enforcement and the experience and well tried practices of the past will be carried forward. The constraints on the FSA's actions, which applied in the past, and which have been shown to be effective, will apply in the future. I am happy to expand on some of those, for example the impact of the possibility of judicial review. One of those constraints, or as I would prefer to put it, contributions to the effectiveness of regulation is a public interest board. But to see why it is effective and can be effective it is important to understand how it operates and in my experience an important part of the effectiveness of the board is that it operates as a unitary board which in turn helps to ensure that it is a strong and united board. As I said, I will be quite happy to elaborate on any of these points if the Committee desires.

341.   Thank you very much. Mr Telford?

(*Mr Telford*)   Thank you, my Lord Chairman. My name is Philip Telford, I am a Senior Policy Researcher with the Consumers' Association. With me is my colleague Francesca Arcidiaco who is our Senior Public Affairs Officer working on personal finance and financial services. I would like to thank you for the opportunity you have given us to present evidence today about the proposed arrangements for accountability of the FSA. As you may imagine this is a theme of great interest to us, accountability of the regulator to consumers and to investors. I would like to say at the outset that we see a key role for consumer involvement at the very heart of regulation, and at the heart of the regulatory structure. Of the FSA's four current statutory objectives, two of them public awareness and the protection of consumers relate specifically to consumer issues. Set against this background, consumer representation, consumer involvement and accountability to consumers is of course vital. We have certainly been pleased with the prompt move by the regulator to establish the FSA Consumer Panel. Certainly we are encouraged by the approach we have seen already of the Panel, as we were by the work we saw from the predecessor of that body, the PIA Consumer Panel. However, there are certainly no grounds for complacency. We do remember that although the Financial Services Act was passed in 1986 it took until 1995 before we had a Consumer Panel at all and then only for one of the regulators, the Personal Investment Authority. For too long the voice of the consumer was marginalised in the regulatory structure. We are convinced that it is vital we put in place a robust system of consumer involvement. We wholeheartedly welcome the fact that the Consumer Panel will be on a statutory basis. But more than this we think it must have an independent budget, its own team of staff. It must be free to make public statements and there must be a requirement for the FSA Board to make formal responses to the Panel's reports and research. The Panel should also be able to undertake research across a broad range of areas and not be restricted to regulated activities. More than this, the Panel is not the only conduit for

consumer involvement and a consumer voice. It is vital that they and the FSA Board involve consumer organisations and individual experts in formal and informal consultation. We would also like to see the use of consumer impact statements by the regulator in the same way that they will issue financial impact statements. We fully support the fact that appointments to the FSA Board should be made in accordance with the Nolan Principles and clearly we would not take issue with the need to recruit competent and experienced individuals. However there should be a recognition that a balance is required between the interests of consumers and the demands of regulated firms. We really feel the time is long overdue for real commitment to consumer representation within the financial services industry.

342.   Thank you very much. Before we move on to the questioning I would like to give Andrew Whittaker and David Roe the opportunity to say anything if they wish to. I realise that ten days has passed since we last met and you might have had a chance to reflect on some of the things that have gone on. We have had two papers from you which we will be making available in the next day or two, one of which deals with some of the comments you have made on some of the evidence we have received so far and the other gives your latest thoughts on the enforcement process. We will be discussing that again on Thursday and we will make those papers available. Is there anything you want to say, Andrew, today?

(*Mr Whittaker*)   Nothing I would like to say at this stage.

343.   David?

(*Mr Roe*)   Thank you, Chairman. I would like to mention a couple of things now. I am sure they are things that we will come back to later but if I have an opportunity to say them now that will be fine. The first point is just to clarify the Government's intention as regards requiring the FSA to maintain Consumer and Practitioner Panels, which a couple of the witnesses have already mentioned. As the Economic Secretary implied in the evidence that she gave to the Committee, Ministers think it is desirable to allow some flexibility to develop the most effective arrangements over time. Therefore it is not the Government's intention to set out in detail in the Bill how the Panels should operate or be constituted. I would like also to say something, if I may, about a couple of other issues. One is the role of the non-executive members of the Board and the other is the question of the role of the Chief Executive and the Chairman, really by way of clarification. There will be a committee of the non-executive members of the Board, who will be in a majority. The chairman of this committee is to be appointed by the Treasury. The committee will have a special role in keeping under review whether the FSA is undertaking its functions in an economic and efficient way. This corresponds to the particular principle in clause 2(3)(a) of the Bill. Related to that, the committee will keep under review the adequacy of the FSA's internal financial controls. It will also determine the remuneration of the chairman and the executive members of the Board. Finally, there will be a requirement on the committee to report on the

[Chairman *Cont*]

performance of its functions within the FSA's annual report. These functions of the non-executive committee will be in addition to the general responsibilities of the Board as a whole for seeing that the FSA acts in a way that is compatible with its statutory objectives. On the role of the Chairman, the Bill currently leaves open, as does indeed the current legislation, whether the Chairman should also be the Chief Executive. Whilst there is no intention to the change the current arrangements whereby Howard Davies is the Chairman and Chief Executive and there is a non-executive Deputy Chairman, Ministers recognise that in the longer term there may be other arrangements which could work. They are however mindful of the fact that parallels with other models of corporate governance are not exact. For example, whereas the shareholders of companies are likely to be fairly diffuse, in the case of the FSA there is clear accountability to Government and Parliament, as well as to stakeholders more generally. There is also a good case for a strong line of direct accountability to Treasury Ministers from the senior executive of the regulator.

　　Chairman: I think that takes us into the first set of questions in relation to the FSA Board that we want to put.

Mr Loughton

344. Could I start with the point about the joint roles of the Chairman and Chief Executive, as David Roe has just said. He has come up with the news there that in the longer term apparently Ministers acknowledge that other arrangements could work. Are you satisfied at the moment that the roles of Chairman and Chief Executive, however trustworthy and upstanding the particular character Howard Davies may be, is a workable concept? Would it be much more desirable that they are separated right from the outset?

　　(Dr McDonald) I will take that question. I think it is important to bear in mind that you are dealing with a public body where the focus of the Board is on fulfilling the objectives of the FSA, in other words it functions differently from the way in which a company board functions. I think that certainly in this interim period, where the amalgamation of the various SROs into one body has been a long and difficult process, and also where at the moment you have below the Chief Executive a triumvirate of senior managers. Probably it has been an efficient way of establishing a new regime and I think the Government is right to take that view on this interim period at least, maybe in the future there will be changes in the structure, indeed some changes in the structure of the FSA have already taken place over the past two years. As you are moving on to become a fully established board, a fully established regulatory authority, so the specific tasks that had to be completed in this two year period will fall away and the main focus will be on the conduct of regulations. I do not think it has presented any particular problems at present. It may be that one wants to look again at the structure in the future, one has to be flexible.

345. Yes. With respect to Dr McDonald the last time from classical history we had a triumvirate it resulted in an emperor emerging from it. Are you realistically suggesting that in a couple of years' time, the timescale you put forward, Howard Davies will be very happy to split his roles? Does not the character of having a joint Chairman and Chief Executive alter perhaps the views of the majority of non executive directors on the board whereby the person chairing that meeting, running an organisation, also sets the agenda and puts the points that he wants to discuss on the agenda. Do you not think it changes the whole character from the outset?

　　(Dr McDonald) I have to say that I have not noticed the difference in character which you suggest. The SIB Board, of course, and SIB itself was a much smaller organisation, that did have an Executive Chairman and Chief Executive as well who obviously had to agree on the agenda presented to the Board. Under Howard Davies, Howard Davies has to operate with the support of the senior managers to carry the business forward and establish fully the new regulatory authority under the new legislation. Whether or not it should take a different structure in the future is an open question one would have to concede.

346. We have had some other views, it is conscious that the view from Howard Davies and the FSA would be not one of timescale, this is the news that has come out now.

　　(Dr McDonald) No, I am not speaking for the FSA, these are my views entirely.

347. Indeed, but one of precedents, based on the Bank of England we are going to have a governor, rather than a chairman of the board or whatever. Is it justified to model the FSA on the Bank of England now or in two years or whenever?

　　(Mr Telford) I think our view is that it does not necessarily cause a problem having the two offices merged into one person, it could do. Of course if the suggestion was put forward that it could cause a problem, that is quite possible. If there is the flexibility to change that structure and to have a division between those two roles I think that is right. I think we see that at the moment there is a big job to do bringing together the different SROs, in setting up the new body and establishing perhaps a consistent theme to the FSA and what it does and that it may be appropriate to have that joint function at the moment. We would take very much the view that it is an evolutionary approach to regulation we have to have and things may look very different in six months never mind six years' time. If the person themselves is not satisfactory then they are accountable for what they are doing and could be replaced. We would not be wedded, I think, to saying that there must be a division over all time or one office for all time. It is reassuring that can change as and when it is necessary and that could be sooner or it could be later.

　　(Ms Saunders) I would just like to supplement that by saying personally I think that the Government is intending to establish a world class regulator which is recognised worldwide as being such. I think the most important thing, therefore, is that the standards that are set within the FSA are perceived externally by the

[Mr Loughton Cont]

public and those to whom the regulators are accountable as setting the highest possible standards of corporate governance. I think it is for others to judge whether the structure that is currently proposed stands up against those tests.

348. Do we know how they do it in other countries?

(Ms Saunders) I do not personally.

Chairman: I think the majority have an executive chairman—that would be my observation.

Lord Haskel

349. It is all very well to have a paid chief executive as chairman when things are going well but of course it is when there is trouble you need a non-executive chairman or a separate person to raise matters on the agenda which maybe the chief executive would find it difficult to raise or would not want to raise. I wonder if you have any observations on that?

(Dr McDonald) I think in my experience there has from time to time been a creative tension, shall we say, between the chairman and the chief executive but that has been all to the good. You are talking about boards with a majority of non-executive directors whose function is to look at broadly speaking two issues, the way in which the authority is actually running itself and of course to focus to a large extent on policy issues which obviously are on the basis of papers put before the board but which require a detailed and thoughtful and open discussion by all members of the board. I think that although the model that people naturally look to nowadays is very appropriate in the case of a commercial company, I do think it is somewhat different and we can afford to be more flexible in the case of a regulatory authority. I do actually think it is not the most important issue to consider as regards the organisation running the regulatory authority.

Lord Poole

350. Perhaps we could ask what the most important issue is? You were talking about the structure and the organisation. What is more important?

(Dr McDonald) There are various important issues but let's focus on two because these two are the two that you are concerned with today. The nature of the board is extremely important; the individuals and the kind of contribution that they bring to the board and the way and extent to which they can help to shape and direct regulatory policy. I am setting aside just for the moment the issues of enforcement and accountability of that because we are focusing on a slightly different area. The second board issues are practitioner and consumer input and both are absolutely vital to the proper functioning of a regulatory authority. In some ways I take the view that, although of course there are often clashes at first, what one needs to do is bring the practitioner and the consumer interest together in such a way that the regulations that one proposes both protect the consumers and are conducive to the conduct of good business and best practice on the industry side. If we

are looking at the general functioning of the authority, then the contribution that the board makes and the contribution of the practitioner and the consumer input is extremely important to the way in which a regulatory authority can function and to its effectiveness.

Lord Haskel

351. Coming back to the question of the board, it has been suggested that the appointments to the FSA board should be subject to confirmation by Parliament—a kind of confirmation hearing I suppose. Do you think this is important? What is your view about it?

(Dr McDonald) Now that we have got the Nolan procedures, we do have very important checks. Secondly, it is important that the process of selection of board members should, of course, be open and fair but also efficient and if we go too much down the American path we could find ourselves waiting for a very long time for members of boards to be appointed. I have on occasion visited some of the American regulatory authorities to find they are well short of a full complement of commissioners because Senate or Congress have not approved them and months and months have gone by, so hopefully we have hit upon a relatively efficient method of appointing persons to the board.

Mr Sheerman

352. Dr McDonald, in her opening statement, did conclude she wanted a strong united board. In some respects that is what some of our participants in these "seminars", as I think we like to call them, are worried about—a strong united board that is really too strong—and that the lines of responsibility run all the way to the FSA, which has a chairman/chief executive as we have just been discussing, whereas other voices have said the accountability should really run through Ministers to Parliament and that should be the route—whether it should be consumers, the protection panel or the Ombudsman. The Ombudsman only this morning was saying to some of us in the Committee that he would like to see that accountability to Parliament through Ministers, not to the FSA. Do our panel think that is an important principle?

(Dr McDonald) There are a couple of points that I would like to make here. When I was talking about a strong and united board, I had a couple of issues in mind. One is it seems to me that some of the questions pre-suppose that consumer "representatives"—which is not the term one should apply to membership of the board—and practitioners or people from practitioner background would be somehow opposed on the board. What one wants on the board is individuals who bring a variety of skills and expertise to the board. One should not split the board into too many sub-committees where sectional interest might develop, if I may put it like that. What I have found in my experience is that, particularly on regulatory policy issues and indeed on a range of issues, there is considerable constructive debate which then leads to a view which the chairman accepts or rejects (or wishes

[Mr Sheerman *Cont*]

he had not but nevertheless accepts) so from that point of view, when you are talking about a strong board, you are looking at the board in relation to the chairman and the executives. Then, from the regulatory authority and from the board, one should be looking from the board through the chairman to the accountability to Parliament and to Ministers but what the chairman is bringing to the Treasury and to Ministers is, in fact, the concerted views of the board and that should be that kind of check and distillation of policy and decisions on other issues.

(Ms Saunders) To go back to the initial question which was the extent to which the FSA should be accountable to Parliament through ministers, in terms of the creative tensions that there are between the four statutory objectives that the FSA is going to fulfil, it is ultimately essential that there be accountability right back to Parliament. However, there are questions—and the discussion today begs them—about the extent to which that is carried through and the ways in which it can most effectively be carried through. The suggestion that one of the ways of delivering that accountability should be through the FSA's annual report and through interrogation of it—either by a scrutiny committee like this or by a Treasury select committee—are sound but in addition it is essential that the FSA be required to respond to the various statements that are made and challenges to the way in which it delivers its performance by both the consumer panel and the practitioner panel.

Lord Poole

353. I do not understand that. Could you expand, please?

(Ms Saunders) When the consumer panel makes recommendations to the board, whether through comments on consultative documents or policy statements, the FSA should be required to respond to those and, indeed, to account for its performance against its consumer protection and awareness objectives in its annual report. If it is dissenting from what the consumer panel is itself recommending, it should make clear why and the basis on which its regulatory judgments are made. I recognise that there will be times when there are balances to be struck but I think it is very important that the FSA board itself is clear about what balances have been struck and the basis on which those have been struck and, if there are trade-offs to be made, that it is prepared to be open about what those are. I would like to supplement this by commenting briefly on the question of consumer expertise within the board itself. There is no doubt that, with the size and scope of the FSA, it will be an executive regulator and the ability of any board to influence day-to-day operation is bound to be limited. It is very important for there to be a majority of public interest people on the board but in addition, if I draw from my experience as a PIA board member, it is extremely helpful to have several members of that board who have a background in consumer matters— consumer research, consumer understanding—so they bring to that board a recognition of the imbalance within the market place and in power within the regulatory structure itself. Certainly within the PIA

board there have been three people coming from precisely that background on what is a very large board and we have, over a period of time, had an influence in the way in which the practitioners themselves approached the issues. However much it is desirable for there to be a unitary board—and without a unitary board regulation cannot function effectively—the fact is that, in the early stages at least, people come carrying their previous baggage and they have to learn to approach this broader set of objectives in a balanced way. From that point of view, if you have only got one potential person who understands the sort of approach a consumer expert can take and the sort of questions that those coming from an investor's perspective can raise, then they are very isolated.

Mrs Blackman

354. Clarifying what you said, you are supportive, then, of dedicated consumer expertise on the board?

(Ms Saunders) People should be appointed on the basis of Nolan principles and on the basis of their previous expertise. I am suggesting that one of the very important elements of expertise is understanding the consumer end of the market and I believe that to have one board member out of twelve or fifteen is simply not enough to deliver that.

355. So are you fully supportive of the Government's response on this issue at present?

(Ms Saunders) It seems to me that the Government's response does not go far enough in recognising that public interest is very broadly drawn and that there are people who have sets of principles based on their consumer understanding and market research techniques who can actually bring added value to a board and whose primary function is consumer and investor protection.

(Mr Telford) Certainly looking at a regulator who has statutory objectives to protect consumers and to deliver good consumer products in the market place and to look at a whole range of consumer issues then yes, while they must appoint competent people with good qualities and in a transparent way, they must give attention to the fact that consumer knowledge and the way the market works for the retail, high street consumer is just as important as it is to understand the way regulated firms operate and their priorities and the criteria they have when they look towards a regulator for success and for bringing something to the market place. Clearly the FSA board and the FSA must be accountable to Parliament absolutely. There must be a strong board. We would probably say more than a united board there must be a questioning board. The job for the board must be to question what the FSA as a body is doing; what policy initiatives it has; where its spending resource is. Part of that is to say to themselves and the FSA board "We must make it clear to our constituents"—whether that is consumers or regulated firms—"what we are doing and why", and if consultation responses or reports are put into them, or research, they must be in a position to respond and say whether they will do something and, if they will not, why not. They must be quite clear and open and that

[Mrs Blackman Cont]

would inform everyone what the FSA is or is not doing and it would also help Parliament in scrutinising the board itself.

Chairman: We must move on. We have two panels this afternoon and a busy agenda so we must move on to the questions of consumer and practitioner panels. A number of people made statements in their introductory remarks about how consumer and practitioner panels operate so let us move on to that.

Lord Montague of Oxford

356. Could we look for a moment at the interaction between the consumer panel, the FSA and the Ombudsman? I will just take you up for a second in that spirit about appointments to the FSA and this strong consumer experience on bodies to which you refer. I am a bit worried in hearing that that it might undermine the consumer panel. Is it not slightly fulfilling the role of the consumer panel and might not a better approach be to have some of the members of the consumer panel as members of the FSA? That is just a thought for you to comment on. Thinking of your role, however, and the interaction of the consumer panel and the FSA and the Ombudsman scheme, perhaps you could tell us how you anticipate that working. Do you, for example, expect the FSA to make a statement about consumers in this activity without reference to yourself?

(Ms Saunders) Can I take the second part first because it will be helpful? In terms of day-to-day operation, the consumer panel would be rightly irritated and feel that an opportunity had been missed if the FSA was making substantial public statements impacting on consumer protection and its attempts to fulfil that role without having had any reference to us. It would have lost an opportunity for consultation and to get support potentially for what it is doing or to consult us in advance on what it was doing. I would genuinely expect, however, that working relationships would be good enough that the FSA would bring such matters to us in advance and already, in terms of practice, we are being consulted in advance on preparations for consultative papers; we are having regular feedback into our meetings on the issues that the consumer relations division are dealing with and we have an opportunity to comment back to staff. Over time, if we build on the experience of the PIA consumer panel, which has been in existence for four years, then I would also expect us to call in FSA staff and discuss with them the issues, challenges and performance of their own duties. That is the only way in which we can get access to the intelligence of what is going on on the ground and feedback about the regulatory lessons that the FSA is learning in order to influence the development of our own policy. The fact of the matter is that it is through monitoring enforcement and surveillance of the market that the FSA will develop a lot of its intelligence. We have to counter that, however, by research of our own which enables us to compare what is actually happening on the ground in the consumer market and the experiences that individual consumers are having with what the FSA tells us it is doing. That is very important indeed. When it comes to the question of whether members of

the consumer panel should be members of the FSA, I am not quite sure whether you mean members of the FSA staff or members of the board.

357. I meant members of the board.

(Ms Saunders) There have been very substantial discussions in the past about that. As chairman of the PIA consumer panel I was, and am, a PIA board member. It is recognised that having the chair of the consumer panel on the board implies a degree of compromise of independence and you can argue it both ways. There is a value in having separate people with consumer expertise on the board—although I have to say that that makes my relationship with the board as chairman of the FSA panel very important indeed because I have to be able to work with that board to influence the board and do so from the outside but, in terms of credibility of the panel as an independent voice, the separation is helpful.

358. Are you envisaging a relationship with the Ombudsman scheme and exchange of information?

(Ms Saunders) Yes. I would certainly expect the panel to receive information from the Ombudsman scheme on the progress of complaints, the volume of complaints and the issues arising out of complaints and we will seek that from the FSA Ombudsman bureau. I would very much hope the gateway to access information will not inhibit that relationship but obviously it is not yet established. It is very important.

(Mr Telford) May I say I would just agree with that. We certainly see a role, of course, for a very strong and independent consumer panel in terms of budget and research, acting very much as an advocate on consumer views—exclusively, you might say—as long as there is consumer involvement and a consumer voice on the board as well. We would not wish to see a model where the only consumer representation on the board was because the consumer panel person was brought on where that was seen as "Well, now we have done enough". We would see a role in both fields for consumer involvement.

359. In your opening statement, Ms Saunders, you talked—and I agree with you totally—about the importance of the one stop image (which I am sure is going to develop, and it is going to be a great disappointment to consumers if it does not prove to be a one stop) and you suggested pensions should come in and long term care, but you made no reference to a very delicate area as far as consumers are concerned—namely, consumer credit. Would you care to comment on that?

(Ms Saunders) The whole area of consumer credit is tied up with the OFT's existing responsibilities under the Consumer Credit Act and with the relationship between that Act and mortgage regulation. We are very strongly of the view that mortgage regulation should be within the scope of the FSA and we will contribute evidence to the Treasury as part of its review. When you then get into the wider area of whether all loans should be subject to FSA jurisdiction, that has not been looked at across the piece and a review of that would need to take place. It is very important for the longer term credibility of the FSA that, when consumers access its helpline or want

[Lord Montague of Oxford *Cont]*

to access the Ombudsman Bureau, they do not get responses which keep saying "We are the Financial Services Authority but we cannot deal with that".

Viscount Trenchard

360. I would like to talk about the membership of the panels but, just before I do, I understand well why Ms Saunders thinks that it is important that the members of the consumer panel probably should not be the same people as the consumer representatives on the board because it might compromise their independence; nevertheless I still think there may be some confusion in the purpose and I am not quite clear myself whether the purpose of the consumer panel is inherently different from the purpose of having a representative element of consumer people on the board—be they executives or be they non-executives. I am still not quite clear about that. Moving on to the question of the membership of the panels, however, how would you select these people? You have said they have to be as representative as possible but which organisations would you look to to put people forward? How would you select them? How would this process be free and fair?

(Ms Saunders) I am very happy to answer that. The process we went through in appointing the current FSA panel, which I think was sound, was openly to advertise using Nolan principles. We had 320 applications from all over the UK and from a wide range of interests and we selected them against clear criteria. The panel was then appointed by the FSA board but I, as chairman designate of the FSA panel, was involved throughout the selection procedure. The panel members come from a wide range of backgrounds—the consumer movement, the voluntary sector, market research, from Northern Ireland and Scotland, from advice agencies—so it is a broadly based panel and has credibility for that. In terms of the difference in the panel's role from that of board members, it seems to me the panel is there to some extent to redress the balance of power. The fact of the matter is that consumer interest outside regulation is diffuse: individual consumers have very little power in relation to the firms from which they buy and consumer organisations resources can be counted on the fingers of one hand in terms of full time officials working on financial services in general. It is very important that there is a properly resourced panel which can actually research the market, identify the issues the public are concerned about and look at their experiences and represent those in an articulate and informed way. The difference between that role and the role of board members is that board members need to look at the statutory objectives across the piece and deliver regulation as Dr McDonald said at the beginning, which is seen to meet, at times, conflicting objectives.

Chairman

361. There are two issues you raised at the beginning about securing the independence of this panel—both in terms of the appointment and in terms of the budget. We have seen that the Government has moved to make the panels statutory. Would you like to see some strengthening of the way the appointments are made and the budget?— This could be either in terms of having them approved by the Treasury or in some other way particularly in relation to the appointment of the chairman and the budget? What do you have in mind?

(Ms Saunders) It could be helpful to have a separate procedure for the appointment of the chairman from that of panel members and it may well be that that would be another of the checks and balances so that the FSA was not seen to appoint all of them. Also it could be helpful in the future either for the consumer panel itself to have a member involved in the appointment of future members and chairs or, indeed, for someone from the external consumer movement to be nominated to be involved in that process. As far as the budget itself is concerned, the best source of resources for the consumer panel has to be regulated firms and what research has been done in the past illustrates that consumers are prepared to pay for regulation where they see it is effective and in their interests to do so. For a small proportion of the total budget to be allocated to that consumer research and consumer panel's work is very important. As to whether there should be some external process involved in the negotiation of the budget, I do not have a strong view on that. It is important that the panel identifies its work priorities and can justify a budget based on those priorities.

(Ms Arcidiaco) Perhaps I can also reinforce this point. We feel quite strongly that the chairman of the consumer panel should be appointed by the Treasury and not by the FSA. We would further wish that this be done according to an open and public procedure. Of course, Nolan principles would apply but we would add, for example, an invitation by the Treasury for a consumer organisation to present nominees or candidates, who would not necessarily be members of the organisation but be "certified", in a way, consumer advocates. It does seem a trivial point but it is very difficult to find people with very good experience in consumer advocacy and often, as the point was made before, there is a confusion between the upholding of public interest principles and consumer interest principles. We would also like to make a point regarding the reinforcement of the independence of the panel by the definition of a formula which would set the budget for the panel. We do not have any problems about the level of funding which has been defined for the present panel but we feel that, in view of further possible increases in inflation or as a way of calculating future allocations, a formula would be very helpful.

Mr Plaskitt

362. That leads me to the area I want to ask you about. You sound relaxed about the £420,000 budget but I would like to ask all witnesses whether they feel as relaxed about it as you do. I would like

[Mr Plaskitt Cont]

to hear more about how that budget should in future be determined. You have just talked about a formula. In your case, perhaps you could expand a bit on that and perhaps the other witnesses could say how they would like to see the budget determined in the future. It looks as if it is determined by the FSA at that point but should it be? Should you have more self-determination over the budget, whether it should be some sort of formula or constraint over lines of accountability and, if so, what?

(Ms Saunders) You are absolutely right: in the first instance the budget of £420,000 was agreed by the FSA board on the advice of its consumer relations division just about the time when the panel was established but that amount does not take account of the staff support that we get which is very significant and I would not want to see the degree of involvement between staff from across the FSA compromised by arguments over how much we should pay for that. However, I do think as a point of principle in the future the panel would wish to identify its own budget and negotiate that with the FSA. The FSA, after all, will have the resources to deliver. On the question whether or not a formula would be helpful, we can always argue for more money but it is very important that priorities against expenditure are clear. If someone could come up with a formula that said "This is an appropriate level of expenditure on consumer protection and an identifiable one", I would be very happy to consider it. At the moment the amount we have is a quarter of one per cent. That seems to me intuitively to be quite low but it is early days and we have to identify the work programme in the context of the FSA's much wider remit before, in a sense, plucking figures out of the air.

363. How soon after this moves on to a statutory basis and this Bill becomes an Act would you like to see the budget reviewed? There has been an indication of willingness to review. How far down the road do you want to go before it is looked at again?

(Ms Saunders) I would say not more than another six months. I am not waiting for N2; I shall be wanting to review this in the third quarter of this year before the FSA sets its fee structure for next year.

(Dr McDonald) When looking at budgetary matters one must also bear in mind the need for flexibility. There will be occasions on which the consumer panel might want to commission far more research in one year than it would in another. For example, I mentioned that I chaired the consumer panel on the pensions review where, of course, a great deal of work needed to be done to make sure, or to try to make sure, that consumers understood the need for a pensions review and that the documentation sent to them was comprehensible and so forth. On other occasions disclosure was introduced for the first time. So I can see that when there are major changes, either in the type of products which are going to be sold—say, the introduction of ISAs—or some major review is taking place, that a consumer panel should be in a

position to say, "X was our budget last year but in this particular year we are going to need to commission a good deal of consumer survey work and it would have, clearly, a beneficial impact on the way the FSA wishes to develop its policy in this matter". It is important, therefore, not to go for too rigid a formula that is going to exclude such possibilities and it is important not to build that in—particularly into a Bill.

(Mr Telford) We are relaxed about that budget as a starting point and we will see how that goes. It is a point well taken: to put an actual formula into the Bill probably is not the way forward, but the formula should be seen as a transparency and we can then decide whether a quarter of one per cent is enough and, if it does not look enough, we can build on that if required.

Chairman

364. For this session there is just one other group of questions I would like to put to you. This is the question of the role of the non-executive committee. Are you happy with the balance of those tasks which have been given specifically to the non-executives as opposed to the tasks that go to the whole board or should the non-executives themselves as a committee have a wider or narrower remit?

(Dr McDonald) I am happy with the tasks that have been assigned to the role of the non-executive committee at the present time but it is very important, as I said before, to make sure that the board is in a position to review a wide range of matters as a board and to come to a consensus view as a board. It is very important, therefore, not to keep restricting things too much to a non-executive committee.

(Mr Telford) Likewise, we are happy with the particular duties given to them but, in the spirit of having a questioning board, we would like them to ask questions on whatever they want and not be restricted by statute or even by practice not to ask certain questions.

(Ms Saunders) I do not have a view.

365. Is there anything pressing anyone wants to say?

(Dr McDonald) I do not think so.

Lord Fraser of Carmyllie

366. Perhaps I can ask this and if you have a view on it you might let us know some time. The Delegated Powers and Deregulation Committee are uncomfortable with the idea that the FSA should be given powers to determine who is a private person for the right to sue. It does seem rather an extraordinary power to give to the FSA. If the consumer panel has any view about that, it might be helpful.

(Dr McDonald) I have no view.

Chairman

367. We will invite your comments in writing on that. Are there any other points anyone wants to raise?

[**Chairman** *Cont*]

(*Mr Telford*) The only point I would like to make is please put mortgages in the scope of the Bill.

Mr Sheerman

368. Is that unanimous amongst the witnesses?

(*Dr McDonald*) No. I really think you have to bear in mind—and perhaps like St Augustine it should definitely be not yet—the enormous scope of that. It would be approximately another 20,000 mortgage intermediaries of various kinds; it is about mortgage advisory firms; between 40-60,000 mortgage advisers have not yet fully benefited from a training and competence regime which one would certainly want to put in place as part of the regulations; and it would mean enormous staff commitment on the part of the FSA. Let it set itself up, get itself going and then look at taking on new tasks. It is a bit soon.

369. You would not want primary legislation necessarily to extend these powers, or would you?

(*Dr McDonald*) The FSA under the Bill already has the power or its remit could be extended but, if you leave it like that, it is the best way to do it.

Chairman

370. There are two approaches to this which have been suggested to us. One is that the powers are in the Bill and then the Treasury does an assessment at some stage in the future as to how the present system is working and decides whether or not there should be changes. The other approach we have had put to us is that this is too important an issue to be left to that process; it is a question of principle and it should be decided as a question of principle and it is the issue of the timing that could be left to another day. It is this is not something which should just be taken argued as a supplementary matter but is so key to the whole question of having a single regulator that the decision should be made as part of the Bill, and the question of timing could be left to another stage.

(*Ms Saunders*) Could I just interject and say that I think your second observation is absolutely right and that there is plenty of scope within the Bill for differing levels of regulation and a different approach to regulation for different sectors of the market. The issue of principle, however, is so important in terms of consumer understanding of what a financial services regulator is and should be that the problems for the FSA, if mortgages are left out, will be greater than the problems and the challenges of how the mortgage market is regulated.

371. Mr Telford?

(*Mr Telford*) Exactly. The point of the one-stop shop is vital and the principle should be established. We do not want to hear that mortgage advisers may not be trained or competent, they are out there selling mortgages so they should be and there can be different levels of regulation. There is already a code of practice out there and that can be used as the basis of regulation. It would give the statutory clout of having the FSA in charge of regulating mortgages.

(*Dr McDonald*) I am still dubious about these extensions.

Mr Plaskitt: But do you agree with the point of principle?

Lord Montague of Oxford

372. It is a matter of timing, is it not?

(*Dr McDonald*) I think there are difficulties involved in extending the principle to mortgages because then it seems to me one would have to extend it to all kinds of consumer credit as well.

Mr Plaskitt

373. When you spoke before you spoke about needing a delay before implementation which implied that you did not have an objection.

(*Dr McDonald*) That was from the point of view really of if Parliament imposes the obligation to regulate mortgages on the FSA then it needs to understand very well that it is a huge task that the FSA would have to undertake in addition to its current tasks.

Chairman

374. In wrapping this session up I would like as usual to ask representatives of the Treasury and the FSA if there is anything they would like to say—particularly on what we have been hearing about just now or anything else that has come up in this session before we move to the next set of witnesses.

(*Mr Whittaker*) Chairman, could I say a few words first of all about accountability and governance. I think we take the position that accountability should be clearly fixed. It should be accountability in the public interest to Parliament through Ministers. We think that governance is a slightly different matter, that governance can change over time according to the circumstances in which you are operating. The optimal governance structure does not need to be fixed for all time. It is interesting, for example, to note that the governance structure in America for the SEC, which is one we have not discussed at all this afternoon, is one which has a full-time Chairman and five full-time commissioners each with their own areas of responsibility. So it is not necessarily the case that any one governance structure that one would adopt now would be the right one for all time. The right approach we would advocate is flexibility in relation to governance and clarity in relation to accountability. As far as the role of the Consumer Panel is concerned, and indeed the Practitioners Panel too, our position is that their value to us lies in their independence. Neither of these organisations will be of any value to us if it appears that they are merely poodles of the organisation we operate. I think that certainly the Consumer Panel has already demonstrated its independence not least in their submissions to this Committee which in a number of respects do not mirror our own submissions to

[**Chairman** *Cont*]

you. In terms of the accountability structure for those two panels our position would be that it is really a question of balance and how you secure the necessary level of independence without increasing bureaucracy and rigidity in the Bill but rather maintain consistency with the Bill principle that accountability should be to Parliament through Ministers. So we see that as being something where there may be some room for further enhancement but within those safeguards. That is all I wanted to say in relation to the main subject of the debate. I think our position in relation to mortgages has already been made clear.

375. David?

(Mr Roe) Nothing.

Mr Sheerman

376. We have had two views on this. Can the Bill as presently drafted be modified over time? Is it flexible enough to take in mortgages at a later date?

(Mr Roe) Yes.

Chairman: Thank you very much.

Examination of witnesses

Mr David Challen, Chairman of the FSA Practitioners Forum, Mr Tim Herrington, Law Society Company Law Committee, Mr Kit Farrow, London Investment Bankers Association, Mr Derek Wanless, NatWest, Mr Mark Boleat, Association of British Insurers, and Ms Angela Knight, Association of Private Client Investment Managers and Stockbrokers, called in and examined.

Chairman

377. Good afternoon and thank you very much for coming. I am sorry it is a bit of crush but I am afraid that the geography of the room, means that we have only so much space. Some of you were present during the previous session. Today we are trying to major on the subject of accountability and to have the views both of the regulated community and of those who have responsibilities towards the consumer side as well. There are a number of issues that we want to cover. I would like to give you the opportunity first of all of introducing yourselves and to make any introductory comments you would like about the subject we are dealing with today. There may be other comments you would like to make about other subjects that may be on your minds but we do want to, as far as possible, deal with the issues of accountability. Mr Challen?

(Mr Challen) I am David Challen and I am the Chairman of the London Investment Bank within the Schroders Group but I am here really as Chairman of what is now called the Practitioners Forum so you may find me using that term as well as the one you have become accustomed to using. I think the issue of accountability as far as practitioners are concerned really raises two pretty different questions. One is does the FSA conduct itself so as to take account of the views of practitioners in arriving at its policies and in the manner in which it handles day-to-day business and, second, the rather different question, and one I know you have spent a lot of time looking at, which is is the FSA properly accountable for the way in which it exercises over practitioners its potentially very great powers of discipline and punishment? Because you have looked at that second one I do not propose to spend any time on it although I would not want to give the impression that it was not a matter of intense importance and interest to practitioners. So let me turn to the first of those questions and perhaps answer it in the light of early practical experience of the operation of the Practitioners Forum. We were established last November, we comprise senior representatives from the businesses which are regulated by the FSA, and we regard it as our role to make representations to the FSA on any matter which we believe is causing concern amongst practitioners about the way the FSA's operations are conducted in practice. We also expect to respond with a practitioners' view on issues which the FSA will come to us with and we aim to play a role in helping the FSA to formulate its policies and develop its appropriate response to issues which are raised during the standard consultation procedures it engages in. All of this we know we should do and wish to do having regard to the statutory duties of the FSA but with particular regard of course to the

fact that the Bill also requires them to take into account considerations such as their efficiency, the need to ensure that the regulatory burden produces commensurate benefits and the need to ensure that the innovation and competitiveness of the British financial services industry is safeguarded and not impaired. I would say that our early experience of working with the FSA suggests to me that with the current management we are making good progress in establishing an open and responsive relationship. Frankly, we ask ourselves what power do we have to enforce accountability in terms of the question we are addressing? The answer of course is none except the threat of public dissent. As things currently stand, however, I think we will exercise real influence. The trouble of course is that arrangements have to be inspected for their durability not just in relation to the present incumbents in the job. In that light I am glad that the Practitioners Panel is to be a requirement of the Act. However, until we see what, if any, duty the FSA will be given to take any notice of it, it is quite difficult to assess the degree to which there is constitutional accountability to practitioners. This means, as far as I can see, that the power of practitioners to exercise influence over the FSA could be limited to their ability to kick up a fuss in the right quarters. With people of goodwill trying to make the regulatory system work fairly I think that is probably enough. If the Government ever appointed the wrong people to the top jobs of the FSA, the FSA might well, I think, be able to ignore balanced representation from practitioners with impunity. In that event the accountability of a rather potentially freewheeling FSA to Parliament will assume great importance because dissatisfied practitioners would have to make the grounds for their dissatisfaction known to the legislators who may have to take action. I think one has to conclude, in other words, that there will be adequate accountability of the FSA in the sense of the question that I first asked if the FSA wants there to be and, if not, not.

(Mr Herrington) I am Tim Herrington, a partner in the London office of Clifford Chance, a leading international law firm. I head up my firm's financial services regulatory practice. I am here today in my capacity as Chairman of the Law Society's Company Law Committee. My Committee is one of the Law Society's specialist standing committees whose work is undertaken in the public interest with the object of maintaining and improving the quality of law and the practice of law. The Company Law Committee consists of specialists in the field of company and financial services law and regulation from both the solicitors and the barristers professions and is, therefore, usually able to speak on behalf of the whole of the practising profession on matters within

[Chairman *Cont]*

its province. Our approach is to comment in great detail on legislative proposals which affect our area of expertise and in that context we have submitted to the Treasury an 80 page memorandum containing many detailed comments on the draft Bill. We are undertaking a similar exercise in relation to the recent Treasury consultation papers on regulated activities and financial promotion, although we do regret the very short period of consultation that has been given in respect of those very important papers. I am pleased to have this opportunity to address the issue of the accountability of the Financial Services Authority and in particular its accountability to the regulated community. We have made the point that the legal structure chosen for the FSA creates challenges in establishing clear accountability arrangements. It is a hybrid; a private body exercising public functions. We have expressed concerns that its private status and the operational independence of the board, coupled with the fact that, unlike the existing system, the FSA does not exercise its powers as a delegate of the Treasury could weaken political accountability. Parliament will clearly need to be vigilant to ensure that does not turn out to be the case. On the other hand, the conventional arrangements for accountability of a board of directors present in a traditional company are absent; there are no shareholders whose views the board needs to have regard to. The draft Bill, as proposed to be strengthened through the measures set out in the Progress Report, seeks to address these issues particularly through the creation of specific roles for the non-executive committee, the establishment of the Consumer and Practitioner Panels, the arrangements for the investigation of complaints and the power to commission periodic independent reports on the FSA's operations. My Committee believes that the improvements to the accountability arrangements set out in the Progress Report do go a long way to address the concerns we have previously raised that arise out of the Authority's legal status. There is, however, one other very important aspect of accountability, namely accountability under the law. We continue to have concerns about the FSA's accountability in this respect and in particular the continuation of its statutory immunity. In paragraph 3.10 of the Progress Report the Government justifies the continuation of the immunity on the grounds that without it "the regulator's staff would be unable to go about their business without being unduly hampered by concerns about legal action". As lawyers, we find that a worrying statement. Accountability under the law is vitally important for any public authority and we do not believe that the case for the continuation of the immunity has been clearly made in the light of the increased powers of the FSA. We are particularly concerned that negligent action taken by the Authority in the execution of its powers could have serious financial effects on a firm's business. These concerns would perhaps be lessened if there was a further strengthening of the arrangements for the independent investigation of complaints and in particular if the investigator had power to award

compensation in cases of maladministration. There is of course a good precedent for this in the form of the Parliamentary Commissioner for Administration whose jurisdiction has recently been extended to cover a large number of quangos; the extension of the Parliamentary Commissioner's jurisdiction in this area therefore merits serious consideration. He does, of course, have power to recommend payment of compensation in serious cases of maladministration, as you will remember from the Barlow Clowes case. I would of course be pleased to elaborate on these points in the course of the afternoon.

378. Thank you very much. Mr Farrow?
  (Mr Farrow) Thank you, my Lord Chairman. My name is Kit Farrow, I am the Director General of the London Investment Banking Association which is the trade association of the investment banking industry in London whose membership includes most of the world scale financial institutions whose presence in London makes London the international financial centre that it is. The principal concern which I shall be speaking from is for the competitive position of London as a financial centre as it is affected by the Bill. I would like to remind the Committee how different a market that is from the retail market that was being discussed with the consumer representatives earlier. The wholesale markets are a world where buyers and sellers are both well informed and both well resourced. They neither need nor want protection from their professional counterparties. If the competitive position of London is to be preserved it needs to be a cost-competitive market and it is very important indeed that the regulatory approach to the protection of retail consumers is so organised that it does not impinge on the competitiveness of a wholesale interprofessional market to which it is of very, very limited relevance. That is not to say that there is any conflict between the two, it is simply that each should be appropriate to the particular circumstances that it is addressing. I had the opportunity to give evidence to you earlier about the enforcement regime and I promised you a supplementary note which I shall be addressing to you tomorrow, so I will not go into that, if I may, today

379. Thank you.
  (Mr Farrow) I should like on the issue of today's agenda of accountability essentially to support very, very briefly the remarks which Tim Herrington and David Challen have already made in relation to consultation. Undoubtedly the announcements in the Progress Report take us a considerable way in the right direction but there are further improvements to be made. I think it is very important to be clear on the distinction between the role of the Practitioner Panel, which David Challen chairs, and which, given the breadth of responsibilities of the FSA, cannot possibly be, as it were, the source of detailed advice about the detail of regulation, about particular facets of the market, it has to deal and it is appropriately equipped to deal with broad, high level issues and the arrangements for consultation about detail, which are also important, need to exist side by side with it. I

[Chairman _Cont_]

would like also to endorse very strongly what Tim Herrington said about investigation of complaints. The constitution of the FSA gives it enormous powers over the livelihoods of all who work in the City. Those powers may be necessary but it is important to ensure that this organisation, as other organisations of wide responsibility, is subject to arrangements which can ensure that it handles its own affairs properly. The particular issue of accountability that I would like to repeat concerns the power of investigation of the FSA, particularly in its capacity as the controller of the ability to do their job of all the people who work in the City. Those are immensely wide powers. At the moment the consultative proposals provide for the FSA to make its own arrangements for the investigation of complaints into it. That seems to me to be inappropriate given the breadth of its powers and I am very clear that the Bill should be more specific in establishing the arrangements for thoroughly independent investigations whether by the Parliamentary Commissioner for Administration or by another individual whose responsibilities and whose own appointment are subject to similar arrangements.

380. Thank you very much.

(Ms Knight) My name is Angela Knight and I am Chief Executive of the Association of Private Clients, Investment Managers and Stockbrokers. So anyone in this room who has bought or sold some shares recently has probably done so through one of our members. We, too, have been heavily engaged in responding to the welter of consultation documents which have come out and requests for information over these last few months. We have already sent to this Committee two documents and I have a have third with me, if you wish Chairman, and can also send each member our clause by clause response to the draft Bill if so requested. However, I would like to concentrate, if I may, specifically on accountability issues which we believe are particularly important to the practitioners who, after all, are going to be paying for it all. We believe that there needs to be far greater emphasis placed upon the requirement for on-going consultation with the regulated community. The FSA does have a duty to consult but there is no such requirement to put the responses into the public domain and if they ignore some of the proposals that have been made to give the reasons why they have so done. It is of interest to note that of the 21 consultation papers issued so far by the FSA they have given a feedback statement on one. We appreciate that they are very busy but even so this is a matter which needs to have very considerable attention paid to it in future. We also think that accountability would be strengthened if the so-called FSA principles on which they are currently consulting were seen as a two-way charter so that principles govern the regulators as well as the regulated community. Just as we have to deal fairly and openly with the regulators and staff up our firms properly so the same should be a requirement of the regulators themselves. There is a widespread concern about the

variety of rule interpretation that currently takes place and, of course, if a rule is interpreted in one direction in one way by the visiting body one year and then the regulators interpret it differently next year it can be very costly for firms. We believe that the opportunity should be taken with the FSA being set up to ensure that there is a record of interpretation in the public domain which is accessible by the regulated community. As with LIBA we believe that the international competitiveness of the UK is of fundamental importance. As a committee of non-executive members the board of the FSA is proposed to have certain responsibilities given to it, we would suggest this is perhaps a third responsibility that should be given to that committee that it has to report either separately on an annual basis or as one of the specified contents of the Annual Report. As Clifford Chance, we have great concern about the issue of statutory immunity and find it rather difficult to understand why the FSA can be empowered to inadvertently but negligently remove the livelihood from a firm or from an individual and that firm or individual has no redress. The disciplinary process is of course very important. That has been covered elsewhere. I will conclude, if I may, by raising our last point which relates to the reasonable exercise of powers which we do think should be incorporated as a requirement of the FSA. We do understand that the Government has responded that all public authorities have to act reasonably. I am not a lawyer but our lawyers have advised us that the law in this instance is based upon something called the _Wednesbury_ decision which says that as long as the public authority has taken into account all relevant matters, even if it reaches an unreasonable decision, it can be believed to have acted reasonably. That sounds to us rather an unfortunate interpretation. If that is an interpretation of the law then we do believe that it is essential that the FSA has reasonable exercise of its powers as laymen understand that expression "reasonable" to be.

381. Thank you very much. Derek?

(Mr Wanless) My name is Derek Wanless and I am Group Chief Executive of NatWest and I am also here as a member of David Challen's Practitioners Panel. I would echo everything that David has said. The fact that the FSA set up the Forum, as they call it, was a very positive step and I think it is a very important step in terms of how consultation should happen and picks up some of the points that previous speakers have made. I think the important issue is that there is openness in the process and the panel has the opportunity to report publicly each year. I believe that one of the panel's important roles will be to ensure that the consultation process is working especially in these early days of the setting up of the FSA. The Practitioners Forum in no way whatsoever takes away the need to consult normal industry channels, normal bodies, but we are there, I think, if the FSA takes a view that is contrary to some of the advice that has been given for them to explain to us why they have taken that view and for us to make further comments. I think

[Chairman *Cont]*

that is a particularly important role to play. As in all the rest of this it depends how well-meaning individuals put that into practice as to whether it works well. I think the ability to report is a particularly important aspect of how we will proceed. As far as NatWest is concerned we welcome the opportunity to comment on the Bill and already have done so. We acknowledge and welcome the Treasury proposals that have been made to increase accountability thus far. We have concerns about the way some of the debates have seemed to be formed, like for example the issue of Chairman and Chief Executive and are they two roles, because it seem to us in that particular case people have picked up Cadbury there. Cadbury is there for public companies who have got shareholders and I personally have a view that the separation of Chairman and Chief Executive, particularly if we are talking about a non-executive Chairman of the FSA, will complicate the issue of accountability rather than clarify it. The important thing is the totality of the checks and balances that work. We expressed a view in our evidence that the National Audit Office might have a role in terms of looking at the FSA, important issues being transparency of information that would then be available and I think transparency of information, both the reports of ourselves, the consumers body, and potentially the NAO, would be important in this. We do also have the belief that the system can be improved if there is a proper appeals system and a proper structure within the FSA (which is probably a matter for the legislation) where those who are responsible for bringing disciplinary proceedings and those who are responsible for adjudicating are kept separate. The issue of the accountability of the FSA needs to be seen in a wider context. We do believe also that the focus they have placed on consumer education is important and will be helpful in terms of them as a body overall being able to carry out the very many responsibilities that they have.

(Mr Boléat) I am Mark Boléat and I am Director-General of the Association of British Insurers. I will be brief, Chairman, because most of the points I wanted to make have been made several times already and I endorse them. I think our concern is not so much accountability to the regulated community but accountability more generally. I do not think you can look at an aspect of it. I very much endorse what Mr Challen said on that. We would like to see stronger accountability to the Government and to Parliament. For example, the Treasury should have a right to comment on rule changes and not merely to be notified of them. We would like to see a power of direction and we would certainly like to see a report to Parliament. As you know, a report to Parliament can in its effect vary from totally nothing to very substantial. It is quite significant how this Committee has probably provided the most valuable forum of debate on these issues because there is actually debate. You can question the officials and they have to answer this on the public record. The rest of the consultation consists of large amounts of paper flowing and while

the officials are very happy to have discussions, and these things are argued, I think that public debate you are having is very important and I would like to see that continue when the Bill comes into effect. What the mechanism is, whether it is a Committee like this or whether it is the Treasury Select Committee, matters less but there needs to be a body of Parliament that is able to challenge in a meaningful way the FSA. As far as industry is concerned, I very much endorse what has been said. The Practitioner Forum has a role but most of the consultation has to be through the usual channels, through the markets, the trade associations, through individual companies. The FSA should be obliged to follow Government best practice on how to consult, which it does not in every respect at present. There is a Cabinet Office document on this. That would also include regulatory impact assessments. Others have said that where a strong industry view is rejected then this should be justified and not simply "we reject the view". There needs to be a reasoned argument. The final point is what matters at the end of the day is not what is in the legislation but actually the attitude of the FSA and the attitude of the regulated community. At the moment I think those attitudes are absolutely correct but that may not continue for all time and if things go wrong that is when the legislation is important and that is where Parliament is important because no quango can ignore Parliament. If it so wishes it can ignore the regulated community, even if it would be unwise to do so, and I am sure the FSA would have no wish to do so.

382. In a moment I would like to move on to the questions of complaints and immunity and the whole question of consultation. It would be helpful for the Committee if we could have responses from each of you on the group of questions that we spent quite some time putting to the previous panel. This would simply get them out of way, for those of you who have not expressed a view. What do you feel about the issue of the governance of the FSA in terms of the chairman and chief executive, the composition of the board, present roles that are given to the non-executives as a separate committee rather than as part of the board as a whole? Do you think the position which the Treasury has taken in the Progress Report largely takes care of these issues of governance and the structure of the board or are there other changes that you would like to see?

(Mr Challen) For my part I do think so. I think it is okay.

(Mr Herrington) As I said, I think we are broadly content with the way it has come out. I do not think we would have ideally liked to have seen the body start in its current form. There is a lot of history here and the FSA has inherited the legal structure under the old regime. I think if you were to start with a clean sheet of paper you would not form this vehicle as a private company limited by guarantee, that is not really an appropriate vehicle which has all the corporate law which is then really stripped away from it. The Government had to be quite clever, I think, in actually devising a structure

[Chairman Cont]

which is going to backtrack from that and also to give it a structure that is going to work and we will have to wait and see whether it does. I think the ingredients are there for a system that can work with goodwill on all sides.

(Mr Farrow) We are happy with the board structure arrangements that the Government has chosen. One small point of detail is that I would think it appropriate that the non- executive board members choose their own chairman rather than for the Treasury to decide who should be their chairman.

(Ms Knight) Again, very similar to that of LIBA. Yes, we do agree that what is being proposed is not unreasonable. As I said in my opening statement, we would like to see an extra responsibility given to the non-executive committee and I think they should choose their chairman, and indeed in the case of the practitioner panel and the consumer panel they should be seen to be independent and so have an independent right to choose which chairman they wish.

(Mr Wanless) Yes.

(Mr Boléat) Yes.

Mr Sheerman

383. That means not one of you really questions the principle of having an FSA, that all of you are perfectly happy with one body?

(Mr Wanless) As a practitioner what we have got to put into context is what was there before. There were so many things wrong with what was there before that all of us within NatWest think this has got a very good chance as long as the structure is right. Of course, the wrong people doing the wrong things could kill it. Yes, it is a lot better than what was there before. The process that we are going through of consultation is capable of making it a very good regulator.

(Ms Knight) I think we have to accept that the policy decision has been made and therefore what we have to do as practitioners is to ensure that we get the best result rather than put up our hands and say "no, we do not want it". One fights the winnable wars, not the ones which there is not any point in fighting.

Chairman

384. Are there any more points on governance of the FSA? Could we move on then to the question of the practitioner panel and ask the general question of each of you to what extent you are now content with the way that is? How far would you like to get some more safeguards built into the Bill? We understand that there is a reluctance to try and legislate for everything. At the same time we have heard that there is some desire in one or two parts to strengthen the position of the panels. It would be helpful to the Committee if you could put to us any suggestions that you would like to make about how that might be tweaked.

(Mr Challen) Can I just perhaps repeat a little bit of the comment I made in my opening remarks and develop it a bit. It depends, of course, how the existence of the Practitioner Panel is to be put into the Bill. It is not in the draft Bill.

385. How would you like it to be?

(Mr Challen) If it simply says "there should be a Practitioner Panel" then, as I said in my opening remarks, it is not clear that gives any obligation to what I describe as a freewheeling FSA perhaps run by different people from the people who run it now to actually take notice of it. That would not be satisfactory. I am quite confident that is not how it will operate at the moment. Therefore, it is for consideration whether in including it in the Bill some words should be used to explain in what way it is to perform its function for the FSA or indeed perhaps in what way the FSA is to report where it has been unable to accept the recommendations which the Practitioner Panel has made to it on certain matters of intense interest to practitioners.

Lord Poole: Might it be helpful if we ask for something in writing from the Practitioner Panel and the Consumer Panel on their thoughts on this rather than to try and develop it now?

Chairman

386. If you would like to do that I am certainly happy for you to do that. We have seen the Treasury's proposal that these should now be statutory, the question is would either of the groups who are responsible or involved with the panels like to put to us any particular suggestions of how to strengthen this when it comes to the legislation or should it just be left in the loosest form? This is an opportunity for you to put your thoughts to us.

(Mr Challen) I would like to take up the suggestion that we come back to you. I am not a parliamentary draftsman even when I have got time to do it, certainly not on the hoof. I think it would be more sensible for us to try to think how it might be done in the Bill and let you have something in writing.

Mr Sheerman

387. Could we have a quick word from the FSA on the question of the 21 Consultation Documents and there being only one response. Is that true and, if so, why?

(Mr Whittaker) Thank you very much.

Chairman

388. This is the result of a rest over the holidays!

(Mr Whittaker) Thank you for the opportunity to respond to that. I think I would probably need to respond to you on that in writing. We have issued a programme indicating when we expect to respond on different documents and it may be that we are only part way through that programme at the moment. If I might I would like to give you some more detail separately.

Mr Sheerman: That was not meant to be aggressive, Chairman.

Chairman

389. Do any witnesses want to comment on this question of the Practitioners Panel and the extent to which they would like to see anything built into the legislation about it?

(Ms Knight) Certainly our group who considered this were rather inclined by the explicit requirement mentioned within the questions we have here of the FSA to consult the panels when making rules or broad policy statements otherwise we wondered what was the point of the Practitioners Panel. There you have a group of people, an expert resource on guidance and policy and rules and you can do your reality checks with them. So we thought that that was a good idea. We also, as I say, believe that the panels should appoint their own chairmen, possibly for a three-year period only, as that would again be a check on the system. Finally, we would expect regular reports coming out for publication where FSA money was being spent, for example with the Consumer Panel, which was discussed earlier, we would expect to see a report on what that money was spent on and how it was spent because, as I said at the start, it is the regulated firms who will be paying for it.

(Mr Wanless) The practitioners will certainly be expected to do research amongst regulated firms and use that research as the basis of a report which is produced annually. The issue about resources for that sort of research is obviously an important issue. Again the attitudes of the FSA so far are rather positive in that respect because they themselves see the benefits they get from it.

Lord Montague of Oxford

390. Has the Practitioners Panel anticipated any relationship with the Ombudsman scheme and the operation of that scheme?

(Mr Challen) To be honest with you, no we have not but that does not mean we should not.

391. Do you think that might warrant a further letter?

(Mr Challen) I am in danger of committing myself to an extended correspondence.

Chairman: And I may say that any correspondence has to be in very quickly if it is to be of any use because we have a deadline to meet!

Mr Loughton

392. In the Progress Report what it actually says is that the FSA is to be required by law to maintain Consumer and Practitioner Panels, fine. "The panels will have a role in assessing the performance of the FSA against its statutory objectives." That is pretty woolly stuff. What if the Practitioners Panel with its not generous budget, as we have heard, commissions research (which is one of the plus points David has touted) amongst practitioners and practitioners come back to say that our fees are 50 per cent too high in our view. What practically do we think the result of that is going to be vis-à-vis the role of the Practitioners Panel with the FSA? Do you need to

have more teeth written into the primary legislation so that the FSA have to take some degree of note and action on that or is it purely going through the motions of being seen to consult and commission research which will not actually come to anything at the end of the day?

(Mr Challen) Your particular example may not be an especially practical one to achieve real movement on because the costs of the FSA are going to be subject to an irreducible minimum. One of the prime responsibilities which the Practitioners Panel feels it has, and indeed I think so do the FSA, is to scrutinise the budget annually and to raise objections if the budget appears to be getting out of hand. The point you make is really the point I made earlier on that unless there is something in the Bill (which I am now committed to trying to draft for you) that says more than it should be a panel and it should be consulted, such as in the case of if we do not take any notice of it then we have to give reasons why, then I think the powers of the Practitioners Panel, with people who are not trying to make this system work, will be very limited.

393. Where do you get the irreducible minimum from?

(Mr Challen) Canary Wharf—I mean the building.

394. Howard Davies would have us believe that if it has been a particularly good year for the FSA fining people then the flip side of that is that the fees to members will be diminished accordingly. That was the whole basis of the fine income going to the FSA rather than going to a central pot in the Treasury.

(Mr Challen) I do not contemplate misdemeanours on such a scale, I must say.

(Mr Farrow) Could I suggest that the two critical ways of ensuring the strength of the panel are a) the calibre of the individuals who are on it and b) an obligation for the FSA to come out in public if they have rejected the advice of those distinguished individuals. If there is then a public issue that will see that the issue is properly debated.

(Ms Knight) Practitioners are not normally shy, retiring souls, Chairman, and if they come across a situation where they feel they are being charged unnecessarily or there is an erroneous rule or something like that, I suspect they would shout very loudly indeed. That does not mean I do not want to ensure that the Practitioners Panel's role is properly strengthened and its views are properly represented to the FSA board, but equally we must be aware that much of the debate will continue to take place in the public domain and if the FSA is seen to act in an incorrect, erroneous or unreasonable manner then that will be very well known and comments will be made.

Chairman

395. What you are saying is that the obligation should be upon the FSA to respond ——

(Ms Knight) Yes, very much so.

[Chairman *Cont*]

396. —— To the points that are being made to them and this should not become a one-way conversation if this is to work.

(Ms Knight) Yes.

Chairman: Could we move on to the question of statutory immunity and complaints.

Mr Kidney

397. Tim Herrington, that was an excellent exposition of your view of statutory immunity for the FSA. Your group thinks that statutory immunity is unjustified but you recognise that different people might have a different view?

(Mr Herrington) Of course. It is a very difficult balancing act here and we have to face the fact that it has been in the legislation, albeit we would say in a rather different context. Those of you, like me, who still have the war wounds from 1986 will remember that there was great debate about statutory immunity at that time and the initial draft of that Bill did not have it for the SROs, for example, it was something that was built into the Bill as it went through. The reason it was felt to be important was because there was great practitioner involvement at that stage and practitioners were not wanting to serve on a body where they might be laying themselves open to personal liabilities. I think it is different now with a body which I regard as purely a public body. We are into the realms of a public body here even though it is considered a private body and there are not many public bodies that actually have an immunity of this kind. It has to be very clearly justified to continue on that basis when one bears in mind the extended powers it has. The sort of example I give——

Chairman

398. The Bank of England has these powers.

(Mr Herrington) The Bank of England has these powers, yes, it is there but that is not to say that it should continue. I am not saying that.

399. It was just you were saying it was unusual for a public body and I made the point that in the case——

(Mr Herrington) The police, for example, I believe do not have statutory immunity. This body will have prosecuting powers similar to the police in some respects so there is a debate here about whether it is appropriate for a body of this type to have this immunity.

Mr Kidney

400. My colleague is going to deal with complaints. I know you say if there is statutory immunity the complaints system needs to be robust and independent and have the power to award compensation but I will leave that to my colleague. Can I move on to the recognised investment exchanges where the Bill proposes a narrower statutory immunity but the exchanges are arguing

that they should have the same one as the FSA. What is your view on that argument?

(Mr Herrington) That is quite a difficult one. The exchanges do not have it at the moment and it was considered inappropriate. The question is what is the role of the exchange? Is the exchange going to have a regulatory role? Essentially it is a market providing a facility for others to do business by and I think at the moment it is unclear in the way the FSA policy is working out how much regulatory responsibility is going to lie with the exchanges. Kit is shaking his head and it would be interesting to know why. I think it is not necessarily an inconsistent position to say that you would have one without the other but I suspect a degree of symmetry is going to be considered desirable here between the two bodies.

401. Not by the Government in the Progress Report who say they stand by the more limited statutory immunity for the RIEs despite the RIEs arguing they should have the same as the FSA. Kit Farrow has got a different view. Can we hear it.

(Mr Farrow) Can I first declare an interest as a board member of an RIE and I suspect the only person in the room who as an unpaid director of a recognised exchange had to go home and say actually we were in receipt of the threat of personal litigation in response to regulatory activity which I had been party to, given the regulatory responsibilities put on exchanges to maintain clean, open, fair, proper markets. It seemed to me quite inappropriate that whereas the other parts of the regulatory regime which are discharging very similar regulatory responsibilities were not open to personal suit for discharging those responsibilities but I was. I do disagree very strongly with what Tim just said in saying that it is not clear what regulatory responsibility exchanges will have in the new regime. They are very clearly specified. There are duties to maintain a proper market which are going to be spelt out in substantially greater detail. The exchanges periodically have to take regulatory decisions which have very big financial implications not merely for the members of the market but for the users of the market. In the case that I referred to it was not a member of the market who was unhappy at the regulatory decision, it was a customer whose activities had been interfered with. I wish to make my point of view known. Could I just say one thing further. I do believe that both for the exchanges and for the FSA that the immunity should not apply in the event of negligence or recklessness.

Chairman: What I heard you all saying was although you had some doubts about statutory immunity, if statutory immunity was there you wanted to make sure that you had a very good complaints procedure which would back it up from the other direction.

Lord Fraser of Carmyllie

402. Just a question on statutory immunity. We have had one legal opinion submitted to us that even if the Government or Parliament wishes to confer

[**Lord Fraser of Carmyllie** *Cont*]

statutory immunity on the FSA, under human rights requirements those will be set aside. What is not clear to me is whether that is a rogue view or whether you would share it?

(*Mr Herrington*) I am aware of it and it is a respectable legal view certainly. There is also a European issue, as I understand it. I believe there are issues on the European front as to whether it is appropriate for statutory immunity to continue for regulators. That would be a debate that we could have all afternoon I suspect.

Mr Beard

403. What kinds of arrangements do you see would be most appropriate for dealing with independent investigation of complaints against the FSA? In particular, do you believe that the Parliamentary Commissioner for Administration could have a role in such arrangements?

(*Mr Herrington*) Yes. I mentioned that as a possibility this afternoon in my opening remarks. What struck me was that I suddenly thought of something that said that the Government has brought into the ambit of the Ombudsman a large number of quasi-governmental bodies and non-departmental governmental organisations or whatever, a very large list, and I thought if it is good enough for the Competition Commission, as it is now called, why is this not something that has been thought of in the context of the FSA? One of the criticisms you might have of the proposals that are in the draft Bill, even as proposed to be strengthened, is that there is perhaps no real independence of this investigator, he is appointed by the FSA, and should we have somebody who is clearly independent of the FSA to carry out this task?

404. You are seeing the Parliamentary Commissioner as being the sole investigator of complaints?

(*Mr Herrington*) That could be the vehicle through which it operates, yes.

405. I wonder if other members of the panel would like to comment on the question.

(*Mr Boléat*) We would certainly see a role for the Parliamentary Commissioner.

406. What particular arrangements would you foresee before you reach those heights?

(*Mr Boléat*) Whether it is the only arrangement or additional is a second order question. I think it is important that there is that additional safeguard.

(*Mr Challen*) I agree with that. I take it we are talking about arrangements which actually could result in compensation in cases where recklessness or negligence have resulted in loss to either individuals or firms?

(*Mr Herrington*) The law allows the recommendation of compensation to be made but I think it is almost invariable practice for people to comply with the recommendations.

(*Mr Farrow*) If there is such a power to award compensation it should not be paid by the FSA out of fees that it has collected from the industry, it is

inherent in the situation that it should be a charge on public funds.

(*Mr Wanless*) In the first instance it is important that the FSA organises itself internally in terms of the appeal system, as I said in the introductory remarks I made, and how in particular it keeps close to the various markets that it operates in and separates out the disciplinary proceedings for adjudicating. After that when those processes are exhausted then it is appropriate for the Parliamentary Commissioner to be involved.

Chairman

407. If that process was strengthened and it was of the nature that you are describing then you feel that you could sleep easier with the whole subject of statutory immunity?

(*Ms Knight*) No. I think we would still wish to see statutory immunity removed under certain circumstances, such as negligence.

Mr Sheerman

408. There is a lot of international experience here. The question we do not often get the chance to ask is here we have had a range of questions asked this afternoon but are there competitor markets that do it better? Are we missing something that we could change at this late stage of our consultation? We have tried to get more international information but some of us accept this is probably where we have been most limited. Is there international experience from the global companies that you are involved with to suggest that we are missing some aspect of it?

(*Mr Challen*) I am told, but I am afraid I cannot vouch for it, that the SEC do not have statutory immunity.

409. They do not have?

(*Mr Challen*) I am told not.

Mr Beard

410. Do you not accept the inhibiting effect there will be?

(*Mr Challen*) I do understand that.

411. If there is no statutory immunity there will be a great aversion to risk taking and a great deal of people looking over their shoulders rather than proceeding with things that ought to be proceeded with.

(*Mr Challen*) I understand that connection.

(*Ms Knight*) That is why you actually limit the areas from which statutory immunity is removed. We do recognise that potentially if statutory immunity was removed altogether there could be that concern which you raise, yes. There are certain circumstances where, for example, the FSA could potentially act negligently, somebody or a firm's livelihood being severely impaired or removed, they have acted negligently and there is no recourse. That does seem to us to be significantly unfair. That is why, recognising that there are difficulties, we still

[Mr Beard Cont]

believe that in certain circumstances immunity ought to be removed.

Mr Heathcoat-Amory

412. Can I just follow that up. Sometimes it seems that we are trying to regulate a national market in this Bill but actually we are regulating an international market which happens to transact in London or the United Kingdom. I am interested in the sensitivity of this market to the regulatory regime. Presumably a good bit of legislation will act as a magnet for customers and suppliers but bad regulation, arbitrary or ambiguous regulation, might act as a deterrent. I would be interested if any of our witnesses have got a feel for how and whether these wholesale markets are sensitive to both the cost and what one might call the regulatory culture we are developing here.
(Mr Challen) Extremely sensitive.
(Mr Farrow) If I might suggest one of the great concerns of my association is the fear of the combination of uncertainty in the definition of offences allied to very stringent penalties. It has been part of the accepted wisdom that it is very important that the market should be flexible to adapt to new circumstances and to be innovative. If you are subject to a regime which says in the most general terms "you must not do anything which is not proper or which is not of high standard" that is such a vague requirement that if you find some innovative opportunity there is a danger that you will be worried that viewed after the event somebody may decide that you were not working to a high enough standard. You create a worry that people will not, in fact, innovate without actually going to the regulator and saying "look, I am thinking of doing things differently, is that all right?" In that way we could bring to the UK the regulatory tradition that in other markets has basically prohibited anything that has not been explicitly endorsed.

Mr Sheerman

413. It occurred to us that it is a very fine balance, is it not? We have your side coming here and they say we have got to be a competitive market and this is a global business. We understand that and all of us in this Committee want London and the United Kingdom to continue as a competitive place to do this sort of business. On the other hand, we have consumers coming in saying we need much more regulation and protection. What seems to be missing is surely what this Bill must deliver is a culture of integrity where business can be done and one knows it is an honest business with the right parameters and that the culture is right. I do not hear that word either from your side or from their side and it is important, is it not?
(Mr Farrow) I absolutely agree with you. In our earlier discussion one of the points we debated was the absence of any reference to "intent" in some of these very broad criteria about you must have high standards and if I disagree with you about what is high in a particular circumstance or proper in a

particular circumstance, it would be an enormous help if there were some notion that behaviour that was innocent in intent was not at the same time criminal or subject to unlimited fines or whatever. I was very encouraged by our previous meeting because Andrew Whittaker indicated that the question of intent was not a yes/no thing. There is very relevant US experience where intent is an element of the offence but proving it is not as difficult as it might seem.
(Ms Knight) Because the need to balance good regulation against the competitiveness of the financial industry is a very sensitive issue, we believe that it ought to be an issue which is given prominent importance and the non-executive committee reporting on it annually we felt was a good way. Not only does one have to recognise that business of a wholesale nature could be lost out of the United Kingdom if we do not get this right but potentially business of a retail nature could be lost out of the United Kingdom and therefore the desire that consumers have which is to have a far more perfect regime, for want of a better description, than the one we have at the moment could well have the effect of moving the business out of the United Kingdom, using the passport regime back in. With all due respect, I have to say it would be much harder for Mrs Jones in Bognor South to get compensation from a Greek firm quartered in Piraeus because the business had moved out there than it would be if that business were kept within the United Kingdom. So we have to be very careful in balancing the cost of regulation, the certainty of regulation and the needs of consumers, which is what is of benefit to the United Kingdom's financial industry, and the problems that could be associated if we regulated ourselves out of the current scenario.
(Mr Boléat) May I support that, my Lord Chairman. It is more important for the wholesale markets but for the retail markets, particularly with a single passport, regulation is capable of pushing business outside the United Kingdom. In the last evidence I gave I mentioned Ireland as an example. At the moment I do not regard it as a problem but it could be.

Lord Poole

414. There has been a great deal of assertion that business can be moved out of the United Kingdom because of the mechanisms or the pressures of regulation. This is the first time that cost has been mentioned. I have circulated around the Committee responses from quite a large number of banks and others involved in the securities industry. Practically nobody could tell us in any meaningful way what the cost of compliance was to them and, furthermore, they find it very difficult, they said, to distinguish between the cost of compliance and what would have been proper management in any event. With only one or two exceptions people were not even prepared to try in great detail. I do not think it would be fair to name them because it was not a public correspondence but it has been shared with my colleagues. It ill becomes the industry to bang

[Lord Poole *Cont]*

on too much about cost unless it is going to stand up and say, "Excuse me, we would like to present you with some really well thought through numbers on this because we are beginning to be extremely concerned about what is happening." I would just say that I am sure the Committee would find it very helpful were you able to go away and come back with something even if it were only from your area of the world to justify the assertion that these costs would be so great that they would risk pushing the business elsewhere because that is not what the correspondence delivered.

(Ms Knight) Chair, if I may respond. I think that is a perfectly valid question as is the point that has been made. Indeed, regulation is not just a burden, it is also part of operating a business in a proper and businesslike manner. However, where costs start to really cause a problem is rule changes, additional rules and in an incremental nature. We actually published, as an association, the results of a survey that we did of our members three months ago about the costs to them of a particular regulatory change that they were having to make. I made the information available to the FSA and I made the information available in the public domain and in fact it was quite widely reported. On a quarterly basis we are now surveying all of our members, we are listing whatever is the latest regulatory change which will impact upon them—obviously not all will impact upon them—because that enables us to get a cost against these specific items rather than in the areas of generality which I do not think would be helpful for the Committee in order to be able to form a proper view of what is the reasonable cost of regulation and where it is that it really starts to cause an adverse effect and a problem upon firms and consequentially to their customers.

(Mr Boléat) I think I said that I do not regard this as a problem at present. It is very difficult to produce general figures. It is not going to happen that an institution is going to say "we have had enough, we are going over there"; it is far more a business looking at expanding and it may be a British institution that is looking at expanding and it is looking at a range of issues—the regulatory environment, what might happen to it in the future—and as a result of this is it going to locate in London or Edinburgh or Dublin or Piraeus. It is very difficult to pin down. I am not certain that for competitive reasons an institution would necessarily say it is for this reason. I understand what you say, it would be helpful to have nice, solid figures but when we have tried to look at this it is very difficult to differentiate out what a company should be doing for itself and what the regulators require it to be doing.

Lord Haskel

415. If the wholesalers find that the cost of regulation is too onerous, is it possible for them to remain in London yet operate in another jurisdiction?

(Mr Farrow) Yes indeed. The more IT improves, the easier it is to have people who represent the British, the French, the Japanese and the German subsidiaries all actually sitting in the same office

and deciding, as circumstances permit, which of those national companies is actually to be designated as the person who conducted the business. We have been discussing this in terms of companies but we are moving to a world in which competition between exchanges is becoming much more real. The cost of doing a transaction on one exchange is extremely easily compared with the cost of doing the same transaction on another exchange. I believe cost competitiveness in international competition between exchanges is something that we do need to be quite alert to.

Mr Beard

416. We have heard an awful lot about cost competitiveness in this respect. There must also be a price if the regulations are so lax that integrity is eroded and the reputation disappears.

(Ms Knight) Absolutely.

417. We do not seem to hear the same emphasis on that side of that argument.

(Ms Knight) With all due respect, we have all said that we need a balance. It is that balance that we are seeking to achieve, be it practitioners, be it yourselves as the Committee and I am sure the Government itself.

Viscount Trenchard

418. You have talked about the need to maintain the international competitiveness of London because that is clearly crucially important, and it has also been acknowledged that too much regulation will stifle innovation and put major international players off doing business here. On the other hand, the consumer representatives in the main are arguing for enhanced regulation in certain respects. Obviously it is a balance, but do you think in fact that the end consumer has gained from the relatively free atmosphere that has existed in London and restricting regulation in the long term is of benefit to the consumer because it encourages innovation which leads to a wider range of products? Whilst there may be dangers there may also be more to choose from? Obviously you need safeguards. Do you mind very much that the need to maintain the international competitiveness of London is not included as one of the statutory objectives of the Bill? Do you think if it were it would actually be in the interests not only of practitioners but also of consumers?

(Mr Farrow) If I might reply, could I recall that my earliest remark was that regulation needed to be appropriate for the particular area that was regulated. I think there is a very sharp distinction to be drawn between inter-professional markets and retail markets so that the costs that are properly put on the regulation of a retail market do not spill over to be subscribed to by people who are transacting in an international market which could just as easily be in another country but happens to be to our benefit located at the moment in this country. If I might comment from your own experience, my Lord, you have a lot of experience of the Japanese market and

[Viscount Trenchard *Cont*]

I think you will have seen there that stifling regulation can be a very, very considerable burden on competitiveness.

419. I would say that in Japan that is absolutely so and that whenever one sought advice from the regulator as to whether one could introduce some innovation or some new product, one never ever got a clear answer and the result was that one was so frightened that one did not do it and one told one's head office you cannot do it.

(Mr Farrow) You cannot do it here, it would be better to arrange it somewhere else.

420. Do it in Hong Kong or wherever, that is true.

(Mr Boléat) Could I add a point on that. The retail markets also hope that the costs of regulating the wholesale markets do not spill over to them. In terms of innovation the retail markets are also important. I would take motor insurance as an example. I have recently been able to look at that in Japan. The British market is the most innovative, the most competitive whereas the Japanese market consists of 28 companies all doing exactly the same business charging the same agreed premiums. Thus the consumer can benefit very substantially through a competitive market. International competitiveness is important for a number of reasons but so is the competitiveness of the market important for consumers within Britain.

(Mr Wanless) I was going to make a point that one aspect of the regulated regime that has been most destructive in the terms of innovation in the consumer market is polarisation which has inhibited organisations from looking at what they say to customers, how they say it and how they present a product.

(Ms Knight) The first safeguard to the consumer is not winding up the regulation which winds down the choice available, it is actually the education of the consumer.

Mr Sheerman

421. Anyone who has looked at the last four crises in financial institutions will see that what we have got that is probably a greater problem than any other financial centre is a press that, if there is a glitch, another mini scandal, will tell the world that this is an unsafe place to operate and invest in. We have got a unique press for that. Post-Barings they said it was the end of London as a place to do business. We have got to be very careful when what I call building a market of integrity many of us on this Committee will err a little bit on one side rather than the other because we know what the ramifications could be for this very important industry to get it slightly wrong and the press comments on it in the way they do in this country.

(Mr Boléat) Brave comment!

(Ms Knight) We are not here to argue regulation of the press!

Chairman

422. I am about to ask for responses from the Treasury and the FSA. There are just two things I would like to put to you very briefly before that. One of the interesting things I have found sitting in this Committee which is a change from my previous role is the way that people come forward and suddenly want the Treasury to take on tasks. In my former position people were always saying why can you not stop the Treasury doing this? First of all, we had the experience of people volunteering that the fines should come to the Treasury rather than be returned to the industry. Then we had the suggestion that the NAO might be brought into this. Then, thirdly, that the Treasury should have some reserve powers whereby if they did not like something that the FSA was doing it could intervene. In my previous role the case that was put to me was "How are you going to stop the Treasury second guessing". Some of this is a surprise, as I sit here, hearing a suggestion that the Treasury should get more and more involved in these issues. To what extent this is a collective view or are they this just thoughts from some of the individuals?

(Mr Boléat) It is our view that the Treasury should be more involved. It is not because there has been a change of management recently. At the end of the day if something is going wrong the accountability ends with Parliament. That is the fact of the matter. If a regulatory body wishes to be extremely awkward it can be awkward and unless you have got the ability to go to a Minister through an MP or directly then I think you have a serious problem. We have certainly had cases where we have found the Treasury to be extremely helpful on matters that regulators have been dealing with because the Treasury officials, who we regard very highly under both existing and previous management, have an extremely wide knowledge and wide vision. I am grovelling enough!

Lord Poole

423. Are you looking for a new job?

(Mr Boléat) From 7 June I am available! That is not a job application! I do think that the Treasury is often able to look at issues in a wider context than a regulatory body in the same way that I think, for example, the DTI can compared with the Office of Fair Trading. It is in the nature of regulatory bodies that they are more narrowly focused than government departments.

(Mr Wanless) The issues in terms of confidence in the UK financial markets, whether it is about the consumer market or about the international competitiveness of London, are so important that the Treasury should have reserve powers.

(Ms Knight) I agree, Chairman, I was absolutely amazed at these calls for reserve powers to be given to the Treasury. I think one has to recognise that people will believe the Treasury to have responsibility for something and whether the Treasury has or has not people will deem that it ought to have that responsibility. So whether the

[**Lord Poole** Cont]

Treasury has reserve powers or not it will still be heavily involved. The problems, if there are any, that are associated will be heavily debated on the floor of the House of Commons, MPs will have 300 people lining up outside their constituencies, so I do not think we can see this as necessary on one side or other. The point that actually concerns me is that if we get to a position where the Treasury has to step in and use its reserve powers to order the FSA to go down route A rather than route B then I think the FSA has failed and regulation has failed in the UK. I am not sure that leaving reserve powers with the Treasury actually is going to do any good or bring any benefit in practical terms.

(Mr Farrow) Could I disabuse you of one of the reasons why people might want to reserve powers, my Lord, and that is if there are overt powers for the Treasury to intervene then there is a prospect that their intervention will be overt. There is quite often a suspicion that they intervene where they have no powers but they do so covertly.

Chairman

424. I do not think I will join in this debate other than to say that all of the time we had the ability for the Treasury to give instructions to the Bank of England, although this was a power that was never used, it nevertheless was present in the background of most of the discussions that took place. We normally make more use of our witnesses from the Treasury and the FSA. I think the time has come for them to comment on what has been said as we move to the end of this session. I would like you both to have an opportunity to respond, particularly on the question of statutory immunity. I think we have an outstanding question which is just how is it limited under the proposals and how could it be limited? How far, when you begin to limit it, does it take away the power that is there? Also I would ask you if there are any other issues you would like to comment on as well.

(Mr Roe) Thank you. Yes, statutory immunity is limited of course to exclude action in bad faith which reflects the existing position. I do think it is instructive to look at comparisons with bodies which are performing similar functions in other countries. That has been suggested today and the FSA at a previous hearing produced a list of countries where there are comparable arrangements. I think that is a very important point. I think it is also worth stressing that the arrangements for statutory immunity reflect existing arrangements. Again, I think that is very important. On the question of the complaints investigation arrangements, we do not believe that the FSA is a body of the type that falls within the remit of the Parliamentary Ombudsman. However, what we are doing is to provide in the Bill for there to be arrangements for the investigation of complaints which are specific to this particular structure with the investigator being able to publish reports and also to publish FSA responses to his reports. I think this is an opportunity to tailor the arrangements to the particular needs of the circumstances that we are all looking at at the

moment and, indeed, one of the improvements which was made recently was to require the FSA to consult publicly on the arrangements it is putting in place. I think we should see the issue very much in that context. I do not think I particularly felt I needed to say anything else except on the point of having a Treasury power to issue directions. I think we should really ask ourselves whether it would be in anybody's interests were the Treasury in a position where it was constantly being asked to second guess decisions which the FSA was making. It seems to us that would not actually be desirable in terms of having an effective regulator not does it seem necessary given all the other things we are doing to build a successful, effective accountability structure.

425. Andrew?

(Mr Whittaker) Could I just pick up, Chairman, on one outstanding point. Obviously I agree with what David said!

Lord Poole: I think all is revealed now!

Chairman

426. But he has not directed you!

(Mr Whittaker) The one outstanding point that I wanted to pick up on was the reference to the idea that an independent complaints commission might have the power to award compensation. I can see why the Committee is attracted to that. I think the scepticism I would have is one that parallels some of the earlier scepticism and whether in fact it would be practical to arrange that so that the costs of paying compensation fell on the Treasury rather than, as I suspect is more likely, on the industry.

427. Do any of the panel or any members of the Committee wish to ask any more questions?

(Mr Challen) You raised a clutch of issues about Treasury involvement and you only got answers about reserve powers. I would not want you to think therefore that there was universal support for the idea of fines going to the Treasury. I do not think there is any support for that on the Practitioners Forum. We think fines should go to mitigate the costs of regulation but as at present the accounting systems of the FSA should make it quite transparent and not make it a budgetary incentive to find fault.

Mr Heathcoat-Amory

428. It seems to me that there is a good intention to reduce the cost of regulation by offsetting the fine income against the fees but in practice over time the budget of the FSA will also become dependent on fine income, whatever the original intention. Is it not objectionable in principle that a fining agency and decider of legal cases should have a financial interest, however indirect, in the outcome? This seems to be an abuse.

(Mr Challen) I am surprised by your assertion that the fine income will be the predominant source of revenue.

429. Obviously not the predominant source but it will become significant. Fines in America are very substantial.

MINUTES OF EVIDENCE TAKEN BEFORE
THE JOINT COMMITTEE ON FINANCIAL SERVICES AND MARKETS

116

13 *April 1999]* Mr David Challen, Mr Tim Herrington, Mr Kit Farrow *[Continued*
Mr Derek Wanless, Mr Mark Boleat and Ms Angela Knight

[Mr Heathcoat-Amory *Cont]*

(*Mr Challen*) Are you suggesting that we should follow that route?

430. We are legislating here for a long period of time. We have to look at the possibility that there should be some very large fines. I am concerned that the people deciding on those fines should have an indirect interest in the outcome. I think this is a curious arrangement. I am not a lawyer. I think it needs defending rather than simply appealing to a precedent.

(*Mr Challen*) I think the defence is that it is reasonable for the regulated industry to have the costs of regulation reduced by those who have transgressed, presumably therefore increasing indirectly the costs falling on the others. As I have said before it seems to me that the present arrangements of keeping the fine income transparently separate will enable those who scrutinise the FSA, and I include the Practitioners Forum and obviously Parliament, to ensure that is not abused. I can see no reason whatsoever for the Treasury to get their hands on it.

(*Mr Herrington*) The half-way house that we suggested was that the fines should go perhaps to the compensation scheme, or the Ombudsman scheme, that keeps it within the system so that the cost of regulation as a whole is reduced but it does not go directly into the FSA's pocket.

(*Mr Farrow*) May I remind you that I earlier suggested that the fines should go to meet the costs of representation of individuals who are subject to disciplinary procedures. I think you are very familiar with some past cases where the individuals have been at risk of enormous costs as a result of exercising their right to have an independent hearing of their case. The income from fines could be used to meet those costs of representation.

(*Ms Knight*) We believe that the fines should be kept within the system. The important thing there is that there is a public record of that, it is in, it is reported on an annual basis, because that actually does keep a check on a ratcheting up of fines for the sake of ratcheting up, whether they are going to Kit Farrow's good cause or whether they are going to keep down the fees of the regulated firms, whichever it may be. We do need to know precisely what is happening and it is part of accountability that should be there and made public.

Chairman

431. There have, of course, been three lots of transactions that have now been raised. One is the question of what happens to the fines on the industry, the question of who should pay for compensation to people through the complaints procedure and then there is the issue of Legal Aid, which is what you are referring to, which in one sense could get the Treasury involved in each of those transactions or some or all of them could be kept within the industry and in a sense accounted for.

(*Mr Wanless*) My preference would be for the fees to be abated. I think the key issue is the total cost of regulation which is the transparency point basically, that there ought to be a look at the total cost of operating the FSA, the issue of the small amount coming from fines and what the licence fees are separate issues and should be seen as separate issues. It should not be a same year issue, it should be a future year mechanism.

Lord Fraser of Carmyllie: That is tied up with the issue of costs as well. It is not unknown sometimes for fines to be relatively small but the costs to be very significant. It might seem somewhat bizarre to have all costs going to the FSA and a relatively small amount of fines going to the Treasury.

Mr Sheerman

432. The mark of a successful FSA will surely be a low fine income?

(*Mr Boléat*) Transparency is the most important point. There must be no hint that fining is done to increase revenue. How that is achieved is secondary. I thought for one moment you were leading us down the road of using the fines to pay the compensation by the FSA, a circular process.

Chairman: Thank you very much for coming here this afternoon and giving us the benefit of your experience. It has been very useful. Thank you very much.

Printed in the UK by The Stationery Office Limited
4/99   423845   78344

ISBN 0-10-433199-2

HOUSE OF LORDS
HOUSE OF COMMONS

SESSION 1998–99

JOINT COMMITTEE ON FINANCIAL SERVICES AND MARKETS

MINUTES OF EVIDENCE

Thursday 15 April 1999

Lord Hobhouse of Woodborough and Lord Lester of Herne Hill

*Mr Andreas Whittam Smith, Mr David Thomas, Mr Brian Murphy,
Mr Walter Merricks, Mr Peter Dean and Mr Tony Holland*

Mr David Roe and Mr Andrew Whittaker in attendance

*Printed pursuant to the Order of the House of Lords of 2 March 1999
Ordered by* The House of Commons *to be printed
15 April 1999*

LONDON: THE STATIONERY OFFICE
£4.65

HL Paper 50-vii
HC 328-vii

THURSDAY 15 APRIL 1999

Present:

Lord Burns(in the Chair)
Lord Fraser of Carmyllie
Lord Haskel
Lord Montague of Oxford
Lord Poole
Lord Taverne

Mr Nigel Beard
Mrs Liz Blackman
Mr David Heathcoat-Amory
Mr David Kidney
Mr Tim Loughton
Mr James Plaskitt
Mr Barry Sheerman

Examination of witnesses

LORD HOBHOUSE OF WOODBOROUGH, a Member of the House of Lords, Lord of Appeal in Ordinary, and LORD LESTER OF HERNE HILL, QC, a Member of the House of Lords, were examined.

MR DAVID ROE, Head of Financial Services and Markets Bill Team, HM Treasury, and MR ANDREW WHITTAKER, Deputy General Counsel, Financial Services Authority, in attendance.

Chairman

433. Good afternoon, Lord Hobhouse and Lord Lester. Welcome to this Joint Committee. We have had a number of sessions now at which we have been exploring the issues in the draft Bill. We have been taking as our text the Treasury Progress Report which is the Treasury's response to the consultation and asking witnesses how far they think that what is being offered there meets their concerns. We have had two quite lengthy sessions on the whole subject of discipline and enforcement. We have had present David Roe from the Treasury and Andrew Whittaker from the FSA, who are sitting to your right, who have at the appropriate moment been asked to comment on some of the things which have been said, so we have been able to have running interaction on some of the matters. We are very pleased you have been able to come this afternoon. We have recently had another three papers given to us, two of which are particularly relevant, one from the Treasury and one from the FSA, dealing with the question of enforcement procedures. They move the story on, partly I think falling under the heading of clarification. We are particularly interested this afternoon to discuss with you the extent to which you feel the discussion that has taken place, the clarifications we have had, take forward the issues which each of you have previously expressed concern about or have offered views on. That is basically our agenda. I would like to begin by asking you to comment, and to respond to what you have now seen in terms of this moving story; how far you think it takes us; whether the issues that are of your greatest concern are being dealt with; and how much further we have to go. Lord Hobhouse?

(Lord Hobhouse of Woodborough) Thank you for inviting me to attend. As you will appreciate as a Law Lord it is not really open to me to answer legal questions which may in due course come before the courts in particular on the effect of the Human Rights Convention but I am happy that you have asked also Lord Lester to attend, so I will defer to him on any question like that if that is acceptable to you. Now the reason why I have accepted your invitation to appear

is because I am concerned, and I continue to be concerned, about the drafting and inclusion in its present form of part 6 of the draft, that is the part which deals with civil fines and market abuse. It first came to my attention last autumn when I attended a seminar of the Financial Law Panel which was also attended by representatives of the Treasury and by members of the judiciary. I am afraid the view that was formed by quite a number of us on that occasion was that it was not yet in a fit state to form part of a Bill to be introduced to the House. That substantially remains the same position today. The only draft in existence is the same draft as was then seen and the only proposals for relevant changes are those which are to be made to Section 60 and following and part 7. You have asked questions about that and you are definitely interested, and if I may leave that to the discussion, but they do in my view go a long way towards meeting the concerns, and that is very helpful because the previous situation was undoubtedly unsatisfactory. It was summarised eloquently by Mr Loughton at one of your hearings as being both policeman, prosecutor, judge and then the person who had the privilege of spending the fine that had been collected. My concerns relate to Clause 56 and they really remain because there have been no changes proposed to Clause 56 and furthermore certain of the suggestions for the improvement of Clause 56 have been specifically rejected by the Minister. If I might just indicate to you very briefly the headings under which those concerns arise. The first is that Section 56 in conjunction with Clause 58 is a power to fine, and it is a power to impose a punishment. Therefore, whatever may be the technicalities, it is essentially criminal and the use of the word civil is not going to alter this. This is not a scheme for the payment of compensation nor is it a scheme for the payment of restitution or restitution. It is a scheme for punishment and indeed that is the intention of the Minister, as she has made perfectly clear. Normally the scheme for punishment would be connected to a declaration if a certain conduct was illegal. Clause 56 subsection (1) does not make any conduct illegal and it specifically

[Chairman *Cont*]

refrains from doing that. Therefore, as it is drafted at present it purports to authorise punishment for what is lawful conduct. That is something which is just wrong in principle. The situation is made more serious by the provision of subclause (9) which says that behaviour can be inaction as well as action. That means somebody who is under no duty to act in a particular way, no legal duty, can nevertheless be punished for failing to act and that again is an extreme example of the consequences of this draft as it presently stands. Furthermore, and this is a point which has been made on many occasions, Clause 56(1) drafts what we might describe as the "offence" in terms which lack certainty and clarity. Now you may feel that in this area it is very important that there should be certainty and clarity and that at present is lacking as a number of witnesses have pointed out to you. The code in my view, and I can amplify this if you wish, does not meet this objection, and indeed the function of a code in this context should be to provide a safe haven rather than to meet deficiencies in the drafting of the Bill itself. In other words, the function of the code ought to be to tell people what is not unlawful so that they know where they stand; if they comply with the code then they are not going to be attacked. Fifthly, it is a matter of deliberate policy, as has been stated by the Minister in her evidence on 18 March this year, pages 33 to 34, that the intention is to punish innocent conduct. There has been a deliberate exclusion of any element of intent and it is justified solely by the effect of the conduct upon confidence in the market. That is again a difficult concept to support and it is difficult to accept a scheme which includes punishing people for innocent conduct. Sixthly, there is a lack of definition to whom these provisions are to apply. They are separate from the regulatory and disciplinary provisions. They are deliberately drafted so as to apply to the non regulated community. There is no necessary problem about that but you must then engage on a much more precise exercise of definition, than has presently been undertaken. The Minister, if I may say so, with respect, in the same passages to which I have already referred seems to be under a misapprehension as to the way in which the Bill has been drafted. She treats it as applying to people who are participants in the market whereas it is going to apply to people who are non participants. I can amplify this if you wish. It is quite clear from subclauses 1(a),(b), (ii) and (iii) and 5 and that is its effect and indeed some witnesses who have appeared before you have pointed that out to you and that leads on to the seventh point I want to make which is that it applies extraterritorially, and that is subclause 4(b). All those things when one adds them together add up to a scheme for punishing people who may be abroad, who may not be taking any active part in any market in this country, who have not done anything illegal, whose conduct is innocent, who are under no duty to act where they are accused of failing to act, and nevertheless punishing them for such conduct. That is something which needs very careful consideration before it can be approved and indeed if the objectives which underlie that scheme are to be achieved then it needs a new approach to the drafting and much more careful understanding of what is involved. May I say that I am not adverse to effective regulatory schemes and I would wish to endorse the general approach and policy of the Bill in so far as it is proper for me to do so. It is very important that we get it right on this occasion. That has been said on previous occasions and it is self-evident. Furthermore, in this area of commercial activity, there is always a need for certainty, that point has been made to you, and that is lacking at present and furthermore the whole object is to create confidence and confidence will not be created where an uncertain arbitrary scheme, which may well prove to be ineffective, is introduced in this Bill. Now this is what I would call a bolt on provision, Section 56 and following. If it cannot be drafted in a satisfactory form before the Bill is introduced to Parliament then one of the things which ought to be considered is whether it ought not to wait to an amending Bill in order that a properly drafted provision can be introduced.

434. Thank you very much, Lord Hobhouse. Lord Lester?

(Lord Lester of Herne Hill)   Thank you very much, Lord Chairman. I too would like to say what a pleasure it is to give evidence to you and I shall try to follow the example of Lord Hobhouse by speaking bluntly and avoiding legal jargon or gobbledegook because I sympathise with the great majority of your Committee who are not lawyers. Can I just make one or two preliminary points. The first is this is an excellent procedure. It is quite excellent for the Government to come to this Joint Committee to have pre-legislative scrutiny and that you are taking evidence. Secondly, like Lord Hobhouse, I enthusiastically in my case support the aims of the Bill. I agree respectfully with every point that he has made, looking at the Bill through the eyes of a British lawyer, using traditional British principles of justice without even thinking of the European Human Rights Convention. I am not going to repeat any of the points that Lord Hobhouse has made. What I shall do, if I may, is briefly to answer your question, looking at the answer mainly through the eyes of the new constitutional standards that will be in force when the Human Rights Act comes into force. A couple of points on that, if I may. These are not alien, foreign, curious European standards; the standards in Article 6 of the Human Rights Convention were drafted by British legal civil servants reflecting ancient British principles of natural justice and fairness and Article 6 is described in Strasbourg as the "British" Article of the Convention. So we can leave to one side any feeling that this is some arcane alien standard. One other generality, if I may. When the Bill is published, the Minister will undoubtedly put on the face of it his or her view that it is compatible with the European Convention on Human Rights; that is because Section 19 of the Human Rights Act requires such a statement. Now one unfortunate feature of Government practice at the moment is that reasons are not given at the outset for that opinion. Therefore, it seems to me very important indeed for this Joint Committee, if I may say so, to seek to persuade the Government to give their reasons now and before the Bill is published for considering that what they propose is compatible with Convention

[Chairman Cont]

rights. I say that because you have my opinion, my advice, the advice of many others with the cards facing upwards on the table. You can understand what we are saying we think the Convention means. What you do not have is the benefit of the Government's response to that. It seems to me unfair to the Joint Committee if you are not provided with some proper response explaining in respect of each of the concerns what the Government's position is; otherwise you are just looking at one side of the picture. May I just say this that the concerns expressed in my joint opinion and the advice were of course concerns expressed because those were the concerns raised by my clients; but in addition to those concerns I have some concerns of my own. You will not have time to go into them now but may I simply say what they are and then pass on to the Convention. Firstly, I doubt very much whether the statutory immunity from liability which the FSA will enjoy will pass muster under Article 6 of the Convention. Similar immunities have been struck down and I doubt whether that one will stand. Secondly, the combination of an FSA power to fine and to use the fine as a clawback for its legal costs seems to me to be wrong in principle. It is improper to use a fine for that purpose and I am sure that anyhow that process should be done by the independent tribunal and not by the FSA themselves who will be self-interested. Thirdly, I am worried—and here I refer to my colleague Charles Flint QC's lecture which the Committee will have been provided with—I am worried, as he is, by what he calls plea bargaining, the pressure upon a person to plead guilty and submit to a massive fine rather than to appeal. I simply remind the Committee that that European principle of "equality of arms", as it is called, says that you must not put a person into an unequal position vis-à-vis an authority like the FSA. Fourthly, I think that giving the FSA the extraordinary power under Section 55(2) to decide the scope of tort liability between who are to be the private persons who can sue seems to me to be a quite extraordinary power to give to a body that is not Parliament or a Minister. That just seems to me constitutionally improper. And lastly, like Charles Flint QC, I think the principle of legal certainty applies not only if the proceedings are classified as criminal in substance for the purposes of Article 6 safeguards but even if they are civil because here people's civil rights to property and to reputation are going to be determined by the FSA at the first instance and that triggers the requirements of fairness and equality in civil proceedings as well as in criminal proceedings. I shall not repeat the other areas of concern. Those are all set out in the opinion and advice. If it is helpful I can respond as to which of those I remain concerned about. I remain concerned that the market abuses regime will be regarded as criminal whatever the Bill may say and therefore will trigger all the procedural safeguards, the full panoply of safeguards required by Article 6. I think it wholly unsatisfactory that that opinion will only ripen into a decision when the Law Lords decide it in three years' time when the Human Rights Act is in force and someone takes the case all the way there upsetting the entire scheme. It seems to me to be lacking in common

sense if the Bill is introduced with that ambiguity in it—and I respectfully agree with Lord Alexander of Weedon's Delegated Powers and Deregulation Committee's view that that uncertainty must be removed—and it should be removed by making it clear that what are called civil fines, are criminal and by taking the consequences in terms of procedural fairness. I remain very concerned indeed and nothing that I have read anywhere has in any way altered my view or those of many others that this is in substance criminal, as Lord Hobhouse himself has said. So far as the right to an independent and impartial tribunal is concerned I commend the fact that the Government and the FSA have moved to the position where there will be an independent and impartial tribunal able to look at the substance afresh and carry out the trial from the beginning. My concern about legal assistance for those who cannot afford representation remains. As regards the presumption of innocence that I regard as a very serious matter. Plainly it has got to be respected both by the FSA and by the statutory scheme. As far as compelled evidence is concerned, I remain concerned that though I believe it is not understood widely, the compelled evidence problem, the Ernest Saunders case problem, extends to no more than compelling oral testimony and then using it in evidence thereafter. What must not happen is that somebody can be compelled to give evidence and then their testimony can be used, as happened in Ernest Saunders' case. That does not mean that it is necessary to stop a search warrant being used to obtain evidence of documents and so on independent of the will of the accused. There I think it is quite clear that the Bill as it stands would allow breaches of Article 6 in that respect. So far as legal certainty is concerned I will not repeat the very full description given by Lord Hobhouse. There is a complete lack of legal certainty but what you may wish to discuss is what to do about it. Finally, the prohibition against double jeopardy also seems to me to be still a serious concern. In brief the one area where my concern has been largely allayed is in the right to an independent and impartial court.

Chairman: Thank you very much. I think you have amply fulfilled your remit of giving us your opinions with an absence of legal jargon. You are quite right there are many of us who are not lawyers. Mrs Blackman?

Mrs Blackman

435. I think I am going to modify my question in the light of the statements made. On the issue of civil and criminal justice, what can be done now in terms of amending the Bill to take account of some of the more certain or convincing opinions that you have given this afternoon, for example, in terms of your view the whole of the market abuse regime as being criminal. Do you see moves that can be made to clarify with certainty through the Bill which aspects are most certainly criminal?

(Lord Lester of Herne Hill) I think there are several layers of the problem. The first is should the Bill admit on its face that this is criminal, to which the answer is yes it should. Once it does that then Parliamentary counsel will easily be able to reflect the

[Mrs Blackman *Cont]*

consequences of that in the subsequent provisions of
the Bill. What has happened, for reasons I understand
but do not agree with, is the sponsors of the Bill are
attempting to avoid the full panoply of criminal justice
by calling the process civil in form even though it is
criminal in its consequences. The policy decision that
has to be taken, and I very much hope the Joint
Committee will say this, is to recognise what Lord
Hobhouse has said so clearly and strongly and will be
likely to say were he sitting as a judge I suspect,
namely that this is criminal in substance. That is
exactly what the French Court of Appeal and Court of
Cassation have done as recently as December and
January in judgements I have read. It is not just a few
practitioners who are saying this. There are courts that
have decided this already. That is the policy decision.
Once that decision has been taken I think certain
matters will flow from that of a technical kind. For
example, there will need to be a restriction on the
admissibility of evidence that violates presumption of
innocence and other matters of that sort. That is the
key thing which can be done. It is not a drafting
problem. It is a policy question.

Lord Taverne

436.   I am sorry if I have not necessarily got all the
points clear but any knowledge I had of the law was
so long ago I have forgotten it all. You say that 56(1)
lacks clarity and certainty and the Code does not meet
the objection. Do you think then that the Code should
be so comprehensive that it deals with all offences
which can be regarded as within the scope of this part
of the Act?
(Lord Hobhouse of Woodborough) The most
useful function of the Code will be to provide guidance
to people in the City and people who are being advised
what is safe conduct. In other words, it provides them
with a code which if they follow then they know they
are acting in accordance with the requirements of the
authority. That is something which people have
stressed the importance of in evidence to this
Committee beforehand and is very important
practically because people participating in these
markets, whether at the disciplinary level or at the
market abuse level, do need to know what conduct is
permissable. So the Code must, in my view, fulfil that
function for reasons of fairness and reasons of
fulfilling the practical need. What I would like to see
in this Bill would be something which would build that
in as part of the scheme, part 6 at least, which said that
it would be a defence to any allegation of market abuse
that a person had *bona fide* acted in accordance with
the Code. That is looking at it from that point of view.
Looking at it from the other point of view of the
positive, defining the criminal activity, the essential
definition must be in the statute, in the primary
legislation, in my view. If you are creating a criminal
offence or something that is tantamount to a criminal
offence, then it ought to be defined in statute although
certain Is may be dotted and Ts may be crossed in
regulations for example. Certain forms of disclosure
that have to be made, certain types of commodity and
transaction that have to be disclosed, that type of thing,
but there must be a free-standing and adequate

definition in the primary legislation itself. May I say
this: that having looked at the proposed Code it does
not set at rest any of my concerns at all.
(Lord Lester of Herne Hill) Would you mind very
much if I also said something on that question in
answer to Lord Taverne because I find the issues about
legal certainty particularly problematic. Would that
be helpful?

Chairman

437.   It would.
(Lord Lester of Herne Hill) The dilemma is that
one does not want to have the bad old days of the
over-detailed rule book approach on the one hand, but
on the other hand, you want people to be able
reasonably to foresee whether their misconduct will
lead to unpleasant consequences in the form of
massive fines and disqualification. This is a very
difficult problem because one wants flexibility and one
wants legal certainty and plainly the primary Act
cannot solve all the problems itself. One other aspect
is that if this is not got right members of the bar like
myself will be employed by dubious clients who will
use every argument they can think of and incur huge
costs because it will be worth it given the massive
nature of the fines in arguing unmeritorious points
because of defects in the scheme. That is why Lord
Taverne's question seemed to me to be extremely
important. If I can have a stab at answering it. It seems
to me that the more one create binding rules the better
because if one has binding rules rather than vague
moral precepts then that enables one to have
reasonable certainty. What is quite clear to me is that
what you cannot do is to treat the moral precepts in
the Code as triggering what is really criminal liability
because of vagueness and you certainly cannot do what
the FSA now contemplate apparently which is to treat
conduct analogous to what is in the Code as being
potentially capable of triggering liability. So there is a
long way to go in dealing with it and I think Lord
Alexander's Committee suggested one way of dealing
with it would be by way of advance clearance to give
you a safe harbour. That is alright up to a point but I
doubt very much whether the FSA will be very keen
(because they will not have the resources) on providing
an early clearance system. If they are not keen on
doing so they cannot have their cake and eat it as well.
If they are not willing to provide that kind of early
warning early clearance system it seems to me one has
got to go for greater legal certainty. Ideally I would go
for both.

Mr Heathcoat-Amory

438.   It seems to me that if the Government
proceed with this Bill as it is quite large parts of it
could turn out to be unenforceable so rather than
improving regulation we could be undermining it. My
question is what might be the consequences if despite
the ministerial certificate the Bill turns out by the court
to be incompatible with the European Convention in a
number of respects? What might happen? Would the
FSA have to withdraw and try and use other parts of
the Bill? Would the Bill have to be amended by

[**Mr Heathcoat-Amory** *Cont*]

Parliament in short order? Could our witnesses perhaps look a little bit ahead at the worst case scenario to find out what might happen and what we can do about it.

(Lord Lester of Herne Hill) When the Human Rights Act comes into force we will be operating under a new constitutional and legal order because the courts will be given the duty under Section 3 of that Act where possible to construe legislation to conform with Convention rights even by means of a strained interpretation and if they cannot do so then they may grant a declaration of incompatibility, where they cannot with their strained interpretation solve the problem which has been left to them by Parliament. That means that there will be great uncertainty in the market-place until the House of Lords has decided whether section so-and-so can be read compatibly with Article 6 of the Convention or not, to take a concrete case, and whether it is criminal or civil in terms of safeguards. This is not hypothetical. There is a case in the Court of Appeal pending judgement, the Dame Shirley Porter case where her case is that the regime under which she was fined £26 million was criminal in nature and one of the issues even without the Human Rights Act the Court has got to decide and the Law Lords may have to decide is that question. Until that question is solved the markets will not have the faintest idea as to the procedural rights which the alleged wrong-doers will enjoy and the House of Lords will have a choice either to reread the statute to solve the problem, to remove the defect or to say we cannot and therefore we declare it to be incompatible with Article 6 which is what the Court of Appeal decided the other day in another case called *Kebilene* when they decided that a reverse onus provision in terrorist legislation violated Article 6 of the Convention. That is also going to the House of Lords. So there will be a tremendous amount of enjoyable litigation at huge expense for me and my colleagues to no public benefit except to ourselves because of the defects in the legislation. That is why my plea is to take the business away from the bar but to make sure that we have a proper scheme.

Chairman

439. Before going on with the questioning of my colleagues could I ask a question which I keep having to ask myself time and time again as we go through this quite complicated area? How far are your concerns related to the proposed market abuse regime and how far do they relate to the enforcement procedures generally and to other things that may be at issue here? Lord Hobhouse suggested that one part of this might be seen as a bolt-on—the part of it which is to do with market abuse. So far as questions arise from that, it seems to me that one can address them separately. And then there is the more general question, in the comments you are making about certainty and the questions about the criminal nature of some of these issues, of how far they apply to the enforcement process in general. I think it would be helpful to the Committee, as we go on with our conversation, if we could be clear how far they apply to both areas.

(Lord Lester of Herne Hill) I am less certain about the position with regard to disciplinary proceedings than market abuse. The way I would put it is that there is certainly a real possibility, given the draconian nature of the penalties, that the courts would regard these proceedings or disciplinary proceedings of a particular kind, certainly where a mental element was involved—dishonesty and matters of that kind—as being criminal in substance. That seems to me to be a very real possibility. The French cases to which I referred were of course dealing with disciplinary proceedings and the French courts held that because of the draconian nature of the fines, which were far more lenient than any we are talking about, there had to be Article 6 safeguards. So there is at the very least a real possibility that for the most heinous of disciplinary offences they would be regarded as criminal in substance. For the less serious ones, my own view is that they are unlikely to be regarded as criminal in substance. There is probably a spectrum of conduct and the gravity of penalty and the seriousness of the wrong-doing probably have to be taken into account. That is not a very helpful answer because it is vague but it is the best I can do.

440. And that is taken into account the papers we have had from the Treasury and the FSA about how they propose the disciplinary procedure should work. They propose a first stage which is an administrative process and then, where there is not a resolution of the issue, it becomes a judicial matter.

(Lord Lester of Herne Hill) I think they have moved admirably well. I have mentioned already my concern about the fines being inflicted by the FSA including their costs, which is one aspect. The other is the coercive element, saying to Mr X, "You can either go quietly and pay up, or you can exercise your right of appeal". That form of plea bargaining has none of the safeguards it has in the criminal process at the moment and could result in great unfairness.

441. How would you take care of that within the outlines of the scheme which is now being put forward by the FSA?

(Lord Lester of Herne Hill) I would like to think about that. I have not got a ready answer but it seems to me the problem needs to be thought about properly.

Lord Taverne

442. Can I ask you a question which is not covered in your Opinion, and that relates to the procedures which apply to the Ombudsman? Is there any danger that the fairness requirements of Article 6 of the Convention can also be invoked against the provisions dealing with the ombudsman? He seems to have a certain amount of arbitrary jurisdiction against which there appears to be no possibility of appeal. He has great powers to impose very large compensation awards. Is there a danger here too?

(Lord Lester of Herne Hill) I do not know whether the Committee have the benefit of yet another Opinion that was done by my colleague—they are in the same chambers, which I should mention for the record is Blackstone Chambers—David Pannick, QC. No, perhaps I cannot quote from that, it is not an Opinion

[Lord Taverne *Cont*]

which is in the public domain. Suffice it to say that there are some problematic features of the Ombudsman but I would not wish to give evidence on that now without further consideration.

Lord Fraser of Carmyllie

443. As I understand your response it is that the progress report that the Treasury published in March is such that you are confident now that the independent external tribunal would meet the Human Rights Convention requirements, but what you are saying is that does not excuse those who operate the system from ensuring at all stages up to appearance before that tribunal that nevertheless requirements under the Convention have to be met; such issues as equality of arms in plea bargaining have to be considered.

(Lord Lester of Herne Hill) That is right, Lord Fraser. I would be happier if there were a legally qualified chair or president of the tribunal, for obvious reasons. Subject to that, it seems to me that it is going to be an independent and impartial tribunal which satisfies the requirement of that part of Article 6, but the FSA will have a duty under the Human Rights Act, section 6, to comply with the Convention rights. It will not be liable necessarily for damages—that is another point—but it will be liable for damages under the Human Rights Act provided the judges somehow read away the immunity that is to be imposed in the FSA Bill. That is another inconsistency that needs to be removed. We do not want judges having to give a declaration of incompatibility of immunity to allow one to sue the FSA if they unreasonably searched my office or coerced me—and I am sure they would not do any such thing—in a way that violates equality of arms. I think Lord Fraser has summed up my position here.

444. What I wonder is if we might be in danger of focusing too much on the FSA. It is not only the FSA which will have these powers under the Act, Part XV of the Bill as it is presently drafted would allow the recognised investment exchanges similarly to have rules and impose draconian fines, deprive people of their livelihood and the like, and I take it in those circumstances the whole of the Human Rights Convention would apply to those processes as well?

(Lord Lester of Herne Hill) Yes, because they would be treated as public authorities for the purpose of the Human Rights Act and of the Convention. Even if they are private in form, their functions are public in substance and therefore they would be, and all the same safeguards must apply.

445. I think you make the point in your supplementary Advice about some of the previous SROs, that the character of the imposition of discipline in those circumstances stems from the contractual relationship within the exchange.

(Lord Lester of Herne Hill) Exactly so.

446. Am I incorrect then in understanding that once this Bill is in place with this framework that will fly off because the authority that the exchange has exercised in imposing discipline will be as its base a statutory one under the umbrella of the FSA?

(Lord Lester of Herne Hill) That is exactly right. I think in the old system they would have been treated as public authorities for judicial review purposes, but now it is certain beyond argument they will be treated as public authorities under the statutory scheme. I see our colleague in the Treasury nodding agreement. I am sure that is their intention as well. So a whole range of other bodies would be required to act in a constitutional way, if I can use that expression, by which I mean in accordance with traditional British principles of fairness which are anchored in the Human Rights Act and the European Convention.

447. Because both you and Lord Hobhouse expressed the view that three years hence this issue might come before the House of Lords and be regarded as incompatible with our obligations under that Convention. What I want to see if I am correct in understanding is, that issue might arise out of an action which is taken in respect of some disciplinary proceedings by one of these exchanges and not just the FSA itself?

(Lord Lester of Herne Hill) Certainly, and of course that applies not only in the context of this Bill but more widely. We have a unique opportunity at the moment with this Bill to get it right in advance. What I am really saying, and I am sure this is why the Committee is working, we should be prophylactic, we should be preventative, we should not really be authorising either as Government or Parliament a scheme that we know is likely to be highly vulnerable to legal challenge.

Chairman

448. I would like at this point to ask Andrew Whittaker and David Roe whether they would like to respond, bearing in mind, and I think we all have to understand this, theirs is a slightly difficult position in these circumstances. They may not be able to respond in all cases particularly when they are matters for Ministers, but it is often helpful to have their responses at this stage.

(Mr Whittaker) Thank you, Chairman. I would like to respond first on a number of points that have been made in relation to ECHR. We are committed to securing the highest standards of fairness in the way in which we operate. We are, therefore, committed to ensuring that we are complying with ECHR and with the ordinary principles of English justice. We are also committed to doing so in a way that is speedy and effective. We support the Government in fulfilling its original commitment, in the Chancellor's May 1997 announcement, to give us by statute all the powers available to the self regulatory organisations by contract and in particular the power to fine. We think it would be a pity if the introduction of a new single regulator were to result in a loss of safeguards for investors and depositors and policy holders rather than an increase in the protection for them. We also support the Government in wanting to create a civil complement to the criminal law for dealing with market abuse. In our view not all conduct which damages markets should be treated as criminal and it is right for the Government to wish to adopt new

[Chairman *Cont*]

means where old ones have been shown unable adequately to cover the ground. Notwithstanding all that, we recognise that it is right that the Government should give further thought to the issues which have been raised given the importance, with which we agree, of getting this right, and we look forward to seeing a further statement from them in due course. If the Government does conclude that there is real concern that some of the provisions which the Bill characterises as civil and disciplinary should be regarded as criminal there are in principle two options for dealing with the situation. The first one would be to ensure that those provisions are more clearly defined as civil, while the second would be to put in place any necessary criminal-style procedures to ensure safeguards on the basis that they are criminal. Since we support the need for a civil complement to criminal law our preference would be the former, but we believe that potentially either could solve the ECHR issues. Moving on to the concerns that have been expressed in relation to market abuse, we want to confirm again what we have said previously to this Committee, that within the FSA we have no desire to use the market abuse regime to cover innocent conduct. We would have no difficulty with the provision being amended to make it clear that that is not the intention. As we see it there are various ways in which you can improve legal certainty and some of those have been raised in earlier sessions of the Committee. We, for our part, have no problem with legal certainty being improved both by changes to the Bill, if changes to the Bill would help, and by increased reliance on what we do ourselves either in terms of the code of conduct or in terms of guidance which we give. I have made comments previously to the Committee about our willingness to give guidance. Can I just clarify a number of smaller points that have also been made. Lord Lester expressed a concern that we had at one point indicated that we wished to take into account analogous provisions when interpreting more general provisions. If I could just explain what was meant by that. When we are looking at the enforcement of generally expressed principles and there are also rules in an analogous area, we would take into account the existence of those rules in an analogous area in interpreting the principles if there were some ambiguity as to what they were to be regarded as covering. The point has been made that the nature of the penalties we can operate would be draconian but the withdrawal of authorisation is also a very serious remedy, a very serious sanction, and I do not think anyone would suggest that needs to be characterised as a criminal remedy or a criminal punishment. We think that in addition to the nature of the penalty, the seriousness of the penalty, its nature and context can be taken into account as well. Finally, in relation to the points that have been made about coercion in relation to settlement procedures, we have no desire to have a structure in which coercion plays any part. We are ourselves content to provide safeguards against coercion should that be a concern. The main option we are currently exploring in that regard would be the involvement of a professional mediator. That is all I would like to say.

449. Thank you very much, that is helpful.

(Mr Roe) I would like to underline that the Government is entirely committed to achieving fairness whilst at the same time not losing sight of the objectives of having effectively regulated markets, which is after all the purpose of the regime. The Economic Secretary when she gave evidence in the Committee did say that there were some issues relating to the Convention on which she would be coming back to you. I would not like my silence or any physical gestures to be interpreted as necessarily implying assent to anything that has been said. On one particular point, on which I would like to look at the record, there was some discussion of the position of recognised investment exchanges and the way that their status would be changed by the current legislation. I am not sure whether that was quite right. I cannot give you a definitive view on that now but it is just something that I would like to flag up as something that when I heard it did not sound quite right to me.

450. Thank you very much. Can I ask one question first for clarification before we move on. In the further memorandum by the Financial Services Authority, Lord Hobhouse, in paragraph four——

(Lord Hobhouse of Woodborough) Can I just find the document.

451. It is FSM 91.[1]

(Lord Lester of Herne Hill) Is that the one attached to the questions we received?

452. No. If you cannot respond immediately maybe you could have a look at it whilst the discussion goes on. In paragraph four they say: "In principle, we would have no difficulty with a provision that made clear that the FSA could not take action to impose a civil fine for market abuse where conduct is in compliance with the Code."

(Lord Hobhouse of Woodborough) I have not yet found the reference, I am sorry.

Chairman: It is paragraph four. This is a response to some of the points that have been raised. I would be interested to know how far they go to meet your concern.

Lord Taverne

453. I was going to ask Lord Hobhouse, or Lord Lester, to respond to a point that was made by Mr Whittaker. Are there circumstances in which fines can be imposed which would not make the conduct a subject of the criminal law? see Q 439

(Lord Hobhouse of Woodborough) My belief is that the answer to that is no in all practical terms. You can fine for civil contempt of court, for example, but I think it would be wrong to build on that analogy in the present context.

(Lord Lester of Herne Hill) Under the Convention there are minor fines, like traffic fines, that are not regarded as triggering criminal safeguards but anything which is a serious fine—sorry, not anything. I will start again. If the fine or potential fine is so

---

[1] Appendix 5.

[Lord Taverne *Cont*]

large, as it would be in this case, then that would tend to trigger criminal safeguards as the French case has illustrated.

Lord Montague of Oxford

454.   Lord Lester, you did state earlier that you were doubtful about the use of fines. Perhaps you could indicate where you think the destiny of the fines would be acceptable?

(Lord Lester of Herne Hill)   What I was doubtful about was not the use of fines, it was about the use of fines to claw back the FSA's legal costs.

455.   Yes, I realise that.

(Lord Lester of Herne Hill)   It is that combination of two completely different interests. Once you allow the FSA to use the fining process to fund itself rather than giving the money to the Treasury the consequence of that is to create a series of vices. One is that the FSA then appears to be self-interested, and indeed is self-interested, in the amount of fines since it is a way of recovering their own expenses which may be massive in a complicated case. The other is that they become, if you like, judge in their own cause, and with this coercive element, although I welcome the recognition that safeguards may be able to be built in by the FSA against that with the mediation process, but still coupled with that it seems to me that one is going to have a very coercive and unfair result if the fine can be used by the FSA to fund itself. That is why I think one should give that function strictly to the tribunal. So I am not against the use of fines in principle, it is the safeguards and purpose for which the fines are used which I think is important.

Chairman

456.   If there was an arrangement whereby the FSA had to budget within its normal budget procedure for its enforcement costs, but there was a system where the fines were used as a rebate back to the people who were paying their fees and it went directly and was not influenced by whatever the costs of enforcement had been, would that still leave you feeling very uncomfortable?

(Lord Lester of Herne Hill)   I would feel less uncomfortable because it would simply be in a sense a formality to route it in that way rather than to the Treasury. My concerns are more with it including their own costs and it being decided by them themselves.

Mr Kidney

457.   Could I just ask a couple of questions, first of all on the whole disciplinary regime? Administrative fines do not necessarily have to be classified as criminal, from what you are saying. We have in this country administrative fines from the Revenue and the Department of Social Security and so on, do you accept they are quite acceptable as a civil alternative to the criminal one?

(Lord Lester of Herne Hill)   I certainly agree, as I think I said at the beginning, that it is a more open question as to when administrative proceedings

involving fines become criminal in substance and when they remain civil, and I said there is a spectrum. So they can remain civil, it is a question of degree.

458.   Is part of the degree the amount? The Inland Revenue, I think, is up to 100 per cent extra of the amount the person fiddled, if you like, and the Department of Social Security is 30 per cent of the amount over-claimed. Would you say they are quite modest things, whereas an open-ended fine under the FSA is huge?

(Lord Lester of Herne Hill)   There are three criteria they use under Article 6. They are, what is the purpose, is it really criminal in substance? Here it seems to me the purpose is very largely a deterrent, it is to win the confidence of the rest of the world that we have procedures for regulating the City of London and matters of that kind, which is very important. Once it becomes punitive as a deterrent, then on the first criterion of the European Court's case law it will be classified as criminal. The second one is whether the wrong is specific to a particular class of people or to the general community, and that is not a very important test, it does not really much affect us. The third one, which really matters, is the degree of severity of the fine and there it seems to me, given the massive fines on those first and third criteria, as I think I said in my advice, it is very possible that they will be regarded as criminal like the market abuse offences.

459.   I would like to move on to market abuse and the whole new civil regime. Again there are countries which have legislated for a civil alternative to the criminal regime. Spain has a civil wrong alongside the criminal wrong, and in the USA they now have a civil remedy alongside the criminal remedy. The SEC can go to a court to impose a civil penalty. Are they all then in danger of being really criminal in nature or are there levels of degree so that the civil regime for market abuse can be acceptable if it is drawn correctly?

(Lord Lester of Herne Hill)   It is complicated to answer questions about comparative law and practice without knowing the full legal regime of the country concerned.   Let me take as an example the United States. You are perfectly right in saying that the SEC is able to use civil as well as criminal sanctions, but the SEC is closely regulated not least by the due process clause in the American Bill of Rights and there have been a number of constitutional cases which have interfered with what the SEC might have wished to do, in a similar way to the examples which Lord Fraser of Carmyllie was suggesting when the Human Rights Act comes into force. Of course the United States is not a party to the European Human Rights Convention and therefore the problem will not be characterised in quite the same way under their system. I know nothing about the Spanish system, except their written constitution I am sure will enshrine the Convention's safeguards and there may well be Spanish case law from its constitutional court about which I am not an expert.

460.   Is it your view that we could draw a civil remedy alongside the criminal one for market abuse in this country which would be completely compatible?

(Lord Lester of Herne Hill)   I would have to see the colour of their money first before I could comment.

[**Mr Kidney** *Cont*]

It is too abstract a question I think for me to be able to answer.

(*Lord Hobhouse of Woodborough*)   The problem is if you go down the fining route you then have to accept the consequences of liberty to impose fines. If you accept all those consequences then you may find at the end of the day you comply with the Convention, that you treat it as effectively a criminal proceeding although it does not go before an ordinary court, that it satisfies the requirements of fairness, protection against self-incrimination and so on. So you can achieve a result of that kind by redrafting and you can also achieve the necessary degree of certainty but you have to decide at the start which route you are going to go down and then comply with the necessary requirements.

Mr Loughton

461.   Does this problem still apply if you are not talking about financial fines but the penalties are in terms of restrictions of membership rights, in terms of suspension of right to trade in financial products or whatever they might be? Does that get away from some of these legal problems if we are not talking about purely financial penalties?

(*Lord Lester of Herne Hill*)   The question is a very general one. English and Scottish fairness requirements will apply as much to disqualification, loss of livelihood and loss of reputation, as they will to fines, so all the requirements of natural justice, fairness, and all the administrative law requirements will apply. As I said before, under the Convention as well, because one is determining someone's civil rights, including the right to a good reputation and their livelihood, that will also trigger many of the procedural safeguards in Article 6 of the Convention. Not all of them, because for example the privilege against self-incrimination may be looked at differently whether it is criminal or civil, both under Convention law and under English law. In both cases the fairness requirements are strong and apply whether it is civil or criminal.

462.   I understand. I am not a lawyer but to take a specific example, a hypothetical case, fund managers to be regulated by the FSA pay their membership dues or whatever and have to be licensed to sell certain products, if an ISA provider did not live up to the expectations and its clients were aggrieved by the way it ran its ISA funds or whatever, and as a consequence the FSA said, "For the next financial year you are not allowed to be a provider of ISAs", which did not involve any fine but did involve taking away the livelihood, which only came about because that financial institution became a member of the club to carry out that chosen nature of business, does that make it any easier under the European angle than being penalised by a heavy fine which tends towards the criminal side, as you are saying?

(*Lord Lester of Herne Hill*)   No. I think what I am saying is that the detriment is as great whether it is financial or putting you out of business for a year or more and blighting your reputation, and the fairness requirements apply with great force in both situations.

But there may be some situations where, and this is rather technical, because there is a fine and because it is a deterrent and penal in its consequences, it has to be classified as criminal and therefore the additional requirements with regard to the presumption of innocence in particular will apply.

(*Lord Hobhouse of Woodborough*)   If I might add to that, there is a distinction between the withdrawal of a privilege and the imposition of a punishment. If you are doing it under the regulatory scheme and saying that somebody requires to be licensed you have to justify the regulatory scheme. In other words, you have to show the need for it and that the regulations which you introduce are appropriate and reasonable and not disproportionate. Then if somebody fails to comply with that reasonable scheme then provided they are subject to a fair procedure which will decide whether or not they have failed to comply you are not getting into the ambit of what most people would regard as punishment. If you start imposing fines then you are potentially in a different area and for practical purposes in the area that we are talking about it looks as though you will almost inevitably be in that area. Just to go back to the market abuse type of situation, if the regime were to be that you could go to court and get an injunction against people who were practising market abuse then you would be in the civil area. If you were saying that we will make it a tort, rather like under Clause 55 in a better format, then that again would be civil, or restitution of unfair enrichment, unjust enrichment. Those would be within a civil scheme but once you introduce the system of fining, which is punishing, then you have these problems.

(*Lord Lester of Herne Hill*)   Could I just add one thing in addition about the Convention. The Bar Council of England and Wales has a disciplinary system and a barrister who was disbarred brought a case in Strasbourg against the United Kingdom on the basis that the procedures were not sufficiently fair and the procedures were revised as a result of the Bar thinking more clearly about Article 6 of the Convention. It is quite a good example of the way in which Article 6 can require full fairness particularly in a professional disciplinary context.

Lord Poole

463.   I find it quite difficult to get my head around some of this. We have heard from the Minister and the FSA a mantra which basically says "Of course we are very concerned to do everything properly and conform with the ECHR" and they are not sitting, as it were, very far away from you and you are saying "Excuse me, I think there are a number of examples of areas in this Bill where I do not think you are going forward". I assume that there is space here for reasonable people to disagree but am I right in saying that really what you are trying to do is to alert us to what you would between you consider to be some very high probabilities, that it would be unwise of the Government to proceed without taking seriously into account?

(*Lord Lester of Herne Hill*)   I am really saying, first of all, that as this is pre-legislative scrutiny the Government should, and I am sure if asked would,

[**Lord Poole** *Cont*]

provide the Joint Committee with its best view about the impact of the European Human Rights Convention and British constitutional principles of law to their scheme. That ought to come now, I think, rather than after the Bill has been published so that the Committee is well informed and can make a report based upon it. Secondly, it must be better for the Bill to be in as perfect a state as possible before it is introduced rather than after and certainly before it has been enacted into law. My experience as someone who worked within Government, not as great as that of you, Lord Chairman, is that the time to improve legislation is before it is introduced into Parliament since what happens thereafter is of much less significance.

Chairman: I think we will have to consider whether we can press the Government to give their views before we come to make our report but, as you know, time is extremely short. One other possibility is that we could try to press them to make their views known after our report has been published but before the Bill is introduced. We will have to discuss with them what the best timetable is for that. I am very grateful for the evidence. I think the Committee has found this session immensely helpful. In the light of the additional document we have shown you this afternoon if there is anything you want to add now or if you would like to let us know at a later point we would of course be enormously grateful for that too. We are adopting an approach of trying to find ways in which we can bring together the evidence that we have had and make suggestions about how the Bill might be improved. We are not adopting an approach of just standing back and saying "This is something that will not work", we are actually looking for solutions to some of these problems but obviously in the very

limited time we have got there is only so much we can do.

Lord Taverne: I have one question. We have very thoroughly explored the provisions about market abuse and I did ask a question about how the Convention might also affect the provisions in this Bill for the Ombudsman. I am not aware of any opinion having been put before this Committee on this also equally important question. Lord Lester mentioned that there was an Opinion which he had which also seemed to think this is a very important question. Could we perhaps have that as well because we may persuade the Government to avoid a dreadful mistake dealing with market abuse and then find that they have made an equal howler in the section dealing with the Ombudsman.

(Lord Lester of Herne Hill) I inadvertently referred to an Opinion of which I have knowledge but it is not my property. The client has ownership of the Opinion and, therefore, I cannot say any more about it except that my own opinion is that the Article 6 provisions undoubtedly apply to the Ombudsman and have serious implications for the way that the Ombudsman system is brought into existence. That is what is now going to be considered, I understand, at your next session.

Chairman

464. It is.

(Lord Lester of Herne Hill) It may be that the FSA might be able to provide you with their view about the impact of Article 6 on the Ombudsman.

Chairman: Thank you both very much, it has been very helpful.

Examination of witnesses

Mr ANDREAS WHITTAM SMITH, Chairman, Financial Services Ombudsman Scheme, Mr DAVID THOMAS, Banking Ombudsman, Mr BRIAN MURPHY, Building Societies Ombudsman, Mr WALTER MERRICKS, Insurance Ombudsman, Mr PETER DEAN, Investment Ombudsman, and Mr TONY HOLLAND, Personal Investment Authority Ombudsman, called in and examined.

Mr DAVID ROE, Head of Financial Services and Markets Bill Team, HM Treasury, and Mr ANDREW WHITTAKER, Deputy General Counsel, Financial Services Authority, in attendance.

Chairman

465. Good afternoon. It is very nice to see you all. I am sorry we are over-running a little but, as you heard, we were dealing with some quite difficult matters. For those of us who are not lawyers it has taken us a little while to get our minds round them. This session is an opportunity to talk about the Ombudsman scheme and we are very pleased to see you all here. I have said to other witnesses that if there is anything else outside the scope of the particular subject we have defined for the session which you wish to offer comments about, we are very happy to have them but our main purpose is to concentrate on the Ombudsman scheme. I suggest the way forward might be to ask you each to introduce yourselves and to give us any introductory remarks you might like to make.

(Mr Whittam Smith) Thank you very much, Chairman. Like everybody who has appeared in front of you, I am extremely glad as an interested party to have a chance to comment on the Bill. I think we have been asked by way of introduction to speak for three or four minutes. I am the Chairman of the Financial Services Ombudsman scheme and therefore not an ombudsman, and not likely to be so either. I thought it might be useful if I just said a little as to how I see the scheme developing. The first point I would like to make is that normally if you are engaged in a merger of some kind or reconstruction it is because what has gone before has not been done very well, but this is not that case at all. What has gone before has been done very well. In the seven weeks in which I have been Chairman I have got to know the schemes as well as one can in that period and they are extremely effective and two of them are voluntary and that is an admirable thing. So the Financial Services Ombudsman Scheme Limited's task is to build on the success of the existing schemes and the question is, in what way can we be better. I think there are a number of points I would like to make here before I hand over to one of my colleagues. What are the advantages to be seized? First of all, of course, that we can provide a single point of entry for complainants. That is extremely important. However, I would not like you to think that it has been a grossly confusing situation up to now, the schemes individually are very used to receiving enquiries and complaints from people who should have turned to another scheme and they are very good at directing people, so there is already a work around if you like, but we shall be able to dispense with the work around and provide a very clear single point of entry. Partly as a consequence of that and partly because of our size, we should be able

to make ourselves much better known, that is extremely important. We will be a single scheme, we will have the ability to make ourselves better known, we will have a single address, a single telephone number, and I shall want us to log and examine how well we are known as we go along, and I hope to find that is a rising curve. Thirdly, as a single scheme we can try—and this is going to be a complicated business—to remove any gaps and overlaps which exist if you look at the eight schemes as they are. We can make a more coherent pattern. That, however, is going to depend upon the whole notion of the compulsory jurisdiction and the voluntary jurisdiction, and as we shall probably come to later on that is not the easiest system in the world to work. Fourthly, there will be some economies of scale. I do not think the economies of scale are going to be huge, they certainly will exist, but the primary job is to be a case worker and there are no economies of scale to be gained from putting case workers together, but in all the support services there clearly are. So there are some gains of efficiency to be sought. I think that putting the schemes together will yield something which I always pay great attention to and find well worth working for, which is there should be a fruitful chemistry when you put together eight schemes which have been independent and know each other rather well at the level of the ombudsman but do not know each other very well below that level, and I think they will learn from each other and will develop the creativity which was not possible before and will result in a better service to the consumers. Finally, although the existing schemes certainly are independent and have run independently, and nobody I think has ever impugned their independence, nonetheless the consumer may believe they are not, that the industry somehow must control them when all is said and done. I think that charge will be less capable of being levied against us because of our arrangements. I think our arrangements are clearly and signally independent and that itself is a virtue. That is as far as I would like to go now and I may have exhausted my four minutes.

(Mr Dean) Chairman, I have been deputed to act as a quasi-spokesman for the Ombudsmen, although others will speak from time to time and answer individual questions. Can I start with some introductions? On my right is Mr Walter Merricks, who is the Insurance Ombudsman. I am the Investment Ombudsman. To my immediate left is Mr Brian Murphy, who is the Building Societies Ombudsman, on his left Mr Tony Holland, the Personal Investment Authority Ombudsman, and on his left Mr David Thomas, the Banking Ombudsman. We are a diverse bunch. Two of us run voluntary schemes, that is to say

[Chairman *Cont]*

the Banking Ombudsman and the Insurance Ombudsman. One of us is a statutory scheme, that is Mr Brian Murphy's Building Societies Ombudsman scheme. The other two, Tony Holland's and mine, are hybrid schemes, we exist by virtue of two of the SROs, the PIA and in my case, IMRO. Despite this diversity and we have come into being at different times over the last 20 years—the Insurance Ombudsman scheme is the oldest, about 18 years old, others more recent— there are more similarities between what we do than there are differences. We are all in the business of resolving complaints and we all seek to do so promptly and fairly and informally. The Ombudsman story is a story of success. It is gratifying that Mr Whittam Smith should say that rather than you simply hear it from our mouths. It is a system which is favoured by consumers and consumer bodies and also by the industries. Against that background of success we are obviously pleased as Ombudsmen that it is an Ombudsman scheme that has been chosen as the method of dispute resolution as part of the new regime, albeit it will imply the extinction of our individual offices. Over the last 12-18 months we have collaborated as far as we can in anticipation of the legislation by making recommendations to the FSA, comments to the Treasury and latterly, of course, a submission to yourselves. In our memorandum to you we have highlighted three points. First, the paramount importance, as we see it, of minimising formality. It is an extremely important feature of the Ombudsman schemes that they do operate very informally and flexibly. We are delighted, therefore, that some of the provisions in the draft Bill relating to appeals on points of law and cost orders and so forth are no longer going to be pursued, but we are left with residual concerns about Article 6 and I am sure you will wish to come on to that later on. The second matter concerns scheme coverage, the coverage of the new scheme, and we remain concerned about gaps, particularly in relation to unauthorised mortgage lending firms and consumer credit firms. Thirdly, we are uneasy about the dependence on a cost benefit analysis as being a prerequisite for the FSA to exercise its discretion in deciding the scope of the compulsory jurisdiction. We are not opposed to cost benefit analyses as a matter of principle, we just question whether they are an adequate means of measuring the value of an Ombudsman system. Simple comparison of cost and benefit does not seem to do that. Lord Chairman, that was all I wanted to say by way of introduction and we will be happy to take any questions which you put to us.

Chairman: Thank you very much.

Mr Loughton

466. Some of us, myself not included, were able to speak to the Chairman the other day. In general terms could you perhaps tell us why the Ombudsman scheme is such a success and what advantages it has over a tribunal system or other systems for example?

(Mr Dean) One of the things that we can do is investigate. We take an active role in investigating, getting at the facts which tribunals typically find it hard to do. We operate an inquisitorial process as opposed to an accusatorial one or adversarial one. Secondly, we are able to conciliate, we are able to take measures during the course of an investigation which mean that a complaint can be resolved sometimes very quickly and amicably without a great deal of fuss and without the need for a formal determination by the Ombudsman. There are advantages of informality. I think that it is a more user friendly process than many tribunals, it is flexible, there are cost advantages, and I have to say that the Ombudsman schemes are a proven success, they have shown that they work.

467. Could you contrast it with, say, the Parliamentary Ombudsman, of which many Members here will have a greater experience, in terms of it is more formal from what you say, the timescale is rather more drawn out, although that has been improved a little one hopes. What can the Parliamentary Ombudsman learn from yourselves? That is one point. Secondly, stemming from that, perhaps you could comment on your different experiences in different roles as statutory bodies or as voluntary bodies as you have been but all coming from slightly different angles.

(Mr Dean) I think we must resist the temptation posed by your first question to tell the Parliamentary Ombudsman how to do his job.

Lord Fraser of Carmyllie

468. Go on.

(Mr Dean) He is actually doing a very different job from us. What we are doing is looking at complaints by customers of firms and arriving at a view typically as to what is fair and reasonable in the circumstances and saying what that is and the firm pays up or does not pay up if it is not fair to do so. The Parliamentary Ombudsman has no power, as I understand it, to fine or indeed to do much except express opinion.

Mr Loughton

469. He can institute penalties.

(Mr Dean) In that case I am wrong about that. As regards timescales I really would not like to comment on that. We have rather different timescales among ourselves as to how quickly we resolve complaints. All I can say is that we do our best to resolve them very quickly.

470. And your different approaches?

(Mr Dean) Others might wish to chip in here. I would say that the different approaches are not so significant as you might think. We do find ourselves all doing substantially the same job irrespective of whether we have voluntary origins or statutory origins, we are all resolving disputes as rapidly as we can. There are some differences in so far as the voluntary schemes may not have within their jurisdiction everybody they might wish whereas the statutory schemes may do so, or in Tony Holland's scheme and mine we do have within our jurisdiction the firms subject to the Personal Investment Authority jurisdiction and IMRO jurisdiction. The similarities are greater than the differences I would say.

[**Mr Loughton** *Cont*]

471. Finally, you mentioned gaps. Could you perhaps comment on some of the complaints that fall outside your remit at the moment and how you think that may now be plugged? Can you give us some examples perhaps of things that you have not been able to tackle.

(Mr Dean) I mentioned two in my opening comments and I will ask one of my colleagues to deal with those. So far as gaps, we do, as Mr Whittam Smith said at the outset, have a pretty crisp system of passing on complaints from one of us that should go to one other and that is really not too much of a serious problem. I think we probably would not be able to give an answer as to how many complaints come to us that actually fall outside the remit, we have not added those figures up. On the two particular matters, consumer credit and mortgage, which are matters of concern perhaps I could ask David Thomas to talk about those.

(Mr Thomas) If I can just pick up one earlier comment. Brian Murphy runs the Building Societies Ombudsman Scheme which is statutory, I run a scheme which is voluntary, but in the nature of the complaints that we deal with they are very much the same. It is the nature of the complaint which typifies the differences, in so far as they exist, between the different schemes. What Brian Murphy and I do is very similar and in so far as it is different from what Peter Dean does or what Tony Holland does it is because of the different nature of the product with which we are dealing. Leading on to the jurisdiction point, we are concerned about three inter-related issues. We are concerned first that the new Ombudsman scheme should have a jurisdiction which is at least as wide as the aggregate of the existing Ombudsman schemes so that nothing which is covered now ought to be left out. Secondly, we are anxious to identify any gaps and to take this opportunity of plugging them or at least providing the legislative framework by which they may be plugged at an appropriate stage in the future. Thirdly, to ensure that the subsequent framework is one which consumers can actually understand, that they will be able to tell without a lot of complicated explanation from us as to whether we will be able to help them or not. There are two areas of particular difficulty which concern us. The first area is the area of lending money. Lending money is something which is often done by organisations which hold a deposit-taking licence, typically banks or building societies, but it is often done by other organisations. Ombudsmen schemes exist to redress the uneven balance between the small consumer and the large institution with whom they are dealing and indeed to replace the feeling that all was not equal between those parties in the courts. It is probably difficult to find a circumstances where parties are more unequal than where one is talking about the relationship between a lender and a borrower and therefore, if there is any area which cries out for comprehensive coverage, it is where money is being lent. We have a situation at the moment where the majority of mortgage lenders are banks or building societies but there are a small number of mortgage lenders, some of them with practices which have been criticised very severely by for example the Office of Fair Trading, who do not fall within our existing jurisdictions and it would appear are likely to fall outside the jurisdiction of the new Ombudsman scheme. Secondly, there are mortgage brokers who introduce business to various lenders. Insofar as they are also authorised for investment business, presently under the Financial Services Act, they will need to be authorised by the Financial Services Authority and the Financial Services Authority will be able to bring them within the scope of the new Ombudsman scheme. But insofar as they do not do other financial services business, the FSA will not be able to bring them into the scope of the compulsory scheme according to the system as it is currently proposed. So if you envisage a typical high street with three mortgage brokers, Mortgage Broker A also sells endowment policies and is forced by the FSA to be in the Ombudsman scheme, Mortgage Broker B does not sell endowment policies but voluntarily decides to join the Ombudsman scheme and come under its jurisdiction, and Mortgage Broker C, who is probably the one who most needs it, decides not to join the Ombudsman scheme at all. Where we are trying to create a scheme that is simpler for consumers to understand, it seems to me that is a situation which is not particularly easy for them to understand. The final area is the area of credit cards and personal loans where at the moment there are some organisations which are providing credit cards which are neither banks or building societies and which are not covered, and there are many organisations out there which are providing personal loans which have licences from the Office of Fair Trading authorising them to provide loans but they will not require that authorisation by the FSA and therefore will fall outside the Ombudsman scheme for compulsory jurisdiction as proposed.

Lord Montague of Oxford

472. I would like to develop what you have been saying a little and slightly change the terminology because it is being summarised now as a one stop shop, and that is certainly the impression the consumer will get and is increasingly getting. You have explained what you want to bring into, as it were, the one stop shop and I am concerned about how all this will be made known. I do not know whether it is the intention of the Ombudsman to produce an annual report, annual guidance, I do not know about your budget and whether you will have sufficient funds to make things clear. I think the combined expenditure of all of you is about £15 million, is that right? Clearly you will need to supplement that. I am also a bit concerned about the impression that the public will get about where it will get help, which is not quite the same as someone resolving a particular dispute. Help it can of course get from the FSA, it is only when there is a dispute they will turn to the Ombudsman, so I would like to hear about how this is likely to be clarified.

(Mr Whittam Smith) Starting with your last point, I think it will be very important for the FSA, which will have the power I think, to compel providers of financial services to make it plain at the point of the transaction that there is an Ombudsman scheme so as part of the basic literature, the basic deal, if you like,

[Lord Montague of Oxford *Cont*]

you are put on notice there is an Ombudsman scheme. Clearly you should first complain to the provider but you should always know the Ombudsman scheme is there as a back up. If that is done, I think it would already be a great improvement. Secondly, we will, indeed must, publish an annual report but I think there must be much more than that and I think it would be very important for us to publish a series of bulletins and perhaps special papers designed not only to inform the public quite often by a secondary route, which is through the financial press, but also we do have a role I think to play in helping the industry to improve its own procedures. I think it would be very important for us to try and do that. But I am absolutely committed to broadcasting the scheme as widely as possible and I think it is very much the responsibility of the board to know that it has to adopt a sort of evangelical, missionary approach to this. Everybody must know about it.

473. The budget?

(Mr Whittam Smith)   No work has been done on the budget yet. From my point of view, I have observed, as you have, that the combined spending is about £15 million, but that is a figure which, if it were the available revenue for a commercial enterprise, would yield on normal considerations enough money to put in hand a reasonable promotional and marketing campaign.

Mr Sheerman

474. Our role as a pre-legislative inquiry is to tease out whether there is at this stage any improvements you would like to see in the Bill as drafted. The big question is, are there? Is the Bill giving you sufficient powers? Are you happy with them? Can you see modifications which could take place at any stage which could make it more effective? I am one of these sceptics who start off thinking almost that this is an alien concept drafted in Scandinavia— and Andrew and I had this conversation the other morning. You do say you are very successful but, representing a constituency which is a fairly average constituency, I do know that the most financially deprived people in my constituency probably have the most trouble getting access to you or knowing about you because you are quite a complex set of people with quite complex rules. I think you still appeal very much to the *Moneybox* type of listener, the professional middle classes, and you have actually failed to get down to the people who pay mostly on credit and get into the most financial trouble because they pay high interest rates and all the rest. You are talking to a sceptic, so can you on the one hand tell me that this new improved Ombudsman is going to get to the parts which have not been reached before, and on the other hand are you content with the Bill as framed?

(Mr Dean)   So far as getting to the parts which have not been reached before is concerned, there is nothing we would wish to add to what Mr Whittam Smith has already said. So far as improvements in the Bill are concerned, I think I said at the outset what our main concerns were. I think that the issue of gaps is

one which possibly is capable of being dealt with. We do not have drafts here to put on the table but I think that possibly is. So far as minimising formality is concerned, that is a more complicated question. The issue revolves largely around, so far as our current concerns go, the effect on Article 6 of the European Convention on Human Rights, about which you have heard a great deal earlier this afternoon. Our perception of the matter is that there is no doubt at all, as we understand it, that Article 6 will apply to the new scheme as it is currently envisaged because it is conceived as a compulsory scheme which will bind and no amount of tinkering with the wording here or there will alter that situation. If that remains the Government's intention then a consequence is going to be that it will be subject to Article 6. Our discussions have proceeded on that footing. The issue therefore is, how does one minimise the effects of Article 6 and that is something upon which we have more work to do. I think so far as this Committee is concerned it would be very helpful if, to the extent you agree with us, you would bear in mind the virtue of and need for informality as the Bill wends its way through Parliament and keep an eye on it. I do not know whether Mr Holland wants to add to that?

(Mr Holland)   Yes, I would. The Article 6 point is the crux, as far as my colleagues and I are concerned, of whatever success we may have had—I appreciate that may be a contentious view—and certainly the success of the new scheme. Just to give you a flavour of what happens at the moment, I can only speak as to my own operation but it is quite a large one, I have 130 staff and of those 70 are case officers and they made over 9,000 decisions last year. The normal process is not that different from that of my colleague's. When a complaint or a dispute comes in— it is quite a cross-section of people who send in complaints ranging from the less well off to the quite well off—the case officer initially tries to mediate between the two parties. That process does not last very long and he then moves to a provisional assessment. In 80 per cent of the cases, 80 per cent of the 9,000 cases I am talking about, that provisional assessment will be accepted by both parties. The remaining 20 per cent go to myself and my colleagues who are the Ombudsmen at my bureau and we then come either to a preliminary conclusion or give room for further argument and then arrive at a decision. We will occasionally have hearings, sometimes that go on for a day or two, but that is the rarity rather than the norm. The benefits of what we do now is first of all what Lord Lester referred to as equality of arms in the sense that whereas before he was concerned about the equality of arms between the regulator and the provider, we are concerned with an equality of arms between the complainant and the provider who may be a big company or may be quite a small independent financial adviser but who has behind him, of course, very often an insurer who is represented by lawyers. We try to avoid any kind of adversarial hearing, and we do not have adversarial hearings. If we do have a hearing it is on the basis that it is an investigative, inquisitorial type hearing and an agenda is set by the Ombudsman. That will be very difficult to sustain in

[Mr Sheerman *Cont*]

that mode in the future. If I can put this in as polite a way as possible for myself and my colleagues who are lawyers, it is going to be very difficult to prevent what is up to now an informal and flexible operation becoming legalistic and effectively becoming a financial services court. That is why we need, and indeed I am praying for, the help of this Committee because it is in this area that we are most exposed to changing what people expect to see at the end of the Bill and what actually will arrive. There are ways around the issue which I will not go into great detail about if you do not wish me to because of the time but certainly it would help us to know that this Committee is alive to these dangers and could explore ways around them.

Chairman

475. Could you give us the headlines of what they would be?

(Mr Holland) Yes. The first issue is when you actually introduce the obligation to have a fair and public hearing, does that mean during the entirety of the process or do you take it as far down the process as possible when you have reduced the original 100 per cent of complaints down to the last 20 per cent that are actually going to an Ombudsman? That is the first point. One has to assume that it is better to introduce the hearing as far down the process as possible to avoid hearings being used in as many cases as the complainants may wish, or indeed the insurers of the IFAs might wish. The second thing is assuming you take it a long way down the process I think one can justifiably do it by saying that everything remains as before, the Ombudsman makes his decision, and then if somebody still wants a hearing you have some kind of review operation at the end ring-fenced which is done by a different Ombudsman which would mean that any concerns the courts may have would be directed towards that review section rather than the process as a whole. At the end of the process it is possible, of course, that there are other issues under the Convention that one can use to minimise even further the necessity to have a hearing. The Convention and the courts in Strasbourg have very clearly said on a number of occasions that it is not always necessary to have a fair and public hearing in the context of how we understand that word to actually comply with Article 6. If, for example, there is no dispute about facts it is unlikely that a hearing would help and it may not be necessary. There are two words I would just like to headline and those two words are "proportionality" and "margin of appreciation". Proportionality means, of course, having regard to what is at stake and the effort involved in having the hearing. The margin of appreciation is the question of the state saying "we actually favour this kind of dispute resolution", so the means of it being done this way are attractive even though it may well be that Article 6 may say otherwise.

Lord Taverne

476. I am very worried about the application of Article 6 in the light of what we heard earlier and the fact that there appear to be some legal opinions which suggest that there may be conflict between the section dealing with the Ombudsman and Article 6. I am worried about it because, like you, I very much hope that it will be possible to retain the informal approach and keep the law out of it as far as possible. I have got certain questions. First, have you had a legal Opinion?

(Mr Dean) We have seen a legal Opinion. I would be amazed if we could not find a way of getting it to you.

(Mr Holland) I think I have got six Opinions which, not surprisingly, do not exactly agree. I can certainly let you have the opinion that my own bureau obtained because that is our property.

477. I think it would be very useful for us if we could have one. The second question is have you had any difficulties with the Convention in the past because this problem is not going to be new unless there are special provisions in this Act which did not exist in the past which raise the question?

(Mr Dean) No. I think with one exception we have not in the past. The reason is that our schemes have not had the characteristic of being binding and compulsory, it is that feature. I think that the PIA Ombudsman is different in that respect.

(Mr Holland) I have always been exposed technically to the risk of someone eventually going to Strasbourg and enforcing their Article 6 rights by that route because I am both binding and compulsory. It is those two features that bring Article 6 into play.

478. Then I have got some particular worries about these provisions. First, I think you have already mentioned the question of equality of treatment or equality of arms between the investor and the practitioner but there are also provisions here—I do not know whether they are normal—at 155(2) saying: "The complaint is to be determined in favour of the complainant if the Ombudsman considers that the matter complained of (a) is contrary to law, or (b) is not fair and reasonable in the circumstances", which suggests that you have *carte blanche* for arbitrary decisions which have nothing to do with the law. It seems to me very sensible but is that not something which may get you into trouble with something or other in the Convention?

(Mr Dean) It is not in itself. On the fair and reasonable provision I do not think so. We have not received any advice that the fair and reasonable criterion would lead to problems with the Convention. It is one, by the way, which exists in four out of five of our schemes already.

479. The fact that you can appeal on a point of law means that you can still appeal on this although it is not subject to the law?

(Mr Dean) One of the comforts which we have drawn from the Progress Report has been that the Treasury is minded to drop the notion of an appeal on a point of law which we were very strongly opposed to and we are glad to see the back of.

Mr Sheerman

480. Could I take you back very quickly to one item. Would you prefer to be accountable to this place through a Minister or to your FSA friends?

[Mr Sheerman *Cont]*

(Mr Whittam Smith) Certainly the FSA are my friends. Accountability is extremely important to me. It is important in a number of ways. It is important, first of all, because of course we have a lot of power and there have to be checks and balances. Secondly, because in forming the ethos of this new organisation it is very important that everybody should understand where accountability lies. How I see accountability, and it would be up to others to judge whether the Act needs to reflect this, is that we are first of all accountable to consumers, we are secondly accountable through Ministers to Parliament, but thirdly we are accountable to the industry. I do not think any regulator or body such as ours can do its business properly without having an eye to the health of the industry. Fourthly, of course, we are accountable to the FSA. We are very accountable to the FSA because they both have to approve our budget and make every appointment to the board.

Lord Fraser of Carmyllie

481.   Do you approve of that appointment by the FSA?

(Mr Whittam Smith) So far I am very pleased with it!

Lord Haskel

482.   Who do you think should appoint you? Do you think the FSA should appoint you?

(Mr Whittam Smith) All I can say is that I think one has to be guided by how matters have turned out so far. I will not say anything about myself but I will say that the board which has been chosen by the FSA is an extremely good one and represents a wide range of interests and, moreover, as I have discovered from the first two board meetings we have held, they are very independent and pugnacious people so we have an exceptionally good board.

Chairman

483.   Is it not the case that your own appointment required the agreement of Ministers?

(Mr Whittam Smith) Yes, it did.

Mr Beard

484.   Several people in consultation made the point that has been made that the provisions look possibly more legalistic and inflexible under the new arrangement than the rather open and flexible arrangements of the voluntary scheme to its detriment. Is Article 6 the only source of this inflexibility and legalism?

(Mr Dean) It is the principal outstanding source. We were earlier concerned about appeal on a point of law and issues of costs. Article 6 remains the single most important aspect of it.

Chairman

485.   Could I ask a slightly naive question on this issue of scope? You are suggesting the scope of your activities should be different from that of the FSA and that you would like to be involved in areas where people are not going to be involved with the FSA. Would this not be a source over the longer term for a good deal of confusion? You are dealing with complaints to do with things where you are seen in some instances as being an FSA Ombudsman and yet you would be responsible for some areas which the FSA is not actually regulating.

(Mr Dean) A number of issues there, Chairman. We do not see ourselves as an FSA Ombudsman. There is a huge distinction in the minds even of those of us who are associated in some way already with the regulator between the process of regulation and the process of an Ombudsman. We are an independent process from that. Secondly, the main source of our concern was simply this, if you take the five of us as we are at the moment we are dealing with disputes not all of which are covered by the regulatory system, therefore unless you are going to have a multiplicity of Ombudsmen or gaps the jurisdiction does need to be extended beyond the proposed scope of the regulation, otherwise you forfeit one of the objectives which is to have a single comprehensive scheme.

486.   You will appreciate that we have covered this in other discussions where people have argued we will need a single comprehensive financial regulator, which I suppose is where these two issues come together.

(Mr Dean) Yes.

(Mr Merricks) Perhaps I could add, Chairman, that because this is going to be a scheme which has to be explained to consumers—and where one is talking about regulators it is basically the industry who has to understand how the regulatory system works—consumers who complain have to know whether this really is a one stop scheme or not. I, as the Insurance Ombudsman, deal with quite a large number of complaints which arise from payment protection insurance, that is insurance against accidents and redundancy if you are taking out a loan. Nearly all those loans are provided by consumer credit providers. I can say that I can deal with the insurance aspect of that at the moment. If I was part of a one stop Financial Services Ombudsman scheme, it would be very odd indeed to say to a consumer, "We can deal with a complaint you have about the insurance that you took up which backs this loan but not about the loan." I would not wish to be the Ombudsman who had to explain to somebody why we could do one but not the other.

487.   But would you like to be the regulator who also had to explain it?

(Mr Merricks) It is possible, and I think it may be sensible—and I do not know if my colleagues entirely share this view—that the remit of the FSA and the remit of the Financial Services Ombudsman scheme do not have to be exactly the same, and indeed because there is going to be a voluntary jurisdiction of the Ombudsman scheme they will not be exactly the same.

Lord Haskel

488.   In your paper you question whether your effectiveness should be judged by a cost benefit analysis. If we do not have a cost benefit analysis how

[**Lord Haskel** *Cont*]

would you judge the effectiveness of your work? How would people know they are getting some sort of value for money, quality of service, et cetera?

(Mr Dean) I will have a go at that. Our concern was about the adequacy of a cost benefit analysis as being the criterion for deciding whether or not this or that area should be subject to compulsory jurisdiction. I do not know that you can judge the value of an Ombudsman purely by adding up the costs and benefits, that was the real point.

489.   Do you have an alternative suggestion?

(Mr Dean) Ultimately it is a matter for either Ministers or indeed the decision-makers rather than just an adding up of costs and benefits.

(Mr Merricks) The reason this problem now arises is because of the amendment the Government perhaps sensibly propose to make. As the Bill stands at the moment it provides that all regulated activities carried out by authorised persons would be subject to compulsory jurisdiction. The Treasury, wishing to provide a more flexible arrangement, decided to give the FSA a discretion as to whether anything or how much should fall within the compulsory jurisdiction as opposed to a principle set out in a Bill, an Act, endorsed by Parliament that everything was a regulated activity. The next sub-section would say that effectively fringe matters could be taken in by a compulsory jurisdiction direction subject to a cost benefit analysis. If it was only the fringe matters which were going to be added in and one could say a cost benefit analysis would be sensible to see whether we add in a few more things, then one can see that is not a serious objection. If it is actually the whole core of the compulsory jurisdiction which has to be subjected to a cost benefit analysis, I think there is a greater objection to that, indeed I have reason to believe the FSA themselves may feel a little uncomfortable about approaching that task.

490.   I can see an awful lot of argument over the basis of a cost benefit analysis and it would be helpful if there was some sort of alternative suggestion.

(Mr Dean) The alternative is that it is decided in the Bill itself by Parliament.

Lord Montague of Oxford

491.   I just wonder whether as your schemes operate at the moment you are completely satisfied with the co-operation you get from all the firms and the people with whom you have to deal. The Bill, of course, is silent on whether people should be required to co-operate with you. Do you regard that as a deficiency?

(Mr Dean) I will start answering insofar as I do run a scheme which deals with complaints against firms regulated by IMRO. I can say that we do not have a problem of non co-operation, there is no problem whatever. That is because the IMRO rules require co-operation and firms would be extraordinarily foolish to ignore that requirement and they do not do so in practice, so there is no problem with non co-operation. I venture to suppose that there would be little problem of non co-operation from any firm that was regulated for the same reason. I do not

know whether any of my colleagues would want to add anything.

(Mr Holland) The only problem I have is not in relation to the big providers or even providers of any product, it is in relation to independent financial advisers who obviously carry professional indemnity insurance. Certainly sometimes, particularly with the smaller ones, there can be some difficulty both at the initial stage and indeed in the tenacity with which the case is then subsequently fought by their lawyers, particularly if there is a large amount at stake. Occasionally, it has not happened more than about half a dozen times, there is then the issue of enforcement and there is, at the present moment, a lacuna in the legislation about enforcement where somebody decides to resign from the PIA, but I think that is taken care of in the Bill.

Chairman

492.   Is there anything that you would like to say, David?

(Mr Roe) Thank you, Chairman. I just want to say a couple of things about scope. The first point is that we do recognise that there is a concern that the scope ought not to be unnecessarily narrower than the sum of the current schemes, although in saying that it is worth bearing in mind that a lot of the current coverage is voluntary. The way that we have approached this is to have two jurisdictions which run alongside each other. The first is the compulsory jurisdiction and what this does is allow the FSA to compel the coverage of all the financial services activities of regulated firms, in other words it is not limited just to regulated activities within the terms of the Bill, if you are an authorised person then your other financial services activities can be covered. Initially the draft Bill took as a starting point regulated activities and allowed that to be added to. The reason that we changed that to make it more flexible was that there were some examples which were brought to our attention of activities where in practice there were unlikely to be a useful role for the Ombudsman. One example might be an activity where it is inconceivable that there would be any retail customers for that activity. So it seemed not terribly useful in legislative terms to bring that automatically within it. The solution that we adopted, therefore, was to give the FSA greater discretion. One of the things that they will need to take into account is cost benefit assessment which we think is a principle which applies in all kinds of areas to do with regulation and complaints handling and it seems to us to be a reasonable one. Andrew may have something to say about the approach that has actually been taken towards making that assessment. The other point I want to mention for completeness is the voluntary scheme which, as I say, will run alongside the compulsory scheme. That means that where there are people who are not regulated under the Bill, and we heard mentioned people in the consumer credit area, there will be the opportunity for their activities to be covered by the Ombudsman scheme if they people agree.

(Mr Whittaker) There are just two points that I would like to add to David's comments, both in

MINUTES OF EVIDENCE TAKEN BEFORE
THE JOINT COMMITTEE ON FINANCIAL SERVICES AND MARKETS

134

15 April 1999] Mr Andreas Whittam Smith, Mr David Thomas, Mr Brian Murphy, Mr Walter Merricks, Mr Peter Dean and Mr Tony Holland *[Continued*

[Chairman *Cont***]**

relation to scope. The first one relates to the idea that, as I understand it, it might be proposed that the scope of the Ombudsman scheme should be extended to some firms which are not authorised under the Financial Services and Markets Bill and that would be done on a compulsory basis rather than merely on the voluntary basis that David has just described and might be done in particular in relation to mortgage providers who are not authorised and in relation to Consumer Credit Act licensees who are not authorised under our legislation. We have some hesitation about this both for the reason you mentioned, Chairman, in relation to the confusion of responsibilities with the Office of Fair Trading who do regulate Consumer Credit Act licence holders but also because of the way in which this might work in practice. Taking Consumer Credit Act licence holders, we believe there are some 400,000 Consumer Credit Act licence holders. We would not want those additional firms and individuals to require authorisation in order to be brought within the Ombudsman scheme but it would be very difficult as we read it to try and bring them within the scheme on a compulsory basis without requiring authorisation because what is currently required as part of the way in which the Ombudsman schemes work at the moment is that there is a prior process, just as with the MP filter for the Parliamentary Commissioner, where the firm itself is required to deal with complaints and required to do so by the rules put in place by the regulator. We would have no jurisdiction to put in place such rules and to monitor and enforce those rules, or indeed rules requiring co-operation with the Ombudsman, if the firms were not authorised. We think the right approach is to go through the voluntary jurisdiction where there can be a contractual arrangement in order to deal with those firms who are not within the authorisation net. Secondly, in relation to our approach on cost benefit analysis, yes it would certainly be the case that it would be much easier if the Ombudsman scheme's jurisdiction were conclusively set by the legislation and we had no work at all to do in determining what

that jurisdiction should be, but we do not take a narrow view on the application of the cost benefit test. It has been suggested, for example, that simply because the amount of determining a particular claim may be more than the amount claimed one would be compelled to take the view that was not cost beneficial. For example, if a claim were only for £100 and you knew that it always cost £200 to determine it. We do not take the view that the cost benefit test means that such claims could not be brought within the scheme. We think that it is possible not to look at each transaction but to look at the overall benefits of bringing a particular sector of business within the scheme as against the overall costs of doing so. So we think the position may not be as bad as some have feared in relation to the application of a cost benefit test.

Lord Montague of Oxford

493. We have not mentioned consumer panels. Do you anticipate co-operation in relationships with the consumer panels?

(Mr Whittam Smith) In principle, yes, I certainly do. I would always wish to consider any particular matter against the notion that we are very independent. It is very important. I think it is a very sensitive area and you have to judge it case by case. Of course, one wants to be as co-operative as possible.

494. I am thinking of general information about what you are learning.

(Mr Whittam Smith) Exactly, I understand that. It would not be to our advantage to be thought to be completely in breach of the FSA and its satraps.

Mr Sheerman

495. Where is your new building?

(Mr Whittam Smith) I do not know yet but I hope it will not be in Canary Wharf.

Chairman: On that note, thank you very much for coming this afternoon, it has been very interesting. You have given us some very useful material.

Printed in the UK by The Stationery Office Limited
5/99   425070   78344

ISBN 0-10-433299-9

9 780104 332993

APPENDICES TO THE MINUTES OF EVIDENCE

TAKEN BEFORE THE JOINT COMMITTEE ON FINANCIAL SERVICES AND MARKETS

APPENDIX 1

Note by HM Treasury on the scope of regulated activities and delegation to Trading Standards Officers

The Committee has sought written evidence on the possibility of extending the scope of the regime, either immediately or in due course to general insurance, motor insurance, occupational pensions and consumer credit. It also sought information on how far the FSA could delegate supervisory and enforcement functions to Trading Standards Officers.

Scope of Regulated Activities

1. Clause 11 of the draft Financial Services and Markets Bill provides that the Treasury may by order prescribe regulated activities for the purposes of the Bill. It would be possible to include a variety of activities related to the areas identified by the Committee.

2. As the Committee is aware, the Treasury published in February 1999 a consultation document entitled "Regulated Activities" which includes a draft order setting out proposals for the scope of regulated activities under the Bill. The closing date for consultation responses is 30 April 1999.

3. The Government is able to keep under review potential changes to the scope of regulated activities. Current intentions as regards the activities identified by the Committee are set our below:

— *General insurance (including motor insurance).* At present, proposed regulation of general insurance is limited to the authorisation and prudential oversight of insurance companies and Lloyd's and to certain other proposals in relation to Lloyd's provided for in Part XVI of the draft Bill. Following consultation in 1998 on the need for statutory regulation of insurance brokers and other general insurance intermediaries, the Government is looking to the insurance industry to develop effective voluntary standards of professional practice that will command widespread support. It has been encouraged in this regard by the work done towards creating a General Insurance Standards Council, now expected to start operations early next year. Under proposals made by the insurance industry for this standards body, membership of the Financial Services Ombudsman Scheme will be a pre-condition of GISC membership, and membership will be open to insurance companies and intermediaries, including brokers, who sell personal lines general insurance.

— *Occupational pensions.* Under the existing legislation, certain persons who carry on investment business in connection with occupational pensions (for example, investment managers or trustees who manage the investment activity of a fund) will need to be regulated by the Financial Services Authority or one of the Self-Regulating Organisations. The Occupational Pensions Regulatory Agency (OPRA) also carries out regulatory functions concerning, amongst other things, the duties and activities of trustees and employers, and the rights of scheme members. The Government has no current plans to change these arrangements.

— *Consumer credit.* Providing consumer credit as such is not regulated by the Financial Services Authority and the Government has no plans to include providing consumer credit within the scope of regulated activities under the draft Financial Services and Markets Bill. The Government does however plan to review the case for regulating the provision of mortgage advice later this year, and there may be implications for those mortgages which fall within the Consumer Credit Act regime.

Delegation of supervisory and enforcement functions to Trading Standards Officers

4. Under Paragraph 6 of Schedule 1 to the draft Bill, the FSA may arrange for monitoring functions, but *not* enforcement functions, to be carried out by another body or person which it believes is competent to perform those functions. The FSA could, in principle, delegate monitoring functions to a range of possible bodies or persons.

13 April 1999

APPENDIX 2

Note by HM Treasury on enforcement procedures

In view of the considerable interest being taken by the Committee in the enforcement procedures and the nature of the tribunal, this memorandum is being submitted in order to provide further clarification of the Government's objectives for this part of the Bill, and the respective roles that are envisaged for the FSA's administrative procedures and the new independent tribunal's judicial procedures.

This memorandum also responds to the Committee's enquiry concerning the possibility of persons who are not employees of the FSA making decisions on behalf of the FSA which have legal force.

THE OBJECTIVES

1.   The Government's overall objectives, which appear to be shared by many of the witnesses the Committee has heard on the subject, are:

   (i)   A procedure that is objectively fair, that secures a person's rights to a fair hearing as enshrined in the ECHR and the Human Rights Act.

  (ii)   Consistent with that basic fairness objective, we also want to avoid unnecessary dependence on the tribunal to rule in all cases, and enable them to be settled to the satisfaction of both parties without recourse to legal procedures which may be expensive and time-consuming. At present the vast majority of cases are decided without recourse to a tribunal, and we would wish to see that pattern continue. But the other party must have adequate opportunity to establish the basis of the proposed action and make representations.

 (iii)   The procedure must also allow justice to be done, and be seen to be done, from the point of view of any victims of regulatory breaches and the wider public, whose confidence in the financial services industry is central to the wider aims of this Bill.

2.   The way in which we have sought to achieve these objectives is by making a distinct separation between the regulatory procedures of the FSA, which are administrative in nature, and the judicial procedures of the tribunal. The Government would welcome the Committee's views on whether that separation is sufficiently clear at present.

3.   This separation of procedures is marked out by the two notices set out in clauses 210 and 211 of the draft Bill, referred to as the "warning notice" and the "decision notice" respectively. The changing nature of the procedures is reflected in the precise functions of these notices.

The administrative stage

4.   The first notice, the "warning notice" marks the transition between the FSA's informal supervisory procedures and the formal stage of the enforcement procedures (see attached diagram). It triggers certain statutory rights for the other party. He has a right to know the basis on which the FSA has formed its view, to make representations, and to see the relevant evidence if he so wishes. However, the existence of this formal stage does not, and should not, preclude there having been less formal discussions prior to the issuing of the notice. Indeed, where the other party is an authorised person we would generally expect the FSA to have raised and discussed emerging problems with him before such formal procedures were initiated. The significance of the warning notice lies in the fact that it defines the point at which the particular statutory rights to see evidence and make representations are triggered.

5.   The second notice, the "decision notice", marks the end of the regulatory procedures, and the point at which the judicial procedures may begin. It is the decision notice that informs the other party that the FSA has heard and considered any representations he may have made, and what action, if any, the FSA has decided is appropriate. So it is at this point that the FSA must decide whether, in their view, there has been a breach, and if there has, by whom it has been committed, and what the appropriate penalty is. That decision is intended to be an administrative decision, for which the FSA must be accountable alongside its other decisions, and which must be taken in a fair and reasonable manner.

The judicial or determinative stage

6.   At the point that the decision notice is issued, the other party has a choice. That notice triggers his right to have the matter referred to the tribunal. If he does not exercise this right, then after a prescribed period the decision must take effect. The FSA must be able to enforce it and be able to take it into account in subsequent regulatory dealings.

7.   If, on the other hand, the other party does choose to have the case referred, the FSA's decision does not take effect. Instead it is the Government's intention that it should become the basis of the FSA's case to be put before the first instance tribunal. Or, to put it another way, the decision is set aside in favour of the decision which the tribunal will reach in due course. The tribunal will then consider the case put before it by the FSA and hear all relevant evidence and representations put before it. It will be able to decide not only on the facts of the case, but also to take its own view as to the correct interpretation of those facts and on the appropriate action (if any) that should be taken in light of its findings. Its decision will be binding on both the FSA and the other party (subject to any appeal to the appropriate appeal court on a point of law). The tribunal will also have discretion whether to award costs against either party.

8.   The precise procedural rules for the tribunal will be a matter for the Lord Chancellor and will be consulted on in draft in due course.

Voting members of committees

9. In the FSA's consultation paper, *Financial services regulation: Enforcing the new regime* (CP17) it was proposed that the decisions to issue either a warning or a decision notice should be taken on behalf of the FSA by an Enforcement Committee, established by the FSA Board, but independent of the FSA's operational supervisory and enforcement staff. The Committee has asked whether in this, or any other context, members of such a committee, who are not employees of the FSA, could vote on or take decisions on behalf of the FSA which have legal force.

10. There is no problem of principle to this, so long as the decisions thus taken are properly those of the FSA. This requires that as a minimum the committee members who can vote or take the decisions are appointed by the board (though that does not require them to be employees), are given some policy directions by the Board as to how the powers should be exercised, and are meaningfully answerable to the Board for the exercise of those powers in accordance with those policy directions. It is, of course, vital that the establishment by the Board of this or any other committee does not detract from the overall accountability framework. Ultimately this must mean that the Board retains a review function in relation to the functioning of the committee, and that its members can be dismissed in appropriate, even if limited, circumstances.

13 April 1999

ANNEX

ENFORCEMENT PROCEDURES

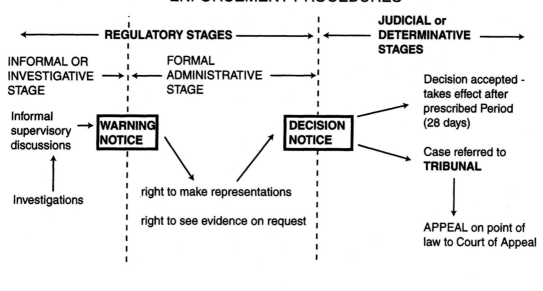

APPENDIX 3

Note by HM Treasury on the protection of employees

See minutes of evidence Q 113

Lord Poole enquired about the protection of the individual when disciplinary action is being taken. He expressed concern that while the FSA and the firm might agree on the most rapid course of action, the individual employee could be disadvantaged as a result.

1. Where the FSA is proposing to take disciplinary action against an employee who is an approved person, clause 51 of the draft Bill requires it to issue him with a warning notice. This allows the individual concerned to make representations. If a decision notice is subsequently issued he can then have the matter reconsidered by the independent Tribunal established under the Bill.

2. The employee has equivalent protection where the FSA proposes, under Clause 47 of the Bill, to withdraw its approval for the employment of a person where he is not considered fit and proper to carry out the function in question. The process of withdrawal is again subject to the employee's full right to make representations to the FSA against the warning notice and, if an adverse decision is nonetheless taken, to appeal to the Tribunal.

3. If such an appeal were unsuccessful and the withdrawal of approval were confirmed by the Tribunal, we recognise that this could be likely to lead to the dismissal of the employee. Moreover, if the employee claimed

unfair dismissal, the reason for the dismissal would appear to be potentially fair because continuing to employ him in a regulated function would result in contravention of a duty or restriction imposed by or under statute (see section 98(2)(d) of the Employment Rights Act 1996). However it would still be necessary as a matter of general employment law for the employer to show that they had followed fair procedures and had acted reasonably in treating the reason as a sufficient reason for dismissing the employee.

4.   For example it would remain open to the employee to argue, before the Employment Tribunal, that the dismissal was unfair on the grounds that it had taken place prior to the outcome of the hearing before the Tribunal established under the Bill, or without making proper attempts to find suitable alternative work (for example work not involving a regulated function) for the employee within the firm.

5.   In other circumstances the FSA may be proposing to take action against the firm and not against the individual, but nevertheless the reasons given in the warning notice issued to the firm may identify an individual employee in prejudicial terms. In those circumstances also the employee generally has a right, under Clause 210, to be given a copy of the warning notice and to make representations to the FSA. If the FSA nonetheless comes to an adverse decision, then again if the reasons identified in the decision notice identify the employee in prejudicial terms he will have a right under Clause 211 of the Bill to have the matter reconsidered by the Tribunal. The employee may use this right to challenge the substance of the decision itself, or to challenge any opinion expressed by the Authority in relation to him.

6.   Criticism of an individual employee might, if confirmed by the Tribunal established by the Bill, lead to internal disciplinary action against him by his employer which might ultimately include the sanction of dismissal. However, such action would be subject to the usual avenues of recourse to the Employment Tribunal, and it would remain open to the employee to argue that, notwithstanding the criticism made of him, it was not reasonable in all the circumstances for him to be dismissed. The employee would be able to make a claim of unfair dismissal to the Employment Tribunal where he has the necessary period of qualifying service (currently two years, but soon to be reduced to one year under the Fairness at Work Bill).

7.   Finally there may be circumstances where the employee is not mentioned in any notice issued by the FSA but where the individual is nonetheless implicated in some way. In particular it is possible that a case may be settled between the firm and the FSA before the formal stage of the disciplinary procedure is reached, and that action may be taken against the employee by the employer, including dismissal. As already mentioned, the Employment Tribunal would consider whether or not the employer acted reasonably in treating the reason as a sufficient one for dismissing the employee in accordance with the requirements of employment legislation.

12 April 1999

APPENDIX 4

Memorandum by the Financial Services Authority

A.   INTRODUCTION AND SUMMARY

1.   This Memorandum is submitted to the Joint Committee in the context of its consideration of the Financial Services and Markets Bill. The FSA looks forward to elaborating on this note in oral evidence on 16 March.

2.   The FSA welcomes the Government's commitment to introduce this legislation in the current Parliamentary session, and in particular the work of the Committee in considering the Bill by way of pre-legislative scrutiny. We recognise that Parliament will wish to take a close interest in this wide-ranging new legislation and in the way in which we propose to exercise the powers to be conferred on us to regulate financial business. The FSA has followed closely the responses to the Government's consultation on the draft Bill and welcomes the recent Progress Report by HMT, summarising the main issues raised and explaining the Government's response.

3.   This Memorandum summarises the FSA's preparations for assuming its new powers (paragraphs 4 to 8) and deals in turn with the six questions on which the Committee has decided to focus its inquiry (paragraphs 9 to 40).

The FSA's preparations for assuming its new powers

4.   The FSA is currently responsible, under the Banking Act 1987 and the Financial Services Act 1986 respectively, for supervising banks and for overseeing the regulation of investment business. Further powers for the regulation of other financial sectors (for example, building societies, insurance (including Lloyd's), credit unions and friendly societies) are to be transferred to the FSA by this Bill. In the meantime, the existing regulators continue to have responsibility under the various statutes for regulating individual sectors. For example, the Boards of the self-regulating organisations (SROs) remain responsible for authorisation and enforcement decisions in relation to the firms which they regulate.

5. The FSA has agreed with the other constituent bodies to integrate relevant staff as quickly as possible, in order to reduce uncertainty for them and so minimise any risk to regulatory effectiveness. This managerial integration was completed in January this year, when the majority of officials from the Insurance Directorate of HM Treasury and the Registry of Friendly Societies transferred their employment to the FSA, joining colleagues formerly employed by the Securities and Investments Board, the Bank of England, and the three SROs. These staff, working under a single FSA management structure, supply services under contract to the other regulators in order to enable them to discharge their responsibilities.

6. This managerial integration is already leading to a more efficient and focused approach to areas of common interest—for example, the response to turbulence in international financial markets, and handling Year 2000 issues. In some areas work will continue to integrate operationally ahead of the new legislation—for example, in consolidating the various complaints-handling arrangements established under current statutes.

7. In its published Plan and Budget for 1999–2000, the FSA has summarised the work which it expects to carry out in the coming year to prepare for the new regime. In particular, in line with our open approach, we will continue to consult publicly on the broad range of policy issues which need to be settled. Annex I to this note lists the further consultation and other papers planned for the coming year.

8. Developing the Handbook of rules and guidance which will apply to regulated institutions in future is a substantial and complex project. Following earlier consultation on the approach to be adopted, and in particular on the balance to be struck between developing fresh material and carrying over existing requirements, the FSA is now working on the various sections of the Handbook. We will take this opportunity to remove unnecessary rules and to adopt a common approach to the regulation of similar business, while maintaining appropriate differentiation for different types of business and for business done with different categories of customer.

B. QUESTIONS ON WHICH THE COMMITTEE HAS DECIDED TO FOCUS

9. The rest of this Memorandum deals with the six specific topics identified by the Committee.

Proposed arrangements for the accountability of the FSA

10. The FSA recognises that the establishment of a single financial regulator with wide-ranging powers raises important questions about the means by which it is to be held accountable for its actions, policies and costs.

11. The draft Bill includes a series of mechanisms for securing the FSA's accountability and establishing checks and balances on its operations. These include:

— the statutory objectives and general duties, referred to below, which can be enforced through judicial review;

— the reporting mechanisms; our Annual Report to the Chancellor is to be laid before Parliament, and we will be required to hold an annual open meeting to present our Annual Report to the full range of stakeholders;

— our governance structures; the Board is appointed, and can be removed, by the Treasury. The Board will have a majority of non-executive members. There is to be a separate non-executive committee with responsibility, among other things, for setting the pay of the executive Board members and overseeing the economic and efficient use of the FSA's resources. That committee will be required to report on its work, as part of the FSA's Annual Report. (The first Chairman of the non-executive committee will be Stewart Boyd QC, recently appointed Deputy Chairman of the FSA);

— a variety of forms of external review. The Bill will require consumer and practitioner panels to be set up, which will contribute to our decision making and report publicly on their views on how we operate. The statute will require the FSA to have in place arrangements for independent investigation of complaints against itself. The Director General of Fair Trading will scrutinise our rules to ensure that they are not unduly restrictive of competition. HM Treasury will be able to commission periodic value for money audits of our operations. And the Treasury will have power to commission inquiries into regulatory matters of public concern;

— procedural safeguards on rule making and policy making. Rule making (including on fees to be paid by regulated institutions) will need to be subject to public consultation. There will be requirements for cost-benefit analysis, and proposed rules and rule changes will need to be accompanied by an explanation of how they relate to the FSA's objectives. Decisions on rule making are reserved to the Board itself;

— powers in the hands of HM Treasury to require the FSA to change our rules and practices when necessary on competition grounds or to achieve compliance with the UK's international obligations;

— an independent tribunal, administered separately by the Lord Chancellor's Department, to resolve disputed cases involving authorisation and enforcement decisions by the FSA.

12. We acknowledge the very high level of interest in these accountability mechanisms and how they will operate. We believe that the mechanisms now in place, including the improvements announced by the Government in January in response to consultation, provide a sound and robust basis for the FSA's accountability.

The proposed statutory objectives and the principles

13.   The establishment of statutory objectives (in the areas of market confidence, public awareness, protection of consumers and reduction of financial crime) for the new single regulator has been widely welcomed. The draft legislation supplements these with a set of general duties; these require, in summary, that the FSA must have regard to:

— the need to use its resources in the most efficient and economic way;

— the responsibilities of those who manage the affairs of authorised persons;

— the need for proportionality;

— the desirability of facilitating innovation;

— the international character of financial services and markets, and the desirability of maintaining the competitive position of the United Kingdom; and

— the principle that competition between authorised persons should not be impeded or distorted unnecessarily.

14.   The FSA believes that these objectives and duties strike the right balance and provide an important means of accountability. We welcome the Government's commitment to consider ways in which the drafting of the consumer protection objective might be clarified or improved to ensure that the FSA's objectives in this area are not open to mis-understanding.

15.   We welcome the imposition of a duty on the FSA to take into account the desirability of maintaining the competitive position of the United Kingdom. Some have argued that we should have an objective to promote the competitiveness of the UK's financial services. We agree with HMT that this is not necessary; we believe that an objective in this area would sit uneasily with our other responsibilities. In particular, we believe that firms might well consider such involvement by the FSA in commercial (rather than regulatory) matters intrusive rather than helpful.

16.   These statutory objectives and duties provide a basis for the FSA's legal accountability; if we mis-construe them, or fail to take them into account, judicial review is available to those affected by our decisions or actions. Ordinary principles of public law will, where a general policy has been announced, require us to act in accordance with it unless there is good reason to depart from it or modify it for the future.

Discipline, enforcement and the Tribunal

17.   Responses to the draft Bill and to the FSA's consultative paper "Financial Services Regulation: Enforcing the New Regime" issued in December 1998 demonstrate a keen interest in the nature and operation of the FSA's enforcement processes in future. Whilst enforcement action is a vital element in the regulatory regime, and will continue to be so in future, it is important to set it in context. By far the greater part of the regulatory authorities' efforts is devoted to work designed to ensure that financial institutions have the systems and processes in place to minimise the risk of any contravention of regulatory requirements—on the basis that prevention is better than cure. Most of the supervision and monitoring work in all the areas coming together in the FSA is therefore a collaborative effort in which the interests of the regulator and of firms' senior management are quite closely aligned. Of the FSA's approximately 1,850 staff, only just over 150 are involved in enforcement work—and about 40 of these are engaged in "perimeter work", ensuring that non-regulated firms or individuals do not undertake business for which they have no authorisation.

18.   We are currently engaged on a major project to design appropriate structures and processes for enforcement work under the new legislation. The focus of this is the consultation paper we published last December, where we are now reviewing the responses received.

19.   The proposals which we have put forward so far incorporate four main features, seeking to balance the requirements of fairness with the desirability of securing a cost-effective, speedy and efficient process (in which firms, individuals and the FSA share an interest):

— a clear separation of functions between operational staff and decision-makers, so that the staff who investigate a case and recommend enforcement proceedings do not take the final decision to proceed;

— the Chair of the Enforcement Committee (whose responsibility includes issuing the notices which begin proceedings and the decision notices imposing sanctions) will be a full-time position. The appointment and removal of that person would be a matter for the Board of the FSA, which would make appointments following an open selection process, with the assistance of external advice. The Chair would report directly to the Board, supported by staff not within the enforcement directorate. Measures such as these are designed to buttress the independence of the Chair from operational staff.

— we propose to involve practitioners and public interest representatives in our enforcement decision-making processes. The Board will appoint a panel, including recently retired practitioners and others who are able to make the time commitment necessary to deal with the larger enforcement cases;

— we propose that the subject of disciplinary action should be able to make representations and, if appropriate, have an oral hearing.

20.   These proposals are consistent with the Treasury's announcement in December of four changes to the Bill to clarify the role of the FSA and the independent appeals tribunal, viz:

— a statutory duty on the FSA to establish and publish procedures on taking disciplinary action, and to act in accordance with them;

— an explicit right for those subject to disciplinary proceedings to request to see the evidence on which a case rests, and a duty on the FSA to disclose such evidence;

— an explicit bar on the FSA publicising enforcement action until the full process, including any tribunal proceedings, has been completed;

— dropping the Lord Chancellor's power to make rules on when relevant evidence might be inadmissible before the Tribunal. The Tribunal will be a tribunal of first instance, and the Government has said that its current working title ("The Financial Services and Markets Appeals Tribunal") may be changed to reflect this.

21.   The FSA Board attaches great importance to its ability to deliver effective enforcement action; such action can be effective only if it is fair and seen to be fair. We recognise the strength of feeling on this subject among the regulated community and will consider carefully the responses to consultation over the coming weeks. In the second quarter of 1999 we will publish a feedback statement, summarising the responses received and announcing any further policy decisions. We would hope to be able to give the Committee an early indication of our latest thinking in this area before they report at the end of April.[1]

Scope of the new regime

22.   The scope of the legislation—deciding which activities and products should be regulated and, broadly, in what ways—is a matter for decision by Government and Parliament. The Government has recently published for consultation draft regulations outlining the scope of the proposed new regime. This reflects the Government's approach, previously announced, to:

— give the FSA jurisdiction over the activities and products currently regulated by the predecessor bodies;

— give the FSA additional powers (for example, in relation to Lloyd's) where the case for change is already made;

— keep under review the case for including certain activities not currently regulated.

23.   As the FSA said in its evidence to the House of Commons Treasury Committee last year, it believes that decisions on any future extension of regulatory scope should be made in the light of a set of well defined criteria. The FSA is conscious of strong views in some quarters, including among some parliamentarians, that the marketing of mortgage products should be included in the legislation. The FSA attaches importance to the applications of cost-benefit analysis to proposals for further regulation of this sector and looks forward to contributing to HMT's review of the operation of the Code of the Council of Mortgage Lenders. Many firms— in particular, banks and building societies—which market mortgage products are already supervised for prudential purposes by the FSA. However, the FSA's very preliminary estimate is that around 6,000 further firms (including estate agents and credit and mortgage brokers) might need authorisation for this line of business.

24.   Discussions continue, to which the FSA looks forward to contributing, on the desirability of incorporating the regulation of some other products—in particular, long-term care insurance products—in the FSA's jurisdiction. Now that the Royal Commission has reported, and has made a specific recommendation that Long-Term Care should be brought within the ambit of conduct of business regulation at the earliest possible date, we are considering with HMT how this line of business should most effectively be regulated in future.

25.   Members of professional bodies (for example, solicitors and accountants) may, under the current legislation, conduct investment business on the basis of certification by their professional body. A large number of professional firms—of the order of 12,000, we estimate—are authorised essentially on a precautionary basis because they may from time to time conduct investment business in connection with their professional business. We note HMT's recent statement proposing a number of changes in the legislation to deal with unnecessary authorisation of members of the professions. We welcome the Treasury Committee's view that the definition of financial advice needs to be drawn as narrowly as possible to prevent unnecessary regulation in this area.

Ombudsman and Compensation Scheme

26.   Ministers announced at an early stage that one of the benefits of regulatory reform would be the opportunity to create "one-stop" shopping for consumers who need to avail themselves of dispute-resolution and

---

[1] See Appendix 9.

compensation arrangements. The draft legislation therefore provides for the establishment of a single Financial Services Ombudsman and a single Compensation Scheme, replacing the multiplicity of existing schemes.

27. The FSA's work in these two areas has been of two kinds: first, to establish the arrangements which will need to be in place when the new legislation is implemented; and, second, to examine the scope for bringing together the current schemes as far as possible operationally in advance of the legislation, in order to provide a more streamlined service to consumers at the earliest possible stage.

28. The FSA has now appointed the Board of the new Ombudsman Scheme, to be chaired by Andreas Whittam Smith. The initial responsibility of the Scheme Board will be to work with the FSA in setting up the new Scheme. It will play a key role in deciding its design and structure. Our objective will be to ensure that the new Scheme delivers a cost-effective, accessible and fair dispute-resolution service. We plan to consult this year on scope, terms of reference and funding.

29. Responses to the Government's consultation on the Bill highlighted a number of concerns about the operation of the proposed scheme. HMT recently announced a number of changes to respond to these concerns, removing the right to appeal on points of law, restricting the costs to which complainants could be subject and widening the potential scope of the compulsory jurisdiction of the Scheme. The FSA will also have the ability to exclude some categories of regulated firms where there is a case to do so (e.g., wholesale businesses which do not have customers who would be eligible to use the Scheme).

30. The FSA and the Scheme Board will take these changes into account in their further work in this area. Proposals relating to the scope of the Scheme's compulsory jurisdiction (which will apply to authorised firms only) will be subject to cost-benefit analysis and consultation. We have considered carefully the potential impact of ECHR requirements on the proposed new statutory Scheme and have sought to establish whether concerns that the new Scheme will have to be more court-like in its procedures are well founded. We believe that it is possible to design an ECHR-compliant scheme which retains the benefits of flexibility and informality, which are key features of the existing non-statutory Ombudsmen Schemes.

31. The FSA will consult shortly on its policy for the new single Compensation Scheme. Our earlier consultation exercise demonstrated broad support for a single Compensation Scheme Board, with division into three sub-schemes covering deposit-taking, insurance and investment business. The FSA will also take account of the strong views expressed by the industry urging us to avoid cross-subsidy between dissimilar business activities within these sub-schemes, except where there is a clearly identified need and the proposals have been the subject of specific consultation.

Market Abuse

32. The proposal in the legislation to give the FSA powers to impose civil fines to deal with abuse of markets, and the Code of Market Conduct which the FSA published in draft for consultation, has attracted much comment.

33. Before turning to the comments received, it is worth restating the rationale for the new regime: to preserve and enhance the efficiency of financial markets. Damage to those markets affects not only market participants but the economy as a whole. The current statutory protections for the major UK markets are widely perceived to be incomplete. On the one hand, the criminal offences of insider dealing and market manipulation cover only a limited range of very serious misconduct. On the other, the regulatory regime covers a wider range of misconduct but only a subset of market participants. There is a gap, in that conduct by unregulated persons which damages the market can only generally be addressed through the criminal law. The Government has decided—and we agree with this approach—that the FSA, in pursuit of its objective of maintaining confidence in financial markets, ought to be able to take administrative action against any market participant who abuses the markets.

34. The Government has made it clear that the new regime is designed to complement the existing criminal offences and is not an alternative. Where people have committed a criminal offence, and where it is appropriate to prosecute, that will be done, following the guidance set out in the Code for Crown Prosecutors. The draft Bill gives the FSA the power to prosecute such offences itself. The FSA is currently drawing up guidelines with the other prosecutors both for determining when cases will be taken the civil or criminal route and for deciding who should take action in a given case. The FSA intends to publish these guidelines.

35. The new regime in the Bill aims to bring about improvements in three areas:
   — to reduce the fragmentation of responsibility, which has sometimes caused problems in the past. The current fragmentation—between the Serious Fraud Office, the DTI, the FSA, the SROs and the Recognised Investment Exchanges, all of whom potentially have an interest in dealing with market misconduct—is unsatisfactory. The FSA will have powers to deal with regulatory breaches, to take action for breaches of the new market abuse provisions in the Bill, and to prosecute the existing criminal offences of insider dealing and market manipulation;
   — to allow the FSA to take effective administrative action where markets have been abused by any market participant. This is in line with the approach adopted in the US and a number of other

overseas jurisdictions. Had the regulators had these powers in 1995, we would have been better equipped to deal with the damage inflicted on the London markets in the Sumitomo case. The effects of this behaviour are estimated to have cost industry many hundreds of millions of dollars in higher copper prices. The existence of civil powers in the US allowed the American regulators to tackle this problem more effectively than we were able to, even though the market directly affected was in London. Other cases currently being considered by the regulators could be handled more effectively if the proposed new powers were already available.

— to introduce greater transparency into the area of market abuse. The regulators can currently take action against regulated investment firms and registered individuals for breach of the FSA Statements of Principle in this area (Principle 3 provides simply that: "A firm should observe high standards of market conduct"). The new regime seeks to make clearer what are acceptable and unacceptable behaviours in this respect. The Bill itself defines abusive behaviour in broad terms, and requires the FSA to issue a Code of Market Conduct to clarify the behaviours which amount, or do not amount to, abuse. Abusive behaviour must be such as to damage confidence that the market is true and fair. The FSA supports the overall approach of establishing framework legislation which allows the FSA to provide clarity in a flexible and evolving Code.

36. The comments received on these aspects of the Bill and on the draft Code reflected five main themes. A number of commentators argued that the FSA needs to be more specific in describing the types of behaviour which it will regard as acceptable or unacceptable. We appreciate this desire for clarity and are working closely with market participants on reviewing comments on the Code and discussing possible changes. We have set up a practitioner group consisting of members nominated by the main trade associations, including the BBA, ISDA, LIBA, and the exchanges. In parallel, the Markets and Exchanges Regulatory Liaison and Information Network (MERLIN) will be considering similar issues. This group consists of representatives from the recognised investment exchanges, the Panel on Takeovers and Mergers, the Bank of England, the DTI and HM Treasury. The industry has made it clear, though, that they do not want a prescriptive rulebook in this area. Overly detailed prescription risks increasing compliance costs and stifling innovation; there is a balance to be struck between the desirability of being specific and the need to produce a regime which is flexible enough to changing market practices.

37. The second strand of comments reflected the desire for the insertion of a general test of intent in the Bill and in the Code. Respondents regarded it as unfair that they could be subject to administrative action if there was no proof of intent. We believe that in some circumstances, where conduct has fallen short of the standards reasonably expected of market participants, it should be possible to take enforcement action where there has been no intent. The economic efficiency of markets can be damaged by the unintended effects of actions, for example, of negligent behaviour.

38. The third main area of comment was on a perceived increase in the "layering" of regulation in the area of market abuse. This broke down into two themes. First, there was some concern about the interaction between the FSA's powers in this area and those of other bodies. We have outlined above the steps we are taking to co-ordinate action with other prosecutors. We are also working with the exchanges and the Takeover Panel to make sure that the appropriate body takes action in individual cases. Our policy is that, where there has been a breach of the rules of a recognised investment exchange or the Takeover Panel, if those bodies have adequate investigative, disciplinary and enforcement powers to address the conduct in question, the FSA would not normally propose to take action. The second area of concern was how the new regime will relate to criminal offences and to the FSA's rules on the conduct of authorised firms. As to the criminal law, we have indicated above that it will remain distinct. In preparing the FSA Handbook, we will ensure maximum coherence and consistency between the Code of Market Conduct and other rules applying to authorised firms. Overall, therefore, there should be no additional layer of regulatory requirements on regulated investment firms.

39. The fourth area of comments concerned the status of the Code itself (which is, of course, a matter for the Treasury). The Code carries evidential weight; some expressed concern that it would be possible for the FSA to take action for breach of the primary legislation even in circumstances where someone had complied with the Code. The FSA made clear in its consultative paper on enforcement policy that, generally, where a person has acted in compliance with the standards set out in the Code, it will not seek to impose a civil fine for market abuse.

40. Finally, a number of respondents expressed a desire for the FSA to issue guidance, or even what are known in the USA as "no action letters", which firms could rely on, since a code cannot by its nature cover all the situations in which market users may find themselves. It has always been the FSA's intention to issue general guidance to supplement the Code. However, it is clearly not possible for regulators to provide no action letters unless they are given very specific details of the transactions envisaged. Any clearance procedures might not always be very rapid, except at very significant cost for regulated firms. So we are exploring ways in which the market's reasonable desire for certainty can be accommodated without excessive bureaucracy, while giving due weight to senior management's primary responsibility for their firms' compliance with regulatory requirements.

12 March 1999

ANNEX I

Forthcoming consultation and other papers

Subject	Type of paper	Planned time of publication
High-level standards		
Principles for businesses (Consultation Paper 13)	Feedback statement	Q2 1999
Principles and Code of Practice for approved persons	Consultation paper	Q2 1999
Senior management responsibilities and high-level systems and controls	Consultation paper	Q2 1999
Authorisation		
Qualifying conditions for authorisation	Consultation paper	Q1 1999
Scope of approved persons regime: fitness and propriety and suitability of individuals	Consultation paper	Q2 1999
Permissions	Consultation paper	Q2 1999
Grandfathering of firms and individuals	Policy statement	Q4 1999
Authorisation manual	Consultation paper	Q4 1999
Collective Investment Schemes sourcebook	Consultation paper	Q1 2000
Prudential standards		
Initial policy on harmonisation	Consultation paper	Q3 1999
Prudential sourcebook	Consultation paper	Q2 2000
Supervision		
Supervision manual	Consultation paper	Q4 1999
New responsibilities		
The future regulation of Lloyd's (Consultation Paper 16)	Feedback statement	Q2 1999
Credit Unions[1]		
Professional firms currently regulated by recognised professional bodies	Consultation paper	[1]Q2 1999
Conduct of business standards		
Conduct of business sourcebook	Consultation paper	Q3 1999
Financial crime objective		
Approach to new anti-money laundering rules	Consultation paper	Q2 1999
Markets and exchanges		
Future regulation of inter-professional business (Discussion paper—October 1998)	Feedback statement	Q2 1999
Market conduct sourcebook	Consultation paper	Q3 1999
Exchanges and clearing houses sourcebook	Consultation paper	Q4 1999
Enforcement		
Financial Services Regulation: enforcing the new regime (Consultation paper 17)	Feedback statement	Q2 1999
Enforcing the general prohibition on unauthorised business	Consultation paper	Q2 1999
Enforcement manual	Consultation paper	Q4 1999
Industry training		
Training and competence sourcebook	Consultation paper	Q3 1999
Consumer relations		
Promoting public understanding of financial services: a strategy for consumer education	Policy statement	Q2 1999
Compensation Scheme: policy	Consultation paper	Q2 1999
Compensation Scheme: rules	Consultation paper	Q4 1999
Ombudsman Scheme: rules	Consultation paper	Q2 1999
Complaints Code	Consultation paper	Q3 1999
Fees		
Fees, once new legislation is in force	Consultation paper	Q2 2000

[1] Contingent on developments in Treasury policy.

APPENDIX 5

Supplementary Memorandum by the Financial Services Authority

INTRODUCTION

1. The Committee has raised with the FSA two issues which have arisen in the course of the oral evidence which it has taken over recent weeks. In addition, the FSA wishes to take this opportunity to comment on some other aspects of evidence given and to amplify its own earlier evidence in specific areas. This note therefore covers the following topics:

— Market abuse (paragraphs 2-18).

— Destination and treatment of fine income (paragraphs 19-21).

— Enforcement of FSA Principles (paragraphs 22–27).

— Involvement of practitioners in FSA's decision-making (paragraph 28).

— The Consumer Panel's budget (paragraph 29).

— Protection of employees (paragraph 30).

— FSA staffing issues (paragraphs 31-46).

The FSA's latest thinking on its internal decision making on disciplinary cases is set out in a separate note.

A. MARKET ABUSE

Rationale

2. The FSA's view is that the need for a new civil framework to tackle market abuse, complementing the existing criminal offences, is clear. There is behaviour which is capable of damaging the integrity and efficiency of markets which does not constitute either insider dealing or market manipulation under the existing criminal regime, but which it would be inappropriate to criminalise. Such behaviour may be the subject of regulatory sanctions when engaged in by the authorised community, but that community does not embrace the full range of market participants. There is thus a gap in the ability of the existing regime to protect UK financial markets and those who use them. The new regime makes clear that all those who take advantage of the organised investment markets recognised in the UK will be required to comply with the same standards of behaviour to safeguard the markets' integrity and efficiency.

Certainty

3. We believe that it is essential that the market abuse regime established under the new legislation should strike the correct balance between, on the one hand, providing flexible arrangements which can adapt to fast-changing markets and, on the other, giving market participants adequate guidance as to whether conduct is likely to fall foul of the regime. Getting this balance right is vital. That is why we have embarked on a lengthy consultation process with market participants.

4. A number of concerns have been expressed over the uncertainty that arises from the status of the Code of Market Conduct ("the Code"). As an "evidential" Code, compliance with, or breach of, its provisions will not be conclusive of compliance with, or breach of, the statutory provisions. In principle, we would have no difficulty with a provision that made clear that the FSA could not take action to impose a civil fine for market abuse where conduct is in compliance with the Code. The effect would be to ensure that those who abided by the provisions of the Code could not be the subject of enforcement action under the general provisions of clause 56.

5. In the same way, the FSA would favour statutory provisions that made clear that breach of the Code would amount to market abuse. A primary provision such as that in clause 56 would then become an enabling provision setting the outer limits of an FSA rule-making power in relation to market abuse. The Code would take the form of a binding code setting out the standards of market conduct. We appreciate that this would be a wide-ranging rule-making power for the FSA to have, especially as the provisions will apply to unauthorised persons. Nevertheless we think that giving the FSA's Code full, binding force would address many of the concerns that have been expressed regarding lack of certainty in the new regime.

6. We continue to believe that it is possible to devise a Code which sets out with clarity the standards of conduct which are to be expected of all those persons who take advantage of the organised investment markets recognised in the UK. We have previously set out for the Committee the extensive consultations in which we are currently engaged with a view to revising the provisions of the Code. This process will, we believe, result in a clearer and more precise text which market participants will find it easier to apply in practice. This is the purpose of the consultative process. We believe that the Code will give Authorised Firms considerably more guidance than is currently available from the regulators as to what constitutes acceptable standards of market conduct.

Intent

7. There has been a great deal of debate about whether the FSA should be required to prove intent before imposing a sanction for market abuse. Considerable confusion exists as to precisely what "intent" means in this context; it is a term which means different things to different people. We set out below a range of different tests which may be adopted in any rule or legislative provision and describe them in a way which may assist the Committee in understanding our approach to the Code:

— "Strict liability"—here liability or sanctions are imposed wherever a person commits certain acts, regardless of his state of mind at the time. Such provisions are generally used where preventing the conduct in question is considered so important in the public interest that it should be sanctioned on a "no fault" basis;

— Negligence—a negligence test is one which requires persons concerned to take reasonable steps to avoid particular acts or events occurring. What are "reasonable steps" is judged on an objective basis according to the standards of a reasonable person in the position of the defendant. On this test, liability or sanctions may be imposed where a person *"knew or ought to have known"* that his conduct would have the unwanted consequence or where the person failed to take reasonable care. Such a standard is appropriate where it is desirable to provide an incentive to persons to take reasonable care not to behave in a manner that will have the undesirable effect in question;

— Recklessness—unlike the objective negligence standard, a recklessness test requires an examination of what was in the mind of the person concerned. In order to show recklessness it is necessary to show that the person concerned acted *without caring* whether his conduct would have the undesirable consequences that it did. A person may be negligent but not reckless in that he may have failed to take reasonable care when judged by the standards of reasonable persons, but he may have genuinely (but unreasonably) believed that his conduct would not have the consequences that it did;

— Intent—like recklessness, this term may be used to describe an entirely subjective test which requires proof that a person intended the consequences of his actions, i.e., that he actually knew or believed they would occur. While intention is often inferred from circumstantial evidence as to what the natural consequences of a person's action would be, the tribunal of fact must still satisfy itself that this is what was in the mind of the person concerned. A genuine belief or ignorance (no matter how unreasonable it may be) may defeat an allegation of intent. Intent and recklessness are tests which are generally reserved for criminal offences which carry the threat of imprisonment because they denote serious moral culpability.

8. It has never been the FSA's intention that the market abuse regime should be capable of being used to punish conduct on a "no fault" or strict liability basis. We do not consider that to be the effect of the draft Code and will be working to ensure that this is made clearer in future drafts of the Code. However, we do not accept, as a general proposition, that conduct that damages the economic integrity and efficiency of the UK's organised investment markets should be capable of being pursued only where recklessness or intent (as described above) can be shown. In order to prevent significant damage to the efficient operation of our investment markets we consider that it is right to expect those who take advantage of those markets to take reasonable care to ensure that they do not act in ways that undermine those markets and damage the interests of all market participants. We therefore consider that, in principle, the adoption of a negligence standard is appropriate in relation to certain types of conduct.

9. The precise degree of fault that should have to be shown on the part of any person accused of abusing the market needs to be considered carefully in the context of each of the different types of conduct that the Code seeks to address. We will be seeking to address this in a more transparent way in future drafts of the Code. We are not convinced that a provision in the primary legislation requiring the proof of intent to commit market abuse would be beneficial, although we do consider that in certain circumstances some form of "due diligence" defence may be appropriate. We will be examining the Code in some detail from that perspective.

Relationship between market abuse and Exchange rules

10. We are concerned to ensure that the market abuse regime interacts in a transparent and coherent way with the rules of the Recognised Investment Exchanges (RIEs). Clearly, however, it would not be appropriate to provide a "safe harbour" for conduct which did not breach the rules of an RIE unless those rules themselves adequately address the various types of misconduct at which the market abuse regime is directed. A detailed examination of the rules and practices of each Exchange is under way. It is important that the legislation does not provide a loophole for market misconduct which cannot be said to breach the rules of any one individual RIE but which nevertheless falls short of the standards set out in the Code. Such loopholes may well exist given that the Code will cover transactions undertaken off-exchange as well as on-exchange.

11. For this reason an attempt to provide a blanket safe harbour in this area in the primary legislation would, in our view, be fraught with difficulty. Instead, we think that the overarching provision in the Bill should place beyond doubt the FSA's ability to include such "safe harbours" in the Code.

Guidance and "pre-clearance"

12. There has been much interest in relation to the new provisions on market abuse in the scope for individual guidance (whether in the form of interpretative letters, no-action letters, or pre-clearances) to be obtained from the FSA. As stated in our memorandum to the Committee of 12 March, it has always been the FSA's intention to issue guidance to supplement the Code, but it is clearly not possible for regulators to provide

no action letters unless they are given very specific details of the transactions envisaged. Such clearance procedures might not always be very rapid, except at significant cost for regulated firms.

13.   There is still detailed work to be done to elaborate the FSA's policies and arrangements for giving guidance to individual firms under the new legislation, particularly with respect to the Code, and to develop guidelines on the status of guidance. The FSA will carry that work forward in consultation with interested parties.

B.   Costs incurred in the course of disciplinary proceedings

14.   One of the objectives of the FSA's proposed disciplinary decision-making process is to keep to a minimum the cost incurred by the firms and individuals concerned and by the FSA itself. Accordingly, the FSA's proposed internal procedures provide the opportunity for a firm or individual to reach an agreed outcome in a disciplinary case rather than refer the case to the statutory tribunal. The respondent firm or individual will have the option to enter into settlement negotiations and to go to mediation. We hope this will lead to a greater number of settlements.

15.   We recognise that significant costs may be incurred, particularly when a case reaches the tribunal stage. The draft Bill provides that the tribunal may order a party to the proceedings to pay to another party to the proceedings the whole or part of the costs or expenses incurred by the other party in connection with the proceedings. This is consistent with the normal practice in civil litigation that "costs follow the event". The draft Bill confers on the Tribunal a broad discretion in relation to costs; the Tribunal is not required to order that all or indeed any of the costs be paid to the successful party.

16.   Concerns have been expressed that this provision could lead to an unsuccessful respondent bearing the whole cost of the proceedings, and that this would deter individuals in particular from exercising their right to contest the FSA's findings. On this basis, it has been contended that it is unfair to expect an individual to face the uncertainty of possibly being required to contribute to the FSA's costs. It is said to be a particular disincentive where a person believes that they may have a good answer to the charges in most respects, but that they may still lose some minor aspect of the case.

17.   The FSA as a regulatory authority is charged with enforcing regulatory requirements in the public interest, and should not, it can be argued, be deterred from reasonably bringing cases in pursuance of its statutory objectives, even where it is ultimately unsuccessful. In general, the FSA should not be required to pay the costs of a respondent, except where it acted unreasonably in bringing the proceedings.

18.   One alternative would be for each party to be responsible for bearing its own costs, whatever the outcome. This would give the parties a greater degree of control over their financial exposure. However, it would have the disadvantage that a party who has been exonerated by the Tribunal would be unable to recover its costs from the FSA. Similarly, the FSA would be unable to recover costs from parties which had been found by the Tribunal to have breached regulatory requirements. The FSA's costs would then fall to be paid by compliant firms through the FSA's fees.

C.   Destination and treatment of fine income

19.   A number of witnesses have given evidence to the Committee on the question of the destination, and the treatment in the FSA's hands, of fine income. The Chairman of the FSA touched on this subject in oral evidence on 16 March. We hope it will be helpful to the Committee if we set out our views in a little more detail, picking up specific concerns raised by other witnesses in the meantime.

20.   The FSA will have power to impose a range of disciplinary sanctions, of which levying a fine is only one. Not every case of misconduct leading to enforcement action will warrant a financial penalty. The FSA believes that it is appropriate for fine income to be used to reduce the direct regulatory costs for the majority of firms which are not fined by the FSA. Alternative approaches, envisaging that fine income would pass to some other destination, would mean that "good" firms would subsidise the costs of investigating and disciplining the "bad"; we do not find that an attractive proposition. The FSA's preferred approach is supported by a number of trade associations and senior industry figures. In response to concerns that such an approach exposes the FSA to real or perceived conflicts of interest, the FSA would make the following points:

— the new legislation will require the FSA to consult on, publish and adhere to transparent procedures and processes for its enforcement work. This will include our policy on fining; in this context we expect to list the factors which we will take into account in determining the level of a fine. External stakeholders will therefore in future be able to assess whether—in specific cases, and more generally—the FSA is acting in accordance with its stated policy in this area. This process of consultancy by FSA is already under way, through the publication of CP17 in November 1998;

— firms or individuals who wish to challenge the imposition or the quantum of a fine which the FSA's Enforcement Committee is minded to impose have the right to have their case considered afresh by the independent Tribunal;

— in accordance with our responsibility under the new legislation to use our resources in the most efficient and economic way (to be monitored and reported on by the non-executive Committee), we have put in place a financial management and reporting framework which we believe provides a clear and robust mechanism to ensure transparency as to the FSA's expenditure. This will ensure that income from fines is not used to mask higher than budgeted expenditure;

— specifically, we identify in our published Plan and Budget for the coming year a "control total" covering our mainstream regulatory costs, including in-house enforcement costs, but excluding external enforcement costs (for example, hiring investigating accountants and instructing outside lawyers on particular cases) which are subject to substantial fluctuations year-on-year. The actual and budgeted "control total" expenditure will therefore not be affected by the incidence of fines. (The alternative approach—budgeting for enforcement costs and taking fines "above the line"— would result in a more volatile "control total".);

— any excess of fine income over external enforcement costs will reduce fees to the regulated industry;

— in our Annual Report and Accounts we will report against this framework; this will have the advantage that external stakeholders can track the FSA's expenditure year-on-year on a like-for-like basis.

21.   We believe that these mechanisms provide proper safeguards against any possible misuse by the FSA of fine income and preserves the advantage, outlined above, of enabling such income to flow back to the regulated industry in reduced fees.

D.   Enforcement of the FSA principles

22.   It has been suggested that the FSA should not have power to take enforcement action for breaches of FSA Principles alone.

23.   The use of Principles has been a feature of the regulatory regime for investment business for the last decade. The introduction in 1989 of a power to make broad statements of principle followed severe criticism from the regulated industry of the compliance costs associated with applying a large body of highly detailed and prescriptive rules.

24.   The use of statements of principle enables the regulator to avoid detailed prescription in certain areas. Principles can provide regulated firms with flexibility in determining how they should comply with regulatory standards. They are capable of being applied to new and changing circumstances and help to prevent "creative compliance" or the exploitation of technical loopholes in more detailed rules. The FSA Principles would not continue to serve their intended purposes if they could not be effectively enforced.

25.   We recognise that the practical application of the Principles needs to be reasonably predictable for those to whom they apply. We will therefore amplify the Principles through a combination of rules, evidential provisions and guidance. The FSA Principles should not therefore be viewed in isolation, but in the broader regulatory context.

26.   Disciplinary action for breach of a Principle may be appropriate where there has been a breach of related detailed rules, evidential provision or guidance. This reflects current SRO practice, where breaches of principles and rules are often pursued together. However, as happens in some cases now, there may also be circumstances in which it will be proper to take disciplinary action, based exclusively on a breach of one or more of the Principles.

27.   If the Principles are to achieve their purpose, it is important the FSA should be able to take action to enforce them where:

— it is clear that the conduct in question violates the Principles, regardless of whether any detailed rule, code or evidential provision has strictly been breached;

— the behaviour in question breaches the Principles because it is closely analogous to behaviour which would constitute a breach of a detailed rule, and would breach the spirit, though not the letter, of the rule. For example, rules may prohibit an authorised entity from holding certain kinds of investment, and a deliberate attempt is made to circumvent the rules by interposing intermediate companies, so that the investments are held indirectly;

— there is evidence of systematic and repeated breach of detailed rules. For example, repeated breaches of rules about recommending suitable products may indicate wider problems, such as a lack of due skill, care and diligence, breaching Principle 2.

E.   Response to the Joint Committee's 1 April letter on FSA's decision making

28.   In response to the Committee's letter of 1 April on the involvement of practitioners in the FSA's decision-making, the position is as follows:

— the FSA Board, appointed by the Treasury, includes a number of industry practitioners as non-executive directors. All directors are, however, appointed in the public interest, and the whole Board is, of course, responsible for the FSA's overall strategic direction and in particular for the exercise of its legislative functions;

— under the FSA's current proposals, the Enforcement Committee (whose members will be appointed by the Board, and will be accountable to the Board) will include practitioner and non-practitioner public interest representatives. An overwhelming number of the responses to CP17 favoured both groups having voting powers in relation to their involvement in the FSA's enforcement process;

— beyond that, as we said in "The Open Approach to Regulation", the FSA will involve practitioners in an advisory capacity through a wide range of groups, such as the Practitioner Forum, the Small Business Practitioner Panel, the Handbook Advisory Group and the Market Conduct Group. Such practitioners do not take decisions on behalf of the FSA.

F. The Consumer Panel's budget

29.   The FSA would take this opportunity to clarify an answer given by Howard Davies in oral evidence on 16 March. The budget of £420,000 for the Consumer Panel is wholly available for the Panel's own use; it does not include the salary and overhead costs of the FSA staff who service and assist the Panel in its work. It is also important to note that the Consumer Panel's own budget is part of a larger effort to understand consumer views, and inform consumers, carried out by our directorate of Consumer Affairs.

G. Protection of employees

30.   We have seen HM Treasury's note to the Committee on the protection of employees where disciplinary action is being taken against a regulated firm, and have nothing to add.

H. Staffing issues

31.   The Committee asked a number of questions in its letter of 24 March about FSA staffing issues. Staffing the new Authority with the right mix and quality of staff has been challenging. Inevitably, we suffered from staff losses in the first few months of our existence. Immediately post merger our turnover rate was unsustainably high, peaking at 19 per cent in the first three months after the merger. As the organisation has settled down post transition we have seen turnover fall to more acceptable levels—turnover (three month rate annualised) is currently running at seven per cent. Since we were established we have been pleased with our record in being able to attract high calibre individuals into the Authority—we have attracted some 360 staff since 1 June. As the Authority becomes established we expect to find it easier to "sell" a period of employment in the regulatory body as a worthwhile career option.

32.   We support our new recruits with a comprehensive training programme, which includes induction and, for our regulatory staff, technical training which encompasses the individual technical training programmes provided in the prior organisations. We supplement our in-house training by sending staff on external courses and to conferences to ensure that they remain up to speed with market developments.

What salaries is the FSA able to offer?

33.   The FSA aims to be competitive in offering a remuneration package which attracts and retains the right mix of staff. We pitch our base pay against median or second-quartile pay levels in the relevant sectors of the financial services market. In benchmarking our pay, we generally compare our salaries to those in the market which we regulate, taking account of the sectors from which we recruit people, and to which we lose them— that is, financial services sector companies and professional services firms. By the "financial services sector" we mean retail banks, investment banks and insurance firms.

34.   Different sectors within the financial services industry can offer very different salary levels, so the pay of our staff is not uniform across the organisation. We accommodate these variances by having very broad indicative pay ranges which are used to manage pay levels across the organisation. The table below sets out the pay ranges for our staff and the number of staff employed at each level:

FSA Employees: Data as at January 1999

Grade	No. Staff	Pay Range
Administrator/Secretary	578	£12–£30k
Associate	886	£20–£60k
Manager	210	£45–£90k
Head of Department	44	Up to £110k
Director	15	Individual Salaries
Total	1,733	

35. In recruiting staff with specialist skills which are crucial to our work and where we are particularly vulnerable to the external market we are prepared to pay individual salaries, sometimes in excess of the indicative pay ranges that we set.

36. We do not try to compete with the external market in making bonus payments. In this first year we have operated a Performance Reward Plan which has paid out, on average, non-pensionable awards of six per cent of salary.

37. In feedback from employees who have resigned from the FSA, pay has rarely featured as the dominant reason for leaving.

What proportion of your senior staff have market experience?

38. Our objective is to recruit from a range of different sources, balancing the need for an understanding of the market with specialist policy making and other skills. As at the end of March 1999, 29 per cent of our senior staff (defined as Heads of Department or above) engaged in front line regulatory work have private sector market experience. A further 16 per cent have experience of operating in a market environment through work in the Bank of England markets (i.e., gilts, money markets and foreign exchange operations) and banking functions. By virtue of our history, a significant number of our senior staff have a public sector background. (The Treasury, Bank of England, Building Societies Commission, Registry of Friendly Societies, Friendly Societies Commission, all recruited primarily from university, and staff were moved in and out of regulatory functions.)

39. Going forward, as a private sector organisation we are and will increasingly be recruiting from the private sector and our experience profile will change accordingly. By way of example, 55 per cent of the management team (including middle managers) in the supervisory areas of our Investment Businesses Division have market experience; of which one quarter of that experience was in the compliance field. We expect this profile to be more typical of the experience of our managers in the future. Since the FSA was established in June last year we have recruited to around 200 front line regulatory posts, for the vast majority of which we have found excellent recruits from the firms that we regulate. At senior levels, we have recently recruited two Heads of Department, one for our Complex Groups Division and the other for the Markets and Exchanges Division. The former comes with considerable compliance experience direct in a major international bank. The latter has been a Director of two major trade associations in the derivatives and investment banking fields.

40. In the parts of the Authority where senior staff typically have less market experience, the prior organisations (in particular the Bank of England and the Insurance Division of the Treasury) recruited "grey panthers" to work directly with the banking and insurance supervisors. These are former senior managers drawn from the industry to work as internal consultants with front line regulatory staff. Collectively they have a wealth of experience drawn from years of specialising in different parts of the financial services industry. Some are employed on a formal consultancy basis to enable them to pursue other external roles (e.g., sitting on industry advisory committees) which maintains their external perspective.

41. In addition, we resource a number of key posts in the regulatory areas of the organisation with inward secondees. We currently have 38 inward secondees, 16 per cent from banking firms and over 60 per cent from professional services firms (law and accountancy firms); together they bring considerable experience from working directly with our regulated firms.

42. On the issue of outward secondments, the Bank of England, which recruited many regulatory staff direct from university, introduced an initiative to improve exposure to the external market by introducing six month placements in regulated institutions. At the FSA we intend to continue to use this approach to enhance the market knowledge base of our existing staff. We also second staff to other regulators (e.g., in Hong Kong) and to other relevant bodies (e.g. DGXV of the European Commission).

What proportion of your senior staff have a regulation or compliance background?

43. Virtually all our senior staff have previous regulatory experience—the majority were appointed from a prior regulatory organisation. Very few have a compliance background in firms. In recruiting senior staff since 1 June we have brought in a number of key players with industry experience who have not previously worked in regulation e.g., Director of Markets and Exchanges; Director, Investment Businesses.

What proportion of your senior staff are lawyers?

44. Given the range of statutory powers which the FSA will exercise, we regard it as important to have access to high quality, prompt legal advice. In addition to the five lawyers at senior level in the General Counsel's Division, 15 per cent of our front line regulatory senior staff are lawyers.

What is the turnover rate of senior staff?

45. Turnover of senior staff since 1 June is 7.9 per cent on an annualised basis.

How far below complement are you?

46. At the end of the 1998–99 budget year we were 85 below complement. Our new budget for 1999–2000 provides for an increase in headcount of 105 reflecting an increase in the volume of our underlying business, the resources required to update the regulatory rulebooks and meeting our new consumer objectives. We are now actively recruiting for a number of these posts. Recruitment will be activated for the others during the course of the year.

13 April 1999

APPENDIX 6

Note by the Financial Services Authority on the jurisdiction of the Financial Services Ombudsman Scheme

1. The draft Bill provides that the Financial Services Ombudsman (FSO) Scheme will have a *compulsory* jurisdiction and a *voluntary* jurisdiction. These will be defined by a combination of rules (and directions) made by the FSA and the FSO Scheme and will be the subject of detailed public consultation later this year.

2. The scope of the new Scheme will be defined by reference to the following factors:

— *Activity*—whether the complaint relates to an activity covered by either the compulsory or voluntary jurisdiction of the scheme;

— *Complainant*—whether the complainant is an "eligible complainant";

— *Complaint*—whether the complaint itself is an "eligible complaint" (e.g., whether it relates to an act or omission giving rise to financial loss/distress or inconvenience; whether it was lodged within the prescribed time limits; whether the firm has attempted to resolve the complaint first etc.).

COMPULSORY JURISDICTION

3. As it currently stands, the draft Bill provides for the Scheme to have compulsory jurisdiction over all regulated activities and over any non-regulated activities (e.g., mortgage lending) listed in Schedule 2 and designated by the FSA for this purpose. However, the Treasury has recently announced that it intends to make the provisions for setting the Scheme's jurisdiction simpler and more flexible.

4. The FSA will have wider discretion over which complaints are to be included in the compulsory jurisdiction. It will now be able:

— to *include* within the compulsory jurisdiction *all* financial services activities carried out by authorised persons, not just those specified in the Bill;

— to *include* within the compulsory jurisdiction complaints which relate to a service which forms part of an activity within the compulsory jurisdiction, even though that service, if looked at in isolation, would not be a financial service (e.g., a complaint about a property valuation, where it was carried out in the course of arranging a mortgage); and

— to *exclude* from the compulsory jurisdiction certain categories of authorised firms where there is a case to do so (e.g., wholesale business where firms do not have customers who would be eligible to use the Scheme).

5. This means that the vast majority of disputes which are currently handled by the existing schemes (set out in the attached annex) will be capable of being brought within the new Scheme's *compulsory* jurisdiction. The Treasury plans to give the FSO Scheme similar discretion over the scope of the voluntary jurisdiction (see paragraph 7 below).

6. Activities will be brought within the compulsory jurisdiction by virtue of a Compulsory Jurisdiction Direction (CJD) made by the FSA. However, this will be subject to cost benefit analysis and consultation. The FSA will therefore be examining the case for including different categories of business within the scope of the compulsory jurisdiction of the new Scheme and will consult on this, and other issues referred to in this note, later in the year.

VOLUNTARY JURISDICTION

7. The voluntary jurisdiction will apply to any firm which has agreed to participate in the Scheme, as extended by a Voluntary Jurisdiction Direction (VJD). VJDs may bring within the scope of the Scheme:

— complaints against unauthorised persons who are carrying on activities which are subject to the compulsory jurisdiction for authorised firms; and

— complaints against authorised or unauthorised persons arising out of activities which are not part of the compulsory jurisdiction.

VJDs will be made by the FSO Scheme following consultation, and with the approval of the FSA.

ELIGIBLE COMPLAINANT

8. The draft Bill envisages that the FSA will define which complainants are eligible to complain in relation to activities covered by the compulsory jurisdiction and that the FSO Scheme (with the approval of the FSA) will define complainant eligibility in relation to the voluntary jurisdiction.

9. The FSA has taken the view that the new Scheme should be designed primarily to assist those who are least able to sustain financial loss and who do not have the resources to pursue their claims before the courts. We therefore proposed, in our earlier consultation paper on this area (Consultation Paper 4 on "Consumer Complaints"), that access to the new Ombudsman arrangements should be restricted to complaints from private individuals, unincorporated bodies, partnerships and small companies. This won general approval and the forthcoming consultation paper will seek to define these terms more precisely.

TERRITORIAL SCOPE

10. We envisage, subject to further consultation, that the new Scheme will deal with unresolved consumer disputes about business or services provided in or from the UK, irrespective of the country of residence of the consumer.

26 March 1999

ANNEX

Current Complaints Handling Schemes in the Financial Services Area

The Banking Ombudsman	Banks[1]
The Building Societies Ombudsman	Building Societies
The Investment Ombudsman	Firms regulated by IMRO
The Insurance Ombudsman	Insurance companies and their tied agents[1]
The Personal Insurance Arbitration Service	Insurance companies[1]
The PIA Ombudsman Bureau	Firms regulated by PIA: life assurance companies and their agents, and independent financial advisers
The SFA Complaints Bureau and Arbitration Service	Firms regulated by SFA
The FSA Direct Regulation Unit and Independent Investigator[1]	Firms regulated by the FSA (formerly known as the SIB)

[1] Participation in these schemes is voluntary.

APPENDIX 7

Note by the Financial Services Authority on the "Wallis Report"

The Final Report of the Financial System Inquiry ("The Wallis Report") was published in Australia in March 1997. Commissioned by the Federal Treasurer, Peter Costello, in June 1996, the inquiry was charged with providing a stocktake of the results arising from the deregulation of the Australian financial system since the early 1980s. In addition, the Report was to make recommendations on the nature of regulatory arrangements in Australia. A key recommendation was the establishment of an integrated financial regulator. The Australian Prudential Regulation Authority was therefore created on 1 July 1998. Chapter 16.6 of the Report covers the Inquiry's work on the cost of regulation. The Inquiry identified three main costs: the direct (or infrastructure) cost of regulators, the compliance costs of those under regulation, and the allocative efficiency costs of benefits forgone. Analysis naturally centres on the cost of regulation in Australia, but the UK figures among the sample of jurisdictions used in the comparison.

The Inquiry found that the UK regulators had the lowest direct cost out of the sample of 8 jurisdictions, with 0.40 basis points of financial sector assets for the period 1994–95 (see Figure 16.4). This compared favourably with the United States (0.99 basis points of assets) and Hong Kong (0.51 basis points of assets). Australia was placed at the opposite end of the spectrum (1.13 basis points of assets).

The Report acknowledged that it is more difficult to assess national aggregates for compliance costs of regulated entities. A comparison of compliance costs in six countries for 1996 was, however, offered (see Figure 16.5). Again, the UK figured at the lower end of the spectrum, with compliance costs of 2.8 basis points of financial sector assets. Only New Zealand had a lower compliance cost than the UK (1.4 basis points of assets). The US had very much the highest compliance costs (10.5 basis points of assets).

Finally, allocative and other efficiency costs were considered. The Report noted the types of allocative costs which exist, but no comparative data was offered, presumably due to the difficulty in effecting such international comparisons.

26 March 1999

APPENDIX 8

Note by the Financial Services Authority on regulating mortgage advice

A   INTRODUCTION

1.   The Joint Committee has expressed interest in whether mortgage advice should be included within the scope of the new legislation.

2.   The Economic Secretary to the Treasury has asked the Financial Services Authority to undertake a cost benefit analysis of the impact of mortgage advice regulation. This will be one input to the Treasury's review of whether the FSA should have powers to regulate mortgage advice. New work will be required to undertake this analysis, since we have not looked at the market since the Council of Mortgage Lending Code of Mortgage Lending Practice came fully into effect in July 1998.

3.   This Memorandum summarises some preliminary work which the FSA has undertaken on the regulation of mortgage advice. Further and more detailed research is under way in response to the request from the Treasury.

B.   MARKET STRUCTURE

4.   In 1998 there were approximately 1.1 million new mortgages for home purchase, with an average loan size of almost £60,000. This excludes remortgages, further advances and top-ups. Including these categories brings the total to around 1.8 million. Mortgages are therefore one of the largest categories of long-term financial products purchased by retail consumers.

5.   Most mortgage providers (for example banks and building societies) and providers of other loans secured on property (banks, buildings societies and some finance houses) are already regulated by the FSA, as are those mortgage advisers who also give financial advice on investments. But this regulation does not currently extend to mortgage advice, although it does cover advising on, and selling, investment products which can be used to repay mortgages. In addition, a large number of firms who currently do not give investment advice and hence are not regulated by the FSA (including many firms of mortgage brokers, estate agents, solicitors and accountants) give mortgage advice to their customers. Other firms not authorised for investment advice (including credit brokers and finance houses) give advice on other loans which are secured on property but where the purpose of the loan is not to purchase property.

6.   It is difficult to be precise about the number of firms which would be affected. Around 20,000 firms currently provide advice on mortgages (most acting as intermediaries but some as providers who advise only on their own in-house mortgage products). Of these 20,000 firms, a few thousand who are not currently authorised for investment business might choose to seek authorisation for mortgage advice; others might choose to become appointed representatives of mortgage providers; and no doubt some firms currently providing mortgage advice would choose to cease that activity if it became subject to statutory regulation.

C.   COSTS AND BENEFITS

7.   The total cost of regulating mortgage advice could be substantial. This would depend in part on whether the regime applied only to loans for home purchase or whether it included all loans secured on people's homes. The second option would be significantly more costly, because credit brokers and finance houses could then come within the scope of the regime.

8.   We assume that the regulation of mortgage advice would involve conduct of business requirements broadly similar to those already applied to the sale of retail investments; and that the existing regulation of the giving of advice on and the sale of endowment policies, and of other investment products which can be used to repay mortgage borrowing, will continue largely unchanged.

9.   At a very speculative illustration of the additional compliance costs that might be involved, let us assume that there are 5,000 firms who are not currently authorised for investment business but who would choose to become authorised for mortgage advice. If the annual additional compliance cost for these firms were to be the same per registered individual as the estimated current additional compliance cost for a one-adviser IFA firm (namely £2,400), then the total annual cost to the industry would be £22 million, in addition to which there could be significant one-off costs. However, this could understate the total annual additional compliance cost

because it takes no account of additional costs for firms who are already authorised to give investment advice or for firms who would choose to become appointed representatives of mortgage providers. An additional cost of £1,000 for each of these firms could add up to a further £15 million per year. But these illustrations could be an overstatement because, for a firm already following the CML code, the additional compliance cost per registered individual should be significantly less than has been assumed. The Code has not been in operation long enough to allow us to assess these costs with any accuracy.

10. In addition to additional compliance costs, there would also be a direct impact on the FSA's own costs, which are met by fees levied on regulated firms. The magnitude of this impact is difficult to estimate but our preliminary work suggests that the regulation of mortgage advice could require something in the region of an additional 100–200 FSA staff.

11. The cost benefit analysis we will be undertaking for the Treasury will aim to establish more precisely the number of firms likely to be affected by the regulation of mortgage advice, how the effect will vary from one type of firm to another and the likely additional costs which regulation would impose on firms. We will also consider the risk that if regulation leads to a reduction in the number of intermediaries in the mortgage market this could impose costs through a reduction in competition and through a reduction in the availability of advice to some consumers.

12. For most consumers, taking out a mortgage is a large, complex and infrequent transaction. The benefits of regulating mortgage advice should include a reduction in the number of consumers entering into inappropriate commitments; and an enhancement in the quantity and quality of the information available to consumers, and thus in their ability to exercise more informed and effective choice in the mortgage market. The CML Code may already be achieving some of these benefits, where firms comply fully with its provisions. The cost-benefit analysis will aim to compare the cost-benefit balance of regulating mortgage advice with the cost-benefit balance of continuing with the CML Code. We will also be able to consider the results of research into consumer detriment being undertaken by the FSA's Consumer Panel.

31 March 1999

APPENDIX 9

Note by the Financial Services Authority on the revised proposals on the disciplinary decision-making process

INTRODUCTION

1. The FSA's proposed decision-making process constituted an important part of Consultation Paper 17 and many of the responses and much of the concurrent public debate have focused on this subject. This memorandum updates the Committee on the FSA's current thinking. A diagram is attached by way of summary.

2. The revised proposals which follow are derived from our consultation responses and recent discussions with a range of interested parties. (They are limited for the time being to discipline. Work continues on an appropriate process for intervention and admissions purposes.)

3. The proposals take account of the Government's clarification of aspects of the statutory framework for discipline set out in its March 1999 Treasury Progress Report, including clarification of the respective roles of the FSA's administrative procedures and the independent Tribunal's judicial ones.

4. However, we do not know whether Government policy will develop in a way which will impact on what is said in this paper. The overall framework within which FSA procedures will operate is, of course, a matter for the Government. We should also stress that our Board has not yet considered these revised proposals. They are necessarily tentative, therefore, and subject to further refinement. Having said that, we believe they meet the objectives we set ourselves, and are capable of commanding general support.

DESIGNING THE DISCIPLINARY DECISION-MAKING PROCESS: THE FSA'S OBJECTIVES

5. Our aims in devising the FSA's decision-making process are to ensure that the arrangements, together with the statutory right to go to the independent Tribunal administered by the Lord Chancellor's Department, provide a process that is:

(a) fair and seen to be fair; and

(b) efficient and effective.

6. In our view this involves:

— providing those subject to FSA disciplinary action with sufficient information as to the reasons for that action, and the evidence on which the action is based, so as to enable them to understand the FSA's grounds and, if they wish, to challenge them;

— providing those subject to FSA action with a reasonable opportunity effectively to challenge the grounds for the proposed action and present any evidence and arguments that are relevant to the decision in question;

— ensuring that decisions to exercise the FSA's enforcement powers are subject to consideration by a person or persons who are able to take a dispassionate and impartial view of the case for FSA action;

— ensuring that decisions are informed by the views of persons with adequate experience and expertise in the subject matter;

— avoiding unnecessary expense (whether to the FSA, those subject to FSA action or the public purse);

— avoiding unnecessary delay to the FSA's ability to take effective action or to bring disputes over FSA action to a conclusion;

— providing a mechanism for determining at an early stage what issues are in dispute and ensuring that the process remains focused on those issues;

— providing an opportunity for the FSA and the firm or individual concerned to reach agreement as to the matters of concern to the FSA and the action to be taken;

— avoiding unnecessary duplication of work (whether by the FSA or the Tribunal) in the consideration of issues which are in dispute;

— providing sufficient flexibility to enable procedures to be tailored to the requirements of each case.

7.   Those who responded to CP17 generally supported these objectives.

8.   In CP17, we proposed to establish an Enforcement Committee capable of operating on a quasi-judicial basis. In the light of the responses to CP17, and the Government's clarifications about the statutory framework, we no longer believe that to be the most appropriate way of delivering our objectives. In particular, it would not serve our objectives if the Enforcement Committee were required to duplicate the function of the first instance, independent statutory Tribunal.

THE ENFORCEMENT COMMITTEE

9.   We propose to establish a process in which an Enforcement Committee would take formal enforcement decisions. The Enforcement Committee would consist of a Chairman and other members appointed by the Board specifically to take decisions on the exercise of the FSA's enforcement powers on the Board's behalf. As such, the Chairman and other members of the Committee would be required to apply the general policies and procedures set by the Board in considering individual cases. As suggested in CP17, we propose that the Committee Chairman would be required to report to the Board on a regular basis on the performance of the Committee's duties.

10.   In CP17, we asked for views on whether the Committee should include practitioner and other public interest representatives who would be able to vote on disciplinary decisions. The clear majority of those who responded believed that it was important that these representatives should be able to vote.

INITIATION OF PROCEEDINGS AND FIRST NOTICE STAGE

11.   Under our revised proposals, the operational staff would make a recommendation to the Enforcement Committee that disciplinary proceedings should be initiated by the Committee on behalf of the Board. At this stage, the Committee would consider the case presented by the staff.

12.   If the Committee considered that there were insufficient grounds or that it was otherwise inappropriate to initiate the case, it would be dismissed at this stage.

13.   If the Committee considered that there were sufficient grounds and that it was appropriate to initiate proceedings, it would decide to issue the first notice (referred to in the draft Bill as a "Warning Notice") setting out:

— the alleged breaches/lack of fitness or properness;

— the grounds for those allegations;

— the action that the FSA considered appropriate (including any proposed penalty).

RESPONSE TO PROCEEDINGS

14.   The respondent firm or individual would then have the opportunity:

— to obtain from the FSA, upon request, details of the evidence upon which the FSA would propose to rely;

— to enter into settlement discussions with FSA staff about the allegations and/or proposed action on a "without prejudice" basis;

— if the settlement discussions reached a deadlock, to enter into mediation. (We are currently considering what particular mediation arrangements might be most useful in this context.) The independent mediator's role would be to seek to facilitate an agreement between the FSA staff and the respondent rather than to arbitrate between them or impose a decision;

— to make written and/or oral representations to the Enforcement Committee in relation to the merits of the case and any proposed penalty;

— not to engage in any of the process described above, in which event the case would proceed directly to the second notice stage below. (At that stage, the respondent would be able to exercise the right to have the case heard by the Tribunal).

SETTLED CASES

15.   In the majority of cases, we anticipate that, as now, settlement discussions would result in agreement between the staff and the firm or individual. In that event, the Enforcement Committee would meet again to consider whether it thought the terms of the agreement were appropriate. If it were duly satisfied, it would issue a second notice (referred to in the draft Bill as a "decision notice") reflecting the terms of the agreement. It should be noted that this second notice could and, generally, would be published: see paragraphs 17-19 below.

DISPUTED CASES

16.   We anticipate that it will be only in the minority of cases that no agreement can be reached between the firm or individual and the FSA staff. In that event, the Enforcement Committee would meet to consider the case in the light of any written or oral representations received. It would then either dismiss the case, or decide that it was still minded to proceed. If the Committee were still minded to proceed (whether on the same basis as before or, in the light of representations made, on a revised basis) the Committee would issue a second notice stating:

— the alleged breaches/lack of fitness or properness;

— the grounds for those allegations;

— the action that the FSA considers appropriate (including any proposed penalty);

— the right of the defendant to have the case heard by the independent Tribunal.

PROCEDURE FOLLOWING THE ISSUE OF THE SECOND NOTICE

17.   The respondent would have a period of 28 days after the issue of the second notice in which to decide whether to exercise the right to have the case heard by the Tribunal.

18.   If that right was not exercised, the notice could be published and the proposed action would take effect. For example, any proposed fine would then become payable.

19.   If the case were referred to the Tribunal, a full judicial hearing would take place and the FSA would not, meanwhile, be able to publish the second notice. Any statements made by the respondent in earlier "without prejudice" settlement discussions would not be revealed to the Tribunal by the FSA.

20.   The process proposed above has the following advantages:

— it is flexible enough to cater for a wide range of cases from the most straightforward to the most complex. For example, it can provide a speedy, fair and effective process for individuals who may wish to address the Enforcement Committee directly but who are prepared to accept the Committee's subsequent decisions without exercising their Tribunal rights. It also provides a fast track for those who do not wish to engage with the various internal options, e.g., to enter into settlement negotiations, but decide from the outset that they will seek a Tribunal hearing.

— the Enforcement Committee would be empowered to conclude, after hearing any representations, that there remained a case to answer, but it would be for the statutory Tribunal, rather than the Committee, to reach a judicial determination. Therefore an expensive and protracted hearing before the Committee involving witness evidence (which could subsequently be duplicated at the statutory Tribunal stage) would be avoided;

— the opportunity for early settlement with the option for mediation is in line with the current trend in civil litigation following Lord Woolf's report. Published settlements are, of course, a common feature of current SRO disciplinary processes. On the other hand, the opportunity to make oral and/or written representations directly to the Enforcement Committee is generally new in the financial services disciplinary process. We believe this will lead to greater confidence in the fairness of the process, as well as potentially a larger proportion of settlements than is presently the case.

12 April 1999

ANNEX

FSA'S DECISION MAKING PROCESS - A POSSIBLE MODEL

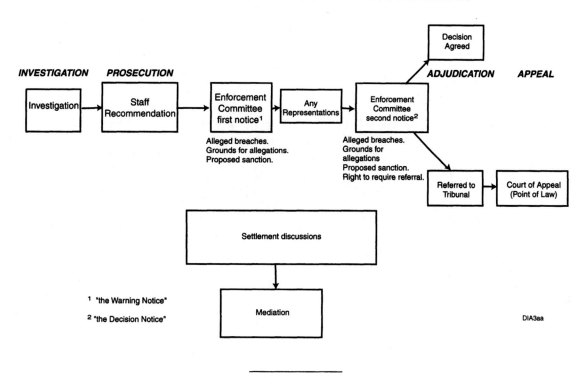

APPENDIX 10

Memorandum by the Financial Services Authority Consumer Panel

INTRODUCTION

1.   This Memorandum is submitted by the FSA Consumer Panel to the Joint Committee on Financial Services and Markets. The Financial Services Authority (FSA) established the Consumer Panel to advise the FSA Board on the interests and concerns of consumers and to report on the FSA's effectiveness in meeting its consumer protection and public awareness statutory objectives. There are 11 members of the Panel representing a broad range of consumer interests. The Panel is independent of the FSA—it can raise its own concerns, initiate its own research and publish its own reports. Membership details of the Panel are attached at Annex A.[1]

2.   The Panel's submission is organised under the following headings:

— Regulatory objectives.

— Accountability and the Consumer Panel.

— Scope of the FSA.

— Authorisation, enforcement and investigative powers.

— Single Ombudsman scheme.

— Compensation scheme.

REGULATORY OBJECTIVES

The protection of consumers

3.   The Panel welcomes the inclusion of a consumer protection objective for the FSA. However, this is undermined by the qualification at Clause 5(2)(c) of the draft Bill: *"the general principle that consumers should take responsibility for their own decisions"*. This should be removed. It introduces a principle that is absent from all consumer protection legislation and undermines the main purpose of the objective. If, as stated in the

---

[1] Not printed.

Treasury's progress report, the purpose of this clause is not to provide absolute protection to consumers, this qualification is unnecessary as Clause 5(2)(a) and (b) already cover this.

4.   We do not support the Treasury's justification for the retention of Clause 5(2)(c):

— the Treasury states that it is intended that this clause is a presumption which will vary according to different circumstances—different circumstances are already covered in Clause 5(2)(a) and (b);

— the Treasury suggests that this clause prevents the risk of the moral hazard of consumers thinking that if they use the services of an authorised person their interests will be fully protected. There is absolutely no evidence of a moral hazard in the past without such legislation.

A suitability requirement

5.   The FSA should have an additional regulatory objective that mirrors existing consumer protection legislation in other areas to ensure that financial services are fit for purpose. We support the proposal made by the National Consumer Council for such an objective. In our view it should be a requirement in the Bill that:

— products are reasonably suitable for the purposes for which they are commonly bought or for any particular purpose which the buyer makes known to the provider (a fitness requirement); and

— products do not put the consumers' investment at risk, other than in ways it can be shown were indicated prominently before purchase (a safety requirement).

6.   The inclusion of such an objective does not involve any radical changes from existing regulation since it is already enshrined in the Personal Investment Authority's suitability requirements. It would not require the FSA to have an explicit statutory role to improve the quality of products. Nor would it require the FSA to pre-vet all products. The Treasury argues that protecting consumers can be achieved by other means but this was not easy with the problem of "unsafe" home income plans, which took time and difficulty to resolve.

Matters the FSA should have regard to

7.   The Panel recommends two additions to the list of matters that the FSA should have regard to in carrying out its general functions. Firstly, we recommend the list of matters should require the FSA to take account of the needs of those consumers who are disadvantaged in the context of the matter under consideration. We recognise that reducing financial exclusion and improving access to financial services raises wider social issues for the Government to address. It is important, nevertheless, that the FSA has regard to the Government's objectives in this area when carrying out its functions.

8.   The second requirement that should be added to the list of matters that the FSA should have regard to in carrying out its general function is whether it should work alone or in partnership with other bodies such as advice agencies and local authorities (e.g., trading standards authorities). Such partnerships could bring a range of benefits including:

— giving the FSA access to information and complaints from consumers experiencing problems on the ground;

— use of local agents to disseminate material to the public.

Accountability and the Consumer Panel

9.   We welcome the Government's announcement that the Bill will contain a statutory requirement for the FSA to establish a Consumer Panel. The FSA has appointed a Consumer Panel following an open recruitment process based on Nolan principles and provided the Panel with staff support and a budget to carry out its own work and commission research. The relevant clause of the Bill should reflect this good practice by securing:

— the independence of the Consumer Panel whose members should be appointed following open competition;

— the Panel's powers to provide advice, to evaluate the effectiveness of the FSA in meeting its statutory public awareness and consumer protection objectives, to make recommendations, to conduct research and to publish its work;

— a requirement on the FSA to provide resources adequate to the Panel's needs;

— the Panel's ability to spend its budget on investigating any aspects of financial services which impact on consumers, in terms of the priorities it sets for itself; and

— a requirement to include in the FSA's annual report, the Panel's assessment of the FSA's effectiveness in meeting its statutory objectives.

10.   In reviewing the effectiveness of the FSA itself, the non-executive committee should have particular regard to the findings of the Consumer Panel and should comment on these.

SCOPE OF THE FSA

11. Despite the Government's rhetoric it is regrettable that the Bill fails to provide a one-stop shop for consumers in terms of the FSA's scope. The Government's announcement to extend the compulsory jurisdiction of the Single Ombudsman scheme recognises the importance of a one-stop shop for redress but the Bill fails to deliver this in other areas of regulation. We acknowledge that the type of regulation can vary between different markets but call for the scope of the FSA to be extended. We recommend that the remit of the FSA is extended to include mortgages and long-term care insurance because of the complexity of these products and the vulnerability of consumers who are purchasing them.

12. We recognise that the Treasury is waiting to evaluate the effectiveness of the Mortgage Code but believe that mortgages must be included in the FSA's remit from the outset for the following reasons:
— a mortgage is one of the most significant financial transactions people make;
— it is estimated there are about 4,000 different mortgages for consumers to choose from—the choice is bewildering and complex;
— mortgages are purchased infrequently by inexperienced consumers who often have to make decisions very quickly;
— there is evidence of the failure of lenders and intermediaries to comply with their own Code;
— a voluntary body is unlikely to be able to take effective action against large companies who are non-compliant (past experience of regulators such as LAUTRO and PIA suggest that it is necessary to fine large organisations for non-compliance);
— there has been a growth in new types of home income plans many of which are on the boundary between investment products which the FSA will regulate and mortgages that may fall outside the FSA's scope; and
— it is difficult for the FSA and non-statutory bodies to provide effective consumer protection because of information sharing problems (see paragraph 20).

If mortgages are regulated by the FSA, account will need to be taken of the relationship with the Consumer Credit Act.

13. Remedying the present confusion about the position of long-term care insurance should not have to wait for the evolution of overall long-term care policy. The Panel strongly endorses the recommendation of the Royal Commission that long-term care insurance should be subject to conduct of business regulation by the FSA for the following reasons:
— most purchasers will be financially naive;
— there will be scope for high pressure selling to a section of the population who are elderly and vulnerable;
— there will be a limited number of products on the market and so most purchasers will be unable to seek alternatives;
— many financial advisers will not have sufficient knowledge of the benefit system to give full advice; and
— many of the products are expensive and complicated.

14. The draft Bill would enable the FSA to extend conduct of business regulation to deposit taking and general insurance if it was justified following a cost benefit analysis. We note that some industry respondents have expressed concern about this. These concerns should already be addressed by changes to strengthen the FSA's accountability. We strongly endorse the retention of the existing flexibility in the Bill to enable the introduction of conduct of business regulation if at some time in the future the voluntary codes of practice covering banking and general insurance are found to be inadequate or inadequately enforced.

15. We welcome the Government's commitment to consult fully on secondary legislation concerning changes to the FSA's scope, which will also be subject to debate and positive approval in Parliament. However, statutory instruments are far from accessible and transparent. We urge that any consultation explains clearly the provisions of the legislation and its impact on consumers.

16. We are concerned about the interface between the FSA and other regulatory bodies. For example, the respective pension functions of OPRA and the FSA appear increasingly obscure. This will create problems in the context of stakeholder pensions because of the lack of a one-stop shop to deal with consumer complaints (see paragraph 23). There may also be problems in providing clear explanations to the public about the nature of protection and regulation given the split between OPRA and the FSA. We recommend that the pension functions of OPRA and the FSA are subject to urgent review and taken account of in the context of the draft Bill.

AUTHORISATION, ENFORCEMENT AND INVESTIGATIVE POWERS

17. We welcome the powers the Bill will give the FSA over individuals who manage and have a significant influence on the work of authorised firms. We recommend that the Bill gives the FSA powers to check criminal records of such persons as a matter of course to provide appropriate consumer protection. The Bill should also require the FSA to establish a public register of approved persons and of prohibited persons so that consumers can check the status of persons they come into contact with.

18.   We strongly support the retention of the range of enforcement powers available to the FSA to provide adequate consumer protection. We note that compliance with the European Convention on Human Rights (ECHR) has been raised by a number of respondents from the industry. Whilst these concerns must be addressed by the Treasury, they must not undermine the powers of the FSA to protect consumers by effectively enforcing its rules. Whilst we appreciate that disciplinary action cannot be published until the conclusion of disciplinary proceedings, there should be a presumption set out in the Bill that the FSA's use of its powers of intervention will be published to make consumers aware of problems. This is of particular importance in the retail investment market. In our response to the FSA's consultation on the enforcement regime we strongly recommended that the FSA put intervention action into the public domain as a matter of course to raise consumer awareness of problems and because of its deterrent effect.

19.   The Government has not yet published the information gateway provisions of the Bill. We recommend that there are information sharing powers to and from the FSA, and OPRA, the OFT, local authority trading standards departments, the Financial Services Ombudsman Scheme and other relevant Ombudsman, amongst others. These will be important sources of information for the FSA's monitoring and enforcement activities. In addition the FSA will be a rich source of intelligence to the OFT in carrying out its competition functions.

20.   We recognise the difficulties of extending the information gateway provisions to non-statutory bodies. However, this must be explored as it will be important that information can be shared between the FSA and non-statutory bodies responsible for monitoring compliance with voluntary codes of practice. For example, if the sale of mortgages is not brought within the scope of the Bill the non-statutory bodies responsible for monitoring compliance with the Mortgage Code should be able to receive information that the FSA may have on non-compliance of mortgage lenders and intermediaries with FSA rules.

SINGLE OMBUDSMAN SCHEME

21.   We welcome the changes to enable the scope of compulsory jurisdiction of the Ombudsman Scheme arrangements to be extended. However, we are concerned that these extensions are at the discretion of the FSA. We recommend that the extensions to scope of the compulsory jurisdiction of the Ombudsman should be set out in primary legislation and not be at the discretion of the FSA or alternatively that the legislation should give the Minister reserve powers to extend the scope of the compulsory jurisdiction.

22.   Although the power allowing the Ombudsman to order complainants to pay costs in certain circumstances has been removed, this has been replaced by a power authorising the FSA to make rules authorising the awarding of costs against complainants. We strongly oppose the retention of any power to enable the Scheme to order complainants to pay any costs. This completely undermines the principle of Ombudsman schemes which to date have been free to complainants. Experience suggests that many consumers who may appear to be acting unreasonably have valid complaints and they must not be deterred from using the Ombudsman Scheme. As the Ombudsman schemes currently have powers to reject claims that are frivolous or vexatious, we do not consider that there is any justification for introducing a power to enable the Ombudsman to recover its costs from consumers.

23.   The advantage of a single Ombudsman Scheme will be undermined by the Government's proposals in the stakeholder pensions Green Paper. Under the Government's proposals for stakeholder pensions, complaints will be dealt with by the Pensions Ombudsman and the Financial Services Ombudsman. In its response to the Green Paper the Panel has recommended that customers are offered a one-stop shop for complaints about pensions.

SINGLE COMPENSATION SCHEME

24.   We support the creation of a single compensation scheme for consumers. It will be important to ensure that smooth transitional arrangements are put in place and that the new scheme commences with the new legislation.

1 April 1999

APPENDIX 11

Memorandum by the All-Party Parliamentary Group on Socially Responsible Investment

We are concerned the draft Bill lacks explicit reference to:

1.   Sustainable development and the role of the financial services regulator.

2.   Consumer education on the social and environmental impact of their investments.

3.   Protection of the green and ethical consumer in regulated activities.

1. SUSTAINABLE DEVELOPMENT AND THE ROLE OF THE FINANCIAL SERVICES REGULATOR

There is a growing awareness among some financial services players that our economic future relies on our environmental future, and that the financial sector has a key role to play.

The FSA as the new single regulator of the industry should in our view be involved in a debate on what is best practice in sustainable development, i.e., environmental protection, social equity and economic development, and ensure that their activities promote rather than inhibit sustainability.

The All Party Parliamentary Group on Socially Responsible Investment believes sustainable development is an essential element of maintaining market confidence through the elimination of risk in financial services and the draft Bill should make this explicit.

The APPG believes that maintaining confidence in the financial system (clause 3(1) of the draft Bill) requires an explicit requirement to ensure that the financial system promotes and enables sustainable development.

We believe that the market confidence objective as drafted in clause 3 of the draft Bill is insufficient to achieve this aim and that a further sub-clause (3) should be added stating:

> "3(3) In considering the factors affecting market confidence, the Authority must have regard to the contribution of the financial system to promoting and enabling sustainable development and to the contribution of sustainable development to the stability of the financial system."

2. CONSUMER EDUCATION ON THE SOCIAL AND ENVIRONMENTAL IMPACT OF THEIR INVESTMENTS

An increasing number of consumers have ethical and social concerns. Green and ethical consumers form a major group within the population. In 1996, MORI identified 41 per cent of the adult British population as green consumers.

We believe the FSA's new remit for consumer education should take on board these legitimate concerns and educate people about the choices they can make about where their money goes. The existing clause 4 of the draft Bill should be amended to include a subclause reading:

> — "4(2)(c) promoting awareness of the range and general nature of impacts of investment and finance on individuals, society, and the environment."

3. PROTECTION OF THE GREEN AND ETHICAL CONSUMER IN REGULATED ACTIVITIES

The increase in ethical consumers is also evidenced by the growth in funds invested ethically which has outstripped all unit and investment trusts in every year except one since 1989. In the past two years to January 1999, the total funds managed by ethical unit and investment trusts has almost doubled from £1.1 billion to £2.1 billion according to the Ethical Investment Research Service (EIRIS).

The Financial Services and Markets Bill should make explicit the protection of green and ethical consumers. We believe that the protection of consumers objective as drafted in Clause 5 is insufficient to address this aim and should be amended to read:

> "5(2)(d) the differing degrees to which consumers wish their ethical, social and environmental concerns to be taken into account in relation to different kinds of regulated activities. Ethical, social and environmental concerns include consideration of the range and nature of impacts of investment and finance on individuals, society, and the environment."

We also hope the FSA will protect the consumer by issuing guidance stating that regulated persons should ask consumers whether they have any ethical, social or environmental concerns which they wish to have taken into account in the financial advice which they receive as part of the routine fact find. I proposed such a move in the Financial Services (Ethical Considerations) Bill I presented to Parliament on 18 November 1998.

9 March 1999

APPENDIX 12

Memorandum by the Association of British Credit Unions Limited

1. The Association of British Credit Unions Limited ("ABCUL") is pleased to provide this submission on behalf of its 434 member credit unions in England, Scotland and Wales. Our member credit unions account for 81 per cent of the individual members and 85 per cent. of the assets of all credit unions in the country, and they represent a cross-section of credit unions of all types and sizes.

2. Credit unions are mutual, self-help, co-operative financial institutions, registered under the Credit Unions Act 1979. They operate under the simple principle of pooling the savings of their individual members to provide

members with low-cost loans. Credit unions are governed by unpaid volunteers, elected by their members on the principle of "one member, one vote." They are regulated by the Registry of Friendly Societies, and, since the beginning of this year, on the Registry's behalf by the Financial Services Authority ("FSA").

3. The purpose of this letter is to propose two amendments to the Financial Services and Markets Bill ("FSMB") which are essential to the future growth and success of credit unions, as discussed more fully below.

4. *Background.* Government has correctly recognised that credit unions offer great potential to meet the financial needs of those millions of Britons who are currently excluded from affordable and accessible financial services. A major impediment to credit unions accomplishing this objective has been the very restrictive limitations on credit union powers under the Credit Unions Act 1979. For the last year and a half, ABCUL and other credit union organisations have been united in seeking major changes to that law.

5. In her preface to a Treasury Consultation Document on Amendments to the Credit Unions Act published last November, the Economic Secretary to the Treasury stated that "Government supports fully [credit unions'] ethos of self help and thrift and is determined to encourage the sector." Last year, 206 Members of the House of Commons signed an Early Day Motion supporting the changes in the law that are being sought by ABCUL.

6. The de-regulation proposals published by Treasury last November are responsive to many of our goals. However, we are informed that two important objectives can only be addressed through primary legislation. Accordingly, we are submitting this letter to propose two specific amendments to the FSMB:

7. *Our first proposal is to amend Section 2(3) of the FSMB to add an additional consideration which FSA must have regard to in discharging its functions: namely, the desirability of maintaining corporate diversity among enterprises providing financial services, in order to widen consumer choice.*

8. FSA has been given the unprecedented challenge of regulating all financial services providers in this country. The entities coming under its authority range from some of the largest financial institutions in the world, with thousands of employees and billions in assets, to small credit unions with only a few hundred members, operated entirely by unpaid volunteers. FSA supervision must therefore accommodate a diverse range of organisational structures: sole traders, not-for-profit credit unions and other mutuals, as well as stock companies, both large and small.

9. This tremendous diversity represents a great strength of the financial services marketplace in Britain, and it must not be lost as a result of consolidating financial supervision under a single regulator. At present, consumers can choose among huge companies that offer a wide range of financial services—but consumers can also choose the alternative of credit unions and other small mutuals that are community owned and democratically controlled by their customers. As Government has recognised, the existence of community-based mutuals such as credit unions helps assure that no one will be left without access to financial services, so that those individuals excluded by the large providers will have an alternative in locally owned financial institutions.

10. Accordingly, it is surprising that the Bill does not impose on FSA any specific duty to assure that its regulation preserves this necessary diversity among providers of financial services. Nothing would appear to require the Authority to adapt its regulatory approach to fit the unique needs and statutory purposes of financial providers of different types. In the absence of such a duty, we fear that predictable bureaucratic tendencies will result over time in a "one size fits all" approach to regulation. Such an outcome would further erode mutuality as an alternative for consumers—to the advantage of large for-profit providers who have the resources to handle any kind of regulation and which already enjoy huge advantages of scale and market dominance.

11. It is therefore imperative that FSA have a clear remit to preserve this diversity, in the interest of all British consumers. We respectfully submit that an obligation to do so should be written into the law.

12. It should be emphasised that in all our discussions with FSA officials we have been impressed by their dedication to this principle. We should also emphasise that credit unions desire effective supervision and regulation and welcome the transfer of supervision for credit unions to FSA. We believe that FSA's expanded resources and expertise will lead to improved supervision. We are concerned, however, that FSA have a clear statutory mandate to consider the differing needs and objectives of the diverse kinds of financial organisations it regulates.

13. *Accordingly, we recommend that the FSMB be amended to add to Clause Two Subsection (3), Page 2 after line 15, the following: "(g) the desirability of maintaining corporate diversity among enterprises providing financial services, in order to widen consumer choice."*

14. Government has correctly perceived credit unions as offering a unique solution to pressing social problems. That credit unions can serve such a role follows directly from them being fundamentally different from other financial institutions. They are, in fact, true mutuals, organised without any profit motive, and directed by volunteers who serve with no compensation. To assure that credit unions remain true to their fundamental social purposes, whilst assuring they are financially sound as well, requires a very different regulatory approach than is appropriate to other financial institutions.

15. For example, credit union members are not merely customers. They have the democratic power to change things if a credit union is not being operated in their best interests. Regulation should encourage and respect that democracy, not discourage it. At a time when mutuality is in the decline elsewhere in the financial sector, Government policy and legislation must assure that it stays alive in credit unions. For it is the mutual ethos of credit unions—not the profit motive—that steers them in the direction of serving those most in need of credit union services.

16. Therefore, it is crucial that the law governing FSA recognise the importance of different regulatory approaches for different types of providers—such as credit unions with a unique ethos of volunteer democracy and service. We believe the change we are suggesting will assure this result, while being entirely consistent with the other considerations and objectives that are proposed for FSA.

17. *Our second proposal is to include a provision in the FSMB to amend the Credit Unions Act 1979 to permit creation of a credit union-owned and controlled central finance facility.*

18. Experience in other countries where credit unions have been most successful demonstrates the essential importance of there being a credit union-owned and controlled central finance facility or similar central service organisation that can provide credit unions with the back-office financial and liquidity management services needed to provide economies of scale. Such an organisation typically contracts with commercial banks to acquire the specialised expertise necessary for such services. By its nature, it is itself a regulated financial services provider, subject to more intensive supervision than the credit unions it serves.

19. Such a central facility is essential if credit unions are to achieve Government's ambitious goals for serving the financially excluded. Compared with other financial services providers, credit unions are relatively small, community-owned and community-controlled institutions.

A central organisation would provide the management expertise and economies of scale required to allow even small credit unions to offer a broad range of services, whilst retaining their community focus and their local governance by unpaid, democratically elected volunteers.

20. We have requested HM Treasury to provide for such a central facility in the de-regulation proposals described above. Treasury has informed us, however, that in its view such a facility could not be provided for under a de-regulation order but would instead require enactment of primary legislation.

21. We believe the most economical way of doing so would be to include a simple provision in the FSMB. Specifically, we request that a new clause be added to the FSMB to amend section 1(3) of the Credit Unions Act 1979 to add a new subsection (e) creating an additional object of a credit union, as follows:

> *"(e) to invest in an authorised central credit union organisation established to provide credit unions with liquidity lending, investment management, information systems and other operational support and administrative services."*

22. *Conclusion.* We believe that these two changes to the Financial Services and Markets Bill are essential if credit unions are to achieve their potential of bringing accessible and reasonably priced financial services to those millions of citizens who are currently not well served by other providers. We respectfully commend these two amendments for consideration by the Joint Committee on Financial Services and Markets.

30 March 1999

APPENDIX 13

Memorandum by the Association of British Insurers (ABI) and the British Bankers Association (BBA)

EXECUTIVE SUMMARY

INTRODUCTION

1. Both the ABI and the BBA welcome the creation of a single regulator for the financial services industry, and believe it is important that good progress is made in underpinning the FSA with a legal framework that will enable it to function and adapt to changing circumstances. As such we endorse the framework approach to legislation in the Bill.

2. A central theme in many of our comments is a concern in the banking and insurance industries that a much more formal system of supervision is being introduced, with a heavy reliance on detailed rules backed by a discipline and enforcement system for breaches of rules. Such an approach will tend to undermine the collaborative and open relationship that has existed, particularly with reference to prudential and control issues, which in the past has encouraged a constructive approach to resolving issues of concern as they arise.

Accountability

3. The FSA will be accountable to Ministers in the first instance and through them to Parliament. Various additional mechanisms such as the FSA's Annual Report and the work of the Treasury Select Committee will further strengthen FSA accountability. In addition we believe the Treasury should have a right to comment on whether rule changes are consistent with the FSA's statutory objectives, and we also believe that the rate of fees set by the FSA should be regarded as a rule change, and therefore made subject to formal consultation.

Statutory Objectives

4. The statutory objectives as proposed are broadly right, and it would be a mistake to caveat them with exemptions and exclusions. The only additional objective for which there is a strong case deals with competition, and would oblige the FSA to take international comparators into account. As advocated below, we believe this would sharpen FSA focus and provide a point of reference against which to judge its rules.

Discipline Enforcement and Market Abuse

5.   Issues related to discipline, enforcement and the Tribunal have been deeply felt by the industry. Although changes have been proposed, further change will be necessary if enforcement is to be fair and effective. A more neutral starting point for enforcement is needed; a stronger recognition that it will normally be inappropriate to discipline on prudential matters, or for breaches of general principles. The market abuse proposals must address the issue of intent and should be able to accept that dealing which fully fulfils the requirements of the code of market abuse should not be subject to fines.

Mortgages

6.   The Mortgage Code delivers an effective alternative to statutory conduct of business regulation, and managing the latter would bring real additional costs for members, and for the FSA. We believe the review of the Mortgage Code, currently under way by HMT, should be concluded before decisions are taken on mortgage regulation.

---

1.   The British Bankers' Association and the Association of British Insurers are the two largest trade associations for the financial services industry, covering together all major insurance, banking and financial services markets at both the retail and wholesale levels. Between them, they represent 96 per cent of insurance business written in the UK and 95 per cent of banking business. Their members are active throughout the UK, within the single European market, internationally in wholesale markets, as well as through a retail presence in some countries.

2.   The brief evidence given below supplements the original submissions of the ABI & BBA, which the Joint Committee has access to, and addresses the particular subjects raised in the Joint Committee's Press Notice 2 of 10 March.

PROPOSED ARRANGEMENTS FOR THE ACCOUNTABILITY OF THE FSA

3.   HM Government has chosen to establish a powerful independent regulator on a statutory basis, covering a wide scope of the financial services industry and most financial markets. To fulfil its objectives the FSA needs considerable rule making powers, and the capacity to enforce these in a manner which is fair and reasonable. The ultimate accountability of the FSA is to Parliament, which can amend its powers by primary legislation and has the opportunity to review its work through such bodies as the Treasury Select Committee. In addition the proposed Annual Report will enable Parliament to debate the FSA's work in full. At the same time, while the FSA must be given room to do its job, and not face operational interference from government, it is right that the general accountability of the FSA should not be delegated lightly.

4.   The proposals on accountability in the draft Bill as summarised in paragraph 3.2 of HM Treasury's Progress Report are necessary. The proposals to enhance consultation in paragraphs 3.6 ff. are broadly welcome, but do not go far enough. Given the importance of this matter it needs to be addressed in primary legislation. Without change, consultation, a key obligation in a statutory system, will be more formal than real. We consider that:

— As well as consulting on proposed rule changes and publishing a statement of alterations as proposed in paragraph 5.2 of the Progress Report, where FSA rejects widely argued positions from practitioners and/or consumers it should be obliged to make clear in full why it has done so.

— The Bill already provides that the FSA should give Treasury copies of any rules or standing guidance that it makes. In addition, Treasury should have the right to state whether or not they agree that any changes or additions are in line with the FSA's statutory objectives.

5.   While the statutory basis for the consumer and practitioner panels is welcome, as is the establishment of a market abuse panel, none of these are substitutes for effective consultation with the industry and with its Trade Associations. Indeed there is a danger that the FSA will come to rely unduly on these Panels, with the danger of indifference to the industry or consumers more generally, or worse the possibility that the Panels will cease to provide an independent view.

6.   The funding of the FSA, whatever mechanism is settled on, will be by the financial services industry via a specific and hypothecated tax. There is therefore a strong case for practitioner involvement in decisions about the setting of the tax rate, and means should be found to establish this in legislation. The solution is to make the rate at which fees are charged, and not just the funding mechanism, a rule change on which the FSA should be obliged to consult. In general the industry seeks a well-funded regulator paying salaries that will retain and motivate the quality of staff it needs for a demanding and important role.

PROPOSED STATUTORY OBJECTIVES AND PRINCIPLES OF THE FSA

7. The thrust of the statutory objectives established in the Bill (clauses 3–6) is right, and it would be a mistake to undermine it by reference in the objectives to the circumstances of any specialised group. Creating enabling legislation which allows the FSA to adapt and amend rules in the face of new circumstances is right, and a restrictive set of statutory objectives would weaken that adaptive capability which is fundamental to regulatory effectiveness in the 21ˢᵗ Century. However, given the key importance of the objectives and the principles to which the FSA should have regard in the performance of its functions, Parliament will expect Ministers to be satisfied that the FSA is acting properly—after all the Rule Book will have the force of law. In delegating such powers to the FSA, there should be accountability that the powers are being exercised in a manner consistent with the statutory objectives.

8. The broad definition of consumer is right for primary legislation and should enable the FSA to draw more carefully the lines between retail and wholesale markets as these develop and change over time. Equally this definition should enable a line to be firmly drawn between transactions undertaken in a personal rather than business capacity. Stressing the importance of consumer protection in general, not merely depositor or policyholder protection, is right, and given meaning by the explicit wording that such a right by consumers to expect protection brings with it a correlative duty to make informed decisions and take responsibility for them (Clause 5.2(c)). Competition is most effective in providing innovative and cost-efficient services when consumers make responsible and rational decisions on the basis of clear and adequate information.

9. The FSA will have a general duty (Clause 2(3)(e) and (f)) to have regard to the international character of the financial services industry and the need for competition between authorised persons, but we believe this is not enough. Specifically there is a strong case for an additional statutory objective that requires the FSA to treat all firms operating in the UK in a like manner to the fullest extent possible, and to promote such competitive neutrality abroad. Her Majesty's Government's argument (4.16 of the Progress Report) talks of their "pervasive influence", but influence is not enough—a statutory objective would oblige the FSA to draft rule changes it could defend as consistent with an international competitiveness objective—something which needs to be established in legislation. In fulfilling this general duty, FSA will need to have regard to the burden its supervisory requirement places on regulated entities, compared to those placed on competitors with equivalent business regulated elsewhere.

DISCIPLINE, ENFORCEMENT AND THE TRIBUNAL

10. We have expressed our concerns about the proposed disciplinary framework to the Government in our response to the draft Bill and to the FSA in response to their Consultation Paper on enforcing the new regime (CP17). Our concerns relate to the fairness of the proposed arrangements, the interaction of the enforcement regime with effective supervision, and compatibility with the European Convention on Human Rights. Our comments here take into account the revisions proposed by the Treasury in its progress report dated March 1999.

11. At the outset it is worth stressing the very considerable enforcement powers that exist at present, and which will not be abolished with the passing of this legislation. It is already the case that banking and insurance supervisors can restrict the range of businesses our firms are involved in, and that they apply capital and solvency rates well above those required by EU legislation. These additional capital and solvency charges cost our members very significant sums, and they are variable by the regulators on the basis of their assessment of the performance of our members in delivering on their regulatory obligations. Powerful enforcement tools exist in the current arrangements, and there is a case for reviewing whether or not they should be retained in their current form, given the major new enforcement tools that are to be introduced under the Bill.

12. Our concern with process of enforcement proposed in the Bill relates to the need to ensure a separation of enforcement into distinct steps, with independent parties involved to ensure that a subsequent step is not tainted by an earlier decision. The steps are

    (i)   investigation of an apparent breach of rules or law;

    (ii) decision to proceed against the relevant person;

    (iii) decision to convict, fine or censure;

    (iv) appeal from this last decision.

13. As proposed, the FSA is empowered to undertake all the first three (except for a criminal offence, when step (iii) will be for a court). The Bill will now require the FSA to establish and publish procedures and to act in accordance with such procedures. However, the FSA will have to work within the Bill framework whereby step (ii) consists of a Warning Notice, which is not just a decision that there is a case to answer but that the person will be fined or censured unless they can prove themselves innocent. This presumption of guilt is uniquely reserved for financial services and does not exist in criminal law. The process proposed is not commensurate with an open and constructive relationship with regulated firms. We believe that the process needs to have a more neutral starting point so that both sides can be heard before any decision to take disciplinary action is taken, even in principle. It is argued that, because the Tribunal will rehear the whole case, the person involved is protected. This ignores the reality of the costs involved in preparing and presenting a case at such a Tribunal, which lead individuals to settle when they should not. Indeed, the whole process needs to incorporate the possibility of legal representation and the reimbursement of costs by the FSA when they instigate proceedings which subsequently fail.

14.   Under the proposed legislation the FSA will be given unique powers to levy unlimited fines for breaches of its rules based on a civil rather than criminal burden of proof. Further efforts must be made to clarify that where very large and damaging fines are proposed, the burden of proof employed should be criminal not civil. While it is accepted that financial services companies deal in sums of money which may appear large to the man in the street, it is nevertheless unfair that they should be subject to arbitrarily large penalties, especially as it appears to be the FSA's intention to assess fines as a deterrent and our experience of SROs adopting a similar attitude is that fines are escalated without regard to the real mischief being penalised. For our members, the reputational damage caused by the publicity surrounding any adverse finding by the regulator is sufficient deterrent. It is even more invidious to increase fines merely in order to increase the point size of the ensuing press headlines. In general, the use of enforcement action should not come to be viewed as a mark of success in regulation and it is not an appropriate way to illustrate public accountability.

15.   Banking and insurance firms have a need for prudential supervision which is quite different from conduct of business regulation. This supervision works best when the supervisor and the institution develop mutual trust and understanding. We are concerned that if, when a firm voluntarily discusses a particular situation frankly with its supervisor, this results in enforcement action, the climate of trust will break down and the supervisory relationship will not function. The sanctions imposed when prudential solvency requirements are breached should focus on corrective action rather than retribution—the imposition of fines is only appropriate in cases of deliberate or reckless misconduct.

16.   There is a concern about privileged and confidential information and documents which continues in the financial services industry. The Government has stated its intention to amend the proposed information gathering and investigation powers of the FSA but it is not clear to us that they have met our concerns. Prudential regulation can often involve the supervisor seeking to assess how a regulated firm may be affected by particular developments, for example when a bank's major customer is in difficulties or an insurer receives many claims relating to a risk which has changed in nature. In these situations, firms will wish to share with their supervisor information which is confidential (because it is part of the banker-customer relationship) or privileged (because it has been prepared to assess the firm's legal position). We have therefore two issues: first where financial institutions hand over information or documents to the FSA, it must be clearly established in law that such material always carries any legal privilege with it. Otherwise financial firms will face uncertainty as to where privilege stops, and be unable to co-operate fully with the FSA.

17.   Second there must be a clear set of rules, underpinned by legislation, about onward disclosure of material by the FSA to third parties, including overseas regulators. Different legal systems or freedom of information requirements in other countries may make disclosure inappropriate. An example would be the disclosure of an insurers claims reserving policy being treated as acceptance of liability, something which can cause serious problems for firms. Disclosure to other regulators, subject to Memoranda of Understanding, should require the FSA to obtain assurance about the end use of any material disclosed—proper prudential purposes and the pursuit of financial crime are both legitimate purposes, broader civil or political actions are not.

18.   As we mention below under Market Abuse, it is one requirement of the ECHR that an individual should know what he is to comply with if he is at risk of a criminal sanction for non-compliance. It seems to us only fair that a similar criterion should apply for the sanctions at the FSA's disposal which, if not criminal, are equally devastating in their effect on individuals and firms. The Bill allows the FSA to make rules and evidential provisions relating to those rules. The FSA is proceeding to make very general rules ("Principles") and then more detailed rules and codes of conduct which are evidential. This provides a structure similar to that for Market Abuse where there is a general offence and an evidential Code established by the FSA. In both cases, the FSA reserves the right to take action on the basis of a breach of the Principle or Clause 56 of the Bill, as qualified by the Code of Market Abuse, even where no other rule or code provision has been breached. We believe that this cannot be fair and that the Bill should restrict the FSA's scope for action to breaches of Rules only. It should be possible to rely on compliance with an evidential code.

Rights of civil action in respect of breaches of the rules

19.   Further, the availability under the Bill of direct rights of action for breaches of rules is unhelpful and unnecessary. It is unhelpful in that it could lead to a legalistic and cautious approach to the drafting of rules (a danger which FSA recognise and feel they can overcome) and unnecessary given rights of access to the Ombudsman or the courts.

20.   The new regulatory regime should not incorporate a civil right of action for breach of a rule. Perhaps more than any other factor, Section 62 of the Financial Services Act, which provides such a right, increased the pressure for detailed provisions, rules and exemptions. There was a strong perception that without plenty of detail and certainty, the rules would lead to dramatically increased litigation. As the then Chairman of the SIB put it:

   —   "[Section 62] had a serious adverse effect on the SIB rulebook . . . the problem was that it focused the attention of practitioners and more particularly their lawyers on amending the rules not to improve them generally, but simply to minimise the possibility of claims. This led to long and complicated provisions, attempting to draw fine distinctions to produce safe harbours for legitimate industry practice, whilst maintaining the essence of the original objective of the rule".

21. If this proposal is retained, it should be more clearly defined by amending Clause 80 (3) of the Bill so that a particular rule would have to positively provide for the right of action by a private person—something which may be more appropriate in specific cases, for example disputes about fair dealing.

SCOPE OF THE NEW REGIME: THE PROVISION OF MORTGAGE ADVICE AND RECOGNISED PROFESSIONAL BODIES

Mortgage advice and the regulation of loans secured on land

22. Although the Committee has said it will be looking at the position of mortgage advice, it is not clear to us that this can be viewed in isolation of the broader question of the regulation of loans secured on land (to use the terminology of Schedule 2 of the Bill). We consider it very important that the regulatory regime under the Bill provides an appropriate level of consumer protection, taking into account, *inter alia*, the nature of the financial service in question and, where appropriate, the existence of alternative means of regulation, such as industry codes of conduct. The conduct of mortgage business is currently governed by such a code of practice, the Mortgage Code. All significant mortgage providers adhere to the Mortgage Code and, since last year, mortgage intermediaries have also been covered by the Code. We consider it to have been an effective alternative to statutory regulation, and the changes to the compliance machinery for the Code, currently in the pipeline, such as an enhanced monitoring and disciplinary role for the Independent Review Body, will further enhance its effectiveness.

23. We recognise that HM Treasury is currently reviewing the efficacy of the Mortgage Code and will decide later this year whether the regulation of loans secured on land should be placed within the scope of FSA. Parliament will also wish to take a view on the desirability of the regulation of mortgage advice, and we would hope that the timing of this decision will be such as to allow the outcome of the Treasury's review to be taken into account.

Recognised Professional Bodies

24. The approach to RPBs as indicated in Section 3 of HM Treasury's "Regulated Activities" paper (February 1999) is right. Where legal and accounting professionals provide investment advice in a manner which is subordinate to their main services, they should not have to seek authorisation. Where they provide financial services as free standing products, it is right that they should have appropriate authorisation from the FSA and be regulated on exactly the same basis as other authorised firms.

OMBUDSMEN AND INVESTOR COMPENSATION

The Financial Services Ombudsman

25. Effective redress arrangements are essential for consumer confidence in financial services. We support the proposals for a single financial services Ombudsman (FSO) scheme for the resolution of complaints which are not capable of being resolved via a firm's own internal complaints procedure. It should help clarify the redress arrangements in the eyes of consumers and should ensure a consistency of standards of redress across the range of financial services to be regulated by the FSA.

26. The existing Ombudsman arrangements available to customers of banks and insurers have provided a fast, effective means of impartial redress binding on the firm and at no cost to the customer. This will continue to be the case under the new FSO scheme, but other advantages of the existing industry Ombudsman schemes will be lost, we fear. This is because a statutory Ombudsman scheme will, inevitably, be more legalistic in its approach compared to the existing voluntary arrangements and this will have a detrimental effect compared to the relative openness and informality with which firms currently deal with the banking and insurance Ombudsmen. This will be a particular danger, if the FSA insists on sharing information received by the FSO.

27. Whilst the new FSO will, as we have noted, provide welcome rationalisation, there will still be anomalies. For example, Treasury ministers recently announced their intention to extend the compulsory scope of the FSO, in respect of FSA-authorised firms, to certain financial services which are not covered by the Financial Services and Markets Bill. For banks this will mean, *inter alia*, that their non-mortgage lending business will fall within the compulsory jurisdiction of the FSO. However, other lenders, not authorised by FSA, will be under no obligation to join the FSO scheme, but may be subject to the Ombudsman's voluntary jurisdiction should they so wish.

Consumer Compensation

28. An effective compensation scheme is fundamental to the Government's proposals for the new single regulator. We support the Government's aims of a single compensation scheme with a single board and a harmonised administration function.

29.   We also agree with proposals which FSA has issued separately (in their consultation paper 5 of January 1998) that there is a need to distinguish between the differing needs of customers of deposit-takers, insurance companies and investment firms. This can best be achieved by having three sub-schemes within the single scheme. This differentiation is currently reflected in the three existing schemes; namely, the Deposit Protection Scheme (and its building society equivalent), the Investors Compensation Scheme and the Policyholder Protection Scheme.

30.   We support the FSA's proposal that there should be no cross-subsidy between the sub-schemes and we would stress, also, the need for the compensation scheme to be seen to be independent of the FSA. Consistent with the statutory objectives set out in the Financial Services and Markets Bill, it is, we believe, fundamental that the FSA should not seek to remove all risk from customers, and some element of co-insurance should be retained.

31.   There is a particular difficulty in the delegation of powers to set the scope of the compensation schemes and the bases for levies. Parliament may prefer that primary or secondary legislation is the appropriate way to define the extent to which the customers of solvent businesses should pay for the losses of other consumers.

MARKET ABUSE

32.   The ABI and BBA agree with the policy objective behind Part VI of the draft Bill, namely to seek to ensure that UK markets operate in an open, transparent and fair manner. That said, the draft Bill gives rise to serious concerns under a number of heads, and needs to be amended in order to ensure fairness and certainty. Fairness and sufficient certainty are essential if firms are to feel confident in operating in UK markets.

Definition of the Offence of Market Abuse—Intent

33.   We strongly believe that there should be a test of intent in the manner in which the offence is drafted in Section 56. The absence of such an objective test has two effects: it means that persons may be unfairly pursued for the unintended consequences of their actions; it also means that the definition of the offence is defined in a highly subjective way. Agencies with a similar role to the FSA in other jurisdictions have to demonstrate intent or show recklessness—and the SEC has shown that it can be done in many hundreds of cases.

34.   In focusing on the effect of behaviour instead of on intent, the definition of market abuse in the draft Bill does not, as the Government concedes, give participants sufficient certainty as to the application of the market abuse regime. The Committee will be aware that, in the opinion of Lord Lester QC, "the Market Abuse offences as defined in the draft Bill are framed at such a high level of generality that they do not satisfy Article 7(1) of the Convention [the European Convention of Human Rights], which requires, in accordance with the principle of legal certainty, that an offence must be clearly defined in law so that a person may foresee the consequences of his or its actions."

Role and Status of the Code of Market Conduct

35.   The Government argues that it is the Code of Market Conduct drawn up under Section 57 by the FSA which is to provide the certainty that the legislation will not. This raises two objections. Firstly, as a matter of principle, as this part of the Bill applies universally and not simply to firms regulated by the FSA, it seems desirable that clarity should be delivered in the legislation itself. Secondly, the evidential status of the Code means that compliance with it is not conclusive, and yet compliance really ought to provide a safe harbour for commercial transactions.

Enforcement

36.   This is covered in a separate section. The concerns about due process have added force in the context of market abuse in that the FSA enforcement regime will be applied to persons not subject to authorisation by the FSA.

Overlap and Layering within the Market Abuse Regime

37.   While we understand that Government and regulators are keen to see compliance which goes beyond "lip service", it is important that there is an overall coherence to the regime, and that the layering of similar but not identical requirements is avoided. We are concerned that in several respects the proposed regime is unnecessarily complex. For example:

  — The interaction of criminal, civil and regulatory provisions causes concern about the complexity of the overall regime which will emerge.

— The general definition of market abuse goes beyond the definitions of the criminal offence of insider dealing in the Criminal Justice Act, and of market manipulation in section 212 of the draft Bill, and does not recognise the defences allowed in those circumstances.

38. Firms will have to consider whether behaviour is criminal or not, as well as whether it complies with the Code. Even if it meets these tests, Section 56 may still be breached. Authorised firms will, moreover, have to consider their behaviour against the FSA's rules and any exchange rules which might be applicable. There are also variations in the way that the various requirements are drafted when dealing with the same matter.

22 March 1999

APPENDIX 14

Memorandum by the Association of Private Client Investment Managers and Stockbrokers (APCIMS)

INTRODUCTION

1.1 The overwhelming majority of private client stockbroking and investment management firms are members of APCIMS and they act for the estimated 12 million individual shareholders in the United Kingdom when they buy or sell shares. Most of our members are currently regulated by the SFA; the remainder are regulated by IMRO.

1.2 APCIMS submitted a detailed response on the Financial Services and Markets Bill in October 1998 and we have commented on most of the Consultation Papers published by the FSA to date. We have also reviewed the recent Consultation Papers published by HM Treasury and the Progress Report on the Bill. Our submissions for the Joint Committee reflect the concerns which we continue to have regarding various elements of the proposed regime. These concerns are set out below:

ACCOUNTABILITY OF THE FSA

2.1 We are pleased by the proposals in the Progress Report regarding the introduction of additional measures to increase the accountability of the FSA not just to Parliament but also to the regulated community. When commenting on FSA Consultation Paper 13 on the Proposed Principles for firms, we suggested that the FSA should also have some Principles on how it should conduct itself. We saw this as an opportunity to create a "Charter for the Financial Services Industry" which would, in effect, be a pact on standards by authorised persons and their regulator. The adoption of this proposal would go a long way to reassure firms of the FSA's commitment to the openness and accountability of its role. It also highlights that firms too have expectations of their regulator and its responsibility to provide a quality service.

2.2 If the suggestion of an industry Charter is adopted, then the FSA's compliance with its Principles could be included in the reports of the Practitioner and Consumer Panels and could also be subject to Treasury scrutiny.

2.3 We suggested that the following Principles could initially be considered for adoption by the FSA. Alternative and/or additional Principles for the FSA will be developed when this suggestion is discussed more widely. (The Principle is set out in bold; the explanatory text is set out underneath in italics.)

A. The FSA will conduct itself with integrity, due diligence and skill in the performance of its objectives.

A1. *This requires FSA staff to conduct themselves in a professional and proper manner. Staff will always take account of the size of an authorised person and the nature of its business and will act appropriately. Every effort will be made to ensure that the staff who have regular dealings with firms or who develop policy or act in an enforcement capacity will have direct experience of the financial services industry. All FSA staff will undergo regular training and will already have, or will acquire, qualifications suitable to their job function.*

B. The FSA will publish all rules interpretations and formal guidance to ensure that rules are understood and applied in a consistent manner and will respond promptly to all requests for advice and guidance from authorised persons.

B1. *FSA staff will not refuse to answer queries or give assistance simply because they have made a subjective decision that the request is unreasonable. It is inevitable that the staff which develop rules will occasionally receive queries from firms which indicate a lack of understanding of the requirements. Such queries could be classed by the staff as unreasonable and yet they may have arisen because the regulatory strictures or requirements have been written in ambiguous language, or because contradictory advice has been given by other FSA staff or because a situation has developed which was not envisaged at the time that the rules were prepared.*

B2. *The best way for any regulator to understand how firms are receiving its regulatory announcements is for it to encourage firms to ask questions and to seek guidance when necessary. Such dialogue quickly exposes ambiguities in rules and misunderstandings which may exist in the market.*

B3. *In the early months of the new regulatory environment, the FSA sends an unfortunate and unacceptable message to its constituent firms when it states that it will only respond to what it considers to be reasonable requests for informal guidance. Under this suggested Principle 2, the FSA will be proactive in encouraging firms to ask about the regulatory regime and to seek guidance when necessary either directly or via their representative trade associations.*

C. **The FSA will ensure that any inspection visit to a firm is conducted under the management of a senior member of FSA staff who is suitable for this task either because he/she has direct experience of the business conducted by that firm or because they have visited the firm before. The FSA report on a firm following this inspection visit shall be issued promptly after the completion of the inspection.**

C1. *This should prevent the continuation of the scenario where a firm is visited/inspected/advised by regulatory staff who have little or no understanding of its business, instruments, systems, organisation or the extent of its international involvement. The presence of a senior manager with suitable direct experience will reassure firms that they are more likely to be given pragmatic, common sense advice which is appropriate and does not entail needless processes and unjustifiable expense.*

MONEY LAUNDERING

3.1 Paragraph 4.14 of the Progress Report fails to address a key concern which we expressed on the Bill, namely the requirement that firms will have to *detect* financial crime. Currently, all firms have a responsibility to deter financial crimes such as money laundering. Firms take this responsibility seriously as is evidenced by the Money Laundering Guidelines which were developed by practitioners and which are updated on a regular basis.

3.2 The new regime requires firms to detect money laundering rather than simply to assist in its deterrence. This change in emphasis places a considerable costs-burden upon firms as they will have to employ and train personnel to ensure the presence of staff with the appropriate set of skills to detect money laundering. Similarly, if the Treasury expects the FSA to seek out this activity then it too will have to employ a highly trained set of individuals who are conversant with the complexities of such transactions or it will have to contract out such expertise to other bodies. One need only speak to NCIS to understand the lengths that money launderers will go to in continuing their activities; it is big business with large sums at stake. It should therefore come as no surprise that such big business employs both highly paid and talented people to cover up their activities. We urge the Treasury to reconsider the stance taken in the Bill and to return to the lesser test of deterrence rather than detection.

MARKET ABUSE AND GUIDANCE

4.1 We are gravely concerned by the Treasury's view that firms can be punished as market abusers for the unintended consequences of their actions.[1] We strongly urge the Treasury to reconsider its stance vis-a-vis the role of "intent" in identifying market abuse as we believe it to be an essential element in the offence. We appreciate that it is impracticable to describe market abuse offences in primary legislation but we believe that the Bill should be amended to include a requirement that the offence of market abuse includes an assessment of the intention or motivation of the firm.

4.2 The offence of market abuse is a combination of action (which may also be a decision not to act) and of motivation. It is a deception practised on the market and is a deliberate and wilful act. The motivation of a firm can be deduced from an objective assessment of its conduct over the relevant period, by ascertaining who would benefit from a particular action and by using tests of reasonableness.

4.3 If the Bill proceeds in the absence of a test of intent, firms will be in the uncomfortable position of having no certainty regarding the assessment of their actions by regulators. Indeed they will be regulated by hindsight as they will be expected to know in advance the exact effect which any trade may have on the market and to decide whether there is any danger of that impact being negative and therefore liable to be deemed "abusive". No market is perfect as it inevitably involves an imbalance of buyers and sellers and it can be affected by many different events and developments both external and internal. All trades have an impact of some kind (especially in an illiquid market) without there being a sinister motive behind them. The assumption that if a trade impacts in a negative way on a market it necessarily involves market abuse is incorrect and potentially damaging for the UK financial markets.

4.4 It will be almost impossible for Compliance Officers to advise trading desks on whether to proceed with various trades. It is likely that this will force firms to seek more guidance from the FSA in advance of trades as they will be striving to establish greater certainty in this area. There is also a danger that innovation may be

---

[1] We note the FSA's plan to use "principal purpose" tests in its Code of Conduct but we believe that primary legislation should also include a reference to a test of intent.

stifled or that firms seeking to create new methods of dealing or new instruments may take their business to another regulatory regime which has more certainty.

4.5   Paragraph 5.8 of the Progress Report states that it is unlikely that the FSA will wish to discipline firms who have followed its guidance. However, the FSA has notified firms that, in general, compliance with the guidance is not a guarantee against subsequent disciplinary action. We suggest that the Treasury and FSA discuss this matter further to agree a common approach which confirms that proven compliance with guidance is sufficient to ward off subsequent actions.

4.6   The Treasury has stated that it is keen to close off all loopholes in order to protect consumers. Whilst this intention is laudable, in practice this leaves firms in a position where any action can be subsequently held to have been abusive. If an act falls outside the scope of the law, the rules or the code then the firm which committed that act cannot be disciplined. We believe that regulators should not twist rules or codes to pursue a firm for an act which was not foreseen or allowed for in the regulatory regime. Instead, we suggest that the regulator should learn from the experience and that the rules and/or code should be amended to address future repetitions of the particular act. We strongly urge the Treasury and the FSA to reconsider the apparent move towards regulating by hindsight and to favour the development of a regulatory regime which is based on certain, clear and simple rules.

4.7   We challenge the statement in paragraph 5.8 of the Progress Report that " . . . it would be [inappropriate] to compel the FSA to provide specific guidance on request". We suggest that the FSA has a responsibility to help firms to understand their regulatory obligations and this involves acting as the provider of guidance on request. It would be unacceptable for the FSA to have the power to choose to reject requests for help from the firms which it regulates. We are not yet sure whether the FSA will be a regulator or a supervisor but the approach being adopted to market abuse and enforcement makes one fear that it will assume the role of a regulator.

ENFORCEMENT AND DISCIPLINE

5.1   We are pleased that the Treasury will ensure that the Bill is in compliance with the European Convention on Human Rights. We look forward to receiving further information about how the re-named tribunal will interact with the Enforcement Committee being established by the FSA.

5.2   We believe that a disciplinary action (for reasons other than deliberate misconduct or criminality) indicates a failure both by the firm and by the FSA. The supervision staff at the FSA play a key role in preventing the initiation of an enforcement/disciplinary action by ensuring that firms know what is expected of them and are well informed about regulatory developments. We firmly believe that the FSA has a role to play in encouraging firms to be compliant. It would be beneficial to the FSA and its regulated community if it assumed the persona of the approachable but pragmatic supervisor which encourages compliance through supervision and inspection teams which are staffed by people who understand the many businesses which they regulate and who are keen to help firms to "get it right".

THE OMBUDSMAN SCHEME

6.1   Paragraph 11.8 of the Progress Report states that the Ombudsman's decision will be binding on the respondent but not the complainant. Whilst this process is possibly acceptable when the claimant is a private individual, it is unacceptable if the claimant is an authorised firm. For example, it could be possible for one of the major banks to be a "customer" and one of our small member firms to be a defendant. We suggest that either the Ombudsman Scheme should not be used by authorised persons or that the Bill be amended to accommodate the possible use of the scheme by firms.

6.2   There is no mechanism which requires the Ombudsman to verify that its interpretation of the rules is consistent with that of the FSA although this may be addressed via future Consultation Papers on this matter.

6.3   We are concerned about the broadening of the scope of the Ombudsman's jurisdiction over services which would not otherwise fall within the scope of the Bill (see paragraph 11.6 of the Progress Report). This removes certainty about the exact scope of the Ombudsman's jurisdiction and leaves firms vulnerable to a challenge on matters which they did not know that the Ombudsman would decide to investigate.

THE INVESTORS COMPENSATION SCHEME

7.1   We accept that a policy decision to have one consumer compensation scheme has been agreed. However, if it is set up as proposed with one pot for deposit taking, one for insurance and the rest for the securities industry, then this will result in significant increases in contributions from prudent and well managed firms to pay for the losses incurred by others whose business is dramatically different. If the new scheme is to be fair then a firm should pay commensurate with the business that it undertakes and the risk involved and it should allow for a reduction in fees when a firm has sufficient insurance to cover its responsibilities to its clients.

MISCELLANEOUS COMMENTS ON THE PROGRESS REPORT

8.1   We are aware of the list of questions upon which the Committee has agreed to focus its inquiry. Nevertheless we have additional observations on the Progress Report which we would like to bring to the attention of the Committee. These are set out briefly below:

(a)   in paragraph 4.11 the report states that regulation should *ensure* that consumers are able to make reasoned decisions. We suggest that this is too burdensome a requirement and that no regulation can ensure such a thing. We suggest instead that the Treasury seek a regulated environment in which consumers can make informed decisions and obtain independent advice to assist them with their investment decisions; and

(b)   in paragraph 5.2 we ask that when the FSA publishes final versions of its rule changes, it should also explain how many comments it received during the consultation and the extent to which those comments influenced the new rule(s). This would highlight the quantity of input received by the FSA and it would let firms know the extent to which they were influencing developments.

29 March 1999

APPENDIX 15

Supplementary Memorandum by the Association of Private Client Investment Managers and Stockbrokers (APCIMS)

1.   MARKET ABUSE AND GUIDANCE

1.1   The Treasury have stated in paragraph 13.5 of the Progress Report that the intention of the market abuse fines is to protect people's confidence in the market (rather than to penalise wrongdoers). In my view, punitive legislation is not an appropriate way to prevent firms doing something which they do not intend or expect to result in the "market abuse" consequences. This is especially the case where those consequences depend on what onlookers may think, which the firm may have never even contemplated; you cannot prevent firms doing something unless they intended to do it. It is unfair to penalise firms (and, indeed, ordinary companies) on this basis.

1.2   It seems to me that the threat of penal sanctions would mean that firms will continually have to ask their compliance officers to take a view on what onlookers may conclude from a particular transaction. This would impose probably unacceptable delays in effecting a particular transaction, and may anyway not avoid the offence being committed, if the compliance officer does not view the transaction in the same way as the market (as it is all subjective). Alternatively, it will penalise firms merely because they are there. This policy will cause major problems not only to regulated firms but also to the wider community. For example, non-UK gold producers will be liable if gold futures traders interpret their conduct as meaning something, even if that impression was not intended; this will be the case even if the gold producer had no idea how its conduct would be interpreted or, indeed, that there is such an offence of market abuse in the UK which can be committed by it inadvertently.

1.3   In relation to discipline generally, it is somewhat unfair that the FSA may discipline firms, which complied with FSA guidance. Although paragraph 5.8 of the Progress Report states that the FSA is not likely to do so, this leaves open the possibility that in certain cases the FSA will wish to discipline firms which follow its guidance, which surely is not an appropriate method of regulation. Indeed, it is not at all clear that (as should be the case) the FSA's restrictive policy on discipline (typically, fines) will apply also to the FSA's exercise of its powers to require restitution or disgorgement.

1.4   More important in practice is the risk that counterparties or clients can successfully sue for contravention of rules (and claim restitution) even though the firm has complied with the FSA's guidance, which surely is all that the Treasury can expect. It is therefore very important that the Bill should provide that Private rights of action (under clause 80) do not apply where the firm has followed FSA guidance; if the firm has nonetheless contravened the "spirit" of the guidance (whatever that means) the FSA can still discipline that firm even if counterparties and clients are not entitled to sue.

2.   ENFORCEMENT AND DISCIPLINE

2.1   The Treasury has stated in paragraph 6.11 of the Progress Report that it will not agree to incorporate a provision in the Bill that the FSA will act "reasonably". It explains that this is because as the FSA is a public authority it will anyway be required to act reasonably. However, the term "reasonable" is used in that context in a different sense.

2.2   The leading case is the *Wednesbury* decision in 1947. Without getting too technical about it, the Court of Appeal held in that case that, assuming that the public authority (in the present context the FSA) takes into account only and all relevant matters, it would not be treated as acting "unreasonably" merely because it reaches an unreasonable decision. Instead, it would only be treated as acting "unreasonably" for this purpose if it reaches a decision that, in the present context, no reasonable regulator could have reached. The Court expressly started that a court would not have the authority to substitute its own view as to what was a reasonable decision for that of the FSA.

2.3   This is surely not enough for regulated firms. They want to know that if they act properly the FSA will also act properly. What this means is that the FSA should not take decisions which are unreasonable (in normal English). For this reason it is important that the FSA should be subject to an express obligation to act reasonably.

9 March 1999

APPENDIX 16

Note by the Association of Private Client Investment Managers and Stockbrokers (APCIMS) on accountability and the FSA

Accountability of the FSA has been improved following the Treasury's announcement at the turn of the year, however further changes need to be made as follows:

1.   ONGOING CONSULTATION

Whilst having a duty to consult on rules, codes and guidance, there is no requirement for the FSA to place in the public domain the responses it receives, nor explain why, for example, it has not taken up suggestions made to it by the industry. Of the 21 consultation papers so far issued by the FSA, and of which APCIMS has responded to all except those relating to the regulation of Lloyds and the pensions review, a feedback statement was published on CP10 on market abuse only. For the remainder, the only responses we have received so far merely say "Thank you for your response". We consider that more feedback on the responses should be published as a matter of urgency.

2.   INTERNATIONAL COMPETITIVENESS OF THE UK

There is already a requirement for a committee of non-executive board members to keep under review whether the FSA is undertaking its functions in an economic and efficient way in addition to considering the adequacy of the FSA's internal financial controls. However, financial regulation can have the result of affecting significantly the ability of UK quartered firms to compete in an international market. Yet there is no requirement for the FSA to address this issue. We propose that a second committee of non-executive members should be set up to address the international competitiveness of UK's firms with the changing financial regulation framework and the ongoing regulatory requirements and report on an annual basis.

3.   STATUTORY IMMUNITY

The FSA has statutory immunity from negligent actions, whilst retaining the ability to remove the means of livelihood of those whom it regulates. The reason given for granting this immunity is that without it the Government considers that regulators would be hampered by concerns of legal action from discharging their duties properly. In view of the fact that other professionals ranging from the police to the medical profession are not immune, we consider that the FSA should not be immune either. However, we also recognise the need to ensure that they are not impeded by continuous unnecessary legal actions and so propose that an action against the FSA can only take place under specific circumstances such as negligence.

4.   FSA PRINCIPLES

As with the SIB before it, the FSA is proposing a set of high level principles to govern the regulated community. APCIMS believes that these principles should be a two way street. So, just as financial firms have to respond quickly to the regulator and be staffed with professional people, so should the FSA be required to do likewise. Current practice, for example, is for a regulatory team to visit a firm but then take three months to send them a follow up letter listing the points found that they wish to see addressed—and then only give them seven days to respond. CP20 proposes that the FSA has up to a year in which to decide whether an applicant firm is to be authorised, but awards an applicant firm only 28 days in which to make representations following a failed application.

There is no requirement for the regulatory teams to be staffed with people who have experience of the business that they are visiting. With the haemorrhaging of staff, particularly from the SFA and from IMRO, firms are already finding that there can be inadequate experience among the staff of visiting teams.

Disciplinary action should be linked to rule breaches only and not breaches of a principle as they are designed to be general statements and are not specific.

5. RULE INTERPRETATION

There needs to be a public record of how rules are interpreted under differing circumstances. It is well documented that at present differing teams will interpret rules differently. For example, SFA Rule 4.112 on reconciliations, required SFA firms to carry out monthly reconciliations on investments which they do not hold against statements issued by the custodians of the investments. IMRO firms had no equivalent requirement. This rule resulted in considerable expense for our firms and for many demands that IMRO and SFA rules be synchronised. The whole investment club fiasco developed from advice issued by enforcement teams without consulting the SFA Policy unit and then subsequently policy had to support them. As a result, APCIMS had to develop the tedious and administratively burdensome route for firms to follow, otherwise the investment club movement would have been severely depleted. We understand that banking supervision keeps such a record and although the existing SROs do not and it would be unreasonable to expect them to start to do so now, with the new FSA rulebook this should be done so there is a Record of Interpretation available to the regulators and regulated alike and accessible on the Internet.

6. THE REASONABLE EXERCISE OF POWERS

The Government has responded that the FSA, like other public authorities, must exercise its powers reasonably and so does not believe it is necessary to include in the legislation a requirement for the FSA to act reasonably.

However, the existing regulatory bodies—public authorities—require an appellant firm or individual to pay their regulators costs if that firm, or person loses their appeal, but if they win the appeal they cannot claim their legal costs back from the regulator.

It is proposed that the FSA can issue guidance which a firm abides by, but it can subsequently prosecute that firm if it believes the firm has not acted in the "right spirit".

Neither action appears to be "reasonable".

The "Wednesbury" decision on this matter says that as long as a public authority has taken into account all relevant matters even if it reached an unreasonable decision, it would not be considered to have acted unreasonably. It could only be considered as acting unreasonably if it reached a decision that no reasonable regulator could have reached. So as a reasonable regulator can reach an unreasonable decision, there is not much comfort here for a regulated firm. Especially as a court would not have the authority to substitute its own view as to what was a reasonable decision for that of the FSA.

For there to be a good relationship between regulator and the regulated, a requirement for the FSA to exercise its powers reasonably should be explicitly included in the Bill. The alternative proposed by Government of Judicial Review is costly and for practical purposes only available to large institutions, those on legal aid or the legal profession acting for itself.

7. THE DISCIPLINARY PROCESS

We consider that a much fairer procedure to that currently proposed would be as follows:

— The FSA notifies a firm that it considered to have acted in breach of the rules and, accordingly, that the FSA is considering taking disciplinary action.

— If it disputes this, the firm has the opportunity to present its case along with the regulators to the FSA Enforcement Committee composed of a majority of external practitioners and with a Chairman from one of the external practitioners.

— The firm or individual would have the option to appear in front of the Committee to make their case should they choose to do so.

— Even after the case has been heard by this Committee, both the FSA and the firm would retain the right to appeal against the decision to the independent tribunal route.

— Only after the final decision on disciplinary action would consideration be given to fines or other penalties by the Enforcement Committee.

— No publicity given to the case until after all procedures have been fulfilled.

8. MARKET ABUSE SHOULD INCLUDE "INTENT"

Market abuse is the combination of action and motivation from those who undertake it, but in so doing other innocent parties can find themselves inadvertently involved. If intent is not specified within the legislation, firms will be regulated by hindsight and expected to know in advance the exact effect that any trade may have on a market. This is a practical impossibility as all trades on a market affect the price of the security.

13 April 1999

APPENDIX 17

Memorandum by the Association of Lloyd's Members (ALM)

The Financial Services and Markets Bill ends the long standing right of Lloyd's to regulate itself. I am writing as Chairman of the Association of Lloyd's Members, which represents the majority of the Names who continue to underwrite. Names, in the broad sense of individual capital providers, supply £3,500 million of capacity to the market, and the regulation of Lloyd's is of vital importance to them.

REGULATION OF LLOYD'S

The last two decades have seen a massive failure of self regulation at Lloyd's, which inflicted losses exceeding £8,000 million on Names, and which brought the market to the brink of insolvency. These losses were not the mere product of misfortune, although they were triggered by a variety of catastrophes and claims arising from asbestosis. However, their magnitude and their concentration on a minority of syndicates at Lloyd's arose from gross negligence and a failure of regulatory supervision. Five separate High Court judgments found that there had been culpable negligence by Lloyd's agencies and awarded the Names involved the most substantial damages in English legal history.

Against that background, the ALM supports the intention of the Financial Services and Markets Bill to bring the regulation of Lloyd's under the Financial Services Authority. However, we are very concerned that the Bill may not enable the FSA to regulate the market effectively and that there may be a dangerous combination of responsibility without effective powers.

Everybody accepts that over the last four years there has been a very substantial improvement in the regulation of Lloyd's. The Regulatory Division has a strong and effective director and a staff who have made great progress in remedying the faults of the past. They should remain in place, and continue to work in close liaison with the market, an essential condition for effective regulation for a market place as idiosyncratic as that of Lloyd's. We do not advocate the creation of a Lloyd's Department at the FSA and the absorption within it of the Lloyd's Regulatory Division.

However, it is clearly time to change the Regulatory Division's reporting lines. At present the Division reports to, and is subordinate to, the Council of Lloyd's. It is, of course, tempting to say that, given the enormous task the FSA faces, it would be much the simplest solution to leave the Council to get on with it, with the FSA merely retaining a degree of oversight, as is currently proposed. The implications of this decision would, however, be very hard to justify. One of the key features of the creation of the FSA is that for the generality of financial services it sets up a regulatory structure clearly separated from the activities and markets regulated, a principle which should obviously be applied to Lloyd's too. If things are left as they are, the Regulatory Division and process will remain subordinate to a Council which can override byelaws or decisions put forward by the Regulatory Division. The Council of Lloyd's always contains a specified number of Working Members who, together with other "insiders", have the power to block byelaws and exercise wide ranging influence more generally. This would mean that at Lloyd's, alone in the FSA's domain, one would perpetuate the inappropriate practice of the regulated employing and controlling the regulators.

This problem is far from theoretical. Not much more than two years ago, a High Court judge found that Stephen Merrett, who had only just ceased to be Deputy Chairman of the Council of Lloyd's, had intentionally deceived both the auditors of his syndicate and the Names on it as to their liabilities. The Names were awarded damages of over £100 million. Other members of the Council have been defendants in similar litigation, or have actually been the subject of disciplinary proceedings brought by Lloyd's itself. We believe that the FSA must be able to control the Regulatory Division at Lloyd's directly.

We are also concerned with the Bill's provision that, banks apart, all the financial institutions to be regulated by the FSA, including Lloyd's, will be authorised *automatically* when the Act is implemented. While this is appropriate and inevitable for the other bodies, the starting position of Lloyd's is different. It has not been subject to the previous 1986 Financial Services Act or any other external scrutiny. Hence there can be no confidence that the Council's constitutional arrangements and practices are appropriate for handling regulatory issues under the new Act. Particularly if it is intended to proceed with the "preferred" solution, there may well be a number of steps and undertakings which it would be appropriate for the FSA or Treasury to require the Council to undertake or commit to before authorisation. Since we understand that the FSA is likely to arrive at its views on how to arrange the regulation of Lloyd's in the relatively near future, this is an urgent issue, which presumably should be recognised in Clause 190 in the legislation.

AMENDMENT TO THE 1982 ACT

We were very concerned to learn that it had been suggested to the Committee at two separate hearings that the Financial Services Bill should be amended to give the Treasury, at the request of the Council of Lloyd's, the power to amend the 1982 Lloyd's Act.

We recognise that the 1982 Act restricts Lloyd's in many ways, some of which may be commercially disadvantageous. So we understand why it can be argued that it is desirable to amend the Act.

However, imperfect though it may be, the 1982 Act also contains vital safeguards for the members of Lloyd's, of whom the Names and other capital providers continue to be a vital part. For example, if the Council passes a byelaw, which is perceived to be against the interests of the members, they have the right to revoke the byelaw at a subsequent General Meeting. It is a vitally important point that the vote at such meetings is conducted on a one member, one vote basis.

Of course, it will be suggested that the intention of giving Lloyd's and the Treasury the power to amend the Lloyd's Act would only be used for financial regulation, since this is the purpose of the Financial Services Bill. The difficulty with this argument is that financial regulation can have a very direct impact on the capital and income of Names at Lloyd's. Indeed much of the regulatory debate since 1995 has revolved around how far regulatory policy should preserve a level playing field or, rather, be tilted to encourage non-aligned capital providers to leave the market.

The creation of any such broad power, with its potentially major implications for the market place and its participants, should be very carefully considered. To avoid controversial and potentially fundamental changes in a private Bill designed to protect the rights of a wide range of private persons, both corporate and individual, every care needs to be taken to ensure that there is *full provision for those individuals to safeguard their rights*.The process of change should be an open and fair one. The best way to achieve this would be to provide that any amendment must have been previously approved by a substantial majority of the members of Lloyd's, say 75 per cent *voting on the one member one vote basis enshrined in the 1982 Lloyd's Act*. If one did this, it would be reasonable to confine the electorate to members currently underwriting at Lloyd's, since these would be the parties affected by any amendment to the Act. A further essential safeguard would be that any such amendments should be approved in advance by the FSA.

29 March 1999

APPENDIX 18

Memorandum by the Association of Solicitor Investment Managers (ASIM)

1. This association has previously made submissions dated 14 August 1998 (provided to David Roe, HM Treasury) and 27 November 1998 (copy enclosed).[1]

2. The recent growth in investment services provided by solicitors' firms (where employees have the necessary qualifications) has been one of the most interesting competitive innovations of the last decade and has provided access to independent, local, high-quality advice with unrivalled investor protection to many people. The FSA is under a duty to encourage such innovative, competitive developments but we are concerned that proposals set out in its consultation papers (or pre-consultation papers) to date would make such an innovation highly unlikely to re-occur in future and would damage the development of this movement amongst solicitors' firms.

3. Our view is that the proposals in FSA Consultation Paper 20—The Qualifying Conditions for Authorisation—will be a severe deterrent to any small organisation which may wish to enter the market for investment services. This is because of the requirements for professional validation of business plans, pre-application commitment to premises, systems and staff and the six-month approval period which will in combination deter even well organised entrepreneurs and constitute a significant barrier to entry.

---

[1] Not printed.

4. We are also concerned at the possible imposition of overburdensome financial resources requirements on agency investment management firms, such as those in solicitors' firms, which would increase costs for no benefit to consumers.

5. ASIM members' customers are already adequately protected by insurance and business continuity arrangements which have long been in place in solicitors' firms under statutory rules. Financial failure of a firm is an unlikely cause of investor loss in solicitor investment managers because:

5.1 the agency structure involves no capital at trading risk;

5.2 solicitors' statutory intervention arrangements come into play in the event of business failure;

5.3 indemnity insurance provides cover against fraud and negligence.

6. Imposing capital adequacy requirements on integrated legal and investment practices will force the expensive demerger of the two business streams in order that the "pure" legal stream is not saddled with the inefficient capital adequacy costs. Demerger will bring about substantial and pointless additional costs—separate premises, separate computer networks, separate administration and separate staff contracts. ASIM believes 30 per cent to 40 per cent of existing solicitor investment managers would close down their businesses, reducing choice for the consumer in these circumstances.

31 March 1999

APPENDIX 19

Memorandum by the Association of Unit Trusts and Investment Funds (AUTIF)

Accountability

— FSA's accountability to Parliament and public needs to be strengthened.

— Treasury Select Committee should review FSA Annual Report and present findings to House of Commons for debate.

— FSA should consult on all significant policy initiatives, not just rule changes.

— FSA should also hold public hearings on important policy proposals.

Enforcement

— FSA needs to promote a culture of mutual trust between regulator and regulated. Discipline should be the exception, not the norm.

— Role of proposed Enforcement Committee should be enshrined in Bill.

— Bill should require FSA to delay publicising disciplinary action against a firm until any parallel investigations into the firm's employees have been completed.

— Enforcement Committee should exercise independent oversight of cost and timescale of disciplinary proceedings.

— There is also a need for independent scrutiny of the FSA's use of fines.

— Both Enforcement Committee and Tribunal should be able to award costs against FSA.

— Statutory immunity of FSA staff from civil suit should be removed.

Scope

— Early publication of missing provisions relating to collective investment schemes is essential.

1. The Association of Unit Trusts and Investment Funds welcomes the opportunity to comment on the issues identified by the Joint Committee. Our main concerns are set out below.

ACCOUNTABILITY

2. The FSA will be independent of both Government and industry. Although accountable to the Treasury, the link is, by design, very weak. There is thus an accountability deficit which is best mitigated by increased, and statutory, openness and consultation requirements.

3. The draft Bill gives the FSA extremely wide ranging powers, especially in the area of enforcement and discipline. Whilst these powers are designed to make the FSA an effective regulator, it is essential that they are balanced by a robust framework of accountability. We therefore welcome the recent announcement by the Economic Secretary, Patricia Hewitt, of further measures to strengthen the FSA's accountability.

4. However, the provisions of the draft Bill largely focus on accountability to Treasury ministers. *We believe there is a pressing need to improve the FSA's accountability to Parliament and the public.* The best way to achieve Parliamentary accountability would be to ask a Committee of the House—probably the Treasury Select Committee—to review the FSA's Annual Report, in order to assess how well the FSA is performing in meeting its statutory objectives. The House of Commons should then have an opportunity to debate the Committee's findings. We believe that this would be a far more effective discipline on the FSA's activities than the procedure currently envisaged by the Treasury, whereby the FSA's Annual Report will simply be laid before Parliament without debate. We are aware that the FSA will be required to hold an annual public meeting, but we doubt whether this will be as effective in maintaining accountability as a debate in the House of Commons.

5. The draft Bill requires the FSA to carry out public consultation whenever it proposes to change its rules. *We think that the Authority should also be required to consult on all policy initiatives affecting one or more sections of the regulated community,* even where they do not involve rule changes. This would be in line with the Inland Revenue's formal practice of consulting "wherever it is practicable to do so".

6. It would also be desirable for the FSA to publish a summary of responses to consultation, with individual responses available for scrutiny, except where respondents specifically request anonymity.

7. Finally, we believe that the FSA should be willing to learn from the practices of overseas regulators in this area. It would improve the openness and transparency of the policy making process if the FSA were to adopt the practice of the US Federal Reserve and Securities and Exchanges Commission of holding public hearings on important policy proposals. This would have the incidental benefit of helping the FSA to raise its public profile, and thus to meet its consumer education objective.

ENFORCEMENT

8. The draft Bill gives the FSA far reaching powers of enforcement and discipline. It is clearly desirable for the FSA to be able to deal swiftly and effectively with those who breach regulatory obligations wilfully or recklessly. At the same time, there is a perception that some of the FSA's constituent organisations—notably IMRO—have sometimes exercised their (more limited) powers in an oppressive manner. Enforcement in the FSA is in the hands of the ex-IMRO team. This has naturally given rise to a concern amongst industry and legal practitioners that the FSA's enforcement regime should contain appropriate checks and balances and adequately protect the rights of firms and individuals. We believe it is important for these safeguards to be incorporated in the Bill itself. In our view, the safeguards announced so far do not go far enough.

9. We recognise that the Treasury and FSA have a difficult balance to strike in this area. The FSA will clearly need to exercise its enforcement powers in a way that is fair and just to those accused. But equally, it is essential that the FSA's procedures do not become inflexible or legalistic. Against this background, we believe there are a number of relatively simple measures that could be taken to improve the fairness and transparency of the proposed enforcement regime whilst leaving the FSA with the required degree of flexibility:

(i) *Most importantly, the FSA needs to promote an atmosphere of mutual trust and dialogue between a firm and its regulators.* It is counter-productive to impose a fine and/or issue a public reprimand for minor or inadvertent rule breaches, since this will inhibit the flow of information between the firm and its regulators. In a recent case, one of the SROs publicly disciplined a firm for a rule breach which the firm itself had brought to its regulators' attention. Public censure should, in our view, be reserved for those who deliberately breach regulatory requirements or act negligently. For occasional, minor rule breaches, the FSA should use private reprimands instead. The need to discipline should be seen as a failure of regulation, not a success.

(ii) AUTIF welcomes the proposal to establish an Enforcement Committee, with practitioner and public interest members, to hear disciplinary cases. *It would help reinforce the separation of powers between the FSA enforcement staff and the Committee if the latter's role were enshrined in the Bill itself (as per the Practitioner and Consumer Panels).*

(iii) In some recent disciplinary cases, there has been a protracted delay between the conclusion of disciplinary proceedings against a firm and the completion of follow up enquiries into the firm's employees. It is very difficult to maintain the presumption of innocence of the individual in these circumstances. *We believe that the Bill should require the FSA to delay publicising the outcome of a disciplinary case against a firm until any related proceedings against the firm's employees—including any appeal to the Tribunal—have been completed.*

(iv) In recent cases, the unnecessarily protracted nature of SRO proceedings has meant that the accused have run out of defence funds. This has introduced an element of injustice for the individuals concerned. We believe, therefore, that the Enforcement Committee should have a formal role in monitoring *the cost and timescale of disciplinary proceedings,* in order to ensure that the FSA enforcement staff conduct their investigations as quickly and efficiently as possible. The Committee should review the progress of active enforcement cases on a regular basis to check whether target service standards are being met.

(v) The proposal that the FSA should use the proceeds of fines to meet its general costs gives the Authority an artificial incentive to use fines as a disciplinary tool. Consequently, we believe there is a need for *independent oversight of the FSA's use of fines*, to ensure that any fine imposed on a firm or individual is proportionate to the nature of the offence. Within the FSA, the Enforcement Committee could provide this oversight, but we would also encourage the Treasury Committee to monitor the FSA's use of fines.

(vi) Legal costs arising from a disciplinary action can be so prohibitive as to deter individuals and firms from taking their case to appeal. It is therefore vital that both the Enforcement Committee and the Tribunal should be able to *award costs against the FSA* if they find in favour of the firm or individual. It is not clear that the Bill makes adequate provision for this.

(vii) We believe that a key check is missing from the Bill in that the FSA staff will enjoy a statutory immunity from civil suit. Given the oppressive manner in which some SROs have acted in the past within powers not dissimilar to those in the Bill, we believe that this statutory immunity should be removed.

SCOPE

10. We are studying the Treasury's Consultation Document on Regulated Activities and will respond separately on this. In our earlier submission to the Joint Committee, dated 2 March, we emphasised the need for the Committee to have an opportunity, and sufficient time, to examine the new draft legislation in its entirety before completing its report. *We remain very concerned that most of the main Bill clauses relating to collective investment schemes (unit trusts and open ended investment companies) have still not been published for comment.* It will be impossible for the Committee to meet its terms of reference if it has no sight of these important parts of the Bill. We would encourage the Committee to press for immediate publication of these missing provisions, which are central to the Government's intentions on savings and pensions.

17 March 1999

APPENDIX 20

Supplementary Memorandum by the Association of Unit Trusts and Investment Funds (AUTIF)

Q1. *Do you believe that there will be sufficient certainty as to what constitutes breach of FSA rules, individual misconduct, and market abuse? If not, what can be put in the Bill to ensure greater certainty?*

Q6. *Do you believe that the enforcement procedures as now proposed, including those for market abuse, meet the standards of natural justice and the ECHR? If not, what more needs to be done? Are the Government in danger of writing in too many safeguards, and rendering the powers ineffective?*

Q7. *Do you find the Government's arguments against putting intent into the Bill, and Mr Davies's assurances, persuasive? If not, how would you like the Bill amended?*

These questions are related, so I will consider them together.

No, we do not believe the rules are sufficient or clear. For two reasons—firstly, something I will call the exaggerated behaviour syndrome, secondly because hindsight plays such an important role.

EXAGGERATED BEHAVIOUR AND HINDSIGHT

In my experience, market abuse is often just an exaggerated form of normal behaviour. Let me give you an example, large City brokers issue research reports every day on stocks. They may also own a position in a stock they write a positive report about. Will the FSA be able to say in advance when the issuance of a glowing report on a stock that the broker owns becomes market abuse? Will not intent come into it? Or will the FSA simply have to show that the price of the stock went up as clear evidence of intent to abuse? I hope not.

How about a company which takes a short position in a stock? If the stock subsequently goes down, is this evidence of market abuse, or simply good investing?

In most markets, the everyday buying and selling of stocks has the effect of moving prices up and down. When does an otherwise normal action become abusive action? How will the FSA know the difference when in both cases the effect of the action may be the same?

This is what concerns me most, that hindsight will be used to determine whether a given behaviour was market abuse or not, when in practice both normal behaviour and intentional market abuse can have the same consequence.

INTENT—PRICING EXAMPLE OF EXAGGERATED BEHAVIOUR

When is selling a loss leader product a legitimate strategy to gain share, and when is it predatory pricing to wipe out your competitor? Consumers benefit from the first, but can lose out if competition is reduced. How will the FSA know when something is OK for consumers and when it becomes market abuse?

INTENT—TRACKER FUNDS EXAMPLE OF HINDSIGHT

The Committee is right to be delving into this matter. In my mind, we are in danger of penalising honest people with 20/20 hindsight. Let me give you a live example. Today tracker or index funds are very popular, but in the future we might well come to believe that they distorted markets because of the way they invest in companies without thinking. Will the marketers of tracker funds be held to account under the market abuse regime even though they had no intention to abuse the market? In my experience, it is not easy to see that unintentional market abuse is taking place except with hindsight.

SHOULD INTENT BE IN THE BILL?

The market abuse regime proposed to introduce a code of behaviour. Like the Committee, I am anxious to see how this is crafted without intent forcing its way in.

While not yet accepting intent, Mr Davies in his response to a question by the Chairman said, "It is quite clear that we *do not* propose to prosecute people for accidental offences". Now the Oxford English Dictionary defines accident as "Anything that happens without foresight or expectation". Sounds like unintentional to me. I think the Committee is wise to continue probing this issue since I fail to see how any concept of natural justice can ignore intent in the financial services world where the chance outcome of risky transactions plays such an important role.

PROPOSALS FOR DEALING WITH MARKET ABUSE?

We recommend that market abuse cases fall to the Enforcement Committee that will have to examine each case based on the facts.

Q3.   *Do you believe that the proposals for guidance and waiver will allow the FSA to give responsible traders enough certainty and comfort? If not, what more needs to be provided for?*

GUIDANCE AND INNOVATION

Guidance is mostly tied to innovation. Firms that plan to do business following normal practice don't need guidance. But if the UK is to be a centre of innovation and if the FSA is to meet its principle of taking innovation into account, then it must have a robust system of guidance on which regulated firms know they can rely. One particular concern for the investment fund industry is that we do not know whether the rule waiver power is intended to cover the investment fund rules. We are severely hampered at the moment because under the present regime it does not.

Firms most often ask for guidance because an existing rule has become obsolete. It's important to be clear here. I am talking here about when the firm isn't asking for guidance on how to comply with a rule. It's asking for the FSA's agreement to actually breach the rule.

For instance a rule that says you have to get something in writing from the consumer will have firms seeking guidance from the FSA about whether a fax is OK, or a recorded phone conversation, or an email. Consumers benefit from such innovation.

Clearly, the FSA can't then turn around and prosecute the firm for breaching the rule. So some certainty is needed here.

In fact because innovation and guidance go hand-in-hand, requests for guidance will often be the FSA's early warning system that a rule has become obsolete. This Committee has already heard about the need for re-writing existing rulebooks. I think it must be accepted that rules do become obsolete because of innovation and firms need to be able to rely on the FSA's guidance in this regard.

Q4.   *Are the FSA's proposed powers coherent? Are they sufficient?*

"PREVENTION IS BETTER THAN CURE" VS COHERENT POWERS

The FSA itself believes strongly that its powers should be used to promote "prevention instead of cure". But I fear they may have confused a firm's duty to *try* and prevent problems, with an *absolute duty* to prevent problems in all cases.

I can tell you from experience that no processing environment is foolproof. No manager can know of every glitch in the system. You solve problems by having a process to identify them quickly, before they can harm consumers, and by refining the process on an on-going basis.

I think we can be certain that if the powers of the FSA are used to fine firms when they themselves find a problem in the normal course of carrying out their controls reviews, then a climate of distrust will grow between the FSA and the regulated.

IT BECOMES CATCH-22 REGULATION BY HINDSIGHT

I am concerned that hindsight will be used to say that when a company's system of controls uncovers a problem (say a dishonest employee) that the failure to prevent the problem in the first place is evidence the controls were weak. It is this Catch-22 logic that is the most dangerous part of the proposed Bill. Who will discipline the FSA if it goes down this regulatory path?

DUE DILIGENCE MUST BE A DEFENCE BY MANAGEMENT

Individual accountability is a good principle. Management should be expected to develop compliance procedures that are reasonably designed.

But plainly, due diligence by management should be a defence against personal liability. Otherwise in the UK your only absolute defence is to be lucky. Anyone who tells you that you can run a financial service business error free every day has never tried to do it.

Q5. *Are you satisfied with the proposals for the Tribunal, as they now stand? Do they make sense?*

THE TRIBUNAL PROCESS

Yes, we welcome the revised proposals for a Tribunal of first instance.

But the Tribunal in procedural terms is after the fact. You get to the Tribunal far too late. Which is why we propose a stronger Enforcement Committee (see below).

We want a fair system for all concerned. Neither the FSA nor industry should decide what is fair. Instead, the Enforcement Committee must be truly independent with a non-FSA Chairman and majority voting by independent members.

In his testimony, in response to a question from Viscount Trenchard, Howard Davies described how firms will want to settle a matter quickly. As Mr Davies said "Sometimes they are not sure how strong their case is or they would like to get things settled and move on . . . "

Isn't this the central issue? That in most cases, we are talking shades of grey. How well supervised was an employee who turns out to be dishonest? Here again hindsight is being used to say that the evidence of his dishonesty is proof that he was badly supervised. How strong is anyone's case where a dishonest employee has been particularly crafty?

PLEA BARGAINING

In his reply to Mr Kidney's question, Mr Thorpe described a process where the "option is then for the parties to sit down and discuss it and determine whether there is agreement about it." That sounds like a plea bargaining session to me.

This is where much more strengthening and balancing of powers is required. Yes, of course, the option of going to a Tribunal exists, but it is expensive, time consuming and drawn out and as Mr Davies himself said firms prefer to "get things settled and move on".

WHY WE NEED AN ENFORCEMENT COMMITTEE

This is why we believe an Enforcement Committee enshrined in the Bill with an independent Chairman is essential. It needs both practitioner and public interest members and all should have votes.

Only this way, can a set of guidelines be developed by the Enforcement Committee about when discipline is called for and when it is not.

ENFORCEMENT—MOST PROBLEMS ARE SMALL, NOT HEADLINE GRABBING

When we talk about the behaviour requiring a sanction by the FSA, many have in the mind the Maxwell, Barings or Morgan Grenfell situations. In fact, often we are talking about breaches of detailed rules, where no consumer lost money, but where firms failed to achieve perfection in the way they carry out their affairs. In many cases the firms find the errors themselves and bring them to the attention of the FSA.

MOST BREACHES ARE MINOR

Many of the regulatory issues that will actually come before such an Enforcement Committee will concern proposals to discipline firms for relatively minor back office and administrative breaches. For this we need an enforcement regime that is quick, efficient and flexible. It needs to be both fair and transparent to those accused and also one that consumers can have confidence in, which I believe our proposals will achieve.

AWARDING OF COSTS AGAINST FSA

We consider it essential that both the Enforcement Committee and the Tribunal are able to award costs against the FSA where there is a finding in favour of the accused. The prospect of high legal costs deters many firms and individuals from exercising their rights, and leads to pressure to settle early—to "plea bargain" in the American terminology.

MEDIATION

In his reply to a question by the Chairman, Mr Thorpe allowed that perhaps another avenue will exist. He mentioned "a form of *mediation* between the party who is accused . . . and the FSA." Clearly, it would be interesting to know more of how this mediation process might work. For instance will the mediator be independent? Does the Enforcement Committee suggest mediation before considering a matter further? I suggest, though, that a truly independent Enforcement Committee could avoid the need for yet another layer.

Q9. *Are the FSA's powers of investigation excessive?*

This is a regulator which has unprecedented powers.

The FSA can enter your house at night without a warrant and take whatever papers it wants. If you try and stop them you commit a criminal offence. They then require you to attend an interview, at which you will not have a right to silence—in fact using your right to silence will be an offence itself. They get no joy from you so they call in your spouse. He or she likewise has no right to silence.

Plainly anyone would find these powers alarming.

Other issues

CAVEAT EMPTOR

There seems to be a great deal of consternation over the question of investor responsibility. We all want to avoid the pitfalls of moral hazard and of mis-selling.

What are we to do?

We think the issue is very simple.

The first principle should be that consumers are accountable for all investment risk so long as they received a fair explanation of what they were buying.

There are two qualifications—*if* a firm gives advice on an investment, the advice should be suitable given the investor's circumstances *at the time*. This last point is quite important. Suitability must be viewed in light of the situation when the advice was given.

HINDSIGHT AND THE CONSUMER "BLAME CULTURE"

All too often again, hindsight is the criterion used to determine if someone was mis-sold. But almost all investment and saving decisions involve making assumptions about the future. For instance, before you tie up your money in a 90-day notice account, you need to be pretty sure you won't need the money in that 90 days. But if you lose your job the next day and now need the money, were you mis-sold?

We have to guard against encouraging financial consumers down the road of "someone else is to blame if I lose money". For example, someone trapped in a negative equity housing situation may well wish to say they had a mortgage foisted on them by a greedy financial services company. Whereas someone who has made money congratulates himself on the wisdom of having borrowed and taken his chances in the housing market.

We have to accept that in the financial world, there is an important difference between a good investment decision and a bad outcome. If with hindsight, bad outcomes are to be used as evidence of poor advice at the time, then consumers will be able to invest risk free, knowing someone else is to blame.

CONSUMER EDUCATION

Much is proposed about consumer education. It is obvious we need the public to understand more about money and financial matters. But if the Treasury is right and a large part of the population doesn't understand what a percentage figure is, then we are talking about a failure of the school system. I don't believe the FSA will ever have a budget large enough to educate consumers sufficiently from such a low level.

Separately, participants in the market, and AUTIF itself, all provide educational materials for consumers. It actually is in the industry's interest for consumers to know how to tell a good product from a poor one.

Much is talked about educating consumers about financial products. And that rules need to make sure that they only buy suitable products. But no one talks about educating consumers about how to purchase a house. Yet, this will likely become their largest financial asset or financial drain.

IS THE BILL ALL BAD?

No. The consolidation of the regulators will have a positive effect on the efficiency of the regulatory system if done properly. Currently all three SROs have published guidance about the Internet, which differs each from the other (e.g., where to put authorisation status of the owner of a website).

The consolidation of five different compensation schemes and eight separate Ombudsmen schemes is also beneficial to the investor and to the industry.

Can you object to a robust enforcement regime given the pensions mis-selling scandal, Barings, Morgan Grenfell and others?

No, but I can object to an unfair one. Any regime which does not provide for a right to be heard, for due diligence to be a defence, for the right to examine the witnesses and evidence against you will never be acceptable. In the end a regime that is not fair will not be respected. In the UK we have long set the standard for justice by demanding that it not only be done but that it manifestly be seen to be done.

WHAT SAFEGUARDS DO YOU FEEL SHOULD BE IN PLACE?

The FSA should not be able to intervene or initiate a prosecution against a firm or an individual except where there was a clear statement of what is required of the firm and there is reasonable evidence that the firm has failed to observe that in a material way and in a way that puts investors at risk.

The various functions of investigator, prosecutor, judge and jury should be clearly split, and a number of them made independent of the FSA executive.

All disciplinary processes should provide for:
— The right to a pre-enforcement hearing.
— Independent composition of the judicial arm (the Enforcement Committee).
— Due diligence as a defence.
— The right to examine witnesses and evidence against you.

31 March 1999

APPENDIX 21

Memorandum by AXA Sun Life

AXA Sun Life wishes to make representations to the Joint Committee in support of the principle of *"Caveat emptor"* which is included in the draft Bill.

The regulatory objective of consumer protection contained in clause 5 requires the Authority to have regard to " . . . the general principle that consumers should take responsibility for their decisions." This is consistent with the Gower report of 1984, which led to the Financial Services Act and stated " . . . it should [not] seek to achieve the impossible task of protecting fools from their own folly. All it should do is try to prevent people being made fools of." We understand that clause 5 has met with a mixed response, with the regulated community generally supporting the provision whilst consumer groups suggest that it is unfair to place the ultimate responsibility on retail consumers who are faced with difficult decisions, often on the basis of little knowledge.

AXA Sun Life believes it is essential that the right of consumers to expect protection is balanced by a duty on consumers to make, and take responsibility for, informed decisions. The aim of regulation should be to put the consumer in a position where he can make a reasoned decision on the basis of clear and adequate information. This will also help stimulate competition in the market to develop innovative and cost effective products and services. If the consumer believed that his interests would be fully protected, even though he took no responsibility, he would have less incentive to make an informed decision and the need for him to seek information would be reduced.

Whilst a consumer may initially have little knowledge, a range of opportunities exist for him to seek information and advice. Indeed another statutory objective is for the Authority to promote public understanding of the financial system. We agree with Stephen Byers, who said "the aim is to ensure customers have the ability to understand and question advice and literature they are given". In addition there is already a requirement for providers of some financial products to issue specified information to consumers before and after the sale is concluded and to provide a "cooling off" period in which the consumer can cancel without penalty. The thrust of legislation should be to ensure that consumers receive full information in a manner that empowers them to make decisions. The recent introduction of the "CAT" mark for Individual Savings Accounts illustrates new ways of providing consumer information in an easy to understand form.

We are particularly concerned that the removal of the *"caveat emptor"* principle from the draft Bill will send the wrong message to consumers and may be misinterpreted by them. Removal at this stage is likely to attract more comment than if the principle had not been included in the initial draft and may encourage some consumers to make reckless decisions in the belief that their interests will be protected whatever happens.

Financial decisions cover a wide spectrum of products and services and the appropriate degree of consumer protection needs to take account of both the type of investment or service and the experience of different consumer groups. Clause 5 of the Bill contains the flexibility necessary to match consumer protection to the range of situations that may arise. Within this framework, it is reasonable for the customer to retain some responsibility, with the product provider having responsibility to provide the information necessary for the customer to make his decision. AXA Sun Life therefore fully supports the principle set out in the Bill.

16 April 1999

APPENDIX 22

Memorandum by Barclays PLC

I write on behalf of Barclays PLC pursuant to your Press Notice No. 2, dated 10 March 1999. I would like to thank you for giving us an opportunity to submit written evidence to you.

As you may be aware, we have also previously submitted a response to the Treasury Select Committee, and understand that you have access to such material. We thought you might find it helpful if we let you have a more focused version of this material. The enclosed submission therefore focuses on the following areas where our response is summarised (*not printed*):

1. PROPOSED ARRANGEMENTS FOR THE ACCOUNTABILITY OF THE FSA

We believe that the Bill should provide adequately for the scrutiny of the Annual Report both through Parliament and through an external audit process—in the latter case as part of the preparation of the Annual Report.

2. PROPOSED STATUTORY OBJECTIVES AND PRINCIPLES OF THE FSA

We broadly welcome these as they should enhance the accountability of the FSA. However, we are not clear how they relate to one another and how conflicts of priority between the different objectives may be resolved.

3. DISCIPLINE, ENFORCEMENT AND THE TRIBUNAL

We have a number of concerns regarding the disciplinary measures contained in Part XII of the Bill. These primarily relate to the transparency and fairness of the investigation procedure and the interaction with the FSA's powers to institute proceedings under clause 215. The FSA has moved some way in recognising these concerns since our submission to the Treasury Select Committee in November 1998.

4. SCOPE OF THE NEW REGIME

We support the Government's decision to allow the self-regulatory approach to the new mortgage code time to bed down before resorting to a statutory regime.

5. OMBUDSMAN AND COMPENSATION SCHEME

We broadly welcome such schemes although we are unsure as to their application and funding. We enclose a copy of our recent letter to the British Bankers Association.

6. MARKET ABUSE

We believe that the current draft needs much re-thinking and re-drafting to take account of the overlaps with the existing law. There is a significant danger that, as currently drafted, the provisions will do little to protect confidence in the integrity of relevant markets and will add much in the way of confusion and complexity.

23 March 1999

ANNEX

Letter from the Group General Counsel and Group Secretary, Barclays PLC, to the Director, British Bankers' Association

Thank you for your letter of 8 March. I have reviewed the proposal with colleagues internally and we have the following comments with reference to the points you raise.

It would be a mistake to remove the right to appeal to the courts on a point of law, both for consumers and providers. Although it is, obviously, very important indeed that consumers understand that appeal is only possible on a point of law (or, indirectly, by way of judicial review) and that the system is not abused it must be right in principle that a wrong decision by the Ombudsman is able to be appealed and that, as a consequence, redress to consumers is delayed.

In principle it seems to be right that there should be consistency of treatment for customers of all non-mortgage lending providers although it also seems difficult to argue that the financial services Ombudsman's jurisdiction should not extend to all financial services whether provided by authorised persons or otherwise—although I do not know whether this would be achievable within the current terms of the FSMB.

On balance we do not think it is right that complainants should not have to bear costs when they have behaved *unreasonably* or *improperly* although we recognise the desirability of attracting complainants to use the Ombudsman system rather than resorting to court. Nevertheless, it seems that where there is abuse of the system by a complainant they should be made to pay the costs of the other parties and I would therefore favour leaving the Bill as currently drafted although it is important to make it clear that this is not intended to be any sort of block to complainants using the Ombudsman system in the normal course of events.

It is right that the FSA should have a discretion to exclude certain categories or regulated firms.

If you wish to discuss any of the above please let me know.

Howard Trust

22 March 1999

APPENDIX 23

Memorandum by the Building Societies Association (BSA)

INTRODUCTION

1. The Building Societies Association has only a few brief points to make to the Joint Committee on Financial Services and Markets on the draft Financial Services and Markets Bill. The Association notes that the Committee has access to material already submitted to the Treasury—our detailed comments on the draft Bill were submitted to the Treasury on 29 October 1998. The BSA represents the 71 building societies in the UK which currently have total assets of over £150 billion, around 19 million investors and nearly 3 million borrowers.

2. There are a number of key issues for building societies arising from the draft Financial Services and Markets Bill. However, the Bill is drafted in very broad and wide ranging terms, with many provisions giving wide powers to the Financial Services Authority or the Treasury. This will undoubtedly provide welcome flexibility in the way in which the regulatory system is operated in practice, and is able to develop in future. Furthermore, the Treasury progress report on the Bill (issued on 5 March 1999) gives some helpful indications that some of the concerns expressed by the BSA and other bodies last year are likely to be met. Our remaining concerns can largely be raised in response to the appropriate more detailed consultations by the FSA and Treasury.

3. The key issues for building societies arising from the draft Bill, relevant to the areas on which the Committee is focussing its inquiry, are referred to briefly below.

PROPOSED ARRANGEMENTS FOR ACCOUNTABILITY OF THE FSA

4. Our original concerns about arrangements for accountability of the FSA have largely been met by the proposed changes to the draft Bill noted in the Treasury's progress report.

PROPOSED STATUTORY OBJECTIVES AND PRINCIPLES OF THE FSA

5. The Association believes that there should be an additional matter to which the FSA must have regard in discharging its general functions (Clause 2(3) of the draft Bill)—the desirability of maintaining corporate diversity among enterprises providing financial services in order to widen consumer choice.

DISCIPLINE, ENFORCEMENT AND THE TRIBUNAL

6. Here again, the proposed changes to the draft Bill noted in the Treasury's progress report, and the FSA's proposals in its Consultation Paper 17, are welcomed. However, the draft Bill would give the FSA very wide powers to intervene in the business of an authorised person if there had been a breach of any requirement imposed by or under the Bill, or if it appeared desirable to do so in order to protect customers or potential customers. The potential impact of using these powers could be significant for the business concerned, and the Association remains concerned that the differences between the requirements of rules for conduct of business regulation (i.e., at the product or individual sales level) and of rules for prudential supervision (i.e., at the institution level) should be appropriately recognised.

7. The public use of intervention powers in relation to a deposit taker could create a serious loss of confidence in the institution with consequent adverse effects on individual depositors. While, in certain circumstances, the powers of control currently available to the Building Societies Commission under the Building Societies Act 1986 are as wide as some of those to be available to the FSA under the draft Bill, the Commission has used its formal statutory powers in only a tiny number of cases. The Association is concerned that the FSA should use its formal statutory powers of intervention in relation to any prudential concerns about a building society only as a last resort.

SCOPE OF THE NEW REGIME

8. The Association believes that conduct of business regulation should not be extended to mortgages or deposits—the Council of Mortgage Lenders *Mortgage Code* and the joint BBA/BSA *Banking Code* provide appropriate safeguards for consumers in these areas and can readily be amended where necessary. Bringing these areas into statutory regulation would create very significant additional costs of compliance which would have to be passed on to consumers.

OMBUDSMAN SCHEME AND COMPENSATION SCHEME

9. The Association's main concerns with the Ombudsman and compensation schemes is that there should be appropriate allocation of the Ombudsman costs and of contributions to compensation sub-schemes between different categories of institutions and business sectors. Factors to be considered in determining such allocation should include the risk profile of particular sectors.

31 March 1999

APPENDIX 24

Note by Mr David Challen, Chairman, the FSA Practitioners Forum

At the hearing of the Joint Committee which I recently attended I was invited to suggest ways in which the FSA's relationship with the Practitioner Panel might be described in the Bill.

I would propose something along the following lines:

"Before proposing new, or revisions to existing, policies and/or associated principles or rules, which could have a material impact on regulated firms, the FSA will consult the Practitioner Panel. Where it decides not to follow any formal guidance offered by the Practitioner Panel, the FSA will report its reasons for so deciding to the Practitioner Panel and in the FSA's Annual Report."

16 April 1999

APPENDIX 25

Memorandum by the Compliance Register Limited

INTRODUCTION

Further to our conversation on Thursday 8 April, I have pleasure in enclosing the following comments and observations for the Committee's consideration. I have tried to contact all members of our Advisory Board ("the Board") but given the short time scale, it has not been possible to get all their views nor to formulate a formal response that would be representative of the Board as a whole.

However, the Board will be very pleased to lend any assistance it can towards the re-drafting of the revised Bill particularly with regard to any areas of difficulty. Please do not hesitate to contact me if such assistance is required.

A. PROGRESS REPORT FROM THE TREASURY

The Treasury's recent Progress Report indicates that although the Government has made many concessions, which go far to redress the lack of balance in the draft Bill, there is nonetheless a feeling among City firms that a number of the concessions are token gestures and that others are about the minimum that they could have done given the strength and loudness of the objections in relation to FSA's power and accountability.

The opportunity now exists to focus on some particular outstanding issues such as those set out below:

B. "NO ACTION" LETTERS

Whilst it is still not yet clear the extent to which FSA will gear itself up to providing *ad-hoc* guidance (and we comment further on this below), they seem to have missed the main point on no action letters. Of course, FSA can issue guidance and interpret its own rules and grant waivers from them. What is clear however, is:

(a) they cannot waive a provision of primary legislation or a related statutory instrument, unless an expressed power is included in the Bill (which is inconceivable);

(b) their guidance about provisions of the Bill and statutory instruments under it is likely to be less helpful, particularly if they continue their traditional approach of responding that it is for the courts to decide.

We all recognise that the courts will decide the meaning of the law, but there is nevertheless a role for the FSA to state its position regarding enforcement. *Here the "no action" letter comes into its own, and is quite distinct from waivers and guidance.*

A "no action" procedure would involve the FSA issuing a letter which states that, in the particular circumstances described, the FSA would not take enforcement action under a particular statutory provision. Of course, one can argue that the Bill does not need to empower the FSA in order for it to do this. However, we would argue strongly that the Bill should make provision for two reasons.

(i) *So that it is formally recognised that such letters will be available*
   — FSA seems to deny or dissemble when asked whether such letters have been issued in the past (we know of at least one occasion which is, of course, confidential);

(ii) *Because the Bill could provide a framework to ensure that, in general, such no action letters are published.*

In relation to such a procedure, and in relation to its own *ad-hoc* guidance (and possible waivers) there seems to be a concern that the FSA will find its resources diverted. What seems not to have been adequately considered, (although mentioned briefly to FSA's chairman before the Joint Committee) at least publicly, is FSA's potential to charge for no action letters, guidance and waivers. This should be seriously considered, and if necessary provision should be made in the Bill.

C. ENFORCEMENT POLICY

(a) Amidst all the arguments about investigation powers, enforcement sanctions, appeals, etc., one important argument seems to have been lost. We are being encouraged to take heart from FSA's public statement of its enforcement policy (at least what will presumably become a public statement once it has taken into account responses to Consultation Paper 17). We cannot take heart from this because FSA has the right to change it (even though it is, of course, obliged to publish information about certain aspects of its approach).

(b) *The important point, therefore, is that the critical elements of enforcement policy should be specified in the Bill.* It could perhaps be a provision which is amendable by statutory instrument subject to positive resolution of both Houses. Alternatively, the policy itself could be specified by statutory instrument, subject to positive resolution of both Houses and subject to prior consultation.

(c) The reference by Antony Hilton in the Evening Standard last month to "bullying, intimidation and seething vindictiveness in the old system" a reference which was raised by the Joint Committee with Howard Davies on 16 March, is a description which many in the industry can relate to. Most do not believe it is all-pervading, but have encountered evidence of it.

(d) Success and career advancement within the FSA should not be dependent upon obtaining guilty pleas and imposition of penalties.

(e) Most compliance professionals have some (if not considerable) sympathy with their erstwhile brethren in Morgan Grenfell. There is considerable concern at the impossibly high standards (retrospectively assessed) being set for senior management and compliance staff.

D. Transparency of regulation

(a) *Exchanges*

— This is a matter which has been of considerable concern to many in the industry over many years, ever since they began to get full details of LIFFE's rules, which before publication of their four-volumed glossy rule book, were extremely opaque.

— Although, now, all the exchanges make their rule books publicly available, there is nevertheless much that affects the rights and obligations of members which is not made publicly available immediately on issue or upon taking effect. We refer to board notices of exchanges, such as the London Metal Exchange's board notices on give ups. In the context of security exchanges, we mention the London Stock Exchange's trade compensation scheme, details of which were circulated to members in October 1997 in connection with the launch of SETS and are considered by the Stock Exchange to be guidance, but do not appear in its official list of guidance.

(b) *FSA et al*

— Unfortunately, the exchanges are not the only regulator guilty in this area. Again, in the area of give ups, one can point to the circular letter issued by FSA/SFA to LME members in August 1998. This is not a one-off omission—the problem goes back at least as far as FSA/SFA's letter to all members years ago concerning the compliance responsibility of senior management, which was subsequently incorporated in SFA Board Notice 87 (in 1992) and now covered by Appendix 38.

— Even in the current consultation agenda of FSA we find that those papers which are not formally designated as consultation papers are given no reference and therefore may not be easily identified at a later date. For example, "Meeting our responsibilities", "The Open Approach to Regulation", and "the Discussion paper on inter-professional business". Other material, such as feed back on consultation seems to have been released selectively.

— Other examples concerning FSA/SIB include standard form, circular letters to:

(i) Internet Service Providers and others in connection with Internet regulation and their potential need to obtain authorisation; and

(ii) traders and others in the new UK gas markets several years ago, again concerning the possible need to obtain regulatory status (e.g., authorisation under the 1986 Act or permission under Schedule 1, paragraph 23).

— Transparent regulation should require that any communication whatsoever which goes to all firms (or members, in the case of a SRO or exchange) or a particular category or categories of members (as distinct from a letter sent to a specific firm and tailored and personalised to the circumstances of that firm) be listed in the official publication listings of the regulator. Thus post inspection visit letters could be based on a template or precedent without requiring either to be published, should be published and listed.

— All of these matters are important in helping firms and their advisors ascertain regulatory attitudes as well as the rights and obligations of regulated firms. This kind of transparency should be incorporated in:

(i) in the Bill itself so far as FSA is concerned; and

(ii) the recognition criteria for exchanges and clearing houses (to be set out by Treasury Statutory Instrument, a draft of which has been published for consultation).

E. User-friendly regulation

(a) Although some improvement in the drafting of the Bill has been promised—for example, to consolidate the many different rule making powers and procedures of FSA, much of the legislation proposed is difficult to track or essentially unclear.

(b) The proposed Regulated Activities Order is a good example of the form. Its approach of repeating essentially the same exclusion several times, once for each activity makes it more difficult to analyse exclusions.

(c) The market abuse provisions in the Bill are examples of uncertainty and lack of clarity.

F. Transitional arrangements

More care needs to be taken about transition to the new regime. For example, FSA seems to assume that its new principles for business can be introduced on N2 date. Presumably, they are seen as so basic as not to have systems implications. Yet dramatic changes have been wrought in the effects of regulation under the 1986 Act, based on the existing 10 principles. Principles do indeed have detailed implications for conduct, which implies (in turn) procedural IT, training and other implications.

G. CORPORATE GOVERNANCE

The FSA should be required, under provisions in the legislation, to abide by corporate governance best practice by separating the roles of Chairman and Chief Executive. It is widely accepted that an independent chairman with a "detached" view can have a considerable "moderating" influence on the actions of the executive arm of the organisation.

H. DISCIPLINARY POWERS

— It is right and proper that the FSA should be given considerable powers in order that it may be an effective regulator "with teeth".

— However, as the saying goes "power corrupts and absolute power corrupts absolutely", important checks and balances must be provided for in the legislation.

— One of the key controls will be to provide for appeals against disciplinary decisions to be heard by an independent commission whose members are not appointed by the FSA. This should include appeals against decisions and awards made by the proposed Ombudsman.

If you require any further information or assistance, please do not hesitate to contact me.

13 April 1999

APPENDIX 26

Note by the Comptroller and Auditor General, National Audit Office

INTRODUCTION

1. This Note has been prepared as a contribution to the inquiry by the Joint Committee on Financial Services and Markets into the Government's proposals for the regulation of financial services.

2. Over the next couple of years, the Financial Services Authority will assume responsibility for regulating many thousands of businesses, including banks, building societies, friendly societies, insurance companies, providers of retail financial services, fund managers, and securities and derivatives firms. It will also regulate the Lloyd's insurance market, which has not before been subject to external regulation.

PLANNED ACCOUNTABILITY ARRANGEMENTS

3. Under the terms of the Bill, the Authority will be required to report annually to the Treasury on the achievement of its statutory objectives, which are to maintain market confidence, promote public understanding, protect consumers, and reduce financial crime. The Government intend these objectives to provide benchmarks against which the performance of the Authority can be measured. The Authority will be accountable to Treasury Ministers and through them to Parliament.

4. The Authority will also be establishing two statutory bodies: a Consumer Panel and a Practitioner Forum, the latter to represent regulated firms and individuals. Both bodies will monitor the work of the Authority and be free to publish their views on the Authority's performance against its statutory objectives. The Consumer Panel will also be able to commission consumer surveys.

5. As a Companies Act company the Authority will, in the normal way, appoint its own external auditors. But the Bill does not make provision for the independent examination and evaluation of the Authority's performance.

6. We understand however that the Treasury intend to strengthen the provision for the independent scrutiny of the Authority by including in the Bill a power for the Treasury to commission and publish independent value for money audits of the Financial Services Authority. As we understand it, these audits would be carried out on each occasion by a private sector firm with relevant expertise selected through a competitive process. The aim would be to provide Parliament and other interested bodies with additional assurance that the FSA is operating efficiently and effectively and with full regard to value for money. Such provisions would clearly be a significant response to the concerns that have been expressed about the need for independent scrutiny of the FSA. But the question is whether they go far enough, in that the timing of such examinations and their terms of reference would not be fixed independently of the executive. There is therefore a risk that the examinations would not be seen to be fully independent. This would put a question mark over the extent of the accountability of the Authority to Parliament.

7. There is a good case for the Comptroller and Auditor General having rights of access to the Financial Services Authority to undertake value for money scrutinies:

— Although constituted as a private sector company, the Authority exists to carry out public policy.

— The Comptroller and Auditor General would bring the necessary authority and independence to the role of independent assessor and would be well placed to report on the Authority's performance against its statutory objectives.

— The Comptroller and Auditor General is the external auditor of a number of regulatory bodies—such as the economic regulators—which share some of the characteristics of the new regulator, and he also has rights of access to a wide range of other bodies exercising regulatory functions whose performance he examines, reporting the results to Parliament. Working with a wide range of external specialists and well respected organisations the National Audit Office have built up considerable expertise in the regulatory field and would be well placed to carry out authoritative studies of the way the FSA is addressing its objectives, through providing reassurance to Parliament and assisting in the accountability of the Authority.

— A number of representative bodies[1] have suggested such a role for the National Audit Office, arguing that, because of the range of responsibilities of the new regulator, and notwithstanding their representation on the Practitioner Forum, regulated firms would not be in a good position to assess the Authority's performance against the statutory objectives or provide pressure for value for money.

POSSIBLE WAYS FORWARD

8. There are various ways in which the arrangements for independent scrutiny of the Authority could be strengthened. For example the legislation could provide the Comptroller and Auditor General with full access rights to the Financial Services Authority on the basis of which he could periodically report to Parliament on the Authority's performance. Alternatively the Comptroller and Auditor General could be given the same powers as the Treasury to carry out or otherwise commission and publish periodic performance audits of the Financial Services Authority. Under that scenario it would be important, of course, for the Comptroller and Auditor General and the Treasury to consult on a case by case basis to avoid any duplication of effort. And this would certainly be possible from the Comptroller and Auditor General's point of view.

7 April 1999

APPENDIX 27

Memorandum by the Confederation of Insurance Trade Unions

We note that the Joint Committee's enquiry is focusing on the issue of discipline, enforcement and the tribunal. We wish to bring to the attention of the Committee the way in which the financial services industry is interpreting the regulation of references for financial advisers which has unfairly excluded a number of our members from the industry over the last few years.

The PIA's rules require that employers provide a reference on a member of a firm's investment staff to another regulated firm of all matters which the firm has reasonable grounds for believing to be relevant and true. This includes whether or not an individual has been the subject of a complaint.

In practice the basis of a complaint may relate to the performance, or administration of a product rather than to the advice or conduct of the financial adviser during the sales process.

Even complaints which are not up-held are recorded as part of the financial adviser's reference and our experience is that such complaints can prevent our members from gaining new employment.

We have raised this matter in our recent submission to the FSA and HM Treasury as part of the Government's consultation exercise. Furthermore we have raised our concerns in meetings with the PIA who have expressed the view that this is an issue for employers rather than for the regulator.

In response to our earlier attempts to raise this matter with the PIA they wrote that:

> *PIA's rules require that a reference provided on a member of a firm's investment staff to another regulated firm, or to an appointed representative firm should make full and frank disclosure of all matters which the firm has reasonable grounds for believing to be relevant and true.*

> *Whether or not an individual has been subject of a complaint (as defined in PIA's rules) will be a matter of fact. The fact that a complaint had been received against an individual would always be relevant information and should therefore be disclosed in a reference. We would expect a reference would disclose in addition, whether the complaint had been upheld, and whether compensation had been paid to the complainant.*

> *PIA's rules do not make any distinction between the way in which complaints received against an individual who is still in a firm's employ and those received against an individual who has left a firm should be treated. Some firms have adopted the practice of seeking comments from ex-advisers when a complaint is received however, such a practice is not required by PIA's rules on complaints handing,*

---

[1] The Association of Private Client Investment Managers and Stockbrokers: Association of Unit Trusts and Investment Funds: the Securities Institute.

since a firm is responsible for the activities of its investment staff ... The responsibility for investigating a complaint will always rest with the firm itself rather than with the individual who is the subject of the complaint.

Whilst the PIA regard this issue as an issue for the employer, it is clear to us that employers believe that they are directly complying with PIA regulations in the supply of reference. A financial adviser can be excluded from the industry on the basis of their reference. Financial advisers have no rights to:

— View their complaints record which forms a part of their reference.

— Comment on a complaint.

— Appeal to an employer or regulator about a reference.

CITU proposes that:

— Financial Advisers should have a right to see their regulatory reference.

— Financial Advisers should have a right to make representations to both the employer and the regulator concerning complaints listed in such a reference.

— Complaints that have not been upheld should not be part of a financial adviser's reference.

CITU is in a position to provide written testimonials from our members who have been adversely affected by references from their employer which they believe are mis-leading or do not reflect the advice that they have given to the consumer.

24 March 1999

APPENDIX 28

Memorandum by the Consumers' Association

INTRODUCTION

Consumers' Association (CA) welcomes the opportunity to respond to the Financial Services Authority (FSA) consultation on enforcement. The ability and willingness of the financial services regulators to take pro-active and effective disciplinary measures has been an area that we have taken interest in from the perspective of consumer confidence in the market and consumer redress. In our response to the Treasury consultation on the draft Financial Services and Markets Bill we stated our view that:

"The regulation of authorised persons must make it clear in practice as well as theory that individuals are responsible for the actions of their organisations. Disciplinary measures of public censure and fining should be used when appropriate."

As a general point CA favours wide ranging disciplinary and enforcement powers for the regulator. In our view it has been the lack of powers, and more specifically the lack of willingness of regulators to use these powers, that has been a detriment to consumer protection.

Therefore we have set out below the areas in which we wish to comment.

SUMMARY

— We regard it as essential that a strong regulator with wide ranging disciplinary and enforcement powers protects consumers.

— The FSA must adopt a pro-active stance in identifying problems before they become serious or widespread matters.

— The powers of the FSA must be practical and usable.

— The FSA powers must be simple and streamlined and not overly legalistic or complex.

— Investigations should be targeted.

— Individual accountability is essential and the FSA must be able to take action against individuals when this is warranted.

— Accountability is important but so is the ability for the FSA to use its powers quickly, efficiently and effectively.

DETAILED COMMENTS

Part 2 *Intervention*

In considering the FSA powers of intervention in the business and affairs of firms, we would first state that we expect the bedrock of this interaction to be an environment of openness and co-operation. Not only should this be expected from regulated firms, as outlined in the Principles of Business, but it is also the most cost effective method of dealing with issues on a day-to-day basis.

In terms of regulatory intervention, we naturally regard it as essential that the FSA has wide powers to deal with firms, against the background of its statutory objectives. But more than this we regard it as essential the FSA adopts a pro-active stance in trying to identify potential problems either before they manifest themselves, or before they manifest themselves on a large scale. CA has been critical of the financial regulators in the past for their inability to position themselves ahead of problems, and has often been in the unfortunate position of having to react to market failures.

So in terms of the FSA's overall approach to intervention we would strongly welcome a high profile pro-active role. In this context we were very encouraged by the recent statement by Howard Davies warning firms about misleading consumers about Individual Savings Accounts (ISAs).

We are pleased to see a clear statement from the FSA that it must co-operate and collaborate with overseas regulators. This is indeed essential for the effective regulation of the international market in financial services, particularly in view of the many challenges that lie ahead in terms of E-Commerce, distance selling and the Euro. It will be imperative to have robust mechanisms in place to cope with cross border jurisdiction and the enforcement of regulations.

While we accept that many instances of intervention can and will be conducted on a regulator to firm basis only, we regard it as essential that the FSA are quick to make details of intervention public where this will benefit the market in terms of confidence and warning consumers.

Part 3   *Investigations*

Investigations should be conducted with regard to the statutory objectives of the FSA, but they should also be targeted so that the weight of enforcement falls where it is most appropriate. By being pro-active in gathering information, the regulator should have a clear understanding as to which sectors and firms may require the most monitoring.

Part 4   *Securing Redress for Consumers*

We strongly support FSA powers to ensure that losses suffered by consumers are made good when they occur as a result of a regulatory breach. In addition to this consumers will still have the right to complain to the firm, and ultimately to take their complaint up with the Financial Services Ombudsman.

In most cases we expect that the FSA will be able to agree with the firm as to the extent of compensation, the form it will take and the timescale for payment. If this is not possible, we strongly support the ability of the FSA to utilise statutory powers.

Part 5   *Discipline of Authorised Firms and Approved Persons*

With regard to disciplinary powers we welcome the ability for the FSA to issue public statements about firms and individuals and to impose fines on firms and individuals.

We have had concerns in the past about fines levied only against firms, in that they have seldom been large enough to damage the institution, they are ultimately paid for by consumers, and they place accountability on the firm rather than on the individual. Nevertheless the sanction of imposing fines against firms and against individuals is an important one, and we do not subscribe to the view that the ability of the FSA to impose fines pushes the regime onto a criminal basis.

We have strongly supported moves towards individual accountability in the industry. There must be effective sanctions to make employees, especially company directors and senior management, responsible for the actions of the companies they are managing. For example, throughout the protracted pension mis-selling review not a single senior manager, board member, director or compliance officer has been censured or fined, even when the regulators have identified internal management failures as a cause of, or contributing factor to, the mis-selling.

As a final sanction, we are fully supportive of powers to withdraw authorisation, and ensure that individuals who are not fit and proper are removed from the industry.

Part 6   *Market Misconduct*

Part 7   *The FSA's Decision-making Process*

The issue of the wide-ranging powers that the FSA will be able to utilise has received much attention and lobbying from certain sections of the industry. As stated earlier CA's general concern has been more about the lack of powers of financial regulators or the lack of use, rather than concerns about over use. However, it is of course correct that the FSA is accountable for its actions.

The existence of an independent Appeal Tribunal is an important safeguard as is the establishment of an FSA Enforcement Committee.

We are clear that within a structure that is accountable and contains procedural safeguards, the FSA must be able to operate a process that is as simple as possible, and that avoids an overly complex legislative approach.

In terms of the actions of the Enforcement Committee, the procedure must be flexible enough to deal with each case before the Committee. However as a general principle we consider it appropriate for the Committee to issue a Warning Notice at outset and then allow the firm or individual to make representations to the FSA. We believe that this mirrors the existing regime for dealing with disciplinary issues.

OTHER ISSUES

In conclusion it is vital that the enforcement regime adopts a pro-active consumer focused approach that delivers against the statutory objectives of protecting consumers, maintaining confidence in the financial system and reducing financial crime. The financial services industry has inflicted many blows to public confidence in recent years, and we regard it as essential that the FSA uses its enforcement powers to ensure a fair and competitive market where consumers can buy with confidence.

February 1999

APPENDIX 29

Memorandum by the Council of Mortgage Lenders (CML)

INTRODUCTION

1. The Council of Mortgage Lenders (CML) is the representative trade association for mortgage lenders in the UK. Its 118 members hold 98 per cent. of the assets of the residential mortgage market and comprise banks, building societies, insurance companies and other specialist mortgage lenders. The CML welcomes this opportunity to comment on the Joint Committee's inquiry into the Financial Services and Markets Bill, particularly with reference to the position of mortgage advice and the scope of the new regime.

SUMMARY OF THE RESPONSE

2. The main points in this submission are as follows:

— The industry believes the regulatory framework for selling mortgages must deliver sufficient consumer protection in an effective and cost effective way. The Mortgage Code provides such a framework and it is a secondary issue whether regulation should be on a voluntary or statutory basis in the longer term.

— The decision whether to incorporate mortgage advice within the scope of the Bill should be undertaken after an analysis of the perceived additional benefits to consumers of a statutory approach, balanced against the potential cost implications. This analysis will be undertaken during the Treasury review later this year.

— The reserve power in Schedule 2 of the Bill does not refer to "mortgage advice", but rather to "loans secured on land". The Treasury review and the analysis of costs/benefits should not, therefore, be limited to consideration of whether mortgage advice should be included within the scope of the Financial Services Authority. It should encompass other secured loans currently regulated under the Consumer Credit Act 1974 and the role of the Office of Fair Trading as the present licensing authority.

— In terms of consumer protection, there would be no logic in adopting an artificial distinction under the Bill between different types of loans secured on land based on the limit of £25,000 in the Consumer Credit Act 1974. A distinction could be drawn, if thought necessary after a cost/benefit analysis, between the regulation of secured loans on the basis of the Code framework under the Bill, and regulation of unsecured loans under the Consumer Credit Act 1974.

— The CML is disappointed that the Government has decided, as announced in its recent Progress Report on the Bill, to remove the option of giving power to the FSA to endorse voluntary Codes. This would have been a way to ensure that the FSA could influence future developments on mortgage market regulation, and would have underpinned the activity of the independent mortgage regulators, the Independent Review Body for the Banking and Mortgage Codes and the Mortgage Code Register of Intermediaries Limited, without the FSA needing to become the statutory regulator.

— The CML believes that the Mortgage Code has already introduced demonstrable benefits for consumers taking out mortgages in the UK since July 1997:

— improved consumer awareness of benchmark standards across the industry;

— registering all mortgage intermediaries active in the market for the first time;

— an advice and written recommendation service across the market for the first time;

— more transparent product information on the financial implications of taking out a mortgage;

— independently verified training and competence arrangements specifically designed for mortgage advisers;

— free, independent redress arrangements for customers with a mortgage complaint, with universal coverage for the first time;

— enhanced compliance monitoring regimes by the independent regulators, the MCRI and the IRB, including prompt responses to compliance concerns raised by recent mystery shopper exercises on the Code.

BACKGROUND

3. The CML provided two detailed submissions to the Treasury Committee on developments in relation to the Code in 1998. In response to the Treasury Committee's Third Report on Financial Services Regulation, the CML has reiterated its support for the Treasury's approach to reviewing the Code in 1999.

COST/BENEFIT ANALYSIS UNDER A TREASURY REVIEW

4. The CML and members have consistently reinforced their support for a regulatory framework for selling mortgages which delivers appropriate consumer protection. In the industry's view, a voluntary code can achieve this in both an effective and cost effective way. The decision whether the Code framework should be on a voluntary or statutory basis in the longer term is a secondary issue. The case for statutory intervention has not been proven, in the light of the tangible benefits which the Code framework has already introduced. A decision to introduce statutory regulation by the FSA should only be undertaken after an appropriate cost/benefit analysis as part of the proposed Treasury review.

THE RESERVE POWER IN THE BILL

5. Moreover, the reserve power in the Financial Services and Markets Bill refers to the FSA potentially being asked to regulate the sale of "loans secured on lending" i.e., it is not limited to first mortgages under the Mortgage Code. The CML therefore believes that the Treasury review and the cost/benefit analysis should encompass all relevant loans that might come within the scope of the Bill—mortgages and other secured loans currently regulated under the Consumer Credit Act 1974. It should cover the role of the Office of Fair Trading as the present licensing authority for secured loans below £25,000.

6. If the objective is to ensure delivery of sufficient consumer protection to borrowers who might potentially suffer detriment through taking out a loan secured on land, the CML suggests that no logical distinction can be drawn between mortgages outside the scope of the Consumer Credit Act, as they are above £25,000, and those which are within the scope of that legislation because they are below £25,000. There would seem to be little logic in the FSA regulating a loan for £25,001 and the OFT licensing regime applying to a loan for £24,999. A distinction could be drawn, if thought necessary after a cost/benefit analysis, between the regulation of all secured loans on the basis of the Code framework under the Bill, and regulation of unsecured loans under the Consumer Credit Act 1974.

FSA ENDORSEMENT OF VOLUNTARY CODES

7. The CML is disappointed that the Government has decided, as announced in its recent Progress Report on the Bill, to remove the option of giving power to the FSA to endorse voluntary Codes under Section 47A of the Financial Services Act 1986. By endorsing the Mortgage Code, this would have been a way to ensure that the FSA could influence future developments on mortgage market regulation, and would have underpinned the activity of the IRB and MCRI, without the FSA needing to become the statutory regulator.

8. In other areas, flexible solutions are being considered, for example the use of local trading standards authorities to assist the FSA in its monitoring work. There is a case for the FSA to be given the power to endorse appropriate codes, and for the recent decision to remove the power from the Bill to be reversed.

CONSUMER PROTECTION UNDER THE CODE

9. The CML believes that the Code has already introduced demonstrable benefits for consumers taking out mortgages in the UK. Firstly, awareness among consumers of the benchmark standards which they should expect to receive from lenders and mortgage intermediaries has increased since the Code was first introduced in July 1997. This is not surprising as over three million copies of the Code, and an additional three million copies of the CML's Code leaflet for consumers, have been disseminated.

10.   The CML has announced that from the end of April 1999 a copy of the leaflet describing the key principles of the Code should be given out by lenders and mortgage intermediaries at the first point of contact with consumers. 12 million copies of the Plain English Campaign crystal-marked leaflet *You and your mortgage* have been produced for the industry's use. Over time, this should continue to add to consumers' awareness and enable prospective borrowers to raise any queries about the mortgage before they have committed themselves.

11.   The Code framework has for the first time identified every mortgage intermediary in the market, through a registration process operated by the Mortgage Code Register of Intermediaries Limited. From its launch in April 1998, the number of MCRI registered intermediaries has increased steadily over the last 12 months so that there are now 47,000 individuals (41,000 April 1998) represented in 20,500 firms (16,000 in April 1998). Lenders have committed not to accept mortgage business from non-registered intermediaries.

12.   The Code has caused all lenders and intermediaries to review their literature to provide information about the key issues of concern to consumers, including the financial implications of taking out a loan. From the end of April, lenders are also required to make explicit reference to the Code in their product literature to set out the levels of service available to consumers under the Code i.e., advice, information or execution only.

13.   The CML has introduced a new statistical return completed by subscribers from which it is clear that the vast majority of lenders who subscribe to the Code offer an advice service and take up of advice through lenders direct is over 40 per cent of their new business in 1998. This advice figure is in addition to advice which would be given by intermediaries, who typically represent around half of new business introductions. Therefore, since the Code was introduced, there has been a significant take up of the advice service by consumers.

14.   In advance of launching the Code, in conjunction with the Chartered Institute of Bankers, the CML and lenders promoted the introduction of a targeted mortgage advice qualification, the Certificate for Mortgage Advice and Practice (CeMAP). Already over 10,000 registrations have been received by the CIB for this qualification. Recently, the CML, the IRB and the MCRI have indicated that they would be consulting on whether it should become a mandatory requirement under the Code to successfully complete an appropriate training qualification. This consultation exercise is due to take place later this year.

15.   The CML has also introduced, with the assistance of the Chartered Institute of Arbitrators, a new Mortgage Code Arbitration Scheme for use by lenders not within the current Ombudsman arrangements, and mortgage intermediaries registered with MCRI. The introduction of this Scheme was recognised in the Government's first annual report as a measure helping to deliver on its manifesto commitment to increase consumer protection for mortgage buyers.

16.   As a result of this new scheme, any individual who has a complaint about a mortgage has a free, independent redress scheme available. Once the Financial Services Ombudsman Scheme arrangements are in place, the CML would wish to investigate the possibility of all mortgage complaints being dealt with by the Financial Services Ombudsman in the future. This would ensure a single point of entry for consumers with a complaint about a mortgage or related financial service, without necessarily requiring the sale of mortgages to be regulated by the FSA.

17.   The CML has also liaised closely with the IRB and MCRI, the independent regulators, on plans to strengthen their compliance monitoring arrangements and enhance their funding under the Code in 1999. This has already led to a number of initiatives, including an MCRI report being published on potential concerns in the area of "accelerator" products sold with a mortgage.

18.   Later this year, the IRB and MCRI will be undertaking their own mystery shopper exercises, the results of which should be known by the time of the Treasury review. This is in addition to planned compliance visits to lenders and mortgage intermediaries, and builds upon the compliance regime which has been in place for lenders since the Code came into effect in July 1997.

CONCLUSION

19.   The CML remains of the view that the objective should be to deliver a regulatory framework which is effective, cost effective and delivers robust and appropriate consumer protection. It believes that through the progress to date it has already demonstrated improvements in consumer protection. If the Treasury review concludes, after an appropriate cost/benefit analysis, that the sale of mortgages and other loans secured on land should be regulated by the Financial Services Authority, the CML believes that the regulatory framework which has been put in place under the Code should be adopted.

20.   To seek to re-write the current regulatory framework would be costly, time consuming and, ultimately, would not add significantly to the consumer protection in place under the voluntary Code.

31 March 1999

APPENDIX 30

Memorandum by Rt Hon David Davis, MP, Chairman, Committee of Public Accounts

I am writing to you about the audit and accountability arrangements for the new Financial Services Authority in connection with your inquiry into the Government's proposals for the regulation of financial services.

I understand that, under the terms of the draft Financial Services and Markets Bill, the Financial Services Authority would be responsible for regulating practically the whole financial services industry in the United Kingdom. It would also take over the functions of some public sector bodies, such as the Building and Friendly Societies Commissions, the Friendly Societies Registry and the Treasury's Insurance Directorate, which the Comptroller and Auditor General currently audits. I also understand that the Authority would be given the statutory objectives of maintaining market confidence, promoting public understanding, protecting consumers, and reducing financial crime. It would be required to report annually to the Treasury on the achievement of these objectives, which would provide a benchmark against which the performance of the Authority could be measured.

The Authority would be accountable to Treasury Ministers and through them to Parliament. The Authority would also be establishing two statutory bodies: a Consumer Panel and a Practitioner Forum, the latter to represent regulated firms and individuals. Both bodies would monitor the work of the Authority and be free to publish their views on the Authority's performance against its statutory objectives. The Consumer Panel would also be able to commission consumer surveys.

Clearly these measures have much to commend them. I note, however, that the draft Bill does not provide for independent validation of the Authority's performance and I am not convinced that the proposals will go far enough towards providing a satisfactory assurance to Parliament, to regulated businesses and to consumers that the Authority is operating efficiently and effectively and with full regard to value for money. Such assurance is necessary because the Authority will have a significant impact on a major area of the economy, on the businesses it regulates and on the consumers who use financial services. Although constituted as a private company, the Authority would have statutory objectives and would exist to carry out public policy. In my view these arrangements call strongly for independent validation of the Authority's performance.

I understand that the Treasury now propose to include a power in the Bill for the Treasury to commission and publish independent value for money audits of the Financial Services Authority. The Treasury's intention is that these audits would be carried out by private sector firms.

The Treasury's new proposals, although an improvement on what was previously proposed, do not go far enough. The Treasury would, in effect, be able to decide if and when to appoint consultants to review the performance of the Financial Services Authority and would be able to lay down the consultants' terms of reference. The proposed arrangement does not provide the independent validation which full accountability to Parliament requires.

The Comptroller and Auditor General already has audit access to a number of bodies which share some of the characteristics of the new regulator, including the regulators of the privatised utilities who are, like the Financial Services Authority, funded from levies on regulated firms. The National Audit Office has built up considerable expertise in the regulatory field, has published a series of reports which have added greatly to consumer confidence, and could provide valuable assistance to the Authority and the Treasury in this area. If the Authority is to get off to a good start, it needs to secure the confidence of the financial services industry, a number of whose representative bodies have suggested a role for the National Audit Office. A clear line of accountability to Parliament and the industry, accompanied by independent validation of performance by the Comptroller and Auditor General, would go a long way to achieving this.

In short, I believe that the Comptroller and Auditor General would be well placed to provide fully independent assessments of the performance of the Financial Services Authority and to report to Parliament. This would enhance accountability to Parliament and other stakeholders.

8 April 1999

APPENDIX 31

Memorandum by Denton Hall

We wish to make a submission to the Joint Committee as set out below and in the attached Annex.

Denton Hall is a leading international law firm, based in the City of London but with over 120 partners in more than a dozen offices around the world. In addition to an active financial markets and regulatory law practice in London, we have advised governments and securities regulators and exchanges in many overseas countries, on capital markets development in general and in particular on the drafting of securities laws and regulations.

We did not respond directly to HM Treasury on last July's Consultation Document on the Financial Services and Markets Bill, but rather were very active in industry and professional groups in preparing their submissions. However, we now wish to pursue a number of specific points which we feel have been inadequately addressed despite the various submissions.

We would draw the Joint Committee's attention to the following five points, each of which is developed further in the Annex to this memorandum.

1. "No action" letters

The response of Treasury and the FSA has so far missed the point, which is that a "no action" letter procedure is needed to deal with problems in the Act (as finally passed) and related statutory instruments. FSA guidance may not help, and FSA is clearly incompetent to waive legislative provisions.

A formal, open and transparent procedure should be enshrined in statute.

2. Transparency of regulation

All rules, guidance, policy statements, and general decisions should be published and be readily accessible except where confidential to a particular firm. The Bill should require this of FSA, and Treasury's standards for the recognition of exchanges should require this of exchanges.

Everyone working with the regime has a right to know as much as possible about the regulators' attitude and thinking on issues, at least once it is being implemented in practice. All too often policy and other decisions affecting particular descriptions or categories of firm, or even all the members of an exchange, are not published but circulated only to the firms which the regulator knows to be affected.

3. Enforcement policy

The key elements of enforcement policy should be specified in the Bill, or perhaps in a statutory instrument subject to prior consultation and to the affirmative resolution procedure. Even if FSA is required to consult on and publish such policy, it is not right that it should have as broad discretion to determine (and change) it as is currently proposed.

4. Scope of Regulation—precautionary authorisation for professional firms

The position of professional firms, such as solicitors, accountants and actuaries, has not been adequately addressed. The Treasury has expressed its intention that such firms should not generally require authorisation but the draft primary and secondary legislation would not significantly alter the current position.

5. User-friendly regulation

There is still scope for much improvement in the form of presentation of and clarity of language in the draft Bill (for example in relation to market abuse) and draft statutory instruments (especially that on regulated activities).

6. Transitional arrangements

FSA must be required or encouraged to have transitional periods for all changes, since even basic changes like the proposed new set of principles for business can have important organisational, systems and training implications.

We trust that this outline together with the attached Annex are sufficiently clear. We should be happy to elaborate further any particular point.

16 April 1999

ANNEX

1. "No action" letters

Both HM Treasury and FSA seem to have missed the main point on no action letters. FSA can issue guidance and interpret its own rules and grant waivers from them. On the other hand:

    (a) FSA cannot waive a provision of primary legislation or a related statutory instrument, unless an expressed power is included in the Bill (which is inconceivable), and

(b) FSA's guidance about provisions of the Bill and statutory instruments under it is likely to be less helpful, particularly if they continue their traditional approach of responding, to the effect that it is for the courts to decide.

Of course, the courts will decide the meaning of the law, but there is nevertheless a role for the FSA to state its position regarding enforcement. *The "no action" letter has a particular value here, quite distinct from waivers and guidance.*

A "no action" procedure would involve the FSA issuing a letter which states that, in the particular circumstances described, the FSA would not take enforcement action under a particular statutory provision. One can argue that the Bill does not need expressly to empower the FSA for it to do this. However, we strongly contend that the Bill should make provision because:

(i) then it will be formally recognised that such letters will be available;

(ii) the Bill could provide that, in general, such no action letters must be published—this would avoid suggestions of unjustified differential treatment.

In relation to such a producer, and in relation to its own ad-hoc guidance (and possible waivers) there seems to be a concern that the FSA will find its resources diverted. What seems not to have been adequately considered, at least publicly (although mentioned briefly by FSA's chairman before the Joint Committee), is FSA's potential to charge for no action letters, guidance and waivers (so its concerns about being unduly distracted by requests for these are over-stated). This should be seriously considered, and if necessary provision should be made in the Bill.

2. ENFORCEMENT POLICY

A very important point risks being forgotten among all the other arguments about investigation powers, enforcement sanctions, appeals, etc. *The point is that the critical elements of enforcement policy should be specified in the Bill.* It could perhaps be a provision which is amendable by statutory instrument subject to affirmative resolution of both Houses. Alternatively, the policy itself could be specified by statutory instrument, subject to positive resolution of both Houses and subject to prior consultation.

The financial sector and its advisers are encouraged to take comfort from the proposed public statement of FSA's enforcement policy. We cannot do so because FSA has the right to change it.

A critical issue which concerns many in the sector (and their advisers) is how Mr Davies and his Board will ensure that success and career advancement in many parts of his organisation will not depend upon obtaining guilty pleas and imposition of penalties. People who have done nothing wrong but, with hindsight, could have performed their job differently are being forced to choose between a ruined career and reputation, if they accept the regulator's charges, and bankruptcy if they fight (and both plights, of course, if they fight and lose).

3. TRANSPARENCY OF REGULATION

Exchanges

This is a matter which has been of considerable concern to us over many years. From our discussions with other lawyers closely involved in advising firms which carry out business on securities and futures exchanges, we know it is of concern to many of them.

Although, now, all the exchanges make their rule books publicly available, there is nevertheless much that affects the rights and obligations of members which is not made publicly available immediately on issue or upon taking effect (if at all). Examples include:

— the London Metal Exchange's board notices on give ups (sent to members only), and

— the London Stock Exchange's trade compensation scheme (details of which were circulated to members in October 1997 in connection with the launch of SETS and are considered by the Stock Exchange to be guidance, but do not appear in its official list of guidance).

Regulators

The Financial Services Authority itself, and the self-regulating organisations, have also been guilty in this respect.

On "give up" arrangements again, FSA/SFA issued a circular letter to LME members last August. This is not a one-off omission—the problem goes back at least as far as FSA/SFA's letter to all members some years ago concerning the compliance responsibility of senior management, which was subsequently incorporated in SFA Board Notice 87 (in 1992) and now covered by Appendix 38 of SFA's rules.

Even in the current consultation agenda of FSA we find that those papers which are not formally designated as consultation papers are given no reference and therefore may not be easily identified at a later date. For example, "Meeting our responsibilities", "The Open Approach to Regulation", and "the Discussion paper on inter-professional business".

A good example of FSA's failure, in the context of the current consultation process, has occurred very recently. At FSA's recent (and expensive) conference on market abuse it released to delegates its feedback statement on the consultation on this subject. No press release was issued nor publication made—indeed both the FSA's Markets Department and FSA's publications unit denied existence of the feedback statement. We ultimately tracked it down on FSA's web-site, where it had been "filed" in a different manner to other feedback statements—an extraordinary approach in relation to one of the more controversial aspects of the new regime.

Other examples concerning FSA/SIB include standard form, circular letters to:

(a) Internet Service Providers and others in connection with Internet regulation and their potential need to obtain authorisation; and

(b) traders and others in the new UK gas markets several years ago, again concerning the possible need to obtain regulatory status (e.g., authorisation under the 1986 Act or permission under Schedule 1, paragraph 23).

Transparent regulation requires that any communication whatsoever which goes to all firms (or members, in the case of an exchange), or to a particular category or categories of firms, should be published and listed in any list of the publications of the regulator concerned. On the other hand a letter sent to a specific firm and tailored and personalised to the circumstances of that firm (even if based on a template or precedent) need not be published.

Publication in a readily identifiable and accessible form is critical to helping firms and their advisors ascertain regulatory attitudes as well as the rights and obligations of regulated firms.

This kind of transparency should be incorporated:

(a) in the Bill itself, so far as FSA is concerned; and

(b) in the recognition criteria, which are to be set by statutory instrument for exchanges and clearing houses.

4. SCOPE OF REGULATION—PRECAUTIONARY AUTHORISATION

Neither the draft Bill nor the draft Regulated Activities Order adequately address the position of businesses such as solicitors, accountants and actuaries, who are, generally, currently authorised by their Recognised Professional Body to carry on investment business. Such business is specifically excluded from the Investment Services Directive. Authorisation is currently regarded as necessary because of a perception that it is unsafe to rely on the exclusion currently contained in paragraph 24 of Schedule 1 to the Financial Services Act 1986 for "advice given or arrangements made in course of profession or non-investment business".

The Treasury proposes to clarify definitions so that authorisation will clearly not be required for such firms where the activities either "may reasonably be regarded as necessary" in providing its professional services or where those activities comprise general advice or certain non-discretionary services. Further clarification in FSA guidance is proposed.

We are concerned that the proposals do not address the activities of the medium and large professional firms which act for businesses rather than private clients, particularly those with substantial practices supporting the corporate and finance sectors. Services include legal and accounting analysis, and advice, valuation, drafting of documents and negotiation of deals. With no substantial change to the terms of the current paragraph 24, it is hard to see how businesses which do not fall within that would fall within the equivalent exclusions proposed in Schedule 3 to the draft Order. The proposals appear to focus on small, high street practices.

5. USER-FRIENDLY REGULATION

The Treasury has promised to improve the drafting of the Bill—for example, to consolidate the many different rule making powers and procedures of FSA. But much of the primary and secondary legislation proposed is difficult to follow or essentially unclear.

The proposed Regulated Activities Order is a good example of the former. Its approach of repeating essentially the same exclusion several times, once for each activity makes it more difficult to analyse exclusions. More imaginative forms of presentation are desirable (for example a matrix indicating the relationships among investments, activities, and exclusions).

We strongly disagree with the approach described in paragraph 2 of Part One of the Regulated Activities Consultation Document. The current need to consider that much in Schedule 1 to the Financial Services Act

1986 is qualified (for some purposes, at least) by reference to the Investment Services Directive (ISD) via the statutory instruments which implemented that directive in the UK is unsatisfactory, and inconsistent with the Government's stated objectives and concerns in Part One, paragraph 2.3 of last July's Consultation Document on the Bill.

We recommend a unified approach. The Government is accustomed to implementing European Community/European Union Directives in other fields through legislation which in effect interprets directives within a UK legal and commercial environment. Whilst we accept that the extreme care is necessary, we see no reason in principle why it should not adopt the same approach here.

The market abuse provisions in the Bill are examples of uncertainty and lack of clarity.

6. TRANSITIONAL ARRANGEMENTS

Greater sensitivity than has so far been evident is necessary in transition to the new regime. For example, FSA seems to assume that its new principles for business can be introduced on N2 (the date upon which the Bill will come into force). Presumably, these principles are seen as so basic as not to have business or organisational implications. Yet the existing 10 Statements of Principle effective from April 1990 have, in their practical application, affected dramatically the regulatory environment (despite purporting to express then existing standards). The new principles are bound to have detailed implications for conduct, which implies (in turn) procedures, IT, training, etc., and consequently time and costs to implement.

APPENDIX 32

Memorandum by Mr Gary Envis

Please find enclosed my evidence which I submit for the consideration of the Joint Committee on Financial Services and Markets.

The views expressed in this paper are my own and do not necessarily represent the views of my employer or previous employer or any other person

For the past 16 months I have been an Adjudicator with the Office of the Banking Ombudsman. Prior to that I was the Senior Legal Adviser with the Personal Investment Ombudsman (I was employed by that office for some $2\frac{1}{2}$ years). My knowledge of the PIA Ombudsman Scheme is vast, having been with that Scheme almost from its very beginning, assisting with the establishment of investigation procedures and co-authoring the internal procedures manual. My knowledge of the Office of the Banking Ombudsman Scheme is also considerable.

22 March 1999

ANNEX

SUMMARY

My submissions relate primarily to the establishment of the Financial Services Ombudsman Scheme and those other provisions which have an indirect impact on its operation. The attached paper is an abridged version of my submissions to the Treasury on its consultation on the Bill. I would strongly urge the committee to read my full paper as it contains my own redraft of the relevant provisions of the Bill.

I start by saying that the success or failure of the legislation and financial services reform will be measured by the failure or success of the complaints regime—the resolution of complaints is the face of the legislation to the consumer. The Government will have at its disposal the considerable experience and enthusiasm of the staff of the existing schemes. I feel strongly that the Financial Ombudsman Scheme should achieve its objective of being a speedy and cost effective alternative to the courts. I do not believe that that has been achieved in the draft legislation. My response attempts to deal with those problems I believe exist.

My evidence deals with:

The provisions other than those relating to the Financial Services Ombudsman—section 10 (Exemption of representatives), sections 14 to 16 (Enforceability of Agreements), section 19 (Financial Promotion), and sections 74 (Endorsement of Codes) and 80 (Action for damages).

The Provisions relating to the creation of the Financial Services Ombudsman, in particular:

(1) The general provisions describing the scheme (section 151);

(2) The jurisdiction of the scheme (both compulsory and voluntary) (sections 152-154);

(3) Determination of complaints (sections 155 and 156);

(4) Costs (section 157);

(5) Power to require information (sections 158 and 159);

(6) Funding/fees (section 160);

(7) Schedule 8.

I am aware that the Government has already proposed changes to:

(a) the way the scheme's jurisdiction is to be expressed;

(b) costs; and

(c) appeals on points of law.

Although I have not seen any draft of the proposed changes, based on information available, I do not believe that the issue of jurisdiction has been satisfactorily resolved. I believe that if a consumer conducts business with a regulated person (be that person a bank, building society or financial adviser) he/she should not have to be concerned about issues of jurisdiction or membership of the scheme before they conduct that business or before their complaint can be considered. In my view the legislation could present regulated firms with many technical objections to complaints being considered.

1. Unless otherwise stated, all section and paragraph references are to the sections and paragraphs in the FSM Bill. The Financial Services Ombudsman will be cited as the FSOmbudsman hereafter.

Part A

PROVISIONS OTHER THAN THOSE RELATING TO THE FINANCIAL SERVICES OMBUDSMAN

SECTION 10—EXEMPTION OF REPRESENTATIVES

2. Section 10 appears to be the equivalent to section 44 of the Financial Services Act 1986, although in much simpler terms.

3. It has been argued by senior counsel before a hearing with the Principal PIA Ombudsman that section 44 of the Financial Act has the effect of excluding the doctrine of ostensible authority. That if there is no acceptance in writing for the conduct complained of, the complainants cannot go further and rely on the common law—they are limited by the agreement made under the statutory scheme. That must be wrong. To say otherwise would lead to some extraordinary results. For example, an authorised person could orally hold a third party out as having authority to conduct regulated business (which was in fact outside the terms of the written agreement), but would then be protected by the statutory scheme if a claim was subsequently made in relation to that unauthorised business.

4. It would be useful, in that it would avoid any further dispute, if section 10 specifically stated that the liability of the principal (authorised person) may still arise by reason of any common law principle giving rise to a liability on the part of a principle for the activities of his agent.

SECTIONS 14 TO 16—ENFORCEABILITY OF AGREEMENTS

(a) Extent of the provisions in sections 14 and 15

5. Under section 14, an agreement made in the course of carrying on a regulated activity (excluding deposit taking) in contravention of the general prohibition is unenforceable by the provider against the purchaser.

6. Under section 15, an agreement made by an authorised person (not in contravention of the general prohibition) in consequence of something said or done by a third party in contravention of the general prohibition is unenforceable against the purchaser (this would not include an appointed representative who has gone beyond his authorisation under section 10 because there would be no breach of the general prohibition—it appears that it would only include an unauthorised intermediary).

7. Under section 34 (1) no *authorised person* may carry on a regulated activity in the United Kingdom, or purport to do so, unless the Authority has granted him permission to carry on *that activity* or unless a provision in the FSM Bill gives him such permission. This section does not provide a specific remedy if an authorised person goes beyond his authorisation—it certainly is not clear that an investor could avoid the agreement

(although there may clearly be a claim for breach of statutory duty). It would not come within section 14 and 15 because there is authorisation and thus no contravention of the "*general prohibition*".

8.   It is my view that the right of the investor/customer in sections 14 and 15 to avoid the agreement and claim compensation should be extended to those sales where the authorised person has gone beyond his authorisation (most importantly this would include an appointed representative who has gone beyond the terms of his section 10 agreement).

(b)   *Compensation under section 16*

9.   Where an agreement is unenforceable by reason of section 14 or section 15, compensation is due for any loss suffered by the purchaser. Under section 16 the compensation recoverable will be that sum agreed by the parties or the amount determined by the court. The court also has a power to allow the agreement to be enforced or allow any money paid or transferred under the agreement to be retained.

10.   In my view, the powers of the court set out in section 16 should also be available to the FSOmbudsman. The investor should not be put to the expense of going to court where his investment agreement was procured by an unauthorised person (or, if my submission above is accepted, by an authorised person who goes beyond his authorisation).

11.   As the power of the FSOmbudsman set out in sections 151 to 160 to consider complaints only relates to authorised persons (or persons who have voluntary agreed to participate in the scheme), amendments are necessary. Rather than amending the FSOmbudsman provisions, which would be a difficult task and unnecessarily complicate the FSOmbudsman scheme provisions, the matter could be resolved by specifically giving the Ombudsman jurisdiction within section 16—e.g., "*Notwithstanding sections 151 to 160 and Schedule 8 of this Act the Ombudsman established under those provisions may exercise the powers of the court set out in this section.*"

Section 19—Financial promotion—enforceability of agreement

12.   Under section 19(1) and (2), if a person enters as a customer into a relevant agreement (or exercises any rights conferred by an investment) as a direct or indirect result of an unlawful communication it is unenforceable against him. That person is also entitled to compensation. Again, the amount of compensation is that sum agreed between the parties of the amount determined by the court (section 19(7)). As with section 16, the FSOmbudsman should specifically be included here as having the same jurisdiction as the court.

Section 74—Endorsement of Codes and section 80—action for damages

13.   Section 74 of the FSM Bill provides for the endorsement of codes (or particular provisions of a code) by the Authority where it is satisfied that the provision made by the code could have been made by the Authority in its *general rules* (general rules are defined in section 70(1) as being rules necessary or expedient for the purpose of protecting the interests of persons who, *inter alia*, use the services provided by an authorised person). Breach of an endorsed code may only lead to intervention or discipline (section 74(3)).

14.   Under section 80 of the Bill (which appears to be the equivalent of section 62 of the Financial Services Act) a private person (who is not yet defined) is given a cause of action where there has been a contravention of "*a rule*" (which I assume includes the general rules). Thus even though the Authority could have made the endorsed code as part of its own rules (thereby giving an investor the cause of action under section 80 for its breach) when those same provisions only form part of an endorsed code there is not a cause of action for breach of that endorsed code.

15.   It is my view that where there has been endorsement of a code (or part of a code) under section 74 the investor/customer should be given the same rights where there has been a breach of those endorsed provisions in the same way as those applicable to a breach of a rule by reason of section 80.

Part B

FINANCIAL SERVICES OMBUDSMAN PROVISIONS

Sections 151 to 160

The Scheme

Section 151

16.   Section 151(1) refers to resolving "*disputes involving authorised persons*". There are two points here. First the remainder of the provisions refer to "*complaint*" and for consistency and correctness, the word "*complaints*" should replace "*disputes*" in section 151(1).

17.   Secondly, an *"authorised person"* has the meaning given in section 20(3) (see section 219), namely *"a person who is authorised for the purposes of this Act"*. As I read the provisions, it is clear that the scheme is not limited to resolving *"disputes involving authorised persons"*. The voluntary jurisdiction is an example of this. It is my view that *"involving authorised persons"* should be replaced by *"involving persons subject to the jurisdiction of the scheme"* which would include those with both compulsory and voluntary membership.

18.   I also believe that some fundamental concepts and definitions should be explained in section 151, thereby setting the scene for the remaining provisions. It is apparent that apart from section 151 (4) there is little cross-referencing between sections 151 to 160 and schedule 8, yet both must work together. This could be improved within this section by inserting some relevant cross-references to the definitions contained in schedule 8, for example, *"scheme rules"* and *"Ombudsman"*, which are referred to throughout the sections in Part XIV.

19.   I also believe that this initial section should explain that the Ombudsman's role is not only to make decisions and awards, but to also act as a conciliator (it is this issue which sets it apart from adversarial litigation). The Ombudsman's duty must be to *"facilitate the satisfaction of complaints"* whether by agreement or by making an award. It should also be explained that the Ombudsman shall, in carrying out his functions, decide his own procedure to be adopted in considering complaints (subject, of course, to the legal obligations on him to act fairly and comply with the Human Rights legislation).

SECTION 152 AND 153—COMPULSORY JURISDICTION

20.   As the draft explanatory notes record (on page 58), there are a number of Ombudsman and arbitration schemes operating in the financial services sector. It is intended that the new provisions will replace those existing schemes. Some of those schemes operate on a voluntary membership basis and some on a compulsory membership basis. Those schemes are respected for the work they undertake.

21.   I am aware that the Government intend to make changes to the jurisdiction provisions contained within the draft bill. I have not seen those changes. The explanation provided in the March 1999 Progress Report suggests that the scheme's jurisdiction will be built around the compulsory jurisdiction direction given by the FSA. In my view the jurisdiction should be set out in the legislation and not left to the discretion of the FSA. Consumers need to know what their rights are to complain in the event of fault. My full response to the Treasury's consultations sets out the format I believe the legislation should take. My evidence in this paper will concentrate on the compulsory and voluntary jurisdiction provisions on the assumption that those will remain substantially unaltered by the Government's proposed changes.

22.   Section 152—In relation to this section my specific comments are:

22.1   In subsection 152(2) the conditions of eligibility are that the complainant is eligible under the scheme rules and that the respondent was authorised. Those conditions read along with section 152(1) provide no scope for excluding the complaint on any of the grounds set out in the scheme rules—as there is no reference to the need to have regard to complaint eligibility under the scheme rules. Subsection 152(2) should also have a requirement that *"the complaint is eligible under the scheme rules."*

22.2   Subsection 152(2)(b) requires that the respondent was *"at the time to which the complaint relates . . . "* This would be much improved and easier to apply if it read *"at the time of the events giving rise to the complaint."*

22.3   In subsection 152(5) it states that a complainant is eligible if he falls within a class of person specified in rules made by the Authority. The Authority's procedural rules (in paragraph 14 of schedule 8) do not provide for complainant eligibility rules (e.g., size of companies or partnerships). In any event, complainant eligibility requirements would be more appropriately contained within the scheme rules.

22.4   As a consequence of the amendment to subsection 152(5), subsection 152(6) should now read *"The scheme rules may make provision for persons other than individuals to be eligible."*

23.   The legislation should also make absolutely clear that it is for the Ombudsman (in my view the Chief Ombudsman), in the first instance, to decide whether or not a complaint falls within his jurisdiction and both the respondent and the complainant must co-operate with the Ombudsman in reaching a jurisdictional decision. My full response to the Treasury's consultation contains a new section dealing with co-operation with the Ombudsman at both jurisdiction and investigation stage, and the consequences of failing to do so.

SECTION 154: VOLUNTARY JURISDICTION

24.   If the necessary amendments are made to section 152 so that all complaints dealt with by the schemes which the FSOmbudsman is to replace are covered by section 152 (as I would suggests), then the voluntary jurisdiction need say no more than it will cover complaints not falling with the compulsory jurisdiction.

25.   In relation to the voluntary jurisdiction, under section 154(3) a voluntary jurisdiction direction may be given where:

25.1   It relates to an activity to which a compulsory direction does not apply because the respondent was not an authorised person at the time to which the complaints relates (section 154(3)(a)).

25.2   It relates to an activity which "*could be*" made the subject of a compulsory jurisdiction direction but which has not been (section 154(3)(b)); or

25.3   It relates to an activity which is not a regulated activity (i.e., it does not fall within the Treasury Order made under section 11), could not be made the subject of a compulsory jurisdiction direction (i.e., because it is an activity outside the terms of Schedule 2) but could be made a regulated activity under section 11 (i.e., it is an activity which relates to an investment or is an activity carried on in relation in property of any kind: section 11(1)(a)(b)).

26.   This seems overly complicated. Surely it need say no more than a voluntary jurisdiction direction may cover any type of complaint or respondent which does not fall within the compulsory jurisdiction.

27.   Under subsection 154(2)(b) and (8) it appears that it is not necessary for participation at the time of events giving rise to the complaints—only that the respondent qualified to participate and agreed to participate when the complaint was made to the scheme. I would have thought that the intention was that the respondent had agreed to participate at the time of the events giving rise to the complaint.

28.   It is not clear whether section 154(3)(a) and (b) are separate factors or cumulative. The lack of the word "and" suggests that they are separate. If that is right, for clarity, the addition of the words "*which would otherwise apply*" should be added to section 154(3)(a) so that it reads "*to which a compulsory direction, which would otherwise apply, does not apply because the respondent was not an authorised person . . . .*"

29.   Additional matters not contained within section 154 are:

29.1   There should be provisions for the giving of notice before a respondent can withdraw from the voluntary jurisdiction and the consequences of cessation.

29.2   There should be provisions for the scheme operator to terminate participation in the voluntary jurisdiction and the consequences of cessation.

29.3   The scheme operator should be obliged to keep a register of those persons who have agreed to participate in the voluntary jurisdiction.

SECTIONS 155 AND 156—DETERMINATION OF COMPLAINTS

Compulsory Jurisdiction

INTRODUCTION

30.   Sections 155 and 156 deal with provisions which the Ombudsman must observe when reaching his determination and making his award. The whole of those sections apply to complaints within the compulsory jurisdiction without regard to the type of complaint or the nature of the respondent.

MAKING THE DETERMINATION

31.   Section 155 should be prefaced with a section which explains that if a complaint is not settled or withdrawn during the conciliation process, the Ombudsman may, after the completion of the investigation of the complaint and considering the submission made, make a determination.

32.   The Ombudsman is obliged to make a statement where he has determined a complaint. The statement must give reasons and be signed—there is no provision requiring the Ombudsman to state the nature of the award. Although this may appear obvious, I believe that specific reference to this requirement should be made.

33.   This section should also deal with all other relevant substantive issues. In particular, specific reference should be made to the principle that:

33.1.1   The Ombudsman shall not be bound by any legal rule of evidence.

33.1.2   The Ombudsman shall not be bound by any previous decision made by him or by any other Ombudsman or by any predecessor in any such office.

THE COMPENSATION

34.   Under section 156(1) and (2), in relation to complaints which fall within the compulsory jurisdiction, where the complaint is determined in favour of the complainant, the determination may include a money award or a direction to take steps. There should be a third option—which is a combination of a money award and a direction to take steps.

35. Subsection 156(2)(a) refers to *"such amount as the Ombudsman considers fair compensation for loss or damage (of a kind falling within subsection (3)) suffered by the complainant . . . "* In my view *"fair compensation"* does not denote sufficient objectivity—assessing loss in a legal sense does not involve fairness. Furthermore, there is no reference to compensation for anything other than loss or damage (e.g., distress or inconvenience).

36. I believe that subsection 156(2)(a) should read: *"the determination may include (a) an award of compensation against the respondent for loss or damage or distress or inconvenience (of a kind falling within subsection (3)) suffered by the complainant . . . "*

37. Subsection 156(3) is divided into:

(a) losses for breach of contract; and

(b) loss or damage of any other specified kind.

I do not see the logic behind this division. Many complaints could be based on two or more causes of action—breach of contract and negligence for example. In relation to regulatory complaints, the most common cause of action will be breach of statutory duty as provided for in section 80 of the FSM Bill. In addition to determining the complaint, will it be necessary to decide the cause of action on which the decision is made so that the award can be calculated? This again seems overly complicated.

38. In my view the split should be between:

(a) compensation for any loss or damage for which the court has a power to award damages (irrespective of the nature of the cause of action); and

(b) compensation for any distress or inconvenience or any loss or damage suffered by the complainant not within (a) for which it is fair and reasonable to award compensation.

In this way there is greater correlation between the compensation provisions and the provisions to which the Ombudsman must have regard when reaching his determination—section 155(2).

39. In subsection (5) *"if he* [the Ombudsman] *considers fair compensation requires payment of a larger amount . . . "* a recommendation may be made. In my view *"fair compensation"* is too vague and subjective. It should read *"if he"* [the Ombudsman] *considers that proper compensation requires payment of a larger amount . . . "* a recommendation may be made. This is a more objective test.

40. For clarity subsection 156(6) should read *"The monetary limit is such amount as may be specified by the Authority under subsection (4)"*.

41. Subsection 156(7) should read *"Different monetary limits may be specified . . . "*

ENFORCING THE AWARD

42. Paragraph 17 obviously brings the money award within Order 25, Rule 12(1) of the County Court Rules (applicable in relation to England and Wales). Under the legislation, before a money award can be enforced it must be *"registered in accordance with scheme rules . . . "*. However, there is no provision in paragraph 15 which requires the scheme operator to create or keep a register of awards. Will the complainant have to produce an extract from the register when applying to the county court or some other declaration from the scheme operator or Ombudsman. This appears to be an unusual requirement. The procedure in Order 25, Rule 12(1) merely requires the production of the original or a copy of the award. I would suggest that the requirement to register the award be removed.

Voluntary Jurisdiction

43. There are no provisions at all detailing how complainants within the voluntary jurisdiction will be determined. I assume that this is a matter which will be considered when issuing a voluntary jurisdiction direction. Nevertheless, I do believe that even at this stage, before the making of a voluntary jurisdiction direction and the specifics as to the basis on which awards will be made, that certain provisions should be set out in the legislation. The most important being the right to enforce an award or the right to take injunctive proceedings in respect of an award made by an Ombudsman under the voluntary jurisdiction. Those rights require legislative force.

44. In respect of the enforcement of a money award, Order 25, Rule 12(1) of the County Court Rules requires an *"enactment"* to provide for an award to be enforceable in the county court. It would not, in my view, be sufficient for such provision to be contained within the voluntary jurisdiction direction.

SECTION 157: COSTS

45. I am aware that positive changes to the costs provisions have been proposed by the Government. I will say no more on this issue.

SECTIONS 158 AND 159: POWER TO REQUIRE INFORMATION

46. Section 158 provides the Ombudsman with a power to request information or documentation. As with section 157 (costs), it is not clear whether this applies to section 152 complaints, the voluntary jurisdiction or both.

47. In relation to section 158(3) it should be made clear that the Ombudsman decision is final. It would not be unusual to get into debates as to what information is necessary for the fair determination of the complaint.

48. Subsection 158(4) says that "*the person to whom* [the document] *is produced may*" take copies, etc. Under section 158(1) it is the Ombudsman making the request for the information. It would be much clearer if "*the person to whom* [the document] *is produced may*" was changed to "*the Ombudsman may*" (even though in practice it may be one of his staff receiving the information). A similar amendment should be made *to "the person requiring its production"* in subsection 158(5) as we know this is also the Ombudsman.

49. Subsection 158(6) states that no person may be required to produce or disclose a privileged document. Who decides this where there is a dispute as to whether a document is privileged?

50. I have expressed a view below that the scheme rules should make provision for information to be provided in confidence. I believe that there should be a cross-reference to such a provision in section 158 with the caution that it is for the Ombudsman to decide to what extent regard is had to information provided in confidence.

51. Section 159 provides that if a person (known as the defaulter) fails to comply with a request for information, an Ombudsman may certify that fact in writing to the court and the court may enquire into the case. If the court is satisfied that the defaulter failed to provide the information without reasonable excuse, it may punish the defaulter as if he had been guilty of contempt of court. I have considerable misgivings that this provision should relate to the complainant. The fear of being unable to provide information may of itself be a considerable deterrent to some complainants wishing to make a complaint. In my view there should be three options set out in section 159:

51.1 Where the defaulter is the complainant, the Ombudsman should have a discretion to terminate his investigation.

51.2 Where the defaulter is the respondent or the complainant, the Ombudsman should have a discretion to continue his investigation without references to the information requested.

51.3 Where the defaulter is the respondent, the Ombudsman should have a discretion to report the matter to the court as set out in section 159.

SECTION 160: FUNDING/FEES

52. Section 160 provides for the Authority to make rules requiring the payment to it, or to the scheme operator, by authorised persons of specified amounts or amounts calculated in a specified way. This provision must be read along with paragraph 16 of Schedule 8, which explains that the Scheme rules may require a respondent to pay to the scheme operator such fees as may be specified in the rules.

53. Subject to my belief that the jurisdiction under section 152 should not be limited by the requirement that respondents under that jurisdiction should be authorised persons (and therefore payment in section 160 should not also be so restricted), as far as section 160 and paragraph 16 of Schedule 8 are currently worded I have no objection.

54. There are no fee charging provisions in relation to the voluntary jurisdiction. It may be that these provisions will be included within the voluntary jurisdiction direction. Nevertheless, in order to put the beyond question the scheme's powers to make charges for voluntary participation, I believe that similar provisions to section 160 and paragraph 16 of Schedule 8 should be included in the legislation.

SCHEDULE 8

SCHEDULE 8: PART I AND PART II—GENERAL AND THE SCHEME OPERATOR

Establishment by the Authority of the Scheme Operator

55. Paragraph 2(1) should surely refer to "*the functions conferred on the scheme operator by or under this Act*". It currently refers to "*by or under this Part*". However, the functions of the scheme are much wider than those set out in Part II of Schedule 8—they are more particularly defined in Sections 151 to 160.

Annual Report

56. Paragraph 8 requires that at least once a year the scheme operator makes a report to the Authority on the discharge of its functions. By reason of paragraph 3(5) the function of the scheme operator in producing that report may be exercised only by the Board.

57. I have no particular objection to a report being produced to the Authority by the board. However, one of the strengths of the existing schemes is the report produced by the *Ombudsmen of the Scheme*. The reports currently produced by the existing schemes explain the approach to case investigation, give guidance on issues of importance and detail the work of the scheme. In this way the report is useful to both respondents and complainants. It would be a great loss to lose the production of such a report.

58. In the case of the PIA Ombudsman scheme, its annual report contains a report from the council (seen to be the equivalent to the FSOmbudsman's schemes board) and the Ombudsmen.

59. I would strongly suggest that the same format be followed. There should be an obligation on both the Ombudsmen and the board to produce a report (although the reality would be that they would be contained within the same document).

Guidance

60. Paragraph 9 states that the scheme operator may publish guidance. As this guidance is most likely to relate to the way the scheme investigates complaints (both generally and in relation to specific types of complaints) the Chief Ombudsman should be responsible for providing advice to the scheme operator with regard to this guidance.

Exemption from Liability in Damages

61. Paragraph 11 provides a protection for claims for damages. I would question why this is limited only to the compulsory jurisdiction. I would like to see this protection being given across the whole of the Ombudsman's jurisdictions.

Privilege

62. Under paragraph 12, for the purpose of the law relating to defamation, proceedings in relation to a complaint which is the subject of the compulsory jurisdiction are treated as if they were proceedings before a court. Again, I would question why this is limited only to the compulsory jurisdiction. I would like to see this protection being given across the whole of the Ombudsman's jurisdictions.

SCHEDULE 8: PART III—THE COMPULSORY JURISDICTION

Authority's procedural rules

63. The discretion given to the Authority in paragraph 14 to make procedural rules contains provisions which will impact on issues of the Ombudsman scheme's jurisdiction to consider complaints, namely sub-paragraphs 14(1), 14(2), 14(3). All of those provisions would be more usefully contained within the Scheme Operators Rules (paragraph 15). In this way, the Authority's rules will not form a jurisdictional document thereby simplifying the resolution of jurisdiction disputes.

64. The Authority's rules should be limited to the provisions of paragraph 14(4) which require the respondent to establish appropriate procedures for the resolution of complaints which may be referred to the scheme (I do not see the need for the reference in (b) to *"arise out of an activity to which the Authority's powers under Part VIII do not apply"*).

65. The Authority's rules will only apply to authorised persons. However, there will be those respondents who have agreed to participate in the scheme's jurisdiction on a voluntary basis. It must be right that they are also obliged to have internal complaints procedures in place for the resolution of complaints. The legislation should apply the Authority's rules in this regard to those respondents who have agreed to participate in the scheme.

Scheme Operators Rules

66. Sub-paragraph 15(2) sets out some of the issues which may form part of the scheme rules. I have only two comments:

66.1 Sub-paragraph 15(2)(c) provides that the scheme rules may include a provision for persons other than the complainant and the respondent who appear to have an interest in the determination to be made parties to the complaint. This is a provision which, as far as I am aware, is new to Ombudsman scheme procedures. I would firstly question whether such a provision is necessary as the Ombudsman is dealing only with the complaint and may only make an award against the respondent (he may request information from a third party—who could provide it on a voluntary basis). Secondly, I would question whether such a provision in the scheme rules would be binding on any person whom the Ombudsman wished to make a party to the complaint—I do not see that the scheme rules would have the legislative power to permit the Ombudsman to join third parties.

66.2   Sub-paragraph 15(2)(d)—should also include reference to the provision of information that may be provided in confidence.

SCHEDULE 8: PART IV—THE VOLUNTARY JURISDICTION

67.   Save for the fact that I believe that provisions regarding fees and the enforcement of awards made under the voluntary jurisdiction should be included within Part IV of schedule 8 (in similar terms to paragraph 16 and 17 of schedule 8), and that the discrepancies between the provisions of the voluntary and compulsory jurisdiction in relation to the exemption of liability in damages and privilege should be removed, I have nothing to add in respect of these provisions.

CONCLUSION

68.   It is my opinion that the draft provisions relating to the Ombudsman Scheme are unnecessarily complicated. Simplification can be achieved by making greater use of the legislation and scheme rules under which the existing schemes operate. I believe that the legislation attempts to reinvent a wheel that has been successfully working for some time.

22 March 1999

APPENDIX 33

Memorandum by the Finance and Leasing Association (FLA)

1.   THE FINANCE AND LEASING ASSOCIATION

The Finance and Leasing Association (FLA) is a trade association representing some 98 major companies in the consumer, motor and asset finance industries. Collectively, their credits outstanding amount to £100 billion. They finance 30 per cent of all consumer credit, one third of all gross capital fixed investment and more than half of all new cars. Our members comprise banks, subsidiaries of banks and building societies, leading retailers, manufacturer-owned finance companies, and a range of independent entities. We are by far the largest trade association representing these sectors.

2.   Most of our members are either authorised institutions or their wholly owned subsidiaries. Very few of them do any business regulated for conduct of business purposes by the Financial Services Authority, other than incidentally. Asset finance and leasing business is unregulated, and consumer finance, including motor finance, is regulated under the Consumer Credit Act up to a ceiling of £25,000.

3.   With the exception of the final point on money laundering, this submission relates to the consumer and motor finance sectors. The products of which our members are specialist providers are unsecured lending, point of sale retail and motor credit (through shops and motor dealers for the most part), revolving credit, store and credit cards, and secured lending (second mortgages).

4.   FLA operates a code of practice, which is binding on its full members. The code is supported by a complaints, conciliation and arbitration scheme. The code is currently being reviewed. Like the Council of Mortgage Lenders we believe that our Code is a good basis for the conduct of the industries we represent.

5.   THE FINANCIAL SERVICES OMBUDSMAN

— The provisions of the Consumer Credit Act 1974, and the licensing powers of the Office of Fair Trading, provide a sound regulatory framework for credit products within a ceiling of £25,000. It has operated effectively for many years and is familiar to credit providers, consumers and trading standards officers. There is therefore no point in bringing it within the regulatory scope of the Financial Services Authority. This appears also to be the Government's view. Consumer credit is, however, manifestly a "financial service". It should therefore be included within the wider definition of financial services for the purposes of determining the scope of the Financial Services Ombudsman to handle complaints.

— FLA does not support the idea which has been mooted of a separate credit Ombudsman. We believe that it would give rise to anomalies, distortions and confusion.

— We strongly support the concept of a wide-ranging Financial Services Ombudsman Scheme with compulsory and voluntary jurisdictions, as proposed in the Bill. It will be possible for unauthorised as well as authorised businesses to submit themselves to the new complaints regime, and for complaints about both regulated and unregulated business to be handled by the Ombudsman, provided the definition of "financial services" is a wide one. There is no particular reason for the Financial Services Ombudsman's scope to be confined to the category of business regulated by the FSA. No broad definition of "financial services" has to our knowledge been published. This is probably not necessary so long as common sense is the guide.

— It is clear from HM Treasury's Progress Report of March 1999 (11.5) that the boundary of the Ombudsman's compulsory regime is to be adjusted to encompass the financial services activities of authorised persons even if they are not regulated by FSA. Specifically, the report offers as an example unsecured lending, which is already included in the Banking Code and falls within the remit of the Banking Ombudsman. We welcome this. Such products are also delivered by unauthorised institutions, just as other consumer credit products (see paragraph 3 above), are provided by both authorised and unauthorised institutions, and are direct substitutes for each other. In our view it would be anomalous to limit the Ombudsman's scope in respect of consumer credit to unsecured loans, and a market distortion if the scope of his (or her) voluntary jurisdiction were not identical to that of the compulsory jurisdiction.

— An equally important argument is that for consumers, a single point of entry for complaints about financial services to a clearly independent Ombudsman would be a huge advance. There would also be a single set of rulings on complaints, a further reinforcement of simplicity.

— Such a framework would provide the most encouraging environment for the continuing evolution of voluntary codes of practice such as our own and that of the Council of Mortgage Lenders into sets of standards for specialised business within a single definition of good practice for the whole financial services industry. It would also provide an incentive for firms outside the compulsory jurisdiction to participate in the Ombudsman scheme, with consequent economies of scale.

6. THE REGULATORY TREATMENT OF SECOND MORTGAGES

— The majority of second mortgages are governed by the Consumer Credit Act 1974 because they fall within the financial ceiling of £25,000. First mortgages have been a major focus of recent political and consumer concern because of their dominant position in the overall financial planning of most families, and because, being first charges, they are not subject to statutory regulation of any kind. This is not the case with regulated second mortgages. We do not share the view of the Council of Mortgage Lenders that HM Treasury's cost benefit analysis later this year should be extended beyond first mortgages. Nor do we see a review of the licensing powers of the Director General of Fair Trading as an issue closely related to the regulation of first mortgages.

7. MONEY LAUNDERING

We note that the FSA's money-laundering powers are intended to extend only to authorised institutions. Our own, FLA Money Laundering Guidelines extend to all full members of the Association, authorised and unauthorised, and will continue to do so. Whilst it makes eminent sense for FSA to be the body with responsibilities in this area, it seems illogical to limit them to authorised institutions. Money-launderers themselves recognise no such boundaries. These powers surely trace their origin to the EU Money Laundering Directive, and there is no particular logic other than tidiness in restricting them to authorised institutions.

13 April 1999

APPENDIX 34

Memorandum by the Financial Services Ombudsmen[1]

1. We are grateful for the opportunity to offer some brief observations to the Committee as it considers the draft Bill.

2. The Financial Services Ombudsman scheme provided for in the Bill is intended to embrace and replace all our schemes. Of these two are voluntary (insurance, banking); one derives authority direct from statute (building societies); and two derive authority from SROs established under the Financial Services Act (investment from IMRO, and personal investment from the PIA).

3. As a group of Ombudsmen principally affected by the Bill, we have worked together to make recommendations to the FSA. We made comments on the July 1998 draft to the Treasury and have had a number of helpful meetings with Treasury officials. We welcome section 11 of the Treasury's progress report.

4. Broadly speaking we had two principal points of concern: first that the new scheme might, with the due process requirements of ECHR, and its provisions for appeals and costs orders, resemble a court or tribunal rather than an Ombudsman scheme; and second that the scope of the scheme might still leave out many aspects of financial services where people would expect them to be covered.

---

[1] The Banking, Building Societies, Insurance, Investment and Personal Investment Authority Ombudsmen.

Minimising formality

5.   To some extent the first concern has now been met by the announcement on 1 March by the Economic Secretary that the provisions for appeals and costs orders between parties would be dropped, and we greatly welcome that. The impact of the due process requirements. of Article 6 the ECHR has remained a matter of concern to us from the start, and we have attempted to consider and plan how reformed procedures might comply with these requirements while retaining the informality and flexibility that are the hallmark of an Ombudsman approach. It will be necessary to offer hearings to parties who request it in any case where there is a dispute of material facts. This will have a substantial, but somewhat unpredictable, impact on the work of the scheme. It could well encourage representation for which no legal aid will be available.

Scheme coverage

6.   As far as the scope of the scheme is concerned, the following practical problems appear to remain: unless mortgage provision is regulated, complaints against unauthorised mortgage lending firms (e.g., centralised lenders) cannot be covered by the compulsory jurisdiction. Consumer credit firms offering personal loans, often linked to payment protection insurance, would also be outside the compulsory scope. There remains no mechanism for bringing activities within the compulsory scope of the scheme if they are carried out by firms that do not require FSA authorisation. A significant number of firms involved in mortgages, credit cards and other loans will not require FSA authorisation. In the nature of things, it is those firms most likely to generate problems that will be least likely to sign up to a voluntary jurisdiction. We have proposed, with support from the Director-General of Fair Trading, that it should be possible to extend the scope to those with consumer credit licences from the OFT.

Dependence on "cost benefit analysis"

7.   The new approach to the scope of the scheme will leave the FSA a wide discretion to decide what, within the whole spectrum of regulated business, is to fall within a "compulsory jurisdiction direction" or indeed whether to make such a direction at all. This discretion is to be exercised after carrying out a cost benefit analysis. While cost benefit analysis may be an appropriate test to apply to the extent of regulation, the value of a complaint handling and dispute resolution scheme cannot be measured by a crude comparison of costs and savings. A case where a small amount is at stake may involve an important point of principle. Complaint resolution is not regulation. We question whether the establishment of the scheme should be dependent on an assessment by the FSA of its costs and benefits. There are public policy judgments to be made as to the value to the public (and to the industry) of independent complaint handling that should be more appropriately made by Ministers or by Parliament.

Transition

8.   Apart from a number of other relatively minor points, our remaining concerns centre on the implementation of the new scheme and the transfer of our existing jurisdictions to the new arrangements. It is important that the service to consumers and to the industry is not unduly disrupted, and that the new scheme should be able to deal with complaints about events in the recent past as well as those arising in the future. These matters are to be the subject of transitional provisions, not yet tabled. We assume that these are outside the scope of the Committee's current work.

9.   We would be pleased to give evidence in person.

25 March 1999

APPENDIX 35

Memorandum by the Futures and Options Association (FOA)

1.   The Futures and Options Association (FOA) is the industry association for some 180 institutions which engage in the carrying on of derivatives business (see Annex 1).[1] This brief submission is designed to focus only on matters relevant to the Bill and not on matters of policy and procedure that are within the discretion of FSA (although the extent of that discretion is relevant to the concerns expressed in this submission).

2.   The FOA supports, in principle and in general, the concept of a single regulatory authority for the UK financial service markets and providers.

[1] Not printed.

3. The concerns of the FOA arising in connection with the evolution of the single regulatory authority are set out in a number of detailed position papers, some of which will have already been seen by the Committee. In the interests of brevity, a few of those concerns are set out below:

(a) It is vitally important not to underestimate the potentially serious impact the new regulatory structure could have on the international reputation of the UK financial services sector and on the competitiveness of UK-based financial service providers. In particular, because of the international and wholesale nature of those providers, they are highly sensitive to any matter which may have an adverse effect on their competitiveness; have no particular ties to the UK; and are very well placed for the purpose of relocating business areas to overseas affiliates.

For this reason, extreme care should be taken in (i) setting the regulatory perimeter so as not to include wholesale, essentially physical, markets/participants within financial services regulation (exacerbated by the removal of Permitted Persons status); and (ii) notwithstanding the understandable urgency to introduce the enabling legislation, ensuring that the innovative role of this Committee—which is addressing primarily matters of principle and policy—is not used as a means of shortening the Committee stage—which is responsible for reviewing the detail of the legislation.

(b) The Bill should express more clearly the need for differentiated regulation for wholesale or inter-professional business (cf provisions in the Investment Services Directive and Commission's policy priorities—which include better expression of the need to differentiate wholesale from retail business—for completing the single market in financial services). For example, the definition of "consumer" is given a variety of different meanings in both EU and UK legislation and is clearly normally directed towards individual retail consumers of various products and services. Its use to include wholesale institutions is misleading.

(c) While welcoming the pragmatic approach of providing for a Bill that will serve as enabling legislation, the FOA believes that too much discretion has been left to secondary legislation and, notwithstanding the fact that it will be subject to an affirmative parliamentary procedure, the Bill is far too imprecise about defining the regulatory perimeter (see the letter attached at Annex 2).[1]

(d) The FOA has had significant concerns over an organisation (i.e., the FSA) having considerable, wide ranging, and in some cases, controversial powers—which can have a serious impact on the livelihood of individuals and the business of authorised firms—having also the benefit of statutory immunity. The recently issued Progress Report on the Bill has introduced a number of new and important checks and balances on the exercise of those powers and this has helped to address those concerns. The suggested statutory amendment in (e) below would help to ensure that a proper balance is struck between individual rights and the need for effective regulation.

(e) In view of the industry furore over the significant and unacceptable degree of regulatory and legal uncertainty that has been generated by the imprecise definitions of market abuse, the use of principles for disciplinary process, the significant increase of powers granted to the FSA, the growing interface (not often clear) between criminal and civil process and concerns that the European Convention of Human rights is not being paid sufficient regard in the process of establishing the investigative, disciplinary and criminal powers of the FSA, the FOA believes that the statute should establish parameters for the exercise of their very considerable powers, e.g., as a Clause 2(3) criterion requiring their exercise to be (to use FSA's own words) "transparent, proportionate, consistent and demonstrably fair".

It is recognised that "fairness" is already required under administrative law, but its inclusion in the Bill will serve as a valued public commitment in the light of the above-mentioned concerns and would not involve any change in policy. It would also help to address the current conflicting views over the continuance of statutory immunity.

(f) The FOA believes that the principal role of market supervision should be a matter for the recognised investment exchanges; that, in carrying out this role, they should be on a par with the FSA in the matter of statutory immunity; and that the FSA should exercise its regulatory discretion in such a way as to avoid intervening in commercial matters and to take full account of the potential damage that the exercise of powers of intervention may cause to international reputation and investment values.

(g) The legislation should provide specifically for periodic rules' review by the FSA to ensure that they remain appropriate, effective and cost-effective, bearing in mind that FSA, in any of its consultation papers, has yet to give due recognition to the need for such reviews.

30 March 1999

---

[1] Not printed.

APPENDIX 36

Memorandum by the Halifax Group

1. INTRODUCTION

Our views of the Bill reflect:

— our experience of being regulated under building societies regulation until June 1997;

— our experience of being regulated under banking regulation since June 1997;

— the Clerical Medical Group's long experience of being regulated under Insurance Companies legislation;

— the experience of Halifax Group subsidiaries of being regulated by each of PIA, and IMRO, and SFA.

2. FSA ACCOUNTABILITY

While we understand the anxieties over the powers which FSA will have, we perceive the real issue as being their accountability in exercising them. In this respect debate has focused on FSA's accountability through the enforcement process *after* disciplinary action is taken. However, insufficient attention has been paid to the question of FSA accountability in exercising its supervisory and enforcement powers *before* disciplinary action is taken.

In practice, badly informed or administered regulation on a day to day basis poses actual and opportunity costs to a regulated firm which can be far greater than those which might result from any subsequent disciplinary action. For example FSA can require firms to:

— take onerous steps to demonstrate compliance with ad-hoc and subsequently overturned interpretations of rules;

— pay for external consultants' reports into areas where there may be no justification for regulatory concern; and

— undertake costly, time consuming and diverting remedial action where there is no real mischief to remedy.

The process of "challenging" FDA's requirements at this stage can aggravate the firm's relationship with FSA and so can be a gamble which management are unwilling to take for fear that perceived resistance will escalate administrative action to disciplinary intervention.

What is missing therefore from current debates is how to create what we would term "real time" accountability by the FSA, that is to say the ability of a regulated firm to seek a review of "requests" or orders from a regulator *before* disciplinary action is even a possibility. This accountability could be delivered through the right of administrative appeal to a Committee (say of non-executive directors) within FSA. Or FSA could establish a mediation/conciliation process under which disagreements between the entity and the regulator can be discussed without fear of reprisal.

3. DISCIPLINARY PROCESS

Much of the fear generated about FSA's powers stems from the way in which these have been perceived to have been exercised by current regulators in certain circumstances (and perceptions can influence opinion more than reality where there is inadequate information about the reality). In particular significant concern has arisen through regulators having inflicted severe punishment on individuals who have acted honestly and with integrity. Using discipline in this way creates an environment in which:

— good quality management, and those with the attributes to serve as high quality non-executive directors, will be deterred from choosing to exercise their talents in the regulated financial services sector; and

— those who do serve in the sector will demand prescriptive and authoritative guidance from FSA on how they should behave in order to ensure safety from disciplinary action. This will obviously frustrate achievement of FSA's ambition to let good management manage, and to rely on the maximum extent possible on high level principles and codes rather than detailed rules as the means for spelling out regulatory expectations.

These fears would largely be dispelled if FSA—and preferably the Bill—were to make it clear that disciplinary action would be taken only where a firm or individual had acted deliberately or recklessly in breaching regulatory requirements. However FSA have made it clear that they see disciplinary action as going beyond this and (a) being appropriate to address issues of competence and aptitude, and (b) serving as an effective means of sending out messages to deter others.

We believe that using disciplinary powers in this way is both unnecessary and self-defeating. There are ample ways in which individuals who lack competence or aptitude can be dealt with through normal employer/employee and market disciplines. And regulators have means, other than disciplinary actions, of sending out effective messages to their audiences. FSA's taking unto itself the power to ruin an individual and his/her family even where the individual has acted honestly and with integrity adds nothing to the prospects of creating the relationship of trust and compliance between regulator and regulated to which FSA (and we) aspire—but it detracts from these prospects very seriously.

And if FSA remain wedded to their current disciplinary policy, that relationship will be worsened further by the fact that the staff employed by the regulator are immune from the personal financial jeopardy to which they can subject those employed within the industry even were they to act incompetently or worse.

31 March 1999

APPENDIX 37

Memorandum by the Independent Financial Advisers Association (IFAA)

In our view there are five questions which should be asked when creating or recreating regulatory architecture. These are:

— Who are you trying to protect?

— What are you trying to protect them against?

— Is it cost-effective?

— Is it fair?

— Can you explain it to the public?

CHECKS AND BALANCES

A general question that needs to be asked, *"Under what circumstances could the Chairman of the FSA refuse to take actions demanded by HM Treasury?"*

The Treasury is not only the sponsoring Ministry for the financial services industry but is also the creator of its own financial services products, the creator of tax regimes and the controller of government welfare spending and policy and the overall controller of the Economy.

This puts the Treasury in control of most of the major factors that could compromise any financial advice given by the industry. We fear that unless there is a framework that clearly delineates the powers of the FSA, the Government might be tempted to use the FSA to cover up embarrassing failures of Government policy or taxation.

SCOPE

We wish to suggest a finessing of the current proposals that might add further clarity and flexibility. Currently there are two options for the FSA namely, either regulate in-house as part of the one-stop shop concept or not regulate at all.

We suggest a third option:

— *Allow voluntary regulators to regulate under an inspection and systems control regime created by the FSA.*

The Regulation of Mortgages and General Insurance

The current voluntary system will not lead to efficient or sustainable regulation.

— *GISC and MCRI are not in the information "matrix"* enjoyed by more formal regulators. Proven miscreants from other regulated areas will therefore be able to invade the voluntary sector without those regulators knowing about it.

— *FSA has no powers to homologate systems and standards* between the voluntary sector and itself thus leaving those who need to be both in the statutory and voluntary forms of regulation to trade with a confusing array of standards. In practice, this will lead to the same information being requested by different regulators in different ways. Three regulators also mean three sets of costs and three sets of overheads.

— *The voluntary regulators suffer from a lack of the legal protection* afforded to other regulators against being sued by the regulated. This can lead to a toothless and lengthy form of regulation and much of the regulatory effort being subsumed in litigation.

— *The voluntary structure is endemically unstable* dependent as it is on the continuing good will of product providers to refuse to deal with those outside the code. Those tasked with regulating under this regime find some of their actions compromised by the will of providers. Independent intermediaries find their independence compromised by such regulation as it gives providers influence over the way intermediaries can go to the market.

Our proposal allows a third way which will not impact too heavily on the structure of FSA but will ensure effective and structured regulation in areas which are deemed to be of a lesser risk. It may be in the fullness of time that areas currently regulated in-house may be better regulated externally by such bodies. Our approach will allow that to happen without further legislation.

Whilst the intellectual argument for the current Bill is the "one-stop shop", intermediaries who trade across the borders of Financial Services, Mortgages and General Insurance will face three regulators and three lots of costs. More importantly their clients will face a confusing array of regulators and complaint schemes. We are fully aware of the danger of overloading the FSA particularly early in its life. Thus our suggestion allows for both MCRI and GSCI to be brought into the "one-stop shop" without the disruption that full integration would bring.

COST

We believe the FSA should be subject to scrutiny by external and independent examiners.

In pursuing the concept of compliance cost assessments, we suggest that the Better Regulation Unit should appoint an independent task force to make regular inspections of the Authority's expenditure and also ad hoc cost assessments of the effect of specific rule changes.

ACCOUNTABILITY

We do not believe it is appropriate for the Treasury, as the FSA's sponsoring department, to appoint the members of the Authority's Board. This function should be carried out by a different department of Government.

We recommend that the Minister for the Cabinet Office should be appointed to this role.

We take the view that the ad hoc reporting of the Securities and Investments Board—(now FSA) and other regulators to the Treasury Select Committee is unsatisfactory. Select Committees have a wide range of issues to address and cannot exercise adequate supervision even of a single financial services regulator.

We suggest that it might be appropriate for the Treasury Select Committee to appoint a sub-committee (as for the Civil Service) for the purpose of parliamentary scrutiny.

We believe that there must be a check on the regulator's actions outside the concept of judicial review. It is our opinion that regulators have expanded beyond their powers confident in the knowledge that the judicial review route is cumbersome and expensive. The previous Act was drawn so widely that any action from the regulator was unlikely to be deemed ultra-vires and the test of reasonableness is often in itself unreasonable.

In essence we wish to see a clear framework of duties and responsibilities enshrined within the Bill so that the regulator's powers are clearly defined.

There is a balance to be achieved between flexibility and the creation of an over mighty being which the current draft singly fails to address.

STATUS DISCLOSURE—POLARISATION

Polarisation is the current process under which all those distributing financial services products must disclose for which party in a transaction they are working. In essence; are they working for the provider (Tied Agent or Company Salesman) or the Client (IFA)?

We therefore suggest that consideration be given to incorporating the disclosure of distribution status in the Bill. This would put an end to the arguments, create certainty for the industry and underpin investor protection.

Other Issues

As suggested earlier the draft is remarkable for what it does not contain as much as what it does. We would wish to add the following areas for consideration.

Basis of Redress

There are lessons to be learnt from the Pensions Review. The most important was the wholesale dismantling of the process of common law by SIB. This opened a Pandora's Box which far from shortening the process, had the reverse effect and prolonged the review.

We cannot see that any reasonable investor would expect to receive redress above and beyond his entitlement in a court of law. That said, we do not wish for those who feel they have a complaint to need to resort to the courts. It is therefore necessary for all redress procedures to offer complainants a parallel system to the courts at less cost.

Any other method of redress is by definition profoundly unfair on the policyholders and shareholders who would effectively fund such payments. It is also unfair to professional advisers who do not have access to policyholders and shareholders money and depend on professional indemnity to pay redress. Any deviation from common law creates a hiatus in the PI market with cover becoming either unavailable or prohibitively expensive.

We believe that all redress procedures must be based on common law and this concept should be enshrined in the Act. This would be an invaluable curb on any regulatory excesses ensuring policyholders and shareholders funds are not raided for inappropriate purposes.

A competitive and healthy market can only be achieved by the involvement of professional advisers. The involvement of professional advisers is only possible by the use of professional indemnity insurance and a regulatory system that in turn is based on the common law.

Both for reasons of asset protection and the continued existence of the professional adviser, we believe that such protection should form part of the Act and be reflected in all the processes of regulation including Ombudsman and Compensation schemes.

The Office of Fair Trading

The current FSA 1986 puts a duty on the OFT to comment and make recommendations on issues of competition. We believe this should continue but be tempered by considerations of investor protection.

Whose side is the FSA on?

This may seem a strange question but an important one. We understand that one of the FSA's major tasks is to protect the investor but it is important that the regulator holds the ring for all stakeholders in the process and is not perceived as favouring any single party.

As both the FSA and its Ombudsman have a judiciary function it would be wrong for them to be anything but independent. This needs to be clarified within the wording of the Bill. It also needs to be both de jure and de facto independent of Government.

Discipline and access to the Industry

The denial of rights to the regulated does not enhance the rights of the consumer

Both parties should be able to rely on due processes, checks and balances which will protect even those who might be an embarrassment either to their employers, the regulators, politicians or the industry.

The current disciplinary regimes fall short of the high standards we are entitled to expect. Hearings do not keep the defendant properly informed and represented. The appeals process is expensive and inaccessible.

The procedure for making a complaint against the regulator also requires revision. Pressure can be applied to dissuade a complainant from pursing a complaint. Furthermore, the process is unduly lengthy and unwieldy.

It is for the common good that those who are unable to come up to the standards of the industry are removed from it but it should be remembered that such processes impact completely on the lives of those in the industry and must be seen to be both fair and timely.

It is likely that a firm that finds itself under regulatory pressure will produce a "sacrificial lamb" which will find itself cast out of the firm without the means financially or evidentially to defend itself.

Thought also needs to be given to the role of compliance officers and whistle blowers and what protection regulation should be offering.

If the fining of top management were to become a regular event consideration would need to be given to the long-term impact on the recruitment of top managers into the sector.

ANNEX 1

SUBJECTS COVERED BY THE EVIDENCE OF THE 23 MARCH

SESSION QUESTIONS

Definition of Consumer

The current division between professional investor and retail consumer is one we would wish to see maintained. The relationship between a professional investor and adviser is one of near equals who are regularly in the market and should need less regulation. The relationship between consumer and adviser is usually one of unequal knowledge and irregular access to the market, therefore the degree of protection should be higher.

We accept the NCC definition of a consumer.

Caveat Emptor

We are unhappy with the phrase "Caveat Emptor" preferring instead "Consumer Responsibility". Whilst we understand that the nature of financial services products does not lend itself to easy comprehension, equally there are many other products that are purchased that are complicated and whose usefulness might change over time.

If we are to have a regime of full disclosure there must be some onus on the consumer to concentrate on what is being advised, to give the adviser correct information on which to base the advice and to seek further advice when circumstances change. We call this "Consumer Responsibility".

We do not wish to place undue onus on the consumer but to make the role of the advised an active one. We do not wish to see consumers encouraged to take a passive role in their financial futures secure in the knowledge that the phrase "I did not understand" would be the perfect form of defence against future changes in circumstances.

All financial advice is based on a balance of possibilities. Advisers are not fortune-tellers and can only be judged on their advice at the time it is given. The outcome of that advice will be subject to a great number of forces, political, fiscal, legal commercial, etc., over which the adviser cannot have any influence.

Whilst we are happy to be judged on the basis that our advice might be negligent, we cannot be expected to act as guarantor of the outcome of the advice. Nor should consumers be able to back one course of action and have a stake in other courses of action should they prove to be more beneficial.

MARKET CONFIDENCE

We are unclear whether an explicit objective to support the Bank of England to manage systemic risk would be helpful. We do wish to see the UK's excellent record of fine prudential regulation be maintained and can see a danger if the roles of the FSA and Bank of England are not clear to all.

COMPETITIVENESS

The inclusion of this area in the principles is we believe the minimum required. The actions of previous regulators in so publicly criticising "the shortcomings" of the industry have done much to give succour to our international competitors. It is also the case that such publicity has done much to undermine public confidence in the UK financial services market.

REGULATORY BURDEN

Whilst we welcome the cost benefit analysis approach it does not give the whole story: many regulatory actions are almost impossible to cost, as on their own there is little apparent cost. However when one views such actions collectively the combined cost is high.

We would also like to see an onus on the regulator to review their existing regime as to its costs and invasiveness on a regular basis. Here again we believe that there is a role for the Better Regulation Unit.

We would also wish to see the regulator substantiating costs it might impose on an individual company in the course of regulating that firm.

PUBLIC AWARENESS

We welcome the new concentration on public awareness. It is in line with the IFAA checklist on regulation.
5. *"Can you explain your proposals to the public?"*

Whilst any education of the public is a good idea we wish to ensure that the FSA is tasked with explaining its role and that of the regulatory regime to the public before embarking on wider forms of financial education. There is little point in creating a regime costing in excess of £300 million and the public being unaware of its scope and benefits.

We are happy with the Chancellor's announcement but have some doubts whether league tables will succeed in comparing like with like on a consistent basis.

FINANCIAL CRIME

Whilst regulated persons may think they are taking adequate steps to prevent financial crime, that does not mean that all financial crime will be prevented. When such crime is discovered whatever steps were taken previously must have been by definition inadequate. There is too much wisdom after the event in these proposals.

OTHER OBJECTIVES AND PRINCIPLES

We note the NCC's wish to insert concepts of "satisfactory quality" into the regime. Whilst we have no real objections to this there are serious issues surrounding how and when such judgments might be made. It might be easier to insert a concept of profoundly poor quality. Is quality the issue or are we really looking at value for money?

Again we note the NCC's views on exclusion. We agree subject to an addition. It is not simply the right to product that should be included but the right to advice.

CONFLICT BETWEEN OBJECTIVES

We understand that there will be tension between objectives and between objectives and principles. Putting them in some priority order might be helpful now but what happens when priorities change as they inevitably will?

We are somewhat concerned that objectives and principles might be used as an excuse for precipitate action against a particular sector.

31 March 1999

APPENDIX 38

Memorandum by the Institute of Chartered Accountants in England and Wales (ICAEW)

1. We welcome the proposed improvements in the reporting requirements and governance structure of the FSA and in particular the number, appointment procedures and reporting responsibilities of the non-executive directors. However, if the Board of the FSA is to operate effectively then the non-executive directors must take a full part in the decision making process and be fully involved in the consensus building that will be necessary. They will thus be, quite rightly, committed to the decisions made. While this has many advantages in improving the quality of decision making and the breadth of experience employed, it also has the effect of reducing the independence of the non-executive committee. It is not realistic to expect non-executive directors to take a neutral stance in preparing a report on the effect of decisions that they have themselves been involved in making.

2. We support the inclusion in statute of the principles for the implementation of regulation contained in Clause 2(3) of the draft Bill. They are important to the achievement of a number of policy objectives, including the continued development of a competitive and successful financial services industry. However, at present they do not appear to have any explicit enforcement or reporting mechanisms relating to them.

3. Our preferred solution to the problems of reporting independently on the effects of the decision making processes of the FSA and of reporting on the fulfilment of the Clause 2(3) principles would have been for the appointment of an oversight board of knowledgeable individuals, without decision making responsibilities, to report on the operations of the FSA. In the absence of such a board, we welcome the Treasury's proposal that it will have the power to commission independent reports, at periodic intervals, into the efficiency and economy

of the FSA's operations. We urge that this power should be extended to reports on the fulfilment of all the Clause 2(3) principles. We also recommend that fulfilment of the principles should be explicitly required to be covered in the FSA's annual report to the Treasury.

1 April 1999

APPENDIX 39

Note by the Institute of Chartered Accountants in England and Wales and others[1] on the draft Regulated Activities Order

1. PRECAUTIONARY AUTHORISATION

This evidence relates only to the proposals made by HM Treasury on avoiding the need for precautionary authorisation. We support the aims of the proposals as stated in the consultation document and agree with the Treasury Committee of the House of Commons who said *"the definition of financial advice needs to be drawn as narrowly as possible to prevent unnecessary regulation"*. We also agree with the Treasury objective stated in the Overview to the draft Financial Services and Markets Bill that *"the need for the costs of regulation [should] be proportionate to the benefits"*.

We are concerned that the detailed provisions of the draft Order do not appear to achieve these agreed policy objectives. We are also concerned that the consultation indicates that the FSA will have an important role in achieving these policy objectives by issuing guidance about what is and what is not investment business, but gives no specific power or duty for the FSA to issue appropriate guidance.

2. NUMBER OF FIRMS INVOLVED

We fear that there may be no real reduction in the 13,000 or more accounting and law firms who currently maintain authorisation on a precautionary basis. In addition, we fear that the lack of clarity in the draft Order combined with the change to a single regulatory body in the FSA could lead to more firms taking out precautionary authorisation. For example, there are currently approximately 15,000 firms of accountants who are unauthorised. Lack of clarity as to the circumstances in which they may advise small family businesses which are incorporated may lead to these firms reconsidering their position.

3. OBJECTIVES

We do not seek to reinvent the RPB regime. We agree that professional firms which intend to provide mainstream investment business services should be authorised by the FSA. We do seek to ensure that legislation which provides for criminal sanctions is clear and is administered in a way which:

(a)   makes it very clear to practitioners which activities are covered;

(b)   does not fetter the ability of clients to discuss their affairs freely with their chosen professional adviser; and

(c)   excludes activities which do not require the expensive panoply of regulation by the FSA.

4. PROPOSAL

The draft Order seeks to avoid the need for precautionary authorisation in many cases through excluding activities which may *"reasonably be regarded as necessary in the course of a professional business"*. The word "necessary" is a very restrictive test and we are unclear whether the addition of the words *"may reasonably be regarded as"* will have any significant effect in relation to precautionary authorisation. By contrast, the Investment Services Directive does not apply to investment services which are provided *"in an incidental manner in the course of a [regulated] professional activity"*. In our view, the most effective way of achieving this aim would be for the legislation to exclude activities which are incidental to the practice of a profession, while giving the FSA power to specify activities which (because they believe that they carry particular risks to consumers) should not receive the benefit of the incidental exclusion.

1 April 1999

---

[1] The Institutes of Chartered Accountants in England and Wales, Scotland and Ireland, The Association of Chartered Certified Accountants, The Law Society, The Law Societies of Scotland and Northern Ireland, and The Institute of Actuaries.

APPENDIX 40

Memorandum by the Institute of Insurance Brokers

We are writing to you as a member of the Special Select Committee, which has been established to make recommendations on the draft Financial Services and Markets Bill.

Our interest concerns those elements of the proposals, which include, "the power to repeal the Insurance Brokers (Registration) Act (IBRA) 1977" and the detrimental effect of same to the public interest.

Firstly, it is appropriate that we declare our interest as the only professional body in the UK, exclusively dedicated to representing the interests of insurance broking practices and in more recent times as administrators of the Act. Furthermore, that at present there is a heated debate within the industry with regard to the proposal to repeal the statue.

Brief details are as follows:

(1) The IBRA 1977 provided for the registration of insurance brokers and for the regulation of their professional standards. At the time of writing over 13,000 individuals and 3,000 firms are regulated thereunder.

(2) By the very nature of the IBRA 1977, it necessitated the establishment of a Council, as a body corporate with *perpetual succession*.

(3) From a public interest point of view the IBRC:

(a) Resolves over 95 per cent of consumer complaints about their brokers/insurers within seven days—the remainder being of a nature which require detailed investigation and are settled later.

(b) Has an Indemnity and Grants Scheme to compensate consumers with a legitimate claim against an insurance broking practice which has ceased trading or is unable to settle.

(c) Holds over 30,000 cubic feet of records (going back many years) which need to be accessed regularly, in order to investigate all manner of consumer related matters (which under the Statutes of Limitation can arise many years after a policy of insurance was issued or "insurance advice" tendered), often involving other statutes, such as those relating to Employer's Liability, Third Party Motor Insurance, etc. Sometimes very considerable sums of damages/compensation are involved, whereby properly maintained IBRC records may be the only source of assisting legitimate claimants to trace the existence of indemnity at the material time—which some insurers faced with a major claim would prefer to have gone missing.

(d) Assists the Financial Services Authority in discharging its responsibilities under the provisions of the Financial Services Act 1986, there being a considerable need for close co-operation, perhaps for many years to come (again, in the consumer interest).

4. Quite simply, the IBRA 1977 cannot just be "switched off like a light bulb", without causing a legally unenforceable "trail of debris" for many, many years to come.

5. It is our belief that the HM Treasury officials responsible for advising the Minister were quite oblivious to the above mentioned matters and many others which would follow a repeal. However, to be fair, at the time they were being lobbied hard by elements of the industry opposed to the statutory regulation of all those who "give insurance advice" and in favour of the establishment of a non-statutory self-regulatory framework instead (i.e., the proposed General Insurance Standards Council).

6. It is our further belief that ultimately, "advising upon/arranging policies of insurance" will be subjected to statutory regulation (whether via powers to be included in the Financial Services and Markets Bill or, an EU Directive—i.e., it is only a matter of time rather than fact). In this regard it would make sound sense to address the matter properly now, whilst the ideal opportunity exists and ensure that there is proper and prudent continuation of consumer protection, which as mentioned above was always intended to *be in perpetuity*.

7. In our opinion, the Financial Services Authority should become the custodians of a suitably amended IBRA 1977, which should be a mandatory requirement for all "independent insurance advisers". Under such a scenario the existing administrative centre could continue operating (reporting to the FSA)—thus avoiding a further administrative burden on the FSA itself at this very busy time for the Authority. Furthermore, we believe that the proposed GISC could be developed (again accountable to the FSA) to regulate insurer direct sales and tied/multi tied agents.

8. Insurance Brokers themselves wish to retain their professional status, of which they are justifiably proud (having been volunteers for statutory regulation for over 20 years). This should not just be taken away from them. A copy of the survey[1] recently conducted by this Institute is enclosed for your information, which clearly illustrates the strength of feeling, which has been further evidenced by the vast majority of brokers who have paid their regulatory retention fees for 1999 against the background of "impending doom" announced by the Treasury.

---

[1] Not printed.

We feel that by way of this communication, we have warned of the serious consequences a repeal of the IBRA 1977 would cause, unless there is some form of *statutory perpetual succession* and in the absence of same, the detrimental effect to the public interest and all those who have transacted business with insurance brokers—acting in reliance of the protections afforded under the Act.

We would be pleased to meet with members of your Committee, in order to elaborate on any of the issues raised and answer any questions you may have on this subject, before you conclude your report to government.

26 March 1999

APPENDIX 41

Memorandum by the Institutional Fund Managers' Association

TIMETABLE

We urge that the Joint Committee be reconvened, not later than September this year, to hear further representations on the revised Bill and further FSA consultation papers.

COSTS

A mechanism should be put in place whereby the FSA can be challenged about their proposed allocation of costs and consideration should be given to the principles for allocation being enshrined in primary legislation.

The Government should be prepared to pay for costs incurred in the educational programme for meeting the objective of public awareness.

ENFORCEMENT

(a) European Convention on Human Rights

It is important for the credibility of FSA that the enforcement regime should not fall foul of ECHR the first time a decision of the FSA is challenged in Court. Accordingly, the Government must be asked to demonstrate (not simply aver) that the proposed regime will meet the requirement of ECHR.

(b) Role of the Enforcement Committee

We strongly believe that there should be practitioners and public interest representatives on the Committee and that such representatives should be able to vote to ensure the independence of the Committee. Consideration should be given to the Chairman and Secretary of the Committee being appointed by the Lord Chancellor or some other external party.

(c) Award of Costs Against Individuals and the FSA

The Bill should be amended so that individuals may not have costs awarded against them (save in egregious cases) or a limit (say £5,000) should be placed on the amount of costs that can be recovered.

We also strongly recommend that costs should be recoverable against the FSA if an individual (or firm) is successful at the Appeal Tribunal.

OBLIGATIONS OF FSA: NO ACTION LETTERS: GUIDANCE

We believe the FSA should be obliged to provide in a timely manner interpretative guidance applying to a particular factual situation and to provide guidance on its rules which is disseminated to authorised persons in a timely manner.

31 March 1999

APPENDIX 42

Memorandum by the Investors Compensation Scheme (ICS)

The ICS Board has considered and responded to the consultation document on the provisions for the new compensation arrangements set out in Sections 142 to 150 to the draft Financial Services and Markets Bill. Amongst its detailed submissions, the Board made comments on clause 142(4) on the appointment of directors of the new management company and clause 148 by which it is intended that by the rules the FSA will be able to control the amount which the new scheme may levy to cover its management costs. These particular points may be of interest to the Joint Committee.

CLAUSE 142(4)

> "ICS notes that the FSA intends to appoint or remove directors. It considers that the present make-up of the Board representing the financial services industry and public interest members should be continued in some form.". . .

> . . . "However the ICS recommends that the Chief Executive of the scheme is both a director and is appointed by the Board. ICS would anticipate that the appointment of a Chief Executive to the scheme would be discussed with FSA in any event."

The Chief Executive is the key link between the Board and Executive. As the new scheme is likely to be a sizeable operation, it would be important for the Chief Executive to take part in Board decisions which is the current state of affairs with the present management company.

CLAUSE 148

> "Whilst the ultimate sanction of the removal of directors lies with the FSA, the scheme manager needs to be able to control its own budget including not just the levy, but also its management expenses. FSA intends to prescribe the maximum amount that the scheme manager may levy in respect of its running costs, which would fetter that ability. The scheme must be in a position to devote the resources necessary to handling any major default or large numbers of claims, should the need arise, in particular (for example) in case a bank were to be declared in default, for which contingency adequate resources may not have been prepared. ICS considers that the mechanism of accountability and annual report would be sufficient, particularly as a Memorandum of Understanding would also be in place, so that this clause is unnecessary and unwarranted."

At present, the Scheme's budget and levy are set by the ICS Board after consulting with the regulators.

31 March 1999

APPENDIX 43

Memorandum by Justice in Financial Service

1. *The FSA needs power to determine whether individuals are "fit and proper". However, the proposed power to discipline individuals is unnecessary, unfair and potentially incompatible with a free economy.*

2. It is unnecessary because the FSA will have the power to discipline firms that fail to control their employees. If a firm is not controlling its employees, laying down proper procedures and disciplining employees who transgress it can and should be punished or, in serious cases, suspended from carrying out business.

3. It is virtually impossible to see how the FSA can exercise a power to impose censure or fines fairly at all and it is certain that this involves disproportionate cost. Establishing individual responsibilities and omissions inside a firm is difficult and complex. There are great difficulties in allowing any form of fair trial. IMRO's attempts to discipline chief executives of three Morgan Grenfell companies ended with massive and hostile coverage of the regulator, widespread sympathy with the victims in the City and the UK being hauled into the European Court of Human Rights. The only beneficiaries are lawyers who have received around £3 million in fees.

4. As pointed out by the Consumers Association, the power to fine individuals or suspend their right to work for a limited period is useful to force executives to do what the regulator says when their firms would otherwise resist pressure in the courts or otherwise. In effect, the FSA is asking for a power to say to the chief executive of the Pru: "We want you to pay money to this group of investors. You have said that the Pru will fight this in the courts as you do not believe we are right and this money will be paid by investors in the Pru's "with profit" funds and shareholders (who are investors in pension funds and unit trusts managed by other firms). If you do not do what we say, we will bring charges against you personally relating to these matters and other failings. You will be unable to work in the industry until they are resolved. You will have to pay lawyers to defend you. You will not be able to get a penny of those costs back from us and you will have to pay our costs if we establish a single charge against you. We have banned the Pru from giving you an indemnity for your costs."

5. *The FSA's rules determining costs are oppressive and one sided. We urge that the ability to recover costs be limited, following proposals by Lord Woolf for the reform of civil litigation. We suggest recovery by any party to disciplinary proceedings should be limited to the higher of £5,000 or 10 per cent of the required capital of the firm.*

6. In the Morgan Grenfell case, Mr Glyn Owen's lawyers had incurred expenditure totalling some £75,000 when IMRO notified them that it had incurred £200,000 legal costs which it expected to recover from Mr Owen. We suggest that this is intolerable and the primary legislation should limit ability to recover costs on both sides. In other cases, IFAs have been forced to pay between £8,000 and £25,000 costs as a condition of settling charges

relating to record keeping and similar matters. Whilst we accept that, in some circumstances, heavy fines may be appropriate, regulators should not be permitted to use huge costs as a punishment or indeed deterrent to defending a case at all.

7. *We believe that it is wrong for the people who in effect act as judges to be appointed by the FSA, to be paid by the FSA and to receive bonuses that may be increased by fines. We urge that all persons acting as judges be appointed by the Lord Chancellor and that he should determine their pay and conditions.*

8. We agree with the FSA that no charges should be served without independent review of the case. But we cannot see how anyone appointed by the FSA can be independent. The European Court of Human Rights has given a clear guidance on this point.

9. *We view with concern the proposed powers of the FSA and the Ombudsman to award compensation when no legal liability exists without rights of appeal to the courts. We believe that in all cases legal liability should be established by the courts.*

10. We do not think that if the right of appeal to the courts is granted, it will be used often if at all—certainly the right of appeal against the PIA Ombudsman is seldom if ever invoked—but if it does not exist, then the FSA and Ombudsman will be under constant pressure to do what the consumer lobby urges, the industry may become uninsurable and the results will be both unfair to the industry and ultimately harmful to investors as IFAs find it impossible to give advice and withdraw from the industry.

11. We also believe that both the SIB and the ICS have on occasion miscalculated compensation when they have stated that the calculated figures are what a court would award. If there is to be no appeal, some steps must be taken to correct this.

12. *We support the Treasury Select Committee's call for effective arrangements for investigating complaints against the FSA to be set out in primary legislation. We believe that the Ombudsman who deals with complaints against Government departments and the NHS should deal with complaints against the FSA and should report to Parliament, not the FSA.*

13. *Lastly, we believe that the structure of the FSA and the absence of effective judicial supervision creates scope for corruption. There is prima facie evidence of financial interest intruding in a quasi judicial process in three high profile cases—West Bromwich Building Society, Knight Williams, Morgan Grenfell Asset Management. The exercise of quasi judicial functions of the FSA by persons appointed by the Lord Chancellor would greatly reduce the scope for repetition of unfortunate episodes.*

17 March 1999

APPENDIX 44

Supplementary Memorandum by Justice in Financial Services

IMMUNITY AND THE CONSUMER

Listening to the discussions on the immunity that it is proposed to give to the FSA, it was clear that none of the witnesses had given the detailed consideration of the subject that comes with preparing actual cases.

As a result, I suspect the Committee has been misled on three very important points.

The first is the difficulty that anybody bringing a case against the FSA will face in persuading a Court to make a finding or award compensation against the regulator. This includes the European Court on Human Rights which allows competent authorities considerable latitude in carrying out their tasks. There is considerable case law on planning applications to support this point. In practical terms, it will be very difficult to persuade a Court to act unless there is clear evidence that the FSA has displayed significant recklessness or carelessness or otherwise behaved quite disproportionately or unreasonably. Anyone who brings a case without showing this will have to pay the FSA's costs.

This is illustrated in the case of *Melton Medes v SIB*, in which case the Judge awarded indemnity costs to SIB. (It must be said that the plaintiffs in Melton Medes do not seem to have had the sort of case that would win general sympathy, in contrast to the position of our founder and others forced into confessing to crimes they had not committed.) Indemnity costs are usually only awarded rarely, against misbehaving litigants. In this case, the Judge appears to have been motivated by the lack of substantial merits in the plaintiff's case.

It also lies behind Lord Denning's remark—quoted by the chairman—that public bodies should not have to look over their shoulders. The Committee has, I believe, been misled into thinking that the immunity is essential to protect a regulator doing its job.

The second point on which the Committee has been misled relates to confidentiality. The chairman suggested that the immunity might not apply to actions, for instance by somebody adversely affected by "leaks". Melton Medes was an action following a "leak" and the Judge held that damages were not available for breach of the statutory duty to maintain confidence. If damages are to be available to victims of "leaks" then there will have to be specific provision in the FSMB making damages available.

The third—and most important—point was not raised at all. The proposed immunity will apply not just to companies. It will also apply to consumers.

There are very real reasons for allowing consumers to take action against the FSA. The FSA will have the power both to award compensation itself and to delay the Ombudsman from hearing cases whilst it considers action itself. It is unlikely that the Ombudsman will award compensation when the FSA does not. This opens up the real possibility that the FSA will make errors that damage consumers.

The FSA may also damage consumers by taking action against their advisers and either requiring or sanctioning a transfer of adviser that damages consumer interests. Again, the consumer will have no redress.

These are not remote possibilities. There are two high profile cases in which the SIB made errors that either threatened or actually did damage consumers. There are other cases where regulators made mistakes harmful to consumers.

THE WEST BROMWICH BUILDING SOCIETY (WBBS) AND HOME INCOME PLANS

The SIB became involved in the dispute between the WBBS and action groups of elderly investors whose home had been put at risk by borrowing from the WBBS on usurious terms to finance investments that had gone terribly wrong.

Ultimately, this case was resolved in the High Court, with damages of around £38 million being awarded against the WBBS. The High Court found that the WBBS had entered into an unlawful arrangement with the investment adviser responsible and was thus liable for losses caused.

However, at an earlier stage of the proceedings, the SIB had "negotiated" a package with the WBBS which it commended to the elderly investors. This package was much less favourable than the compensation awarded by the High Court.

Plainly, investors who accepted the package recommended by the SIB would not have obtained the compensation due in law. These investors, elderly people with low incomes, are universally regarded as meritorious claimants, the very people that the SIB was meant to protect.

It seems to us very clear that an immunity would protect the FSA from claims in the High Court should it make a similar, massive error. (It should be noted that immunity is not the only issue—see below.)

KNIGHT WILLIAMS

The Knight Williams affair started with the SIB ignoring the advice of the regulator directly involved, FIMBRA, and assuming that Knight Williams and Company Limited had caused clients to suffer heavy losses. In early 1994, when the SIB became involved, it plainly believed that these losses ran into many millions. It now turns out, following investigation by the ICS, that the actual losses were on a far smaller scale that SIB envisaged. It is possible that litigation will eventually establish that losses were below £500,000. Given the size of the Knight Williams client base, this is not a substantial sum and is close to compensation that the firm wanted to offer but was prevented from offering by SIB. Even the sum paid by the ICS under heavy political pressure from Mrs Angela Knight, a former minister, is well within what the firm could have afforded in 1994.

However, instead of encouraging the use of the proper complaints procedure, SIB forced the firm to establish a special complaints handling procedure. In November 1994 Mr Jeremy Orme, SIB's then head of enforcement, urged all unhappy investors to make use of the procedure and have confidence in the SIB.

The result was disastrous. Nobody "who had confidence in the SIB" received compensation until 1997. Some have only just received compensation from the ICS—over four years after SIB urged them to trust it.

The real victims were not unhappy investors, numbering at that point around 400. Approaching 20,000 investors have incurred losses as a result of the SIB putting Knight Williams and Company Limited into liquidation. These are the investors who had no complaints but, because SIB had destroyed their firm, had to transfer the management of their funds.

The transfer was overseen by SIB: Mr Orme was present in person when the arrangements to transfer management were negotiated and concluded. So there can be no doubt of the SIB's close involvement in every step of this affair.

The 20,000 investors whose investments were transferred suffered losses for the following reason. All these investors had a contract with Knight Williams and Company Limited which provided for discretionary fund management. Knight Williams and Company Limited was able and indeed did use the discretion to alter exposures to particular markets. The investments were structured so that a reduction in exposure to, say, Japan and an increase in exposure to, say, America did not require the investors to act and did not expose them to any liability for CGT or income tax.

Under the transfer arrangements made with the full knowledge of SIB, the investments managed by Knight Williams were replaced by investments managed by another firm. But those investments which were not in a PEP were split into separate holdings—so much in the UK, so much in America, so much in Japan, so much in the Far East. Altering the balance of the investments required investors to act and exposed them to CGT. Those investments in PEPs remained in a structure that allowed adjustment of the exposures.

As a result of work done by the ICS, we know that the investments in PEPs performed substantially better than the portfolios which were not in PEPs. As the same fund management firm handled both sets of investments and as the initial exposures of the PEP and non-PEP investments were similar, the under performance of the non-PEP element seems entirely due to investors being locked into Japan and the Far East as a result of arrangements approved by the SIB and only made necessary by the SIB. The losses that have resulted by the SIB breaking up the discretionary management arrangement would appear to be in the order of £90 million— over £4,000 for each of 20,000 elderly investors.

There are, we believe, other cases where investors have suffered losses as a result of regulators deciding to close firms, but none, we think, on this scale.

SHOULD THE FSA BE PROTECTED BY IMMUNITY?

The losses incurred by investors in Knight Williams as a result of what can at best be regarded as gross incompetence on the part of a senior employee of the SIB must give rise to doubt as to whether the FSA should enjoy an extensive immunity from action. The FSA will have far greater powers to intervene than the SIB does. The risk of errors must be higher.

The Knight Williams case has been the subject of detailed work by a QC whose opinion has been made available to the Clerks to the Joint Committee. This opinion shows that there are complex legal issues that need to be considered, relating not just to the immunity but to the duties that are to be laid on the FSA and its legal liabilities.

Although it may involve considerable further work, we believe that the interests of consumers cannot be adequately protected unless the FSA is made liable for the consequences of reckless, thoughtless or incompetent actions that cause heavy losses for consumers. We have examined advice by a QC on the scope for consumers to form action groups and use the Courts and are entirely convinced that, were Parliament to allow consumers to bring actions against the FSA in circumstances in which its actions had caused losses, then this would be a realistic remedy.

We urge the Committee to consider this problem most carefully. As the Committee has been told, firms (and individuals) may well be able to overturn a statutory immunity by application to the European Court of Human Rights as it appears to contravene Article 6 of the Convention (which states that everyone has a right to a fair trial). However, unless the Bill is carefully drafted to give consumers adequate rights against a blundering FSA, they may well be unable to make an application to Strasbourg.

13 April 1999

APPENDIX 45

Memorandum from Kensington Mortgage Company (KMC)

1. KMC welcomes the Committee's decision to examine the position of mortgage advice and for the opportunity to respond to the Committee's inquiry. KMC supports the extension of statutory regulation to cover mortgage products.

2. KMC is the UK's largest "non-conforming" mortgage company providing mortgages to those people who do not meet the increasingly stringent criteria laid down by most high street banks and building societies.

3. KMC provides mortgages to 14,000 customers in the UK. The current total value of its lending is £750 million.These loans are securitised and KMC has received an AAA rating from the markets;

4. KMC was the first "non-conforming" mortgage company to sign up to the Council of Mortgage Lenders Code of Mortgage Lending Practice and the Office of Fair Trading's non-status lending guidelines.

5. The CML's Code has been in operation for a relatively short period of time; since July 1997 in the case of lenders and April 1998 in the case of intermediaries. Some may assess that it is too early to guess the degree of compliance with the Code, although the Treasury intends to carry out a review later this year. It is not within the scope of this submission to comment on the level of compliance with the Code.

6. The case for statutory regulation should not rest on the extent to which those who sign up to the Code comply with it. Voluntary regulation is ineffective because by definition not all lenders and mortgage intermediaries fall within it. For example, in the specialist "non-conforming" sector of the mortgage market

there are nine lenders operating. Eight have signed up to the CML Code, one has not. There are other overseas lenders who tend to come into the market for short periods and then exit again. Moreover, there are many reputable financial institutions that remain outside the CML because there is a waiting period before companies can become full members.

7. If regulation is to be effective its coverage must be total, not partial. Even if 90 per cent of the industry is covered by the CML Code (as is the case in the "non-conforming" sector), it is surely unacceptable that customers run the risk of being mis-sold a mortgage because they find themselves dealing with the 10 per cent of the industry that does not adhere to the highest standards of disclosure and transparency.

8. The best means for disciplining and regulating the market is to ensure that consumers have the necessary information to make effective choices. The information must, therefore, be disclosed in a consistent form that enables customers to make meaningful comparisons of the true costs of credit inherent with different products.

9. There are still too many instances of where charges are not clear, compulsory insurance products are bundled in with the other costs of the mortgage or where customers are unaware that their financial adviser is receiving a substantial commission to sell a particular product. A mortgage is one of the largest commitments individuals will take-on throughout their life. It is surely right that they should enjoy similar levels of protection to those they would enjoy in other sectors of the financial services industry.

10. "Non-conforming" mortgage lending is a specialist sector of the market. It is, however, becoming increasingly important. The world of work is changing. Eight and a half million people are in less secure forms of employment. Temporary and contract workers, divorced men and women, single parents and those suffering illness can all suffer from poor credit ratings through no fault of their own. While at the same time High Street Banks are excluding more and more people as they increasingly make use of inflexible computerised credit-scoring techniques in the drive for cost savings. Non-conforming lending can, therefore, provide short-term bridging measures to allow borrowers to prove their credit-worthiness. They are also a tailored product for the self-employed, consultants and others with irregular work patterns.

11. Suitability is a critical issue in the selling of any mortgage product. It is particularly important in the non-conforming sector. "Non-conforming" lenders should not accept customers who could get a standard mortgage and equally should not hesitate to turn down applications from those at high risk of defaulting.

12. In summary, therefore:
— the vast majority of non-conforming UK mortgage lenders have voluntarily signed-up to the CML Code;
— voluntary regulation will continue to be ineffective because its coverage is partial;
— effective disclosure and transparency is essential if customers are to be able to make informed choices about suitable products;
— customers will not be able to make like-for-like comparisons unless the whole industry adheres to the same standards;
— this can only be achieved through statutory regulation.

APPENDIX 46

Memorandum by the Knight Williams Investors' Action Group (KWIAG)

This evidence is submitted by Kenneth Jordan on behalf of the hundreds of investors whom he represents as co-founder and Chairman of the Knight Williams Investors' Action Group (KWIAG).

The purpose of this submission of written evidence is to bring to light what has happened in the past so that the mistakes and flaws of implementation of the 1986 Financial Services Act will not be repeated in the Financial Services and Markets Bill. That consideration is of over-riding importance in this evidence.

This submission, while written in the first person, is based materially on hard written evidence to be found in thousands of letters to HM Treasury, Members of Parliament, FIMBRA, SIB, FSA, and ICS, and of course to KWIAG.

ANNEX

1. This evidence is directed principally to the first question referred to in the Press Notice No. 2 of 2 March 1999 *"Proposed arrangements for the accountability of the FSA"*.

2. *Accountability:* The lack of accountability by the Financial regulators—FSA, SIB, and most especially the ICS, continues to be the chief cause for complaints from private investors. Whereas of course it is recognised that the ICS is not a financial regulator per se, because of its seamless join with the FSA it attracts an equal share of the criticisms which follow hereafter.

3.1 *Accountability of KWIAG:* It is relevant to the integrity of this evidence that the Joint Committee (especially those members who are among the "new entry" of May 1997) may be fully aware of the credentials of KWIAG members.

We are mostly in our 70s and 80s; some are older. In the 1940s and thereabouts many of us in what should have been our "salad days" were variously engaged in the Armed Services, in Industry, and in Agriculture, in fighting for democracy and natural justice. In what should be our "tranquil twilight days" we find ourselves tired, mentally and physically, with having once again to fight for democracy and natural justice—this time against the very organisations which we had been given to understand were formed to protect our interests.

3.2 KWIAG has no political affiliation. We are the only genuinely voluntary action group to have been invited by a Minister of HM Treasury to give our views (September 1995), in person.

4.1 *Accountability of Government:* On 18 April 1994 Mr Anthony Nelson (MP), the then Economic Secretary to Her Majesty's Treasury, in a letter to Sir Anthony Grant (MP) wrote, *inter alia, "The chief concern of the Government in drafting the Financial Services Act was to provide a high standard of protection for investors"*. I and my KWIAG colleagues took that unequivocal statement by the Minister absolutely at its face value.

4.2 We also note that, *"the detailed ways in which the system is operated are matters for the regulators"*. (See Addendum ONE).[1]

4.3 Had the 1986 Financial Services Act functioned as the then Government intended—"to provide a high standard of protection for investors"—there would never have been the need for the formation of the Knight Williams' Investors Action Group. (Anyone who still thinks otherwise is palpably ignorant of what has happened in financial regulations over the past decade).

4.4 So what went wrong? This is a question which needs to be answered in the past as well as the present tense—the past tense referring to matters of regulation under the 1986 FSA, and the present tense in relation to the draft Financial Services and Markets Bill.

4.5 It is important to remember that the undertaking that "the chief concern . . . was to provide a high standard of protection for investors" has never been repudiated by the previous Government, nor by the present Government.

5.1 ACCOUNTABILITY OF SIB/FSA

5.2 To answer first 4.4 above, this is what went wrong with the operation of the 1986 FSA by the Regulators:

5.3 In rapid order, the Boards of Directors of, certainly, SIB, PIA, ICS, and especially the FSA, were infiltrated (with the consent of HM Treasury) and thus dominated by representatives from the boards of City organisations. As a consequence the FSA Board's impartiality in the matter of protection for investors was compromised.

5.4 To its credit, the present Government has identified the need—prior to the Draft Bill being debated by Parliament—for matters to be scrutinised by an unprecedented Lords/Commons Committee.

5.5 In a letter to the London Evening Standard on Monday 22 March 1999 Mr Michael Blair QC, General Counsel to the Board of the FSA, hastened to put the FSA interpretation of ACCOUNTABILITY. (See Addendum TWO).[1]

5.6 Had Mr Blair seen Mr Anthony Nelson's letter to Sir Anthony Grant (referred to in paragraphs 4.1–4.2 above), he—Mr Blair—might have modified the optimism expressed in the final paragraph of his letter to the Evening Standard. In this connection Mr Nelson, himself, underlined the weazel words "look again".

5.7 So in 1994 even a Treasury Minister was having problems with the lack of accountability shown by the then Chairman of the Government's Chief Financial Regulator. Nothing has changed.

6.1 ACCOUNTABILITY OF FSA AND ICS: It has been the experience of KWIAG members that the ICS, in particular, frequently adopts an adversarial posture when posed with a challenge which it finds difficult to defend. Invariably, it reminds private investors that they have a remedy in the Courts or that they can apply for a "judicial review". As the ICS knows full well both of those options are denied to most private investors because of the cost of litigation and the excessive time involved.

6.2 On the other hand, when KWIAG has invited Sir John Wickerson (the ICS Chairman) to put the ICS manipulation of the Quantification Date to a test case in Court, he has backed off from doing so.

6.3 Last year Sir John Wickerson was asked the perfectly legitimate question as to who, on the Board of the FSA, nominated and seconded Ms Foster-Back for a directorship of the ICS. (The response to the simple request for information may be read in Addendum THREE).[1]

6.4 If one could only choose a single example of the FSA's total opposition to the concept of accountability, then one need look no further than the final sentence of Mr Michael Blair's letter of 10 March 1998 (see

---

[1] Not printed.

Addendum FOUR)[1] in response to Kenneth Jordan's letter of 3 March to the Chairman of the FSA (see Addendum FIVE).[1] (Mr Jordan's letter of 12 March 1998—Addendum SIX[1]—concluded that particular correspondence).

6.5   Therefore, I would earnestly ask that the recommendation contained in the Third Report Volume 1 of the Report and Proceedings of the Treasury Committee (page vi, paragraph (r)) be enforced forthwith. It reads: *"We recommend that minutes of FSA board meetings should be published, with the minimum of deletions for reason of confidentiality"*. It is something we in KWIAG have asked for on many occasions.

7.1   *In Conclusion:* Lord Acton, a Liberal MP and friend of Gladstone, would have understood the problems private investors have with the Regulators, who use their unprecedented immunity from prosecution for damages by reason of their private limited company status. I am certain he would have condemned the use of secrecy by the ICS and the FSA as a means of denying even-handed justice to private investors.

7.2   Lord Acton said: *"The nation that keeps its archives secret has its history written by its enemies"*.

7.3   On behalf of the members of KWIAG and other private investors I do hope that the Joint Committee will endorse the spirit of the sentiment expressed in Mr Anthony Nelson's letter of 18 April 1994 and will seek to ensure that the flaws which have arisen from the 1986 FSA will not be repeated in the Financial Services and Markets Bill.

7.4   Above all, I would urge that the status of private limited company for Regulators (see paragraph 3 of Addendum SEVEN),[1] which does nothing in the way of protection for private investors be SCRAPPED.

March 1999

APPENDIX 47

Memorandum by the Law Society's Company Law Committee

A.   INTRODUCTION AND SUMMARY

1.   This memorandum is submitted to the Joint Committee in the context of its consideration of the draft Financial Services and Markets Bill. The Joint Committee has received our November 1998 Memorandum submitted to HM Treasury. This Memorandum supplements the points we made in our November 1998 Memorandum in respect of certain questions on which the Joint Committee is focusing its inquiry, taking into account HM Treasury's recently published Progress Report.

2.   We have no additional comments to offer at this stage on Questions 2 (Statutory Objectives) 5 (Ombudsman and Compensation Scheme) and 6 (Market Abuse). With regard to market abuse, the comments we expressed in detail in our November 1998 Memorandum, and in particular:

2.1   The general lack of a mental element in the ingredients of the offence is unduly severe and will give rise to great uncertainty and potential injustice. The draft legislation opens up the possibility that a person who reasonably believed that his behaviour would not distort the market could still be penalised. In these situations the regulator will have the considerable benefit of hindsight;

2.2   The provisions designed to prevent use of unpublished information are so wide that they raise the risk that a person can be penalised for acting while in possession of information which is so imprecise that its significance can only be judged with hindsight;

remain and nothing in the Progress Report or the recent report of the FSA on the response they received to Consultation Paper 10 lead us to change the view we previously expressed.

3.   We therefore offer in Part B of this Memorandum further comments on questions 1 (proposed arrangements of accountability of the FSA), 3 (Discipline, enforcement and the Tribunal) and 4 (Scope of the new regime). Our comments are summarised in paragraphs 4 to 17 below.

4.   We believe that the blanket statutory immunity for the FSA is no longer justified and should be limited, if at all, to an immunity for staff and officers of the FSA rather than the body itself (see paragraphs 8 to 11 below).

5.   The FSA's abilities to keep the fines it imposes creates a clear conflict of interest. They should be paid either into the Ombudsman Scheme or the Compensation Scheme (see paragraph 14 below).

---

[1] Not printed.

6.   The scope of the new regime should be clearly limited in the face of the Bill, to business activities, except within strictly defined exceptions (see paragraph 16 below).

7.   The Treasury should, like the FSA, be under a statutory duty to consult on changes to the scope of the regime (see paragraph 17 below).

B.   QUESTIONS ON WHICH THE COMMITTEE HAS DECIDED TO FOCUS

Proposed arrangements for the accountability of the FSA

8.   We welcome the additional provisions to be built into the Bill, as set out in paragraph 3.7 of the Progress Report.

9.   We are now broadly content with the arrangements proposed, subject to one issue. We question the justification for the continuation of the FSA's blanket statutory immunity bearing in mind its significantly increased powers (particularly with regard to prosecutions and rights to enter premises). In paragraph 3.10 of the Progress Report the Government justifies the continuation of the immunity on the grounds that without it "the regulator's staff would be unable to go about their business without being unduly hampered by concerns about legal action". As lawyers, we find that a remarkable statement. Accountability under the law is vitally important for any public authority. It is our understanding that other Public Authorities such as the Police, the Serious Fraud Office and the Customs and Excise do not have such a wide ranging immunity and this does not seem to hamper these authorities in carrying out their legal functions.

10.   We are aware of the argument that if the FSA were made liable for damages, then this is a cost that the regulated community will have to bear, so that the regulated community will end up bearing the cost of paying its own damages claim. This is rather similar to the argument that mutual insurance companies should not be fined because those who end up paying the costs are the policyholders themselves, an argument that the FSA has rejected on the grounds that this risk is one the policyholder takes when acquiring such a policy. The effect of a damages claim where the immunity exists is that the aggrieved party bears the loss; where immunity does not exist the cost is effectively shared across the whole regulated community. It seems obvious to us what is the fairer result.

11.   We therefore strongly urge that the draft Bill be amended to remove the statutory immunity for the FSA itself. We accept that different considerations may apply in relation to individual officers or members of the FSA's staff. The argument for the statutory immunity in the case of SRO board members and staff enshrined in the Financial Services Act 1986 was that without it individuals would be discouraged from filling regulatory positions. This may still be a valid consideration, although it does not seem to be a deterrent as far as the Police and other authorities referred to above are concerned. The financial risk can of course be covered by insurance. It would therefore be possible to retain the immunity for individual officers and staff members whilst removing it for the FSA itself.

12.   We should also mention that we are aware of legal action before the European Court of Justice questioning the legality of the current statutory immunity regarding banking regulators and whether such immunity is consistent with the EU Banking Directives.

Discipline and Enforcement

13.   A representative of our Committee will be giving oral evidence to the Joint Committee relating to the issues on which we have expressed concerns.

14.   We continue to have concerns in that all fine income is retained by the FSA. As we stated in our November 1998 Memorandum, we regard the ability of the FSA to keep fines levied as giving rise to a serious conflict of interest and will appear to undermine its impartiality as the FSA, and potentially its staff have a direct interest in the monies collected by it. We are disappointed that our suggestion, made in discussions with Treasury Officials, that fines be paid to the Ombudsman or Compensation Schemes, thus removing the conflict whilst at the same time helping to fund the costs of the regulatory system has not been taken up.

15.   We welcome the Government's proposal to impose a new statutory duty upon the FSA to establish and publish procedures and to act in accordance with those procedures. FSA Consultation Paper 17 indicated that these procedures would be detailed in a Broad Resolution of the FSA. We consider that this is too informal; we believe that the rules of procedure should be set out in formal rules of procedure, which would be subject to the specific requirements of the Bill regarding consultation.

Scope of the new regime

16.   We have previously expressed concerns that the potential scope of the new regime was far too widely drawn in the draft Bill and, in particular, did not limit the scope to activities carried on by way of business. This concern remains. The Treasury has recently consulted on the secondary legislation regarding scope and except in one instance relating to trustees of occupational pension schemes (mirrored in the current law) the scope is limited to activities carried on by way of business. We therefore see no difficulty in this limitation being contained in the Bill itself; the extension of the legislation to activities of a private character is something which in our view should properly be a matter of primarily legislation except in clearly defined circumstances.

17. The Progress Report contains a commitment by the Treasury to consult fully not only on the initial secondary legislation but on future changes. We are therefore disappointed that there is no statutory duty imposed upon the Treasury to consult in these matters, equivalent to that imposed upon the FSA in relation to its legislative powers. Our concerns appear justified in the light of the fact that the Treasury published on 17 March a very important consultation paper on Financial Promotion with a deadline for comments of 30 April which is totally inadequate for a subject of this importance. We are concerned that without a clear statutory duty to consult within adequate procedures the temptation to pay lip-service to the principle of consultation will easily arise.

22 March 1999

APPENDIX 48

Memorandum by the Law Society of Scotland

INTRODUCTION

1. This paper sets out the submission of the Law Society of Scotland on the Government's proposals for regulation of financial services, embodied in the draft Financial Services & Markets Bill which is to be considered by the Joint Committee.

2. The Society is the recognised professional body for Scottish solicitors and is recognised as such under the Financial Services Act 1986. The Society presently regulates 550 firms of solicitors, who provide a wide range of financial services in many cases, integrated with legal advice.

3. The Society recognises that the creation of the Financial Services Authority will provide a single financial regulator for the industry and consumers which should bring the benefits of clarity and uniformity. However, the Society is concerned that these objectives of clarity and uniformity may not be achieved in respect of Scottish solicitors who may conduct investment business under the new regime.

4. The Society has already expressed its concern to the Economic Secretary at the Treasury on the interplay between the Scottish and Westminster Parliaments on the future regulation of investment business for Scottish solicitors. While financial services regulation is a reserved area for the Westminster Parliament, the Scottish Parliament will have responsibility for the regulation of Scottish solicitors. The draft Bill seeks no amendments to the existing primary legislation governing Scottish solicitors contained in the Solicitors (Scotland) Act 1980. The existing compensation, disciplinary and Ombudsman arrangements governing all aspects of a Scottish solicitor's work will continue in parallel with the proposed arrangements under the draft Bill. Scottish solicitors will therefore be subject to two compensation, disciplinary and Ombudsman's schemes in respect of their investment business and such schemes will be regulated by different Parliaments. More importantly consumers will be confused.

5. The Society has raised these concerns in greater detail with the Treasury and the FSA.

ARRANGEMENTS FOR THE ACCOUNTABILITY OF THE FSA

6. The Society has serious concerns about the accountability and powers of the FSA. The draft Bill has been so constructed that it is in essence an enabling Bill and will provide the FSA with such powers as it deems necessary to regulate, discipline and supervise the financial community. It is essential that such powers should be balanced with an appropriate degree of responsibility to Parliament and to the financial services community and consumers. The Society is not aware of any other body with such wide policy-making and enforcement powers conferred by Statute which is not a direct Ministerial responsibility. While the FSA has addressed some of these concerns, there still appears to be a lack of an effective control mechanism built into the FSA structure whereby an effective and quick review of the FSA's decisions could be made to ensure that the FSA does not act ultra vires.

7. The Society believes that the FSA may wish to consider some of the following measures to increase its own accountability:

— The FSA should be asked to explain the methodology used in its cost/benefit exercises;
— The FSA has established a Practitioner Forum and Consumer Panel—these should be provided for by Statute in the Bill;
— The FSA should be subject to an annual audit by the National Audit Office.

OBJECTIVES OF THE FINANCIAL SERVICES AUTHORITY

8. The Society welcomes the inclusion in the draft Bill of the statement of the statutory objectives of the FSA.

9. The Society suggests that an annual assessment should be undertaken by the FSA to demonstrate whether or not in each year the FSA has met its stated statutory objectives. A report on this assessment should be published annually.

10. The Society believes the Treasury should give consideration to including as an additional objective the maintenance of the international competitiveness of the UK's financial services and markets.

FSA DISCIPLINE AND ENFORCEMENT

11.   The Society is concerned that the FSA may be able to exercise its disciplinary and enforcement powers in a punitative manner. Furthermore, the FSA disciplinary regime would appear to have a criminal rather than civil character and should, in accordance with the European Convention on Human Rights, respect the rights to fair trial and due process which the criminal law provides for defenders.

12.   The Society further believes that the FSA's approach to discipline and enforcement should not solely be directed at the detection and punishment of breaches of Rules but rather that the focus should be on achieving and maintaining compliance. The Society believes that insufficient consideration has been given to compliance through self-assessment which is a philosophy which this Society, through its own experience, believes raises compliance standards considerably.

13.   The FSA should base any enforcement action on the principles of proportionality and consistency so that the cost of compliance for any firm is minimised by ensuring that any action required is proportionate to the risks.

SCOPE OF THE NEW REGIME UNDER THE DRAFT BILL

14.   The Government, on 7 April 1998, announced its initial decision on the future regulation of mortgage advice. The Treasury will be taking a reserved power to extend the FSA's responsibility to include mortgages, as part of the draft Bill. The Society has some difficulty in understanding how a mortgage, which is a debt over heritable property, could be defined as an investment in terms of the draft Bill.

15.   The Society supports the extensions to the Mortgage Code as a means of ensuring adequate protection for consumers where mortgage advice is given.

16.   The Society supports the Council of Mortgage Lenders' approach to the evolving nature of mortgage regulation in the UK. The Society believes that the extension of the Mortgage Code to cover mortgage intermediaries from 30 April 1998 should be subject to a formal review in 1999 to assess whether the Code is working.

17.   The Society is concerned that the definition of "investment" proposed under Clause 1(4) which, taken together with the terms of Schedule 2, may significantly widen the definition of an investment and investment business. The definitions proposed for both terms appear contrary to the Treasury's stated intention of narrowing the scope of investment business to eliminate the need for "precautionary authorisation" currently undertaken by many professional firms. There is a real concern that general business advice, particularly that provided by solicitors to small and medium sized enterprises may be inadvertently caught by the new regulatory system. This could result in significant investment business compliance costs being incurred which may price such advice beyond the scope of many small and medium sized enterprises.

18.   While the Society recognises the Treasury's wish for flexibility for the future in terms of the absence of precise definitions within the draft Bill, the Society is concerned about this approach given that Parliament will be asked to approve the new regulatory structure when the scope is still uncertain. This uncertainty would appear to breach two fundamental principles of regulation that such regulation should be clear and legally certain.

19.   The Society has grave concerns as to the practicality of dual regulation which will apply to Scottish solicitors who conduct investment business. The Society will still, act as a regulator for all areas of a Scottish solicitor's practice bar investment business. This regulation will be subject to oversight by the Scottish Parliament. The investment business activities of Scottish solicitors will be subject to the regulation of the FSA under its powers delegated and provided for by the Westminster Parliament.

20.   The Society is concerned that little, if any, regard has been given to the interplay of the two Parliaments in their future regulation of Scottish solicitors. For example, the Scottish Solicitors Discipline Tribunal is charged with the ultimate responsibility for the disciplining of Scottish solicitors. This Tribunal has powers to discipline Scottish solicitors in respect of their conduct of investment business. However, the draft Bill also proposes that a separate Tribunal be established under the auspices of the FSA which will also be able to discipline Scottish solicitors in their conduct of investment business. As no amendments have been sought to the Solicitors (Scotland) Act 1980, Scottish solicitors will in this and other areas be subject to two regulatory systems determined by separate Parliaments which will neither create certainty or clarity for such solicitors and consumers. This duplication and potential conflict also arises in the interface between the Society's complaints handling, compensation and professional indemnity insurance schemes as determined by the Scottish Parliament and those of the FSA as determined by the Westminster Parliament.

21.   The Society has raised these concerns in greater detail with the Treasury and the FSA.

OMBUDSMAN AND COMPENSATION SCHEMES

22.   The existing Ombudsman Scheme, covering all aspects of a Scottish solicitor's work is that of the Scottish Legal Services Ombudsman. This Ombudsman Scheme is established under the Solicitors (Scotland) Act 1980. The Society's concerns on the interplay of this Scheme and that of the FSA Ombudsman Scheme are similar to the concerns raised in paragraph 21.

23. The Society's compensation scheme is a guarantee fund of unlimited liability which, under the system of dual regulation, will continue to apply through the Scottish Parliament to Scottish solicitors who conduct investment business. This again will result in Scottish solicitors who conduct investment business being subject to two compensation schemes. Consumers will be confused which compensation scheme will handle particular compensation claims and there is a danger that some claims may "fall between" the two schemes.

SUMMARY

The Society's principal concerns which it wishes to identify to the Joint Committee on Financial Services and Markets as contained within this Memorandum are as follows:
— Greater accountability of the FSA should be enshrined in the Financial Services and Markets Bill;
— An annual audit of the FSA to be conducted by the National Audit Office;
— An annual assessment by the FSA as to whether it has met its statutory objectives;
— The principles of proportionality and consistency to be applied by the FSA to its enforcement philosophy to ensure that the cost of compliance for firms should be minimised by ensuring that any enforcement action required is proportionate to the risks;
— The definition of an investment and what activities constitute investment business should be clear and legally certain;
— Urgent steps to be undertaken to ensure that there is not constitutional conflict between the Scottish and Westminster Parliaments in their respective regulation of Scottish solicitors.

March 1999

APPENDIX 49

Memorandum by London Investment Banking Association (LIBA)

Q1. *The Government has made several proposals for enhancing the accountability of the FSA. Are you now happy with the FSA's proposed level of accountability?*
— *Do you think making the establishment of the Enforcement Committee a statutory requirement would improve accountability?*

While agreeing that the measures announced by the Treasury are important steps forward we would like to see the following additional steps:
(i) Annual Report: We would like to see FSA required to include in its annual report:
— an explanation of any occasion on which it has introduced a rule (or other obligation) more onerous than required by the relevant international or European standard;
— the level of expenditure on the public awareness objective;
— an account of FSA's international work.
(ii) Consultation: There should be an obligation to provide a feedback statement on all consultations (see also paragraph 19 below).

Where rules are introduced without consultation because of urgency FSA should seek views after the event and provide feedback.

FSA should be required to explain the methodology used in cost/benefit analyses, and also to give some analysis of alternatives to the rule chosen.

The essential purpose of the Enforcement Committee is to ensure that decisions to take enforcement action are taken by appropriate persons who are independent of the regulator and investigatory authority—in the same way as decisions to prosecute criminal offences are taken by the Crown Prosecution Service. The persons should include someone with appropriate legal experience and someone with commercial experience relevant to the type of business concerned. The importance of their role is such that it is desirable those points should be included in the Bill.

Q2. *What type of arrangements for independent investigation of complaints made against the FSA do you think would be most effective?*

The independent investigator should not be appointed by the FSA or the Treasury. If the PCA is not the investigator the process of appointment should be similar to that for appointment of the PCA.

Q3. *The draft Bill requires the FSA to carry out public consultation whenever it proposes to change its rules. The Association of Unit Trusts and Investment Funds (AUTIF) has suggested that the FSA should also be required to consult on all policy initiatives affecting one or more sections of the regulated community. Do you think there is a need to require the FSA to consult on matters going beyond proposed rule changes?*

LIBA considers that consultation should cover all requirements which are in practice mandatory and potentially the subject of enforcement action.

There is little substantive difference between a rule, a principle, a code and guidance if breach of any of them is subject to the same enforcement process. For example, if there is a principle that persons are to maintain proper standards of market conduct, and breach of that principle is a disciplinary offence subject to unlimited fine or removal of authorisaiton, "guidance" which lays down what is and what is not considered proper conduct is in effect a rule under another name.

Q4. *The AUTIF has also suggested that the FSA should hold public hearings on important policy proposals. Do you think that would be a useful step towards increasing the FSA's accountability?*

Yes. Public debate is a useful discipline

Q5. *Are you satisfied that the rule-making procedures fully accord with the Better Regulation Unit's principles of good regulation?*

No. A few quotations from the Guide indicate areas where the FSA proposals do not seem to match up:

"A full Regulatory Impact Statement should accompany any external consultation . . . " 2.1.

"[In consultation documents] include a statement that responses will normally be made public." 2.6.

"Integrate with previous regulations. If the regulation overlaps with another measure, try to replace it with a combined and streamlined regulation . . . How will those who are being regulated get the full picture of what is required." 3.6

"Helping business and others comply in the most effective way should . . . be one of your key aims. This cannot be achieved solely by detection and punishment of breaches by enforcement officials. Neither do you want the enforcement and sanctions to be so strict that you are effectively discouraging those who are being regulated from performing legitimate activities or forcing them through fear or uncertainty, to go to unnecessary lengths to comply." 4.4

Q6. *Several bodies have suggested that the FSA should be subject to periodic efficiency audit by the NAO. What is your view?*

LIBA considers both that the financial audit of FSA should be conducted by the National Audit Office(NAO) and that NAO should conduct periodic value-for-money scrutiny. FSA has a breadth of power which would more normally be within a government department. NAO has experience both of auditing departments and of conducting value-for-money scrutiny of public policy organisations such as departments and public corporations, and it is wholly appropriate that it should perform both roles in respect of FSA.

14 April 1999

APPENDIX 50

Note by the London Metal Exchange on the statutory immunity for Recognised Investment Exchanges and clearing houses for their regulatory functions

SUMMARY

The draft Bill largely continues the current regulatory regime for investment exchanges and clearing houses whereby Recognised Investment Exchanges (RIEs) have regulatory duties derived from statute, to maintain fair and proper markets. The RIEs are the front-line regulators against market manipulation and other abuse.

The LME fully supports this regime. Market abuse can be effectively deterred only by the exchanges. The FSA is, necessarily, too distant from the markets to act to deter manipulation and to stop it in its tracks. The FSA can act after the event and discipline those found to have manipulated the market: but by then substantial damage could have been inflicted on the market, market participants and market users.

The LME is determined to carry out its regulatory responsibilities. In doing so, however, it is subject to a substantial risk of litigation. The financial strength of the market participants and the financial stakes involved could threaten the commercial viability of the Exchange.

The FSA enjoys statutory immunity for its regulatory actions taken in good faith. The LME's proposal is to limit immunity for RIEs and RCHs to regulatory actions taken in good faith to fulfil their statutory regulatory obligations under the new legislation. It would therefore do no more than treat consistently any given regulatory actions whether taken by an Exchange/Clearing House or the FSA.

The draft Bill proposes limiting immunity to actions from the Exchange's members. This would substantially restrict the LME's capacity and effectiveness with which it is able to fulfil its regulatory functions. The danger of suit from customers of the Exchange, approved warehouses and employees of member firms (none of whom are members of the Exchange) is far greater than from our members.

We understand that there may be some concern about giving commercial organisations statutory immunity or that immunity in these cases may remove civil rights. We believe these concerns to be misplaced. Under our proposal, immunity from civil suit would be heavily circumscribed. Exchanges would still be open to legal challenge that particular actions had been taken for commercial, not regulatory purposes or were taken in bad faith. Exchanges would still be subject to judicial review. Currently the LME is in the unique position of being subject to civil suit and judicial review for the same regulatory action.

8 March 1999

APPENDIX 51

Memorandum by Mr Michael Marks

I welcome the opportunity to provide you with some personal observations upon the Financial Services and Markets Bill.

I should emphasise a few points before I start. Whilst I am Chairman of LIBA and also Chairman of the European businesses of Merrill Lynch, the comments I am making are expressed in my capacity as someone who has been in the City for around 40 years, during which time I've witnessed a fundamental change in the financial services industry in general and the City in particular. Nevertheless, there are core features and virtues of the City which have survived and which subtly bestow its distinctive character and strength. Changes in the past have not eradicated these core values and it is imperative that future changes don't either.

I should perhaps also mention that I am neither a lawyer nor a professional regulator and so my views do not necessarily have the forensic and technical depth that those of my colleagues on the Panel may possess. Therefore I approach the issues as a practitioner and one who wants to see a thriving and fair market in which consumers get what they want and participants are able to make a profit—so far as the markets will allow!

I think that the Bill presents a very exciting opportunity. Self regulation and the SROs have served us well, but I agree that it is time to look at the creation of a unified regulator. I have seen the statutory objectives and criteria which have been set out in the Bill and they are very commendable. However, if the Bill, when it comes out of the Parliamentary process, does not lend itself to cost effective and straightforward *implementation* then the FSA will not be in a position to meet those objectives and criteria, however well intentioned.

Moreover the Act when it emerges has to be *seen* to be right. It must inspire confidence both in consumers and participants. And to do that it must strike various balances along the way.

There must be the correct balance of weight of regulation between the retail and wholesale sector.

There must be the correct balance between flexibility and certainty.

There must be the correct balance between robustness of regulatory power and the fear which will stifle the taking of financial risk and innovation and push business offshore and weaken markets.

There are many balances to be struck, but the common thread that is running through all these issues, is that they are being determined in *public* and with the opportunity for informed debate and inevitable disagreement over detail and in some cases substantive issues. I cannot recall in my career such an open and indepth process. This is very welcome and I wouldn't have it any other way. However, it means that there is an even greater responsibility on all of us to ensure that the results make sense. Of course, not everyone is going to agree about everything but it is clear that some real issues have emerged in the consultation process which must be addressed in a sensible way, if the FSA is to inspire confidence from day one.

I am glad the theme for today is Discipline, Enforcement, the Tribunal and Market Abuse, because I detect that this is an area where there are some real issues to be addressed.

To me there are a number of key points.

1. Have we really got the balance right between the criminal regime and the regulatory regime? I appreciate that there is a dilemma: on the one hand there has been a none too brilliant record on prosecutions for insider dealing and S47 offences. Because of the need for intent and meeting the "beyond reasonable doubt" burden of proof, we are told that a significant volume of prosecutions is not achievable and that therefore the deterrent virtues of the provisions are lost. On the other hand we hear the howls of protest that the civil Market Abuse is criminal in nature—hence the European Convention on Human Rights arguments—and that all the criminal-type protections should follow and that intent should be part of the "offence". We are also told that the Market Abuse regime is not to "replace" the criminal offences and is there to catch those things which wouldn't otherwise be caught.

In my humble view we are in danger of getting to a stage where there is a risk one will need a degree in law to trade in the UK market. This could still the heartbeat of the City.

I think we need to accept a basic fact: an individual who is found against under something like the Market Abuse regime is likely (though, I concede, not inevitably) to be finished. They will not work in mainstream financial markets in this country again. It doesn't matter whether it is a civil or criminal code, whether there is a fine or not. Therefore, *whatever* characterisation is given to the "offence", the process must be fair and seen to be fair if we are to deprive people of their livelihood.

I think it follows from this that the boundaries of the acceptable have to be set as clearly as possible. My sense is that the code supporting the statutory provision is drawn too widely although I accept that, if we *are* to proceed on the basis of a code, then there will always be a risk that its slipstream will catch activity which with hindsight was acceptable.

Three things follow from this: first, it is imperative that realtime guidance from FSA is forthcoming (by the way I don't think it should be charged for!) and moreover is binding—so that firms and individuals at least have the opportunity to know how far they can go in their activities; second, there should be no question that someone who has followed the code should be subjected to "prosecution" and thirdly the current process of consultation should flush out those areas which might otherwise fall foul of the code and the Government can decide whether these constitute acceptable behaviour. If they do: make a safe harbour for them, if not leave them where they fall. In any event let's have some clarity.

I think it also follows that there should be some element of intent required. I understand that the FSA are saying that they have put in a concept in the code which is tantamount to an intent (although not as strong) with the concept of Principal Purpose. I'm not a draftsman but surely we can find a way of putting at least some level of intent enshrined in the Bill.

2. A second key point is the impression which has been generated that the powers of the FSA are too oppressive.

I have a broad understanding of the kind of powers that are proposed to be afforded to FSA and would say that if these powers (or even a watered down version of them) are to be conferred then we need to ensure that the natural justice and procedural niceties are especially well enshrined. It seems to me that some of these issues go in step with each other—the wider the offences or the more draconian the action or investigative powers that can be exercised, then there is more of an imperative to have concepts such as Intent or Binding Guidance woven into the fabric of the regime. Also, for example, I think that the propensity to prosecute in relation to breach of General Principles rather than specific rules is fraught with dangers and, without proper protections, is open to abuse.

In short: if there are to be very strong powers then the protections must be commensurate with them.

I have focused on disciplinary matters because that is the theme for today, but I also think that this area illustrates the need for us to get the overall structure right. If it is too weak and open to abuse by practitioners then consumers lose out and in the end will seek alternative ways to save and spend their money. If the system is capricious or oppressive then it will drive business away from London. Whole markets can disappear in the blink of an eye. This is not just about nationalistic view of keeping London strong, it is about not fragmenting one of the most powerful financial engine rooms in the world, where everyone comes to service their financial needs.

If I were to sum up my view, I suppose I would say, the financial services industry needs to be fair and well regulated to provide protection where needed and a unified regulator is a good move; but do not underestimate the need to have transparent fairness and clarity for the participants—otherwise it might be impossible to rebuild the incredible foundation we have in London and which might be lost if businesses thought that it was more convenient to carry out their activities elsewhere.

30 March 1999

APPENDIX 52

Memorandum by Dr Oonagh McDonald CBE

ACCOUNTABILITY AND THE FSA

1. INTRODUCTION

Concern has been expressed about the breadth of the FSA's powers and its dual role as supervisory authority and the body responsible for enforcing rules and regulations governing the financial services industry. I wish to deal with these concerns from the point of view of a former Board member of the Securities and Investments Board and subsequently the Financial Services Authority, and a member of the Enforcement Committee.

Establishing a single regulatory authority does concentrate the powers of enforcement, which were previously dispersed amongst several entities, thus giving rise to the perception that they are more formidable than the powers under the old regime. That observation has to be qualified by the fact that certain enforcement powers in the field of market abuse have been added, such as the power to investigate insider dealing and market abuse and manipulation together with a civil standard of conduct of universal application. The arguments for extending the civil powers of the regulatory authorities remain as valid as they were when the SIB sought to extend its powers and received the support of the then Government and the Opposition, which now forms the present Government.

Concern has also been expressed about the accountability of the FSA. The lines of accountability have been clearly set out both in the Bill and the FSA documents. The FSA has been set objectives for the first time and will be accountable to the Treasury and to Parliament for the way in which it has achieved those objectives. The legislation also contains a set of general duties, which provide a basis for Parliamentary scrutiny.

PRACTICAL IMPLICATIONS

The first consideration is the breadth of the FSA powers and the perceived lack of accountability both to Parliament and the financial services industry. The temptation with the establishment of a large and powerful regulatory authority is to continue to add to the layers of accountability without understanding the effectiveness of the constraints already properly placed on the authority.

Obviously the Board of the FSA has the ultimate responsibility for the full range of decisions and policies of the FSA. The FSA is itself subject to judicial review on both the achievement of statutory objectives and the general duties laid down in the Bill as well as on specific decisions (e.g., enforcement decisions). Of course, one's duties as a director oblige one to act in the public interest.

That commitment is strengthened by the possibility of judicial review. My experience both as a Member of the Board of the Investors Compensation Scheme and as a member of the Securities and Investments Board, and subsequently the FSA, taught me that such a Board takes its decisions impartially on the basis of the evidence before it. The Board (and its committees) are aware that the decisions must be taken according to Wednesbury criteria of "reasonableness", and such "reasonableness", must be demonstrable.

Both the practitioner panel and the consumer panel will have a significant role to play in determining FSA policies and regulations. A strong and well-informed consumer panel can have a vital role to play in ensuring that regulation protects the investor. Although I was not a member of the consumer panel of the PIA, I chaired the *ad hoc* consumer panel which was set up to assist SIB in the preparation of the Guidance for the Pensions Review. I was a member of the Board at the time but other members of the Panel were not. The Panel had full access to all the papers on the range of issues, which had to be considered and the views of the Panel were taken into account by the Board in the final formulation of the Guidance. These are also important elements in the accountability framework of the FSA and should not be overlooked.

The Practitioner Forum will have an important role to play in ensuring accountability in terms of reporting annually on the FSA's performance and will also have privileged access to the Board and to the staff. But that is not the only form practitioner involvement should and will take. Thorough consultation both formally and informally with practitioners in the development of regulatory policy is essential. Regulations must be designed to protect the investor and the integrity of the markets; but must also be both practicable and feasible, and extensive practitioner consultation is essential to achieve this.

ENFORCEMENT

Most of the debate has focused on the FSA's enforcement procedures and, in particular, that the FSA will act as "prosecutor, judge and jury". It is important to appreciate the nature of the boundaries drawn within the FSA to ensure that full and proper procedures are in place. The structure of supervision and enforcement has been designed to ensure there is separation of function and that the principles of natural justice are preserved. These have been set out in the FSA's Consultation paper on Enforcement and subsequently. These safeguards are important; they separate the operational staff from decision-makers, leaving the enforcement staff to recommend issuing disciplinary proceedings to a separate Enforcement Committee, which makes the decision. The Chair of the Enforcement Committee, once the committee has reached its conclusions, issues the warning notices, which start the proceedings and the decision notices, which impose sanctions.

The Chair of the Committee will be a full-time position, appointed (and removable by the Board) after an open selection process. The Chair would report directly to the Board and would have support staff separate from the enforcement directorate. Practitioners and public interest directors would be involved in the decision-making process, and the subjects of disciplinary action would be able to make representations and have an oral hearing. In the light of pressures from certain quarters, it is tempting to create ever more elaborate structures with increasingly opaque Chinese walls. But there must be a balance between avoiding conflicts of interests, and demonstrating that they have been avoided and an effective means of enforcement, which will both protect the individual or company in the sense that decisions are reached in a reasonable period of time, and protecting investors, who also need to know that the problems within a firm are going to be put right within a reasonable period of time.

The FSA can draw on the considerable experience of the SROs and the SIB in enforcement action. I was a member of the SIB enforcement committee for three years. That Committee was responsible for overseeing the enforcement actions of the SROs and, on occasion, for enforcement actions against companies directly regulated by SIB; as well as for banning individuals from the industry in certain circumstances. As regards investor protection, SIB's hands were tied in that the current Act does not generally allow the regulators to name the individual, who had been banned from the industry. (If the case went to the Financial Services Tribunal and the tribunal upheld the decision to ban that individual from the industry, then the SIB could publish their report).

The Committee was chaired by a lawyer, a non-executive director of the Board. The manner of its deliberations (bearing in mind the possibility of judicial review and other legal challenges such as the failure of the case to stand up in court) are important factors to take into account, when considering whether the proposed system has adequate safeguards built into it.

The SIB committee was able to question and test our staff recommendations, modify them, insist that charges or an enforcement case in its entirety was dropped, guide policy and consider issues of costs and benefits of pursuing enforcement actions in certain cases. Open and frank discussion between staff and non-executive members of the committee were the order of the day. It was a question of weighing the evidence as a committee and coming to conclusions, which could and did lead to the rejection or modification of staff recommendations. All of these safeguards are implicit or explicit in the new legislation.

It is also important to bear in mind the purpose of enforcement actions. The overriding aim is to ensure that the company recognises its failings and to put them right. Those failures are not always some relatively minor breach of the rules, but can, for example, in the case of a direct sales force, involve far-reaching management failures, leading to a poorly trained and poorly supervised sales force engaged in selling inappropriate products to customers. It is vital both to secure the company's co-operation in developing an appropriate strategy for putting the management and training of its sales force in order, and through the fine and public reprimand, making sure that they take the obligation to carry out remedial work seriously. A formal judicial process will not achieve those aims.

Of course, the process of enforcement must conform to the requirements of Article 6 of ECHR. Those requirements are as follows:

    (i)   A fair and public hearing within a reasonable time.

    (ii) An independent and impartial tribunal established by law.

    (iii) The right to be present.

    (iv) Balanced procedures (equality of arms).

    (v)   Access to the court.

    (vi) Permitted to examine and cross-examine witnesses.

Sometimes, those who argue that the FSA's enforcement procedures do not conform to Article 6, seem to suggest that Article 6 implies that the procedures must be judicial procedures. The Article does not define a "tribunal" and the Court has itself stated:

"The Contracting States enjoy a wide discretion as regards the choice of means calculated to ensure that their legal systems are in compliance with the requirements of Article 6(1) in this field. The Court's task is not to indicate those means to the States, but to determine whether the result called for by the Convention has been achieved". (Colozza v. Italy, 1985, 7, E H H R 516). It would seem that the Court is much more concerned with the fairness of the procedures, not with the particular form that they take. The emphasis in the debate over conformity to ECHR should be on achieving the objectives of "fairness".

The Court recognises that an offence may be designated as a disciplinary offence by a contracting state. This will not necessarily be accepted by the Court. In coming to its decision, the Court will consider whether the provisions defining the so-called "disciplinary offence" belong to the legal system of the respondent state, to criminal law, disciplinary law or both. It will also consider the nature of the offence, and that will be the most important consideration. The Court will also consider the severity of the penalty, which the person concerned faces. This suggests that there is considerable scope for the enforcement actions of the FSA to be regarded as *disciplinary actions*.

The other criteria for a fair hearing are much more straightforward: "equality of arms" and a "reasonable" length of time both for the initial hearing and for any appeal. The first criterion refers to the requirement that each party has to be given a reasonable opportunity to present his case, including the presentation of evidence, in conditions, which do not place him at a substantial disadvantage. Obviously, the FSA must always take care that its procedures are designed to give the individual, or the company a proper chance to present relevant evidence.

There is, of course, one clear advantage, which the use of the FSA's proposed enforcement procedures has. One of the Court's judgments indicated that the length of time from charge to appeal is an important consideration in "fairness". Three and a half years was considered to be too long for that process to be completed under Article 6 (Zimmermann and Steiner v Switzerland, 1979). The latest average figures for judicial procedures in England and Wales are better than that. The average length of time from charge to completion in indictable cases in magistrates courts is approximately three months, and, if committed, the average waiting time in the Crown Court is about four months. The waiting time for appeals at the Court of Appeal is approximately 11 months. The defendant can, if there is reason to suspect a miscarriage of justice, take his case to the recently established Criminal Cases Review Commission but would no doubt face further delays, since the Commission currently has over 2,000 cases pending.

The Bill also establishes an independent tribunal, a tribunal of first instance to which all enforcement decisions may be referred. It will be able to consider the full merits of cases referred to it. It is important to have such safeguards, but it is also vital that the regulators and the regulated do not lose sight of the purpose of disciplinary action. Its purpose is to begin the process within the firm of putting the training and management procedures into place to ensure that investors are protected in the future.

The FSA, including its constituent bodies, has consistently sought to achieve the agreement of the firms concerned. For example, in 1997–98, 97 SAO "cases" were concluded; that is, a warning notice has been issued to a firm with some disciplinary action to follow. Of the 97 cases, 57 were settled between the regulator and the firm, 36 were decided by a disciplinary committee and four were decided by the tribunal.

The process of enforcement must, *inter alia,* be efficient and speedy if it is to be effective. The FSA supports that. It must be able to provide an efficient and cost-effective service. The public perception must be that the firm or individual has been disciplined and that the appropriate actions have been taken to prevent the recurrence of the problem. That has by no means always been the case when the procedures involved have been entirely judicial. The trail of Roger Levitt is a case in point. He was charged with 62 counts of fraud after this financial empire collapsed with debts of £34 million, but was finally convicted (which caused some controversy at the time) on a single lesser charge and sentenced to 180 hours community service in 1993. The case cost over £2 million in legal aid.

Whatever the reasons for the outcome of that particular trial, the fact remains that many in the industry feel that their honour and their attempts to provide a proper service have been impugned by the failure to punish fraud. Of course, whilst the public perception of a judgment of that kind will affect the industry, it does little or nothing to protect investors as it suggests that such activities can be undertaken with impunity.

3 March 1999

APPENDIX 53

Memorandum by Money Management Council

Response to Government proposals for regulation of services as included in the draft Financial Services and Markets Bill.

The Money Management Council is the independent financial charity which campaigns for clarity in financial matters to help alleviate the general financial ignorance.

We have responded briefly to the Joint Committee on Financial Services and Markets as follows:

Overview. The Council welcomes the statutory objects for FSA to aid public understanding. It believes this is best fulfilled by acting as a facilitator to existing consumer education bodies and initiatives wherever possible.

1. We were encouraged to see the more precise definition of accountability with the original autonomy being passed more to the Treasury and then to Parliament. The retention of the statutory immunity concurs with our thinking as this provides the strength to operate.

2. Even after explanations the worry is that the objectives are so wide that there could be a diminution of resources to tackle the major objectives.

3. We are pleased to see the withdrawal of the option to endorse individual codes and welcome the proposed improvements clarifying the roles of the tribunal and the FSA.

4. We accept the need to examine the position of other bodies, i.e., Lloyds mortgage advisors and professions currently regulated by RCBs.

5. We agree with the minor variations being proposed.

6. We await with interest the evidential code of conduct from the FSA in respect of Market abuse.

30 March 1999

APPENDIX 54

Memorandum by the National Consumer Council

Having read the transcript of the evidence given to the Joint Committee on Financial Services and Markets. I thought it would be helpful if I summarised the points we wish to make.

The consumer protection objective should be expanded to make clear that consumers are entitled to buy products of satisfactory quality. This would exclude investment performance.

We were not asked our views on the role of the Authority in promoting access to financial services, although this was contained in our response to the Treasury's consultation. As an alternative to what was suggested there, it would be possible to give firms a duty to offer reasonable access to financial services as a further part of the consumer protection principle. The FSA should then have a duty to monitor adherence to this principle.

Retail consumers need more protection than wholesale. Despite the fact that some retail consumers are more expert than others, we think the division should be made between those who buy for purposes outside their trade or profession and those whose business involves buying. This would be in line with other consumer protection legislation.

If this distinction were made it would assist with defining what consumer protection should mean. It would also help with clause 2(2)(c) (caveat emptor). Wholesale consumers can be responsible for their own decisions. Even under current regulation retail consumers are entitled to be sold products which are suitable. This is a long way from taking responsibility for their own decisions. We would like caveat emptor to go in relation to retail consumers. If it does not, then it should be qualified.

We support the proposal that improving competition should be an objective of the Authority. This is different from improving competitiveness. Although there are many competing businesses in the industry it does not seem to have the effect of forcing out products which are poor value for money. The Authority needs to have an objective to address this problem. It again could be considered part of the consumer protection objective.

Anther area we did not discuss in our oral evidence is mortgages. There are overlays between mortgages and the investment products which will be regulated by the FSA. Mortgages are often sold with investment vehicles to repay them or used to buy annuities that are used to pay the interest on the loan. We are publishing a report on the need for improved protection of consumers of equity release schemes on 8 April. It is our view that the FSA should regulate conduct of business in relation to mortgages.

30 March 1999

APPENDIX 55

Memorandum by the Securities Institute

INTRODUCTION

The Securities Institute is the major examining body for the securities and derivatives industry and provides a wide range of industry qualifications which attract over 30,000 entries each year. The Institute is also a substantial provider of training courses and of relevant publications. Unlike the regulatory bodies and trade associations, it is focused on individuals not corporations. Its prime purpose is to set and maintain professional standards and promote excellence in matters of integrity, skill and competence. With 12,000 members in 1,800 firms, the Institute's additional purposes are to promote, for the public benefit, the advancement of knowledge in the field of securities and investments and to consult and research in matters of public interest concerning investment in securities. As such, it is deeply interested in regulatory and other issues which touch on public investment in securities.

As noted above, the Securities Institute is an association of individuals. The draft Bill puts emphasis on individual responsibility and will recognise individuals who will have to be "fit and proper" to carry out their designated responsibilities. These individuals include senior executive officers and we welcome this emphasis on individual responsibility. People not companies are ultimately responsible for conducting the affairs of a firm and having clear and defined personal responsibility for the way in which it is run strengthens the commitment of individuals to run a compliant business.

This submission addresses the issues raised by the Scrutiny Committee and is presented in the order requested.

As a preamble, however, the Institute emphasises that its most important issues are the training and competence of individuals, consumer education and the recognition of specific individuals in regulated firms. In particular, we draw the Committee's attention to the dual role played by Compliance Officers and the need for this to be recognised.

FSA ACCOUNTABILITY

The Securities Institute acknowledges the additional accountability which has now been introduced into the new FSA regime since the publication of the draft Bill and we welcome the changes. The additional arrangements outlined in the Progress Report have clearly taken account of the comments made after the Bill was first published.

We note recent comments from Howard Davies and that the FSA is regarded as being subject to judicial review and welcome this clarification.

However the Securities Institute continues to recommend that the FSA should be subject to review by the National Audit Office and that this requirement should be included in the Bill. This audit should not be simply an audit of the accounts but should include the FSA's effectiveness and whether it provides value for money in regulatory terms. In making this proposal, we note that various component organisations of FSA including the Friendly Societies Commission and the Building Societies Commission are themselves currently subject to audit by the Office.

PROPOSED STATUTORY OBJECTIVES AND PRINCIPLES OF FSA

Consumer education

Consumer education and consumer protection go hand in hand. The Securities Institute therefore warmly welcomes the inclusion of consumer education in the objectives of the FSA. We firmly believe that a financially literate consumer is an essential building block for effective financial services regulation. The FSA itself can do a number of things directly including:

— providing easy to absorb information on the basics of regulated activities;

— providing general information on the suitability of particular products for different groups of savers.

Given the finite nature of its resources the FSA's priority should be to identify organisations and material which meet the needs of consumers, to sponsor approved courses, to encourage and stimulate the development of such material where gaps exist and to orchestrate the provision of information, not attempt to provide it all. FSA's direct resources should be used only to fill gaps which are not being adequately filled by others.

We believe that the FSA might consider "badging" approved products and services in the education field and encouraging companies to work with the Plain English Campaign. In this way, the regulator could stimulate a wide range of material from many suppliers, catering for individual needs and providing a wide range of choice for users. In this context, the Securities Institute stands ready to play its part in achieving this important goal.

Given the FSA's regulatory objective of promoting public awareness of financial products, the Securities Institute also suggests that the FSA should report at least annually to the Secretary of State for Education and Employment on the progress it is making so as to co-ordinate its initiatives with those of the DfEE in this area. This report to the Secretary of State should also be published as part of the FSA's Annual Report.

Recognition of Individuals

The Securities Institute supports the FSA in its proposals that principles as well as detailed rules should guide regulated firms in the conduct of their affairs. Among the principles outlined by the FSA are requirements that firms must conduct their businesses with integrity and that they must organise and control their affairs effectively.

In supporting these aims, the Securities Institute places great emphasis on individual responsibility being taken by those who run and control firms. While a firm's directors have collective responsibility for the actions of the firm, individual responsibilities should be clearly defined so that individuals know what they are and take those responsibilities seriously in the course of their work.

The purpose of the Securities Institute is to help individuals acquire the knowledge and skills to discharge those responsibilities effectively. We also emphasise the importance of integrity to our membership as something beyond mere compliance. "Is it right?" is a more powerful question than "Is it allowed by the Rule Book?".

Keeping advisers up to date

At present there is no clear requirement either in the Bill or in the FSA's proposals for advisers to demonstrate continuing professional development in terms of keeping up to date with changes in products and market practice.

Professor Jim Gower, one of the leading influences on modern financial regulatory thinking, said in his Report[1] "the investor is entitled to some protection from ignorant fools as well as from convicted crooks". We agree. As an investor what I need to know above all is: Can I be sure that this adviser has the information I need? Is that information up to date? Is it relevant to me? Are there better alternatives? Can I rely on his skill and judgment? These are questions that uninformed savers cannot judge easily for themselves but on which they need to be reassured.

The use of computer-based methods of carrying out transactions will continue to develop, bringing cheaper and more efficient dealing services for those who are confident in their own judgments and do not require advice. For many, the provision of good, customer-focused advice on financial products will become an even more critical element in delivering the right financial services to them.

The Institute also emphasises its continuing support for individual regulation. A qualification to demonstrate basic competence is an essential part of a benchmark to ensure that individuals justify being approved to engage in investment business. The draft Bill refers to the holding of a qualification or undergoing training as evidence of being "fit and proper". The Institute is pleased to note that the FSA, in *"Meeting our responsibilities"* recognises that individual qualification, in terms of knowledge and skills, as well as awareness of regulatory requirements and obligations, will form the basis of individuals being allowed to fill key roles in the industry. In our view this regime should extend to all those who advise customers on the choice of investments.

This element of the regulatory regime is of particular interest to the Securities Institute. We shall seek to work closely with the FSA in building on the existing training and competence framework. We shall play our full part, using our past experience of developing successful and widely used examinations and training, to help develop and deliver the necessary qualifications and the means of attaining them, both in attaining basic competencies and in developing professional expertise, whether in the front office or in operations. We support the FSA view that demonstration of competence is no less than consumers have a right to expect and that it will help maintain confidence in the system and provide effective protection. Knowledge and skills are necessary building blocks; an ethical approach to putting the customer's interest first is a further essential element.

The position of Compliance Officers

The Compliance Officer of a regulated firm is in the position of being recognised as the regulatory point of contact by the regulator and has to comply with requests for information from the regulator. Compliance Officers can thus face a major conflict of interest between their duty to the regulator and that to their own firm. Yet Compliance Officers have no legal standing within the regulatory framework as to their particular duties when complying with regulatory demands. The Securities Institute urges that Compliance Officers and their dual responsibility both to the regulator and to the firm be recognised in the legislation. As an example, recent Jersey law defines the duties of a Compliance Officer as being responsible for:

(a) ensuring that the registered person, i.e., the company, has robust arrangements for compliance with law, any orders made under it and the Jersey Codes (of practice);

(b) securing appropriate monitoring of operational performance and promptly instigating action to remedy any deficiencies; and

(c) being the principal point of contact on regulatory matters.

This provides a suitable framework for his duties.

An extract from the Jersey law is attached in an Annex.

Product design

The Bill sets the overall agenda for the reform of financial services regulation and basic standards and includes the duty on FSA to have regard to innovation. But competition in the market place will better serve the interests of savers and investors than regulatory control of products. FSA should concentrate on being the market regulator, not the designer of products. We support the Treasury's views, expressed in the recent Progress Report, that product design should not be a primary objective of the FSA.

DISCIPLINE, ENFORCEMENT AND THE TRIBUNAL

Enforcement and discipline

To work effectively in protecting investors, an enforcement system must command the respect of the regulated community. To do this, it must be fair, seen to be fair, transparent and consistent. A regulatory regime in which time, money and effort are spent by regulated firms fighting the regulator will ultimately harm the consumer's interests.

---

[1] Review of Investor Protection: 1982.

Differentiating retail and wholesale markets

Howard Davies in his evidence to the Committee, outlined a three-way approach:

(1) market professional to market professional;

(2) market professionals to expert investors (e.g., Corporate Treasurers);

(3) the retail market.

The intention is that elements of the regulatory burden would be disapplied in the cases of 1 and 2. However, one important area appears to be missing from this analysis: that is market professional dealing with an expert counter-party who in turn has responsibilities to the retail market, e.g., a fund manager. It remains unclear where such a transaction would fit.

We appreciate that both the legislation and the FSA seek to uphold the London market's competitive position, but definitions of different types of customer and the extent of the protection offered must be clarified as quickly as possible. Over-regulation will drive business from London.

The enforcement process

— There appears to be no right of redress if the FSA takes action which is subsequently found to be wrong.

— The impact of regulatory action should be proportionate to the concerns being addressed. Greater safeguards from punitive action for small transgressions are needed.

— Co-operation with overseas regulators should be subject to reciprocity.

— Intervention and enforcement activities should be carried out without publicity until the matter has been resolved. This is acknowledged by the FSA in its enforcement paper and the Securities Institute strongly supports this stance.

— We welcome the FSA's attempts to clarify the uncertainty surrounding criminal and civil remedies. In particular we welcome the proposal not to pursue a civil case if a criminal one fails. However, the criterion still appears to be almost exclusively whether the regulator has enough evidence for a criminal conviction rather than the seriousness of the case.

— The fining policy should be fair and consistent. FSA should carry out an annual review of the year to make sure that consistency is being followed. It is proposed to allow FSA to levy unlimited fines on a civil law standard of probabilities. This open-ended regime is potentially subject to abuse.

— The public interest and practitioner members of the Enforcement Committee should have full voting rights.

MARKET ABUSE

— We applaud the intention to introduce legislation to curb market abuse which will be more effective and flexible than its predecessors.

— The Securities Institute welcomes the introduction of a proposed Code intended to be more effective than earlier legislation in tackling abuse and in building confidence in the market process.

— We accept the points made by FSA that the level of proof in a serious civil case will be very close to the criminal measure and that no civil action will be pursued once a criminal charge has failed. However there remains no clear view on what is a civil offence and what is a criminal one.

— The proposed regime appears draconian. A course of conduct might be subject to a 7-fold jeopardy if it breached the Code of Market Conduct.

— Notwithstanding the comment in paragraph 13.5 of the Progress Report, the Securities Institute believes that the concept of "intent" should be introduced into the legislation. In general, the law deems a person to intend the consequences of an action. At the moment, however the Precepts and Code can be breached where conduct has an effect of breaching the Code even if there is no intention to do so. To introduce the concept of intent would not destroy the enforceability of the Code, but would offer a measure of protection to practitioners who seek to devise legitimate new and untested market strategies.

— We welcome Howard Davies's comment in evidence to the Scrutiny Committee that the FSA may be prepared to look at innovatory developments in advance.

— With the prospect of draconian action being taken against them and with the possibility of unlimited fines (FS Bill Clause 58), it is important that practitioners should have the assurance that they can discuss in advance proposed courses of market action with the FSA to obtain a clearance or otherwise. Alternatively, there should be a number of well defined "safe harbours" from the operation of the Rule.

March 1999

ANNEX

Extract from Jersey Financial Services Commission Investment Business (Jersey) Law 1998 Code of Practice.

COMPLIANCE

3.6   Paragraph 3.1.4 also includes the requirement for a registered person to designate an appropriately qualified individual, by experience and/or examination, as its compliance officer.

3.6.1   Duties can be delegated either internally or externally.

3.6.2   The compliance officer is responsible for:

3.6.2.1   ensuring the registered person has robust arrangements for compliance with Law, any Orders made under it and the Codes;

3.6.2.2   securing appropriate monitoring or operational performance and promptly instigating action to remedy any deficiencies; and

3.6.2.3   providing the principal point of contact on regulatory matters.

APPENDIX 56

Memorandum by the UK Social Investment Forum (UKSIF)

1.   The UK Social Investment Forum's primary purpose is to promote and encourage the development and positive impact of socially responsible investment throughout the UK. Our membership of stakeholders in ethical, green and socially directed investment includes 25 major financial institutions. UKSIF also provides the secretariat for the All-Party Parliamentary Group on Socially Responsible Investment, chaired by Tony Colman MP.

2.   We welcome the opportunity to give evidence to the Joint Committee on Financial Services and Markets. UKSIF has also submitted evidence to the Treasury Select Committee inquiry last November and responded to the Treasury's consultation document.

3.   We were however disappointed to see no mention of our concerns in the Treasury's March progress report. These concerns focus on three key areas: the lack of any mention of the regulator's role in contributing to sustainable development; the need to ensure consumers are educated about the social and environmental impact of their investments; and the need to protect the green and ethical consumer.

4.   There is a growing awareness among some financial services players that our economic future relies on our environmental future, and that the financial sector has a key role to play. The FSA as the new single regulator of the industry should in our view be involved in a debate on what is best practice in sustainable development, i.e., environmental protection, social equity and economic development, and ensure that their activities promote rather than inhibit sustainability.

5.   UKSIF believes the draft Bill should be amended to integrate a regard to sustainable development as an essential element of maintaining market confidence through the elimination of risk in financial services and the draft Bill should make this explicit.

6.   An increasing number of consumers have ethical and social concerns. Green and ethical consumers form a major group within the population. In 1996, MORI identified 41 per cent of the adult British population as green consumers. We believe that FSA's new remit for consumer education should take on board these legitimate concerns and educate people about the choices they can make about where their money goes. The existing clause 4 of the draft Bill should be amended to include a subclause to promote awareness of the range and general nature of impacts and finance on individuals, society, and the environment.

7.   The increase in ethical consumers is also evidenced by the growth in funds invested ethically which has outstripped all unit and investment trusts in every year except one since 1989. In the past two years to January 1999, the total funds managed by ethical unit and investment trusts has almost doubled from £1.1 billion to £2.1 billion according to the Ethical Investment Research Service (EIRIS).

8.   The Financial Services and Markets Bill should make explicit the protection of green and ethical consumers. We believe that the protection of consumers objective as drafted in Clause 5 is insufficient to address this aim and should be amended to include the differing degrees to which consumers wish their ethical, social and environmental concerns to be taken into account in relation to different kinds of regulated activities. Ethical, social and environmental concerns include consideration of the range and nature of impacts of investment and finance on individuals, society, and the environment.

9. We also hope the FSA will protect the consumer by issuing guidance stating that regulated persons should ask consumers whether they have any ethical, social and environmental concerns which they wish to have taken into account in the financial advice which they receive as part of the routine fact find.

March 1999

APPENDIX 57

Memorandum by Mr C M Williams

This submission focuses on the proposed accountability of the FSA in the light of its conduct to date and that of its predecessor, the SIB.

SUMMARY

1. Despite all the claims to the contrary the structure of the proposed regulatory organisations, the FSA, and therefore ultimately its actions and its accountability will be little different from those of the past. The appointment of board members and their removal, the making of rules and the annual report are similar to the present, and previous, regimes. Of particular significance is the structure as a private limited company with immunity from claims for damages. This in the past has enabled the regulators to disregard the justifiable criticisms of the private investor and in the view of many the regulators are discredited.

2. The structure for regulation with many of the staff recruited from the industry which it regulates and who expect their future career to be back in that industry is biased towards that industry.

3. The structure used by the present system and proposed for the new system makes regulation unaccountable to either the public it is supposed to protect or to government.

4. Regulation structured as proposed has been shown not to work satisfactorily in the past and there is no reason to think that it will be any different in the future.

5. This opinion and the evidence to support it comes as a result of seven years of personal experience of the workings of the regulatory bodies, initially as a private individual and latterly as a member of an action group and is therefore based on actual events and experience. This submission is made as a private individual.

6. The documentary evidence to support this opinion is in my possession but for reason explained in my letter of 17 February 1999 to the Clerk of the Treasury Committee I am unable to quote directly from the documents.

Basis for the opinion expressed above

7. The minutes of evidence of the Treasury Committee held on Tuesday 8 December 1998 contain Mr Davies' response to a question put by Mr Kidney concerning the rationale for the FSA to be structured as a private limited company. Mr Davies' reply gives credence to the view that the structure of the FSA needs a fundamental change if it is to be accountable, particularly to those it is supposed to protect. His answer at paragraph 232, final sentence was: "That is what our institutions want us to do, they want us to employ people who understand their business and go in and out, and that would be facilitated by the private company model . . . "

So the rationale for the FSA to be structured as a private limited company with immunity from actions for damages is:

(a) that this is what *our* industry wants;

(b) so that staff move more easily from the financial services industry to the FSA and back out again.

The first priority of the FSA is therefore to satisfy the financial services industry, a rather peculiar first priority for a regulator. It must be the first priority in Mr Davies' mind because it is fundamental to the structure of the FSA from which all else flows.

8. Mr Davies' comment reveals all too clearly that the regulators are and will continue to be too close to those they are supposed to regulate. The problem in the past was not the FSA86, it was the failure of the regulators to carry out their responsibilities. Once the new broom enthusiasm has died down we shall be back to the same situation as before.

9. To suggest that the private limited company format allows staff to move more easily from the financial services industry to the FSA and back out again overlooks a very important point. When a regulator has found it necessary to use the full regulatory powers on a number of firms in the financial services industry, what will be the chances of employment back in that industry?

10. There is another important feature that inevitably follows on from the structure of a private limited company.

With no outside shareholders the board of directors is only answerable to itself and, as in the past, once appointed is able to act autonomously. Accountability to any other body is difficult to enforce. This was the case in the past and the Treasury was powerless to act. I have letters from officials which prove this point. Once the Delegation Order of the Financial Services Act 1986 came into effect the Treasury was virtually powerless to control the actions of the SIB in any more than a general way. The new legislation contains little to stop this happening again.

11. The Chairman of the Treasury Committee, Mr Radice, in a recent letter to me states that the proposed legislation now takes accountability into consideration. This is not my view. The Treasury may "expect" its appointees to the FSA board to "take account of the need to pursue the objective of protecting consumers . . ." but with members of the financial services industry prominent on the board we know from experience that they have other far more pressing priorities.

12. None of the appointments to any of the boards of the regulatory bodies in the financial service industry including the FSA, come under the remit of the Commissioner for Public Appointments, though lip service is paid to the "guidance" issued by the Commissioner.

13. Consumer Panels, which have an advisory function, are claimed to give the private investor influence in the operations of the regulator. Those of us with experience of organisations know only too well that it is the board that holds and uses the power.

Bodies which only have advisory powers are very easily "fobbed off" and become nothing more than "talking shops".

14. My experience of the operation of the regulators reveals a catalogue of regulatory events which some would describe as incompetence, others that it reveals too close a relationship with those who were supposed to be regulated. What is certain is that the regulators showed a reluctance to act and when they eventually did it was too little as well as too late.

Two agreements negotiated by SIB, contained fatal flaws. There are other examples of a failure to safeguard the interests of the private investors.

When finally it came to paying compensation the "rules" were invoked to ensure that as little as possible was paid out. The iniquitous formulae used to calculate compensation was only possible with a structure which makes the regulatory body, in this case the ICS, virtually unassailable by private individuals. The FSA which now has the responsibility for the ICS "rules", refused to intervene despite numerous requests. At the meetings at which this problem was discussed, the first with the ICS and the second with both the ICS and the FSA we met with prevarication and claims that the "rules" allowed the particular stance being taken.

This, I believe, was due to the structure of the regulators as private limited companies and their close relationship with the industry.

15. It appears that the Government is relying on the FSA annual report and the Treasury Committee to monitor and control the actions of the FSA. Annual reports are notorious for being smokescreens and are often little more than vehicles for self congratulation. They are also historic, but many situations in the financial services industry require immediate action. The Treasury Committee, powerful body that it is, is unlikely to get at the grass roots level of regulation.

19 March 1999

APPENDIX 58

Memorandum by Wise Speke

I write on behalf of a number of Northern stockbrokers who are very concerned about the speed with which your Committee has been charged to consider the various issues connected with the content of what is a very complex Bill. Bearing in mind the time it has taken since the announcement of the Government's views and the production of the Bill, it would seem unrealistic to expect your Committee to consider and determine the various issues raised within the proposed time scale. Whilst it is perfectly understandable that the markets would like to have the certainty of knowing what the position is likely to be, nevertheless the solution needs careful thought, and in our view it would be quite inappropriate to rush such important matters through to legislation because of time pressures.

The FSA proposed eight principles which it plans to impose on authorised firms—these place responsibilities on firms to co-operate with their regulator and to treat clients in a fair manner. We suggest that the FSA should also be bound to observe the same general principles which would describe its responsibilities *vis-a-vis* the authorised community. This is an opportunity to create a "Financial Services Industry Charter", applicable to all who work in this area including the Regulator.

We continue to feel that the FSA should not have the absolute power enabling it to investigate, make judgments, and impose fines without more accountability. Constraints might take the form of publishing the evidence upon which they make a decision to ensure that the rights of defenders and lawyers are safeguarded and that their actions are not in conflict with the European Convention on Human Rights. We feel also that there should be an internal review panel within the FSA, made up of market practitioners, to consider appeals against any FSA decision before an Independent Appeal Tribunal becomes involved, because many of the smaller firms could not face the costs of a full Independent Appeal Tribunal should they find themselves in such a position. The overriding principle should be that any firm facing disciplinary action should be presumed innocent until found guilty.

On the subject of consumer compensation there is a proposal only to have "one" Investors Compensation Scheme. We feel that this is particularly unfair as the Broking Community would be lumped into one of the three proposed sub divisions, namely the rump of the Securities Industry. this would include the PIA members, and it is worth pointing out that IMRO and SFA firms by the end of the year 1996–97 have paid out only 1/10th of the compensation which was paid out to customers of PIA regulated firms.

We are further concerned about the Ombudsman Scheme whereby a decision would be binding on the defendant, but if the complainant is not satisfied then they would have the ability to go to court for redress, which would be unacceptable if the claimant were an authorised firm. In the event of both parties being authorised persons, then either both parties should be able to take it to court or neither party, except on a point of law or fact.

We feel as a group very unhappy that the cost of establishing and operating the FSA is already significant and is likely to rise. We believe that the FSA needs to be required to consider the costs arising from its activities and that it should be required to undertake a detailed cost benefit analysis in relation to all policy and rule proposals. Clearly there must be some mechanism to make the FSA accountable to the authorised community and to Parliament, and we suggest that it should be the responsibility of either the FSA non executive directors or the Treasury to ensure that the FSA is accountable.

Many small firms are particularly concerned about the proposal to require firms to "detect and deter" money laundering, as currently they do not have the staff or the skills to undertake this "detection". This is a completely new development, and quite unfair to place this criminal investigation responsibility on individual firms. Clearly we all want to deter money laundering but cannot accept the responsibility or costs for "detection".

We have noted the four regulatory objectives of the FSA, but bearing in mind the proposed London Stock Exchange Alliance with Frankfurt, we believe that the FSA must have responsibility for representing the interests of the UK Financial Services Industry in both the EU and Non EU countries on a pro-active basis and that this should be incorporated in the Act.

I suppose the overriding concern is that the accountability of the FSA needs to be set out quite clearly in view of the extremely wide powers that are going to be given to it.

I shall be most grateful if you should consider our concerns and relay the strength of them to your Joint Committee.

8 March 1999

APPENDIX 59

Memorandum by World Wide Fund for Nature (WWF)

I am writing to highlight a number of concerns in relation to the above draft bill. I hope that, as Chair of the Joint Scrutiny Committee considering this proposed legislation, you will consider these concerns in your deliberations.

WWF (World Wide Fund for Nature) is the world's largest and most effective conservation organisation. We believe that the draft bill in its current form is a missed opportunity.

Financial services have a highly significant impact on the environment. Five hundred of the world's largest businesses currently control 25 per cent of the planet's output in terms of GDP. Among the world's top 100 economies in 1995–96, no fewer than 51 were businesses and 49 were countries. These businesses are at the core of global environmental concerns, yet they could be a force for positive change rather than destructive practice.

WWF believes that socially responsible investment has enormous potential to conserve endangered species and habitats, and to change the way business and industry operate. It is highly disappointing, therefore, that the draft bill fails to make any reference to the way in which regulation of financial services and markets could help to promote sustainable development, as highlighted by the Rio Earth Summit in 1992.

There are a number of ways in which WWF believes the draft bill could be amended to do this as follows:

— *It should include an explicit requirement to ensure that the financial system promotes and enhances sustainable development.*

— *It should include provision to enhance public understanding of the impacts of their investment on individuals, society and the natural environment*—impacts such as climate change, acidification and deforestation. The draft bill already has a focus on "public awareness and the protection of consumers" which WWF welcomes, given the increasing number of consumers who have ethical, social and environmental concerns. However, this could be strengthened to "incorporate the right for consumers to know that their investments may conflict with their principles."

— *It should include provision to protect green and ethical consumers.* Protection of consumers is already referred to in the draft bill (see above) but it does not reflect the differing degrees to which consumers wish their social, ethical and environmental concerns to be taken into account. While surveys show that many people would wish to invest ethically, few have heard of the option. WWF believes that consumers have a right to know this option exists and that the Financial Services Authority should issue guidance to Independent Financial Advisers to ask consumers about their concerns on these issues.

12 March 1999

APPENDIX 60

Note by Lord Hobhouse of Woodborough

Thank you for inviting me to give evidence to the Joint Committee on Thursday. Towards the end of the hearing, Lord Lester and I were referred to a document, "FSM 91",[1] which we had not seen before. You invited further comments based upon the parts of the document relevant to the evidence which had been given. You also stressed that the Committee was concerned to try and achieve an acceptable draft, an objective which I would share.

I agree that FSM 91 is most certainly relevant. Section A addresses points raised during my evidence.

To recapitulate, the present (and only existing) draft of Part VI proposes to punish (by way of fines) "behaviour" which the FSA considers may affect confidence in the relevant markets. Such a scheme for punishment brings into play a number of principles (as well as Human Rights points) to which the drafting of the legislation must, on that hypothesis, have regard. The existing draft does not do this.

The previous Progress Report of March 1999 had recognised the need for an independent and fair adjudication procedure and therefore accepted one of the fundamental objections to the existing draft. However a significant number of other points of varying importance remained, some very important. My remarks concerning cl.56 were directed to some of these.

An important point which still has to be faced is the ambit of cl.56. Three questions can be asked: Who does it apply to? What conduct does it punish? Will it punish innocent conduct?

The first of these questions is fundamental. The present draft applies to anyone, wherever they may be and whether or not they actually participate in the relevant market. The conduct merely has to be behaviour *in relation to* a relevant investment and that includes, for example, any commodity which may be the subject of permitted trades on a futures or derivatives market. The intention of the FSA and the Minister is, apparently, that cl.56 should apply to "market participants", those who "take advantage" of the market (FSM 91 §2), "market participants", "individual player of the market place" (Evidence 18 March pages 33–34). The present language does not reflect this intention. It is far wider; its effect will be indiscriminate and arbitrary. The draft code does not (and is not appropriate to) remedy this deficiency in the drafting of c.56. The redrafting exercise will not be too difficult once the actual intended ambit has been thought through. Paragraph 2 of FSM 91 ("*Rationale*") still does not understand the discrepancy and is an inadequate response.

The second question is related to the first. Cl.56(1)(b) presently applies to conduct which may be wholly independent of any market transaction to which the relevant person is a party; for example, he may simply have market sensitive information which he does not make public; he may as a producer or consumer simply be resisting pressure being put on him by speculators. A definition is needed which ties the conduct liable to be held abusive into some market (or market directed) activity of the relevant person. Here again the necessary redrafting exercise is not too difficult; drafting techniques exist which can be used to provide the necessary focus to the subclause and enable it to fulfil its purpose of providing a workable definition (and set the limits of the FSA's code making power).

This in turn leads on to the third question—culpability. The Minister unequivocally rejected any concept of culpability in her evidence (18 March pages 33–34). FSM 91, paragraph 8, however, recognises the difficulties inherent in that view and states the intention not to punish conduct on a no fault basis. It will be appreciated that, if the application of cl. 56 is tightened up so as to require some actual direct or indirect participation in the market and the definitions of punishable conduct are redrafted using words like "designed to" or "calculated to", the definition of the mental element will be much easier to formulate. It might even suffice to have a subclause stating that a person's conduct shall not amount to market abuse if it was bona fide and without any intent to undermine confidence in the relevant market.

---

[1] Appendix 5.

Paragraphs 4 and 5 of FSM 91 include statements which should prove useful in evolving an acceptable and effective draft. It is recognised that compliance with the code can mean that conduct is not abusive and it is also recognised that the code making power is in effect a rule-making power and that therefore the power must be properly defined, including a clear definition of "market abuse".

Thus, my response to your question is that FSM 91 represents useful and encouraging progress. But much more needs still to be done to recast and redraft Part VI. Time is very short. There is still not even the beginnings of a satisfactory draft. I hope that my contribution has increased the chances of workable and effective outcome: ineffective or unworkable provisions will benefit no one except those who wish to get away with improperly manipulating the markets.

19 April 1999

APPENDIX 61

Second Supplementary Memorandum by the Financial Services Authority

1. This Memorandum deals with a number of topics which have arisen in recent evidence where the FSA believes it may be helpful for the Committee to have further views and background information. The note covers the following topics:

— the application of Articles 6 and 7 to certain aspects of the FSA's work (paragraphs 2–11);

— defining "private persons" for purposes of suing for damages (paragraph 12));

— double jeopardy (paragraph 13);

— investigation of complaints against the FSA (paragraph 14);

— the FSA's feedback statements following consultation (paragraph 15).

A. *Application of Articles 6 and 7 of the European Convention on Human Rights (ECHR) to the proposed market abuse regime and to FSA's regulatory enforcement activity.*

2. The FSA is concerned that the provisions of the Bill should be compatible with the requirements of the ECHR. We agree with those witnesses who have said that the credibility of the new regulatory regime would be seriously damaged by early litigation successfully challenging the compatibility of the legislation with the ECHR.

3. There are two main outstanding issues in the context of the draft Financial Services and Markets Bill. First, whether the power to impose financial penalties for market abuse, and/or for breach of the FSA's rules amounts to a "criminal" sanction for the purposes of Article 6 ECHR. Second, if so, whether the definition of "market abuse" (together with the proposed Code of Market Conduct) or the proposed FSA Principles are sufficiently certain in their application to comply with the requirements of Article 7 ECHR (the rule against retrospective punishment).

4. In drafting the Bill, the task of ensuring ECHR compatibility falls to the Government. This section draws the attention of the Committee to certain additional points which they may find helpful in preparing their report.

Civil fines for market abuse, disciplinary fines and Article 6 ECHR

5. The question here is whether the legislation should incorporate the protections that Article 6 affords to "criminal proceedings" in relation to the FSA's power to impose fines or financial penalties under the proposed market abuse regime and/or under the proposed disciplinary regime for authorised firms and approved persons. The Treasury has indicated that it is considering the position carefully in the light of the responses to the consultation on the draft Bill.

6. While there are clearly arguments that the proposed fining powers would be criminal sanctions for ECHR purposes, it should not be assumed that any sanction which has a punitive or deterrent effect is treated as a criminal sanction for the purposes of Article 6. In *Air Canada v United Kingdom* (1995) 20 EHRR 150, for example, the European Court of Human Rights considered the imposition by HM Customs & Excise on Air Canada of a requirement to pay £50,000. The payment was required in order to secure the release of an airliner which had (unknown to Air Canada) been used for the importation of illegal drugs and them seized by Customs & Excise. Although in that case the Government appeared to accept that part of the purpose of the £50,000 charge was to punish/deter laxness in Air Canada's security arrangements, the Court of Human Rights held that the sanction was not a "criminal" one for the purposes of Article 6. The Commission has described the requirement to pay £50,000 as "a normal incident of the exercise of regulatory powers which generally accompany international air traffic". Similarly, in *Ravensborg v Sweden* (18 EHRR 38) a fine for contempt of court, convertible into a term of imprisonment in the event of non-payment, was held not to involve a "criminal charge". In *Pierre-Bloch* (21 October 1997) the Court considered a sanction which was clearly punitive in its effect—an election candidate was required to pay to the French Treasury an amount equal to that by which he

had exceeded statutory limits on election expenditure. Although the candidate could also have been prosecuted in the ordinary criminal courts for precisely the same conduct, the court held the administrative sanction was not criminal. This was partly on the grounds that it was "in the nature of a payment to the community of the sum of which the candidate in question improperly took advantage to seek the votes of his fellow citizens and . . . forms part of the measures designed to ensure the proper conduct of parliamentary elections and, in particular, equality of candidates".

7.   We do not suggest that these cases are conclusive of the issues that arise in relation to the draft Bill. They do, however, demonstrate that determining whether proceedings involve a "criminal charge" for ECHR purposes is not straightforward. It requires an examination of a wide range of different factors. These include whether the "offence" in question applies to a limited class (as is the case in relation to the proposed FSA disciplinary regime) or to the population as a whole (see *Ravensborg*). There are a number of cases in which the Strasbourg authorities have held that sanctions which are imposed for the purpose of dealing with the misconduct of a regulated profession are nevertheless to be treated as disciplinary rather than criminal sanctions for the purposes of Article 6. (See, for example, the Commission's decision in *Le Compte v Belgium*, where the imposition of a suspension from the right to practise medicine following disciplinary offences was not considered "criminal").

8.   There is, moreover, clear authority to suggest that the withdrawal of a firm's authorisation would not involve the determination of a criminal charge for Article 6 purposes (see, for example, *The Traktorer Aktlebolag v Sweden* A 159 (1989)—revocation of liquor licence is not "criminal"). In the context of the regulated community in particular, it would seem odd if the less serious sanction of a financial penalty were considered "criminal", while the more serious sanction of withdrawal of a firm's authorisation were not.

Article 7 ECHR

9.   If such sanctions were to constitute "criminal" measures for ECHR purposes, then the principle of legal certainty that is implicit in Article 7 would apply.

10.   Striking the correct balance between certainty and flexibility in the provisions of the legislation, the Code of Market Conduct and the FSA's rules is of vital importance—regardless of the strict requirements of Article 7.

11.   The Strasbourg authorities have made clear that, while the rule against retrospective criminal penalties does incorporate the principle of legal certainty, it is acceptable for broad provisions to be left to the courts to interpret on a case by case basis. Thus, in the case of *Handyside v United Kingdom* the statutory obscenity test in the Obscene Publications Act (i.e., publications whose effect is such as to "tend to deprave and corrupt" persons who are likely to read them) was upheld as being sufficiently certain for ECHR purposes. In that case, the Commission made clear that "the requirements of certainty in law cannot mean that the concrete facts giving rise to criminal liability should be set out in the statute concerned. This is satisfied where it is possible to determine from the relevant statutory provision what act or omission is subject to criminal liability, even if such determination derives from the courts' interpretation of the provision concerned".

B.   *Defining "private persons" for purposes of suing for damages*

12.   We are aware that concern has been expressed about the provision in the draft Bill which would allow FSA to determine who is to be taken to be a "private person" who may sue for damages for breach of an FSA rule. We think that this is a helpful provision, in that it would allow us to ensure, in the interests of firms and consumers, that the same definition of private person is used to determine both who is a private person protected by particular rules, and who is a private person able to sue for breach of those (or other applicable) rules. This is a useful contribution to our ability to distinguish between the different levels of protection appropriate for different categories of consumer.

C.   *Double jeopardy*

13.   The Committee invited the FSA to let it have its views on the subject of double jeopardy. We have seen HM Treasury's note to the Committee[1] on this subject and have nothing to add.

D.   *Investigation of complaints against the FSA*

14.   Some witnesses have suggested to the Committee that the proposal for the FSA to be protected from liability in damages should be counter-balanced by a strengthening of the Bill's provisions relating to the independent investigation of complaints against the FSA. One particular suggestion is that the independent investigator should have power to recommend or award compensation against the FSA. As we indicated at the Committee's hearings, we recognise that the organisation and resources of the Complaints Commissioner will need to be commensurate with the demands placed upon him. But we are concerned that if the compensation suggestion were adopted, this could lead to the same kinds of difficulties as liability in damages before the Court. In any case where a major institution needed to be closed, for example, there would be complaints from

---

[1] Appendix 62.

consumers who lost out as a result, as well as from commercial counterparties and others affected. This could arise however modest the basis for complaint against the FSA, simply because the Commissioner would provide a cost-free means to recover loss. We are concerned that this would be likely to reduce our readiness to take difficult decisions. We believe that the statutory compensation scheme provides the proper safety net for consumers in such circumstances and that commercial counterparties should be encouraged to make their own judgments about those with whom they deal rather than relying on the regulator. Similarly, we think that the right mechanism for a firm to challenge a Decision to close it down would be the independent tribunal, or an application for judicial review of our decision by the courts. The scope for award of damages in such circumstances could, again, impact adversely on the FSA's decision-taking.

E. *The FSA's feedback statements following consultation*

15.   In evidence to the Committee on 13 April, the Chief Executive of APCIMS said that the FSA had published 21 consultative papers so far but only one feedback statement. Details of all the FSA's consultative papers and subsequent feedback/policy statements are set out in Annex 1 to this Memorandum. In summary, the position is:

— In July 1998 in its "Open Approach to Regulation" the FSA set out its approach to consultation. An extract is attached (Annex 2).

— Of the 21 consultative papers published since October 1997, the FSA has issued feedback or policy statements in relation to seven; in relation to a further five, FSA's decided policy has been published or communicated in some other way; and in relation to the remaining nine, feedback or policy statements are already in production or are promised;

— in line with our commitment in "The Open Approach to Regulation", we make available for inspection all non-confidential responses to consultation papers.

23 April 1999

ANNEX 1

FSA consultation and feedback/policy statements consultative papers 1–21

Consultation Paper No.	Topic	Date and Nature of Feedback/Policy Statement
CP1	Consumer involvement	Feedback and Policy Statement: "The Open Approach to Regulation" July 1998
CP2	Practitoner involvement	Feedback and Policy Statement: "The Open Approach to Regulation" July 1998
CP3	Paying for banking supervison	Responses taken into account in CP6—FSA's consultation on fees for 1998–99
CP4	Consumer complaints	Policy Statement issued March 1998
CP5	Consumer compensation	Feedback to be included in a feedback statement by end of Q2 1999
CP6	Fees 1998–99	Fees made and published March 1998, following consideration of responses
CP7	Pensions transfers and opt-outs review (phase 2)	Statements of policy and feedback statements in August 1998 and January 1999
CP8	Designing the FSA handbook of rules and guidance	Feedback Statement October 1998
CP9	The regulation of Individual Saving s Accounts	Policy Statement October 1998
CP10	Market abuse	Feedback Statement March 1999
CP11	Limited issue and limited redemption funds	Policy Statement to be issued in due course
CP12	The implementation of the Investors Compensation Directive (ICD)	Revised rules implementing ICD issued September 1998
CP13	The FSA Principles for businesses	Feedback Statement due in the second quarter 1999
CP14	Collective Investment Schemes: Single Pricing and other amendments to the regulations	Letter issued January 1999 to relevant firms and associations
CP15	Promoting Public Understanding of Financial Services: A strategy for consumer education	Action plan/policy statement due Q2 1999
C16	The future regulation of Lloyd's	Feedback Statement due second quarter 1999
CP17	Financial services regulation: Enforcing the new regime	Feedback Statement due second quarter 1999
CP18	Fees for 1999–2000	Small number of responses received. FSA's Finance Director responded personally to all
CP19	Simplification of the pension review loss assessment calculations for transfers	Policy Statement due Q2 1999; feedback statement due Q3 1999
CP20	Qualifying conditions for authorisation	Feedback Statement due Q3 1999
CP21	Pension transfers and opt outs review Phase 2: optional compliance test for transfer cases	Policy Statement due Q2 1999; feedback statement due Q3 1999

ANNEX 2

EXTRACT FROM "THE OPEN APPROACH TO REGULATION", JULY 1998

THE FSA's APPROACH TO CONSULTATION

1. The FSA is committed to carrying out its responsibilities in an open, transparent and accountable way. This statement describes the approach which we will take to consulting on our policies and plans. We will keep this approach under review, in line with evolving good consultation practice.

2. The FSA expects the forthcoming legislation to require it to consult publicly on proposals to exercise certain of its formal powers (unless the need for urgency does not allow sufficient time) and to carry out, and publish, cost-benefit analysis of regulatory proposals. We will therefore consult on material changes in regulatory requirements, policy or procedure and on our annual plan, budget and fees. Where proposed changes arise from a requirement to comply with EC Directives, we will make this clear.

3. We will consult in a range of ways in order to:
— obtain information and views to help the FSA take well-informed decisions, bearing in mind in particular the costs, benefits, and practical implications of proposed changes to regulatory requirements;
— receive alternative suggestions for achieving particular regulatory objectives;
— promote understanding of the FSA's overall objectives and the reasons for the policies and procedures it adopts;
— obtain feedback on the FSA's existing policies, practices and performance.

4. Consultation will be public and will target the full range of interested parties, including:
— consumers, and their representative bodies;
— individuals, firms or groups with relevant expertise;
— trade associations;
— advisory groups established by the FSA;
— voluntary organisations;
— academics and professional training bodies;
— the media.

5. The FSA will consult according to a number of general principles. It will seek to:
— have informal discussions at an early stage with those likely to be directly affected;
— consult at an early enough stage to enable it to take the responses into account;
— produce reasoned consultative proposals, expressed in plain concise language appropriate for the audience;
— include in consultation papers, and invite views on, preliminary cost-benefit information commensurate with the significance of the proposals in question;
— allow those consulted adequate time to respond;
— provide opportunities, where appropriate, for views and comments to be obtained in structured open hearing-type meetings;
— make all responses to formal consultation available for public inspection, unless the respondent requests otherwise;
— following public consultation on major policy issues, publish a reasoned explanation of our decisions.

6. In the interests of efficiency and avoiding undue burdens on those whom it consults, the FSA's general approach to establishing advisory groups will be:
— to establish such groups only where there is a specific need for advice on a particular topic or area;
— in identifying members with appropriate expertise, to draw on suggestions from a wide range of sources, including trade associations, consumer bodies, interest groups, and by providing opportunities for self-nomination and recommendation by individuals and firms;
— to maintain a group only so long as is necessary for the task.

APPENDIX 62

Note by HM Treasury on double jeopardy

The Committee has asked for a note on the issue of double jeopardy, and on two issues in particular

The phrase "double jeopardy" is used to express concern that people should not be tried or punished twice for the same offence. In practice, it is sometimes used loosely, and there is no general legal principle that the same conduct may never result both in criminal action and in civil or regulatory action. For example, if a doctor is tried for manslaughter as a result of his recklessness in treating a patient, this does not prevent action by the General Medical Council to remove him from practice, or civil action by the patient's family. What double jeopardy means is that the courts will sometimes stay one set of proceedings in order to allow another to be resolved first, particularly where the person concerned could not otherwise fairly prepare their defence. It also suggests that enforcement authorities should organise themselves efficiently to avoid imposing unnecessary burdens on those affected by their actions. The creation of a single regulator significantly reduces the exposure of firms to multiple jeopardy from the different constituent organisations of the FSA. The Bill also contains express provision allowing the FSA to limit the scope of concurrent investigations by exchanges or clearing houses, which would also have the effect of reducing exposure to double jeopardy in the loose sense.

I. *The basis on which decisions are taken as to whether cases should be civil or criminal and the factors that are taken into account in making this decision*

In cases where the evidence available might support either a civil case or a criminal prosecution, the FSA would initially consider whether criminal proceedings were appropriate. In doing this, it will apply the principles of the Crown Prosecution Service's Code for Crown Prosecutors. This will require the FSA to consider:

> Firstly, whether there is sufficient evidence to provide a realistic prospect of conviction against each defendant on each criminal charge. (Which will mean, in practice, that the FSA must be satisfied that the evidence is such that a jury, properly directed in accordance with the law, is more likely than not to convict the defendant of the charge alleged.)

> Secondly, assuming the above test has been satisfied, the FSA must consider whether, having regard to the seriousness of the offence, and all the circumstances, criminal prosecution is in the public interest.

If, in the light of these criteria, the FSA decides that it is not appropriate to prosecute, or to refer possible offences to another prosecuting authority—see below—it would consider the possibility of using its civil enforcement powers.

The FSA has proposed—in its consultation paper CP17 "Financial services regulation: Enforcing the new regime"—to adopt a general policy that cases may be subject to either criminal prosecution or a civil fine, but not to both. However, it may nevertheless be appropriate to pursue other forms of civil or regulatory action in parallel with criminal proceedings. Examples might include an injunction to prevent a continuation of the behaviour concerned, or an order for restitution for the victims. In such circumstances, in deciding whether to take action, the FSA would have regard to the relationship between the civil and criminal proceedings. It would consider, in particular:

> Whether taking civil action might unfairly prejudice the criminal prosecution.

> Whether taking civil action might unfairly prejudice the defendants in the criminal proceedings.

> Whether it is appropriate to take civil action, having regard to the scope of the criminal proceedings and the powers available to criminal courts.

The FSA, in consultation with other prosecuting agencies, is now working on guidelines on dealing with cases which might be taken down either the criminal or civil route. If guidelines cannot be agreed, then there is a reserve power, in clause 65 of the Bill, for the Treasury, with the consent of the Attorney General and the Secretary of State, to issue guidance.

II. *How the overlap between bodies such as the FSA, SFO and the OFT will be avoided*

The FSA, together with other investigative and prosecuting authorities, e.g., the police, the CPS, the SFO, is currently working on draft guidelines covering the investigation of cases which might be of interest to two or more agencies. The intention behind the guidelines is to ensure close liaison and co-operation between these agencies, and avoid any unnecessary duplication of effort. When a case arises which appears to merit further investigation, this should allow for an early decision, in the light of the facts of the case, as to which agency is best placed to take the lead.

Decisions on who should prosecute will, likewise, depend upon the facts of particular cases. If the FSA has taken the lead in investigation of the conduct concerned, then once it is satisfied that a prosecution is appropriate, it will liaise with other criminal prosecution authorities who have an interest and agree with them which would be the most appropriate body to pursue the prosecution. Similarly, if another agency believes that it has evidence to justify a prosecution for an offence which the FSA also has powers to prosecute, it will consult with the FSA to decide who should take the matter forward.

APPENDIX 63

Supplementary Memorandum by the Association of British Insurers

ACCOUNTABILITY TO THE REGULATED COMMUNITY

1. INTRODUCTION

1.1   The Association, jointly with the British Bankers' Association, has already made a written submission to the Committee. We recognise that improvements to the Bill have been made in response to earlier consultation, but, for the reasons given in the answers to questions below, we do not yet consider that all our concerns on accountability have been fully met. Parliament is delegating a unique set of powers to lay rules which will have the force of law and to enforce the regulatory regime. There needs to be a proper balance in the accountability of FSA for the exercise of these powers.

2. ANSWERS TO SPECIFIC QUESTIONS

2.1   *The Government has made several proposals for enhancing the accountability of the FSA. Are you now happy with the FSA's proposed level of accountability?*

We recognise that changes have been proposed to the Bill in response to concerns expressed during the earlier consultation. Treasury, in its Progress Report considered questions of accountability under three main headings; accountability to Ministers and Parliament; ensuring the regulator takes account of the views of practitioners and consumers and discipline and enforcement.

The regulated community will look to the Government and Parliament to ensure that the FSA is operating in an open and fair manner. We set out below ways in which the accountability of FSA under the first two headings could be addressed. In particular:

— As well as consulting on proposed rule changes and publishing a statement of alterations we consider that where the FSA rejects positions widely argued by practitioners and/or consumers it should be obliged to make clear in full why it has done so.

— The Bill already provides that the FSA should give Treasury copies of any rules or standing guidance that it makes. In addition, Treasury should have the right to state whether or not they agree that any changes or additions are in line with the FSA's statutory objectives. In doing this, they would clearly take into account any statements made by the FSA on the results of its consultation.

— We further consider that there needs to be a government power of direction on specific policy issues. As a last resort, this could be used by Treasury in instances where they consider that rule or policy changes are not in line with the FSA's statutory objectives.

— We welcome the proposal that the FSA will be required to provide an annual report to Parliament through Treasury Ministers and that the content of the report will be agreed between Treasury and FSA. The report should be debated by Parliament or by a Committee.

— Changes to the fees are to be treated as rule changes. However, this may mean that only the mechanism by which these are set and not the actual level will be subject to consultation. Consultation on the actual level of fees would be desirable. To date, this has not existed in the setting of insurance fees but in the initial years of FSA it may be more important in order to ensure that FSA takes account of the costs of its proposals.

— The joint BBA/ABI submission to the Committee suggested that there should be an additional statutory objective, in addition to the general duty set out in Clause 2(3)(e)(f) requiring the FSA to have regard to the impact on the competitive position of the industry of any proposed rule changes. This may become more important if the requirements for FSA to report on the impact of its proposals on its statutory objectives are strengthened.

2.2   *Do you think making the establishment of the Enforcement Committee a statutory requirement would improve accountability?*

We see no reason why the establishment of the Enforcement Committee should not be a statutory requirement. However, we consider that the role played by the Enforcement Committee in the enforcement process is more important than whether or not its existence is enshrined in statute. The Enforcement Committee should be in a position to make robust and well informed decisions.

We consider that, as a point of principle, enforcement decisions should be made at the lowest competent level possible within FSA. We are concerned that the procedure currently set out will not result in a hearing by the Enforcement Committee of the case presented which is perceived to be impartial and may thus result in more cases than necessary being referred to the Tribunal.

This is because the Warning Notice (the notice to the regulated entity that FSA considers there may be a case for disciplinary action) will be issued after the Enforcement Committee has reached a view on whether there is a case to answer. The person under review has no opportunity to put his case before that decision is reached. We would suggest that the Warning Notice should give notice that an alleged breach is to be referred to the Enforcement Committee. The Enforcement Committee would then consider the case presented both by the regulated entity and by FSA before issuing a "Decision Notice", rather than satisfying itself that a possible breach has occurred on the basis of evidence presented by the operational divisions only.

2.3 *The Bill requires only that the FSA should have a Chairman. What do you see as the advantages and disadvantages of combining this role with that of Chief Executive? Do you think it will enhance the FSA's accountability?*

The Hampel Committee devised principles of good governance. Among these are that there are two key tasks at the top of every public company—the running of the Board and the executive responsibility for the running of the company's business. There should be a clear division of responsibilities at the head of the company which will ensure a balance of power and authority, such that no one individual has unfettered powers of decision. This predicates against the combination of the role of Chairman and Chief Executive.

We recognise that there is not an exact parallel between the FSA and public company models but consider that FSA should be able to justify the structure adopted. We welcome the suggestion that other models may be examined in future.

2.4 *It has been suggested that appointments to the FSA Board should be subject to confirmation by Parliament? What is your view?*

We do not consider it essential that all appointments to the Board should be subject to confirmation by Parliament.

2.5 *It has also been suggested that some seats on the Board should be reserved for dedicated consumer experts. What do you think of that suggestion? Do you agree with the Government's view that the Board will be most effective if appointments are made on the basis of people's experience and qualities as individuals?*

We consider that appointments should be made on the basis of experience and qualities as individuals and also that consideration should also be given to the balance of backgrounds, views and experience on the Board as a whole.

2.6 *What do you see as the main role of the Consumer/Practitioner Panels? Should there be an explicit requirement on the FSA to consult the Panels when making rules and broad policy statements?*

The Consumer and Practitioner Panels will have the role of providing independent input from the consumer and practitioner point of view, and in assessing FSA's performance against its statutory objectives.

We consider that the FSA should consult the Panels when making rules and broad policy statements. However, we do not consider that the FSA's obligation to consult is met by consulting with the Consumer and Practitioner Panels alone. They are not substitutes for effective consultation with the areas of industry particularly affected by proposals and with their trade associations. The FSA should be able to demonstrate that it has specifically sought the views of market sectors affected by proposals as part of its consultation process.

2.7 *Should the Bill require the Treasury to maintain an appropriate balance between consumer and practitioner representatives? If so, what would you regard as an appropriate balance?*

Given that the Consumer and Practioner Panels are intended to be composed of consumers or practioners, we assume that this question relates to the Board as a whole. Our views are set out above.

2.8 *The Chairman of the Panels are appointed by the FSA. What do you see as the advantages and disadvantages of this? Do you think it would be more appropriate for the Chairman to be appointed by some other body, for example the Treasury, or the non-executive committee, or for the FSA's nominations to require the approval of the Treasury?*

We consider that a mechanism should exist whereby there can be independent review of appointments made. Thus, if appointments are made by FSA, they should be subject to approval by Treasury.

2.9 *The budget for the Consumer Panel has been set by the FSA at £420,000. The FSA has committed itself to an early review of the budget. Are you concerned that the budget will prove inadequate? Are you content with the way in which the budgets of the Panels are set?*

We have no strong views on this issue. We note that the FSA needs to be adequately resourced to do the work it has to do, but at the same time should have due regard to considerations of economy and efficiency. Review of the budget will doubtless be necessary in the light of experience.

2.10 *How do you consider the independence of the Panels can be best safeguarded?*

Mechanisms such as rotation of membership, independence of chairmen and scrutiny of the functions of the Panels, possibly via the FSA annual report, are important.

2.11 *Howard Davies said that the Practitioners Panel in particular was likely to launch quickly some surveys of industry opinion which would provide a sort of benchmark about regulatory sensitivity and regulatory intensity against which they could measure the FSA in the future. Will the Panels be carrying out any such surveys and, if so, when will the first survey be held?*

We welcome Howard Davies' proposal. The timing and running of such surveys is in the hands of the FSA.

2.12 *How do you regard the role of the non-executive committee? Are there any other responsibilities which you would like the committee to fulfil?*

The role of the Non-Executive Committee is set out as being to keep a watch on value for money aspects of FSA's performance. The Committee will also be required to determine the remuneration of the Chairman and executive members of the Board and will be required to report within FSA's annual report. The Chairman of the Board is to be appointed by Treasury.

We do not at the moment see any further role for this committee, but we recognise that it should have an important role in monitoring the cost effectiveness of FSA's operation.

2.13 *Some concern has been expressed at the proposal that income from fines should be returned to the industry as a discount against fees. Do you share this concern? What do you think should happen to the income from fines?*

The key point is that there should be transparency in the use of the income from fines. The income from fines should not be used to offset current years running costs, as we fear that could prejudice the independence of the fine setting process.

2.14 *What type of arrangements for independent investigation of complaints made against the FSA do you think would be most effective?*

We consider it crucial that there should be a robust independent investigation of complaints, particularly given that the Bill proposes that the FSA should have statutory immunity. The independent complaints body should have the power to publish findings, and to order redress, and we look forward to commenting on the FSA's detailed proposals.

Our submission on the Financial Services and Markets Bill recognised that the FSA will need to be robust in its decision making but that there are natural concerns in authorised firms that its immunity is too wide and that appeal procedures are expensive and time consuming and too late in the process to reflect the necessary balance of interests between the regulator and regulated. If there is a gap it is in respect of negligence in the exercise of FSA powers.

2.15 *It is not intended that the FSA should be subject to the jurisdiction of the Parliamentary Commissioner for Administration. Do you think it would be useful if the FSA were brought within the PCA's remit? Do you think such a move would be of benefit to aggrieved "consumers"/investors?*

We understand that, if an individual's complaint related to the operation of Treasury oversight of the FSA, this would come within the PCA's existing remit.

We recognise that there would be benefits in bringing the FSA within the PCA's remit. Of particular importance are the PCA's wide powers to investigate, and its power to order administrative changes. The PCA's normal procedures mean that complaints could only be made to the PCA via an MP and after FSA's internal complaints procedures have been used.

2.16 *The draft Bill requires the FSA to carry out public consultation, whenever it proposed to change its rules. The Association of Unit Trusts and Investment Funds (AUTIF) has suggested that the FSA should also be required to consult on all policy initiatives affecting one or more sections of the regulated community. Do you think there is a need to require the FSA to consult on matters going beyond proposed rule changes?*

We consider that the FSA should consult on policy initiatives affecting one or more sections of the regulated community. At the very least, this should smooth-out the process of rule change by allowing a dialogue on the policy behind the rule change before any detailed drafting is undertaken.

2.17 The AUTIF has also suggested that the FSA should hold public hearings on important policy proposals. Do you think that would be a useful step towards increasing the FSA's accountability?

We consider that public hearings on important policy proposals could be useful, and that FSA should use all appropriate routes of consultation.

2.18 Are you satisfied that the rule making procedures fully accord with the Better Regulation Unit's principles of good regulation?

The Better Regulation Task Force commented in October 1998 on the consultation draft of the Bill, using as a template its "Principles of Good Regulation" and expressed a number of concerns about the Bill. Some of their concerns, notably on the penalty regime and accountability, have not yet fully been addressed. The Task Force will no doubt be commenting on further drafts of the Bill.

2.19 Several bodies have suggested that the FSA should be subject to periodic efficiency audit by the NAO. What is your view?

We consider it essential that the efficiency and cost effectiveness of the FSA should be subject to periodic assessment. The NAO, with extensive experience of public sector bodies, may be well-equipped to do this.

2.20 Several submissions have suggested that the Treasury should retain in reserve powers of direction over the FSA. Do you agree?

As mentioned above, we are strongly of the view that Treasury should retain reserve powers of direction over the FSA, although they would only be used in extreme circumstances. The existence of such powers is an important factor in ensuring that the FSA remains fully accountable to Treasury and through them to Parliament. This is a necessary balance to the sweeping powers of rule making with the force of law which are being delegated by Parliament to FSA.

15 April 1999

APPENDIX 64

Supplementary Memorandum by the London Investment Banking Association

DISCIPLINARY AND ENFORCEMENT ISSUES

A. INTRODUCTION

1. This submission has been prepared in response to Lord Burns' request, at the Committee's 25 March hearing, that it would be helpful if LIBA could prepare a list of specific areas in the legislation where its Members continue to believe that changes are necessary. In preparing this submission we have taken into account policy developments already referred to in the Treasury's 6 March Progress Report, and we have also tried to take subsequent developments into account.

2. The submission concentrates on the disciplinary and enforcement issues which were discussed at the 25 March hearing.[1] We recognise, however, that these issues cannot be considered in isolation: improvements in FSA's accountability—and clarification of the objectives and the principles to which it must have regard—might reduce the need for some of the specific safeguards on the disciplinary front which we still consider to be necessary at this stage. There are some other issues—which we have not yet been able to raise separately with the Committee—which are also important in assessing the overall acceptability of the new regime and its implications for the competitiveness of UK firms. Examples include the drafting of the provisions on the reduction of financial crime objective, FSA's financing arrangements and the arrangements for setting FSA's "public awareness" budget, and the establishment of Ombudsman and compensation schemes which must ensure that wholesale international businesses do not finance expenditure for the benefit of UK retail consumers. (We can provide further details if this would be helpful.) In addition, the Treasury are consulting separately on other important areas such as the scope of the legislation and the new promotion regime, and FSA is due to publish a consultative paper over the next few months on their plans for the regime to apply to "approved person" and senior executives.

3. In this paper we summarise, first, the areas where we think that the general safeguards in the Bill should be enhanced; we then turn to aspects of the disciplinary process itself. We shall comment separately on the proposed market abuse regime. As for *FSA's intervention powers*, at this stage we have nothing to add to section E of the second part of our November submission.

---

[1] We will be providing a separate paper on Market Abuse.

B. FSA's APPROACH TO DISCIPLINARY MATTERS AND CONSTITUTION OF THE TRIBUNAL: HELPING TO SECURE A REASONABLE APPROACH

4.   We believe that the provisions in the Bill on FSA's Annual Report and on the "independent investigator" should be amended so as to enhance external scrutiny of the regulator's procedures which will reduce the risk of inappropriate or unfair proceedings being launched: the Economic Secretary—at the 18 March hearing of the Committee—confirmed that the Bill provided the powers to take the necessary "drastic action [if] FSA ran amok"—but it is clearly in everybody's interest to have the measures in place to prevent such an occurrence.

5.   First, and with regard to *the independent investigator*, we do not think that the announcements made by the Treasury and FSA so far address the concerns raised in our November representations about the investigator's independence: the Progress Report indicates only that the FSA will be required to consult upon its arrangements and that the investigator, as well as being able to report publicly on his investigations, will have the power to publish the FSA's responses to his recommendations. *We continue to believe that the investigator should be appointed by a body other than the FSA, perhaps by the Parliamentary Commissioner or by the same process as for the appointment of the Parliamentary Commissioner, so as to ensure independent scrutiny at least as extensive as that applied to Government.* For example, the way in which FSA chooses to interpret its rules and guidance, and whether an investigation/disciplinary process has been unduly protracted, should be subject to independent review so that "maladministration" can be addressed satisfactorily. (We think that the *validity* of particular enforcement decisions—which will be challengeable at the Tribunal—can be distinguished from the *manner* in which these decisions have been taken and would, therefore, be excluded from this process.) *It will also be important to ensure that the investigator provides a public report each year on his activities. In addition, we believe that the Non-executive Committee's functions should include reviewing any concerns raised about the efficient/fair conduct of FSA's operations: this could be achieved by amendments to Schedule 1 to the draft Bill. We also believe that the Committee should periodically scrutinise the costs and timescale of disciplinary proceedings to ensure that these are conducted efficiently (again, we believe that the Bill should explicitly provide for this).*

6.   A related point concerns *FSA's exemption from liability in damages.* We agree that the regulator should not be inhibited from taking decisive action when this is necessary but, equally, it cannot be right that compensation should not be payable when maladministration has occurred: if necessary, *paragraph 17 of Schedule 1 should be amended accordingly.* (There is, incidentally, an European Convention on Human Rights (ECHR) aspect here: see Paragraphs 10 and 11 of Lord Lester's Opinion.)[1] With regard to the *financing of compensation orders made against FSA,* it is clear that the annual fees paid to FSA by the regulated community should not be used for this purpose (on this see Clifford Chance's evidence at the 25 March hearing).

7.   With regard to the *FSA's Annual Report,* the Treasury have confirmed that there will be an agreed list of the contents (which they are discussing with the FSA currently). As we explained in our November submission on the Bill, *we believe that the legislation should prescribe a number of issues which the FSA would be required to cover in the Report—we continue to believe that one such issue is the regulator's management of disciplinary and enforcement issues during the year.*

8.   We do not question the need for a flexible system, so that the regulator can respond promptly to market developments, and we agree with the Government's wish to establish a structure which is clear, robust, accountable and fair: our main objective has been to seek to establish clear ground rules *in the legislation* to ensure that FSA applies its discretion reasonably. We believe that the approach we advocate is supported by the Government's Better Regulation Guide principles.[2]

9.   The *Bill should be amended to ensure that practitioners are involved in Tribunal hearings*—currently Schedule 10 simply provides that the "President *may,* for the purposes of the appeal, appoint such further members of the . . . lay panel as he thinks appropriate"[3]—and the composition of the lay panel should involve consultations with practitioner bodies (see, for example, for provisions of regulation 5 of the 1993 Industrial Tribunals (Constitution and Rules of Procedures) Regulations).

C. FSA's COSTS

10.   As discussed at the 25 March hearing, there is a major concern that individuals and small firms in particular will be deterred from seeking a full hearing of a case by the fear that they will have to finance FSA's investigatory costs if they lose the case, as well as paying any fine. Clearly, to an individual or firm, it is the amount of penalty overall that matters—not whether it is characterised as a fine or as a contribution to costs. *We think it is essential that FSA's fining powers in the legislation do not extend to the imposition of awards of*

---

[1] The Economic Secretary, at the 18 March hearing, agreed that there would not be immunity if the FSA or its staff had acted in breach of the ECHR: the draft Bill does not appear to recognise this at present.

[2] See the Annex. In addition, we note—from 31 March press stories—that the Government is taking further steps to prevent legislation that imposes a disproportionate burden on business.

[3] Compare with Section 96 of the Financial Services Act which provides that three Members of the Panel should be appointed to hear appeals and that, as far as practicable, "at least one . . . shall be a person with recent practical experience in business relevant to the case".

costs of the investigation, except in cases where it is held that the "offender" has behaved vexatiously (it may be that the legislation, as drafted, already has this effect but the discussion in FSA's Consultation Paper 17— Enforcing the New Regime—suggests that the intention is to impose costs orders). *At the very least, the Bill should allow for costs to be awarded against the FSA (currently Schedule 10 only allows the Tribunal to make orders in respect of costs incurred in connection with its proceedings alone).*

D. EUROPEAN CONVENTION ON HUMAN RIGHTS; THE ENFORCEMENT COMMITTEE

11. The Committee is aware of the debate about whether FSA's disciplinary processes—as regards the market abuse regime in particular—should be regarded as "criminal" for the purposes of the ECHR: we believe that the continued emphasis on "discipline as a deterrent" reinforces the view that the processes should, indeed, be regarded as criminal.

12. Our November submission outlined what the due process implications of this analysis would be but, as we have stressed previously, we hope that the Government would wish to recognise these principles regardless of whether, in strict law, they are required to do so under the Convention.

13. The Treasury have already indicated a number of areas where the framework sketched out in the draft Bill is to be amended:[1] *we believe that the following points still need to be explicitly recognised in legislation* (either primary or secondary):

— *the right of an accused person to be provided with the regulator's evidence;*

— the role of the "enforcement committee", the involvement of practitioners in the committee's work, and the right to be heard before the committee;

— restriction on the use of evidence obtained under compulsion (as entailed by the Conventions);

— the equality of arms principle and the right to be legally represented;

— the "sliding scale" burden of proof.

14. We discuss the Convention's rule on the "foreseeability" of an offence below.

E. FSA'S APPROACH TO DISCIPLINE

15. We continue to be concerned about the lack of consistency with regard to FSA's fundamental approach to disciplinary proceedings: although Consultation Paper 17 stresses the importance of an open and co-operative relationship between firms and the regulator, transparent, proportionate and consistent exercise of power and fair treatment for those in the enforcement process, it also states that "it is equitable that those who breach regulatory obligations should *generally* pay a penalty". This seems to imply that fines will always be sought except in exceptional cases. We believe that the primary objective should be to provide strong incentives for firms to establish efficient internal compliance arrangements and to provide remedies to clients if, as a result of a rule breach, they are put at disadvantage. Fines or censure are only appropriate for firms—or individuals— who egregiously ignore their responsibilities. We acknowledge that enshrining these principles in the Bill is not without difficulty but *we suggest that one way of doing so would be for the Bill to require FSA to prepare and comply with a code matching the relevant provisions of the code for Crown Prosecutors* in determining whether proceedings should be brought forward (the Crown Prosecution Code provides, for example, that prosecutions are less likely to be needed if the defendant has put right the loss or harm that was caused or if the offence was committed as a result of a mistake or misunderstanding).

F. FORESEEABILITY OF OFFENCES

16. In his Opinion Lord Lester stressed that the ECHR requires "offences"—if criminal—to be foreseeable. Whether or not in strict law the Convention applies in this way to FSA, it can only be right for firms or individuals to be censured or fined if it was possible at the time "the behaviour" occurred for them to establish whether or not it would be subject to sanction. (The Better Regulation Guide adopts a similar approach.)[2]

17. This point arises most acutely with regard to the Bill's market abuse provisions and FSA's wish to be able to mount disciplinary proceedings for breaches of their Principles alone. (A separate paper will be submitted on the former.)

18. As we explained in our submissions on the draft Bill, the "light touch" wholesale regime has been a key element in maintaining the City's international competitiveness: the absence of detailed rules has been an important element in this and wholesale clients/counterparties such as large corporations—who neither need nor

---

[1] For example, that FSA will be required to publish procedures and act in accordance with them and that evidence will be disclosed on request to the firms and individuals involved (although, on the latter, we are not clear whether this is to be a legislative requirement).

[2] See the Annex. In this context it is interesting to note the recent Enforcement Statement issued by the Data Protection Registrar which reflects the Guide's principles: "To be effective any piece of legislation must be understood by those to whom it applies . . . understanding and compliance are always preferable to enforcement . . . ".

want the protection provided by retail rules—have no wish to change the current structure. However, the FSA has made clear that it wishes to be able to mount disciplinary proceedings for breaches of the Principles alone in spite of the objections to this approach which firms and their trade associations have already made over recent years to the SROs pursuing a similar tack. (As we made clear at the 25 March hearing, firms had not anticipated that breaches of the Principles alone would be cited in disciplinary procedures when the "new settlement" was introduced in 1991–92.)

19. We believe that, in the wholesale markets at least, there is no need for FSA to adopt such an approach, given the ability of clients/counterparties to look after their own interests, and that to do so will lead firms to press for the introduction of detailed rule to provide the certainty that they need—which will undermine the UK's competitiveness in due course[1]. In addition, FSA do not need to impose disciplinary sanctions for breaches of Principles: if there is some sort of unforeseen gap in the rules which is exploited by a firm in some way in a particular case then the regulator can change the rules as soon as it becomes apparent to prevent other firms pursuing a similar course and, as far as the "offending" firm itself is concerned, a history of such occurrences would colour the regulator's attitude to its assessment of the firm's compliance culture.

20. *Currently the draft Bill provides that the contravention of certain rules will not be actionable at the suit of private persons—Clause 80(3)—and FSA's Consultation Paper 13 (on the new Principles) stresses that this provision is designed to cover the breaches of the Principles. We suggest that the Bill should also provide that censure or fines should not be imposed in respect of breaches of any rule designated under Section 80(3).*

G.   GUIDANCE ON TRANSACTIONS/CLEARANCES/"NO ACTION" PROCEDURES

21. As explained in our November submission, we continue to believe that *the Bill should oblige FSA to provide firms seeking guidance about the regulatory treatment of transactions with a binding view of the regulator's assessment* of their compatibility with the rule book. The greater the extent to which FSA is able to impose disciplinary sanctions for breaches of rules which fail to impose clear guidance on expected behaviour, the more important this matter will be[2] although we agree that the financing of this activity will need to be discussed further.

22. A related issue is the need to ensure that general rules do not override specific ones: we believe that the *Bill should make clear that where a firm has complied with a specific FSA rule, or with the rules of an Exchange, then it should not be vulnerable to disciplinary action for breach of a more general precept.* We cannot believe that such a principle is problematic and our Members—not least those from other countries—would be very concerned if this approach were to be regarded as controversial by the Treasury or FSA.

H.   SETTLEMENTS WITHOUT ADMISSION OF GUILT

23. In our November submission, we explained why our Members, drawing in particular on their experience in the USA, thought that a "settlements without admission of guilt" procedure would be valuable—primarily because it allows the regulator to indicate its disapproval of a firm's behaviour whilst by-passing the potentially lengthy adjudication process when a firm disagrees with the regulator's analysis. We continue to believe that *the Bill should provide for such a procedure* here and we do not understand why the UK authorities are unwilling to accept the point.

14 April 1999

ANNEX

PRINCIPLES OF GOOD REGULATION

This paper summarises some important areas highlighted in the Better Regulation Guide as contributing to good regulatory practice. A review of the framework proposed in the draft Financial Services and Markets Bill in the light of the Better Regulation Task Force's "Principles of Good Regulation" is particularly appropriate

---

[1] The Committee considered competitiveness issues at the 16 March session with FSA and Mr Michael Foot said, citing inter alia the regulator's discussions with LIBA, that the evidence suggested that the cost of compliance with UK regulation did not provide a disincentive for business to be conducted here. It should be noted, though, that our November submission on the compliance cost assessment accompanying the draft Bill stated that "we have little doubt that savings will not be achieved if the new regime creates greater uncertainty than the current framework: we are concerned that—as the Bill is currently drafted—this seems likely to be the outcome: see, in particular, our discussion on Part VI of the Bill . . . ".
   A similar issue arose in the tax field in connection with the Government's proposal to introduce a General Anti Avoidance Rule drafted at a very high level of generality. In that case the Government has decided not to proceed with the proposal but to introduce targeted provisions if gaps in the legislation are exploited. It is not clear why a different approach should be followed in financial services regulation.
[2] With regard to the Government's consultation on the introduction of a GAAR in the tax field (see footnote 6)—we understand that the great majority of bodies responding stressed the need for a pre-clearance procedure.

given the recent publication by the Cabinet Office of the Better Regulation Guide—with the Prime Minister's Foreword—and the Task Force's 1997–98 Annual Report.

THE BETTER REGULATION GUIDE

The Task Force has established five key principles for good regulation: transparency, accountability, targeting, consistency and proportionality. The objective is to ensure that Regulations are necessary, fair, effective and balanced, and that they enjoy a broad degree of public confidence. In particular, Regulations should be properly targeted and clearly defined, and must balance risk, cost and practical benefit ("it is not practical for regulators to seek to exclude all risk. . . fit the remedy to the risk . . . only regulate where you need to . . ."). A copy of the Task Force's effectiveness tests is attached (not printed).

The Better Regulation Guide, published on 10 August, requires Departments to use Regulatory Impact Assessments[1] whenever new legislation or consultation papers on regulatory proposals are published.

The Assessments should include a clear statement of the objectives of the regulatory proposal and its likely effects, and an Assessment should demonstrate that the proposal envisaged is the most effective means of meeting the stated objectives, set out the benefits—and costs—of the proposal, and identify who will be affected (although the Guide notes that the process will not necessarily follow a set pattern). Long term economic benefits and the international dimension should also be considered, as should the danger that a particular rule could give rise to an unintended or perverse result (for example, prohibiting a product could lead consumers to switch to substitutes which pose equal—or even greater–risks). In particular, the Assessment should contain an explanation of why non-regulatory action, such as a code of conduct, would be insufficient.

The Guide discusses drafting, consultation, implementation and achieving compliance, and it gives guidance on reviewing and monitoring. Particular points made in the Guide include:

— The need to avoid Regulations which cause disruption to markets and trade.

— Those being regulated must understand their obligations and there are important costs implications for businesses if requirements are uncertain (although the Guide also stresses the need to avoid overly prescriptive rules and to consider goal-based regulation).[2]

— The importance of regulation being clear and legally certain ("be predictable, people should know where they stand").

— The importance of focusing on achieving compliance rather than just punishing breaches ("make sure the system . . . is designed to bring about compliance, not just to generate enforcement activity . . . Consider compliance through self assessment, i.e., give affected persons an enforceable right to challenge the businesses' compliance. . .": also see below on Enforcement more generally).

— The importance of regulation being properly targeted and not "scatter gun" or universal ("define the exact nature of the problem . . . and match regulation to it as closely as you can . . . Regulation should focus on the problem and minimise side effects . . .").

— The importance of consultation—which is a key element in accountability: adequate time for consultation should be allowed and feedback provided to consultees (in particular, Assessments should be available on request to interested parties, and should be sent *automatically* to those who helped in their preparation).

— The production of consolidated Regulations: if a new Regulation overlaps with another measure, thought should be given to introducing a combined and streamlined regulation.

— Transitional phasing-in periods should be considered.

— Regulations must continue to be relevant: thus, prior to the implementation of a Regulation, the establishment of a procedure for assessing and monitoring the efficacy of the measure should be devised. (Annex 4 of the Guide provides advice on reviewing Regulations.) As part of this process clear regulatory objectives are needed.

— The potential benefits of self-regulation should be considered (on this the Task Force is undertaking further work).

— The benefits of enhancing consumer choice and understanding through information disclosure should be considered (although the costs for businesses of disclosure should also be borne in mind).

— Unnecessary gold plating of international requirements should be avoided.

---

[1] In his Foreword the Prime Minister states that "no regulatory proposal which has an impact on businesses . . . should be considered by the Government without a thorough assessment of the risks, costs and benefits, a clear analysis of who will be affected and an explanation of why non-regulatory action would be insufficient. This requirement applies whenever Ministers or their officials are seeking to clear a new proposal for legislation. Without a prior assessment of the kind described in this Guide, clearance for such proposals will not be given".

[2] The Guide states that where regulation is goal-based, it may help to provide certainty if details are set out of how those affected can comply, while leaving it open to them to find acceptable alternatives.

In addition, *Annex 3* of the Guide sets out *Principles of Good Enforcement*. The Government wishes the principles and procedures to be followed by all appropriate enforcement authorities. The Guide stresses that adherence to these principles should benefit business by reducing the uncertainty of firms about whether they are getting it right, by cutting the overall cost of complying with Regulations, and by assuring businesses that they are competing with one another on level terms.

The Guide stresses, in particular, that helping business to comply in the most effective way should be a key aim. The Guide says that this cannot be achieved solely by detection and punishment of breaches, and neither should enforcement and sanctions be so strict that they effectively discourage those who are being regulated from performing legitimate activities or force them—through fear or uncertainty—to go to unnecessary lengths to comply. The sanctions regime should be proportionate, fair and effective.

The enforcement principles set out in the Guide include:

— Proportionality and consistency: the cost of compliance for business should be minimised by ensuring that any action required is proportionate to the risks. The regulator/authority should carry out its duties in a fair, equitable and consistent manner and, as far as the law allows, it should take account of the circumstances of the case and the attitude of the operator when considering action. Before formal enforcement action is taken, officers should provide an opportunity to discuss the circumstances of the case and, if possible, resolve points of difference (unless immediate action is required, for example in order to protect the public).

— Information and advice in plain language on the rules that are being applied should be provided, and the authority should be open about how it sets about its work. It should take particular care to work with small businesses so that they can meet their legal obligations without unnecessary expense.

— The authority should encourage business to seek advice/information, because prevention is better than cure, and it should clearly distinguish best practice advice from legal requirements.

— The need for clear enforcement standards, setting out the level of service performance that the public and business can expect to receive, should be drawn up in consultation with business and other relevant interested parties, and should be published: those being regulated should know what to expect from the enforcing authorities.

APPENDIX 65

Supplmentary Memorandum by the London Investment Banking Association

MARKET ABUSE

1. Where sanctions may be imposed, we believe that it is very important for firms and individuals that the behaviour expected of them should be clearly described. Given that the proposed market abuse "civil" offence is to apply to all persons—and not just to authorised persons or approved individuals—it seems particularly important that the types of behaviour which are to be subject to fines and other sanctions should be foreseeable in advance. Indeed, since the primary purpose of the proposed new offence is to deter behaviour which is damaging to UK markets, it would be perverse if there was uncertainty about the conduct which would be subject to FSA disciplinary action because that would be liable to deter acceptable market activity.

2. However, if Part VI of the Bill were to be adopted in the form proposed last summer all the existing layers of provisions which could apply to market abuse offences would remain in existence:

— authorised firms and their employees would be subject to FSA rules, Principles and guidance;

— members of an Exchange would be subject to the Exchange's rules;

— *all persons* would be subject to the criminal offences of insider dealing and market manipulation;

but, in addition,

— *all persons* would be subject to the new market abuse offence.

3. There is thus a danger that behaviour which meets all the requirements of the detailed rules may nevertheless be open to sanction under the less clearly specified new offence.

4. The new offence is defined in the Bill in very broad terms, and the Code which is designed to describe types of behaviour considered to be unacceptable under it will have only evidential weight. Further, in some areas the present draft of the Code is also very vague. In addition, although the market abuse offence will generally encompass the kinds of conduct covered by the criminal offences this will not be the case in all circumstances (for example, an essential element in the market abuse offence is the impact of the behaviour on the perceptions of market users about the fairness of the market in question).

5. We believe that the Bill should address the following points:

— that compliance with the Code will provide a safe harbour against prosecutions;[1]

— that the market abuse offence will not be used as an inappropriate alternative to the mounting of prosecutions for the criminal offences;[2]

— that the fact that behaviour was in compliance with an Exchange or FSA rule should provide a safe harbour against a market abuse "prosecution";

— that compliance with a statutory requirement should also provide a safe harbour;

— that FSA should establish a mechanism for providing formal and timely pre-clearances;

— that, if a market abuse by an Exchange member is in breach of Exchange rules, that Exchange rather than FSA should take disciplinary action;

— that once the decision has been taken to mount a criminal prosecution, then FSA should not be able to mount a civil market abuse action subsequently if a conviction is not secured (and vice versa);

— for authorised persons and approved individuals found guilty of market abuse offences, FSA should be prevented from imposing additional fines for "regulatory offences" in respect of the same behaviour.

6. The other changes we are seeking are more fundamental in that they are concerned with the nature and rationale of the new offence proposed.

7. The Government—so far as we are aware—has never provided a statement setting out in detail why a new offence is needed and what the compliance cost implications might be. However, there seem to be two distinct themes. The first is that deterrent sanctions are needed in respect of behaviour which is not criminal but which damages markets (paragraphs 15.5 and 15.11 of Part One of HM Treasury's Consultation Document on the draft Bill). The second is that there are shortcomings in the drafting of the current criminal offences and difficulties in securing convictions under them (in particular, it seems, because of the difficulty of proving intention). We believe that these two distinct concerns should be looked at separately and that there needs to be a proper debate about whether amending the existing offences would not be a better way of meeting the Government's purposes. The examples provided of the sort of behaviour which is being targeted under the new offence—the use of privileged information or giving market participants a mistaken impression of the market in an investment or distorting the market in an investment[3]—already seem potentially to fall within the current criminal offences, with the exception, perhaps, of abusive market squeezes. Moreover, given the breadth of the regulator's rules governing authorised firms and employees, it is not apparent that there is a need for any new offence to apply to them. (On this, the Economic Secretary's comments at the 18th March hearing seem to confirm that it is with regard to the behaviour of non-authorised market participants that there is a gap in the regulatory system which gives rise to the need for the new offences: see Q117.)

8. We are unpersuaded, on the basis of the material that we have seen so far, that the Government's objectives can be secured only by the introduction of a new wide-ranging and very broadly drafted market abuse offence. To the extent that it is a response to the difficulty of proving intent in the present statutory offences it seems that it should be possible to amend the current legislation so that a person's state of mind can be inferred from their behaviour. Our understanding of the position in the US[4] is that a person's state of mind can be inferred from their behaviour: thus, unless an alternative explanation can be provided, the intent element of market abuse could be proved by demonstrating that the person gained from the transaction or series of transactions which he undertook and that that gain was the predicable consequence of his actions.

9. It may be that the main purpose of introducing a new market abuse offence which does not include any concept of intent within its definition is to cover reckless or negligent behaviour (in his evidence at the Committee's 16 March hearing Mr Howard Davies said that FSA "do not intend to prosecute people for accidental offences"). If that is the intention, we believe that the implications of this substantial departure from the normal principles of criminal law should be debated fully before the proposed provisions are proceeded with.

10. We recognise that there may be a deficiency in the criminal law in respect of abusive squeezes conducted by persons who are not members of the relevant exchange or otherwise authorised under the other provisions of the Bill. However, we believe that any such deficiency could be better met by a provision specific to that issue, rather than by the proposed, very widely drafted provision which gives rise to such difficulties of vagueness and consequent uncertainty for market users.

---

[1] We are particularly concerned that the Treasury's Progress Report does not provide comfort on this: "it seems unlikely that the FSA would [take action against someone who had complied with the Code] unless it considered that the person had failed to comply with the *spirit of the new regime*".

[2] It has been stressed by the FSA that criminal prosecutions *will* be mounted where appropriate but since an essential element in the decision on whether to mount a criminal prosecution is whether there is sufficient evidence to do so—the "evidential test"—we are not clear that in practice actions for market abuse will not be used as an easy option.

[3] See paras 15.2 and 15.6 of Part One of HM Treasury's Consultation Document on the draft Bill.

[4] For example, see the transcript of the presentation by Mr Thomas Sjoblom of the SEC at the FSA's 11 March conference on Market Abuse, *not printed.*

ANNEX 1

OUTDATED SECTIONS OF LLOYD'S ACT (1982)

1. *Divestment*: s10–12. The divestment provisions contained in the Act prohibit the cross ownership of Lloyd's Brokers, who bring the business to the market, and managing agents who employ the active underwriter who accepts the insurance risk on behalf of the capital for whom the managing agent acts. This restriction was incorporated in the Act as a protection for the individual member of the Society whose interests might have been harmed by such a relationship. With the introduction of corporate capital there has been a rapid movement towards the alignment of managing agents and the capital for which they underwrite. This trend will result in these restrictions becoming irrelevant since the members they were designed to protect are under common ownership with the managing agent. As many businesses in the insurance industry integrate vertically to secure their distribution networks, and new participants enter the industry unhampered by such restrictions, Lloyd's ability to compete is reduced.

2. *Exclusivity of Lloyds Brokers*: s8(3). The requirement that all insurance transactions at Lloyd's, whether risks being underwritten in the market or outgoing reinsurance, should be passed through a Lloyd's Broker places those underwriting at Lloyd's at a unique commercial disadvantage. All other insurers are at liberty to freely choose the intermediaries they use or, as is increasingly common, deal directly with the assured. At a time when distribution is a key competitive issue for the Lloyd's market this restriction in the Act greatly reduces the Lloyd's market's ability to keep pace with international developments. The Council's ability to relax the requirements is limited.

An additional problem is that the existence of an approved group of intermediaries, Lloyd's Brokers, imports the need to police and regulate them. This contrasts with Her Majesty's Government's decision not to yield to pressure for statutory regulations of other insurance brokers.

3. *Underwriting through an agent*: s8(2). The Act requires that all underwriting should be undertaken through the medium of an underwriting agent. This was a sensible precaution when the membership of the Society was exclusively composed of individual members, few of whom were insurance professionals. However now this requirement has no relevance for those units at Lloyd's who have simplified and modernised their structures by full alignment with the capital for which they underwrite. The Act requirement produces unnecessarily complicated arrangements, which are expensive for those who have to operate them and potentially embarrassing for those responsible for their policing.

ANNEX 2

Proposed drafting of provision to be inserted:

Financial Services and Markets

Power to amend Lloyd's Acts 1871 To 1982	**194A**—(1) The Treasury may, on the written application of the Society, by order amend any provision of the Lloyd's Acts 1871 to 1982 which concerns or relates to the regulation of any activities carried on at Lloyd's.

      (2) The power to make an order under subsection (1) shall be exercisable for the purpose of giving effect to any proposals of the Society which—

      (a) are contained in the application; and

      (b) have been approved by the Authority.

Printed in the UK by The Stationery Office Limited
5/99   424208   78344